800 sketches at Dirken Mnds, Ill.

> main culture rebuilt 1200 AD

iv... annos 16 → 647

... lith Exp 26 → 19 !

GJ Armelajos (1936:14)

Both mo.

I Caloric... March
? Mobility Oct-Nov

1.0 m when 45-60 ...
... LB!

... ~1/LB 2000:16

Hispanic Pueblo
...
...

Life under Pressure

The MIT Press Eurasian Population and Family History Series
Editorial Board: Marco Breschi, Cameron Campbell, Akira Hayami (honorary), Christer Lundh, Michel Oris, and Noriko O. Tsuya
Series Editors: James Z. Lee, Tommy Bengtsson, and George Alter

Life under Pressure: Mortality and Living Standards in Europe and Asia, 1700–1900
Tommy Bengtsson, Cameron Campbell, James Z. Lee, et al.

Forthcoming
Prudence and Pressure: Reproduction in Europe and Asia, 1700–1900
George Alter, Noriko O. Tsuya, Wang Feng, et al.

Life under Pressure

Mortality and Living
Standards in Europe and
Asia, 1700–1900

Tommy Bengtsson, Cameron
Campbell, James Z. Lee, et al.

The MIT Press
Cambridge, Massachusetts
London, England

This book was set in Palatino on 3B2 by Asco Typesetters, Hong Kong.
Printed and bound in the United States of America.

Library of Congress Cataloging-in-Publication Data

Life under pressure : mortality and living standards in Europe and Asia, 1700–1900 /
Tommy Bengtsson ... [et al.].
    p.   cm. — (The MIT Press Eurasian population and family history series)
Includes bibliographical references and index.
ISBN 0-262-02551-5 (hc : alk. paper)
    1. Europe—Population. 2. Asian—Population. 3. Mortality—Europe. 4. Mortality—
Asia. 5. Europe—Economic conditions. 6. Asia—Economic conditions. I. Bengtsson,
Tommy. II. EurAsian Project on Population and Family History. III. Series.

HB3581.L545   2004
304.6′4′09509033—dc22   2003060235

10 9 8 7 6 5 4 3 2 1

Contents

Series Foreword

The study of human behavior at aggregate and individual levels defines the core of all social sciences and some of the humanities. Demography, the mathematical study of human populations, provides a tool kit to do so. Concerned largely with the development and application of quantitative methodologies with which to analyze human populations, demographers make grindstones for many humanistic and social scientific mills.

As a discipline, demography has long been concerned largely with understanding and describing the large-scale processes and implications of the fertility and mortality transitions that together constitute the demographic transition, and the interrelationship of these processes with resources, be they economic or environmental, as well as with other social processes. Historical demography has been central to these endeavors.

Only recently, however, has historical demography begun to change our basic understanding of population behavior. For over two centuries, the Malthusian model has dominated our understanding of population processes. Malthus distinguished two ideal models of population processes: one dominated largely by mortality, which he called the *positive check*, the other by nuptiality and fertility, which he called the *preventive check*. Positive check populations experienced persistent poverty, while preventive check populations prospered. In a magisterial overview, he summarized the available knowledge of his time to demonstrate that while the first process was typical of much of human history, including the non-Western world, the second process was characteristic of "modern" Europe, particularly the England of his time.

For Malthus, what we today term *family planning* requires a uniquely Western ability to calculate consciously the costs and benefits of having children and to decide deliberately to delay or abstain from marriage. Western economic prosperity, in other words, is a product of Western individualism and Western rationality. The confirmation that this preventive check indeed operated for England and began even earlier than Malthus had thought has inspired a major revival of Malthusian theory (Wrigley and Schofield 1981). Such scholars as John Hajnal (1965, 1982) and Alan Macfarlane (1978, 1986, 1987) have suggested that the European origins of the fertility transition, the European roots of individualism, and even the European development of nineteenth-century capitalism are all intertwined and embedded in a European family and demographic culture that encouraged such revolutionary social and economic changes. By identifying and linking demographic systems more explicitly and systematically than Malthus, these and other contemporary social theorists have elevated and amplified the theoretical implications of Malthusian formulations (Goody 1996, Schofield 1989).

Recent findings on demographic behavior outside the West have suggested that elsewhere, other forms of preventive checks were equally important. James Lee, Cameron Campbell, and Wang Feng have shown that a significant proportion of the non-Western population followed a demographic system with fewer positive and more preventive checks than Malthus and his followers had thought (Lee and Campbell 1997, Lee and Wang 1999). These findings, which provide some of the first robust aggregate demographic indices for a variety of historical Chinese populations, challenge many Malthusian assumptions about comparative socioeconomic as well as demographic processes and have been challenged in turn by neo-Malthusians from both sides of the Pacific (Brenner and Isett 2002; Campbell, Wang, and Lee 2002; Cao and Chen 2002; Huang 2002, 2003; Lavely and Wong 1998; Lee, Campbell, and Wang 2002; Pomeranz 2002, 2003; Wang and Lee 2002; Wolf 2001; Zhao 1997a, 1997b, 2002).

New data and new methods, meanwhile, have begun to illuminate the complexities of demographic responses to exogenous stress, economic and otherwise. Whereas Malthus and his successors focused on relationships between economic conditions and demographic behavior at the aggregate level, combined time-series and event-history analyses of longitudinal, nominative, microlevel data now allow for the finely grained differentiation of mortality, fertility, and other demographic responses by social class, household context, and other dimensions at the individual level (Bengtsson 1989, 1993b). Appropriately detailed historical population register data exist for selected communities in at least five countries—Belgium, China, Italy, Japan, and Sweden—and have already been analyzed in a variety of publications (Bengtsson and Saito 2000a; Derosas and Oris 2002).

The Eurasian Population and Family History Project is a collaborative effort by scholars in a variety of countries and disciplines to use these new data and methods to reexamine the Malthusian paradigm, explicitly contrasting populations at the extreme Eastern and Western ends of the Eurasian land mass. By carrying out nearly identical analyses on similar data from Europe and Asia, we compare patterns of demographic responses to economic conditions in a variety of contexts represented by the specific communities in the study, identifying both unity and diversity. By combining the increased resolution of individual-level event-history analysis with formal Malthusian models of demographic behavior under economic stress, we achieve a deeper understanding of human behavior. In this series on Eurasian Population and Family History, we examine and compare in successive volumes the patterns of mortality, fertility, nuptiality, and migration at the individual level.

These books demonstrate that patterns of demographic outcomes are determined by society, not biology. While demographic outcomes at the aggregate level may be subject to the influence of economic conditions, climatic factors, or geography, they are shaped at the level of the community by specific institutional policies and at the level of the household by explicit decisions about the individual allocation of resources and responsibilities. Demographic behavior in the past accordingly varied by geographic location, socioeconomic status, household composition, and position with the household (Lee and Campbell 1997), and demographic responses to short-term stress varied as well (Bengtsson 1993). At both ends of Eurasia, individual demographic actions were the products of political and social negotiation. In that sense, the Eurasia Population and Family History Project advances and reaffirms the importance of social action and human agency.

Our efforts suggest that the grand narratives of classic behavioral theory overestimate the uniformity of human responses to exogenous forces. Different people, defined by age, gender, geographic location, family organization, local institutions, specific occupation, regional history, wealth, and much else, in fact respond differently to different economic constraints and opportunities. As a result, while differences by age, sex, and socioeconomic status are virtually universal in mortality responses to economic change, patterns of response by age, sex, and social class differ dramatically.

Our work, in other words, bridges the apparent contradiction between two classes of social theory: one that emphasizes universalism and similarity—cognitive psychology, economics, social biology—and one that emphasizes contingency and difference: anthropology, cultural studies, history. On the one hand, we show that social action and human agency are virtually universal when confronted with specific constraints, producing patterns of differential demographic behavior that reflect ageism, sexism, and other forms of favoritism and particularism. On the other hand, we also demonstrate that these patterns are products of institutional arrangements, social relationships, and specific preferences that vary by population. As a result, while exogenous forces elicit human responses everywhere, the patterns of response also vary, conditioned by national, regional, and community context as well as by kin, family, and individual circumstances.

Acknowledgments

Big projects and long gestations mean many debts. This is certainly the case for the Eurasia Population and Family History Project and for *Life under Pressure*.

Akira Hayami initially conceived the idea of a large-scale comparative project based on coordinated analyses of nominative household registers from Europe and Asia. In 1993, he initiated discussions with Tommy Bengtsson to organize this effort, and in June 1994 he hosted the initial organizational meeting of the Eurasia Project at the International Research Center for Japanese Studies in Kyoto, Japan. We are very grateful for his leadership, his organizational support, as well as his financial assistance to a number of participants in this project.

Many meetings followed: a second organizational meeting in November 1994 at Lund to finalize project membership, an initial workshop in January 1995 at Venice to design the standard comparative mortality models, a workshop in 1997 at Bloomington to tweak these models, and public presentations in 1997 and 2000 at Kyoto of the initial and final results of our mortality analyses. We also presented early calculations and draft chapters of *Life under Pressure* at the quadrennial meeting of the International Economic History Congress in 1998, the International Congress of Historical Sciences in 2000, and the International Union for the Scientific Study of Population in 2001, as well as at annual meetings of the Social Science History Association in 1995, 1996, 1998, and 2000 and of the Population Association of America in 1998, 1999, and 2000. Without such numerous opportunities to present, discuss, and rethink our research with others and with each other, our analysis and this book would be far less complete.

We thank the following discussants and participants for their valuable advice on our project and our presentations: Jan deVries, Robert Fogel, Myron Gutmann, Michael Haines, Shigemi Kono, Ronald Lee,

/(t 92b-13) dr2w 1783

Kiyomi Morioka, Mari C. Nelson, David Reher, James Riley, Osamu Saito, Roger Schofield, G. William Skinner, Charles Tilly, Donald Treiman, Frans van Poppel, and David Weir. We are especially grateful to Ronald Lee and six anonymous readers for MIT Press who read the book manuscript in its entirety. Their detailed and lengthy comments were very helpful, as were Jack Goldstone's, Daniel Little's, and Ken Sylvester's comments on the series foreword. Many people also commented on individual chapters. We thank them separately in the acknowledgments to each chapter.

We owe a tremendous debt to the institutions that hosted these meetings, as well as to the Ministry of Education in Japan for a Grant-in-Aid for Scientific Research, which funded many of the meetings and some of the research; the National Institute of Child Health and Human Development (R13 HD34883-01), the East Asia Regional Research Working Group of the Social Science Research Council, and the Joint Committee on Chinese Studies of the American Council of Learned Societies, which together funded the 1997 Bloomington Workshop; the Swedish Council for Working Life and Social Research, which funded the second organizational meeting; and a network grant from the European Science Foundation, which funded some of our informal discussions on this book as well as other project activities. Many individuals helped with these activities and we thank them collectively here, especially Catherine Capron, Shannon Russell, Genevieve Schaenger, and John Smith. Other agencies and individuals provided crucial support for related projects or specific research teams and are acknowledged in individual chapters.

The Swedish Council for Working Life and Social Research and the California Institute of Technology provided important financial support for editorial work. Sabrina Boschetti provided crucial and extensive editorial support during the final year of editing and manuscript preparation. We thank Sabrina for her tremendous efforts, as well as Barbara Calli, Heather Guyett, and Madeleine Jarl for their additional assistance.

Finally, we would like to acknowledge David Weir, who in 1984 published "Life under Pressure: France and England, 1670–1870," *Journal of Economic History* 44:27–47, both for his scholarship and his support as well as his felicitous prose.

Contributors

George Alter
Professor
Indiana University

Tommy Bengtsson
Professor of Economic History
and Demography
Lund University

Marco Breschi
Professore di Demografia
Università di Udine

Göran Broström
Professor
Umeå University

Cameron Campbell
Associate Professor
University of California at Los
Angeles

Renzo Derosas
Ricercatore
Università Ca' Foscari di Venezia

Martin Dribe
Research Associate
Lund University

Satomi Kurosu
Associate Professor
Reitaku University

James Z. Lee
Professor of History and
Sociology
California Institute of
Technology
University of Michigan

Matteo Manfredini
Ricercatore
Università di Parma

Hideki Nakazato
Associate Professor
Konan University

Muriel Neven
Chargée de Recherche
Université de Liège

Paul Nystedt
Senior Lecturer
Linköping University

Emiko Ochiai
Associate Professor
Kyoto University

Michel Oris
Professeur Ordinaire
University of Geneva

Rossella Rettaroli
Professore Associato di

Demografia
Università di Bologna

Noriko O. Tsuya
Professor
Keio University

Wang Feng
Associate Professor
University of California, Irvine

MALTHUS'S PERSPECTIVE

[T]here are few states in which there is not a constant effort in the population to increase beyond the means of subsistence. This constant effort as constantly tends to subject the lower classes of society to distress, and to prevent any great permanent melioration of their condition.

(Malthus 1826/1986, 17)

During this season of distress, the discouragements to marriage and the difficulty of rearing a family are so great, that the progress of population is retarded. In the meantime, the cheapness of labour, the plenty of labourers, and the necessity of an increased industry among them, encourage cultivators to employ more labour upon their land ... till ultimately the means of subsistence may become in the same proportion to the population, as at the period from which we set out. The situation of the labourer being then again tolerably comfortable, the restraints to population are in some degree loosened; and, after a short period, the same retrograde and progressive movements, with respect to happiness, are repeated.

This sort of oscillation will not probably be obvious to common view; and it may be difficult even for the most attentive observer to calculate its periods. Yet that,... some alteration of this kind does exist ... no reflecting man, who considers the subject deeply, can well doubt.

One principal reason why this oscillation has been less remarked, and less decidedly conformed by experience than might naturally be expected, is, that the histories of mankind which we possess are, in general, histories only of the higher classes. We have not many accounts that can be depended upon, of the manners and customs of that part of mankind, where these retrograde and progressive movements chiefly take place. A satisfactory history of this kind, of one people and of one period, would require the constant and minute attention of many observing minds in local and general remarks on the state of the lower classes of society, and the causes that influenced it; and, to draw accurate inferences upon this subject, a succession of such historians for some centuries would be necessary.

(1826/1986, 17–18)

[T]his science may be said yet to be in its infancy, and many of the objects, on which it would be desirable to have information, have been either omitted or not stated with sufficient accuracy. Among these, perhaps, may be reckoned ...; the comparative mortality among the children of the most distressed part of the community, and of those who live rather more at their ease; the variations in the real price of labour; the observable differences in the state of the lower classes of society, with respect to ease and happiness, at different times during a certain period; and very accurate registers of births, deaths, and marriages, which are of the utmost importance in this subject.

A faithful history, including such particulars, would tend greatly to elucidate the manner in which the constant check upon population acts; and would probably prove the existence of the retrograde and progressive movements that have been mentioned.

(1826/1986, 19)

1

New Malthusian Perspectives

James Z. Lee, Cameron Campbell, and Tommy Bengtsson

With the publication of *An Essay on the Principle of Population* in 1798 and his expanded second edition in 1803, Thomas Robert Malthus (1766–1834) focused scholarly and popular attention on the comparative poverty of much of human history and the importance of differential demographic processes in determining both population size and living standards. Malthus distinguished two ideal models of population processes: one dominated largely by mortality, which he called the *positive check*, the other by nuptiality and fertility, which he called the *preventive check*. Positive check populations experienced persistent poverty, while preventive check populations prospered. Malthus summarized available data to demonstrate that while the first process was typical of much of human history, including the non-Western world of his time, the second process was characteristic only of "modern" Europe, particularly England. Finally, in spite of the absence then of similarly hard historical data, he outlined a personal vision of a "satisfactory" history of the human condition, or at least of "one people and one period" (Malthus 1826/1986, 18), which, he thought, should differentiate by age group, class, and gender, comparing changes in population, living standards, and other social behavior in terms of the oscillations over the short and long term of the positive and preventive checks.

While we know much about the West, the aggregate, and the long term, we know relatively little about the East, the microlevel, and the short term. Thus, in spite of the attention devoted by Malthus and subsequently by many others to the study of population, our understanding of comparative historical population dynamics remains incomplete. Although we have reconstructed in detail the economic demographic processes of "one people and one period," that is, the Western world, particularly from the eighteenth century onward,[1] we are only beginning to understand the contrasting processes of the non-Western world. We have reconstructed indices of demographic behavior for a small number of countries, but have yet to differentiate these rates by region, community, class, gender, and ethnicity. Similarly, although we know much about worldwide secular changes in demographic behavior during the past two centuries, with the exception of econometric studies of aggregate fluctuations, we know little about short-term oscillations, especially their differential impact along these dimensions.

Our study fills this gap. It is an international comparison of short-term mortality responses at the microlevel in past times, the first in a collective series by the Eurasia Project in Population and Family History, designed to improve our understanding of the individual and family demographic responses to social and economic pressure. Its hallmarks are geographic breadth, temporal depth, and detailed longitudinal data. It examines not just one people, but a variety of micro-populations in West Europe and East Asia; not just one period, but a period of 80 to 150 years, largely from the nineteenth century; not just one community but one hundred communities with 2.5 million longitudinally linked individual-level records; and not just mortality, the subject of this book, but in later volumes of this series, the entire range of demographic behavior, including reproduction, nuptiality, and migration. It is the collective product not just of this trio of authors, but of over a dozen demographers, economists, historians, sociologists, and statisticians from five different countries who have worked collaboratively on this book for ten years beginning in 1994.[2]

Our comparative analyses of historical demographic processes in southern Sweden, eastern Belgium, northern Italy, northeastern Japan, and northeastern China yield insight into the universality of Malthusian principles of human behavior and illuminate similarities and differences in the socioeconomic and demographic history of populations from opposite ends of the Eurasia. We substantiate Malthus's original observation that at the macrolevel, there were two distinct demographic systems—one more characteristic of the East and the other more characteristic of the West—and confirm his assumption that patterns of behavior at the microlevel illuminate social organization and family choices (Goody 1996; Lee and Wang 1999b). At the same time, we refute or qualify many of the specific assumptions and claims that Malthus and neo-Malthusians have made about the behavior of the positive check (Hajnal 1965, 1982; Laslett 1983; Macfarlane 1978, 1987;

Schofield 1989; Wrigley et al. 1997). Contrary to the Malthusian claim that the positive check was more important in the East than in the West, we demonstrate that mortality responses at least to short-term economic pressure were just as great, indeed often greater, in the West as in the East. Contrary to the neo-Malthusian characterization of mortality as a function of ecology and human biology, we demonstrate the importance of human agency not just in the East, but in the West as well. In particular, we show that social and political organization were key determinants of mortality levels and responses as the family, the community, and the state controlled most resource allocation, especially in times of stress. In so doing, we reassert the relevance of Malthusian social theory and at the same time demonstrate the importance of inductive empirical analyses.

Methods

Our project studies how changing economic conditions—food prices, and wages—and different socioeconomic contexts—household, kin, and class composition—affect individual demographic outcomes. By comparing the patterns of demographic responses, we can understand better the socially and culturally conditioned decisions that families and individuals make as they struggle to cope with changing conditions. We begin our comparison with examinations of death because death is less susceptible to cultural construction and data distortion. In later phases, we move on to more complex events: birth, marriage, and migration.[3] We demonstrate in this book that such economic-demographic models enable us to compare individuals, households, kin groups, and communities from widely differing centuries, countries, cultures, and even continents.

Our analysis of population responses to exogenous stress depends on recent advances in methods for the analysis of longitudinal individual-level data (Aalen 1978; Cox 1972; Hosmer and Lemeshow 1999; Kalbfleich and Prentice 1980; Trussell and Guinnane 1993). We have used these methods to construct a number of detailed, dynamic models of demographic behavior that situate each individual within multiple overlapping contexts at different levels of aggregation and in different kinds of settings.[4] We study historical change at the individual, household, kin group, and community levels and explore their relationships to each other and to the economy. By considering the demographic effects of changing economic and social conditions, we measure dynamic processes, not static relationships.[5] Moreover, by focusing on the demographic response to short-term economic stress rather than long-term secular change, we study truly comparable situations. We apply the same model to similarly formatted data from widely different societies. To interpret our results, we then develop a new analytic framework for such well-known sociological concepts as the family, as well as new analytic approaches for such important economic measures as living standards.

This approach distinguishes our study from traditional population history. Whereas population historians emphasize the computation, collection, and assessment of aggregate statistics, we construct and analyze large longitudinal databases of household and individual records. Whereas population historians focus on narrative interpretations of aggregate trends and patterns, we seek insight into the social and economic behavior of individuals and families. Specifically, we measure and identify which patterns of individual demographic behavior are different and which are inherently similar, in spite of the vast differences in space between these populations. We accordingly move beyond writing the demographic histories of specific communities to seek insight into the broad interconnections of society, economy, and population.

We also move beyond traditional economic history, which measures well-being in terms of production, consumption, and real wages and more recently in terms of demography, literacy, and other outcomes. These measures are not only aggregate; they are static, as they refer to specific time periods. Our concept of well-being, in contrast, is dynamic. We focus on how individuals respond to short-term variations in the community and the domestic environment, especially food prices and real wages. The ability to overcome such short-term stress reveals information about what Amartya Sen (1987) has called human "functionings" and "capabilities," that is, about human living standards. Our approach makes full use of individual demographic data as well as household and community socioeconomic data to study well-being by sex, age, socioeconomic status, household structure, and position within the household. We link demographic and economic information, and relate our findings not only to the Malthusian concern over demographic processes and living standards, but also to current economic debates over differences in living standards in the East and the West.

Our focus on comparison of communities, not countries, represents a new approach in social science history. While we generalize about certain aspects of human behavior, we do so within the cultural, economic, and historical contexts of specific communities, not at the national level. In contrast with the dominant thrust in academic research, we ignore contemporary nation-state boundaries and standard historical chronologies (Duara 1995). Thus, while our results illuminate the behavior of specific Belgian, Chinese, Italian, Japanese, and Swedish populations identified in map 1.1 from the early eighteenth to the early twentieth century, we draw from them implications for the demography not of specific countries, but of social and economic systems. This strategy of comparing individual contexts rather than countries avoids the problem of representativeness normally inherent in community studies. Moreover, by selecting communities that are roughly similar in terms of material well-being, we compare community contexts that are roughly comparable. In each region, we select rural communities that are not well-off and are not atypical from their surrounding locations. Whereas some historians compare wealthy areas, we compare ordinary ones, as the poverty of preindustrial communities is more comparable than their wealth (Pomeranz 2000). This is especially true for rural communities, which have fewer institutional safety nets and fewer reserves than cities, and especially true for the biometric implications of low living standards.

In addition, while the previous philosophy of much social science has often been reductionist, striving to reduce the diversity of human experience to simple measures and explanations, our approach is holistic and attempts to embrace the diversity of living conditions and living standards. In contrast to previous calculations that collapse periods of decades and sometimes even centuries of human behavior into single indices, we consider the full range of year-to-year experience. In contrast to previous analyses that condense the experience of entire countries into means and other measures, we account for the diversity of contexts within each population. In contrast to previous demographic models that recognize aggregate behavioral differences only by sex and age, we differentiate behavior at the individual level by household structure and composition, by such socioeconomic indicators as occupation, state appointment, and landholding, as well as by such economic indicators as grain prices and real wages. We thus attempt to capture the full range of variation in individual experience to explain different responses to changing economic conditions.[6]

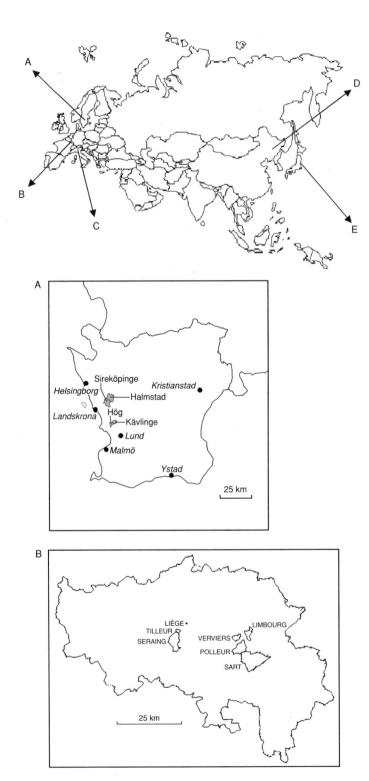

Map 1.1
Eurasian Population and Family History Communities

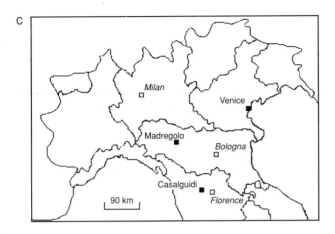

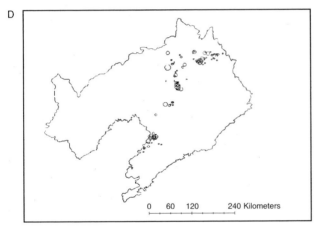

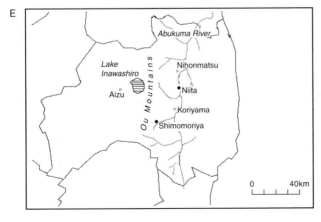

Map 1.1
(continued)

Our analyses, as a result, do not seek to explain demographic outcomes in terms of single causes but rather allow for *webs of causation* in which they are subject to multiple overlapping and, in many cases, interacting influences (McMahon, Pugh, and Ipsen 1960). We distinguish in our analyses among three categories of influences on mortality, illustrated in figure 1.1: individual, household, and relationship. In the *individual model*, we examine the effects of age, gender, marital status, and socioeconomic status. For the *household model*, we also consider effects of household labor capacity and dependency ratio. For the *relationship model*, we examine the role of the presence or absence of specific kin.[7] Thus, for example, we consider the effects of parental presence on children, the effects of presence of parents, spouse, and children for adults, and the presence of adult children for the elderly. For each of the three categories—individual, household, and relationship—we estimate two submodels, the first of which considers influences on *levels* of mortality and the second of which measures influences on *the responsiveness* of mortality to short-term stress.[8]

Analysis of the results of these multiple calculations requires the patience and ability to recognize broad patterns as well as specific findings—the ability, in other words, to recognize forests as well as trees. It is an unfortunate fact of such an approach that the more complete the explanatory model, the less transparent are the substantive implications of the results. Thus, instead of simple indices or familiar cross-tabulations, we present coefficients from identical event-history models that test hypotheses about the effects of wealth, family formation, and intrafamily transfers on the demographic response to short-term economic stress within different economic and cultural contexts. In interpreting coefficients, we focus on comparison not so much of magnitudes but of directions of effects. That is, we emphasize less the relative strengths of specific relationships and more the patterns of responses.

Our approach means that we avoid the teleological trap of computing indices to identify whose measures are bigger, an artificial and invariably political comparison. Instead, we compare patterns of behavior to identify differences and similarities in mortality responses to exogenous pressure and, by extension, compare the demographic vulnerabilities, social choices, and allocation decisions of different communities. As a result, we can observe through the patterns of revealed relationships striking differences in socioeconomic configurations as well as hitherto unidentified universalities in human response to pressure. This is true regardless of the tremendous differences in our communities, located as they are at opposite ends of Eurasia.

Our approach also resolves a major limitation of historical models of change over time. Although it is well established that empirical validation of such models requires longitudinal panel data, such information is typically available for only a few contemporary populations, mainly in developed countries and usually with a time depth of at most half a century, beginning in the mid- to late twentieth century.[9] As a result, most historical studies of earlier periods use cross-sectional data, which are insufficient to document a consistent process of historical change and rely on narratives derived from incomplete, qualitative, and quantitatively crude data, sacrificing precision as well as the modern standards of scientific proof (Mahoney 1999).[10] We avoid such problems by the creation of large, long, longitudinal individual-level data for a variety of communities that have been standardized to allow for valid comparisons. These data, which generally include the entire community, provide the geographic breadth, temporal depth, and level of detail to allow us to generalize with confidence about rural life under pressure in western Europe and East Asia and about the population responses of farm communities in the eighteenth and nineteenth centuries to changing economic conditions.

Data

The data requirements for such an analysis are even more severe than those envisaged by Malthus to produce his "satisfactory history." We need longitudinal individual-level data for large communities over long sweeps of time that include information on occupation, household structure and composition, and individual or household status and that have parallel time series information on either grain prices or farm wages. To allow for event-history analysis, such data must include reliable records of the timing of demographic events and identify at each point in time those individuals who are in the community and those who are at risk of experiencing such events.

The data traditionally relied on by historical demographers are inadequate for these purposes. Fifty years ago, demographers began to develop methods to reconstruct individual and family demographic histories from church records. While these yield counts of vital events and in some cases can be used to produce estimates of vital rates (Fleury and Henry 1985), they neither provide detail on the

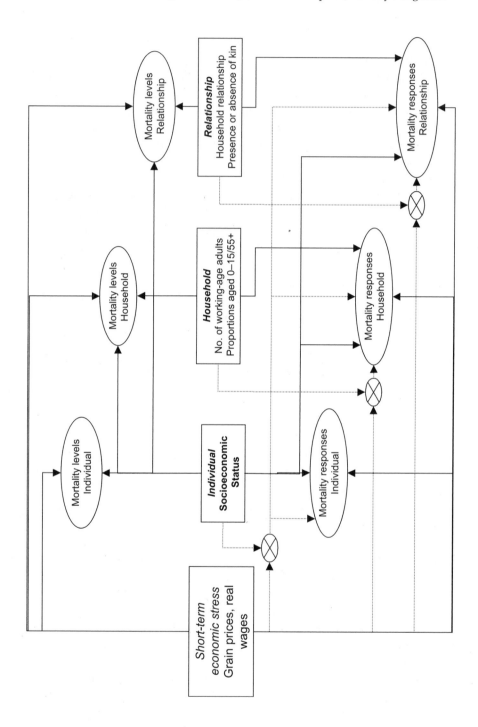

Figure 1.1 Eurasia models of the determinants of mortality levels and responses. *Note:* In each community, these six models were estimated separately for each of eight combinations of gender and age group (0–1, 2–14, 15–54, 55–74).

An Explanation of Our Analytical Method. To examine the influence of socioeconomic status, household composition, and household context on mortality risks and their sensitivity to economic stress, we apply event-history methods. Chapter 2 and the appendix discuss these methods in more detail. In this approach, a mathematical transformation of the risk of dying is a *dependent variable* that is specified to be a function of *explanatory variables* that are part of a model.* The relationship between the transformed risk and the explanatory variables is assumed to be linear, in the sense that the transformed risk can be expressed as the sum of the products of explanatory variables and associated coefficients.

To construct the variables used to estimate the coefficients for each model, we make use of data on individuals, households, and communities. From these data, we construct numeric measurements of the individual and household characteristics to use as explanatory variables. In some cases, these are direct measures, for example, counts of the numbers of adults used in the household model. In situations where the underlying variable is categorical or qualitative, these numeric variables indicate whether a particular condition is true. Thus, in the relationship model, the variable for presence of father takes on one value if he is present and another if he is not.

Our analysis largely consists of the estimation of these coefficients from the data and their substantive interpretation. Each coefficient represents the effect on the transformed risk of dying of a change in the associated explanatory variable, assuming that the other variables in the model are held constant, that is, left unchanged. When the explanatory variable is a quantity, the coefficient reflects the effects of a one-unit change. When the explanatory variable is categorical or qualitative, the coefficient reflects the difference in the transformed risk of dying according to whether the condition is true or false.

We use statistical packages to estimate the coefficients for the variables. The procedures used by these packages are complex. Here, we provide only some basics for the layperson. Essentially, the estimation identifies the coefficients that maximize the likelihood of the observed outcomes. The program makes an initial guess as to the values of the coefficients and evaluates how well this accounts for the observed outcomes. It then makes adjustments to the coefficients and reevaluates. Iteration continues until it is impossible to find a set of coefficients that do a better job of predicting the observed outcomes from the available data. Measures of statistical significance calculated for each coefficient assess the possibility that the calculated relationship may be accounted for by chance, as opposed to a true relationship.

In our presentation of results, we convert estimated coefficients into proportional changes in the risk of dying associated with changes in the explanatory variables. Typically we present the percentage increase or decrease in the chances of dying or proportional changes in the risk of dying associated with a change in an explanatory variable, assuming that the other variables in the model were unchanged. For our measures of economic stress, whether food prices or real wages, the risk ratios reflect the effects on mortality of proportional changes in the underlying variable, not absolute changes.**

To measure differences in the mortality response to economic stress according to individual or household characteristics, we make use of interactions. The results that we present measure the change in the sensitivity of mortality to price associated with a change in individual or household characteristics, for example if a father is present or not. Explanatory variables are sometimes referred to as *right-hand side* or *independent* variables. Dependent variables are also referred to as *left-hand side* variables.

*This is because the variables used in the analysis are actually logarithms of the original prices or wages. By transforming the original variables to measure the effects of proportional changes in prices, we eliminate problems associated with the incomparability across contexts of the units of measurement.

characteristics of households nor allow us to identify who is actually in the community and who is at risk. Conversely, while cross-sectional microdata from censuses and related sources yield detailed and complete reconstructions of household structure and composition (Laslett and Wall 1972), they are not longitudinal and in most cases do not record the timing of vital events.

Longitudinal population register data satisfy these requirements,[11] but are not readily available for most countries.[12] Historical demographers using such data, however, have recently begun to apply quantitative methods from sociology and economics to measure and compare the relationships between family organization and demographic behavior, controlling for economic and social circumstances (Lee and Campbell 1997). In this book, we make use of robust population register data assembled for locations in five different regions of Eurasia. Working in separate teams, we then construct databases for these specific communities from eastern Belgium, northeastern China, northern Italy, northeastern Japan, and southern Sweden; they span two continents, three centuries, and five countries and currently encompass over thirty separate populations with 0.5 million household-level observations and 2.5 million individual-level observations.[13] Acquiring, entering, and organizing these data has taken each team at least a decade, in some cases several decades. Harmonizing the data and completing the calculations and interpretations presented here of mortality and other demographic responses to exogenous pressure have taken another decade.

Design

Data construction alone has been a long, laborious, iterative process. First, each team reconstructed individual, household, and community histories from historical population registers with continuous or almost continuous recording that included details on individual demographic events, individual occupation, individual household position, individual or household socioeconomic status, household structure, and village composition. This required a painstaking process of data location, data entry, and a laborious and time-consuming process of record linkage and data cleaning. Then each team had to identify, collect, and construct parallel serial grain price or farm wage data for these localities or their immediate surrounding area. Finally, each team had to reconfigure this price and population information into similar data structures with identical and identically defined variables and categories. Since remaining differences in the organization of the data from different regions preclude pooling them and estimating a single model on all of the data with region as a covariate,[14] we worked together to develop a common model that each group of participants can estimate by themselves on their own data.[15] Only then were we ready as a group for the collective estimation, evaluation, and comparison of analytical results.

This process of consultation, comparison, and consensus has taken almost as long and has required an intensity, frequency, and diversity of participation that further distinguish our project. Since we began working together in 1994, we have met as an entire group over twenty times to understand each other's data, harmonize approaches, develop common models, adjust calculations, and discuss the implications of results.[16] In addition to these larger meetings, there have been innumerable smaller meetings, mostly of main authors, as well as of individual teams themselves.[17]

Our project requires a higher level of collaboration and cooperation than other historical comparative studies and has yielded results that are more standardized and therefore more comparable. We compute and contrast quantitative results from explicitly similar comparative models using similar primary data. Moreover, we do so for a variety of settings given the combination of the individual, household, and relationship models, with and without price interactions. We can consequently compare and contrast a variety of phenomena and processes across a number of spatial contexts with confidence. This reliance on explicit intensive, iterative, interactive, and collaborative computation of similar primary data marks a departure from the usual approach to historical comparisons, in which individual scholars rely on a more qualitative and intuitive process of synthesis and interpretation of related, though rarely identical, individual research results, often derived from dissimilar data, to compare contexts with which they are not familiar.[18] As a result, while previous comparative histories based on aggregate measures tend to emphasize similarities in quantitative measures, our use of individual measures allows us to identify differences. While previous comparative history based on qualitative findings tend to emphasize differences, we can identify underlying similarities as we transcend the boundaries of community, region, and even country.

In some sense, our efforts in social science history resemble the progression toward "big science" in the physical sciences. Just as the physical sciences require an ever decreasing scale of analysis to achieve greater luminosity, so too have demographers reduced the scale of comparison from national to regional aggregates, as in the Princeton European Fertility Project,[19] and now to individuals and from broad measures to specific calculations. Just as continued progress in the natural sciences now relies heavily, almost exclusively, on complex collaborations of large numbers of scientists and engineers with complementary but highly specialized skills and interests, so too our effort has relied on the intensive and prolonged interaction of scholars from different disciplines with knowledge of different local contexts and facility with specific methods. And just as many big science facilities have yielded both important predicted and unpredicted results, so we too in the course of our ten years of collaboration not only confirm and contradict specific hypotheses we sought to test; in the process, we also achieve unanticipated insights into comparative human behavior and their consequences under short-term stress.

Organization

We begin with mortality, the positive check, and the first of the models proposed by Malthus. In contrast with most other studies of mortality in historical populations, we examine and compare differences in level not only by age and gender, but also by socioeconomic status, as well as by household structure and composition. Because differences in mortality levels reflect socially determined differences in exposure and resistance to disease, they illuminate the economic and social organization of preindustrial communities and families, especially the assignment of responsibilities and the allocation of resources. From the results, we can assess whether socioeconomic status translated into improved survival chances in past times as it does today (Kitagawa and Hauser 1973), and locate the individuals in each society that decisions at the state, community, or family level made vulnerable.

We engage Malthus directly with an examination of differences in the mortality response to short-term economic stress. In spite of the tremendous attention devoted by Malthus and subsequent researchers to what has become known as the "Malthusian crisis"—the impact of scarcity on mortality—we still know relatively little about the impact of changing economic conditions on different segments of the population in the short term. Population and social historians have focused on the causes and consequences of exceptional or great mortality crises, and historical demographers have centered their attention on famine demography and the consequences of famine mortality for long-term population growth (Dyson and Ó Gráda 2002; Menken and Campbell 1992; Watkins and Menken 1985). Economic historians who have measured the response of death rates to short-term variations in prices and wages mostly have done so at the level of the country or region, not within communities or households (Galloway 1988, 1993; R. Lee 1981). As a result, the story of specific mortality crises is now well known, and it is clear that mortality responded systematically to smaller short-term variations in prices and wages. We are, however, less familiar with the everyday choices made within each society that determined who would live or die. While Malthus thought that the lower classes and children were especially vulnerable, we show that some societies discriminated more by gender than class or age, and that in other societies, the aged, working-age males, and even the elite were vulnerable.

We organize the book into three parts. In part one, we use the results of our comparative analysis to illuminate a new comparative geography of human organization and response to economic pressure. We accomplish this in two two-chapter sets. Chapter 2 introduces the current debate over comparative East-West differences in living standards and discusses the advantages of our microapproach over the standard macromeasures, while chapter 3 uses our comparative results to evaluate both the Malthusian claim that mortality levels and responsiveness to economic conditions were greater in the East than the West and the Malthusian understanding that the selectivity of mortality was greater in the West than in the East. Chapter 4 then contrasts the family and community organization of our populations along this East-West divide and shows that these differences affected potential responses to bad times, while chapter 5 uses these comparative results to evaluate recent social theory or explanations of the East-West divide especially as it relates to mortality. We confirm Malthus's observation that mortality patterns differed considerably between East and West, but also show that his and most subsequent social theoretical understanding of the nature and sources of such differences have been incorrect (Das Gupta 1997, 1998; Davis 1955; Hajnal 1982; Macfarlane 1997; Schofield 1989; Skinner 1997; Wrigley and Schofield 1981). Instead, we conclude that mortality responses reflect different traditions of social justice and different patterns of community resources and recourses in times of need.

In part two, we turn from the general to the specific, and present case studies of mortality, secular change, and social organization in our five regions. In chapters 6 through 10, we present five individual local histories from Scania in southern Sweden; Liège and the Ardennes in eastern Belgium; Emilia, Toscana, and Venetia in northern Italy; Ou in northeastern Japan; and Liaodong in northeastern China. Although each of these histories is also a collective product, they differ from the other chapters of the book in that the history they tell is oriented to the specific conditions of their localities rather than to their comparative and relative interest. Almost all the sites are highly rural, but their circumstances and significance vary considerably. As a result, the models developed in these chapters are more detailed and tailored for local circumstances than the common models in parts one and three. Although the studies of the five regions all cover much of the nineteenth century, their specific histories differ considerably. At one end of the spectrum, eastern Belgium was already well embarked on the industrial revolution by the middle of the nineteenth century. At the other end, northeast China and Japan were becoming increasingly commercialized, but they would not become industrialized until later. Northern Italy and southern Sweden lay in between.

In part three, we summarize the contributions our studies make to the comparative understanding of demographic behavior. These studies, as in part one, use the results from the common models to address current issues and debates in social demography. Chapter 11 on gender relies on our results to assess explanations that have been advanced for patterns of sex differences observed in historical and contemporary populations. Chapter 12 on infant and child mortality investigates the implications of our findings for our understanding of the role of social, ecological, and economic and other distal determinants (Mosley and Chen 1984) at different stages in the first years of life. Finally, chapter 13, on old age, examines our results in the light of theoretical accounts of intergenerational relations and care for the aged in traditional societies. While all three chapters make use of results from the standard Eurasia comparative models, chapter 12 extends the analysis with additional calculations for these populations as well as others, and demonstrates that social organization could be as important as human biology in determining the fatality of even the "fatal years" of infant and childhood.

Throughout the book, we contrast our findings with the expectations and assumptions of Malthus and later social scientists. As we shall see, the results of this project challenge our current theoretical understanding of the interrelationships among economic conditions, social organization, and demographic behavior in the past. In particular, patterns of sensitivity to short-term economic stress appear to have differed fundamentally between East and West. In the East, *power*, particularly gender, conditioned the mortality response to changing economic conditions. In the West, socioeconomic status, especially *property*, mattered more.

Overall, we conclude that human agency was at least as important as human biology in determining the patterns of mortality responses to short-term stress. There was no single pattern of mortality differentials by age, sex, socioeconomic status, or even household context that characterized all or even most of our sites but rather a diversity of patterns. Similarly, there was no single pattern of responses to short-term stress apparent for all or even most of our sites, but again a diversity of response patterns. In both cases, these patterns were too complex and diverse to be accounted for by underlying commonalities of biology and physiology; rather, they had to reflect choices made by individuals, households, communities, and states about the allocation of resources and the assignment of work roles that affect the risk of dying.

This study accordingly marks a radical departure from earlier historical studies of mortality that have treated it as exogenous to the individual and household. Such studies, instead of using individual-level data, mostly rely on aggregate measures of mortality, and consequently explain mortality patterns and trends also in terms of such aggregates as the economy or the society on the one hand, and biology, the characteristics of pathogens, or climate, on the other.[20] While such work recognized the endogeneity of mortality, it did so only at the macrolevel, in terms of adjustments by society and the economy. Our approach, which differentiates not only by age and sex but also by socioeconomic status, household composition, and household relationship, more closely resembles studies of contemporary mortality trends and patterns that make use of individual-level data. Rather than claiming single underlying causes for the patterns we observe, we acknowledge the diversity of influences on mortality risks, identify the multiple overlapping and interacting factors that affect mortality, and weigh their relative importance.

Our analysis reveals that mortality patterns were complex, reflective of decisions made by individuals, households, communities, and states. Although every society had certain groups who were a priori more vulnerable—abandoned and orphaned children, the widowed, the disabled, the poor, the childless elderly, and the sick—we find that the effects of stress on these groups varied from one context to the next. In the European populations, the people who responded to stress were generally the landless, whose mortality rose, while the mortality of the landed was often unresponsive and in some cases declined. In the Asian populations, by contrast, the people who responded to stress were very young females and privileged males, both of whose mortality rose. The processes behind these mortality responses, moreover, were different. In the European populations, landlords were buffered and even benefited from their stored wealth, while the landless were not. In the Asian populations, baby girls and female children were either killed directly through infanticide or indirectly through neglect. Wealthy males died in larger numbers because of the erosion of their privileges—benefits that had previously insulated them from economic conditions. In either case, the vulnerable and the processes of vulnerability varied between the East, where ageism and sexism prevailed, and the West, where class was at least as important. There was no universal concept of social justice, no similar system of entitlements, and no common pattern of mortality response to changing conditions.

Life under Pressure belongs to a social scientific historical tradition that differs from traditional history (Kousser 1980). Whereas traditional history emphasizes a narrative approach in which facts are selected and arranged to support a specific interpretation, social scientific history emphasizes rigorous deduction or cautious induction, along with the consideration of all available evidence. Whereas traditional history uses quantification largely to measure specific phenomena, quantification in social scientific history is at the heart of the deductive or inductive processes. As a result, whereas traditional history relies on assertion and illustration to interpret relationships, social scientific history requires clearly specified models and systematic tests of hypotheses not only to provide support for one interpretation but also to rule out others.

Life under Pressure, in other words, also belongs to a scientific tradition with a different methodology from contemporary social science, especially historical social theory. This is especially true in terms of our use of evidence (Mahoney 1999). Whereas much historical sociological theory consists of stylized deduction from selected facts, we derive our conclusions from a process of induction based on a multiplicity of empirical facts. Whereas many historical theorists rely on narrative and plausibility to validate their conclusions, we require a consistent pattern of behavior from rigorously specified models. Whereas historical theorists achieve parsimony by ignoring complexity, we embrace it and seek parsimonious explanations for diverse outcomes. Using our holistic approach, we seek to identify the simplicity that underlies the multiplicity of our results rather than the simple tautology inherent in a reductionist approach.

Our results underline both the importance of local context and the weakness of historical social theory. In spite of the current emphasis in the social sciences on the importance of class, gender, family systems, political institutions, or social relations as sources of inequality and determinants of well-being, few of the associated predictions about differences in mortality levels or responses to stress survive empirical scrutiny. The claims made by Malthus and his successors that the family systems characteristic of the East led to overpopulation, higher levels of mortality, and greater sensitivity to economic stress are just one example of the overall poverty of even very longstanding social scientific explanations. Though social theory and empirical results parted company some time ago, our work indicates that a rapprochement is in order.

This book is the first step in an attempt to reexamine and rebuild comparative social theory. We present findings from a set of models for five different regions over a century to a century and a half of time and show how their results validate some explanations and invalidate others. While these results may not be fully sufficient for us to specify simple laws that account for all of the complex patterns of mortality and mortality responses to short-term stress, they reveal the shortcomings of existing theory and identify a new set of empirical phenomena. They represent the first systematic results of ten years of collaboration of many authors and researchers and much collective effort.

Notes

We thank George Alter, Göran Broström, Martin Dribe, Morgan Kousser, Andrew Lee, Ron Lee, and Wang Feng for their comments on previous drafts of this chapter.

1. This is especially true for northwestern Europe, particularly England and France. See Wrigley and Schofield (1981) and Wrigley et al. (1997), as well as Flinn (1981) and Livi Bacci (1999).

2. We identify different authorship for each specific chapter. These attributions cannot, however, capture the full range of collaborative contributions from project members, and we thank any unnamed members.

3. Birth, for example, is defined quite differently in some societies, with important consequences for reproductive culture. Alter, Tsuya, and Wang, which is currently in preparation, analyzes these consequences and their broader implications in great detail. See too our various symposia volumes: Allen, Bengtsson, and Dribe (forthcoming), Bengtsson and Saito (2000a), Derosas and Oris (2002), J. Lee, Guo, and Ding (2000), and Van Poppel, Oris, and Lee (forthcoming).

4. Our specific approach, which combines time series and event-history analysis, provides for estimation of how time-varying covariates at community level affect individuals. See Bengtsson (1989, 1993b) for the first examples of an application of these techniques to historical demographic data.

5. The word *dynamic* is used to express the influence of one variable on another over time—for example, how bad harvests influence births and deaths during the following years. Generally, dynamic analysis in historical demography has been applied to aggregated data of births, marriages, and deaths to analyze short-term effects of economic variations or long-term relationships between population and living standards. This has been done with a variety of models and methods. See Bengtsson et al. (1998) for an overview. Historical studies at the microlevel are usually static, often because they have to collapse long time periods in order to produce enough events to support statistical analysis.

6. While some details such as the institutional economic arrangements of extraction and relief are also highly relevant, we could not include them in our quantitative calculations of individual-level response as these institutions vary only between communities, not individuals. We therefore compare them systematically but qualitatively in separate chapters.

7. The individual model is nested within both the household and relationship models. While it would also have been preferable for the household models to be nested within the relationship model, in practice it proved impossible, because in some of the data sets, the household and relationship variables were too highly correlated.

8. The former summarizes the main effects of relevant variables and prices or wages, while the latter includes interactions between the two. See the book appendix for a detailed discussion of the models.

9. Such panel studies are largely limited to contemporary America beginning from the 1960s. A well-known example is the Panel Study of Income Dynamics, which began in 1968 (Hill 1992).

10. Cross-sectional data have tremendous problems of exogeneity as they cannot explain the prior processes that produce the cross section. This is why at least one historian has gone so far as to claim that "history has no theory because there are no satisfactory models for theorizing over time, over flux and change.... Theory building in social sciences and humanities is essentially synchronic" (Duara 1998, 106). The problem has been at least as much with the data as with the limitations of theory and methods of analysis.

11. By *population registers*, we mean census-type register data with short time intervals that record demographic events or can be combined with such records as church books of births and deaths to produce continuous information about the entire population living in the communities we analyze.

12. In addition to the five regions included in the current iteration of the Eurasian Project, similar data are also available for the Netherlands and the Republic of China, which

have a separate, ongoing collaborative comparative project of their own and exist in a variety of Eastern European countries as well.

13. These numbers represent the currently available data. Many of the chapters in this book, however, compare only the twenty of these populations that were available earlier, which account for 1.5 million individual level observations. See table A.2 in the book appendix for details on numbers and precise time periods.

14. In a later comparative project of Tokugawa and Qing social demography, we hope to pool these data and estimate directly village and regional coefficients.

15. See the book appendix for an introduction to the data for the various regions. For the northeast Chinese and Japanese data, discrete-time event history methods were most appropriate, but for the eastern Belgian and southern Swedish data, continuous-time methods were most appropriate. The Italian data were compatible with both.

16. This has included two initial organizational meetings at Kyoto and Lund (1994); eight conferences in Arild, Beijing, Bloomington, the Hague, Kyoto, Liège, Osaka, and Venice (1997, 1998, 1999, 2000, and 2001); seven panel presentations and organizational meetings at annual meetings of the Population Association of America (1998, 1999, 2000) and the Social Science History Association (1998, 1999, 2000, 2001); and three panel presentations and organizational meetings at the quadrennial meetings of the International Economic History Congress (1997), the International Congress of Historical Sciences (2000), and the International Union for the Scientific Study of Population (2001); as well as sundry smaller international meetings, of which the most important, held in Venice (1996), produced our initial template model for mortality analysis.

17. In between these face-to-face meetings, we interact regularly by e-mail, phone calls, faxes, and express mail and share documents and results over the Web. We communicate frequently because we rely heavily on consultation and consensus to develop the models used in this book. Thus, while lead authors set the intellectual agenda for a specific volume or chapter and specify the calculations for each team to carry out, the development of the comparative models has been iterative. It begins with proposals for models from lead authors, often distributed electronically. At meetings, participants evaluate the models in the light of their knowledge of their own data. Some covariates are discarded because the relevant data are not available for all regions or else their specifications are adjusted. Some covariates are added based on suggestions from participants who have carried out experiments with their own data. After the meeting, participants return home and estimate the models. At the next meeting, they present and compare results, leading to further discussion and refinement. In some cases, several iterations are necessary before the lead authors can define the final comparative model. While time-consuming, this process has resulted in an approach that fully takes into account the diversity of the contexts and their data.

18. Kolchin (1987) is a good example of this sort of individual comparative history, while Cooper, Holt, and Scott (2000) exemplifies the collaborative comparative history.

19. A comparable previous effort would be the Princeton Fertility Project, formally known as the European Fertility Project. This was a collaborative, comparative effort undertaken by European and American scholars to describe and explain the European fertility transition of the late nineteenth century by analysis of aggregated demographic and socioeconomic data for 1,229 provinces and districts in Europe at various points in time from the late eighteenth century to the middle of the twentieth century. The results challenged widespread assumptions about the role of economic development and other

factors in the causes of transition. Unexpectedly, results also showed that fertility fell at the same time for areas with a common language in different countries and at different times for areas with different languages in the same country, suggesting an important role for the diffusion of new attitudes and techniques among speakers of the same language. The comparative conclusions are summarized in Coale and Watkins (1986), and seven other monographs published between 1971 and 1984 describe the results for specific countries.

20. For example, the authors in Schofield, Reher, and Bideau (1991) focus largely on the potential contribution of changes in aggregate features of economies and societies to the European decline in mortality. See chapter 2 of this book for a detailed review of historical studies of the association between economic conditions and mortality.

I

Comparative Geographies

2   Living Standards and Economic Stress

Tommy Bengtsson

Standard of living is a central concept in studies of the relationship between population and the economy, past and present. It was a main concept in the UN discussions about the large differences in social conditions between its member countries during the 1950s, as well as in the scientific analyses that followed. It is a key point of discussion in the present debate about how far back in time we can trace these differences. The chief question is whether the divergence in living standards existed already before the industrial revolution or was a result thereof, a topic strongly related to this book, as is evident from chapter 1.

Living standard has an impact on most demographic behavior, including marriage, household formation, and childbearing. Migration is also determined by living standards, since the destination is often chosen after comparing present and future differences in standard of living if staying or leaving. Living standards not only constrain everyone, but influence the poor more directly. Malnutrition, whether a result of low nutritional intake or disease, may affect the outcome of lethal diseases and fecundity. Several other important factors, like spread of and exposure to disease, hygiene, sanitation, and medical care, are similarly influenced by economic factors. Living standards are therefore likely to have a strong impact on demographic behavior, particularly in the past, when a considerable part of the population lived close to the margins.

While the analysis of living standards in studies of demographic behavior is essential, the actual performance of such analysis is difficult, especially when working with historical conditions due to problems with data. Production and consumption data are scarce for preindustrial settings, as are income data, particularly at the household level. Contemporary standard-of-living measures are therefore difficult to use in historical studies. In this book, we propose a new, dynamic concept designed for longitudinal microstudies and comparative purposes. We argue that the demographic responses of individuals and households to short-term economic stress depended on their access to resources. Effects of short-term economic stress on migration, nuptiality, fertility, and mortality can therefore be used as an indirect measure of individual living standards. We analyze the standard of living for men and women of various ages, socioeconomic groups, and household settings through their ability to overcome short-term economic stress.

This chapter is divided into six sections followed by a brief summary. We begin with the debate about differences in historical living standards between East and West, continue with a brief examination of different concepts of standard of living, and introduce our alternative concept: the ability to overcome short-term economic stress. The empirical motivation for the new concept, which arises from the studies of demographic response to short-term economic stress at the macrolevel, is reviewed in the next section. We then turn to the link between short-term economic stress and mortality, and ask whether malnutrition or increased exposure was the determinant of mortality during bad years. In the final two sections, we discuss how different social groups and individuals, at different stages in both their own and the family's life cycle, are likely to be affected by short-term economic stress.

The Divergence in Standard of Living between East and West

Adam Smith (1776), Thomas Malthus (1803), and Karl Marx (1853) all claimed that the differences between East and West date back to long before industrialization. Landes (1998) draws the same conclusion in his recent book on world economic history, *The Wealth and Poverty of Nations*. According to Landes, the origins of the Western economic advantage stem from a set of cultural, political, and economic changes initiated by the natural and political philosophy of the Greeks, augmented by technical improvements in the Middle Ages, and reinforced by borrowings from Asia. Thus, prior to the industrial revolution, Western Europe had emerged as a civilization uniquely qualified to conquer science, technology, and the rest of the world (Macfarlane 1978, 1987; Macfarlane and Martin 2002). Technological innovations in the development of guns, sails (Cipolla 1965a), and the chronometer, which aided navigation (Landes 1983), contributed to the European advantage. As a result, the gross domestic product (GDP) per capita difference was already tremendous at the dawn of the industrial revolution (Maddison 2001, 42). This conclusion has, as we soon shall see, been challenged by a number of today's scholars studying Asia.[1]

The classical economists all believed that consumption in Asia was less favorable than in Europe for the majority of the people. Malthus argued that almost all that other kingdoms could afford was also present in China. In addition, there were "an infinite number of things which are to be found nowhere else" (Malthus 1826/1986, 126). In the East, the soil and the climate were advantageous for farming, and agriculture was promoted by the state from early on. Consequently, agriculture was very well developed, and no arable land lay fallow. The low standards of living for the great majority of the Chinese population derived not from a neglect of agriculture but from population pressure generated by extraordinary encouragement of marriage and high fertility. Conditions in Japan were much the same, except that the Japanese were "much more warlike, seditious, dissolute, and ambitious" (Malthus 1826/1986, 138).[2] Evidently, Malthus had the same view of overpopulated China as Smith (Smith 1776/1970, 174–175). Marx added to this portrayal with his characterization of the Asiatic mode of production as static and one in which despots ruled a servile peasantry (Marx 1853).[3]

Smith and Malthus based their conclusions on two sorts of evidence. One was direct evidence in the form of reports from Jesuit priests and other Westerners visiting the East. The other was indirect evidence, such as the cheap cotton products from India entering into the European market. Smith, in particular, argued that the cotton products from India were cheap because wages were low compared to Europe. Food prices were also low compared to Europe, but not as low as wages. Thus, real wages were lower in India than in Europe according to Smith.

Prasannan Parthasarathi (1998, forthcoming) challenges Smith's conclusion. Parthasarathi compares wages and grain prices for spinners and weavers in southern India and Bengal with English ones and finds that the standard of living was at least as high for the Indian workers as their English counterparts. Wages in India were lower, but food prices were even lower due to higher productivity. Robert Allen (forthcoming), using scattered evidence on wages for Japan, India, and the Yangzi, concludes that in the middle of the eighteenth century, Asian standards of living were as high as those in Italy, Germany, and France. Thus, Allen too rejects the traditional view of the great standard of living gap between Europe and Asia, though he does not find any place in Asia with living standards as high as in the most successful parts of Europe.

China was rich but "stationary" according to Smith, because of lack of broad markets and insecure property rights. Li Bozhong (forthcoming) challenges Smith's description of China as stationary. In detailed analysis, based on agricultural handbooks, he shows that labor productivity rose by 30 to 40 percent in the Yangzi Delta during the seventeenth and eighteenth centuries. Kenneth Pomeranz (2000) also disagrees with Smith and argues that markets and households allocated resources as efficiently as in the West. Pomeranz argues that as late as 1800, Chinese living standards compared quite well with those in Europe. In fact, China's richest regions, Yangzi and Lingnan, compared well even with England and Holland. The conclusion is based on comparisons of caloric intake and composition of diets, spending on other consumables than food, such as furnishings, estimations of yields, and so forth. The proportion of income spent on food as well as the income distribution was also similar in the Yangzi Delta and England. Furthermore, Pomeranz argues, the level of consumption was quite stable across China (Pomeranz forthcoming).

Reevaluations of the standard of living in Japan in the mid-nineteenth century also argue that the gap with the West has been overstated (Kuznets 1971, tables 1–2). Based on farm accounts of one wealthy farmer in an "advanced" region, Osamu Saito (1978) shows that the real wage rate for agricultural day labor rose at 2.6 percent annually from 1730 to the 1760s. After the eighteenth century, however, especially after the 1820s, the agrarian economy entered a different phase, in which wages lagged behind the price increase. While producers might have benefited from this price increase, laborers did not. Susan Hanley (1997) draws similar conclusions about Japanese consumption as Pomeranz does for China, using data on diets, furniture, and household goods. The picture of low standards of living and a stationary economy is on its way toward revision for Japan as well.

Turning to demographic indicators of well-being, recent work by James Z. Lee and Wang Feng (1999b) and William Lavely and Bin Wong (1998) has challenged the classical view of overpopulation in East Asia, especially Malthus's understanding of the Chinese population system recently reiterated by Tony Wrigley and Roger Schofield (1981). Lee and Wang argue that Malthus's characterization of the Chinese population system was fundamentally incorrect. Based on a variety of recent historical studies using individual-level data, they demonstrate that deliberate infanticide was a more important check on population size than famines and other catastrophes. Early marriages, meanwhile, did not lead to high birthrates. The reason was that imbalances in the marriage market, created by female infanticide, meant that many men would never marry. In addition, remarriage among widows was not allowed. Furthermore, they show that the fertility of married couples was lower than in Europe because intervals between marriage and first birth were long by intention, as were subsequent birth intervals. Although family institutions were entirely different in China compared to Western Europe, the outcome in terms of life expectancy and population growth was about the same.

Thus, in the new view, the differences in standard of living between East and West do not stem from differences prior to the industrial revolution but are a result of it. Economic conditions in China, Japan, and India were much the same as in Western Europe prior to the industrial revolution; so were population growth and, consequently, the standard of living.[4] Evidently, a number of contemporary specialists on Asian history, demographers and economic historians, have an understanding of well-being in Asia that is very different from the conventional wisdom expressed by the classical economists and later by Landes and Maddison. The question is how they can arrive at such different views about the historical differences between East and West. One answer is that scholars focus on different aspects of standard of living; another is that better data have become available through laborious work.[5]

Thus, the concept of standard of living has several dimensions that need to be discussed further before being used for comparisons between countries or over time. Equally important is that we take into account the geographic areas and the social groups we are comparing. A set of recent findings shows great divergences in economic performance between south and central Europe, between various parts within England and the Netherlands, and between various social groups in the 250-year period before the industrial revolution. Taken together, a number of authors show that economic development in Europe during the seventeenth and eighteenth centuries was very diverse with regard to countries, regions, and social groups (Allen forthcoming; van Zanden forthcoming; Hoffman et al. forthcoming; Williamson 1998a, 1998b). Pomeranz and Parthasarathi are in a similar way analyzing specific regions and social groups for China and India, respectively

(Pomeranz 2000, forthcoming; Parthasarathi 1998, forthcoming). Evidently any comparison between the East and the West, as any comparison of countries within these regions, must therefore take into account the diversity of development by analyzing specific areas and the living standards for specific social groups.

The Concept of Standard of Living

It is desirable to define standard of living as the total utility a person derives from consuming a set of goods as a result of labor, investments, or transfers. Since the utility of various goods depends on personal characteristics, it is difficult to use for comparisons across persons or over time. Therefore, most concepts of standard of living focus on goods themselves and the ability to access them, often measured by income, not on utility. Since the amount of goods accessible with a certain income depends on the prices of these goods, income is deflated by a cost-of-living index. Some concepts focus instead on the particular goods that are consumed, such as food, housing, and clothing.[6] Others include health, education, and sanitation as well. The Basic Need Index, developed in the 1970s, is such an index,[7] and the Human Development Index, which includes fewer items, adds life expectancy instead.[8] These indexes share some characteristics in that they are all aggregated measures; they all amalgamate income or various goods with education and health. They face two problems: one regarding how to weight the various items, the other that the items included often measure living standard at different levels. Income can, for example, be used to buy goods, education, or health. The items therefore overlap and should not be included in the same index. Other indexes measure living standards through the share of household income spent on food[9] or the ability to pay tax.[10] Thus, standard of living can be measured in a number of different ways, with income at one end of the spectrum and utility at the other.

Amartya Sen uses two other concepts to define the standard of living: *functionings* and *capabilities*. Living standard is a matter of functionings (beings and doings), not opulence (income), commodities (goods), or utilities (Sen 1987, 26). *Functionings* are defined as the "various living conditions we can or cannot achieve" and *capabilities* as "our ability to achieve them" (Sen 1987, 16).[11] The set of functionings varies from such elementary things as being adequately nourished, being in good health, avoiding escapable morbidity, and premature mortality to more complex ones such as happiness and self-respect (Sen 1992, 39). Capabilities represent the various sets of functionings a person can achieve due to personal characteristics. Figure 2.1 is based on a summary of Sen's concept of the standard of living by John Muellbauer (1987, 40). We have added income and prices to the original figure. The figure shows how private goods are transformed into intermediate goods, such as calories and proteins, which Sen calls *material characteristics*. Environmental factors, which also have an impact on these characteristics, include both individual liberty and public goods, such as climate, clean air, and the absence of crime. These factors can be goods themselves or represent a set of institutional constraints.

The material characteristics, together with individual characteristics such as metabolism, determine a person's capability to achieve functionings. In the next step, a person's psychological state, for example, possession of religious faith, together with individual capability, determines the functionings he or she will achieve. Thus, the upper boxes could be treated as transfers from income to utility, while the ones at the bottom could be considered constraints or conditional factors. An important point in Sen's argument is that utility cannot be used for comparative measures (Sen 1987, 14). Neither are incomes or goods appropriate measures of living standards since needs and wants vary due to personal and societal characteristics.

We now turn to the concept of standard of living in this book. It bears some similarities to functionings, in the sense that we focus on neither utilities nor goods but rather something in between, which is very dependent on a person's or household's capabilities. We measure the standard of living as the ability to overcome short-term economic stress, that is, variations in income or food prices from one year to the next or even within shorter time spans, as well as income loss after the death of a wage-earning household head. If you can fulfill your long-term plans—to marry, have children, and survive—in the face of acute short-term changes in your environment, then you have a high standard of living. Sensitivity to short-term economic stress, conversely, reveals a lower standard of living.

From numerous historical studies at country and regional levels, we know that food price variation had a strong impact on population, particularly on fertility but also on mortality rates. Variations in food prices were often substantial, and possibilities to compensate by increasing income were few. This study analyzes how changes in food prices, as well as other forms of short-term economic stress, influenced

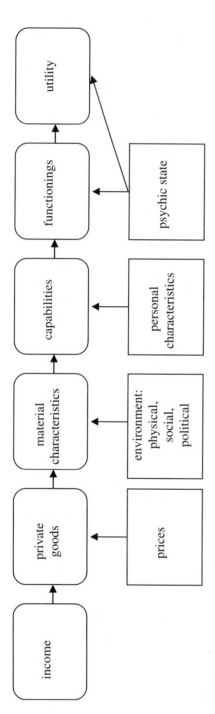

Figure 2.1
The transformation of income to utility through capabilities and functionings in the spirit of Amartya Sen

Table 2.1
Economic and demographic responses to short-term economic stress

---

1. Spending of savings (foodstuff, money, and salable items)
2. Borrow from kin, neighbors, employer, church, or bank
3. Receive relief (rent, tax, poor)
4. Adjust household labor supply (firing servants, out migration of family members)
5. Postpone consumption (marriage, births)
6. Reallocate consumption within the family (mortality)

---

demographic behavior, not of the entire population, but of individuals with certain characteristics. Some characteristics, like sex and birth order, follow people over their life courses, while others, like social and economic resources, might change. Furthermore, we emphasize the impact of the short-term changes in food prices—short-term economic stress—not the long swings in the economy and the population.[12] We are, in other words, interested in the individual response to a repeated phenomenon, which we would expect to be planned and provided for.

Table 2.1 summarizes the strategic range of economic and demographic actions or responses in rural societies to short-term economic stress. The most obvious defensive measure would be to store food, but storage was very costly (Will and Wong with Lee 1991). A granary was not only costly to build but also costly to run. It was similarly costly for farmers to store food from one year to the next, as much food, 20 percent or more, was lost through wastage and nutritional degradation. Moreover, such foods as potatoes could not be stored until the next harvest. Saving money was not as effective as one would anticipate due to inflation in harsh years. Diversification of production was another way to create a stable income, but this was a long-term measure that lowered average production. Similarly, other strategies to smooth effects of variations in harvests and food prices, including rent and tax relief, were mostly available only to those who owned or rented land. Landed households, for example, could stabilize consumption by lowering labor costs in harsh years and thus smoothing annual farm costs. Since loans often required real security, they were typically available only to the landed, so the landless could depend only on poor relief and therefore had greater problems in maintaining a stable standard of living. They were accordingly more vulnerable to short-term economic stress and more likely than the landed to respond demographically. Table 2.1, in other words, represents a social ladder.

The lower the standard of living, the further down the list of possible options each group would have to descend, while the higher the standard of living, the higher such social groups could climb.

Aggregated mortality measures, like age-specific mortality by socioeconomic status, reveal information about the standard of living similar to our new concept but only partly. The more vulnerable to short-term economic stress a certain group is, the higher is that group's level of mortality. Thus, by analyzing the mortality level in certain age groups by sex and socioeconomic status, one should receive information about well-being. This is possibly true, but this approach has some potential drawbacks. First, the level of mortality might be dominated by factors other than standard of living. Merchants, clergymen, and lawyers might, for example, have been more exposed to diseases than farmers and crofters. Some farmers involved in transportation were more exposed to diseases than those who were not. Certain occupations, like fishermen, pose higher risks than the average person faces. Women face certain risks of dying when pregnant. Thus, it is difficult to control for the actual exposure to diseases or accidents with information only on occupation or socioeconomic status. Second, since the model of differences in mortality levels is descriptive rather than causal, it is difficult to interpret the results. There is no reason, however, not to use the information about mortality levels for various groups, but one must be careful and use it as complementary information since it measures various other factors than the response to short-term economic stress does.

Thus, the measure of standard of living that we propose—ability to overcome short-term economic stress—is more precise than mortality levels and therefore easier to interpret. It allows us to analyze the extent and timing of demographic response to economic change for individuals. The more isolated from the negative impact of economic variability, the higher the standard of living. Whether this isolation comes from savings or from the flexibility of the household, or from kin or a larger social context, is as interesting as the causal mechanisms and should therefore be studied in detail. Individuals who respond the same way are, however, assumed to have the same standard of living regardless of how consumption is smoothed.[13] The empirical motivation for the new living standard concept comes from a large number of analyses of the effects of economic stress, measured by food price variation, on mortality, fertility, and nuptiality carried out at a macrolevel. Since these form an important basis for the new concept and what we currently know about the response to short-term economic stress, they will be reviewed in the next section.

Studies of Mortality and Short-Term Economic Stress

Studies of excess mortality can be divided into two schools: studies of famines and mortality crises and studies of effects of variations in harvests on mortality. In studies of the former type, the focus is on extreme situations. This area has received considerable attention from historical demographers and historians beginning with Meuvret in 1946, who analyzed the relationship between famines and mortality crises. The analysis by Goubert in 1960 is in the same tradition, as are a number of studies from the early 1970s. Massimo Livi Bacci, surveying the effects of European famines from the sixteenth to the beginning of the nineteenth century, concluded that large increases in the price of grain often gave rise to marked increases in mortality, less in England than on the Continent (Livi Bacci 1991, 55). These effects were almost always caused by outbreaks of specific diseases such as typhus. Famines played a major role even if the outcome of the diseases was not dependent on nutritional status since people in dire times moved around more looking for employment and food and thereby augmented the spread of diseases. In the analysis of effects of starvation on mortality, the experience of populations of the provinces of Treviso, Venice, and Vicenza during World War I and the populations in Holland and in the Warsaw ghetto during World War II are frequently cited (Livi Bacci 1991, 43–47), as are the studies by Sen (1981) of developing countries. In all these cases, starvation caused many additional deaths, either directly or indirectly through infectious diseases. Similar studies have focused on the reproduction process in times of nutrition crises.[14]

Typical of these studies is a focus on extreme situations. Often, only years with mortality crises are considered, which makes it impossible to estimate the effects of short-term economic stress like harvest failure. Sen's studies of the famines in Asia and Africa can be criticized for the same reason. Instead of asking if a harvest failure of a certain size develops into a famine and a mortality crisis, these studies first identify certain famines and mortality crises and then try to establish whether the harvest was particularly bad that year. They are, however, unable to draw any conclusions about causality since they are sampling on the dependent variable. The merits of these studies are instead the detailed descriptions of famines that they give. Furthermore, the a priori assumption that by studying "cases that are extreme but neither abnormal nor infrequent ... we gain a better insight into the mechanisms of resistance and adaptability" (Livi Bacci 1991, 40) is not well underpinned. Due to unequal income distribution, not a famine but simply high food prices could cause problems. By analyzing all situations and not only the extreme ones, we therefore gain insight into how much variation in the economy it takes to cause problems and for which groups.

The studies of aggregated demographic time series, which constitute the other school, differ markedly from analyses of famines and other extreme situations. This econometric school, which predominates among economic historians, focuses on the systematic variations in economic cycles and their impact on mortality, nuptiality, fertility, and, in a few cases, migration. The first statistical analysis came during the late nineteenth century, but Yule was the first to put it into a solid basis, in 1906 (see R. Lee 1993). Dorothy Swain Thomas became a figurehead within this area of analysis in the interwar period (Thomas 1941). Ronald D. Lee's study in 1981 of short-term variation in population and prices in England, which also became very influential, is much in the same tradition. In that same year, an international symposium took place in Lund, where a number of papers focused on short-term population change.[15] A large number of similar studies have since been published.[16]

These econometric studies show a considerable demographic response to yearly changes in food prices in the past.[17] Mortality, fertility, nuptiality, and migration were all affected by variations in food prices. Not only severe famines but also smaller changes in food supply and prices affected the populations. The response was often distributed over some years, showing a fairly regular pattern, particularly for fertility, which was very sensitive to price variation. The mortality response was much weaker and varied more from country to country (Galloway 1988). At least for Sweden, it is also clear that the fertility response was not an indirect result of the effect of harvests on nuptiality (Carlsson 1970), a fact supported by evidence that the marriage rate varies only half as much as the birthrate. Marriages do not produce very strong short-term effects on birthrates but they do affect them over a twenty-year period. Furthermore, birth figures are influenced more noticeably than nuptiality by fluctuations in the economy.

The analysis of aggregated economic and demographic time series also has its pitfalls. One problem comes from the high levels of aggregation. They have covered the whole of England, France, Sweden, or other countries, or else rather large areas within countries.[18] They show the average response for large populations and cannot reflect the various age, gender, or social differences within the populations. The reason for this limitation is lack of data. It is for the same reason that, with few exceptions, mortality has not been analyzed by cause of death.[19]

In recent years, there have been attempts to overcome the problem with some of these limitations, for example, by studying the mortality response in different age groups. The results from these studies have been very interesting but not always conclusive. A case in point is mortality for infants and children. For Sweden (Bengtsson and Ohlsson 1985) and Italy (Livi Bacci 1991), economic variations had an effect on childhood deaths but not on infant deaths. For Latin America (Palloni, Pérez-Brignoli, and Arias 2000) and England (Schofield 2000), both infant and child mortality were sensitive to economic fluctuations. Thus, for some countries, but not others, we find a relation between economic cycles and infant mortality. At first, one might speculate that these differences are due to variations in breast-feeding habits, since breast-feeding protects infants from certain diseases. However, this cannot explain these geographic differences since we know that breast-feeding was common in England. Only one of these studies analyzes the mortality response by all age groups and by gender.[20]

Researchers have devised several ways to circumvent this problem and allow an analysis of social differences in short-term demographic responses to economic fluctuations. The most frequently used has been to make use of parallel analysis of socially homogeneous regions that differ from each other with respect to prosperity. For example, Galloway (1986, 1988, 1993) looked at rich and poor areas of Rouen and Jutland and classified responses by income levels in different European countries. Reher assessed differences in response by rich and poor districts of Spanish towns (1990) and by ethnicity and race in colonial Mexico (1991). An essay by Hammel and Galloway (2000) compares groups of villages populated mainly by military personnel with other villages during a period of intermittent wars and dramatic shifts in the social structure of Croatia during the eighteenth and nineteenth centuries. In most of these cases, the results have confirmed expectations: mortality in particular has been shown to be much more sensitive to economic fluctuations in poorer areas and fertility in richer areas (R. Lee 1990). These results are not surprising and suggest there are social and economic constraints that condition the demographic responses to economic jolts. However, this approach does not lack difficulties. Similar attempts for Sweden, for example, have run into considerable problems due to random variation (Bengtsson 1984), mainly due to great difficulties in finding homogeneous regions of appropriate size to allow an analysis of mortality by sex and age.

To sum up, from analysis of aggregated data, we know that certain groups were vulnerable to short-term economic stress to such an extent that mortality increased as a result. Thus, at least some households in the past were unable to manage short-term risks. Although the average mortality response to food prices was not that strong, and certainly much weaker than the fertility response, it may well have been much stronger for certain age groups and for certain socioeconomic groups. This is also what the results based on age-specific mortality and mortality for smaller areas indicate. The study of age-specific mortality for Sweden shows that the mortality response among the working adults was very strong indeed. Some European studies also show that people in poor areas were more affected than in rich areas, but we do not know how the impact varied within areas. Only in a few cases has the response been analyzed simultaneously by age, sex, social class, and cause of death, and only once has it been analyzed by household characteristics (Lee, Campbell, and Tan 1992, 163–176). When it comes to the causal link, studies of mortality by cause of death show that the outcome of common endemic air- and waterborne infectious diseases was dependent on short-term economic stress, while for epidemic diseases, like smallpox, it was not (Fridlizius and Ohlsson 1984). Still, the causal links for air- and waterborne infectious diseases are disputable. Some argue that malnutrition reduced immunity, while others argue that short-term economic stress made people move around, so that diseases were more likely to spread in bad than in good years.

Thus, it is fair to say that these studies, taken together, have shown that people in the past could not always overcome short-term variations in production and income and that consumption varied sharply from year to year, but they have not provided much detail beyond that. We have only some indications, and for few areas, about who suffered the most and who died. Generally, we know very little about differences in life expectancy among different social groups and households. We know even less about the underlying causal mechanisms that link economic conditions and mortality together.

For this reason, Bengtsson (1989) has developed an entirely different method, combining longitudinal microdemographic data with macro-economic data using an event-history framework. For a single parish in the middle of Sweden with a high degree of socioeconomic stratification and a large amount of immigration, Bengtsson has shown how different groups were affected by variations in community-wide real wages (Bengtsson 1989, 1993b). The Eurasia Project has developed this idea by analyzing not only differences due to socioeconomic status, sex, and age but also by following the family life cycle as well as a person's position within the household, adding to work by Alter (1988), Lee and Campbell (1997), and others. This approach will not only allow us to analyze standards of living at the microlevel by identifying who is vulnerable to short-term economic stress but also to identify causal links, which is rarely done in the macrolevel time-series analysis we have reviewed above. The major issue—whether nutrition or exposure to diseases caused mortality to increase in years of high food prices—will be discussed in more detail in the next section.

Nutrition, Exposure, and Mortality

In our analysis, we discuss how short-term economic stress influenced mortality by affecting access to nutrients, exposure, spread of diseases, personal care, medical care, heating of houses, and other factors. Our concept of living standard, the demographic response to short-term economic stress, could be used without considering the causal link. The focus is instead on whether the effect is moderated by age, sex, socioeconomic status, family, and household structure. We are none-theless interested in understanding the links between food prices and mortality since it will give us a deeper knowledge about living conditions in the past. If we can show whether the response is due to malnourishment or spread of diseases, or due to temporary labor migration and crowding in the cities, it will also help us to understand other responses, like the fertility response, which was strong throughout Europe. While no one questions the importance of nutrition for mortality in developing countries of today and even for developed countries during extreme situations, as in Warsaw and Amsterdam during World War II when people died from starvation, many historical demographers would argue that nutrition was not a primary cause of deaths in the past. Undoubtedly, this raises the question, If nutrition is very important today, why was it less so in the past? Were populations in the past relatively well fed, or were factors other than nutrition much more important then? One of the scholars who put these issues on the agenda is Robert Fogel, who has devoted much of his work to possible connections between living standards, nutrition (emphasizing the difference between net and gross nutrition), conditions in early life, height, and mortality (Fogel 1996, 1997). Before turning to a more detailed discussion of the past, we review some of the results from studies of contemporary populations regarding nutrition and mortality and ask how they could be applied to historical studies.

Neville Scrimshaw firmly believes, based on contemporary experience, that nutrition must also have been important in the past. The known adverse effects of famine, hunger, chronic energy deficiency, and protein-calorie malnutrition on morbidity as well as mortality, work capacity, cognitive ability, and fertility are strong arguments for this (Scrimshaw 1985, 331). Scrimshaw also points out a number of topics worthy of special consideration by historians, including interaction of nutrition and infection and effects of chronic energy deficiency, vitamin deficiency, and mineral deficiency.

The interaction of nutrition and infections, often referred to as the synergy, is well understood today. All infections, regardless of the agent, affect nutritional status by reducing appetite, worsening the quality of diet ingested, increasing metabolic loss of nutrients, and raising metabolic needs. When the gastrointestinal tract is involved, infections also decrease absorption of nutrients (Rotberg and Rabb 1985, 305–307). Conversely, nutritional deficiencies reduce resistance to infections by weakening the human defense system (Rotberg and Rabb 1985, 307).[21]

While infections always influence nutritional status, the reverse is not always true. Some infections are so virulent that they spread and become lethal regardless of how well nourished a person is. They are, in other words, indiscriminant. Smallpox, malaria, plague, typhoid, tetanus, yellow fever, encephalitis, and poliomyelitis belong to this group (Rotberg and Rabb 1985, 308). The outcomes of many other infections are to varying degrees dependent on resistance. Some are so avirulent that they occur only in very weak persons. One of the main points here is that all infections can create deficiencies of any nutrient that is already on the borderline in a malnourished person (Scrimshaw 1985, 332). Thus, even very nonaggressive infections can be harmful for someone who is already malnourished.

As for the effects of chronic energy deficiency, contemporary studies show that it mainly affects work output. The reason is that metabolic adaptation to lower energy intakes than previously experienced is limited. One could argue that children adapt to lower energy intake by not fully developing their height. Thus, in the future, they require less food (Fogel 1994). Even so, the result is still a lowering of work potential, which may have effects at both the household and societal levels (Dasgupta 1993).

Vitamin deficiencies regardless of eventual calorie deficiencies can manifest themselves in specific well-known diseases. Deficiency of ascorbic acid leads to scurvy. Niacin-tryptophan deficiency can cause pellagra, thiamine deficiency can cause beri-beri, and vitamin D deficiency can cause rickets. Mineral deficiencies can lead to diseases as well. Iron deficiency, for example, can cause anemia and have significant effects on physical capacity and resistance to infections.

Why, then, do historical demographers not find any direct evidence of effects of malnutrition on mortality in the past? One reason is that there exists little information about consumption in the past, and even less about needs, which are determined not only by the work load and maintenance and development of our bodies but also by the disease load. Therefore, any evidence of effects of nourishment on mortality must be indirect. The evidence that is used instead are data on disease patterns, socioeconomic differences, and effects of historical and contemporary famines. Further proof comes from econometric estimates of the effects of grain prices on mortality and results from studies of real wages and heights.

Based on such evidence, Livi Bacci (1991) argues that mortality from indiscriminant diseases for which the nutritional influence on outcomes is minimal (smallpox, malaria, plague, typhoid) was much more common during the sixteenth to eighteenth centuries than later. These diseases were so virulent that they produced illness regardless of differences in resistance within the population. Livi Bacci argues that the relationship between famines and mortality crises most often is a result of outbreaks of such diseases rather than of malnutrition. Diffusion is therefore more important than resistance, and quarantines are consequently effective preventive measures. Still, the spread of such diseases might be a result of bad harvests since they often create crowding and disorder.

It is important to note, as Livi Bacci correctly does, that the disease pattern changed in several key respects during the eighteenth century.

First, by the middle of the eighteenth century, several highly virulent diseases became less prevalent or disappeared. Plague disappeared from Western Europe by the beginning of the eighteenth century. Smallpox, which used to affect all age groups, had become a childhood disease as early as in the mid-eighteenth century. Malaria, another disease that was insensitive to the nutritional status of the host, became less common, mainly due to drainage of swamps. In general, there appears to have been a shift away from highly virulent diseases during the eighteenth century and a rise in the importance of diseases sensitive to the nutritional status of the host.

Second, virulent diseases became less virulent. Smallpox, for example, had become less aggressive even by the end of the eighteenth century.[22] Since the age pattern of smallpox deaths remained unchanged during this stage, it is unlikely that it was spread less efficiently than before. Other diseases, like measles, rubella, and mumps, also shifted from being virulent diseases of adults to less virulent diseases of children.

Thus, two important changes took place sometime during the eighteenth century: highly virulent and nonnutrition-related diseases like plague and malaria become less abundant or disappeared, and some highly virulent diseases became less virulent than before.[23] What happened was thus a change in the distribution of death causes and a shift in the long-term mortality level. Whether the influence of short-term economic stress on mortality stems from malnutrition or spread of diseases is still an open question. Some low-virulence diseases are spread easily (for example, pertussis and cholera), while others are not (including tuberculosis and leprosy). Some of them (like gastrointestinal and respiratory diseases) are with us all of the time. Either way, their outcome is influenced by nutritional status. Conditional upon exposure, mortality among the better nourished is low. This is the key point. Few die of starvation, but diseases that are around most of the time become lethal for malnourished persons. That is also why we can expect to find effects among certain socioeconomic strata, especially the poor, but not the entire population. To answer the question how food prices influence mortality, we must determine whether the mortality upswing is selective or indiscriminant.

The Eurasia Project data are ideally suited for the detection of such effects since we can analyze socioeconomic differentials in mortality risk. Although the precise time periods covered for each site differ, data in most cases are available from roughly 1800 to 1870.[24] The data for the sites in Japan are the earliest, dating back to the 1710s. The data cover late preindustrial and early industrial rural populations that are less exposed to highly virulent, nonnutrition-related diseases, and we therefore expect mortality to be selective. In the next section, we discuss in more detail how we anticipate that different socioeconomic groups responded to short-term economic stress.

Food Prices and Their Influence on Various Socioeconomic Groups

People in the past faced uncertainty from factors both external and internal to the household. Regardless of source of economic stress, the household was often in a precarious situation and had to take immediate actions to maintain consumption in the short run. Stress, even of limited duration, might also have influenced the household in the long run by having an impact on future births and marriages and thus security at old age.[25] A major source of external stress is related to food access. Harvests varied a great deal from one year to the next, often dependent on the weather and thus difficult to forecast. Since the weather affected regions rather than single farmers or villages, bad harvests drove up the price of food. A bad harvest may also have caused a decline in the demand for clothes, household utensils, and other nonconsumables, since ordinary people gave priority to food. Thereby, incomes of artisans and others also declined. High food prices were, however, a stimulus to investment by surplus-producing farmers, which might have increased the demand for goods from this group.

The most commonly used indicator of external stress related to access to food is the price of grain. The basic argument is that for most people, the lion's share of their income was spent on food, and grain products dominated the diet. In Antwerp at the end of the sixteenth century, for example, a working-class family spent 78 percent of its income on food, 50 percent on bread alone (Scholliers 1960, 174; see Abel 1966/1980, 142). In various parts of Italy between 1890 and 1906, the food cost was 52 to 95 percent of the budget (Somogyi 1973; see Livi Bacci 1991, 87). Evidently bread constituted the main intake in terms of calories in Italy. In nineteenth-century Sweden, foodstuffs accounted for 83 percent of the budget according to Gunnar Myrdal's estimate (Myrdal 1933, 115), and Lennart Jörberg estimated that 59 percent of the food costs were attributed to grain (Jörberg 1972. 18[?]) These figures refer to the lower social classes. A correspondin

Table 2.2
Production and price change of grain

Production decline	Price increase according to:		
	Davenant/King (1699)	Jevons (1871–1970)	Parenti (1942)
10%	30%	35%	5%
20	80	78	11
30	160	145	18
40	280	258	27

for farm laborers in the Yangzi Delta suggests that they spent 54 percent of their cash and in kind earnings on basic grain supplies in the early nineteenth century, roughly the same as in Sweden and elsewhere in Europe (Fang 1996, 93, 95; see Pomeranz forthcoming).

It is important to consider the relation between food prices and production, that is, the price elasticity of demand for grain, since it reflects the scale of food availability through price data. Charles Davenant (1699), using data from Gregory King, argued for the late seventeenth century that a 10 percent reduction in production led to a price increase of 30 percent, a 20 percent reduction led to an increase of 80 percent, and so on (see table 2.2 and Wrigley 1987, 93). Stanley Jevons (1871/1970, 182) accepted Davenant's calculations but sought a more general formula, suggesting that the price of corn was roughly the reciprocal of the square of the supply. His more precise formula is close to Davenant's result, as shown in table 2.2. For Siena between 1560 and 1666, G. Parenti found that a 10 percent harvest reduction corresponded to a price increase of 5 percent, and a decrease of 20 percent led to a price increase of 11 percent, as shown in table 2.2 (Parenti 1942; see Livi Bacci 1991, 57). An increase in prices by 27 percent in Siena, which would correspond to a decrease of 40 percent in harvest, was by no means an extreme situation (Livi Bacci 1991, 52–53).

Another important factor was that a large fraction of the production never entered the market (Wrigley 1987; Fogel 1992). The part of the production that was used by the farmers themselves for seed, fodder, and their own consumption was substantial (Fogel 1992, 259; Wrigley 1987, 93–108), and most likely rather inelastic. Consequently, the variability in production affected primarily consumers on the food market.

The question is, then, how food prices were determined locally. One may argue that short-term variations in prices largely reflect the size of the harvests since demand changes only slowly. This is also true in wartime, when farming is impossible in certain areas or people are cut off from the market. Since the grain market was well integrated far back in time, the influence of local variations in harvests on prices was weak. It has also been argued that the harvest was regionally uniform since it is largely determined by the weather, which is similar in large areas (Richards 1984). Thus, it seems fair to assume that grain prices should be considered as exogenously determined when analyzing small communities that are integrated into a larger market such as the areas we study.[26]

How much, then, was consumption affected by food prices? Estimates from developing countries show that the elasticities of household consumption with respect to food crop prices are between −0.37 for Thailand and −0.66 for Sierra Leone (see Dasgupta 1993, 223). Thus, an increase of food prices by 30 percent reduced consumption by 12 to 20 percent.[27] In Paul Thestrup's estimates of the standard of living in Copenhagen, the yearly decline in calorie intake per head was 14 percent in 1763, a bad harvest year (Thestrup 1971, 258–259). Since not all Copenhageners had to lower their consumption that year, some inhabitants saw declines of more than 14 percent. Thus, a decrease in the annual caloric intake for the poorer parts of the population of around 10 to 20 percent is the likely outcome of quite typical price increases during the preindustrial period. Fogel (1992) argues along the same line in his calculations of the effects of changes in food supply and prices on consumption for various social groups. While the share of consumption varied much more for the laborers than for farmers and landlords, their price elasticity regarding food grain was high and stable, since they had to buy food regardless of prices (Fogel 1992, 258–259). Thus, in years of harvest failure, the effects on consumption are bound to be much bigger for these groups, while other groups certainly benefited from high prices.

We expect the vulnerability to short-term economic stress to be affected by the consumption needs of both the individual and the household, which we shall get back to later, and its ability to save. The latter is much a consequence of access to resources other than labor, and particularly land. It is therefore important whether the household was a net producer of food or a net consumer.

How much the group of net consumers was affected depends on if they had any land at all or bought all their food. The larger the share they bought, the more they should have been affected. We should also expect them to be more affected if they were paid in money than in kind, since wages were more stable than food prices. If they were paid in kind, their response to high food prices would have been dependent on the type and length of contract. The category that should have been most disadvantaged by a price increase consisted of artisans who produced common goods, since large groups could not afford their products as food became more expensive. Artisans who produced goods for the agricultural sector could, however, experience an increased demand for their products since farmers generally gain from high prices. Given that prices are determined externally, which we believe they were in the locations we study, net producers were positively affected by high food prices.[28] They benefited more if they paid tax or rent in money than in kind, labor, or share of harvest, and the same if they had long-term rather than short-term contracts. If at all, they should respond positively to high food prices. The most well off among the net producers should not in any way be affected by short-term changes in food prices since they should be able to save or at least borrow. The way it works depends, however, very much on how the tax or rent on land was paid. It therefore differs depending on tenure arrangements—in other words, whether a farmer is freeholder, tenant, sharecropper, or in another category. We shall therefore discuss how the grain price might influence each of these groups separately, assuming that prices are exogenously determined.

There are several groups to consider, each of which had different arrangements for land tenure and each of which may have had a different response to prices, as shown in table 2.3. Freeholders paid a fixed tax in money. Tenants with long-term contracts paid a fixed rent in kind or in money. Tenants with short-term contracts paid a fixed rent in kind or money. Sharecroppers with short-term contracts paid a share of the harvest in rent. Crofters with small plots needed to work as day laborers. Servants were mainly paid in kind. Day laborers were usually paid with money, as were artisans. Except for servants and day laborers who lived in the household where they worked, all other groups had access to some land, where they could grow vegetables and perhaps also keep some hens. Not only the relation to land would be of great potential importance but also the size of the farms for those who owned land. In the beginning of the nineteenth century, for example, the number of freeholders increased in Sweden and Denmark, while the average parcel size declined. Many of those who bought land came from a proletariat background and had to sell off some of

Table 2.3
Influence of high food prices on household budget by socioeconomic group

Net producers	
Freeholders paying a fixed tax in money	Very favorable
Tenants with long-term contracts paying a fixed rent in kind	Favorable
Tenants with long-term contracts paying a fixed rent in money	Very favorable
Tenants with short-term contracts paying a fixed rent in kind	Less favorable
Tenants with short-term contracts paying a fixed rent in money	Favorable
Sharecroppers with short-term contracts paying a share of the harvest in rent	Favorable
Sharecroppers of nonstaple cash crops (e.g., tobacco, cotton, olives)	Not favorable
Net consumers	
Crofters with small plots who needed to work as day laborers	Unfavorable
Servants mainly paid in kind	Neither
Day laborers mainly paid in cash	Very unfavorable
Artisans	Unfavorable

the land of the farms they had bought in order to maintain owner-ship. Therefore, some landowners still depended on income as wage earners.

Basically tenants with a long-term contract gained since the owner of the land could not increase the rent even if prices and incomes for farmers went up (Abel 1966/1980). If the contract was on a short-term basis, the owner might have been able to increase the rent as prices went up, though with a certain time lag. Generally, the best arrangement for the tenants was if the rent was paid in money, since high prices meant that less grain needed to be sold for that purpose. The advantage for sharecroppers was that whatever was left for sale would go at high prices, which meant that they would get more money. However, if sharecroppers produce nonstaple goods, the demand for these goods may have declined as the cost of living went up due to higher grain prices. Thus, this group would have suffered from high prices, in particular if they did not produce food for their own consumption in addition to the marketed crop.

In conclusion, we have a priori expectations that various socioeconomic groups responded in different ways to short-term economic stress caused by harvest or food price variations. The response tells us much about under what conditions they lived, that is, their standard of living. Access to land and ability to store wealth are obvious reasons for differences in response. But as we argue below, the response is not entirely dependent on these factors; the stage of the family life cycle, the size and complexity of the household, and its larger social context are also important.

Consumption and Production over the Individual and Family Life Cycle

All family systems, especially historically, must solve the same basic problem of maintaining consumption over the life course of individual members. The crux of the matter is that basic needs for necessities such as food, clothing, and shelter are relatively constant over the life course, while productive capacity varies much more. Figure 2.2 illustrates the situation by contrasting needs and capabilities by age in a farming population. The fundamental relationships suggested are quite universal.[29] People produce less than they consume at both ends of the life span and produce more than they consume in the middle. This constrains the range of possible family arrangements. If people produced more than they consumed while young, parenting would be unnecessary. If people produced more than they consumed even after they reached old age, arrangements to support the aged would also be unnecessary.

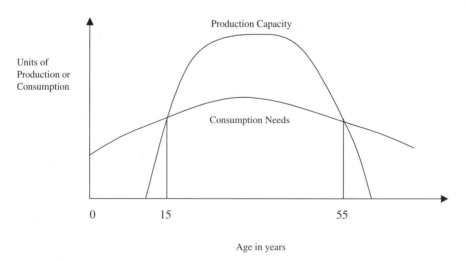

Figure 2.2
Consumption and production over the individual life cycle

Starting with infants, many studies have come to the conclusion that during their earliest stage of life, children were mainly affected by the conditions and practice of their mothers and exposure to epidemic diseases. For this reason, one rarely finds any connection between food prices and infant mortality, as we showed above. The major argument is that children were isolated from external factors as long as they were breast-fed; when infants were weaned, they became vulnerable to short-term economic stress. Ideally, we should divide children into two groups based on their age of weaning. Unfortunately, we cannot do this, for two reasons. First, we do not know the precise age of weaning since it changes a lot over time and between families and societies. Second, the way the data are organized in our Asian locations makes this impossible. We therefore chose to study children during the first two years of life separately from the third to the fifteenth years. Since many children are breast-fed for less than two years, we also expect children belonging to the lowest age group to be vulnerable to short-term economic stress in some degree. Several alternative division lines to address this issue are used in chapter 12, which focuses on children.

For children, several years elapse after their birth before they can work, and even more before they are self-sufficient. The length of the period depends mainly on the type of production and the need for education. In a preindustrial setting, children often started to contribute by age 5 or 6 years and could become self-supporting at 10 to 12 years of age. Boys usually began to work and became self-supporting earlier than girls.[30] In contemporary modern society, much to the chagrin of many parents, children may remain dependent until they are in their mid-twenties. There is little direct evidence on the age at which children in the past became self-sufficient, but there is some indirect evidence. In areas with servant systems, age at leaving home may approximate the age at which children became self-sufficient. In one southern Swedish rural area, for example, the median age at leaving home was 16.2 years for boys and 16.6 for girls.[31] Often children had few opportunities to work at home and had to seek outside employment as soon as they were able.[32] Children of landless parents left home at an even lower age since they had relatively few opportunities to work for the family. There also seems to have been another dividing line at age 15 that lasted until the mid-nineteenth century. It was at that age that children were treated as adults by the law. For example, that was when they began paying personal taxes as adults.[33] Overall, it seems that children in the Swedish countryside were certainly self-supporting by age 15.[34] This is also the dividing age we use throughout this book.

Later in life, productive capacity declines. Although individuals may continue to work, as most did, they are no longer able to provide completely for themselves. Again, there are few hard facts on when individuals in preindustrial societies became dependent, but there is some indirect evidence. The average age at retirement among those leaseholders who received pension privileges on one of the estates in southern Sweden was 63 years for men and 57 years for women.[35] According to records of tenants of state farms in Liaoning province in northeast China during the Qing (1644–1911), men were classified as retired (*tui*) at around 60 years of age and as elderly (*lao*) when they were 65 (Lee and Campbell 1997, 167). At this point, the elderly become dependent on savings they had accumulated earlier in life and on children and kin. In some contexts, the elders might also rely on former employers and society at large, most likely the village or parish. If they were fortunate enough to have savings, they could maintain their earlier standard of living by drawing on them. In some societies, if the elderly owned land, they could write a contract that handed over the right to use it to a relative, an outside individual, or even an institution such as a convent or monastery (Bengtsson and Fridlizius 1994; Gaunt 1983; Odén 1987). In return, they would be provided with food, clothing, and shelter for the rest of their lives. An alternative was to keep the land until they died.[36] These were, of course, options for only the upper class and successful farmers. The landless had to depend on their children, employers, and society.

Responsibility for care of children and the elderly rested primarily, and in several countries legally, on the individual and the family. It was only when they failed that other institutions stepped in. In some societies, the church or other specialized institutions took care of orphans (Lynch 2000, 142–144). In other countries, for example, China, adoption and fosterage were widespread (Wolf and Huang 1980; Wang and Lee 1998). Families were more likely to encounter problems taking care of the elderly, especially if they were landless or semi-landless. Even among the landed, arrangements for the elderly caused many disputes. In some societies, elderly with no other sources of support could receive poor relief. In other cases, responsibility for relief was devolved from the local community to the employer.[37] Thus, the form of transfers from adults to children and elderly varied with the resources of the household and community, which we develop in chapter 4. It is therefore likely that social arrangements were as important as biological needs for health and vulnerability to short-term economic stress.

Since children and elderly depend on transfers from working adults, most often their own relatives but sometimes society at large, it is obvious that these groups must be examined separately in our analysis. When food prices increased, they were likely to have suffered the most. Not only were children and the elderly the most frail to begin with, but they were often perceived as the least valuable members of the household. Both were net consumers—children for at least a few more years and the elderly until the end of their life. Very young children, meanwhile, could be replaced if reductions in their allocations eventually caused their death. Chapter 13 examines the experiences of the elderly in great detail, and chapter 12 focuses on children.

In times of economic stress, families may favor one sex over the other. The reason is that males and females, even as children, performed different tasks both within and outside the household (Tilly and Scott 1975; Hudson and Lee 1990). Demand for their labor and its perceived value might vary, as shown by Cain (1977, 1978) and others for contemporary developing countries. While differences in the value of male and female labor in agricultural settings are difficult to measure directly, there is some indirect evidence. Tenant contracts can sometimes provide some hints. On one estate in rural Sweden, for example, females were valued as two-thirds of a male when rents in labor were set and the owner could decide whether the tenants had to pay with male or female labor.[38] Moreover, in some societies, possible household responses to stress, such as sending members out to work, could affect one sex or the other disproportionately. The labor market outside the household was as segmented as the one inside the household, if not more so. Gender issues are thus important and are analyzed in chapter 11.

We now turn to the vulnerability to short-term economic stress over the family life cycle. Since children are net consumers, family needs increase in the years immediately after formation because couples begin to have children. This increased burden is eventually taken care of when children begin to work and the consumer/worker ratio begins to fall. Until then, the parents have to enlarge the household's labor supply. According to Alexander Chayanov's model, they must either self-exploit by working harder or add working adult relatives, such as siblings (Chayanov 1923/1986). They may also have to borrow, seek poor relief, or consume less. In this simple model, families are assumed to consist of only two generations. Access to land and labor intensity are also assumed to be very elastic so that families could actually expand production to meet increasing needs.

Family forms vary considerably in historical Europe (Wall, Robin, and Laslett 1983); hence, while Chayanov's assumptions are relevant for Russia, for which he developed the model, they are less relevant for Western Europe, where households could add servants when needed. Indeed, Lutz Berkner (1972) developed a model that includes servants. He argued that servants were a labor substitute for children during the years they were growing up. The consumer/worker ratio, which rose rapidly for the first fifteen years after marriage in Chayanov's model, could therefore be flatter, as shown for southern Sweden by Christer Lundh (1995). Overall, family forms varied greatly in historic Europe, making Chayanov's model too simplistic. There were additional complications not addressed in Chayanov's model, mainly dealing with additional adults living in the household. In many rural societies in the past, a married couple also had to take care of their parents. In China, married brothers and even cousins might live together in the same household (Lee and Campbell 1997). In Japan, families could adopt adults. Other studies that use the standard Hammel-Laslett framework to describe the complexity of households also reveal this. These complexities had important implications for mortality, and accordingly must be considered in our analysis.

If the family supports the elderly and infirm, the consumer/worker ratio will be even less favorable than if only small children are present. Overall, responsibilities toward the young and the elderly cause a family's economic situation to vary over the life cycle, and it is not at all given that they can be fulfilled. Mead Cain (1981) suggests that in present-day developing countries, adult children are a form of security against short-term economic stress for the elderly. According to Cain, widowers with small children often lose control of the family farm once they become dependent on relatives and neighbors. This could also have been true in the past since families in both types of societies experienced considerable insecurity, which would then be transferred to dependent elderly within the family. In the West, one alternative institution to prevent such a situation was the custom of remarriage. Without further investigating these institutions, we can safely conclude that the family played a central role for the transfers required to smooth individual consumption over the life cycle.

Our basic hypothesis is that the higher the consumer/worker ratio, the more vulnerable are the members of the family to short-term economic stress. Families with a higher ratio live closer to the margin. To test this hypothesis, we can consider the age composition of the household in the analysis. To assess whether families in different socioeconomic strata are more or less vulnerable to short-term economic stress at particular locations in the domestic cycle, one would examine the separate effects on sensitivity of the numbers of children and elderly in the household. Chapter 5 accordingly examines the influence of household age composition on sensitivity to economic stress.

Anthropologists have hypothesized that Asian family structures influenced mortality outcomes for particular family members (Skinner 1997). For China, the importance of family structure for mortality has even been demonstrated empirically. In their analysis of household organization and population behavior in northeast China, Lee and Campbell (1997) demonstrate that characteristics of the household, as well as the individual's location within the household, affect a number of demographic outcomes, including mortality. Location in the family life cycle should be less important for sensitivity to short-term stress in societies with more complex households. More complex household types had more opportunities to smooth the consumer/worker ratio, including households with servants. We are able to investigate this since there is considerable variation among countries in the complexity of household systems. The main axis is between Asia and Europe, but variation between communities within the same continent and country was also substantial. This will also be discussed in detail in chapter 4 of this book.

Summary

At first glance, it may look as if we are reinventing the wheel by placing so much emphasis on mortality as the ultimate measurement in comparisons of living standards in different countries, just as Malthus and many of his contemporaries did. We are indeed putting a great deal of emphasis on deaths and other demographic events, and for very good reason. The information is rich, solid, and valid. As we see it, the academic endeavor will be to use it in a rather innovative way, by analyzing the demographic response to short-term economic stress. Nonetheless, this attempt also carries ideas from Malthus, referred to in chapter 1, and also in his analysis of specific countries. The development of such a dynamic concept of living standards should become useful for research on historical populations for which data on consumption and production are less abundant. The new concept bears some resemblance to Amartya Sen's concepts, in particular, his definitions of capabilities and functionings. We use as a welfare indicator the outcome of individual capabilities, constrained by household and village characteristics, in situations when food is expensive. We are, in other words, analyzing certain functionings, namely, the most important ones—to stay alive, to marry, and to have children—in situations of economic hardship.

My review of previous findings clearly shows that the mortality response to short-term economic stress is seldom a function of biology; human agency might be equally or even more important. Some social groups have the means to isolate themselves from short-term economic stress; others have not. The premises for empirical analysis of these issues have been the focus of this chapter, and in the next chapter the comparative analyses will follow.

Notes

This work was accomplished as part of the project From Hunger to Modern Economic Growth. Demography and Family Behavior in Sweden, 1650–1900, with financial support from the Bank of Sweden Tercentenary Foundation and the Swedish Council for Social Research. I gratefully acknowledge the opportunity to carry out this study while guest professor at the California Institute of Technology in winter 1999 and value highly my discussions with James Z. Lee throughout the progress of the chapter. I am also thankful to participants at the European Science Foundation conference, "New Evidence of Standard of Living in Europe and Asia," in Arild, Sweden, August 2000, for valuable comments and suggestions on an earlier version of this chapter and in particular to Cameron Campbell, Martin Dribe, Ronald Lee, and Kirk Scott.

1. This group of scholars includes Goody (1996), Hanley (1997), Laveley and Wong (1998), Lee and Wang (1999b), Li (forthcoming), Parthasarathi (1998, forthcoming), Pomeranz (2000, forthcoming), and Wong (1997).

2. In Malthus's chapter on China and Japan, he primarily cites three sources: Du Halde (1738–1741), a collection of letters from other Jesuits, and Staunton's account of an embassy to China (1797). These sources are not only collections of anecdotes. They attempt to give overviews of population totals, production, and other facets of the economy. Thus, the aim of both Du Halde's and Staunton's work was to give an overall picture of living conditions, population, and economic factors in China. There seem to be no major differences in the views expressed by Malthus and Smith, on the one hand, and

Landes on the other. While Malthus used highly relevant sources for China, reflecting the knowledge of his time, he did not do so when he analyzed Japan. In a one-page summary of conditions in Japan, he refers only to Montesquieu, Kaempfer, and Thunberg, a Linnaeus disciple who was in Japan to study the fauna and flora (Malthus, 1826/1986, 137–138). It is somewhat surprising that he did not make use of evidence like that which he used for China, since the sources of information about Japan and China were similar (Lach and Van Kley 1993, 1828–1888).

3. For further discussion about the evidence used by these classical economists, see the introduction in Allen, Bengtsson, and Dribé (forthcoming).

4. The discussion of living standards in the East and the West is strikingly similar to the one that has taken place regarding Europe in past decades. François Crouzet (1966) argued that the differences between England and France in GDP per capita at the beginning of the eighteenth century never were that great and in fact did not even widen as England became industrialized. Instead, it is not until the very end of the eighteenth century that the two countries diverge, as a result of the twenty years of turmoil created by the French Revolution (Crouzet 1966). Generally, later reviews of the peripheral countries in Europe have also tended to upgrade their economies and to question the large differences in comparison with England. They have also received assistance from later investigations, which have tended to revise downward the advance of the English economy relative to other Western European countries (Crafts 1996).

5. Still another answer to the question is that scholars reassess the same evidence in the light of a new theory or paradigm. Malthus, for example, revaluated Thunberg's (1791–1793) description of the living conditions in Japan and drew a conclusion opposite to his.

6. See, for example, Hanley (1997), who uses the concept of "physical well-being" to summarize these aspects of life.

7. The index developed by the International Labor Organization includes food, clothing, shelter, health, education, water, and sanitation (Ghai et al. 1977). It offers no solution of how to weight these measures. Food alone could be weighted by its nutritional content, as proposed by Lagrange (Sen 1987), though not easily, and goods in general could be weighted by prices, but how should health, education, water, and sanitation be weighted? Also, it turned out that a ranking of countries based on Basic Need Indicators gives almost the same results as using income per capita, for the reason that the basic needs end up being a very large proportion of national income.

8. The Human Development Index, created by the UN, has three components: longevity, knowledge, and income (UN 1994). The general problems with this index are similar to the ones faced by the Basic Need Index. Both indexes are highly correlated with each other and GDP per capita (World Bank 1994). Using data back to 1870, Nicholas Crafts (1996) shows that the two measures are also highly correlated historically. Partha Dasgupta and Martin Weale (1992, 120) have extended the Human Development Index to include indices of political and civil liberties. The new index is highly correlated with the Human Development Index.

9. This measure, proposed by Engels in 1857, is based on the fact that when income increases, the share spent on food decreases given that the composition of the household is not changing. See Deaton and Muellbauer (1980).

10. The latter is really a low-end measurement, since typically only a small percentage of the population is entitled. See Lundsjö (1975) and Söderberg (1978).

11. One such functioning that Sen discusses is not being "ashamed to appear in public," referring to Adam Smith (Sen 1987, 17). Smith exemplified this with the person who, in order not to be ashamed to appear in public, needed to wear a white linen shirt.

12. Consequently, we are removing possible long swings and trends from the economic time series that we use as indicators of short-term economic stress.

13. This line of thought, first developed by Bengtsson (1989, 1993b), has been refined within this project, in particular the importance of household characteristics and transfers within the household in conditioning the response to stress. Recent attempts to make use of it include Alter and Oris (2000a), Bengtsson (2000), Breschi, Derosas, and Manfredini (2000), Campbell and Lee (2000), and Tsuya and Kurosu (2000).

14. In particular, Le Roy Ladurie (1975), Frisch (1978), and Bongaarts (1980).

15. See Bengtsson, Fridlizius, and Ohlsson (1984).

16. Originally, analysis of relationships between economic conditions and demographic rates was restricted to northern Europe, with the English and the Swedish experiences among the first to be scrutinized. Since then, considerable work has been done on other areas in southern and central-eastern Europe and in Latin America. For overviews, see Galloway (1988), R. Lee (1991, 1993), and Bengtsson et al. (1998).

17. In almost all of them, the price of grain (usually wheat) has been used as an indicator of harvests, while the temperature during certain periods of the year has been taken as an index of climatic conditions. For a more detailed discussion, see Bengtsson et al. (1998).

18. Some exceptions are found, including one for northern China in which a group of villages is analyzed (Campbell and Lee 1996, 31–39). Another is the analyses of Sweden by sex and age (Bengtsson and Ohlsson 1985).

19. One such exception is Fridlizius and Ohlsson (1984).

20. Bengtsson and Ohlsson (1985).

21. This is done by reducing the production of humoral antibodies, impairing cell-mediated immunity, lessening the effectiveness of phagocytosis, weakening epithelial barriers, and lowering lysozyme production.

22. In Sweden, smallpox mortality went down well before vaccinations started despite evidence that inoculation never was widespread (Fridlizius 1984; Sköld 1997).

23. A comparison of Hollingsworth's results on the life expectancies of English peers with those from Wrigley and Schofield's (1981) study of the total population of England from 1550 to 1800 point in the same direction. It shows that the peers seemed to live shorter, due to higher exposure than the average population before 1700, but longer thereafter as epidemics became less severe (Livi Bacci 1991, 65).

24. See chapter 4 for additional detail on the data used in the analysis.

25. In fact, the situation in the past seems to have been very similar to some of today's developing societies (Bengtsson and Gunnarsson 1994; Cain 1977).

26. This has also been shown for our site in southern Sweden (Dribe 2000).

27. Examples can be found in which food consumption increased with higher prices (Dasgupta 1993, 223).

28. If food prices are endogenously determined and thus dependent mainly on the local harvest, we expect all groups to respond negatively to high prices since they reflect bad harvests. Again, we expect the landed groups to be able to smooth their consumption by storing or borrowing and thus be less affected by short-term economic stress.

29. Hunters and gatherers are exceptions to this according to Kaplan (1994).

30. These are the figures for some of the developing countries in the 1970s and 1980s, and they are likely to be similar for any society during the period prior to industrialization, since they have similar modes of production (Cain 1978, 1982).

31. The figures refer to four rural parishes in southern Sweden, 1829–1866; see Dribe (2000, 112).

32. For example, in urban areas, such as Venice, where children worked outside the home while still living with their families (Derosas 1999) and in areas where they stayed at home until they married.

33. The age when they start to pay tax increased to 17 years in 1841 and 18 years between 1856 and 1858 in Sweden. See Dribe (2000, 120–122) for a detailed discussion.

34. It may have been even earlier. Many served as *lillpiga* and *lilldräng* (young servants) in other households at ages as low as 12 years.

35. The figures refer to pension contracts at Duveke estate, 1834–1889. The figures for freeholders in other areas in Sweden are similar; see Lundh and Olsson (2001, table 1).

36. An investigation of inheritance practices in three parishes in western Sweden shows that only a small fraction of the parents transferred their farms to the next generation during their lifetime (Winberg 1981).

37. See Skoglund (1992) for Sweden.

38. The estate archives at Axelvold, Sweden, 1830–1850.

3   Economic Stress and Mortality

Cameron Campbell, James Z.
Lee, and Tommy Bengtsson
in collaboration with Göran
Broström, Rosella Rettaroli,
and Noriko O. Tsuya

A faithful history, [of long and short oscillations] ... would tend greatly to elucidate the manner in which the constant check upon population acts; and would probably prove the existence of the retrograde and progressive movements that have been mentioned; ...

A circumstance which has, perhaps, more than any other, contributed to conceal this oscillation from common view, is the difference between the nominal and real price of labour. It very rarely happens that the nominal price of labour universally falls; but we well know that it frequently remains the same, while the nominal price of provisions has been gradually rising. ... [A]n increased number of labourers receiving the same money wages will necessarily, by their competition, increase the money price of corn. This is, in fact, a real fall in the price of labour; and, during this period, the condition of the lower classes of the community must be gradually growing worse. But the farmers and capitalists are growing rich from the real cheapness of labour. Their increasing capitals enable them to employ a greater number of men; and, as the population had probably suffered some check from the greater difficulty supporting a family, the demand for labour, after a certain period, would be great in proportion to the supply, and its price would of course rise, if left to find its natural level; and thus the wages of labour, and consequently the condition of the lower classes of society, might have progressive and retrograde movements. ...

In savage life, where there is no regular price of labour, it is little to be doubted that similar oscillations took place. When population has increased nearly to the utmost limits of the food, all the preventive and the positive checks will naturally operate with increased force. Vicious habits with respect to the sex will be more general, the exposing of children more frequent, and both the probability and fatality of wars and epidemics will be considerably greater; and these causes will probably continue their operation till the population is sunk below the level of food; and then the return to comparative plenty will again produce an increase, and, after a certain period, its further progress will again be checked by the same causes.

(Malthus 1826/1986, 19–20)

According to Malthus, the positive check was more common in the East than in the West. Even in the West, however, Malthus wrote that the operation of the positive check can be seen "in the comparative mortality among the children of the most distressed part of the community and of those living rather more at their ease, the variation in the real price of labor, and the observable differences in the state of the lower classes of society with regard to ease and happiness" (1826/ 1986, 19). By contrast, in the East, in "savage life, where there is no regular price of labor, . . . the exposing of children [will be] more frequent and both the probability and fatality of wars and epidemics will be considerable greater" (1826/1986, 20). For Malthus, in other words, the mechanism as well as the magnitude of the positive check differed between East and West. In the West, the magnitude was lower and the process was selective and linked to variation in the price of labor, the differential well-being of the poor and the well-off, and consequent differential patterns of infant and child mortality. In the East, the magnitude was higher, and the process was both selective and indiscriminate: selective, as mortality might rise through increased infanticide and neglect, indiscriminate, as mortality might also rise through exogenous calamity. Those people in the path of pestilence, war, and disease, died; those spared such exposure survived.

Malthus's portrayal of the positive check in the East as intense and indiscriminate has influenced historical narratives of social and economic development ever since (Cao and Chen 2002; Huang 2002; Lee, Campbell, and Wang 2002; Wang and Lee 2002). This is especially true for China, which Malthus singled out as an example of a society dominated by the positive check. Scholars typically take the strength of the positive check for granted in their interpretations of China's population, economic, and social history (Chao 1986; Elvin 1973; Huang 1990).[1] Thus, for example, Cao (2001) interprets changes in Chinese population in the eighteenth and especially nineteenth centuries almost entirely in terms of the Malthusian positive check, emphasizing the frequency and intensity of wars, famines, and epidemics triggered by overpopulation. Indeed, an assumption that the positive check predominated in the East and left it mired in a "high-pressure" (Wrigley and Schofield 1981, 473) or "Asiatic" (459) equilibrium underlies many, if not most, of the claims about poor living standards there.[2]

Recent studies, however, raise the possibility that Malthus and his successors overstated the strength and pervasiveness of the positive check in the Eastern demographic system (Lavely and Wong 1998; Lee, Campbell, and Wang 2002). It is now increasingly apparent that preventive checks, as well as a focused and deliberate form of the positive check, were much more important in the East than previously thought (Lee and Wang 1999b; Macfarlane 1997). Widespread fertility limitation within marriage, as well as infanticide, countered the effects on birthrates of early and universal female marriage, leading to moderate population growth rates. If this is correct, Eastern populations may not have been any more prone to an intense and indiscriminate positive check than Western ones.

In this chapter, we use the results of our comparative analyses to further evaluate Malthus's original claim that the positive check was more intense in the East than in the West, as well as more recent claims that the positive check was just as indiscriminate in the West as in the East. We divide our discussion into three sections. First, we summarize these recent claims and their largely epidemiological explanations of indiscriminate mortality. We then compare mortality levels in our Eastern and Western populations in the next section to show that the scale of mortality was broadly similar, and contrast mortality responses in the third section to demonstrate that mortality in the East and West was equally selective. We document that while selectivity in the West was as much a function of class as age and gender, selectivity in the East was almost entirely a result of age and gender discrimination. We substantiate, in other words, Malthus's original understanding that the positive check was endogenous and selective in the West and challenge more recent claims that the check was exogenous and indiscriminate in the East. At the same time, we dispute Malthus's longstanding claim that the Eastern positive check was stronger and less selective.

Theory

Recent advances in epidemiology have identified the mechanisms by which an indiscriminate positive check would have operated. As discussed in chapter 2, Massimo Livi Bacci (1991, 40–62) has argued that in historical Europe, the positive check was primarily indiscriminate. In his account, the social response to dramatic increases in food prices made conditions ripe for epidemics of lethal diseases. In particular, crowding and migration made it easy for virulent diseases such as typhus and cholera to spread and kill indiscriminately, without regard to socioeconomic or other characteristics.[3] Since such social responses occurred only when price increases were extreme and conditions were especially bad, mild increases in prices had little or no effect on mortality. Support for this view comes largely from the observation that epidemics in historical Europe often coincided with or immediately followed great famines and that such epidemics often killed both the poor and the well-off (Livi Bacci 1991, 46). For China, much of the evidence comes from chronologies of epidemics and other natural disasters (Cao 2001).

Findings on the importance of nutritional status to the ability to resist infection reviewed in chapter 2 raise the possibility, however, of a selective positive check. Based on evidence from contemporary developing countries, Neville Scrimshaw (1983) argued that the deterioration in nutritional status associated with even mild penury impaired immune function, increasing the lethality of already common diseases such as diarrhea and respiratory infections. In this framework, the mortality response to economic stress should have been graduated, so that a slight worsening of conditions could precipitate a small increase in death risks. Empirical findings from econometric studies of the mortality response to prices in historical Europe confirm that while extreme price fluctuations may have provoked disproportionate mortality responses, even very small fluctuations could generate a measurable response (R. Lee 1981, Weir 1984b).[4] Since community and family allocation decisions conditioned the effects of bad times on nutritional status, the resulting increases in mortality should not have been indiscriminate within a population. Since priorities by socioeconomic status, gender, and age were socially determined, patterns of responses should have varied selectively.

The design of previous studies has precluded detailed comparison of East and West, as well as adjudication between selective and indiscriminate positive checks. Studies of the associations between economic conditions and death rates in past times have almost all been based on aggregated data for countries and regions in historical Europe, not Asia (Bengtsson and Ohlsson 1985; R. Lee 1981, 1990, 1997; Livi Bacci 1991; Weir 1984b).[5] Even the studies that have sought to identify socioeconomic differences in mortality responses to economic conditions in past times have relied on comparisons of rich and poor countries or districts (Galloway 1986, 1993; Reher 1990) or ethnicities and races (Reher 1991). While results from such studies may be interpreted to support an indiscriminate positive check, they are ill equipped by their very nature to refute a selective check: the aggregated nature of the data precludes detection of the differences in responses within populations that would be expected from a selective response. The few recent mortality studies that make use of event-history techniques, mainly by Eurasia participants and published in Bengtsson and Saito (2000a), meanwhile, are not useful for comparison between East and West because the models they estimate are not identical.

Our study tests Malthus's claims about differences between East and West in the magnitude and selectivity of the positive check through a comparison of results from our comparative individual-level models. Because of the nature of our holistic approach, which compares mortality responses by age, family relationships, household composition, occupation, sex, and socioeconomic status, the results are complicated, reflecting the complexity of the determinants of mortality itself. Exogenous exposure to infection and illness played an important role in the mortality response in our northeastern Chinese and Japanese populations, just as reduced circumstances, preferential consumption, and reduced resistance were important in southern Sweden, eastern Belgium, and northern Italy. Nevertheless, while we find evidence of both selective endogeneity and indiscriminate exogeneity in all regions, the diversity of responses underlines the importance of particularism, not principles, in accounting for them.

Levels

While aggregated data cannot capture such diversity, it is important to note that the overall magnitude of mortality in our Eastern and Western communities was roughly similar. Table 3.1 summarizes male and female life expectancies for our populations at ages 0, 1, 15, 25, and 55. While life expectancy at birth is not comparable between East and West for reasons we explain below, life expectancies at other ages are comparable across communities and typical of preindustrial populations.[6] Life expectancies at age 1, for example, ranged from the low 40s to around 50. Male and female values were similar, except in northern Italy and Liaodong, where females were at a substantial disadvantage.[7] Children at age 15 could expect to live another forty years or so everywhere except Madregolo, where they could expect to live slightly longer.[8] Differences between populations and by gender narrowed in old age, so that male and female life expectancies at age 55 ranged for the most part between 14 and 17.[9]

Consistency of the gender patterns at different ages confirms that with the exception of female infants, mortality in our Eastern and

Table 3.1
Life expectancies at selected ages

	Age 0		Age 1		Age 15		Age 25		Age 55	
	M	F	M	F	M	F	M	F	M	F
Belgium										
Sart	42.8	42.5	51.8	48.4	45.3	43.3	38.1	35.8	16.0	15.8
China[a]										
Dami	39.0[b]	36.7[b]	47.7	44.8	41.8	38.0	34.4	34.6	17.7	21.4
Daoyi	35.0[b]	29.9[b]	42.7	36.3	42.7	39.3	35.1	34.5	14.7	17.3
Feicheng	37.3[b]	30.0[b]	45.6	36.4	45.6	40.5	37.3	35.0	16.7	17.1
Gaizhou	43.0[b]	40.6[b]	52.6	49.6	44.8	45.5	37.9	40.3	18.6	21.3
Gaizhou Manhan	36.9[b]	34.9[b]	46.3	42.5	44.1	41.2	36.9	36.3	17.2	18.0
Gaizhou Mianding	40.3[b]	34.5[b]	49.3	42.0	41.8	42.7	33.9	37.0	12.7	16.7
Niuzhuang	37.3[b]	41.4[b]	45.6	50.7	45.0	43.9	37.8	38.0	15.9	17.4
Italy										
Casalguidi	36.0	33.6	44.2	40.8	44.9	43.3	36.8	35.8	15.9	17.4
Madregolo	36.0	34.4	46.0	42.2	47.4	43.8	39.0	36.2	15.8	16.1
Japan[c]										
Niita and Shimomoriya	35.1[d]	35.0[d]	42.2	42.1	44.8	41.8	38.3	35.5	16.4	16.3
Sweden										
Four Scanian parishes	40.2	41.2	49.4	49.3	45.8	45.7	37.5	38.2	15.2	14.8

[a] The figures for ages 1, 15, 25, and 55 are actually life expectancies at the most closely corresponding ages in Chinese *sui*: 1, 16, 26, and 56 *sui*, respectively. In the Chinese system of age reckoning, individuals are considered to be 1 *sui* at birth, and their age is incremented every Lunar New Year.

[b] Since the Chinese data do not allow for direct calculation of life expectancy at birth, these estimates were produced from life expectancies at age 1 by assuming that 20 percent of infants died in the first year of life.

[c] For the Japanese figures, age is not chronological age, but *ninbetsu-aratame-cho* (NAC) age—the consecutive number of NAC registrations a person went through after birth.

[d] Estimated from life expectancy at age 1 by assuming that 17 percent of infants died before they could be registered.

Table 3.2
Probabilities of dying in selected age intervals (per 1,000)

Population	Age 0–1		Age 1–15		Age 15–25		Age 25–55		Age 55–75	
	M	F	M	F	M	F	M	F	M	F
Belgium										
Sart	184	142	146	167	64	63	272	328	668	686
China[a]										
Dami			178	178	67	164	435	420	663	638
Daoyi			281	361	61	132	358	392	751	644
Feicheng Yimiancheng			270	376	39	113	338	379	698	666
Gaizhou			133	198	72	105	351	313	606	511
Gaizhou Manhan			237	267	65	122	390	356	743	681
Gaizhou Mianding			143	291	54	101	360	319	800	638
Niuzhuang Liuerbao			261	155	64	97	292	298	711	644
Italy										
Casalguidi	202	200	262	303	41	61	314	357	683	616
Madregolo	236	205	264	286	32	66	256	335	638	696
Japan[b]										
Niita and Shimomoriya			300	260	81	94	281	336	643	667
Sweden										
Four Scanian parishes	202	183	186	183	38	55	306	256	721	718

[a] The figures for ages 1, 15, 25, and 55 are actually values at the most closely corresponding ages in Chinese *sui*: 1, 16, 26, and 56 *sui*, respectively. In the Chinese system of age reckoning, individuals are considered to be 1 *sui* at birth, and their age is incremented every Lunar New Year.
[b] For the Japanese figures, age is not chronological age, but *ninbetsu-aratame-cho* (NAC) age—a consecutive number of NAC registrations a person went through after birth.

Western populations was largely indiscriminate. Table 3.2 compares the probabilities of dying in particular age groups, conditional on survival to the beginning of the age group. Patterns were typical of nineteenth-century populations. Thus, the diverse pattern of life expectancies by gender in table 3.1—a female advantage in Sart, nearly identical life expectancies for men and women in Scania, and a male advantage everywhere else—was the product not of fundamentally different regimes but rather subtle variations on an underlying theme. Where infant mortality could be calculated directly and was not deliberate, it was higher for boys than for girls, as is common in both historical and contemporary populations.[10] In childhood and early adulthood, meanwhile, females had higher death rates than males, as was common for these ages in nineteenth-century populations (Perrenoud 1981). Such excesses are typically attributed to higher female death rates from infectious diseases, especially tuberculosis (Preston 1976).[11] At later ages, as is typical in both historical and contemporary populations, females had lower death rates.

The only examples of selective mortality that emerge from the examination of levels are among children and especially infants. Although the Chinese and Japanese data do not allow for direct calculation of infant mortality, indirect calculations summarized in detail elsewhere suggest that in Daoyi, our largest Liaodong community, excess female infant and child mortality accounted for as much as 20 percent of female births (Lee and Campbell 1997). Moreover, while it is impossible to infer directly how many of these daughters died due to infanticide as opposed to child neglect, parents clearly selectively killed or ignored daughters to achieve goals for the number and sex composition of their children (Lee, Wang, and Campbell 1994; G. W. Skinner 1993; Smith 1977).

Responses

While mortality levels in our Eastern and Western communities were roughly similar, mortality responses to changing economic conditions differed considerably, at least over the short term. To compare the strength of the positive check in our five regional populations, we examine associations between mortality risks and economic conditions captured in the individual models estimated for our respective populations.[12] These individual models include only socioeconomic status and logged grain prices or, in the case of Scania, logged real wages, as covariates.[13] We carry out separate analyses by age group and sex, resulting in eight estimations for each population. The four age groups were infants (0–24 months), children (2–15 years), working-age adults (15–55 years), and the elderly (55 and above).[14] Although participants estimated separate models for the never married and ever married for adults, we consider only the results for the ever married, because several of the populations had too few never married to allow comparison.[15]

Tables 3.3 and 3.4 present elasticities that represent the percentage change in the chances of dying associated with a 10 percent increase in

Table 3.3
Percentage change in infant and child mortality associated with a 10 percent price increase

Country	Site	Infants (0–24 months) Females (%)	(p)	Males (%)	(p)	Children (2–15 years) Females (%)	(p)	Males (%)	(p)
Belgium	Sart	5.07	0.14	−0.60	0.83	7.91	0.06	13.51	0.00
China	Liaodong North					−0.42	0.79	−0.32	0.74
	Liaodong South							2.27	0.08
Italy	Casalguidi	0.21	0.94	8.29	0.00	12.84	0.00	10.55	0.04
	Madregolo	−3.73	0.10	5.72	0.00	4.95	0.16	11.83	0.00
Japan	Niita and Shimomoriya	7.80	0.00	−0.87	0.83	4.00	0.00	0.88	0.61
Sweden	Four Scanian parishes	5.61	0.04	5.39	0.02	8.28	0.02	7.80	0.02

Note: Based on results from the comparative individual models.

Table 3.4
Percentage change in adult and elderly mortality associated with a 10 percent price increase

Country	Site	Ever-married adults Females (%)	(p)	Males (%)	(p)	Ever-married elderly Females (%)	(p)	Males (%)	(p)
Belgium	Sart	6.85	0.10	0.71	0.88	−3.72	0.35	−5.50	0.11
China	Liaodong North	1.62	0.02	2.62	0.00	−0.12	0.88	2.05	0.01
	Liaodong South	−0.09	0.93	−2.39	0.01	−0.24	0.82	−1.51	0.13
Italy	Casalguidi	14.02	0.00	16.91	0.00	15.69	0.00	−0.22	0.96
	Madregolo	5.66	0.07	13.65	0.00	8.24	0.05	4.20	0.27
Japan	Niita and Shimomoriya	1.67	0.29	4.59	0.00	0.81	0.64	7.59	0.00
Sweden	Four Scanian parishes	7.77	0.03	4.62	0.22	6.23	0.08	5.32	0.13

Note: Based on results from the comparative individual models.

grain prices.[16] A value of 12, for example, indicates that for every 10 percent increase in prices, the risk of dying is increased by 12 percent.[17] The underlying scale, of course, is continuous, so in this example, a 20 percent increase in prices would increase the risk of dying by 25.4 percent.[18] Annual price fluctuations of 30 percent were not unusual, and there were examples of even more violent fluctuations; thus, a 10 percent change in prices is modest. Table 3.3 presents results for infants and children, distinguishing between males and females. Table 3.4 presents results for adults and the elderly, distinguishing between men and women and restricting to the ever married.[19]

At least in the short term, mortality responses to price increases were much more pronounced in our Western communities than our Eastern ones. By this measure, in other words, the positive check operated with greater force in the West. The Liaodong populations were the least responsive, with small but statistically significant price effects on mortality risks apparent only among adults. Ten percent increases in price led to no more than 1 or 2 percent changes in the risks of dying. Responses in Niita and Shimomoriya were also weak, except among female infants and elderly males. In Europe, by contrast, 7 to 8 percent increases were not uncommon, even among working-age adults. In Casalguidi and Madregolo, 10 to 15 percent increases were apparent at most ages. In Sart, when prices rose by 10 percent, male child mortality increased by more than 13 percent.

Even more important than these differences in the magnitude of mortality response were the patterns of these responses. Examination of response patterns by age, gender, and marital status confirms that mechanisms were selective, not indiscriminate. In stark contrast with results on famine mortality that suggest that male death rates were affected the most when times were especially bad (Kane 1987; Ó Grada 1999; Sen 1981; Watkins and Menken 1985), the results in Tables 3.3 and 3.4 indicate that either males or females could be more vulnerable, depending on age and location. Results from additional calculations for Scania, Casalguidi, and Madregolo reported in chapters 6 and 8 suggest that although there was evidence of a threshold effect of prices on mortality in some locations—extremely high prices appear to have had a disproportionate impact in these locations—mortality responses for the most part were linear, in the sense that mild increases in price provoked moderate increases in mortality. Moreover, responses tended to be immediate in all locations: additional examinations found little evidence of lags, often found in studies based on aggregated data.

The selectivity of the mechanisms is apparent in the variability of gender patterns of response for infants and children. In Scania, both males and females were vulnerable, only females were vulnerable in Niita and Shimomoriya, and only males were vulnerable in Casalguidi and Madregolo. As for Liaodong, though there are no data to allow direct calculations of infant mortality, indirect evidence suggests that because of infanticide, females were especially vulnerable to price fluctuations (Lee and Campbell 1997; Lee, Campbell, and Tan 1992). So while the magnitudes of the price effects apparent in table 3.3 tend to be consistent—if a 10 percent increase in prices did have an effect, it typically raised the chances that an infant would die by 5 to 8 percent—the variability in the pattern of infant mortality responses by sex suggests that the demographic impact of economic pressure was directed selectively by parents who favored or discriminated against one sex or another when tough times forced reductions in consumption.

But while Western parents may have favored particular infants according to their sex, this does not appear to have been the case for children. The mechanisms governing child mortality there appear to have been indiscriminate, in that males and females were affected similarly everywhere. In Casalguidi, where the effect of prices on infant mortality was apparent only among males, a 10 percent rise in prices increased child mortality for both sexes: by 10.6 percent for males and 4.8 percent for females. In the Scania parishes, a 10 percent reduction in real wages raised child mortality by 7.8 percent for males and 8.3 percent for females. In Sart, prices affected child mortality though not infant mortality. The similarity of response patterns by location and gender within the West indicates that whatever the mechanisms were, they were endogenous, in the sense that features of family organization common to the Western sites underlay them.

Child mortality responses in our Eastern communities were selective, confirming that the uniformity of responses in our Western communities was due to common features of Western social and family organization, not some universal characteristic of child mortality related to biology. The clearest evidence of the selectivity of the Eastern responses was from Niita and Shimomoriya. Children there were clearly less vulnerable to price fluctuations than infants, but the response was still sex specific. Whereas a 10 increase in prices raised female infant mortality by 7.8 percent, it raised female child mortality by only 4.0 percent. In northern Liaodong, there was no statistically significant response for either boys or girls. In southern Liaodong, the weak response for males was statistically significant only according to very liberal criteria.

For working-age adults in table 3.4, the underlying mechanisms were also clearly selective, with pronounced variation from one region to the next in the gender pattern of responses and no clear pattern of differences between our Eastern and Western communities. In some cases, both sexes were affected; in other cases, it was one or the other. In the Scanian parishes and especially in Sart, females were more vulnerable. In Scania, a 10 percent increase in prices raised female mortality by 7.8 percent but male mortality by only 4.6 percent.[20] In Sart, a similar price increase raised adult female mortality by 6.9 percent but had almost no effect on male mortality. Males were only slightly more sensitive than females in Casalguidi, a 16.9 percent increase versus a 14 percent increase, but much more sensitive in Madregolo, where a 10 percent increase in prices increased male mortality by 13.7 percent but female mortality by only 5.7 percent. Males in Niita and Shimomoriya were also more vulnerable than females. In north Liaodong, males and females were both affected by increases, with males slightly more so, but the magnitude of the effect for both was small: a 10 percent increase in prices raised mortality by only 1 or 2 percent.

The response of the elderly appears also to have been highly selective. Moreover, in many regions, including Liaodong, Casalguidi, Madregolo, and Scania, the elderly responded differently than did adults. In Scania, magnitudes of effects for males and females were similar, with 10 percent increases in price raising mortality risks by 5 or 6 percent.[21] In rural Casalguidi and Madregolo, only females were affected by price increases. The female response in Casalguidi was especially strong, with a 10 percent increase in prices triggering a nearly 16 percent increase in mortality risks. In north Liaodong, only males were affected, and the magnitude of the effect was small. Only in Niita and Shimomoriya did the gender patterns of response resemble those of adults: males were once again the only ones affected by price increases. The response was slightly stronger than in the working ages, so that a 10 percent increase in prices raised the death rates of ever-married males by 7.6 percent.

As Malthus predicted, socioeconomic variations in mortality response were more pronounced in our Western communities than in our Eastern ones. We use here the socioeconomic categories from our respective population registers.[22] Tables 3.5 and 3.6 differentiate mortality responses by socioeconomic status, based on results from the estimation of the individual models with price interactions. Originally, estimated hazard ratios for interaction terms in the original results compare effects of prices on mortality for each subcategory to effects for an omitted reference category. For Tables 3.5 and 3.6, we translated these ratios into elasticities representing the total effect of a price increase for the members of a specified category by multiplying hazard ratios for the reference category and the interaction term. For the reference category, the statistical significance summarized in the p-value represents the results of a test of the null hypothesis that there is no effect, against the alternative that there is one. The p-values for the remaining categories, meanwhile, are results from a test of the null hypothesis that price effects are the same as in the reference category, against the alternative that they differ. In Niita and Shimomoriya, where socioeconomic status was measured with household landholding, the ratios in the table represent the effect on price sensitivity of one unit increase in landholding.[23]

The results for socioeconomic status confirm the importance of selective mechanisms in accounting for the mortality response to economic pressure. Whereas response patterns by age and gender reflect the variability of household priorities, the response patterns by socioeconomic status suggest the importance of societal priorities. In particular, they reflect differences across societies, especially between East and West, in the existence or at least the effectiveness of institutions or mechanisms to help insulate less fortunate groups against the consequences of economic pressure. In the East, the societal safety net discussed in chapter 4 helped to prevent the adverse impact of bad times from falling disproportionately on specific socioeconomic strata. In the West, however, a different sense of entitlements meant that socioeconomic status was a more important determinant of sensitivity.

As Malthus suspected, infants and children's socioeconomic differences in the response to economic hardship affected children the most. In some cases, as anticipated in chapter 2, the marginally better-off middle-class households were so much better off that when prices were high, the death rates of their infants and children fell, while the death rates for the poor rose and those of the rich remained constant. Thus, for middle-class households in Casalguidi, a 10 percent increase in prices reduced female infant mortality by 31.5 percent and male child mortality by 31.8 percent. Child mortality and male infant mortality in sharecropper households, meanwhile, rose when prices did. Effects on infants and children in the households of artisans and paid laborers were more erratic. Similarly, in Sart, a 10 percent price

Table 3.5
Effects of prices on infant and child mortality by household socioeconomic status

Country	Site	Status	Infants (0–24 months)				Children (2–15 years)			
			Females		Males		Females		Males	
			(%)	(p)	(%)	(p)	(%)	(p)	(%)	(p)
Belgium	Sart	Cultivator (reference)	4.57	0.23	-0.76	0.80	6.73	0.16	12.92	0.01
		Functionary	3.00	0.97			-33.31	0.36		
		Artisans and industrial workers	-22.71	0.01	-3.70	0.86	14.38	0.65	2.52	0.69
		Day laborers	-3.34	0.46	17.06	0.14	-19.55	0.07	-18.40	0.02
		Miscellaneous	19.31	0.82			82.98	0.54		
China	Liaodong North	Farmer					0.20	0.91	-0.28	0.79
		Artisan					25.20	0.15	-4.17	0.31
		Soldier					-2.39	0.57	3.07	0.42
		Functionary					-14.11	0.10	2.30	0.71
	Liaodong South	Farmer							2.22	0.09
		Artisan								
		Soldier							56.23	0.28
		Functionary							-0.49	0.72
Italy	Casalguidi	Sharecroppers/farmers	0.42	0.89	7.66	0.02	12.77	0.02	13.94	0.03
		Paid farm laborers	4.56	0.56	7.78	0.99	-8.03	0.14	18.80	0.78
		Artisans and not farmers	-2.71	0.69	14.47	0.34	20.61	0.51	-0.22	0.31
		Middle class	-31.48	0.10	-8.65	0.24	37.64	0.29	-31.81	0.00
Japan	Niita and Shimomoriya	Household landholding (in *koku*)	-0.94	0.05	-0.20	0.68	0.10	0.68	0.25	0.23

		Sweden				Four Scanian parishes			
Freeholder		2.95	0.74	7.42	0.39	9.40	0.45	1.80	0.88
Noble tenants		−0.25	0.79	−0.24	0.49	8.47	0.96	1.29	0.98
Semilandless		0.48	0.80	−3.15	0.27	−4.40	0.30	16.79	0.20
Landless		3.87	0.92	5.52	0.83	−1.53	0.38	5.42	0.77

Note: Based on results from the comparative individual models with price interactions. For each category, the percentage change is the total effect of a price change. Thus, the results for reference categories are the main effect of price, and the results for remaining categories are the combined main and interaction effects. For the omitted category, the *p*-value is from a test of the hypothesis that there is a price effect for it. For the remaining categories, *p*-values are from a test of the hypothesis that the price effects differ from that of the omitted category.

Table 3.6
Effects of prices on adult and elderly mortality by household socioeconomic status

Country	Site	Occupation	Ever-married adults				Ever-married elderly			
			Females		Males		Females		Males	
			(%)	(p)	(%)	(p)	(%)	(p)	(%)	(p)
Belgium	Sart	Cultivator (reference)	11.38	0.03	-1.38	0.78	-4.23	0.29	-5.20	0.15
		Functionary	53.82	0.40					-37.33	0.04
		Artisans and industrial workers	18.11	0.74	-25.40	0.22	10.24	0.38	-14.09	0.47
		Day laborers	54.08	0.09	-9.90	0.59	-13.56	0.60	8.53	0.47
		Miscellaneous	101.77	0.45						
China	Liaodong North	Farmer	1.66	0.02	2.77	0.00	-0.27	0.74	1.95	0.01
		Artisan	-6.06	0.32	5.94	0.59	19.57	0.24	-1.65	0.63
		Soldier	3.25	0.77	-3.27	0.19	11.53	0.22	0.58	0.75
		Functionary	1.17	0.95	-0.20	0.65	4.99	0.57	15.91	0.03
	Liaodong South	Farmer	-0.11	0.90	-2.22	0.02	-0.28	0.78	-1.57	0.12
		Artisan								
		Soldier	-7.51	0.42	-17.31	0.01	4.38	0.67	3.67	0.40
		Functionary	11.39	0.39	-9.22	0.21				
Italy	Casalguidi	Sharecroppers/farmers	8.09	0.11	16.09	0.01	10.05	0.05	1.07	0.83
		Paid farm laborers	25.43	0.11	28.56	0.37	29.26	0.17	3.92	0.83
		Artisans and not farmers	23.22	0.19	18.18	0.89	27.57	0.12	6.46	0.69
		Middle class	10.68	0.90	-29.63	0.00	-6.55	0.66	-50.51	0.01
Japan	Niita and Shimomoriya	Household landholding (in *koku*)	0.26	0.18	0.04	0.87	0.00	1.00	0.20	0.46

		Sweden				Four Scanian parishes			
Freeholder		13.83	0.26	12.87	0.26	7.85	0.54	0.68	0.96
Noble tenants		−11.93	0.19	−16.64	0.17	2.20	0.75	12.37	0.48
Semilandless		2.97	0.40	−10.44	0.10	7.91	1.00	−1.99	0.86
Landless		25.29	0.25	9.60	0.78	7.64	0.99	9.39	0.49

Note: Based on results from the comparative individual models with price interactions. For each category, the percentage change is the total effect of a price change. Thus, the results for reference categories are the main effect of price, and the results for remaining categories are the combined main and interaction effects. For the omitted category, the *p*-value is from a test of the hypothesis that there is a price effect for it. For the remaining categories, *p*-values are from a test of the hypothesis that the price effects differ from that of the omitted category.

increase reduced female infant mortality in the households of artisans and industrial workers by 22.7 percent and lowered child mortality for the families of day laborers, even though such price increases raised the child mortality of cultivators.

Socioeconomic differences in the sensitivity of infant and child mortality were much less pronounced in our Eastern communities. In Niita and Shimomoriya, for example, every additional unit of land reduced the response of female infant mortality to a price increase by 0.9 percent. Thus, whereas households with few or no *koku* saw substantial increases in infant female mortality when prices rose, households with ample land saw rates fall.[24] No effects were apparent among male infants or among children. Similarly, in Liaodong, there was only one example of a socioeconomic difference. In northern Liaodong, a 10 percent increase in prices lowered the death rates of the daughters of functionaries by 14.1 percent.

In our Eastern and Western communities, socioeconomic status was less important as a determinant of the sensitivity of mortality among adults.[25] According to table 3.6, where socioeconomic status had a discernible effect, it appeared that higher status reduced or even reversed the effects of prices, even when mortality was rising for other social groups. Thus, working adult males in middle-class households in Casalguidi saw their death rates fall by 29.6 when prices rose by 10 percent, even though the same price increase triggered a 16.1 percent increase in the death rates of their counterparts in sharecropper households. In our Eastern communities, there was only one example of a socioeconomic gradient in the response to prices. In south Liaodong, soldiers saw their mortality fall when prices rose.

As for the response of the elderly, effects of socioeconomic status were apparent only in Sart, Casalguidi, and north Liaodong. In Sart and Casalguidi, the effect was as expected. In Sart, elderly men in households headed by functionaries saw their mortality rates fall by one-third when prices rose 10 percent. In Casalguidi, elderly men in middle-class households also saw their mortality fall: a 10 percent price increase halved the risk of dying. The same price increase raised the mortality of elderly women in sharecropper households by 10 percent. The direction of effects was not always as expected. In north Liaodong, death rates among elderly functionaries were actually more sensitive than among farmers.

Mortality responses in bad times were not only higher in our Western communities than in the East; they were, if anything, more selective and therefore more complicated. Tables 3.7 and 3.8 summarize the diversity of mortality responses to bad times by gender and socioeconomic status for all five regions. Taken together, they suggest that selective preferences, while common in our Chinese and Japanese communities, were equally pervasive in our Swedish, Belgian, and Italian communities as well. Such preferences cut deep, and they cut along class lines as well as along gender, such that when times were bad, the mortality response depended on the interaction of socioeconomic status and gender. In Casalguidi, among the families of sharecroppers, for example, a 10 percent increase in prices resulted in increases of 7.7, 13.9, and 12.8 percent, respectively, for male infants and children and female children, but no change in the mortality of female infants. Among the middle class, rates actually fell 31.5 and 31.8 percent for female infants and male children, respectively, but not for male infants. Both middle-class and sharecropper households, in other words, gave some form of preferential treatment to female infants. The middle class shared their largesse when times were good. The sharecroppers protected them when times were bad.

In our Western populations, such gender-preferential behavior was temporary and is identifiable only when we compare the sensitivity of various age groups by gender and socioeconomic status to changing economic conditions over the short term of a year or two. This is why previous scholars have not been able to confirm gender-differentiated mortality in the rural West before (Johansson 1984, 1987, 1991; Lynch 2000; Wall 1981), not because it was not there (it was), but because it was temporary, was preferential rather than discriminatory, affected only small numbers of girls, and was accordingly elusive. By contrast, in our Eastern populations, while there is virtually no evidence of any selective mortality response to changes in economic conditions by socioeconomic status, there is a sustained selectivity bias by gender that was discriminatory rather than preferential and common in good times as well as bad. Young girls in Liaodong and Ou, regardless of their socioeconomic status, were routinely discriminated against, especially during bad times and especially in their infancy.

Implications

Our results suggest that mortality responses to bad times were a complex equation of age, gender, and socioeconomic status, on the one hand, and presumably family and community preferences and

Table 3.7
Price responses by age and gender

Country	Site	Infants		Children		Ever-married working-age adults		Ever-married elderly adults	
		F	M	F	M	F	M	F	M
Belgium	Sart	No	No	Yes	Yes	Yes	No	No	No
China	Liaodong North			No	No	Yes	Yes	No	Yes
	Liaodong South				Yes	No	Yes	No	No
Italy	Casalguidi	No	Yes	Yes	Yes	Yes	Yes	Yes	No
	Madregolo	Yes	Yes	No	Yes	Yes	Yes	Yes	No
Japan	Niita and Shimomoriya	Yes	No	Yes	No	No	Yes	No	Yes
Sweden	Four Scanian parishes	Yes	Yes	Yes	Yes	Yes	No	Yes	No

Note: Based on results from comparative individual models summarized in tables 3.3 and 3.4. Price effects were considered statistically significant if $p < 0.10$.

Table 3.8
Differences by socioeconomic status in the response to prices

Country	Site	Infants		Children		Ever-married working-age adults		Ever-married elderly adults	
		F	M	F	M	F	M	F	M
Belgium	Sart	Yes	No	Yes	Yes	Yes	No	No	Yes
China	Liaodong North			Yes	No	No	No	No	Yes
	Liaodong South				No	No	Yes	No	No
Italy	Casalguidi Madregolo	No	Yes	No	Yes	No	Yes	No	Yes
Japan	Niita and Shimomoriya	Yes	No	No	No	No	No	No	No
Sweden	Four Scanian parishes[a]	No	No	Yes[a]	Yes[a]	Yes[a]	Yes[a]	No	No

Note: Based on results from individual models with price interactions summarized in tables 3.5 and 3.6. Price effects were considered statistically significant if $p < 0.10$.

[a] In Sweden, differences in price responses by socioeconomic status emerged in the period 1815–1865. See chapter 6, especially tables 6.2 through 6.5, and the accompanying discussion in the text. These differences are not apparent in tables 3.5 and 3.6 because the calculations for those tables are for the shorter period from 1829 to 1865.

resources, on the other. There was, in other words, no one universal pattern of mortality responses by age, sex, or even socioeconomic status. In our Eastern communities, the response appears to have been more exogenous and indiscriminate, while in our Western communities, it was endogenous and particularistic. Thus, conjunctions of circumstances produced an overall pattern characterized by less sensitivity, more consistent preferences, and weak socioeconomic selectivity in the East, as well as the greater responsiveness, more complex preferences, greater socioeconomic differences, and preferential as well as discriminatory behavior in the West.

Human agency, not human biology, must have shaped such mortality responses. Only agency could have accounted for such a diversity of response patterns, not only between East and West, but within them as well. Accordingly, we turn in chapter 4 to a comparison of relevant features of household, community, and societal organization, identifying the potential role each may have played in conditioning the mortality response to economic stress. We then examine in chapter 5 the results from our comparative *household* and *relationship* models to assess empirically claims about the importance of each of these forms of social organization in accounting for differences in the response to economic conditions between East and West. In particular, we assess claims that the conjugal and joint household systems played an instrumental role in our Western and Eastern populations in shielding individuals against the effects of economic stress, by examining how household characteristics conditioned individual mortality responses to changes in economic conditions.

Notes

We thank Ronald Lee for his detailed comments on a previous version of this chapter.

1. Thus Wrigley et al. (1997) conclude, "Had he but known it, Malthus might well have dubbed a preventive-check society, in which marriage acted as the demographic regulator, as 'English' to balance his designation of a positive-check society, where the regular was mortality, as 'Chinese'" (549).

2. The logic is summarized in the suggestion by Wrigley and Schofield (1981) that "in pre-industrial west European societies where fertility levels were modest because age at marriage was high ... the resulting equilibrium population for this reason alone would be lower and real incomes higher than would be possible under an 'Asiatic' regime where fertility was at a high absolute level" (459).

3. Livi Bacci (1991, 49) argues, "Famines, as we know, increased disproportionately the already conspicuous mass of beggars and vagrants. It swelled the numbers migrating to

towns, it packed the poorhouses, hospices, and hospitals, it made easier the spread of epidemic diseases such as typhus." On the role of migration in the mortality response, see Dupâquier (1989), Meuvret (1965), and Pitkänen and Mielke (1993).

4. See Livi Bacci (1991, 55–62) for a critique of these results.

5. The only comparisons between Asia and Europe of which we are aware rely on aggregated data for countries or regions (R. Lee 1990, 1997). For Asia and especially China, moreover, the data in the comparison were from the twentieth century (R. Lee 1990, 1997). One time series for China consisted of annual data for the country as a whole between 1953 and 1964, which includes the famine associated with the Great Leap Forward. The other consisted of data for the province of Taiwan between 1914 and 1938, when it was under Japanese colonial rule. The mortality analysis of Japanese responses was also based on twentieth-century data (R. Lee 1990, 8).

6. Caveats about the comparison of life expectancies between East and West aside, these values are in line with those for other preindustrial populations. From the sixteenth to the eighteenth centuries, life expectancy at birth in England ranged from the low 30s to the low 40s (Wrigley and Schofield 1981, 528). Similarly, in the last half of the eighteenth century and the first half of the nineteenth, life expectancy in Sweden ranged from the mid-30s to the low 40s (Statistiska Centralbyrån 1969, 118). In France, life expectancy during the last of the eighteenth century and the beginning of the nineteenth ranged from the high 20s to the high 30s (Blayo 1975).

7. See chapter 11 for a detailed discussion of gender differences in mortality.

8. In Sweden, life expectancy at age 15 in the last half of the eighteenth century and the first half of the nineteenth was in the low 40s (Statistiska Centralbyrån 1969, 118). In France during the eighteenth century, it was close to 40 (Blayo 1975).

9. See chapter 13 for a detailed discussion of old-age mortality.

10. Some evidence suggests that such gender gaps in infant mortality have a genetic origin, but it is not conclusive (Waldron 1983a, 1983b, 1986, 1987).

11. Maternal mortality, that is, deaths occurring as the result of childbirth, appears to have played only a small role in accounting for female excess mortality in early adulthood. See Schofield (1986) as well as chapter 11.

12. These models do not include effects for lagged prices or wages. Each team carried out its own investigations of such effects and reports the relevant results in their local history chapters.

13. Since the Japanese and Chinese data required use of discrete-time as opposed to continuous-time event-history methods, age was also included as a covariate in their analyses. See chapter 6 for a discussion of the use of real wage data for Scania.

14. See the appendix for a detailed discussion of the data, models, and the construction of the variables for each population. Infancy was defined to include the first twenty-four months of life instead of the first twelve to account for the variability between populations in the length of breast-feeding, as well as problems in the Japanese data in identifying ages in months for the very young.

15. We estimate separate models for the ever married and never married because in the West European populations, especially Scania and Sart, data on the mortality of never-married adults were inadequate for this purpose.

16. In the case of the Scania parishes, they represent the effect of a 10 percent reduction in real wages.

17. Because the original results were hazard ratios that represented changes in the risks of dying associated with one unit increases in logged prices, we calculated the elasticities by multiplying the original coefficients (i.e., the logged hazard ratios) by the log of 1.1, exponentiating, and then converting the resulting proportion to a percentage. In other words, if the original coefficient was b, so that the hazard ratio was e^b, the percentage presented in the tables is calculated as $100 * (e^{b \log(1.1)} - 1)$.

18. $100 * (1.12 * 1.12 - 1) = 25.4$.

19. We do not consider results for the never-married here because in several populations, there were too few to support reliable estimations of the models, making comparison of responses impossible.

20. If the period from 1815 onward is considered, however, the difference between the responses by sex in Scania is not significant. See chapter 6.

21. The effect for males, though almost as large as that for females, was not quite statistically significant.

22. See chapters 6 through 10 for discussion of these categories in the respective local histories.

23. A *koku*, a measure of volume equivalent to 180 liters, refers to the normal rice yield used to compute tribute or tax. All property, including dry fields and homesteads, was converted into *koku* equivalents for tax and tribute purposes; see Ooms 1996.

24. The coefficient for the main effect of price, not shown in the table, implies that a 10 percent increase in prices led to an 18.8 percent increase in death rates for infant females in households with no *koku*. Calculations from the coefficients for the main and interaction effects imply that a 10 percent increase in prices increased mortality risks by 17.7 percent in a household with 1 *koku* and by only 5.7 percent in a household with 12.4 *koku*, the average. Households with 19 or more *koku* would have seen infant female death rates fall when prices rose.

25. Though it is not apparent in table 3.6, Scania was an exception. According to results in tables 6.2 and 6.4, socioeconomic differences in the mortality response to short-term economic stress were highly significant for adults and nearly significant for children.

4   Family and Community

James Z. Lee, Tommy
Bengtsson, and Cameron
Campbell
in collaboration with Marco
Breschi, Martin Dribe, Satomi
Kurosu, Emiko Ochiai, Michel
Oris, and Noriko O. Tsuya

It is a general complaint among master manufacturers, that high wages ruin all their workmen; but it is difficult to conceive that these men would not save a part of their high wages for the future support of their families, instead of spending it in drunkenness and dissipation, if they did not rely on parish assistance for support in case of accidents.

(Malthus 1826/1986, 366)

A man who might not be deterred from going to the alehouse from the consideration that on his death or sickness he should leave his wife and family upon the parish, might yet hesitate in thus dissipating his earnings, if he were assured, that in either of these cases his family must starve, or be left to the support of casual bounty.

(Malthus 1826/1986, 367)

The small number of families in proportion to the number of persons able to bear arms, . . . is accounted for by a custom noticed by Sir George Staunton as general in China. In the enclosure belonging to one dwelling, he observes that a whole family of three generations, with all their respective wives and children, will frequently be found.

(Malthus 1826/1986, 126)

For Malthus, there were only two recourses in bad times: the family and the community. But while Malthus recognized that the family was smaller in the West than in the East and that familial affect was less intense in the East than in the West, he also believed that familial obligations were stronger in China than in England. Whereas Malthus lamented that working men would spend, not save, their wages, if they thought that the community would care for their dependents when times were bad, he believed that in China, the family took care of its own. The thrust of much of his writings about social policy was therefore directed at the West, and at England in particular, both to regulate poor relief so as to force workers to save and to restrict family formation in general.

In fact, the East-West contrasts were much sharper than Malthus realized. Not only were East Asian families larger and more complex than West European families, their organization was more hierarchical and their resources more concentrated under the control of senior members, especially the head (Lee and Campbell 1997). Equally striking, Chinese states were based on a political ideology of human entitlement that required them to "nourish the people" in bad times. European political ideology had no such requirements. As a result, while the Chinese state went to considerable effort to establish a national welfare system to regulate the national food supply, Western states left the food supply largely in private hands. European governments contributed relatively little money or effort to provision the poor in good or bad times. Poor relief, according to Western norms, was an act of Christian charity. According to long-standing and deeply rooted Asian beliefs, it was a central function of good government (Will, Wong, and Lee 1991).[1]

This chapter on the social and economic organization of our populations surveys and compares available responses to economic stress in the various locales, emphasizing the overarching contrasts between our Eastern and Western communities, and by extension, the East and the West. We divide the chapter into two sections. First, we compare community organization, focusing on the different levels of inequality and the different degree of protection from bad times. Then we contrast household organization, including size and structure. We demonstrate that there were remarkable differences between our East Asian and West European populations. East Asians lived in larger households, inequality between households was mild, and there were considerable forms of protection from bad times. West Europeans lived in smaller households, inequality between households was pronounced, and there was little available in the form of social welfare.

Community Organization

We begin with community organization as it had the largest potential impact on mortality responses to short-term stress. Although we know much about the demographic characteristics of the populations we study, we know far less about them as communities. We know their institutional arrangements for famine and poor relief at the national or even regional level, but are less clear about the specific details of each village. This is especially true for our Liaodong populations, who lived scattered among some 400 villages. By contrast, there is far more systematic detailed information available for our four parishes in Scania and two villages in Ou.

At first glance, several commonalities are apparent. All communities were rural. Table 4.1 summarizes the major crops, as well as the arrangements for land tenure. Coincidentally, all were situated close to cities. Though at roughly comparable levels of commercialization, the local economies varied. Liaodong and Scania were particularly productive and exported large quantities of grain. By contrast, Casalguidi and Sart depended on grain imports paid for by commercial agriculture and rural industry. None of these regions or communities was unusually well off or advanced. All were vulnerable to changing economic conditions reflected or caused by variations in grain prices and wages.

Overall, it is the differences, especially those between East and West, that stand out. First and foremost is the distribution of wealth as reflected in landholding. Our Western communities were much less egalitarian than their Eastern counterparts. Figure 4.1 compares the distribution of landownership among families and farmers in our communities in Ou, Sart, Scania, and Tuscana based on late eighteenth- and early nineteenth-century real estate and personal income tax records with land distribution province-wide in Liaoning around 1948. The contrasts are clearest at the opposite ends of the social spectrum. At the top, the richest 5 percent of all families in Sart, Scania, and Tuscana used 31, 36, and 25 percent of the land, respectively, compared to 15 percent in Ou. At the bottom, not only did the poorest 5 percent of all households in all four regions own no land, landless households accounted for 40, 50, and 30 percent of all households in Sart, Scania, and Tuscana, respectively, but only 15 percent of all households in Ou. Although precise figures are not available for our Liaodong communities, the provincial averages at the time of land reform in 1948 were remarkably similar to Ou. Only 15 percent of rural population had no land at all (Liaoning Land Bureau private communication).[2]

Although there were far more landless in our Western communities than in our Eastern ones, the institutional arrangements to protect rural communities in bad times were more extensive in the East than in the West. While the measures to dampen food prices fluctuations were strikingly similar in the East and the West during the eighteenth

Table 4.1
Economic characteristics

Site	Urban/rural	Major crops	% males 15–55 with nonfarm occupation	Land tenure		
Belgium						
Sart	Rural	Wheat, forestry, livestock	39.54	Smallholders, little tenants, and users of common lands, with most people sharing these statuses		
China						
Liaodong Grain state farm systems			4.5			
Daoyi, Feicheng Yimian cheng, Gaizhou Manhan, Gaizhou Rending	Rural	Sorghum		Fixed in-kind rents, paid in grain		
Liaodong Specialized state farm systems						
Dami	Rural	Honey, sorghum		Fixed in-kind rents, paid in specialized produce		
Gaizhou Mianding	Rural	Cotton				
Niuzhuang Liuerbao	Rural	Fish, sorghum				
Italy				Farmers and sharecroppers %	Agricultural day laborers %	
Casalguidi	Rural	Grapes, olives, wheat	11.1	53.4[a]	19.3[a]	
Madregolo	Rural	Wheat, legumes, corn	NA	38.1[a]	34.0[a]	
Japan						
Ou (Niita and Shimomoriya)	Rural	Rice	Nearly 0			

Sweden			Freeholders and crown tenants %	Tenants on noble land %	Semilandless %	Landless and artisans %
Hög	Rural	Rye	47	0	22	31
Kävlinge	Rural	Rye	46	0	15	39
Halmstad	Rural	Rye	1	23	23	53
Sireköpinge	Rural	Rye	0	41	17	42

[a] Information on the profession is only for heads of family and comes from two censuses (1841 for Casalguidi, 1849 for Madregolo). At the moment, for Madregolo this is the only source for data on occupation, while for Casalguidi parish registers also provide some information. Nonetheless, the indication of the profession is rarely precise, not allowing a clear distinction of the different typologies of land tenure.

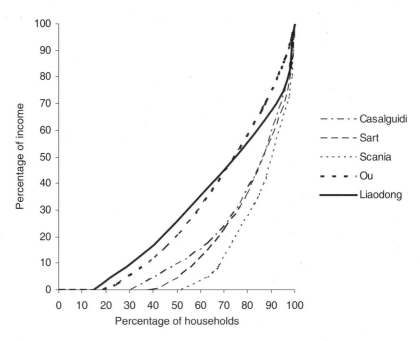

Figure 4.1
Inequality in five Eurasia populations: Wealth reflected from tax records
Sources: Casalguidi: Archivio di Stato di Pistoia, Comunità di Serravalle Pistoiese, Tasse di famiglia, 1830–1837. Ou: for Niita village, Mizuyama Family Documents, Koriyama-shi Historical Records Archive in Fukushima Prefecture (Shimomoriya), 1716–1869; for Shimomoriya village, Endo Family Private Documents (Niita), 1720–1870. Liaodong: Private communication from the Liaoning Land Bureau. Figures from 1948 Provincial Land Reform. Sart: 1822: Archives de l'Etat à Liège, "Rôles de repartition des taxes communales pour l'année 1822," Fonds hollandais, number 2423. Scania: Mantalslängder (Taxation Records), Malmöhus läns landskontors arkiv, Vol. E III: 52, Lunds landsarkiv (The Regional Archives in Lund).

century, they diverged in the beginning of the nineteenth century as the system started to dissolve in the West. Sweden, for example, abandoned the system in 1823 due to the belief that price interventions had a negative impact on the market. In northern Italy, it was abandoned after the Napoleonic Wars, and in Belgium it was last used in 1846–1847. Thus, our communities in the East retained the ability to dampen price increases in years of bad harvests, while the communities in the West lost this ability sometime during the first half of the nineteenth century.

Furthermore, even when governments were committed to stabilizing food prices, the purpose of such market intervention in the West was to help producers, not consumers, while the opposite was true in the

East.[3] As a result, while the goal of Western state food policy was primarily to keep grain prices from falling too much in good harvest years, the purpose of Eastern state policies was to prevent prices from increasing too rapidly in years of poor harvests.

Chinese society focused not only on price interventions but also on famine relief, which was largely the responsibility of the state and organized by the provincial and national as well as local governments. While famine relief also existed in the West, the system was less extensive. Western European society instead focused largely on poor relief, which was the responsibility of the parish and organized at the local community level, often in conjunction with the church.[4] As a result, when times were bad, local communities were often left to their own resources in the West, whereas they could regularly call on provincial and even national reserves in China.

The targets of Western aid were not the landless or the poor, but rather the long-term needy, that is orphans, widows, the sick, and elderly, who were considered worthy recipients of Christian agape, or charity.[5] In other words, Western charity was organized largely to care for the vulnerable, who constituted only a few percent of the population, and not the landless poor, who comprised one-third to half of our Western rural populations. In theory, most of the poor were life cycle servants whose well-being and even taxes were the responsibility of their employer. In reality, a growing number of lifetime married servants and rural employees replaced life cycle servants during the course of the eighteenth century. This expanding group of landless married laborers remained outside most Western systems of poor relief until the arrival of the "new" poor laws from the middle of the nineteenth century onward.

Indeed, the economic organization of our Western communities meant that economic inequality could feed on itself. Since tax and rental arrangements were organized largely to enforce the rights of property owners and the state to be paid, rather than to protect renters from such predatory interests, rent reductions or relief were uncommon. Landlords might allow renters to defer payment, in effect giving them loans, but they did not reduce or cancel rent (see chapters 2 and 6 of this book). While the state might be more forgiving and postpone taxes in bad years, this magnanimity was very carefully scrutinized and restricted to the truly economically exhausted. The net effect was that when times were hard, they were particularly hard in the West. As a consequence, improvements to take care of the landless poor in years of bad harvests were badly needed. In Sweden, for example, the state initiated road and railroad works in bad years to increase employment (Olofsson 1996, 127–129), and the poor law system was reorganized in the 1840s to provide additional relief (Skoglund 1992).

In the East, by contrast, the focus of government efforts was to guarantee adequate food supply for all and the poor in particular. Thus, the Qing state organized a national system of civilian granary reserves, which procured and redistributed grain through two parallel organizations.[6] *Ever-normal granaries* bought and sold grain largely in urban markets in an effort to stabilize prices. *Community granaries* acquired and disbursed grain largely in rural settings through loans and outright gifts to the poor. Both systems were especially prominent in Liaodong, the designated rice bowl of China and a major mobilization area for relief grain to be shipped elsewhere in north China. According to Qing records, the Chinese government stored more grain in Liaodong on a per capita basis than any other province in China, approximately 0.5 *shi* per person or two-month food supply per adult, far greater than the national average of 0.1 *shi* or 3 percent of the annual food supply (Will and Wong with Lee 1991).

As a result, the proportion of the population affected by relief measures during bad times was much higher in our northeast Chinese communities than in our West European communities. In Sart, according to a special investigation in 1846, a particularly bad year, fewer than 5 percent of all men and women received poor relief from the local charity office, the *bureau de bienfaisance.*[7] In Scania, the proportion of families who received parish allowances was if anything even smaller: around 2 to 3 percent of the local population, that is, perhaps 5 percent of the landless.[8] By contrast, the proportion of families who received some form of assistance in bad times in Liaodong could be greater by orders of magnitude. Depending on the specific measures— for example, the release of grain from reserves that lowered the market price—everyone could benefit. Similarly, the measures that followed the great famines in Japan affected everybody, not just the most vulnerable segments of the population.

While the overall scale of government relief mobilized in the East was roughly similar to the scale of Western charity, its organization made it more effective at insulating the poor against the effects of bad times. The West largely provided monetary assistance to vulnerable individuals who were perceived as being incapable of supporting themselves whether times were bad or good. The East largely provided foodstuffs and other necessities directly to the economic poor, and largely in bad times. Since the Chinese state discounted sales of grain from their granaries to targeted poor families with the size of the discounts and the number of targeted individuals rising and falling in tandem with the market price of grain prices, Chinese grain transfers did not have the unwanted effect of exacerbating shortfalls. Since the Chinese state discounted tax rates and required landlords to similarly discount rental rates, bad times did not create a permanent underclass fed by ever increasing debt.

Domestic Group Organization

While community mechanisms for relieving economic stress may have been more pervasive and effective in the East than the West, nowhere were they perfect. Short-term economic fluctuations were a fact of life everywhere in past times, and final responsibility for dealing with them lay with the family. Ironically, however, the societies with the most elaborate community institutions for responding to economic stress also had the family systems theoretically best equipped to protect family members in bad times. East Asian households were in principle larger and in particular more complex than West European ones. Whereas in the West, responsibility for care for the vulnerable such as widows and orphans during normal times lay with the community, in East Asia, it was the responsibility of these families. Similarly, whereas in the West, conjugal families were left to fend for themselves when times were bad, especially if they did not have the means or foresight to save when times were good, kin in the East were supposed to assist each other when times were bad.

Assessment of the potential role of the family system in responding to economic stress requires a detailed comparison of households between East and West. Fortunately, the formal differences between households and family systems have already been identified through standard taxonomies. In 1983, Peter Laslett proposed four sets of criteria to contrast different tendencies in European domestic group organization that embrace differences in Eurasia as well.[9] While other scholars, notably Hajnal (1982) and Todd (1990), have proposed more influential or refined models, no one else has proposed as systematic or as thoughtful a set of model tables for analyzing families, households, or what Laslett referred to as "housefuls." Altogether, Laslett recommends thirty-three measures of domestic organization reproduced in table 4.2, assembled into four groups,[10] and identifies four sets of European tendencies, or ideal regional models, which he labels

Table 4.2
Sets of tendencies in domestic group organization in traditional Europe

Overall criterion	Sets 1 and 2: Northern and Western		Sets 3 and 4: Southern and Eastern	
	1 Western	2 Western/ central or middle	3 Mediterranean	4 Eastern
Occasion and method of domestic group formation				
a1 Formed at marriage of household head	Always	Usually	Seldom	Never
a2 Formed by fission or fusion of extent household(s)	Never	Sometimes	Frequently	Always
a3 Marriage important to household formation	Always	Usually	(Seldom)[a]	Never
a4 Takeover of existent household by new head	Occasional	Frequent	Frequent	Usual
Procreational and demographic criteria				
b1 Age at marriage, female	High	High	Low	Low
b2 Age at marriage, male	High	High	High	Low
b3 Proportions marrying	Low	Low	High	High
b4 Age gap between spouses at first marriage	Narrow	Narrow	Wide	Narrow
b5 Proportion of wives older than husbands	High	Very high	Low	High
b6 Proportion of widows remarrying	High	Very high	Very low	Very low
Criteria of kin composition of groups				
c1 Proportion of resident kin	Very low	Low	High	High
c2 Proportion of multigenerational households	Low	Low	High	Very high
c3 Proportion of households headed by never-married women	High	High	(Low)[a]	High
c4 Proportion of solitaries	Very high	High	Low	Absent
c5 Proportion of no-family households	High	High	Low	Absent

c6 Proportion of simple-family households	High	High	Low	Low
c7 Proportion of extended-family households	Quite high	High	Low	Low
c8 Proportion of multiple-family households	Very low	Low	High	Very high
c9 Proportion of complex-family households (c7 + c8)	Very low	Low	High	Very high
c10 Proportion of frérèches	Absent	Low	High	Very high
c11 Proportion of stem-family households	Very low	High	Low	Low
c12 Proportion of joint-family households	Absent	Low	Very high	Very high
Criteria of organization of work and welfare				
d1 Addition to household of kin as workers	Rare	Common	Very common	Universal
d2 Added working kin called servants	Rare	Common	?	Irrelevant
d3 Addition to household life cycle servants	Very common	Very common	Not uncommon	Irrelevant
d4 Married servants	Uncommon	Common	?	Irrelevant
d5 Attachment to household of inmates as workers	Very rare	Common	?	Occasional
d6 Mean number of adults per household	Low	High	Very high	Maximal
d7 Mean number of households ≤3 persons	Very high	High	Very low	Very low
d8 Mean number of persons of working age (15–65)	Low	Medium	Very high	Very high
d9 Household head described as laborer, journeyman, out-servant, cottager	Often	Sometimes	Never	Never
d10 Household head described as pauper	Often	Sometimes	?	?
d11 Attachment of secondary household to household	Absent	Common	Absent	Absent

Source: Laslett 1983, 526–527.
Note: For the meaning of entries in this table and the character of supposed regions, see the text.
[a] Exceptions to the suggested classification are known to exist.

Western, Central, Mediterranean, and Eastern. While these measures are sometimes inadequately designed[11] or defined,[12] and other times frustratingly impressionistic,[13] taken together they provide a means to map the overall similarities and differences between our Eurasian communities.

When we compare our Eurasian communities by many of Laslett's criteria in table 4.3, we can typically distinguish three groups, with the Liaodong and Ou communities together at one end of the spectrum, the Liegeois and Scanian communities at the other end of the spectrum, and the Emilian and Toscanan communities somewhere in between. While this is less apparent in terms of the organization of work and welfare, an important but complicated criterion where we know less about the role of the domestic group,[14] this is true in terms of kin composition, nuptiality, and group formation.[15] Our data, in other words, suggest that in spite of intellectual traditions that tend to emphasize variation within Europe or Asia at the national or population level,[16] there may also be important metageographic differences that we need to recognize and understand, differences that the Eurasia Project can identify in greater detail in part two of this book and elsewhere.

Three Laslettian criteria, summarized in table 4.3, measure the gap between our populations. The first is the kin composition of the domestic group. Laslett identifies twelve dimensions of kin criteria, listed as c1 through c12, distinguishing a variety of household forms, including stem households—that is, households organized vertically with only one resident heir, and joint households—that is, married heirs living together. In spite of some marked differences between specific populations, which we address later, a high to very high proportion of the northwestern European households are relatively simple, with only one or two coresident generations, while a high to very high proportion of the northeast Asian households are comparatively complex with far more households of three or more coresident generations.[17] Northeast Asian households, while not necessarily larger than northwest European households,[18] are more complicated in terms of their familial relations, as are Mediterranean households.

Our Eurasian communities also differ in terms of their marital patterns. Laslett proposes six dimensions, b1 through b6, of what he calls procreational and demographic criteria. While several have surprisingly similar values in all our populations,[19] there are at least two important differences between East and West: northeast Asian women marry more universally than their northwest European counterparts,[20] and northeast Asian men and women also marry earlier.[21]

Most important, marriage plays a very different role in domestic group formation, measured by Laslett as a1 through a4. In northwestern Europe, the domestic group is formed at the marriage of the household head, a process of creation.[22] By contrast, marriage is largely irrelevant to northeast Asian domestic group formation. Instead, headship in all the Asian populations is typically a process of succession, with a new head succeeding to the headship of the domestic group on the death or retirement of the previous head (Lee and Campbell 1998a,b; Okada and Kurosu 1998). While new domestic groups in all the northeast Asian populations can also form through the fission of existing households, this occurs only occasionally and is often tied to the availability of sufficient land (Lee and Campbell 1997, 1998a,b). Household formation is therefore less frequent in these northeast Asian communities than in the northwest European communities under consideration.[23] Households endure longer and are more important to the organization of the Liaodong and Ou economy, polity, and society.[24] These differences in domestic process, in formation rates, and in symbolic and, as we shall see in part two, substantive demographic importance, more than anything else differentiate Eastern from Western society.

Differences also exist between and within our specific Asian and European populations, with our eastern Belgian populations typically at one end of the spectra and our northeastern Chinese populations at the other. Our northern Italian populations, in particular, often seem to fluctuate from one extreme to another due to the high proportion of sharecroppers and the consequently higher degree of complexity in domestic organization, resembling sometimes the one side, sometimes the other, and sometimes in between.

But at a continental scale, similarities prevail and predominate over differences that would be more pronounced at a lower scale of investigation. Indeed, according to Laslett's own criteria, the differences between our European populations are largely the differences between Western and Mediterranean European populations, with simpler households in the West and more complex family households in the Mediterranean.[25] Even then, tables 4.2 and 4.3 suggest that the Italian populations we study actually resemble the Western model far more than Laslett thought.[26] This similarity between our European populations is also demonstrated in table 4.4, which lists the

Table 4.3
Households in the study populations according to Laslett's criteria

	Sart	Liaodong	Northern Italy	Ou	Scania
Occasion and method of domestic group formation					
a1 Formed at marriage of household head	Usually	Rare	Sometimes	Rare	Usually
a2 Formed by fission or fusion of extent household(s)	Seldom	Occasional	Sometimes	Occasional	Never
a3 Marriage important to household formation	Always	Seldom	Sometimes	Seldom	Always
a4 Takeover of existent household by new head	Seldom	Always	Usually	Usually	Occasional
Procreational and demographic criteria					
b1 Age at marriage, female	High	Low	High	Low	High
b2 Age at marriage, male	High	Low	High	Low	High
b3 Proportions marrying	High 87%	Very high	High 85%	Very high	High 87%
b4 Age gap between spouses at first marriage	Narrow	Narrow	Narrow	Narrow	Narrow
b5 Proportion of wives older than husbands	High 26%	Very Low	High 21%	Low	High 25%
b6 Proportion of widows remarrying	Low	Very Low	Low	High	High
Criteria of kin composition of groups					
c1 Proportion of resident kin	Low 20%	High	High	High	Very low
c2 Proportion of multigenerational households	Low	High	Low	Very high	Low
c3 Proportion of households headed by never-married women	Very low	Very low 2%	Very low	Very low	Very low
c4 Proportion of solitaries	Low	Low 15%	Low	Low 8%	Low
c5 Proportion of no-family households	Low	Very low	Low	Low	Low
c6 Proportion of simple-family households	Very high 71%	Low 23%	High 54–58%	Low 31%	Very high 90%
c7 Proportion of extended-family households	15%	14%	11–22%	20%	Low
c8 Proportion of multiple-family households	Very low	Very high	Low 13–21%	High	Very low

c9 Proportion of complex-family households (c7 + c8)	Low	Very high	Low 31–35%	High	Very low
c10 Proportion of *frérèches*	Absent	High 25%	Very low	Absent	Absent
c11 Proportion of stem-family households	0.6%	13%		36%	Low 20%
c12 Proportion of joint-family households	Absent	High 48%	Low	Low 3	Absent
Criteria of organization of work and welfare					
d1 Addition to household of kin as workers	Sometimes	Usually	Sometimes	Irrelevant	Sometimes
d2 Added working kin called servants	Sometimes	Never	Sometimes	Irrelevant	Sometimes
d3 Addition to household life cycle servants	Occasional	Never	Occasional	Occasional	Common 50%
d4 Married servants	Rare	Never	Rare	Common	Uncommon
d5 Attachment to household of inmates as workers	Rare	Never		Irrelevant	Very rare
d6 Mean number of adults per household	3	4.7	3.5	3.6	4.3
d7 Mean number of households ≤3 persons	35%	40%	30%	36%	Low
d8 Mean number of persons of working age (15–65)	2.75	4.2	3.2	3.2	3.8
d9 Household head described as laborer, journeyman, out-servant, cottager	11%	Never		Not rare	Very rare

Table 4.4
Household members by relationship to head in the study populations

Relation	Sart[a]	Liaodong	Ou	Northern Italy	Scania
Head		15.3	20.3	19.4	21.5
Spouse		10.5	16.4	13.8	17.7
Stem kin		36.4	48.4	50	38.4
Nonstem kin		37.8	10.0	5	0.4
Servants			5.4	5.8	15.2
Others				6	6.7
Total		269,575	119,029	135,876	93,299

[a] In Belgium, "head, spouse, and children account for 90 to 94 percent of all men and 83 to 92 percent of all women. Children-in-law, parents, cousins, uncle or aunt, nephew, niece, are very insignificant. While there occasionally were some siblings they ranged from less than 1 to 5 percent (more females than males). The remaining people in the household were servants who accounted for no more than 1.4 to 5 percent of males and 5 percent of females, but 12 to 14 percent of females age 15–24" (Capron and Oris 1997).

proportions of household relations by sex. In spite of regional differences in family formation, the proportions of nonnuclear and nonstem coresident kin are low, except perhaps among the Italian sharecroppers of Madregolo, near Parma in Emilia-Romagna, the most complex Eurasian European population.[27] In our European, and northwestern European, communities in particular, most household members are members of the same nuclear family.

In our northeast Asian, and Liaodong, communities in particular, they are not. While nuclear families account for the majority of our European households, 74, 58, and 78 percent in eastern Belgium, northern Italy, and southern Sweden, respectively, they account for only 23 and 31 percent in northeast China and Japan, respectively. Instead, coresident parents, grandchildren, children-in-law, uncles, aunts, siblings, siblings-in-law, nephews, nieces, and cousins, virtually nonexistent in our eastern Belgian and southern Swedish populations and no more than 20 percent of our northern Italians,[28] account for an even larger minority, 27 percent of our northeastern Japanese populations, and a majority, over 50 percent, of our northeastern Chinese populations. As a result, both the Liaodong and Ou communities have high levels, 62 and 60 percent, respectively, of complex family households compared with the communities in eastern Belgium, northern Italy, and southern Sweden, where the proportions are 13, 33, and 18 percent, respectively. But while most of these northeastern Chinese complex households are organized laterally and diagonally,[29] the northeastern Japanese complex household is overwhelmingly vertical. Ou households, in other words, have far fewer nonstem kin of the head than Liaodong households. Summarizing table 4.4, the proportion of uncles and aunts, siblings, nephews, nieces, and cousins in northeastern Japan is much closer to northern Italy, 4 and 8 percent, respectively,[30] than to northeastern China, where nonstem kin make up some 40 percent of household members.[31]

These similarities and dissimilarities in kin composition and other criteria are a product of the respective family formation and other principles followed by each population. The northern Italian and northeastern Japanese populations followed a stem primogenitorial system[32] and therefore resemble each other in some ways. So do the eastern Belgian and southern Swedish populations, who follow largely neolocal and partible principles of family formation and inheritance,[33] while the northeastern Chinese populations, who follow joint principles of family formation combined with partible inheritance, stand at the other extreme of social complexity. Other similarities in male patriarchy may explain other cross-continental similarities, such as the low rates of widow remarriage in northeast China and northern Italy and the high rates of widow remarriage in northeast Japan and southern Sweden.[34] Several scholars have drawn attention to these and other similarities in an attempt to identify common Eurasian experiences in terms of gender, health, property, social formation, state formation, and especially demographic behavior.[35]

Implications

The stark differences in East-West mortality responses to bad times can be a consequence of the differences in community recourses, household resources, or both. Indeed, the lower responsiveness of our East Asian communities apparent in chapter 3 appears to reflect overlapping safety nets: not only were community institutions, in particular the state, better organized to ameliorate the effects of economic stress, so were family systems.

Whereas in this chapter we focused on the description of differences in household form, in chapter 5 we examine anthropological accounts of the interactions among kin in our East Asian communities to clarify how the complex joint households actually responded to economic stress and identify testable predictions about how specific characteristics of the household should have influenced mortality levels and responses. To the extent that household characteristics do not in fact condition mortality levels or responses or condition them in unexpected ways, we suggest that community institutions may have been more important in accounting for the contrasting responsiveness of mortality. We conclude with a brief overview of our contributions to the current theoretical understanding of East-West differences in social and political organization, living standards, and demographic behavior.

Notes

1. One reason that Malthus did not emphasize the difference in poor relief systems between East and West may be that the English poor law system differed considerably from other European states. Benefits in England were larger than elsewhere in Europe, and more people in England received them. In the Essex parish of Ardleigh, for example, three-quarters of the population in 1796 received some poor relief, if only for periods as short as three weeks (Wall 2002, 8). In southern Sweden, by contrast, only 1.4 percent of the population, the paupers, received public support in 1827 (Skoglund 1992, 214), while in the village of Sart in the Ardennes, the figure in 1846 was 4.8 percent (Statistique de la Belgique, "Recensement de la population du Royaume de Belgique au 15 Octobre 1846," Bruxelles, 1849). See Solar (1995) for a comparison of the poor law systems in England with those of the Continent.

2. The figures are based on tax records for all locations. Although the landless households did not have access to any land for grain production, almost all of them had small plots of land for growing vegetables. In Sart, they also had access to the common land, the forest.

3. This was the case in Sweden, for example, where farmers could borrow grain from the estate owner or the regional government but day laborers had no such recourse until the mid-nineteenth century.

4. This was the case in Sweden until the 1830s, when reforms started to take place. In Belgium, the local community provided poor relief from the seventeenth century. After the French Revolution, this responsibility was moved from the parish to the municipalities each of which had to establish a *bureau de bienfaisance* (Haesenne-Peremans 1981).

5. There already exists a substantial literature on this point. See Woolf (1986) for a general depiction and Oris and Ochiai (2002) for a specific discussion of the Eurasian populations.

6. While state and community granaries existed in at least some parts of Europe, their purpose differed, their scope was narrower, and they changed over time. In Sweden, there were state granaries in fourteen cities as of 1720, as well as some storehouses devoted to the military (Åmark 1915, 195). Community granaries were also established to complement the state granaries, but in only 15 percent of all villages (Olofsson 1996, 125). The General Storage Institution was established in 1786 to trade grain for the state, take care of taxes paid in grain, and handle grain for the army (Olofsson 1996, 125). Local governors could apply to it for relief during famine. The rules, however, were strict. Relief had to be paid back with interest. This system was oriented primarily toward

farmers, not the poor. The General Storage Institution also intervened in markets, buying grain when prices were low and selling when they were high (Olofsson 1996, 126). In 1823, however, a new law was introduced to forbid it from doing this. It was not until the 1840s that new institutions were developed to provide food and jobs during bad years, to help not just farmers but the poor as well (Olofsson 1996, 127–129).

7. Statistique de la Belgique, "Recensement de la population du Royaume de Belgique au 15 octobre 1846," Bruxelles, 1849.

8. Others, of course, also received relief from former employers, as documented in chapter 6.

9. Laslett (1983, 526–527). See also his earlier influential measures of household morphology presented in Laslett and Wall (1972) and Hammel and Laslett (1974), as well as a critique by G. William Skinner (1997, 56–57).

10. The four groups are (1) the processes of domestic group formation, (2) the patterns of nuptiality, (3) the kin composition of households, and (4) the organization of work and welfare. We discuss only the first three groups in this chapter, as our data do not permit a full comparison of the organization of work and welfare.

11. The most common problem, cited in Saito (1998), is that Laslett's tables do not distinguish adequately among lateral, vertical, or diagonal principles of organization. Like Saito, we therefore follow Wall, Robin, and Laslett (1983) and supplement them with a list of family relations. See Lee and Gjerde (1986) for an alternative approach.

12. This is especially true of the criteria used to measure the organization of work and welfare since they assume a registration system that categorizes household members by their domestic function (worker or servant), their occupation (laborer, journeyman, outservant, or cottager), and their financial status, as well as their family relationships.

13. Laslett uses two sets of scales with twenty-two different terms to differentiate each measure in a spectra that runs the gamut from Irrelevant, Absent, or Never, to Very Rare, Rare, Uncommon, Seldom, Sometimes, Occasional, Not Uncommon, Frequent, Usually, Very Common, Universal, and Always. Not only is it hard to differentiate between Irrelevant and Absent, or Occasional and Sometimes, Very Low, Low, Medium, High, Quite High, Very High, and Maximal are, by definition, subjective terms. We therefore include the precise quantitative measures wherever appropriate to complement his more impressionistic measures.

14. See the respective local histories and their citations in chapters 6 through 10. Although we will know more about the organization of work and welfare once we have completed our ongoing analyses of fertility, nuptiality, and migration, we will never be able to compare these populations formally according to several important criteria since the roles of coresident and nonresident workers as household kin, of working kin as servants, of life cycle servants, of married servants, and of other forms of labor differ considerably in terms of both our populations and our data.

15. While this is generally true, there are, of course, exceptions. See, for example, the values for B5 proportion of wives older than husbands and c10 proportion of *frereches*, married brothers living together, where our northeastern Chinese populations differ substantially not only from our European populations, but also from our northeastern Japanese populations.

16. Many publications mostly associated with Peter Laslett, Richard Wall, and the Cambridge Group for the Study of Population and Social Structure have mapped the variety

of domestic organization in Europe. While less has been done for Asia, especially China, see the very influential article by Wolf and Hanley (1985), as well as Macfarlane (1997), which contrast China and Japan, and Hayami and Ochiai (2001), Ochiai (1998), and Saito (1998), which identify different regional patterns in Japan.

17. *Very high* and *High* here are relative terms. The proportion of multigenerational households (three or more generations) is 35 percent of northeastern Chinese households and 46 percent of northeastern Japanese households, while the proportion of complex family households, that is, extended and multiple family households, is 62 and 60 percent respectively. These values are only for our specific populations under consideration. There are other regions of China and Japan with less complex domestic organization.

18. The mean number of adults per household is larger in most of the Chinese populations: 4.2 in Chengnei, 3.9 in Dami, 5 in Daoyi, 4.1 in Feicheng, 5.4 in Gaizhou, and 4.9 among the Gaizhou Mianding, compared with 3.5 in Casalguidi, 3.8 in Madregolo, 3.6 in Niita and Shimamoriya, 3 in Saart, and 3.5 in Scania. Even Dami, however, with approximately the same number of adults as Madregolo, has a far more complicated household structure.

19. Surprisingly, the proportions of males marrying and the age gap between spouses at first marriage appear to have been roughly similar for all our populations.

20. While the proportion of unmarried men is roughly similar in China and Europe, the proportion of unmarried women is quite different, with virtually no unmarried women in China (Lee and Wang 1999b). In Japan, the situation is less clear-cut, with nearly universal marriage in our Ou villages but more European proportions, around 10 percent, male and female celibacy in other villages elsewhere in Japan (Hamano, Kurosu, and Morimoto, forthcoming). These northeastern Japanese villages, moreover, resemble our northeastern Chinese villages, with virtually no female celibacy: 0.1 percent compared to 2.2 percent male celibacy at ages 45 to 49 (Tsuya and Kurosu 1998).

21. Marriage age fluctuates in our populations by class, by period, and by much else. The area reports, however, supply the following mean or Singulate Mean Ages for first marriage for females and males, respectively: 19.8 and 22.3 in Daoyi, 1774–1873; and 16.3 and 19.3 in Niita and Shimomoriya, 1716–1870, compared with 25.4 and 28.7 in Sart, 1811–1890, 25.4 and 30.7 in Casalguidi, 1819–1858; 23.9 and 28.4 in Madregolo, 1800–1899; and 29.0 and 26.0, respectively, in Scania 1811–1860.

22. The major exception among the Eurasian populations is the sharecropping families of Madregolo in Emilia-Romagna, where new households tended to be created by fission rather than marriage, but this is acknowledged to be atypical. By contrast, marriage was more important to household formation in the more representative Tuscan village, Casalguidi, but even there, not all newly married couples established new households.

23. Czap (1982, 1983) makes a variety of similar points describing domestic group formation in imperial Russia, as does Hoch (1986).

24. There is an enormous literature on the importance of the household in Chinese and Japanese society. See Nakane (1967, 1990), Ochiai (1996), and Yonemura and Nagata (1998) on Japan and Lee and Wang (1999b) on China for an introduction to this literature.

25. Thus, the proportion of simple family households, that is, elementary and sub-elementary households, is 86 percent in Scania and 88 percent in Liège, compared with 66 percent in Toscana and Emilia-Romagna. Similarly, while the proportion of complex family households is low in eastern Belgium and southern Sweden, it is higher in northern Italy, with 33 percent of all households.

26. Contrast the different values for a2, b1, b4, b5, c2, c8, c10, d6, d7, d8 in tables 4.1 and 4.2 for the Mediterranean and Italian populations. We should point out that when Laslett proposed these values in 1983, there had been little scholarly work on the Mediterranean family, thus the many question marks under the Mediterranean model. This is less true now, especially for the western Mediterranean. See, for example, Barbagli (1984) and Reher (1997).

27. Exactly how low is unclear. Twelve percent of all males and 13 percent of all females in Madregolo are listed as *nipote*, that is, nephews, nieces, and grandchildren. Most *nipote*, however, were grandchildren. While we cannot determine the precise proportions for all *nipote*, we can for the very vast majority, of whom 77 percent in Madregolo and 61 percent in Casalguidi were grandchildren (Manfredini, private communication). Nephews and nieces, in other words, account for perhaps 3 percent of the population in Madregolo and 4 percent in Casalguidi.

28. According to Pier Paolo Viazzo (private communication), these proportions are atypical even of much of northern Italy.

29. In Daoyi, for example, the proportions of vertical, horizontal, and diagonally oriented multiple family households, were 27, 53, and 20 percent, respectively (Lee and Campbell 1997, 110).

30. The Italian proportions of nonstem kin vary from approximately 12 percent for Casalguidi to 7 percent for Madregolo and are greater than in Japan. Nevertheless, the proportion of complex family households (c9) is almost twice as high in Japan, 60 percent, as in Italy, 33 percent, because of the much larger number of multiple family households (c8) in Japan, 40 percent, than in Italy, 17 percent. As Ochiai (1998) and Saito (1998) have pointed out, these multiple family Japanese households were almost always arranged vertically and did not therefore depend on nonstem kin.

31. The high proportion of nonstem kin may be a feature of Liaodong banner households who were tied to the land and had little opportunities for migration. Please see chapter 10 for details on the institutional setting of the banner households. Recent studies of household division suggest that nonstem kin were less common in other Chinese populations, where households typically divided earlier (Finegan 1988, Wakefield 1998, Wolf 1985).

32. Saito (1998) demonstrates that Japanese stem households were composed differently from European stem households, with more vertical relatives and more persistent vestiges in contemporary society today, while Ochiai (1998) distinguishes between two types of Japanese stem households, one in the Northeast and the other in the Southwest. Exactly how different the Japanese stem households are from the Italians awaits more finely tuned analyses of both populations.

33. Inheritance in Belgium was largely partible under the old regime, especially in eastern Belgium (Godding 1987).

34. See Tien (1988) and Kertzer (1993) on the parallels between Chinese and Italian patriarchy and Mosk (1983) on the parallels between Japan and Sweden.

35. The most influential examples are Wolf and Hanley (1985) and Macfarlane (1997), which equate the early modern English and Japanese experiences.

5   Society and Mortality

James Z. Lee, Cameron
Campbell, and Wang Feng
in collaboration with Matteo
Manfredini, Michel Oris, and
Noriko O. Tsuya

The Jesuit Parennin, writing to a member of the Royal Academy of Sciences, says, "Another thing that you can scarcely believe is, that dearths should be so frequent in China;... in a time of dearth." ... He then describes the delays and artifices, which often defeat the emperor's intentions to assist, from the public granaries, those parts of the country which are the most distressed. When a harvest fails in any province, either from excessive drought or a sudden inundation, the great mandarins have recourse to the public granaries; but often find them empty, owing to the dishonesty of the inferior mandarins, who have the charge of them. Examinations and researches are then made, and an unwillingness prevails to inform the court of such disagreeable intelligence. Memorials are however at length presented. These memorials pass through many hands, and do not reach the emperor till after many days. The great officers of state are then ordered to assemble, and to deliberate on the means of relieving the misery of the people. Declarations full of expressions of compassion for the people are in the meantime published throughout the empire. The resolution of the tribunal is at length made known; but numberless other ceremonies delay its execution; while those who are suffering have time to die with hunger, before the remedy arrives. Those who do not wait for this last extremity crawl as well as they can into other districts, where they hope to get support, but leave the greatest part of their number dead on the road.

(Malthus 1826/1986, 135–136)

Families were larger and more complex in the East and mortality was less responsive to bad times than in the West.[1] Had he known this, Malthus would have attributed the lower responsiveness of the East to family organization, for he clearly did not believe in the effectiveness of community transfers, at least not in China. While subsequent examinations have confirmed the potential of family organization to account for the reduced sensitivity of the East, they also suggest that Malthus's skepticism about community transfers was overdone. On the one hand, a number of anthropological historians and historical sociologists, following Malthus, have elaborated the rationale that the larger joint households characteristic of East Asian societies were more able to

insulate members against risk than the smaller conjugal families characteristic of Western Europe (Das Gupta 1997, 1998; Davis 1955; G. W.
Skinner 1997). On the other hand, at least one major study of community transfers during the Qing concluded that they were actually effective due to the success of the very national granary system, which
Malthus and others derided as ineffective (Will and Wong with Lee
1991).

In this chapter, we examine the role of family organization in
accounting for the lower sensitivity of our East Asian populations. We
review evidence from the Eurasia standard comparative models on the
role of household organization in conditioning the mortality response
to short-term economic stress. To the extent that the larger and more
complex East Asian households were more successful than the smaller,
conjugal West European households at insulating their members from
short-term stress, we should find that death rates in households with
more working-age adults were less sensitive to price fluctuations. To
the extent that larger households were better off overall, we should
see lower mortality levels for their members. Moreover, to the extent
that East Asian households played an important role in protecting the
most vulnerable members of society, in particular orphans and widows, their mortality should have been lower and less sensitive to
economic fluctuation in our East Asian communities than our West
European communities. A finding that household size had no effect
and that orphans and widows in the East had no advantage over their
Western counterparts would rule out differences in family organization
as the source of the weaker Eastern response and imply that community transfers were responsible.

We divide our chapter into three sections. First, we review social
theory about the role of the complex and conjugal families in providing
security to their members. We identify predictions from these theories
for results on the effects of household characteristics and context from
the Eurasia standard comparative models. We test these theories in the
following two sections by investigating whether empirical results are
consistent with predictions. After examining the role of household
characteristics in determining mortality levels, we look at the role of
household characteristics in determining mortality responses.

Social Theory

The social implications of a more individualistically organized West
and a more collectively organized East are relatively straightforward,

although largely unexplored in academic research.[2] Europeans live in relatively small social units created largely through marriage and typically organize their lives at the individual or conjugal level. Asians live in comparatively more complex social units and often have to accommodate their behavior within the context of a larger coresident group and more competing interests.[3] As a result, whereas European individuals are relatively free to decide on their own to consume, love, marry, move, produce, purchase, retire, and work, Asian individuals often have to negotiate and plan these decisions with others—typically parents in Japan and other senior and fraternal relatives as well in China.[4] Consequently, individual freedom, the right to make and act on individual and individually maximizing decisions, is considered more characteristic of western Europe, especially England and beyond,[5] while cooperation and deference are more typical of East Asia.

The demographic implications of these differences in domestic group composition are less clear. Recently, however, a number of anthropological demographers and demographic historians have traced regional differences in demographic behavior to differences in family formation and different patterns of labor.[6] By linking these cultural and demographic differences to differences in domestic group formation, they have raised our understanding of the social context of human demographic behavior and forced us to expand our disciplinary and spatial horizons well beyond conventional academic, social, or political boundaries.[7] Their theories merit our attention for their logic and testable specificity, as well as their intellectual ambition. Previously, much historical demography and social demography has tended to focus on the economic implications of positive and preventive checks.[8] Increasingly, in the "new" social theory, they also take social context as well as economic factors into consideration.

Generally, social demographers distinguish between two ideal model family systems: a relatively simple conjugal family system characteristic of western, particularly northwestern, Europe,[9] and a comparatively more complex joint household system characteristic of a much wider geographic area stretching from East Asia and South Asia to eastern and southern Europe. Most demographic historians have focused on describing the European conjugal family system and the preventive population check that characterized its demographic behavior.[10] Their general conclusion is that while the social organization of such societies was relatively simple, their demography, and particularly their nuptiality, were sensitive to economic circumstances.[11]

Most anthropological demographers, by contrast, have focused on the rationales and patterns of demographic control in the Eurasian joint households, where demographic behavior was more responsive to social circumstances. On the one hand, since larger and more complicated domestic groups should have wider resource bases, they should also have higher rates of nuptiality and lower rates of mortality.[12] On the other hand, since individuals in joint multiple family households are entitled to more collective support, such households are also more likely to restrict household size and composition and control nuptiality, fertility, and mortality according to the individual's sex, household position, and birth order.[13] These tendencies toward protectionism and particularism underlie most social theory about the relationship in joint households between domestic organization and demographic behavior.

The most important principles in the joint family system to determine the pattern of demographic control are the age-gender hierarchies characteristic of patrilineal and patriarchal joint household family systems, with the aged and males at the top and females and the young at the bottom.[14] According to this logic, a young child's survival depends on his or her sex, birth order, and sibling size. A young adult married woman's survival depends on her marital and fertility status, improving in China if she gives birth to a son and worsening if she gives birth to many daughters.[15] Moreover, while female mortality in patrilineal joint or stem family systems is generally high compared with conjugal and uxorilocal stem family systems,[16] this pattern reverses in old age, particularly among widows, who were better treated in a joint than conjugal family system.[17] G. William Skinner, drawing on his own analysis of historical Japanese populations, further identifies a number of elaborate consequences of such age-gender hierarchies, whereby in the Japanese stem family, for example, the early death of mother-in-law decreases the mortality of daughters-in-law. The early death or retirement of father-in-law decreases the mortality of uxorilocal sons-in-law (1997, 77). He uses similar rationales in other analyses of contemporary Indian, Korean, and Taiwanese populations to explain why couples have distinctive starting, stopping, and cumulative fertility patterns and to emphasize the beneficial presence of grandparents on the fertility of young couples (1997, 69, 74). Such familial principles of demographic behavior are so important, Skinner implies, that they even transcend geography and time to characterize societies that stretch across Eurasia and Africa, before, during, and after the demographic transition.[18]

Recent analyses of demographic behavior by the Eurasian Project provide important new empirical evidence that confirm, challenge, and confound some of these hypotheses about the interrelationships of economic context, family systems, individual position, and population behavior. By applying multivariate models to microlevel data, these analyses can test specific hypotheses about the relationships between such variables as childbearing status and young mothers' mortality, while controlling for such other variables as household economic status, household structure, and marital status, which may confound or specify such a relationship. We can use results from the comparative models to discriminate between such competing explanations as the protectionist and particularistic East. We first verify the importance of the household as a locus by examining the effects of its characteristics on mortality levels. If the household system was important in accounting for the lower responsiveness of the East, then we should find that larger households were less sensitive and that vulnerable individuals such as orphans and widows were better protected.

Methods

We test these claims through examination of results from the comparative models for our populations.[19] Whereas chapter 3 focused on results from the individual models, with and without price interactions, here we make use of results from the household and relationship models, again with and without price interactions. The household models included as covariates aggregate measures of the characteristics of the household, in particular, the number of working-age adults, the proportion of members aged 15 or below, and the proportion of members aged 55 and above. We included the count of working-age adults to test hypotheses about the role of household size in affecting mortality levels and their sensitivity to economic stress and included proportions of young and old to examine the effects of the household dependency burden. We intend for the proportions of young and old to capture the effects of location in the family life cycle discussed in chapter 2, as reflected in the dependency ratio.

The relationship model, by contrast, includes variables for household context measured from the perspective of the individual. Most of these are indicators of the presence or absence of specific kin of the index individual. Since in most of the populations such measures were correlated with aggregate measures of household characteristics, we could not nest the relationship model in the household model, only in the individual model. Models for different age groups included different sets of indicators. For example, only the models for infants, children, and adults included indicators of whether parents were present, while only the models for adults and the elderly included indicators of whether spouses and children were present. While the relationship model included a large number of such measures, here we restrict our discussion to the variables directly relevant to our hypotheses, leaving the discussion of other results to the country and comparative chapters.

Levels

Contrary to anthropological claims, members of larger households were not better off, at least not in the sense of having lower mortality levels. Table 5.1 translates coefficients from the household model into proportional increases in mortality associated with adding a working-age adult to the household in each of the study populations. Differences were apparent both between and within East and West. On the one hand, in Casalguidi and Sart, additional working-age adults appear to have been associated with lower mortality for certain combinations of age, sex, and marital status. Thus, for example, each additional working-age adult lowered the death rates of ever-married elderly females in Sart by 11 percent. On the other hand, additional working-age adults appear to have raised mortality not only among the primarily conjugal households of Scania, but also among the more complex households of Niita and Shimomoriya. Thus, an additional adult raised the death rates of ever-married elderly males in Niita and Shimomoriya by 8 percent and the death rates of ever-married adult females by 5. In Liaodong, where households were the most complex, additional adults had contradictory effects on the death rates of men and women: each additional adult raised ever-married adult female mortality by 1 percent but lowered ever-married adult male mortality by 1 percent.

Effects of age composition are generally but not completely consistent with a life cycle model of the household in which the well-being of members depended on the balance between producers and consumers. Table 5.2 translates coefficients from the household model into the multiplicative effects on mortality risks of increasing the proportion of children in the household by 0.2, or twenty percentage points. This corresponds roughly, but not exactly, to adding a dependent to a

Table 5.1
Proportional change in mortality associated with adding one adult to the household

Country	Site		Infants		Children		Ever-married adults		Ever-married elderly	
			(Ratio)	(p)	(Ratio)	(p)	(Ratio)	(p)	(Ratio)	(p)
Belgium	Sart	Female	0.97	0.65	0.95	0.50	0.95	0.32	0.89	0.05
		Male	1.04	0.48	0.90	0.15	0.92	0.23	0.97	0.49
China	Liaodong	Female			0.98	0.11	1.01	0.06	1.00	0.62
		Male			1.01	0.17	0.99	0.03	1.00	0.39
Italy	Casalguidi	Female	0.96	0.26	0.89	0.07	0.93	0.12	1.08	0.22
		Male	0.94	0.05	0.93	0.30	0.95	0.38	0.91	0.15
	Madregolo	Female	0.98	0.51	1.01	0.89	1.02	0.60	1.04	0.54
		Male	0.97	0.25	1.00	0.95	0.99	0.87	0.98	0.69
Japan	Niita and Shimomoriya	Female	0.85	0.18	1.08	0.08	1.05	0.05	0.98	0.75
		Male	0.90	0.22	1.00	0.96	1.00	0.89	1.08	0.05
Sweden	Four Scanian parishes	Female	0.96	0.13	1.07	0.02	1.04	0.18	1.06	0.18
		Male	0.98	0.32	0.99	0.82	0.95	0.24	1.07	0.01

Source: Comparative household model.

Table 5.2
Proportional change in mortality associated with increasing the proportion of household members aged 0–15 by 20 percentage points

Country	Site		Infants		Children		Ever-married adults		Ever-married elderly	
			(Ratio)	(p)	(Ratio)	(p)	(Ratio)	(p)	(Ratio)	(p)
Belgium	Sart	Female	1.07	0.37	0.97	0.78	0.86	0.01	1.05	0.49
		Male	0.99	0.91	0.86	0.16	0.92	0.23	1.09	0.16
China	Liaodong	Female			1.16	0.20	0.98	0.57	1.03	0.50
		Male			1.14	0.01	0.96	0.25	0.99	0.74
Italy	Casalguidi	Female	1.16	0.04	1.25	0.08	0.91	0.23	1.18	0.11
		Male	1.05	0.54	0.98	0.89	1.15	0.17	0.86	0.18
	Madregolo	Female	0.96	0.71	0.98	0.94	0.79	0.03	1.22	0.21
		Male	0.93	0.48	1.05	0.77	1.29	0.10	1.17	0.33
Japan	Niita and Shimomoriya	Female	0.88	0.76	1.13	0.10	0.98	0.81	0.94	0.62
		Male	0.80	0.74	0.88	0.57	0.93	0.59	1.07	0.28
Sweden	Four Scanian parishes	Female	0.89	0.19	1.15	0.34	1.12	0.21	0.92	0.45
		Male	0.93	0.38	0.96	0.74	1.11	0.23	1.04	0.73

Source: Authors' calculations from coefficients reported by participants from the comparative household models. Adding a child to a household with two adults and a child would increase the proportion below age 15 by 0.17, that is, from 0.33 to 0.50.

household with two working-age adults and one dependent.[20] Effects were most apparent in the populations characterized by more complex households: Niita and Shimomoriya, Liaodong, and Casalguidi and Madregolo. Effects of the proportion young in table 5.2 were most apparent for child mortality, suggesting that children competed with each other for household resources: increasing the proportion of household members below age 15 by 0.20 raised female child mortality by 13 percent in Niita and Shimomoriya and 25 percent in Casalguidi, female infant mortality by 16 percent in Casalguidi, and male child mortality by 14 percent in Liaodong. In Sart and Madregolo, meanwhile, death rates for married adult women actually decreased as the proportion of children increased, suggesting that at least in these two locations, women in their roles as mothers could lay claim to more resources.

Similarly, increases in the proportion elderly raised their death rates in some locations, suggesting competition among them, but had mixed effects on the mortality of household members at other ages. Table 5.3 translates coefficients from the household model into the multiplicative effects on mortality risks of increasing the proportion of elderly household members aged 55 and above in the household by 0.2, or twenty percentage points. In Niita and Shimomoriya, such an increase raised the death rates of ever-married elderly males by 13 percent. In Casalguidi, it raised the death rates of elderly females by 20 percent.

As G. W. Skinner (1997, 75) predicted, the death rates of married adult women and daughters reflected the burden of caring for the elderly: increases in the proportion of elderly raised the death rates of both in Liaodong as well as in Niita and Shimomoriya. In Casalguidi, daughters seem to have competed with the elderly for resources: increases in the proportion elderly raised the death rates of female infants. The exception to this pattern was in Scania, where increases in the proportion elderly lowered female infant mortality. In at least a few cases, boys actually benefited from the presence of the elderly. In Sart and Casalguidi, higher proportions of elderly were associated with lower male child mortality.

Turning to the results from the relationship models, we found virtually no evidence to suggest that children who had lost one or both parents were better off in complex as opposed to conjugal household societies. Table 5.4 summarizes the proportional changes in infant and child mortality associated with effects of missing one or both parents. In theory, the mortality effects of losing a parent should have been most pronounced in the conjugal household European populations, in

Table 5.3
Proportional change in mortality associated with increasing the proportion of household members aged 55 and above by 20 percentage points

Country	Site		Infants (Ratio)	(p)	Children (Ratio)	(p)	Ever-married adults (Ratio)	(p)	Ever-married elderly (Ratio)	(p)
Belgium	Sart	Female	1.18	0.20	1.10	0.58	0.91	0.44	0.91	0.17
		Male	0.95	0.70	0.64	0.05	1.17	0.29	0.99	0.83
China	Liaodong	Female			1.30	0.06	1.06	0.08	0.98	0.54
		Male			0.99	0.80	1.01	0.81	0.96	0.11
Italy	Casalguidi	Female	1.43	0.00	1.13	0.44	1.06	0.57	1.20	0.10
		Male	0.86	0.28	0.52	0.00	1.16	0.41	0.86	0.24
	Madregolo	Female	1.04	0.84	0.96	0.87	0.92	0.71	1.18	0.32
		Male	0.84	0.29	0.70	0.26	0.98	0.95	1.05	0.73
Japan	Niita and Shimomoriya	Female	0.54	0.90	1.30	0.00	1.09	0.09	1.01	0.92
		Male	1.02	0.93	0.95	0.71	0.98	0.83	1.13	0.00
Sweden	Four Scanian parishes	Female	0.58	0.02	1.06	0.83	0.94	0.74	1.06	0.66
		Male	0.93	0.67	0.84	0.52	1.31	0.19	1.13	0.37

Source: Authors' calculations from coefficients reported by participants from the comparative household models. Adding a person above age 55 to a household with two adults and a person above age 55 would increase the proportion above age 55 by 0.17, that is, from 0.33 to 0.50.

Table 5.4
Effects of presence of parents on infant and child mortality

Country	Site	Parents (Ref: Both)	Infants (0–24 months)				Children (2–15 years)			
			Females		Males		Females		Males	
			(Ratio)	(p)	(Ratio)	(p)	(Ratio)	(p)	(Ratio)	(p)
Belgium	Sart	Father	3.23	0.00	2.01	0.01	1.07	0.78	1.53	0.09
		Mother	2.00	0.00	1.57	0.01	1.14	0.52	1.45	0.11
		Neither	1.72	0.11	1.51	0.19	0.38	0.11	1.34	0.51
China	Liaodong	Father					1.00	0.99	1.30	0.03
		Mother					0.89	0.74	1.02	0.89
		Neither					3.29	0.00	1.15	0.50
Italy	Casalguidi	Father	2.10	0.06	2.54	0.02	1.55	0.22	2.01	0.08
		Mother	0.79	0.69	0.42	0.22	0.93	0.84	0.88	0.78
		Neither					4.14	0.05	2.00	0.53
	Madregolo	Father	1.24	0.42	1.47	0.15	2.19	0.16	1.36	0.62
		Mother	1.22	0.48	1.85	0.01	2.68	0.03	1.71	0.27
		Neither								
Japan	Niita and Shimomoriya	Father	0.54	0.76	0.73	0.75	0.90	0.80	0.53	0.38
		Mother	0.91	0.84	0.83	0.74	1.26	0.20	0.81	0.49
		Neither					1.52	0.05	1.52	0.01
Sweden	Four Scanian parishes	Either or none	2.44	0.01	3.00	0.00	1.16	0.67	0.78	0.50

Source: Comparative relationship model.

Table 5.5
Effects of widowhood on adult and elderly mortality

| | | Adults | | | | Elderly | | | |
| | | Females | | Males | | Females | | Males | |
Country	Site	(Ratio)	(p)	(Ratio)	(p)	(Ratio)	(p)	(Ratio)	(p)
Belgium	Sart	1.08	0.68	1.61	0.02	1.09	0.37	1.21	0.03
China	Liaodong	1.40	0.00	1.15	0.05	1.23	0.00	1.10	0.06
Italy	Casalguidi	0.77	0.03	1.12	0.23	0.82	0.15	0.97	0.56
	Madregolo	3.01	0.03	1.31	0.59	0.23	0.17	0.69	0.20
Japan	Niita and Shimomoriya	1.40	0.12	1.33	0.20	1.31	0.01	1.50	0.00

Source: Comparative relationship model.

particular, Sart and Scania, and least apparent in the complex household Asian populations, where other adult kin could fill in for the missing parents. While problems with the data for Ou and Liaodong preclude comparison of infant mortality there with Europe, the results for child mortality certainly fail to reveal a clear divide between East and West. Losing one or both parents affected mortality everywhere. In Liaodong, the loss of both parents more than tripled the death rates of daughters. The loss of a mother raised the death rates of sons by 30 percent. In Ou, being orphaned raised child mortality rates by 50 percent.

Similarly, our results provide no evidence to confirm the suggestion by G. W. Skinner (1997, 78) that widowhood had more severe mortality consequences in conjugal than in complex household systems. Table 5.5 compares the effect of widowhood on adult and elderly mortality.[21] Contrary to the common anthropological hypothesis that these effects should be lower among our northeastern Chinese and Japanese populations, our results suggest, if anything, the opposite. Widowhood had a strong, adverse, and nearly uniform effect in Liaodong and Ou, increasing mortality for adult and elderly men and women. In the West, effects were less apparent. In Sart, widowers but not widows had elevated mortality. In Casalguidi, widows had lower death rates, but in Madregolo their death rates were higher.

Nor do the results confirm the hypothesized link between birth order and child mortality in the complex households of the East. Table 5.6 summarizes mortality differences by the presence of older and young brothers and sisters. There are few significant effects among our northeastern Chinese and Japanese populations. One exception is the mortality of young boys aged 2 to 16 *sui* (1 to 15 Western years) in Liaodong, where having an older sister increases mortality risks by 28 percent. Coincidentally, in Ou, the presence of an older brother raised male child mortality by 28 percent. Contrary to the assumption that female survival in childhood in East Asia was affected by total family size, birth order, and the sex of previous children, having an older sibling had no effect on female child mortality in Ou.[22]

If anything, the presence of siblings was more important as a determinant of child mortality in the European conjugal populations. Although the results on the mortality effects of the proportion young in table 5.2 indicated that children in the household competed with each other for resources, in a number of instances specific configurations of siblings by sex and seniority actually seemed to have a protective effect. Family choices, in other words, could in some situations counteract the mechanical effects of the dependency ratio. Local context conditioned the precise pattern of effects: which siblings mattered and which infants and children were affected varied from one site to the next. In Casalguidi, for example, an older brother lowered female child mortality by nearly 40 percent. In Madregolo, a younger brother nearly halved male child mortality, and a younger sister reduced female child mortality by one-third. Similarly, in Sart, having a younger sister lowered female child mortality by 25 percent. In Scania, the presence of a younger sister lowered male child mortality by one-quarter, although an older sister raised female child mortality by 50 percent.

Confirming the risks associated with a short subsequent birth interval, where the effects on infant mortality of having a younger sibling could be calculated, they were adverse. Again, the gender pattern of effects varied across sites, confirming the importance of behaviors modulated by local context. In Scania, for example, a younger brother more than tripled the death rates of both boys and girls in the first twenty-four months of life. In Madregolo, a younger sibling of either sex more than doubled female mortality in the first twenty-four months of life. In Casalguidi, a younger brother raised the chances that a boy would die by 40 percent.

Results on the effects of presence or absence of kin in the complex household societies yielded mixed results on anthropological hypotheses about the mortality effects of household relationships. In Liaodong, the relationship between a mother's and particularly a widow's chances of survival and whether she had sons was as expected by

Table 5.6
Effects of presence of siblings on infant and child mortality

Country	Site	Sibling	Infants				Children			
			Females		Males		Females		Males	
			(Ratio)	(p)	(Ratio)	(p)	(Ratio)	(p)	(Ratio)	(p)
Belgium	Sart	Older brother	0.92	0.50	0.96	0.74	0.80	0.11	0.92	0.61
		Older sister	0.91	0.46	0.91	0.40	0.91	0.52	1.04	0.78
		Younger brother					0.81	0.12	1.05	0.74
		Younger sister					0.75	0.03	0.99	0.92
China	Liaodong	Older brother					0.89	0.46	0.89	0.16
		Older sister					1.05	0.77	1.28	0.01
		Younger brother					0.83	0.33	1.01	0.90
		Younger sister					0.97	0.89	0.98	0.88
Italy	Casalguidi	Older brother	0.83	0.10	0.93	0.55	0.62	0.00	1.35	0.14
		Older sister	0.94	0.56	0.87	0.20	1.03	0.88	0.66	0.03
		Younger brother	1.30	0.45	1.41	0.09	0.97	0.88	0.76	0.19
		Younger sister	1.31	0.31	1.19	0.43	1.09	0.66	0.79	0.25
	Madregolo	Older brother	1.20	0.36	0.83	0.29	0.87	0.63	1.20	0.51
		Older sister	1.14	0.48	0.75	0.11	0.88	0.65	0.91	0.73
		Younger brother	3.24	0.00	1.63	0.36	0.69	0.18	0.57	0.05
		Younger sister	2.37	0.04	1.60	0.32	0.63	0.08	0.69	0.16
Japan	Niita and Shimomoriya	Older brother	1.08	0.81	0.69	0.38	1.19	0.25	1.28	0.05
		Older sister	0.89	0.76	0.78	0.52	1.03	0.86	0.91	0.64
		Younger brother					0.86	0.62	1.29	0.13
		Younger sister					0.91	0.77	0.99	0.97

Sweden	Four Scanian parishes								
	Older brother	1.05	0.77	1.07	0.64	1.14	0.52	0.98	0.90
	Older sister	1.16	0.35	1.18	0.23	1.50	0.05	1.13	0.49
	Younger brother	3.79	0.03	3.68	0.01	0.96	0.83	0.81	0.21
	Younger sister	1.11	0.92	0.60	0.61	0.87	0.48	0.74	0.08

Source: Comparative relationship model.

G. W. Skinner (1997, 75). Ever-married women in Liaodong aged 15 to
55 *sui* with no living sons have death rates 12.2 percent higher than
those with at least one living son (table 5.4). Similarly, a widow with
no living sons has death rates 55 percent higher than a widow with
at least one living son.[23] However, contrary to expectations, the presence of a mother-in-law actually benefited a married woman in Liaodong, lowering her chances of dying by 15.7 percent (table 5.4).

Responses

The anthropological prediction that larger, more complicated households shielded their members against external shocks does not seem
to be true. For the effects of number of working-age adults in table 5.7,
we present the proportional change in sensitivity of mortality to price
associated with the addition of a working-age adult to the household.
According to table 5.7, increases in the number of working-age adults
actually increased the sensitivity of mortality in several sites, at least
among infants and children. The effect was most extreme in Niita and
Shimomoriya, where each additional adult dramatically increased the
response of infant mortality and had a more moderate but statistically
significant effect on the sensitivity of male child mortality. In Sart,
additional adults raised the sensitivity of female infant and male child
mortality. Only in Scania did additional adults have the expected
effects, moderately reducing the sensitivity of female infant mortality.

Results on the sensitivity of adult and elderly mortality in table 5.7
also fail to support the claim that larger households were better able to
shield their members against the effects of short-term economic stress.
Among ever-married adults, effects of household size on sensitivity
were rare. In the two cases they were apparent, however, they were in
the expected direction. Thus, every additional adult reduced the sensitivity of ever-married female mortality by two-thirds in Sart. In Niita
and Shimomoriya, the effect was also in the expected direction, with
every additional adult reducing the sensitivity of ever-married male
mortality by about one-quarter. Among the elderly, effects of household size and age composition were apparent in Niita-Shimomoriya,
Scania, south Liaodong, and Casalguidi but also inconsistent. Additional working-age adults increased sensitivity in Niita-Shimomoriya
and Scania but reduced it in Casalguidi and south Liaodong.

Effects of the dependency burden on sensitivity to short-term stress
were similarly inconsistent, confirming the importance of local context
in shaping outcomes. Tables 5.8 and 5.9 translate the original results

Table 5.7
Effects of adding an adult on sensitivity of mortality to price

Country	Site		Infants (Ratio)	(p)	Children (Ratio)	(p)	Ever-married adults (Ratio)	(p)	Ever-married elderly (Ratio)	(p)
Belgium	Sart	Female	2.49	0.08	1.15	0.78	0.34	0.00	2.68	0.13
		Male	0.65	0.22	3.11	0.04	1.41	0.53	1.18	0.66
China	North Liaodong	Female			0.98	0.72	1.00	0.70	1.02	0.27
		Male			1.01	0.71	1.01	0.46	0.99	0.45
	South Liaodong	Female					1.01	0.39	1.02	0.24
		Male			0.99	0.44	0.99	0.40	0.98	0.10
Italy	Casalguidi	Female	0.81	0.30	1.67	0.17	1.12	0.64	0.58	0.07
		Male	0.90	0.55	1.34	0.50	0.75	0.36	1.42	0.36
	Madregolo	Female	1.10	0.28	1.16	0.15	0.96	0.69	0.90	0.52
		Male	1.09	0.14	0.99	0.92	1.18	0.12	0.95	0.69
Japan	Niita and Shimomoriya	Female	9.47	0.00	1.04	0.78	0.83	0.11	1.39	0.00
		Male	9.93	0.00	1.26	0.02	0.77	0.09	1.06	0.00
Sweden	Four Scanian parishes	Female	0.81	0.09	1.06	0.63	1.00	0.98	0.87	0.52
		Male	0.50	0.34	0.88	0.52	5.33	0.60	1.61	0.00

Source: Comparative household model with price interactions.

Table 5.8
Effects of adding a child age 0–15 on sensitivity of mortality to price

Country	Site		Infants (Ratio)	(p)	Children (Ratio)	(p)	Ever-married adults (Ratio)	(p)	Ever-married elderly (Ratio)	(p)
Belgium	Sart	Female	2.11	0.14	0.29	0.10	0.48	0.05	0.86	0.78
		Male	0.81	0.62	1.75	0.43	1.02	0.97	0.82	0.70
China	North Liaodong	Female			0.88	0.68	1.07	0.50	1.08	0.53
		Male			0.93	0.66	0.92	0.41	0.92	0.52
	South Liaodong	Female					0.85	0.13	1.12	0.39
		Male			1.06	0.76	0.93	0.50	1.12	0.40
Italy	Casalguidi	Female	0.65	0.30	0.82	0.76	1.06	0.88	0.33	0.04
		Male	1.10	0.81	0.83	0.81	0.68	0.46	1.50	0.58
	Madregolo	Female	1.16	0.76	1.16	0.80	1.20	0.54	0.61	0.42
		Male	2.46	0.00	1.16	0.73	0.85	0.61	1.62	0.39
Japan	Niita and Shimomoriya	Female	1.34	0.05	1.08	0.75	0.89	0.79	1.38	0.00
		Male	0.79	0.92	2.23	0.00	1.00	0.99	1.11	0.00
Sweden	Four Scanian parishes	Female	0.47	0.08	1.16	0.82	1.06	0.88	0.46	0.12
		Male	0.75	0.76	1.05	0.93	0.88	0.54	1.72	0.28

Source: Comparative household model with price interactions.

Table 5.9
Effects of adding an elderly person on sensitivity of mortality to price

Country	Site		Infants (Ratio)	(p)	Children (Ratio)	(p)	Ever-married adults (Ratio)	(p)	Ever-married elderly (Ratio)	(p)
Belgium	Sart	Female	1.49	0.61	0.17	0.09	0.10	0.00	3.03	0.13
		Male	0.73	0.69	0.89	0.93	0.24	0.14	0.89	0.86
China	North Liaodong	Female			1.00	0.99	1.19	0.08	1.02	0.86
		Male			1.02	0.89	0.87	0.25	1.02	0.80
	South Liaodong	Female			1.07	0.72	1.12	0.31	1.20	0.07
		Male					1.01	0.94	1.03	0.73
Italy	Casalguidi	Female	3.23	0.10	0.45	0.30	0.52	0.24	0.35	0.06
		Male	0.73	0.67	5.19	0.13	3.23	0.18	2.07	0.35
	Madregolo	Female	1.68	0.40	2.38	0.32	2.76	0.10	0.65	0.42
		Male	1.82	0.16	0.96	0.96	0.45	0.32	1.49	0.41
Japan	Niita and Shimomoriya	Female	1.10	0.01	1.17	0.37	1.05	0.82	1.65	0.00
		Male	1.01	0.86	1.67	0.00	0.60	0.90	1.18	0.00
Sweden	Four Scanian parishes	Female			2.08	0.57	1.80	0.48	0.43	0.15
		Male			0.82	0.87	0.74	0.07	1.96	0.30

Source: Comparative household model with price interactions.

from the comparative household model with price interactions into the proportional change in mortality sensitivity associated with a 20 percentage point increase in the proportion of household members in these age groups. In some but not all cases, increases in the proportion of household members who were infants, children, or elderly raised the sensitivity of infant or child mortality. This was most clearly the case for female infant and male child mortality in Niita and Shimomoriya. In both cases, sensitivity rose when the proportions young or old increased. In Madregolo, increases in the proportion young raised the sensitivity of male infant mortality, and in Casalguidi, increases in the proportion elderly raised the sensitivity of female infant mortality. This pattern was by no means universal, however. In Sart and Scania, higher proportions of members who were very young or very old actually appeared to reduce sensitivity to price fluctuations.

Effects of age composition on the sensitivity of adult mortality were also apparent but again inconsistent. In Sart, increases in the proportions young or old reduced the sensitivity of ever-married female mortality. In north Liaodong, increases in the proportion elderly raised the sensitivity of ever-married female mortality. In Madregolo, increases in the proportion elderly raised the sensitivity of ever-married female mortality. In the Scania parishes, increases in the proportion elderly dramatically reduced the sensitivity of ever-married male mortality. Effects on the sensitivity of the mortality of the elderly were similarly inconsistent, with increases in the dependency ratio raising sensitivity in Ou but lowering it in Casalguidi.

Nor did complex households protect the most vulnerable members of society, children who had lost a parent, against economic stress. Table 5.10 summarizes the proportional change in the sensitivity of mortality to price associated with the loss of one or both parents. If anything, children who had lost a parent were more vulnerable in complex family systems than they were in conjugal family systems. According to the results for child mortality in table 5.10, death rates of boys in Liaodong who had lost their mothers were more than twice as sensitive to price fluctuations as those of boys with both parents. Similarly, in Ou, orphanhood more than doubled the sensitivity of child mortality rates, and the loss of a mother also had strong effects. In Europe, by contrast, there were no statistically significant effects of loss of parents on the sensitivity of child mortality.

Similarly, when it came to sensitivity, widows were no more vulnerable in conjugal family systems than in joint family systems. Table 5.11 presents the proportional changes in the sensitivity of mortality asso-

Table 5.10
Effects of presence of parents on sensitivity of infant and child mortality to price

Country	Site	Parents (Ref: Both)	Infants (0–24 months)				Children (2–15 years)			
			Females		Males		Females		Males	
			(Ratio)	(p)	(Ratio)	(p)	(Ratio)	(p)	(Ratio)	(p)
Belgium	Sart	Father	0.32	0.43	2.65	0.47			4.79	0.29
		Mother	1.48	0.77	0.89	0.93	0.32	0.36		
		Neither			1.03	0.99				
China	Liaodong North	Father					6.86	0.04	2.22	0.03
		Mother					1.87	0.52	0.92	0.83
		Neither					0.75	0.74	2.60	0.14
	Liaodong South	Father							1.47	0.37
		Mother							0.78	0.56
		Neither							1.26	0.72
Italy	Casalguidi	Father	0.47	0.71	0.14	0.39	0.20	0.34	2.42	0.63
		Mother	3.17	0.78	0.00	0.12	7.33	0.32	0.60	0.80
		Neither					0.71	0.94		
	Madregolo	Father	5.63	0.05	0.89	0.91	3.09	0.36	0.28	0.31
		Mother	0.46	0.62	2.92	0.16	7.00	0.13	2.31	0.39
		Neither								
Japan	Niita and Shimomoriya	Father	0.00	1.00	0.02	0.99	9.44	0.00	3.03	0.00
		Mother	1.55	0.56	0.92	0.94	0.72	0.73	0.89	0.85
		Neither					2.14	0.05	2.82	0.00
Sweden	Four Scanian parishes	Either or none	0.11	0.26	0.02	0.05	0.19	0.31	2.14	0.63

Source: Comparative relationship model with price interactions.

Table 5.11
Effects of widowhood on sensitivity of adult and elderly mortality to price

Country	Site	Adults				Elderly			
		Females		Males		Females		Males	
		(Ratio)	(p)	(Ratio)	(p)	(Ratio)	(p)	(Ratio)	(p)
Belgium	Sart	0.83	0.90	5.57	0.30	0.55	0.51	0.76	0.72
China	Liaodong North	0.79	0.28	0.95	0.81	0.89	0.59	0.78	0.09
	Liaodong South	0.76	0.20	1.45	0.16	0.67	0.08	1.01	0.94
Italy	Casalguidi	4.12	0.45	3.70	0.36	0.05	0.14	1.39	0.76
	Madregolo	1.67	0.69	3.15	0.53	177.73	0.06	0.38	0.16
Japan	Niita and Shimomoriya	0.43	0.78	0.78	0.87	0.54	0.46	0.72	0.53

Source: Comparative relationship model with price interactions.

ciated with being widowed. According to the results, widowhood did not affect the sensitivity of adult widows or widowers. Among the elderly, being widowed seems to have reduced the vulnerability of men in north Liaodong and women in south Liaodong.

Conclusion

The results in this chapter and chapter 4 demonstrate the striking contrast in the domestic organization and the demographic behavior of eastern and western Eurasia. Although many aspects of the demographic implications are still unclear,[24] the basic dimensions of this dichotomy are apparent. Northeast Asian and Mediterranean households were more complex than northwest European households. Mortality was also more controlled and more differentiated in northeast Asia and the Mediterranean according to domestic group organization, while in northwest Europe, mortality was more susceptible to economic conditions. The hoary images of the familial Chinese, Japanese, and Italians, on the one hand, and the individualistic Belgians and especially Swedes, on the other, ring true.

Our results, in other words, seem to confirm our intuitive understanding of meta-geography, as well as some claims about the demographic implications of household organization. Tables 5.2, 5.3, 5.8, and 5.9, for example, confirm that the family life cycle, measured as the proportions of young and old, had the expected effects on individual living standards, reflected in mortality. Households at early stages of the family life cycle seem to have suffered from the dependency burden associated with having a higher proportion of members who were young (Chayanov 1923/1986).[25] At later stages of the family life cycle, as shown in table 5.3, the burden of caring for elderly household members appears to have fallen on married women and daughters.

In spite of the powerful logic and systemic beauty of anthropological models of family systems, however, many of the hypothesized patterns of behavior are not apparent in our Eurasian communities. Most important, results on the effects of numbers of working-age adults in tables 5.1 and 5.7 demonstrated that larger households in Asia were not better off, in the sense of having either lower mortality levels or being less sensitive to short-term economic stress. Differences in household organization are accordingly unlikely to have accounted for the lower sensitivity of the Eastern populations observed in chapter 3.

Others results are inconclusive or even opposite to expectations. For example, tables 5.4, 5.5, 5.10, and 5.11 demonstrated that widowhood or loss of a parent seemed to be a disaster in the East as in the West, if not more so. The larger and more complex households of the East, in other words, appear not to have been effective at caring for the most vulnerable members of the family. Table 5.6, meanwhile, revealed that the presence of certain siblings actually had a protective effect for children, with the precise pattern varying from one context to another. Thus, while our findings confirm the significance of domestic organization for demographic behavior, this significance clearly varies by geographic location, and effects are often counterintuitive.

The effect of geography, moreover, does not solely reflect a simple divide between Western conjugal and Eastern complex family systems.[26] While results from the Eurasian standard comparative models identify a number of situations where household size, composition, and relationship had effects on individual mortality and its sensitivity to short-term stress, the direction and strength of the effects varied not only between East and West, but within them as well.

Household systems may be less important in explaining differences in demographic behavior than geographic location and specific regional or continental histories of family and family behavior.[27] David Reher (1998), writing on Western Europe, has described the importance of local familial traditions over formal family systems and family organization in defining some enduring contrasts in European family ties. Similarly, our results, although still preliminary and incomplete, suggest that there may be other equally enduring contrasts between Eurasian family ties, especially between East Asia and western Europe.

In spite of the popularity of convergence theory, human society remains divergent, a product of specific historical processes. This divergence transcends national boundaries between the northeast Asian and northwest European communities, respectively, but persists between continental boundaries. The irony, of course, is that while the Eurasian Project is an initial step to produce a nonnational history based on individual data, not aggregate data, written at the community level, not the country level, our preliminary efforts to produce a social scientific history for the twenty-first century have to some extent also reconfirmed the meta-geography of the nineteenth century.

Notes

1. See chapter 3 on East-West differences in the responsiveness of mortality to short-term stress and chapter 4 on differences in community and household organization.

2. For whatever reason, in both East Asia and the West, this topic has been the preserve of pundits. See Doi (1973), Huntington (1995), and Nakane (1973) for recent examples. The most objective scholarly analyses are probably from the perspective of clinical psychology. See Triandis (1995) for a summary of the state of this field.

3. See Lee and Wang (1999b) for a discussion of Chinese demographic behavior within the context of this comparative framework.

4. In rural China, such collective organization was largely at the level of the household. In rural Japan, however, village organization also played a major role in such decision making (Ooms 1996). Such organization is beyond the scope of the Laslett model tables and cannot be discussed here.

5. The English origins of Western individualism are a major theme in Macfarlane (1978, 1986, 1987). See Berlin (1958) and Q. Skinner (1997) for the English roots of the Western concepts of liberty and freedom.

6. While the founding father of this field may be John Hajnal (1965, 1982), most subsequent work has been in anthropological demography by Das Gupta (1995, 1997, 1998), Goody (1983, 1990, 1996), Harrell (1997), Macfarlane (1978, 1986, 1987), G. W. Skinner (1993, 1997), Wolf (1995, 1998), and Wolf and Huang (1980).

7. In some cases, notably Wolf (1995), as far as social biology not just of humans, but of primates as well.

8. Wrigley and Schofield (1981) and Wrigley et al. (1997) are most responsible for the very successful revival of this Malthusian tradition during the past two decades. Malthusian theory has also been particularly influential in studies of China (Chao 1986; Elvin 1973; Ho 1959; Huang 1985, 1990; Perkins 1969), but less influential in studies of Japan, thanks to the many contributions by Akira Hayami and his colleagues (Hayami 1986).

9. According to Hajnal (1982, 449), northwest Europe covers the Scandinavian countries (including Ireland but not Finland), the British Isles, the Low Countries, the German-speaking area, and northern France.

10. These are roughly the twin agendas and achievements of the Cambridge Group for the History of Population and Social Structure.

11. Schofield, drawing on Hajnal (1982) as well as his own work with Wrigley and Lee, has summarized these findings in several articles (1984, 1985a, 1985b) and places them in an East-West individualist-collectivist context in Schofield (1989). See too the important elaborations by Goldstone (1986), Levine (1987), and Weir (1984a) of nuptiality behavior in England.

12. This logic dates back to Davis's (1955) analysis of fertility and nuptiality. See Das Gupta (1997, 1998), and especially G. W. Skinner's (1997) elaboration of these ideas, as well as Wolf (1998).

13. Monica Das Gupta (1998, 453), for example, has hypothesized that joint households may consequently have wider mortality differentials between siblings in early childhood and narrower mortality differentials in late childhood than in stem or nuclear family systems. Similarly, G. William Skinner (1997, 72) has postulated that a child's chance of surviving depends on his or her sex and the number and sex of the preceding children.

14. According to G. W. Skinner, "Gender bias informs [all] three types of family systems in contingent fashion. In general, structural bias is pronounced in joint family systems and minimal in conjugal family systems.... Patrilineal joint family systems, which obtain in one variant or another in a continuous belt of agrarian societies stretching from China across South Asia and the Middle East into Eastern Europe and North Africa, present the extreme examples of consistent, thoroughgoing male bias " (1997, 58–59).

15. "In a word, her life is usually (and normatively) miserable, and until she has a child (preferably of course a male child) her life is unlikely to improve. If she should bear a string of daughters, it will get much worse" (G. W. Skinner 1997, 75).

16. "Whereas in conjugal family systems and in uxorilocal stem family systems, the status of the 'young married women' is very often a happy one, in the patrilineal joint family systems of East and South Asia it is the status of highest stress.... Thus, we may expect the elevated age-specific female mortality rates often associated with the child-bearing years to have a characteristic trajectory in populations with patrilineal joint family systems" (G. W. Skinner 1997, 75).

17. "I propose that, other things being equal, the mortality of the elderly widowed will be highest in conjugal family systems and lowest in joint family systems, with stem family systems generally intermediate and highly variable" (G. W. Skinner 1997, 78).

18. Such schemes of course can be traced back to Goody's heroic (1976) comparison of Eurasian and African domestic organization, which sought to identify important differences. More recent work of Das Gupta (1997, 1998) and G. W. Skinner (1997), while recognizing such differences especially between conjugal and joint family systems, tends to emphasize similarities within family systems.

19. See the appendix for a detailed discussion of the models, the data, and the construction of the variables for the different populations.

20. For example, adding a child to a household with two adults and a child increases the proportion of members below age 15 by 0.17, raising it from 0.33 to 0.50.

21. See also chapter 13 for an examination of the mortality consequences of widowhood.

22. It does, of course, have an enormous impact on infant survivorship due to the common practice of female infanticide, which we describe in Lee and Campbell (1997) for one specific Liaodong population and Lee and Wang (1999b) for China in general during the past three centuries.

23. See chapter 13 for a more detailed discussion of results from the Eurasia standard comparative models on the determinants of elderly mortality.

24. The geographic boundaries are probably relatively similar to those first identified by Hajnal (1965).

25. This effect was more apparent for the mortality of the young than the old. See chapter 13 for a more detailed examination of the effects of the dependency burden on the mortality of the elderly.

26. See also the many results on mortality in Campbell and Lee (1996, 2000) and Tsuya and Kurosu (2000). We develop this further in our forthcoming books on reproduction, marriage, and migration in the MIT Press Eurasian Population and Family History Series.

27. Goody (1983) is a model of such large-scale explanation.

II   Local Histories

6

Mortality and Social Class in Four Scanian Parishes, 1766–1865

Tommy Bengtsson

In years of poor harvests in the past, hordes of hungry people took to the road in search of food and work. According to both contemporary Swedes such as Pehr Wargentin (1772/1976), renowned astronomer and statistician, and to visitors, such as Thomas Malthus (1803/1826/1986), the demographic toll during such years was heavy. Wargentin (1772) demonstrated a distinct correlation between harvests and mortality, fertility and nuptiality.[1] Based on this work and his own experience during his travels in Sweden in 1799, Malthus postulated that Sweden's population was strongly affected by harvest variations and worse off than its neighbors Norway and Denmark, the result of the Swedish government's mercantilistic, pronatal policy (Malthus 1803/1826/1986, 168).

The causality between harvests and mortality has not gone unquestioned. Gustav Utterström claimed, in his debate with Eli Heckscher, who took the same view as Wargentin and Malthus, that at least infant mortality had a rhythm of its own, independent of harvest outcome and food prices (Heckscher 1949, 42–44; Utterström 1957, 207–208). That infants were unaffected by food prices has been confirmed in later studies, but recent research has yielded additional evidence for causality between economic cycles and mortality in almost all other age groups (Bengtsson and Ohlsson 1985). Later studies have also shown that, as in other parts of Europe, births were rather more affected than deaths, and marriages less (Bengtsson 1993a, Galloway 1988).

The demographic response to short-term economic variations changed as the Swedish economy developed (Bengtsson and Ohlsson 1978, 1985). The effect of short-term economic stress on mortality diminished, starting in the first half of the nineteenth century with a transformation of agriculture characterized by enclosures, new crops, technical change, and an increase in commercialization and globalization. Thus, the answer to the long-debated question of whether the economic development in the first half of the nineteenth century led to improved social conditions was affirmative.[2] The mortality response weakened further in the latter part of the nineteenth century as job opportunities became better and real wages started to increase. The specific mechanisms underlying this change and the social dimensions of the mortality response are, however, largely unknown.

These questions of causality mechanisms and possible social differentiation in mortality impact have been tackled at the microlevel by combining longitudinal individual data and community-wide information on food prices and wages (Bengtsson 1989, 1993b). Such studies used annual time series of local grain prices and real wages for agricultural workers as covariates in an event-history analysis. Bengtsson (1989, 1993b) first demonstrated the advantage of the method by comparing the effects of short-term economic stress on mortality of various social groups in a single mining parish in central Sweden. Bengtsson (2000) and Dribe (2000) later used this method on a larger set of parishes in southern Sweden.

The results from southern Sweden show that the landless were affected the most (Bengtsson 2000). Mortality from air- and waterborne diseases went up after years with low real wages (high food prices), though actual cause of death in different age groups differed (Bengtsson 2000). The short-term economic stress of the landless did not diminish alongside the rural transformation and commercialization of the early 1800s, contrary to the overall national pattern. It was not until new labor markets opened up, at home and abroad, and industrialization brought with it long-term increase in real wages (after 1860) that the landless in southern Sweden became less vulnerable to fluctuations in food prices (Bengtsson and Dribe forthcoming).

This chapter investigates how hitherto unexamined aspects like family size and structure mediated the impact of food prices on mortality. Following the approach outlined in chapter 2, I will examine the effect on survival chances of having access to land, changes over the family life cycle, and the individual's position within the household. The hypothesis is that families in their initial stage are particularly vulnerable to short-term economic stress since the consumer/worker ratio increases during the first fifteen years after marriage as a result of childbirth. Household structure might also influence the vulnerability of members to short-term economic stress; persons living in a household that has become fragmentary or otherwise incomplete should suffer more from short-term economic stress than others. The mortality of small children, for example, might increase if a parent dies. When decreasing consumption put pressure on a household, its members did not share the burden equally. The position of the individual within the household likely influenced his or her chances of survival. Public institutions, granary systems, and, in particular, the poor relief system, might, however, dampen the negative impact on well-being in years of high food prices, as discussed in chapter 4.

This chapter will first describe the local community safety nets available in the four parishes of our study: Hög, Kävlinge, Halmstad, and Sireköpinge, shown in map 6.1. This is followed by an analysis of

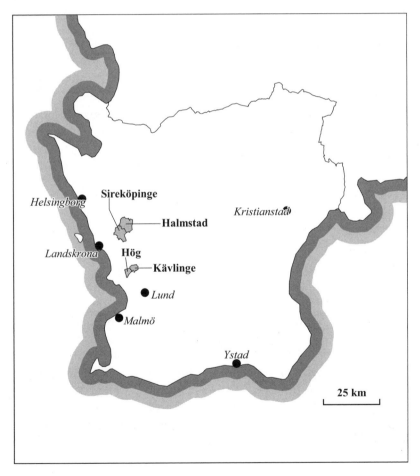

Map 6.1
Southern Sweden

economic development and social structure of the parishes and a discussion of models and data. Finally, I present the results of my analysis. I map the social gradient of the mortality response to short-term economic stress and discuss the causal mechanisms. I pay special attention to how economic stress affects causes of death. Then, I discuss whether families with small children were particularly vulnerable, and whether a person's socioeconomic status or their position in the household affected their vulnerability.

The four parishes analyzed in this study are located about 10 kilometers from the coast in the western part of Scania, the southernmost province of Sweden.[3] Nearby towns, Lund, Landskrona, and Helsingborg, are all very small and 10 to 30 kilometers away. The parishes are compact in their geographic location but vary in size, topography, and socioeconomic conditions. During the period studied here, Kävlinge, Hög, Sireköpinge, and southern Halmstad were open-country farmland, and northern Halmstad was more wooded. The parish populations numbered between 200 and 500 inhabitants each in 1800. For obvious reasons, they are not fully representative of Sweden or even Scania. They do, however, as a group, represent the type of economic and social diversity that existed at that time and geographic setting. They were ordinary rural parishes, presenting no atypical characteristics, and the life courses of people living and working in these communities, consequently, very likely resembled that of most men and families.

Poor Relief

One tends to believe that public systems for taking care of the poor were more developed in Western Europe, including Sweden, than in Asian countries such as China and Japan, where more complex family and kin group structures provided social security for their members. The public poor relief system is well documented for preindustrial Europe, in particular for England, as shown in chapter 4.[4] Throughout Europe, various institutions, religious and others, often at the parish level, took care of the sick and poor. The old poor relief system in England gave, in addition, temporary relief during sickness and seasonal and cyclical spells of unemployment, prior to its reorganization in the 1830s (Solar 1995, 6; Wall 2002). The Swedish poor relief system in the first half of the nineteenth century was organized similarly, with one important exception: it was not designed to give temporary relief during sickness and unemployment. The Swedish system involved the state, the county administration, the local community and church, the employer, and the family (Skoglund 1992, Åmark 1915).

Transfers over the life cycle were based on the family. Responsibility for the care of children lay almost entirely in the hands of parents, unlike, for example, Italy, where institutions for foundling children could ease the burden of parents, as shown in chapters 8 and 12. The local communities transferred a small amount of taxes to children by building schoolhouses and providing for health care at childbirth by trained nurses. The main costs of bringing up children were, however, paid by their parents. In return, when children grew up, they became responsible for their parents.[5] Thus, transfers over the life cycle were primarily a family issue.[6]

If the family failed, according to laws from 1763 to 1766, the local community was responsible for the sick and miserably poor, the orphans, and the elderly. The parish was free to organize such poor relief in various ways. In most cases, it was the parish itself that arranged the relief. In others, the poor were rotated among the farmers, or allowed to go begging. In the parishes included in this study, the estate owners, the freeholders, and the tenants were responsible for relief (Skoglund 1992; Banggaard 2002).

In Hög and Kävlinge, the freeholders and Crown tenants were responsible for the poor relief, while in Halmstad and Sireköpinge, the responsibility belonged to the owners of the estates, their tenants, and, toward the end of the period, the freeholders (Banggaard 2002). Relief could be administered as indoor relief, as it was in Sireköpinge in 1850 when a new poorhouse was built, and in the other three parishes, where poorhouses had already been built in the beginning of the nineteenth century, sometimes in combination with the schoolhouse, or as outdoor relief. Outdoor relief meant either that the employers took care of elderly former employees or their widows or that the local community paid someone to do it (Tuvestrand, Lövgren, and Danielson 1995, 73–74; Banggaard 2002). This was often the case for orphans. Disputes often arose between farmers and authorities over whether a person was permanently employed by the farmer himself, in which case, the local community, not the farmer, bore the costs.[7]

Tenant contracts in Sireköpinge and Halmstad often stipulated that the tenant, in addition to his normal rent, also had to give support to the poorhouse. This could be done by providing a certain yearly amount of firewood or food (Lundh and Olsson 2001, 124–127). Sometimes the contract instead stated that the new tenant had to take care of the former, retired tenant who still lived on the farm.

On average, only a small fraction of the population—in all, sixteen persons in the four parishes in 1800—received parish indoor relief.[8] The pattern was the same throughout Sweden, as shown by a public investigation in 1829 in which only 2.1 percent of the Swedish population received public poor relief (Skoglund 1992). The figure for Malmöhus County, in which the four parishes in this study are located, was 1.4 percent. These figures, however, incorporate only those who directly received parish indoor relief, not those who received relief from their former employers. Either way, the Swedish poor relief system at the beginning of the nineteenth century was not designed to take care of large groups of people in temporary need during years of high food prices, but only the small fraction in permanent need of assistance.

The church could provide temporary help in bad years from its repair fund or its poor-relief funds (Svensson 2001). The problem for many in need was that such loans were only given against security, which meant that only the landed and others with solid assets could get loans. While the landless poor could not rely on temporary assistance in years when employment was low and food prices high, they could at least be exempted from paying taxes. Some 20 percent were, for example, exempted from paying any tax at all in this area in the 1820s (Söderberg 1978, 41). The number varied from one year to the next and could sometimes be much higher. Tenants on noble land could also temporarily be released from paying rents, and the amount of rents thus postponed could be substantial. In 1773, for example, the Bjersgård estate reported that in that year alone, farmers paid back 1,034 daler silver coins, which corresponded to the total amount of rents for one year (Olsson 2002, 124). Thus, the tenants, as well as the freeholders, could store a large share of their harvests even in bad years and also borrow money to buy grain if needed, while the landless at best could only rely on not having to pay taxes.

The government took certain measures to ease the burden on people during bad years. It built granaries to give support during years of bad harvests and to level out prices (Åmark 1915, 195), and in the 1820s and 1830s, it initiated roadworks to provide employment opportunities when the rural labor market failed (Olofsson 1996, 127–129). A general complaint about the granaries, though, was that there was not enough grain during bad years (Utterström 1957). Much of the grain was spoiled, and the cost of storing as much as needed was simply too high. As for public expenditure to lower unemployment in years of bad harvests, only about 1 percent of total expenditure went into such efforts, although outlays in specific years could be higher (Olofsson 1996, 121). Furthermore, the state granary system and the funds for public works were effective mainly in middle and northern Sweden.

The amount of grain bought and sold by the granaries also influenced prices. Indeed, this was one of its purposes. According to the statutes, granaries were obligated to buy grain to prevent prices from falling too low, since this would otherwise cause problems for the producers (Åmark 1915). The unintended but positive effect for consumers was that this prevented prices from increasing too much as grain was sold in years with bad harvests. The system was, however, abandoned in 1823 as a result of complaints that it interfered with market mechanisms (Olofsson 1996, 26).

To sum up, measures were taken at various levels—the family, the employer, the local community including the church, and the state—to give support to persons who could not provide for themselves. Support was given to the permanently sick or disabled whose families were too poor to support them and the elderly without relatives who could take care of them. Only a small fraction of the population received public support. Overall, the poor relief system was not well developed, and total expenditures accounted for only a few percent of the total gross domestic production and thus were insufficient to eliminate the problems related to variations in harvests, which often were of an entirely different magnitude. A bad harvest might be one-third of a normal one, with imports compensating for only a fraction of it. Instead, loans and reductions in taxes and rents took care of problems caused by harvest variation. Loans were, however, given only against security, regardless of whether the parish or the provincial government granted them, implying that they were available only to the landed. Furthermore, the granary systems were not used for stabilizing food prices after 1823. Inevitably, neither the different public systems nor capital markets or other private institutions could ease the burdens for the landless in years of high food prices.

The growing numbers of married day laborers who were hired on temporary bases were particularly vulnerable, not having the same security as the farmhands and servants, often unmarried, who were hired on annual contracts. The group of married landless had been growing throughout most of the eighteenth century and constituted a large part of the population in the beginning of the nineteenth century. Social tensions grew and the state made efforts to create jobs for them in years of bad harvests. Finally, a new poor law system was introduced in 1847 (Banggaard 2002). Thereafter, not only producers but also consumers could receive some temporary assistance. While the Swedish poor law system shared many similarities with the English, their developments were reversed: the English system moved away from temporary relief to the unemployed supplied by the landlords in the 1830s, while such a system was introduced in Scania and the rest of Sweden in the 1840s.

Economic Development and Social Structure

Scania is known as the granary of Sweden.[9] When Sweden acquired Scania from Denmark in 1658, 54 percent of the land was owned by the noble class and exempted from tax, 27 percent belonged to the Crown, and 11 percent was church land. Only 8 percent belonged to freeholders (Weibull 1923, 63). During the latter part of the seventeenth century, the Crown reacquired considerable tracts of land that had earlier been sold or given to the nobles in exchange for war duties. In the eighteenth century the Crown sold land to tenants or others, who thus became freeholders. These sales were initiated by a statute of 1701 and had a fiscal motive: to finance the Great Nordic War (Heckscher 1944, 116–117). Although the values of the sales were insignificant at the beginning, the statute marked a change in economic policy. The idea was to encourage the development of agriculture in order to reduce imports of grain to Sweden and enable more people to live off the land. Rapid population increase lowered the cost of labor, which benefited domestic industry. The sale of state land was further promoted during the eighteenth century (Weibull 1923, 64), and as a consequence, 30 percent of Scania belonged to freeholders, 44 percent was manorial, and 26 percent was Crown land by 1801. The subdivision of farm holdings (*hemmansklyvning*), enabled through partible inheritance and sale of land parcels (legalized in the mid-eighteenth century), further stimulated population growth. This was an adjustment to increasing productivity, rendering it possible for a family to make a living on smaller farms than before. In reality, it meant that farms were subdivided even further, which also took place from the beginning of the nineteenth century onward. The underlying idea was mercantilistic, and the purpose was to promote economic growth in Sweden, in the manufacturing industry as well as in the agricultural sector. This was the policy Malthus had complained about, since he thought that it would only lead to misery of the laborers.

Agricultural development was characterized by land reclamation, enclosures, new crops and new technology, and labor reorganization. The eighteenth and early nineteenth centuries were periods of continuous land reclamation. New land was brought under the plough, mainly by the conversion of pastureland. For a very long time, agriculture had been organized in an open field system whereby each peasant worked a number of strips in different parts of the village land. Pasture and woodlands were used as commons for grazing livestock and sundry other purposes. Rye, barley, and oats were the dominant crops. Potatoes spread to various parts of Scania by the end of the eighteenth century but were grown on a small scale (Weibull 1923, 103). Animal husbandry was of somewhat limited importance relative to grain production. Still, it did have a certain weight for the large estates since export of live oxen from Scania was allowed during the eighteenth century, while grain was not. Enclosure movements began with the *Storskifte* Act of 1749/1757, in an attempt to reduce the number of strips. The effects were limited, and some villages were not involved in this movement at all. Enclosure legislation did not have the same importance for noble land since the estate owner often owned entire villages, which made legal authorization easier (Fridlizius 1979).

Sweden experienced an agricultural revolution during the early nineteenth century. Total production increased rapidly, as did land productivity, owing to improved tools and equipment, new crops and crop rotations, and further enclosure movements. The *Enskifte* enclosure was initiated in 1803, and by 1823, more than half of Scania's agricultural land had been enclosed. This statute was followed in 1827 by the *Laga* (parliamentary) Enclosure Act. The two peasant parishes in our study, Hög and Kävlinge, were enclosed in 1804, and the two noble parishes were enclosed later. Halmstad was enclosed in 1827, and the production system entirely reorganized in 1844. In Sireköpinge, which was enclosed in 1849, most of the land was sold to the tenants.

The period also saw a commercialization and globalization of agriculture following the lifting of restrictions on the grain trade in Scania. Whereas Scania's grain surplus could be sold on only the Swedish market until the early nineteenth century, it now became legal to export it. New markets, together with increased prices and secure

property rights, provided a strong stimulus to agricultural transformation (Fridlizius 1979). New crops were introduced, and beans, peas,
and vetches were grown on the fallow (Weibull 1923, 96). The farmers
responded so strongly to the demands of the new markets in the Netherlands and England that grain became Sweden's third most important
export, after iron and timber. The high prices prevailing during the
Napoleonic Wars also boosted investment in agriculture. When prices
dropped in the 1820s, many farmers faced great problems but enclosures resumed, partly as a result of a parliamentary decision in 1827.
Throughout this period, villages were split up and families moved out
to the contiguous tracts of land allotted to each farm.

Swedish industrialization took its first steps in the early nineteenth
century, but the industrial revolution did not start until the latter part
of the century. Its most notable feature, as far as Scania was concerned,
was the expansion of the textile industry, which took place mainly
after 1865, some of it close to Kävlinge.

The source of wealth in rural Scania was access to land that was very
unequally distributed, as shown in figure 4.1. As a result of the transformation of the agricultural sector, in 1800 half of the families were
landless or had only small plots of land insufficient to support a family.
The social structure of the agricultural sector is often difficult to analyze in detail. Due to changes in productivity, differences of wealth
between the various categories of farmers and occupations are unclear
and subject to change with the passage of time. Data on occupations
must therefore be combined with information about types of tenure
(from land registers) and farm size (from poll tax records), in order to
arrive at a better understanding of the social structure.

Farm size was recorded in *mantal*. This was not a measure of the
actual size of the farm but a tax assessment unit based on potential
productive capacity. The measure is difficult to use for comparisons
over time since land reclamation, introduction of new crops, and
other improvements changed the productive capacity, while the *mantal*
stayed the same. For example, a farm with a *mantal* of one-quarter was
considered to be the smallest taxable unit in the early eighteenth century, and further subdivision was prohibited. However, by the end of
the eighteenth century, the minimum size had been lowered to one-
eighth of a *mantal* and by the beginning of the nineteenth century
to one-sixteenth of a *mantal*. It was not until the nineteenth century,
though, that the farms were split up into plots too small to support a
family.

Table 6.1
Four Scanian parishes 1766–1865: Families by socioeconomic status

Social group	1766–1815	1815–1865
Higher occupations and nobility	1.3%	1.2%
1. Freeholders and Crown tenants > 1/16 *mantal*	12.7	13.0
2. Noble tenants > 1/16 *mantal*	25.1	11.9
3. Freeholders and Crown tenants < 1/16 *mantal*	0.1	6.5
3. Noble tenants < 1/16 *mantal*	0.0	2.4
3. Crofters	0.6	12.8
4. Laborers and cottagers	45.8	38.5
4. Artisans and qualified laborers	2.1	4.1
4. Soldiers	3.8	4.7
4. Lodgers	0.6	3.8
4. Others/not available	7.7	1.1
Total	100.0	100.0

Note: The numbering of the social groups refers to the categorization used in this study: (1) freeholders and Crown tenants, (2) tenants on noble land, (3) semilandless, and (4) landless. These tabulations do not include unmarried servants working and living on the farms.
Source: Scanian Demographic Database.

From these poll tax records, it is evident that the nobility and persons with higher education, like clergymen, constituted the upper class of rural society and, as shown in table 6.1, that only a few percent of the families belonged to this group. The estate owned by the nobility was often of high value. Sireköpinge estate, for example, owned all the land of the parish in 1765, taxed at 23.875 *mantal* (Gillberg 1765, 228, 271). Most of it was rented out to tenants; the estate itself farmed only 3.5 *mantal*. The farmstead used by the clergymen was often among the largest in the parish, as in the Italian parishes included in this book, with a value of up to one *mantal*.[10] The peasants, generally with farms between one-eighth and one-half of a *mantal*, can be divided into three categories: freeholders, tenants on Crown land, and tenants on noble land.[11] Freeholders owned their land and paid tax to the Crown in cash or kind. They could sell their land or transfer it to the next generation. Tenants on Crown land had security of tenure and could also transfer land to the next generation as long as their rents to the Crown were paid satisfactorily. Tenants on noble land often paid their rent in the form of labor but sometimes in cash or in kind. In Halmstad and Sireköpinge, rent was paid only in the form of labor until the 1860s.

Tenancy could be for life or for a fixed term. Examination of tenant holdings in Scania and an in-depth study of the Duveke estate in Halmstad parish show that tenant leases during the nineteenth century switched from lifetime to limited duration contracts (Bengtsson and Dribe 1997; Olsson 2002, 96–98). In this way, the owners of the land could raise the rents as the prices of grain increased. Households with farms with less than one-sixteenth of a *mantal* are considered semi-landless, since they were unable to support a family and were thus dependent on work outside the farm. Due to legislation, this group came into existence only after the enclosure reforms in the beginning of the nineteenth century. Before then, all families with farmsteads that were taxed were regarded as being able to live off their land.

Crofters (*torpare*) were semilandless since their plots were usually not large enough to support their families. They also depended on cash income earned by laboring for others. In addition, the rent paid to the landowner was often in the form of labor. Still, the difference between freeholders and tenants with small farms, on the one hand, and croft-ers, on the other hand, could be very small. Most cottagers (*gatehus-män*) belonged to the landless group, being almost entirely dependent on the income of their labor, though some had plots of land. The dif-ference between this group and the crofters could be marginal. In the nineteenth century, it became common in Scania to marry while still in domestic service, thus giving rise to a new social group called *statare*. This group is included in the same category as cottagers, although they did not necessarily live in a cottage. These groups derived their main income directly from agriculture. In addition to these groups, artisans, soldiers, fishermen, and others lived in the countryside. The numerous unmarried servants living and working on farms are not included in table 6.1.[12]

The number of families in the four parishes increased substantially over the 100-year period of analysis, but the proportion landed stayed the same, at about 30 percent. Instead, the proportion of peasants with small farms (less than 1/16 *mantal*) increased, and so did the propor-tion of crofters. Thus, the proportion of families with small plots of land increased more rapidly than the groups of larger landowners and landless. The social groups are unevenly spread over the four parishes since Halmstad and Sireköpinge comprised primarily noble land, while freehold and Crown land predominated in Kävlinge and Hög.

Population trends in the province of Scania were broadly similar to those in Sweden as a whole. So were the levels and trends in life expectancy, which rose from roughly 35 years in 1750 to 45 years in

1850. Infant mortality was slightly higher than the Swedish average in the latter part of the eighteenth century but declined faster and was slightly lower from the mid-nineteenth century onward. Mortality among working adults and the elderly declined later and more slowly. Population growth was faster in the four parishes than in the country at large. Until the mid-1700s, the population of these four parishes grew at an average rate of 0.9 percent per year, but for the next 100 years, the growth rate was between 1.3 and 1.4 percent per year. After this, growth rates dropped again to an annual average of 0.9 percent. These figures are taken from family reconstitution data and therefore reflect only families, not unmarried individuals such as farmhands or single-person households. Since marriage among the landless became more common in the first part of the eighteenth century, it is likely that the growth rate during this period is slightly overestimated. In a comparison between censuses, family data account for 80 percent of all individuals in 1850 but only 65 percent in 1750 (Bengtsson and Dribe 1997). This means that the proportion of unmarried maidservants and farmhands declined in the 1800s, signifying earlier family formation and lower numbers never marrying (Lundh 1995).

Figure 6.1 shows the population totals for an expanded sample of more than twenty-five Scanian parishes along with real wages.[13] The latter are defined as the nominal wages of agricultural laborers deflated

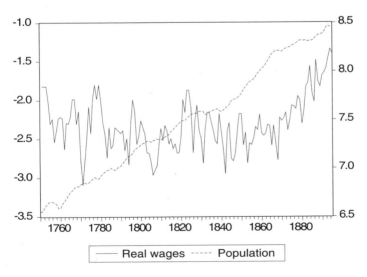

Figure 6.1
Population and real wages, twenty-five Scanian parishes, 1750–1895 (log values)

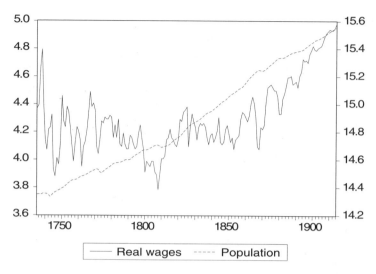

Figure 6.2
Real wages and population, Sweden 1736–1914 (log values)

by the price of rye, the dominant crop, from 1750 to 1895. The price of rye was the local price reported to the provincial authorities. They used it to work out the market price scale, which was then used to translate contracts written in kind into money. As with the rest of Sweden, shown in figure 6.2, Scanian prices increased rapidly between 1750 and 1810, then more slowly until 1870, when they started to decline. Wage data for agricultural laborers show a pattern similar to that for the country as a whole. Thus, wages followed grain prices and living costs quite well until the mid-nineteenth century, when real wages increased simultaneously with population totals, though a certain temporary decline took place around the last decades of the eighteenth century.[14]

Overall, there is no evidence when using conventional measures that the substantial population increase of the eighteenth and nineteenth centuries led to declines in standards of living. Certain periods, some of them lasting up to thirty years, exhibit declines in living standards, followed by increases in the next period. In fact, the level of real wages in Sweden was fairly stable from the early eighteenth century until the industrial revolution, when it started to rise. Therefore, there is no point in analyzing the possible long-term population response. Nevertheless, a quick look shows that while life expectancy at birth increased with 10 years from between 1750 and 1850, both nuptiality and fertility were stable.

To summarize, economic structure changed rapidly in Scania in the early years of the nineteenth century when grain exports to international markets grew, enclosures were in progress, and new agricultural methods were coming into widespread use. The Scanian port towns grew faster than in any other part of the country due to their involvement in the grain trade (Bengtsson 1990, 186–187). At the same time, population was increasing and real wages remained stable. As the industrial sector expanded toward the end of the century, work opportunities were generated outside agriculture. Kävlinge, for example, grew rapidly in the closing decades of the nineteenth century because of the many new factories established after it was connected to the railway (Bengtsson and Dribe 1997). During this period, real wages grew at the same time as population was increasing. The changes in social structure started as far back as the eighteenth century when the number of married landless started to increase. Being a servant or day laborer was no longer a part of life constrained to youth but became a lifelong destiny for many.

Models and Data

The data have been extracted from the Scanian Demographic Database, which consists of records of births, marriages, deaths, and migration (Reutersward and Olsson 1993). As described in the appendix, the material for Sireköpinge and Halmstad goes back to 1646 and for the other two parishes to the 1680s. The parish register material is of high quality and shows no gaps for births, deaths, or marriages except for a few years. Information about farm size and tenure, from the poll tax records and land registers, are linked to the family reconstitutions based on the parish records of marriages, births, and deaths. Finally, additional information regarding household composition and size from the catechetical records is added for the period 1829 to 1865.

We have modified the Eurasia standard comparative model, presented in chapters 2 and 3 as well as in the appendix, to fit the Scanian reality better. Some variables are defined somewhat differently, and some categories are impossible to use because there are too few cases.[15] Another deviation from the standard model is that both sexes are analyzed in the same model in this chapter since they share many similarities in regard to influences of other covariates.

The major difference from the general model is the choice of community variable to measure short-term economic stress. While observed or detrended food price series are used in the other studies of the project, this study uses the real wages of agricultural day laborers. The advantage of the real wage series over prices to us is that real wages were almost stationary up until the 1860s (Bengtsson 2000, 304–349). Nominal wages, however, changed very slowly in the short run, which means that short-term variation in real wages was mainly determined by food prices. The difference, when comparing results, is that the sign of the effect on mortality is the opposite since real wages are falling when prices are rising. Thus, the estimated coefficient for the influence of short-term economic stress on mortality will have the opposite interpretation of the other studies in the Eurasia project. The wage and price data are collected locally, just after the harvest in the fall, to be used for prices set by the government for each county of Sweden. The wage is the day rate for agricultural workers. It stems from the same source as rye prices, which are used as a proxy for food costs since it was the main crop used for food.

The division into separate age groups in the Eurasia standard model differs slightly from the one used in this chapter. Breast-feeding was common but generally of short duration in this part of Scania.[16] Infants therefore had some protection against infectious diseases during the first year of life but less during the second year. Experiments show that the ages 1 to 5, 5 to 10, and 10 to 15 years are quite similar with respect to vulnerability to short-term economic stress and are therefore grouped together. The upper age limit of 15 years is chosen because children normally left home around that age (Dribe 2000). This is also their last year of not paying tax. Adults are divided into two age groups as well: 25 to 55 years and 55 years and above. After about 55 years of age, adults became more and more dependent on other people (Bengtsson and Dribe 1997). Retirement, often partial, took place at ages 55 to 60 (Gaunt 1983).

For all age groups except the elderly, the mortality response that occurs in the year after the harvest is modeled. In the case of the elderly, lags of as long as two years have been considered in previous work. In contrast to results from analysis of aggregated data, there is no evidence to indicate any response to longer lags (Bengtsson 1989, 1993b). This chapter focuses mainly on children aged 1 to 15 years and married adults aged 25 to 55 years, groups that are more vulnerable to short-term economic stress than infants and elderly.[17]

The population is divided into four socioeconomic groups since several of the groups shown in table 6.1 are too small to analyze: (1)

freeholders and Crown tenants,[18] (2) tenants on noble land, (3) semi-landless, and (4) landless. The group consisting of nobles and highly educated has been excluded from the analysis since it is too small to be included in the general model. A farm of less than 1/16 *mantal* is considered to be too small for a family to live on, as previously argued. Freeholders and tenants with smaller farms have therefore been put into the semilanded group, which also includes crofters. The fourth group includes agricultural laborers, artisans, soldiers, and others who have no access to land other than small gardens.

Not all of the social groups would necessarily suffer from low real wages, as this was synonymous with high grain prices. Farmers with a surplus for the market could actually benefit, as argued in chapter 2. The same might also apply to tenants, such as those with fixed long-term rents. We therefore expect the two landed groups to benefit from low real wages. Families with small farms or only small plots of land depended on working for others and could suffer hardship when real wages were low. We therefore expect the semilandless and in particular the landless to suffer from low real wages.

A Cox proportional hazards model with time-varying covariates is used. The time-varying covariates are treated by right-censoring and left-truncating the spells every time a covariate changes. The effects of time-varying community variables such as the price of rye and time periods are treated the same way.[19] Before estimating models, the question of whether the assumption of proportional hazards required by the Cox regression model is fulfilled must be considered. This has been done by evaluating the logarithm of the cumulative hazard function by social class, gender, and parish. Generally, the assumption of proportional hazards is fulfilled except for the cumulative hazards function for the parish; the curves cross each other not only over the entire period but also in the subperiods. For this reason, previous analyses have been stratified by parish. This chapter follows a multilevel approach procedure instead, with fixed covariates for the parishes. Some of the other curves, such as the curves for social class, cross slightly or in some cases run very closely together. It would have been possible to improve the estimations by changing the categories and the age interval, but keeping the definitions as they are is of value for comparative reasons. Moreover, the crossings are not all that systematic, and some element of crossing occasioned by similarities and randomness does not alter the estimations much.

Results

Adults of both sexes were, to a similar degree, vulnerable to short-term economic stress prior to the agricultural reforms of the early nineteenth century, as shown by the parameter estimates in table 6.2. While the overall effect of logged real wages is highly significant, the interaction effect is not significant even though the estimate of the gender difference is rather large in the first period. A test for social differences in the response is shown in the same table. Although the relative risks differ considerably between the groups, both the overall likelihood ratio test and the Wald test of the individual socioeconomic group show no significant effect. Certainly some individuals and some families must have been able to overcome short-term economic stress, but it is not possible to detect any social difference in the response. Mortality increased after years with low real wages.

The results for the period 1815–1865 confirm the conclusion that the agricultural reforms in the beginning of the nineteenth century increased the social stratification of the countryside. This is particularly true when it comes to the response among adults in working ages. While the response among the freeholders and tenants was not statistically significant, mortality among adult day laborers and artisans increased by 12.9 percent when real wages declined by 10 percent, as shown in table 6.2. The likelihood ratio test shows that the social gradient in the response is highly significant. Again, no difference is found between men and women.

Since the group consisting of crofters and smallholders varies so much in size from the first to the second period, a set of alternative calculations for various combinations of socioeconomic groups has been made. The result is shown in table 6.3. In addition to the two periods analyzed in table 6.2, a subperiod, 1829–1865, is shown. The reason is that the models that include household size and composition use this period due to data limitations. Each line represents a separate regression. The first line shows the results for all social groups and the following ones for various combinations. It is clearly shown that all social groups suffered from economic stress during the period 1766–1815 to such a degree that it affected the mortality of married adults in working ages. The results for the period 1815 to 1865 show a strong social gradient in the response to short-term economic stress. The landless suffered from low real wages to a larger extent than previously. The landed responded in the opposite way, indicating abilities to smooth consumption in the short run. The group of crofters and small-holders seems to fall in between. The difference between the groups still holds true for the shorter period, 1829 to 1865. Evidently the conditions changed in different directions for the landed and the landless after the agricultural reforms in the beginning of the nineteenth century.

Table 6.4 shows the same calculations for children aged 1 to 15 years as for their parents. Again, a strong mortality response to short-term economic stress is found during both periods. For the first period, no differences due to sex and social group are found. So far, the results are the same as for their parents. Although a fair number of events, 518 deaths, are analyzed during the second period and rather large differences in relative risks exist between the two sexes and the social groups, these differences are still not significant, though it seems that girls suffer more than boys from short-term economic stress. In table 6.5, which shows the results when the population is split according to social group, some social differences in the mortality response to short-term economic stress can be detected during the period 1766 to 1815; children of landless and semilandless suffered more from short-term economic stress than children of landowners. The difference becomes more pronounced during the period 1815 to 1865 as the children of landless show no significant response at all. Overall, the results are much in line with the finding for their parents, except for the gender differences during the nineteenth century.

The general relationship between economic fluctuations and mortality was neither symmetrical nor linear (Bengtsson 2000, 324–325). Mortality did not decrease as much when wages were high as much as it increased when wages were low. Minor deviations from the average real wage had only a minor effect.

Cause-specific mortality is analyzed using a competing risk model, in which mortality from causes other than the one analyzed is treated as censoring events.[20] The models are estimated for the entire period, 1766 to 1865, since the number of events would otherwise have been too small. For the same reason, mortality is aggregated into five categories: airborne infectious diseases, waterborne infectious diseases, other infectious diseases, other specified diseases, and nonspecified diseases. Although we analyze the entire 1766 to 1865 year period, we must keep in mind that the disease panorama changed over time when interpreting the results in table 6.6. In the first period, children and, to a minor extent, adults died mainly from epidemic diseases, which

Table 6.2
Effects of sex, socioeconomic group, and declines in real wages on relative risks of mortality, married adults, in ages 25–55 years

| | 1766–1815 | | | | | | |
| | Interaction with gender | | | | Interaction with socioeconomic status | | |
	Mean	LR p	Relative risk	Wald p	LR p	Relative risk	Wald p
Sex		0.50			0.85		
Male (Ref.)	49.60		1.00			1.00	
Female	50.40		0.90	0.46		0.98	0.85
Socioeconomic group		0.00			0.66		
Freeholders and Crown tenants (Ref.)	16.60		1.00			1.00	
Tenants on noble land	32.10		0.82	0.44		0.88	0.65
Crofters and smallholders	1.00		2.25	0.13		2.56	0.25
Landless	50.30		0.97	0.87		1.06	0.81
10% decline in real wages	−2.30	0.00	1.04	0.14	0.00	1.10	0.06
10% decline in real wages							
× Sex		0.24					
Male (Ref.)			1.04				
Female			1.08	0.24			
× Socioeconomic group					0.41		
Freeholders and Crown tenants (Ref.)						1.10	
Tenants on noble land						1.06	0.55
Crofters and smallholders						1.04	0.81
Landless						1.04	0.40
Chi-square		36.89			36.25		
Degrees of freedom		10			12		
Overall p-value		0.00			0.00		
Number of deaths		282			282		

Note: Controls for year of birth and parish were included but the results are not presented here.

1815–1865						
Interaction with gender				Interaction with socioeconomic status		
Mean	LR p	Relative risk	Wald p	LR p	Relative risk	Wald p
	0.85			0.66		
52.00		1.00			1.00	
48.00		0.98	0.88		0.96	0.66
	0.00			0.00		
22.80		1.00			1.00	
23.40		0.52	0.01		0.55	0.02
14.60		0.97	0.87		0.99	0.98
39.30		1.03	0.87		0.81	0.29
−2.30	0.01	1.06	0.02	0.00	0.99	0.86
	0.71					
		1.06				
		1.05	0.71			
				0.00		
					0.99	
					0.87	0.25
					0.88	0.83
					1.13	0.02
	64.41			83.23		
	10			12		
	0.00			0.00		
	369			369		

Table 6.3
Effects of a 10 percent decline in real wages on relative risks of dying among married adults in ages 25–55 years in different socioeconomic groups

	1766–1815			1815–1865			1829–1865		
	Relative risk	LR p	Deaths	Relative risk	LR p	Deaths	Relative risk	LR p	Deaths
All socioeconomic groups	1.06	0.00	282	0.94	0.01	369	1.06	0.02	289
Landed (1 and 2)	1.07	0.02	111	0.95	0.22	89	1.04	0.45	63
Landed and crofters (1, 2, and 3)	1.07	0.02	115	0.96	0.22	162	0.98	0.68	129
Landless and crofters (3 and 4)	1.05	0.06	171	1.09	0.00	280	1.07	0.02	226
Landless (4)	1.05	0.06	167	1.13	0.00	207	1.12	0.00	160

Note: For classification of socioeconomic groups, see table 6.1. Controls were included for gender, year of birth, and parish, but the results are not presented here. Each row represents a separate model estimation for each period. Relative risk shows the effect of a 10 percent decline in real wages.

explains why we do not find a social gradient in the response to short-term economic stress during the first period. The relative importance of nutrition-related diseases, however, grew over time, as discussed in chapter 2. Smallpox, the major nonnutritional disease among children, for example, became less common in the latter part of the eighteenth century and was almost eliminated by the time vaccination started in the first decade of the nineteenth century.

Mortality from all causes of death is shown in table 6.6 for comparison. The overall response was of the same magnitude for children and adults. A 10 percent decline in real wages increased mortality from all causes of death among adults by 5.4 percent and among children by 6.2 percent. The strongest response was for mortality from food and waterborne infectious diseases, as shown in table 6.6. A 10 percent decline in real wages increased mortality more than 20 percent. The particular cause of death was, however, not the same for children and adults: adults died from typhoid and other fevers, both communicable diseases, after a decline in real wages, and children died from gastrointestinal diseases such as diarrhea, and other nutrition-related diseases (Bengtsson 2000, table 11.3). Even though the response to short-term economic stress is very strong for this group of diseases, the numbers of deaths are still much smaller than from airborne infectious diseases, as shown in table 6.6. The most common airborne infection that children died of was smallpox, and the most common for adults was pneumonia (Bengtsson 2000, table 11.3). While smallpox was a disease for which the nutritional influence on the outcome was known to be minimal, the nutritional influence on the outcome of having pneumonia was strong.

Although Meuvret (1965, 510–513) argues that diseases like smallpox do not need the surplus of people who wandered around to find jobs after bad harvests in order to spread, a close connection is still found between short-term economic stress and mortality from smallpox. This is evident from the estimations for the four parishes (Bengtsson 2000, table 11.3). It has also been shown for another area of Sweden (Bengtsson 1999). We cannot therefore exclude the possibility that the effects of changes in real wages on mortality in airborne infectious diseases among children shown in table 6.6 reflect the spread of epidemic diseases (smallpox) during the latter half of the eighteenth century. This would explain why it does not discriminate against social status. The social differences in the mortality response to short-term economic stress during the second period indicate that nutritional

Table 6.4
Effects of sex, socioeconomic group, and real wages on relative risks of mortality among children aged 1–15 years

	1766–1815						
	Interaction with gender				Interaction with socioeconomic status		
	Mean	LR p	Relative risk	Wald p	LR p	Relative risk	Wald p
Sex		0.06			0.03		
Male (Ref.)	51.80		1.00			1.00	
Female	48.20		1.19	0.17		1.27	0.03
Socioeconomic group		0.00			0.00		
Freeholders and Crown tenants (Ref.)	18.60		1.00			1.00	
Tenants on noble land	36.60		0.52	0.00		0.51	0.00
Crofters and smallholders	0.90		0.88	0.86		0.34	0.42
Landless	43.90		0.92	0.64		0.84	0.36
10% decline in real wages	−2.30	0.00	1.06	0.02	0.00	1.05	0.00
10% decline in real wages							
× Sex		0.33					
Male (Ref.)			1.06				
Female			1.10	0.33			
× Socioeconomic group					0.41		
Freeholders and Crown tenants (Ref.)						1.05	
Tenants on noble land						1.05	0.98
Crofters and smallholders						1.32	0.28
Landless						1.10	0.31
Chi-square		49.51			51.42		
Degrees of freedom		10			12		
Overall p-value		0.00			0.00		
Number of deaths		337			337		

Note: Controls for year of birth and parish were included, but the results are not presented here.

1815–1865						
	Interaction with gender			Interaction with socioeconomic status		
Mean	LR p	Relative risk	Wald p	LR p	Relative risk	Wald p
	0.03			0.05		
51.10		1.00			1.00	
48.90		0.76	0.01		0.84	0.05
	0.00			0.00		
16.80		1.00			1.00	
23.40		1.74	0.01		1.99	0.00
18.90		1.57	0.01		1.54	0.04
41.00		1.79	0.00		1.75	0.00
−2.30	0.00	1.03	0.19	0.00	1.06	0.23
	0.09					
		1.03				
		1.09	0.09			
				0.12		
					1.06	
					−0.96	0.15
					1.07	0.88
					1.07	0.81
	39.04			41.93		
	10			12		
	0.00			0.00		
	518			518		

Table 6.5
Effects of a 10 percent decline in real wages on relative risks of dying among children aged 1–15 years in various socioeconomic groups

	1766–1815			1815–1865			1829–1865		
	Relative risk	LR p	Deaths	Relative risk	LR p	Deaths	Relative risk	LR p	Deaths
All socioeconomic groups	1.07	0.00	337	1.06	0.00	518	1.06	0.01	414
Landed (1 and 2)	1.05	0.09	150	1.01	0.78	134	1.04	0.37	89
Landed and crofters (1, 2, and 3)	1.05	0.07	152	1.04	0.16	254	1.05	0.09	201
Landless and crofters (3 and 4)	1.10	0.00	187	1.07	0.00	384	1.07	0.01	325
Landless (4)	1.10	0.00	185	1.08	0.00	264	1.07	0.02	213

Note: For classification of socioeconomic groups, see table 6.1. Controls were included for gender, year of birth, and parish, but the results are not presented here. Each row represents a separate model estimation for each period. Relative risk shows the effect of a 10 percent decline in real wages.

Table 6.6
Effects of a 10 percent decline in real wages and socioeconomic status on relative risks of mortality from different types of diseases, adults ages 25–55 and children ages 1–15, 1766–1865.

	Adults 25–55 years						Children 1–15 years					
	All deaths	Air-borne infections	Water-borne infections	Other infections	Other specified	Un-specified	All deaths	Air-borne infections	Water-borne infections	Other infections	Other specified	Un-specified
Socioeconomic group												
Freeholders and Crown ten. (Ref.)	1.00	1.00	1.00	1.00	1.00	1.00	1.00	1.00	1.00	1.00	1.00	1.00
Tenants on noble land	0.70	0.87	0.68	0.57	0.70	1.73	1.00	0.99	0.86	2.20	1.18	0.84
Crofters and smallholders	1.08	1.41	0.27	0.43	1.21	4.06	1.22	1.32	0.63	1.57	0.95	1.01
Landless	1.02	0.98	0.78	0.84	0.67	4.37	1.34	1.25	1.17	1.97	1.31	1.23
LR p-value	*0.01*	*0.03*	*0.16*	*0.32*	*0.32*	*0.00*	*0.00*	*0.15*	*0.69*	*0.46*	*0.67*	*0.24*
10% decline in real wages	1.05	1.04	1.21	1.06	1.02	1.05	1.06	1.06	1.24	1.06	1.05	1.04
LR p-value	*0.00*	*0.07*	*0.01*	*0.12*	*0.43*	*0.25*	*0.00*	*0.00*	*0.00*	*0.31*	*0.07*	*0.18*
Chi-square	98.09	70.81	50.87	32.63	59.98	139.73	56.35	71.81	30.03	22.38	76.97	162.58
Degrees of freedom	9	9	9	9	9	9	9	9	9	9	9	9
Overall p-value	0.00	0.00	0.00	0.00	0.00	0.00	0.00	0.00	0.00	0.01	0.00	0.00
Number of deaths	651	217	78	73	112	105	855	429	41	46	119	183

Note: Controls for sex, year of birth, and parish were included, but the results are not presented here.

factors became more important for the outcome of diseases, as the highly virulent epidemic diseases become uncommon.

Table 6.7 shows the estimations of models, which investigate whether the families were more vulnerable to short-term economic stress in their initial stages, when dependency rates increased. Two indicators of the family life cycle are used: a young-age dependency ratio and an old-age dependency ratio. The two covariates are defined as the proportions of persons below age 15 and above age 55, respectively. Since families can increase the size of the workforce by hiring servants or having relatives live with them, this indicator is measured at the household rather than family level. As shown in table 6.7, the proportion of elderly is around 4 percent, while the proportion of young is 49 percent when sampling on children and 38 percent when sampling on adults. The reason for the lower figure for adults is that the parents are followed until they are 55 years of age, an age by which most of their children have left home. Evidently, the overall consumer/worker ratio or the overall dependency ratio for the family is almost entirely determined by the pace at which the children arrived. The proportion of young is thus used as an indicator of the family life cycle. Since the size of the household increases as children are born and as additional adults are added, household size is controlled for. The idea is that household size itself might affect the risk of dying, either due to crowding or as an indicator of wealth. Thus, by controlling for household size, the net effect of changes in the consumer/worker ratio on the response to short-term economic stress can be estimated.

While no effect of the proportion of young on mortality is found for children, their parents are affected. A 20 percent increase in the proportion of young will increase the level of mortality among their parents by 14 percent. The effects are the same for mothers and fathers (not reported here). No effect of the young-age dependency ratio on vulnerability to short-term economic stress can be found, however, as shown in table 6.7. Additional experiments, which categorize the covariate young-age dependency ratio to allow for step-wise effects, do not change the result (not reported here), nor do experiments with models for single socioeconomic groups (not reported here).

From contemporary records, such as court records of disputes between children and their aged parents regarding set-aside contracts and from bank records, we know that the elderly could be a heavy burden for the family. The results, however, show no general effect of high proportions of the elderly on other members of the family.

Thus, there is no support found for the hypotheses that the family was more vulnerable to short-term economic stress in its initial stages, when consumers but not producers were added as children were born. Furthermore, no support is found for the hypothesis that a higher proportion of elderly made the household more vulnerable to short-term economic stress.

Several other findings tell a very similar story: that life was precarious and that families lived with great uncertainties. For example, if the birth interval was extremely short, the risk of dying was higher for the older child, particularly if the newborn was a boy. If a previously born child had died, the risk for the next child was also higher. Thus, parents with the possible assistance of servants, kin, or public health still could not provide for their children under difficult circumstances. Quite obviously, as shown in table 6.8, infants missing one or both parents had much higher mortality than if both parents were alive and present. Therefore, not only short-term economic stress but also other unfavorable conditions regarding the family and household structure determined the outcome of diseases. Even more significant is that not only children but also adults in working ages experienced higher mortality than normal in years of economic stress. Both the landed and the landless faced severe problems of short-term economic stress during the period 1766 to 1815, while only the landless were affected in the period thereafter, and the social network around the families could not make up for problems facing them. It was not until after the 1860s, when real wages for agricultural workers increased, that the link between short-term economic stress and mortality disappeared among the landless as well (Bengtsson and Dribe forthcoming).

Conclusion

This study examines living conditions in four rural Scanian parishes during the periods before and after the large-scale reforms that took place in agriculture in the beginning of the nineteenth century. The reforms changed the production structure and made farming more commercial. The source of wealth was land, which was very unequally distributed. When the reforms started, only half of the families owned or rented farms that were large enough to support a family, and the others were at least partly dependent on labor income to support their families. The problem was that their wages did not keep up with sudden increases in food prices. It was also more difficult to find jobs in

Table 6.7
Effects of real wages, proportion young and old, number of persons in working ages, sex, and socioeconomic group on relative risks of dying, 1829–1865

	Children 1–15 years						
	No interaction				Interaction with proportion young		
	Mean	LR p	Relative risk	Wald p	LR p	Relative risk	Wald p
Sex		0.08			0.08		
Male (Ref.)	50.7		1.00			1.00	
Female	49.3		0.84	0.09		0.84	0.09
Socioeconomic group		0.01			0.01		
Freeholders and Crown tenants (Ref.)	16.2		1.00			1.00	
Tenants on noble land	25.3		1.51	0.08		1.51	0.08
Crofters and smallholders	22.5		1.65	0.01		1.65	0.01
Landless	36.0		1.85	0.00		1.85	0.00
Working age, number of persons	4.7	0.25	1.02	0.23	0.25	1.02	0.23
Proportion young (20% increase)	49.1	0.20	1.10	0.20	0.15	1.06	0.47
Proportion old (20% increase)	3.8	0.47	1.10	0.47	0.48	1.10	0.47
10% decline in real wages	−2.3	0.01	1.06	0.01	0.05	1.06	0.01
× proportion young					0.50	1.06	0.50
Chi-square		37.8			38.26		
Degrees of freedom		12			13		
Overall p-value		0.00			0.00		
Number of deaths		410			410		

Note: Controls were included for year of birth and parish, but the results are not presented here.

Adults 25–55 years						
No interaction				Interaction with proportion young		
Mean	LR p	Relative risk	Wald p	LR p	Relative risk	Wald p
	0.81			0.81		
48.8		1.00			1.00	
51.2		0.97	0.81		0.97	0.81
	0.13			0.14		
15.2		1.00			1.00	
23.6		0.59	0.06		0.59	0.07
22.0		0.72	0.17		0.72	0.17
39.2		0.87	0.53		0.87	0.53
4.9	0.69	1.01	0.68	0.67	1.01	0.66
38.2	0.02	1.14	0.03	0.01	1.20	0.01
4.3	0.59	1.06	0.59	0.59	1.06	0.59
−2.3	0.01	1.07	0.01	0.00	1.07	0.01
				0.17	1.07	0.17
	54.56			56.44		
	12			13		
	0.00			0.00		
	278			278		

Table 6.8
Effects of real wages, presence of family members, sex, and socioeconomic group on relative risks of dying, 1829–1865

| | Children 1–15 years | | | | | | | Infants 0–1 years | | | |
| | Presence of parents | | | | Presence of siblings | | | Presence of parents | | | |
	Mean	LR p	Relative risk	Wald p	LR p	Relative risk	Wald p	Mean	LR p	Relative risk	Wald p
Sex		0.08			0.07				0.09		
Male (Ref.)	50.7		1.00			1.00		51.2		1.00	
Female	49.3		0.84	0.08		0.84	0.07	48.8		0.89	0.19
Socioeconomic group		0.02			0.05				0.89		
Freeholders and Crown tenants (Ref.)	16.2		1.00			1.00		15.3		1.00	
Tenants on noble land	25.3		1.51	0.08		1.51	0.08	22.2		0.91	0.63
Crofters and smallholders	22.5		1.60	0.02		1.55	0.03	21.6		0.97	0.84
Landless	36.0		1.78	0.01		1.71	0.01	40.8		0.90	0.52
Older brothers	0.5				0.33	0.90	0.33				
Older sisters	0.5				0.38	1.1	0.38				
Younger brothers	0.5				0.35	0.89	0.35				
Younger sisters	0.5				0.04	0.76	0.04				
Parents		0.36							0.02		
Both present	94.3		1.00					98.6		1.00	
Both not present	5.7		1.90					1.4		6.33	0.02
10% decline in real wages	−2.3	0.01	1.06	0.01	0.01	1.06	0.01	−2.3	0.82	1.01	0.82
Chi-square	37.06				42.83			40.68			
Degrees of freedom	24				14			12			
Overall p-value	0.00				0.00			0.00			
Number of deaths	410				410			501			

Note: Controls were included for year of birth, parish, and proportion of young household members, but the results are not presented here.

such years. Families were therefore dependent on their savings to keep up the consumption in years with high food prices and low real wages. Although destitute families could get tax cuts and rent postponements, they had difficulties borrowing, since they did not have the security required for loans. Instead, they had to rely on assistance from relatives, neighbors, employers, and the local community, as well as their own ability to find solutions. We have analyzed the effects of access to land, changes over the family life cycle, household structure, and the individual's position within the household on the mortality response to short-term economic stress in order to find out how successful they were in smoothing out variations in real wages.

We find that all socioeconomic groups were vulnerable to short-term economic stress before the agricultural reforms were implemented. Parents and their children suffered likewise. This was a period in which epidemic diseases still flourished. Infants and children died, for example, from smallpox and whooping cough, while adults died from typhoid fever, all highly virulent diseases for which the outcome was only minimally dependent on nutritional status. Although, according to Meuvret (1965), smallpox did not need the temporary migration of workers and beggars to produce an outbreak, the link between short-term economic stress and the mortality in this disease is documented for this area (Bengtsson 2000) and an area from the middle of Sweden (Bengtsson 1999). Thus, the similarity in response to short-term economic stress between the landed and the landless in this period may have been due, at least partly, to the increased spread of epidemic diseases by temporary work migration.

After the agricultural reforms took place, only the landless and semi-landless were still vulnerable to short-term economic stress. Again, both parents and their children experienced access mortality in years with low real wages. This was a period in which mortality from epidemic diseases was rare among both adults and children. Smallpox, for example, had almost disappeared, and whooping cough caused extra mortality only in a few years. Instead, adults and children died of almost any common air- and waterborne infectious disease—in other words, diseases for which the outcome is known to be dependent on nutrition. The socioeconomic differences became evident since they grew not only in the mortality response to short-term economic stress, but also in the mortality level.

The similarity of the response, but the difference in cause of death, between landless parents and their children in this period makes it hard to believe that the causal link between short-term economic stress and mortality was due to increased exposure to diseases attributable to temporary migration. If this had been the case, then men of working age would have been more vulnerable, since they were the ones who moved around looking for work. Of course, increasing temporary migration may have affected everybody since diseases could be more easily spread when people moved around trying to find work. Then one would expect certain specific diseases to become more common in years of economic stress, which is contradicted by the fact that children and adults died from different diseases in these years.

The inescapable conclusion is that families without land or with only small plots and in need of labor incomes lived in conditions of dire scarcity in the beginning of the nineteenth century. They were unable to smooth their consumption and thus were vulnerable to short-term economic stress, just as Malthus and Wargentin observed. While the changes in agriculture improved economic conditions for the landed, the landless classes became even more vulnerable to short-term economic stress than before, as is shown by their mortality response. Why then did relatives, employers, the local community, or the state not give support to overcome the economically harsh conditions when food prices were high and not compensated for by wages?

Starting with the state, the granary system—the storing of grain and smoothing of prices—was primarily designed to help the producers, the landed. It was to keep up the price in years of good harvests by buying grain and selling it back to the producers in years of bad harvests. Complaints that the system disturbed the market mechanisms led to its abandonment in 1823. Instead, the government took the initiative to start public works to increase employment in bad harvest years, though most of these went to the middle and northern parts of Sweden.

Why then did the local community not assist? Parish relief was designed to help the poor and destitute, the sick and disabled, and the elderly who had no families or employers to support them. Thus, it was designed to assist only a small percentage of the population and did not have the resources to give temporary relief to the many landless during years of economic stress, unlike in England. The parish could lend out money, even for consumption, but only against security, which the landless often lacked.

Why then did their employers not help them? The landlords were responsible for workers with annual contracts, who were mainly unmarried servants before the mid-nineteenth century. They were also responsible for the married day laborers and cottagers living on their farm and working exclusively for them. However, the laborers most often had more than one employer, which meant that they had to rely on themselves in harsh times. Relatives certainly helped to the extent they could, but many, particularly the landless, came from outside the parish and therefore had no relatives in the vicinity to help them.

Thus, the landless poor had to cope with short-term economic stress themselves the best way they could. We find no evidence of age or gender discrimination in years of harsh conditions. We do find that the mortality of both parents increased as they had children. The mortality also increased for an infant if either of the parents died. Thus, the social network for the landless was not strong enough to make up for pressure related to changes in family composition; neither remarriages nor relatives and neighbors could make up for the loss of a parent.

What could the semilandless and landless have done to escape from hunger? Since they were unable to save to the extent they needed and were unable to borrow or get financial aid, one would expect them to move away to find a job in another sector of the economy or at least to migrate to areas where the economic conditions were not as harsh. The problem was that those alternatives did not exist in southern Sweden in the beginning of the nineteenth century. Scania was almost exclusively a rural economy, and conditions were similar throughout the province in years of low real wages. Since the landless had only small plots of land, they had no other choice but to try to find jobs if times were harsh. Consequently, their children left home as soon as they could, often before their parents had to start paying tax for them. They could not adjust costs by delaying marriages of their children, since they left home much earlier. Either way, this opportunity was available only at later stages of the family life cycle, when children were old enough to marry. Thus, the landless were almost trapped. What they could do was to delay births after years with bad harvests, and indeed it seems that they did, but that was evidently not enough. The mortality of the landless increased when real wages turned down also after the agricultural reforms and increased commercialization and globalization in the beginning of the nineteenth century. The result is the opposite to what was found at aggregated level (Bengtsson and Ohlsson 1978, 1985) in the debated question of whether the economic development in the first half of the nineteenth century led to improved social conditions. Taking the findings together, conditions did improve during the period of commercialization but not for the semilandless and landless groups, only for the landlords, merchants, and other social groups that benefited from the growing trade.

The problematic situation of the landless in the beginning of the nineteenth century had its roots in the eighteenth century when the government promoted population growth and it became possible for the landless to marry, just as Malthus argued, but also in the growing commercialization of agriculture. The various systems that gave social security to the poor or to employees were not shaped for giving temporary relief to the large masses of landless families in harsh years. Social tensions grew, and the state started to take action, first, by trying to provide jobs and then by reforming the poor laws. In the 1840s, local communities were made responsible for giving assistance also in case of temporary need, not only in case of total poverty, and also for those migrating into the parish, not only for those residing in it. As jobs outside the agricultural sector became available after the mid-nineteenth century by industrial growth and overseas migration, wages started to follow food prices more closely and consumption started to increase. Consequently, the landless rural workers finally became less vulnerable to short-term economic stress.

Notes

This work was accomplished as part of the project "From Hunger to Modern Economic Growth: Demography and Family Behaviour in Sweden, 1650–1900," with financial support from the Swedish Council for Working Life and Social Research and the Bank of Sweden Tercentenary Foundation. I am grateful to James Z. Lee, Cameron Campbell, Martin Dribe, Patrick Svensson, and Grethe Banggaard for their most valuable comments.

1. Johan Hellstenius (1871) demonstrated that the influence of harvest was not only temporal but affected persons later in life. He showed, for example, a strong influence of harvests in the year prior to birth on later fitness for military service.

2. See Lundh (1983) for an overview of the standard of living debate in Sweden and England.

3. The data are from the Scanian Demographic Database, a collaborative project of the Research Group in Population Economics, Department of Economic History, Lund University, and the Regional Archives in Lund.

4. See Solar (1995) for an overview.

5. The obligation for adult children to take care of their elderly parents was a custom that dates far back in time and is documented by poor relief records (Banggaard 2002). It did not become formal codified law until 1918 and was removed in 1956.

6. Elderly without surviving children could, if they were farm owners, arrange for their own retirement in various ways (Bengtsson and Fridlizius 1994).

7. In appeals against decisions regarding poor relief taken at parish level, higher authorities often took the view that the parish had the ultimate responsibility, which they could never deny. However, they often tried to find an employer or relative to take responsibility. Many examples of such disputes can be found in Banggaard (2002).

8. Tabellverket. Folkmängd. Tabell IV. Riksarkivet and the Demographic Database in Umeå. Only two to three persons received parish relief in each of Hög and Kävlinge; the number in Halmstad and Sireköping was higher (Banggaard 2002).

9. For more details, see Bengtsson and Dribe (1997).

10. Mantalslängder (Taxation Records), Malmöhus läns landskontors arkiv, Vol. E III: 52, Lunds landsarkiv (The Regional Archives in Lund).

11. There were also a few tenants on church land with situations similar to those of the Crown tenants.

12. Children of most social groups often worked as servants after leaving home and prior to marriage (Lundh 1995).

13. For a discussion of the sample and results, see Bengtsson and Oeppen (1993).

14. A closer look at periods of rapidly rising living costs reveals that prices rose most quickly during wars (Bengtsson 2000). This was partly due to the fact that Sweden's monetary system was based on a paper standard for a large part of the eighteenth century. For more details, see Bengtsson (2000), Jörberg (1972), and Åmark (1961, 1–19).

15. A major problem in estimating the Eurasia standard comparative models with Scanian data is that the number of cases is in some instances insufficient to permit robust estimations. This is the case for the presence of parents in the models for children. The proportion of children with only the father or only the mother present is just a few percent. Infants without any parents present are an even smaller group. Thus, this variable had to be defined into two categories: one for children with both parents present and one for children with at least one parent missing. The indicator for presence of younger sisters has caused similar problems when analyzing infant mortality.

16. An investigation of breast-feeding in 1869, performed by the Swedish Medical Board, shows that children in Scania were breast-fed or partly breast-fed (see Broström, Brändström, and Persson 1984). Analysis of mortality by age shows a peak during the seventh month of life, which likely stems from weaning (see Fridlizius 1984, figure 6).

17. The reason for not analyzing unmarried adults is that data on their presence are of poor quality until after 1829.

18. This group also includes a few church tenants renting land under similar conditions as Crown tenants.

19. The statistical program utilized, LIFE, was developed by Göran Broström, Department of Statistics, University of Umeå, partly within the framework of a methodological project being conducted by the Research Group in Population Economics at Lund.

20. For a discussion on causes of death in Scania, see Bengtsson and Lindström (2000).

7

Mortality and
Modernization in Sart and
Surroundings, 1812–1900

George Alter, Muriel Neven,
and Michel Oris

Eastern Belgium covers a relatively small area, but it includes a number of distinct subregions: three different agricultural areas and two separate industrial agglomerations. Our contribution to the Eurasia Project, the commune of Sart (also called Sart-lez-Spa), is located in the Ardennes, the least favored agricultural area, depicted in map 7.1. Although Sart was in some ways relatively isolated, its history cannot be understood apart from the history of the region in which it was located. Indeed, some aspects of Sart's demographic history would appear unexceptional if they were not so different from such nearby communities as the industrial suburbs of Tilleur compared in table 7.1.

The period covered by our demographic data (1812 to 1900) was a time of rapid change in the economy, the society, and the population. It falls between the industrial revolution (1788 to 1850) and the last phase of the demographic transition, including the decisive declines of fertility and mortality (approximately 1873 to 1910). At the dawn of the nineteenth century (1799), two rich families of clothiers, the Simonis and the Biolleys, brought English engineer William Cockerill to build textile machinery in Verviers (Desama and Bauwens 1995, 87). A few years later, his son John established an industrial empire in metallurgy and engineering based on the abundant coal in the subsoil around the city of Liège (Soete 1995, 145). Two rapidly growing urban agglomerations emerged from these developments. From 1806 to 1910, Verviers and its textile suburbs grew from 10,000 to 90,000 inhabitants. Simultaneously, the industrial basin surrounding Liège reached 422,000 inhabitants in 1910, compared to only 50,000 a century earlier. Towns represented only 20 percent of the population of the Province of Liège in 1805, but by 1900 the urban population had grown to 60 percent (Oris 1990, 90).

This radical change in settlement patterns cannot be explained without massive out-migration from the countryside. However, the process

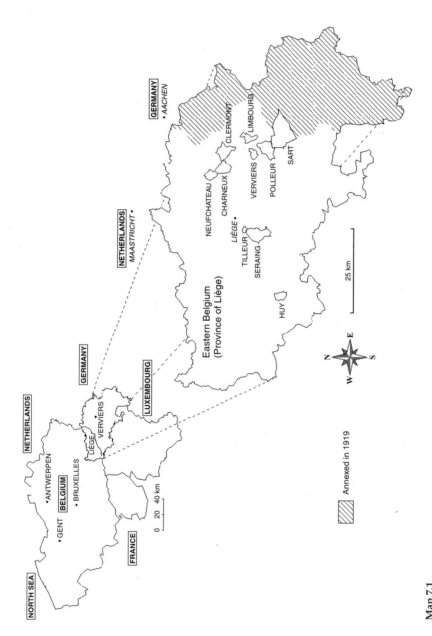

Map 7.1
Eastern Belgium

Table 7.1
Characteristics of Sart and Tilleur

	Sart	Tilleur
Principal economic activity	Agriculture	Coal, iron, and steel
Population 1806	1,791	496
Population 1846	2,380	1,356
Population 1910	2,175	6,750
Period of observation	1812–1900[a]	1846–1880
Person-years	199,196	101,416
Deaths	4,250	2,620

[a] Sart had registers before Belgium became independent in 1830. These were nominative lists that identified all migrations as well as new households. After linkage and comparisons with vital registration, the population from 1812 to 1846 was reconstructed.

was neither smooth nor simple. Most industrial towns experienced an initial phase of explosive growth due to the sudden appearance and development of the modern industry in a predominantly rural landscape. A slow process of maturation followed this period of foundation. The pace of demographic growth gradually slowed, and the proportion of urban population born in towns went up. In this phase, natural increase due to a surplus of births over deaths produced two-thirds of population growth; in-migration produced the other third. In eastern Belgium, the transition between these two phases occurred between 1856 and 1866, and former villages were irrevocably transformed into a landscape of "black country" and factory towns (Eggerickx and Poulain 1995, Oris 1995a). After the economic crisis of 1873, a protracted industrial depression reduced or even eliminated net urban migration and ushered in a new transition for these urban-industrial-proletarian populations. The Liège area successfully introduced the new technology of steel production and began to recover after 1890. The woolen textile industry in Verviers was not able to adapt to new competition, and its demographic decline began in the last decade of the nineteenth century.

Similarly, the fate of the countryside cannot be summarized simply in terms of rural exodus. Two rural areas surround the textile center of Verviers: the Pays de Herve and the Ardennes. The Pays de Herve to the north of Verviers is a region of rich meadows and intensive cattle and dairy production. As early as the seventeenth century, the Pays de Herve was transformed from subsistence farming based on cereals to a commercial agriculture based on grazing, meat, milk, butter, and cheese. These new activities required less labor and developed in conjunction with a very dynamic proto-industry of woolen textiles (Gutman 1988, Neven 2000a).

The Ardennes to the south is a vast region, and we are considering only the area extending from the border of the province of Luxemburg to the Vesdre valley, where the towns of Verviers and Eupen are located. Topographically, it is the highest part of Belgium, culminating at the Signal de Botrange (694 m) and the massif of the Hautes-Fagnes. The latter is a region of peat bogs and forests with damp peaty, schistose, and sandstone soils (Hoyois 1981, 22–29). Much of the territory of Sart belongs to this zone, but the inhabitants were concentrated along its borders in the Theux depression, where soils and climatic conditions are better. They lived in hamlets scattered like agricultural islands in the forests (Montulet 1955).

Proto-industry was not as widespread in Sart as in the Pays de Herve, but it was significant in the eighteenth century. Several iron forges used charcoal from its abundant forests, but these disappeared as coke-based production expanded around Liège. Spinners in Sart also participated in a complex putting-out system organized by the "merchant-clothiers" of Verviers (Haesenne-Peremans 1981, 58; Leboutte 1996, 167; Servais 1982, 236–237). Of course, when these entrepreneurs decided to build modern factories and promote mechanization at the end of the eighteenth century, rural workers could not resist. By 1830, spinning had practically disappeared from the countryside. Handloom weaving persisted longer, but it became a marginal activity by 1850 to 1860 (Neven and Oris 1998).

Peasant properties were small in the Ardennes, but extensive communally owned lands played a vital role in the economy of rural households. Considering them an anachronism that inhibited modernization, the Belgian Parliament enacted legislation in 1847 requiring municipalities to divide and sell their common lands (Lefebvre 1947). Between 1847 and 1873, attempts to develop large commercial farms failed, and this strategy became futile after 1873, when the massive influx of American cereals created a long depression in the rural world. Nevertheless, this ordeal resulted in a transformation from subsistence to commercial agriculture, and the Ardennes finally adopted the mixed agriculture perfected a century earlier in the Pays de Herve (Hoyois 1981, 266; Verstraelen 1972, 24).

After the severe crisis of 1816–1817, the population of Sart increased significantly over the next thirty-five years (from 1,800 to 2,400), but a major change occurred around midcentury. After 1851, the number of inhabitants declined, and by 1900 it had returned to almost exactly the same size as a century before (1,815). Initially rooted in their hamlets and resistant to the attraction of urban and industrial development around Verviers, the inhabitants of Sart started to escape in the 1850s. Out-migration resulted in a loss of 1 to 2 percent of the population per year, even though births always exceeded deaths. Throughout the nineteenth century, the demographic regime was characterized by high marital fertility (total marital fertility rate between 9 and 10 children) and a very rigid Malthusian system of late marriage (average age at first union above age 28 for women) and high definitive celibacy (between 18 and 25 percent) (Alter and Oris 1999).

At the opposite extreme, the demography of industrial towns was largely determined by migratory flows that resulted in highly unbalanced marriage markets: disproportionately female in the textile area and heavily male in the coal and iron basin. In Tilleur, a suburb of Liège, the female average age at first marriage was 26 between 1847 and 1880, and definitive celibacy was under 10 percent. However, the total marital fertility rate (ages 20 to 49) was as high as in the countryside (9.2 children per married woman). Consequently, the total fertility rate in Tilleur was 6.8 compared to only 4.99 in Sart. Thus, the gap between urban and rural fertility was essentially due to the greater weight of Malthusian marriage behavior in the countryside. Birth control did not become a substitute until the last decade of the nineteenth century. We find it diffusing slowly in industrial areas after 1870, but the decisive decline in birthrates occurred between 1895 and 1914. This is late in comparison to more traditional bourgeois towns, where couples started to control their reproduction around 1850, and perhaps even earlier (Oris 1995b).

The Data

Multivariate Individual Analysis

Since the creation of the Central Commission for Statistics under the leadership of the famous scientist Adolphe Quetelet in 1841, Belgium has benefited from good aggregate statistics. These sources have already yielded a large amount of historical research on mortality, especially on causes of death and infant and child mortality.[1] Those results serve as background for our intensive research on the local level. After five years of methodological research and case studies, we can tap the richness of the population registers.[2] Although well described in the international literature (Alter 1988, chap. 1; Gutman and van de Walle 1978; Watkins and Gutman 1983), this source is not always well known abroad. In fact, the complexity of these documents makes them difficult to exploit, especially over long time periods. Furthermore, many Belgian communities have unfortunately lost some or even all of their registers.

The Laboratory of Demography at the University of Liège is constructing a database that will include communities representing all of the distinctive subregions of eastern Belgium. In addition to the commune of Sart, for which we have estimated the common Eurasia Project comparative mortality models, this chapter also benefits from studies of other areas that are being added to this regional database. Muriel Neven (2000a) has recently completed a first analysis of three villages in the Pays de Herve: Charneux, Clermont, and Neufchâteau. Catherine Capron (1996) is reconstructing the history of Limbourg, a small administrative center under the old regime that became integrated as part of the industrial agglomeration surrounding Verviers in the nineteenth century. George Alter (1988, 1996, 1999; Alter, Cliggett, and Urbiel 1996) has studied the female life course and residence patterns of the elderly in Verviers. Michel Oris (1996) has been examining Tilleur, a coal and iron-working suburb of Liège, which was an industrial boomtown when we observe it between 1846 and 1880. Tilleur provides a case study of the consequences of rapid urbanization. Between 1831 and 1866, it grew from 617 to 2,219 inhabitants, an annual growth rate of 3.7 percent per year.

These studies help us to put our results from Sart in a broader geographic context. No single community can represent the diversity of eastern Belgium and the multiplicity of its ways of life. As a consequence, this analysis is not a summary of mortality patterns in eastern Belgium but more often a comparison of extremes. This comparison is not only useful but necessary, because the developing towns in the region, like Tilleur and Limbourg, were fed by poor migrants from the countryside, such as Sart. A dynamic system of relationships tied rural and urban areas together, and migration flows were determined by mortality and in turn determined mortality.

Reconstructing a Population from Population Registers

Population registers were created in the entire Kingdom of Belgium after the 1846 census. Each commune transcribed all the data collected in the census—last name, first name, marital status, birthdate (or age), birthplace, profession, and sometimes relationship to the household head—into volumes with individuals arranged by household. These registers were then updated until the next census. Births, deaths, and migrations into and out of the commune during the period between censuses were added to the registers, as well as any new households formed by marriage or division. In principle, this source allows us to follow all the people who lived in a given locality from one census to the next. Its distinctiveness and richness are due to its dynamic character.

Though rich, the population registers suffer from some weaknesses, most of which are rectifiable, even if the corrections are time-consuming and tedious. Often there was some underregistration of births, deaths, and marriages, but this can easily be detected by comparisons with registers of vital events (*état civil*). Missing events or individuals are then added to the household where they should have been recorded. The most common omissions are infants who died shortly after birth. Indeed, an essential point must be kept in mind: although the Belgian Central Commission for Statistics created the population registers as a basic source of demographic statistics, they were used in daily life by the municipalities as an administrative document. In this context, the administration paid attention only to the living, which explains the absence of stillbirths and a clear underregistration of children who died at very young ages (Alter 1988, 55; Neven 2000a, 10–13).[3] After a series of checks and corrections, our source appears to be very complete with regard to births, deaths, and marriages, even if we know that some small problems remain, such as the classic issue of "false stillbirths" (see Poulain and Tabutin 1977).[4]

Another problem is distinguishing between the de jure and the de facto population. Theoretically, population registers and the deaths we add to them concern only the de jure population. But in practice, those definitions are sometimes unclear and can depend on the interpretation of the local civil servant. In Sart, it appears that domestic servants were underregistered, being considered as de facto population. In contrast, the censuses in towns were more likely to record servants as members of their employers' households, but a few years later, when they left the locality, they often forgot to inform the local authorities. Consequently, the next census often found that the population registers included too many temporary migrants in urban areas, because out-migration had been underregistered. It is interesting to note that the Belgian Central Commission for Statistics was commissioned to clarify the notions of de jure and de facto almost immediately after its creation in 1841 (Heuschling 1841). The problem was thus real, and efforts to solve it did not succeed immediately.

Underregistration of migration is a more difficult problem to solve, since we have few ways to fill in the gaps. When people leave the locality without notifying the local authorities, we notice their absence only when we do not find them in the following census. In these cases, we assign dates of "removal," which are chosen at random from the existing dates of exit.[5] Underregistration of in-migration, which was less important, is treated in a similar way. Most of the time, these disappearances or appearances do not create any statistical problem because only a small percentage of people are affected.[6]

From Old to New Crises: The Demographic Cost of Economic Progress

During the eighteenth century, by 1750 at the latest, population growth became permanent in the future territory of Belgium (born in 1830). This rapid and sustained movement is older than the industrial revolution. A slow but undeniable drop in mortality appeared first in the north of the country, but the Walloon regions followed a short while later (Bruneel et al. 1987, 298). Although mortality diminished because traditional crises occurred less frequently, the junction of the eighteenth and nineteenth centuries was a period of general distress and severe crises. Under the French Regime (1795–1815), food shortages followed an agricultural crisis in 1811–1812. Defeat at Waterloo, a bad harvest, and a typhus epidemic produced a new crisis in 1816–1817, which appears as the last traditional crisis in our region.

Trouble returned in 1830–1831, when nine provinces of the Netherlands revolted and the new Kingdom of Belgium was created. Fifteen years later, the potato blight created an emergency, known in Belgium as the "Flemish crisis," because it was particularly severe in the northern provinces (Desama 1985, 49–53, 104–105). In reality, the last two events did not really affect daily life in eastern Belgium (Alter and Oris

2000a). The industrial revolution had broken the close link between population and subsistence described by Malthus. From then on, resources tended to grow more quickly than population. On the other side of the coin, precocious industrialization also entailed unprecedented and costly urbanization.

At home as well as at work, the new urban population was more likely to be contaminated by infection. Many people crowded into insalubrious houses and worked in harsh conditions. While the eighteenth century was still at the mercy of the triad of war, hunger, and epidemics, part of the nineteenth century is characterized by a depression that is exclusively epidemiological without any links to economic adversity. In fact, the industrial revolution had a twofold influence on mortality: the creation of new forms of employment put an end to starvation, but urbanization and new means of communication created a place where diseases could develop and spread. Consequently, in spite of the poor diet of many urban workers, famines disappeared, but infectious and epidemic diseases proliferated.

Over the course of the nineteenth century, .the epidemiological depression led to a stagnation or even an increase of the crude death rates.[7] This deterioration of mortality follows the chronology and geography of the industrial revolution. For example, the typhus fever of 1816–1817 affected Verviers, the pioneer of the industrial revolution, more severely than other areas of the country (Desama 1985). In this city, the last "traditional" crisis was also the first modern calamity! Indeed, due to its pioneering position in the industrialization process, Verviers experienced high mortality levels linked to urbanization from the 1820s—twenty years before its followers. Mortality worsened in the suburbs of the four main cities in Belgium between 1846 and the last quarter of the nineteenth century (Desama 1976, 105–106). Expectation of life fell to 26 years in Seraing (1856), 29 to 31 in Tilleur (1855–1859), and as low as 23 years during the 1866 cholera epidemic in Dison, an industrial suburb of Verviers (Oris 1998a, 291).

During this period of deteriorating living conditions, the countryside enjoyed an advantage over the towns in both the level and variability of mortality. Annual fluctuations in mortality were much lower in rural areas such as Sart, and crises appear to have been both less frequent and less pronounced (figures 7.1 and 7.2). Until 1871, a turning point in the mortality transition, mortality rates in Tilleur exceeded those in the countryside in more than two years out of three. Limbourg, the small textile center near Verviers, was in an intermediate

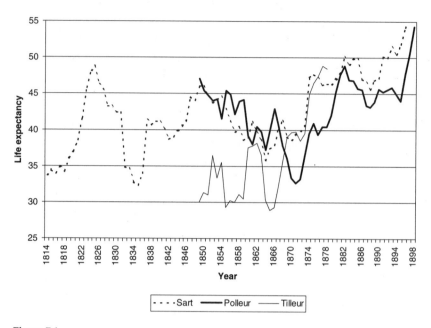

Figure 7.1
Life expectancies at birth in Tilleur, Polleur and Sart in the nineteenth century (five-year moving averages)

position, both benefiting from the development of its larger neighbor and avoiding some of the bad consequences of urbanization because of its out-of-the-way location (Capron 1998, 47). Nevertheless, the urban character of Limbourg is evident in its mortality rates. Its irregular profile is similar though less pronounced than that of Tilleur, the coal and metallurgy center.

The urban penalty emerges clearly from figure 7.2. Life expectancy in Tilleur was lower than in our rural samples from 1847 to 1867. In 1849 the difference was sixteen to seventeen years, because of the cholera outbreak. Although the discrepancy decreased in the following years, the gap remained important until the cholera epidemic of 1866.

Urban epidemics resulted in some appallingly high peaks of mortality: 4 to 6 percent of the population dying suddenly in two or three months. Crises also affected the countryside, but their intensity was much lower. Indeed, rural areas in east Belgium were not protected against epidemic diseases. Sart did not escape the 1834 epidemic of cholera, which may have been combined with influenza and dysentery (Alter and Oris 2000a, 5; Lafosse 1977, 188–197), and typhoid fever

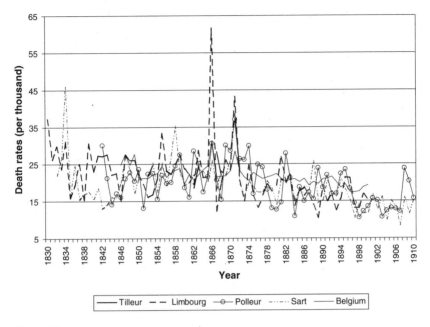

Figure 7.2
Annual crude mortality rates in Tilleur, Limbourg, Polleur, Sart, and all of Belgium in the nineteenth century

was probably responsible for thirty-five deaths per 1,000 inhabitants in 1858. Yet the same village escaped the worst epidemic of the century: the 1866 cholera outbreak (only 1 death in 362 inhabitants). On the whole, the mortality transition appears to have been more continuous in Sart, in spite of some fluctuations between 1857 and 1871, when the expectation of life at birth fluctuated between 35 and 41 years. The village of Polleur, between Sart and Verviers, appears to have been in an intermediate position—not totally safe from the consequences of the industrial revolution a few kilometers away but not as seriously affected as more industrialized suburbs.

The relatively favorable conditions in Sart are explained by its distinctive isolation. Sart was indeed known to be an "isolate," that is, a locality with weak relations with other places and little in-migration (Hélin 1960). Peter Sköld (1997, 109) also observes that remote areas in Sweden often escaped smallpox epidemics. Its relative isolation resolves the paradox of Sart, a place that became poorer and even depopulated after 1851, but where life expectancy improved throughout the nineteenth century. In fact, migration was important in this

Ardennes village, but only in one direction. People left for the towns, and those exits were usually definitive. These departures for jobs in Limbourg, Tilleur, Liège, or Verviers prevented the Ardennes from becoming a rural slum. From this point of view, the rural experience was similar to Ireland after the Great Famine, where population survived and even improved its living standards thanks to massive out-migration to England and North America (Guinanne 1997, esp. pp. 4–6; Ó Grada 1993). However, in eastern Belgium, a new way of life was a few dozen, not hundreds or even thousands of, kilometers away.

The infamous cholera epidemics have undoubtedly stimulated the imagination and can be considered emblematic of the epidemiological depression, but smallpox, measles, and scarlet fever were probably more deadly. Obviously, epidemics dominated the epidemiological landscape. Cholera raged seven times in Belgium during the nineteenth century, but its intensity varied (1832–1834, 1848, 1854, 1859, 1866, 1874, and 1892–1994) (Oris 1988). Some incursions were very localized; those of 1848 and above all 1866 were the most severe. From a strictly demographic point of view, those forays did not really affect population growth, because cholera was particularly intense in urban and industrial centers, where immigrants quickly replaced the dead (Oris 1988, 85; Poulain 1977). A previous study of six east Belgian towns during the period 1847 to 1910, as well as Polleur and Sart, has found four causes of major deviations from the mortality trend: cholera and smallpox share the limelight (twenty-seven crises), and typhoid fever and measles were responsible (together or separately) for four other crises (Neven 1997, 72).

A look at causes of death also sheds light on the use of the term *epidemiological depression*. This analysis, which is discussed at length in Neven (1997) and Capron (1998), reveals two main contributors to the urban/rural differential: digestive complaints and childhood and respiratory diseases. Digestive diseases explain a quarter of the deaths in two urban centers (Limbourg 1846–1866 and Verviers 1851–1876) and can be considered responsible for the towns' excess mortality. Seasonal patterns of death in Tilleur also implicate diarrheal and other water-borne diseases. These problems are typical of uncontrolled urbanization in which the ecology is totally disrupted. Improvements in hygiene follow with a long delay.[8]

Deteriorating living conditions also increased the importance of childhood diseases and respiratory complaints. Although these diseases were present in both urban and rural areas, crowding increased the risks of contagion. The propagation of microbes is mainly due to saliva, and poorly ventilated, overcrowded houses and factories undoubtedly spread infections (Bernhardt 1992, 16–17; Williams 1992; Williams and Mooney 1994). The high proportion of deaths due to respiratory illnesses, 24.2 percent in Limbourg and 27 percent in Verviers, implicates housing conditions (see also Neven and Oris 1995, 228–230).

In eastern Belgium, the turning point of the mortality transition is 1871. That year, a smallpox epidemic raged throughout the region, including all of the localities in our sample, even though it had less effect on the death rate than cholera. This simultaneous attack in both rural and urban areas is a completely new phenomenon. Indeed, in 1871, crude death rates were exactly the same in Polleur and Tilleur (37 per 1,000) and very similar in Sart (38.6 per 1,000) and Limbourg (43.2 per 1,000). This epidemic crystallizes the change from "an epidemiological depression that increased the gap between town and countryside" to "an epidemiological transition at a local and worldwide scale" (Neven 1997, 65–69). Until 1871, the rural villages had remained more or less protected against smallpox, surviving only weak and local crises. Prophylactic measures taken by local authorities (such as revaccination and closing schools) had been enough to prevent great harm. But that year, neither the towns nor the countryside escaped the disease. The link between microbial unification and the fall of mortality remains unclear, but it must not be seen as a coincidence. From the beginning of the 1870s, according to figures 7.1 and 7.2, a real and clear decline of mortality had begun, and differences between town and countryside diminished.

In all the areas that we have studied, there are responses to the changing social and economic context, and an important lesson has emerged from these case studies. In eastern Belgium, the epidemiological depression, which was experienced to some extent in nearly every locality, resulted more from ecology than from economy and more from urbanization than from industrialization. Of course, ecology was transformed by economy, and the industrial revolution had created a new human environment that fundamentally differed from the natural habitat. In fact, the main victims of the depression were children, not their parents, who actually worked in the new factories. It appears that lack of hygiene in a broad sense killed more people than work did.[9]

Indeed, we face a double paradox: deindustrialization in the countryside coincided with falling mortality, while industrial development caused a sharp rise in death rates in towns. Thus, during the nineteenth century, the economic resources of Sart declined but mortality decreased, in part because excess population moved to the towns. Towns such as Tilleur paid for these migration flows with deteriorating public hygiene and the epidemiological depression. In short, rural pauperization went hand in hand with gradually improving life expectancy, while the industrial revolution, though having broken the old Malthusian dilemma and increased available resources, began by increasing mortality. All the parts would seem paradoxical separately, but the whole is coherent.

The Economy of Death: Interactions among Prices, Wages, and Socioeconomic Structures

The Ardennes: Poverty, Prices, and Mortality

All observers agree that life was hard in the Ardennes villages of Sart. During the first half of the nineteenth century, proto-industry was disappearing, and agricultural techniques remained relatively primitive. Indeed, the practice of slash-and-burn agriculture, in which seeds were planted in areas cleared by burning, seems to have persisted well into the century. The steep terrain and poor soil were not suitable for more modern agricultural techniques. Overall, agriculture in the Ardennes was not able to feed its sparse population. The region had to import additional food and was consequently dependent on the market (Hoyois 1981, 135).

These harsh living conditions are reflected in two quantitative indicators of poverty: human height and responses to prices. Men from Sart and from the adjacent village of Polleur were unusually short. A large literature has developed linking adult height to economic and social conditions in childhood. While height can be affected by disease and work effort as well as lack of food, there is little question that poor nutrition will result in short stature. During the nineteenth century, every young man in Belgium was examined for military service at age 20, and we have collected the heights of men from Sart and Polleur who were born from 1816 to 1830 (examined between 1836 and 1850). The average height in this sample is only 160 centimeters, and one in four was exempted from military service for being shorter than the 155 centimeter minimum (Alter and Oris 2000b). In contrast, Quetelet (1869, 354) computed an average height of 164 centimeters for all Belgian men examined between 1842 and 1865, and even this is below the averages of other contemporary European countries.[10]

Mid-nineteenth-century death rates for Sart do not show signs of the epidemiological depression that is evident in much of east Belgium. After the disastrous conditions from 1815 to 1820, mortality was low during the 1820s and rose after cholera struck in the 1830s. But Sart escaped the cholera epidemic of 1849, and expectation of life at birth remained unchanged between the 1812–1846 (40.6 years) and 1847–1866 (40.4 years) periods. In the next period, expectation of life at birth increased by six years to 46.2, and it rose by almost the same amount to reach 51.8 years in the 1890s.

Mortality decline in Sart did not affect every age group at the same time. The data suggest that mortality decline began at the younger ages, perhaps as early as the 1820s among children aged 1 to 9, and then spread to older ages. Figure 7.3 shows age-specific probabilities of dying (q_x) in Sart in four time periods (1812–1846, 1847–1866, 1867–1890, 1891–1899). It is clear that the largest decreases in mortality were in childhood (ages 1 to 14). Mortality did decline at older ages, but the reductions were smaller and appear to have been later in time. This pattern is confirmed by the event-history analysis in table 7.2. Dummy variables for the periods 1847–1874 and 1875–1899 show changes relative to 1812–1846. Relative risks in the middle period were much lower at younger ages, while these improvements spread to other age groups after 1875.

This pattern of differential mortality decline by age is a general finding of research on Belgium (André and Pereira-Roque 1974, 87, 106; Leboutte 1988, 413; Oris 1998a, 305). In Sart and elsewhere in Belgium, infants were the only age group that did not benefit from lower mortality until the end of the century (Lesthaege 1977, 174–175). The probability of dying before age 1 was 160 per 1,000 from 1812 to 1846 and 183 per 1,000 from 1866 to 1890. There appears to have been a decrease in infant mortality after 1890, but we are unable to be sure about this because we cannot check infant deaths against the death registers in that period.

Event-history models also suggest the prevalence of poverty and hunger in Sart by showing a strong association between food prices and mortality, especially among children and adult women. Table 7.2 shows the estimates of the Eurasian individual model, which includes

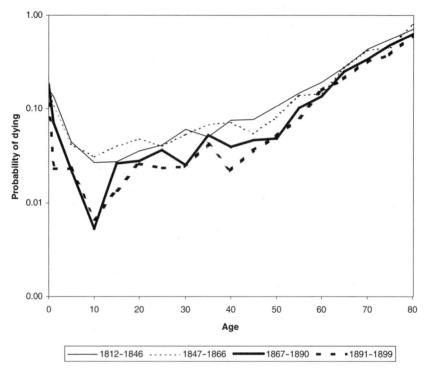

Figure 7.3
Life table probabilities of dying by age and period, Sart, 1812–1899

covariates for prices, occupations, and time periods, for Sart during the period 1812 to 1899. Although annual prices of several other grains are available for east Belgium, we have chosen the price of oats as an indicator of harvest conditions and food availability. As we have explained elsewhere (Alter, Oris, and Servais 1999), the analysis of mortality responses to prices is complicated by the early industrialization and urbanization of this region and its participation in world markets. Local grain prices did not necessarily reflect local agricultural conditions, because food could be shipped in and out of the area in response to market conditions elsewhere in Europe. After experimenting with several price indices,[11] we found the strongest correlation between mortality and the price of oats. In fact, some grain prices appear to have been inversely related to mortality, suggesting that the farmers in Sart were able to benefit from higher prices by selling those grains. Oats were most strongly related to mortality—not because they were

Table 7.2
Effects of prices, time periods, and socioeconomic status on relative risks of dying by gender, age, and marital status, Sart

Subpopulations	Relative risks				Occupation of household head (farmer omitted)			
	Lagged oats price, 1812–1846[a]	Lagged oats price, 1847–1899[a]	Period effect, 1847–1874	Period effect, 1875–1899	Functionary	Artisan and industrial workers	Day laborers	Other
Female infants (0–1 years of life)	1.05	0.90	*0.64*	*0.64*	1.53	0.92	*1.41*	1.06
Male infants (0–1 years of life)	0.99	0.95	0.83	0.78	0.92	1.15	1.28	1.42
Female children (2–14 years of life)	1.08	0.88	*0.71*	0.33	1.64	1.07	1.11	1.46
Male children (2–14 years of life)	*1.14*	0.99	0.84	0.39	0.59	0.97	1.06	1.31
Ever-married adult females (15–54)	1.07	1.02	1.04	0.55	0.98	0.80	0.83	1.17
Ever-married adult males (15–54)	1.01	*0.87*	*0.74*	*0.37*	*1.80*	1.04	*1.58*	*1.80*
Never-married adult females (15–54)	1.02	0.97	1.15	*0.57*	1.33	0.92	0.97	1.23
Never-married adult males (15–54)	1.11	1.01	1.10	0.80	1.44	1.35	1.25	1.07
Ever-married elderly females (55–75)	0.96	1.06	0.88	*0.73*	*0.39*	1.39	1.24	1.02
Ever-married elderly males (55–75)	0.94	1.03	0.94	0.70	1.01	0.87	0.98	*1.53*
Never-married elderly females (55–75)	0.63	1.07	0.70	0.50	2.23	1.23	*0.52*	1.75
Never-married elderly males (55–75)	1.06	0.96	1.25	1.37	0.78	0.92	*3.81*	0.96
Mean	1.02	0.93	0.90	0.64	1.22	1.05	1.34	1.32

Note: Computed from the comparative individual model. Entries in italics are statistically significant at $p < 0.05$.
[a] Effect of a 10 percent increase in the price of oats.

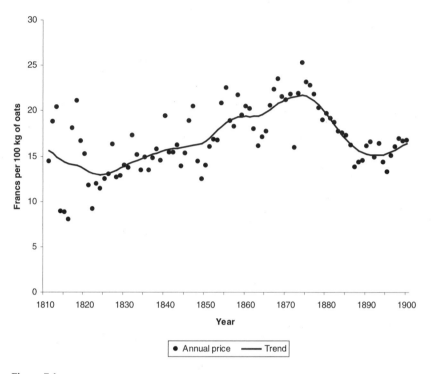

Figure 7.4
Annual prices of oats in east Belgium, 1811–1900
Sources: Deprez (1948), Gadisseur (1990).

the preferred food in Sart, but rather because they were the food of the poor. If conditions were good, households in Sart might afford bread from more appetizing grains, like rye and even wheat, or additional protein from meat or milk products, but in hard times they were forced to eat oats, which were the least expensive source of nutrition. Thus, when the price of oats rose, they had nowhere else to go, and hunger was imminent.

Figure 7.4 shows the course of annual prices of oats in east Belgium during the nineteenth century. The series begins with a period of very high prices during and after the Napoleonic Wars. This is followed by relatively low prices in the 1820s and a steady increase until the 1870s. The economic crisis beginning in 1873 foreshadowed a period of falling prices due to the depression and growing competition from American grain. We have also computed the trend of oats prices using the Hodrick-Prescott procedure. The covariate used in the event-history models is the difference between the logarithm of the observed price of oats and the logarithm of the corresponding price on the trend line. This covariate focuses on short-term fluctuations around the trend and ignores the long-term movements in price levels.

Our categories of occupations in Sart are limited by the small size of the population and its lack of social differentiation. Almost three-quarters of the population lived in households headed by "Farmers," our reference category.[12] In the 1843 population register, which lists landholdings, almost three-quarters of "Farmers" are listed with land, although some of this land may have been rented. "Functionary" refers to a diverse assortment of officials, merchants, and other nonmanual occupations, who comprised about 4 percent of the households. Sart was not large enough to have a substantial middle class, but it did have an array of government officials connected with a customs post on the border with Germany. Some of the persons classified in this category were wealthy, but it also includes low-level officials, like border guards. Consequently, it is often difficult to interpret the results obtained from this category. The category of "Artisans and Industrial Workers" (about 8 percent) is also diverse, including both traditional trades (like blacksmiths and carpenters) and some workers in the textile industry. Many of those listed with artisanal occupations also have land in the 1843 register, but their holdings are smaller than those of the farmers. The 9 percent of heads of household reported as "Day Laborers" (*journalier* in French) were mostly landless, unskilled workers. Finally, the "Other" category includes occupations that were difficult to classify, as well as some households headed by women described as *menagères* (housewives).

The event-history models shown in table 7.2 and elsewhere in this book distinguish between the effect of prices in the period between 1812 and 1846 and the period from 1847 to 1899. We find evidence of strong fluctuations in mortality following years of high prices in the first half of the century but not after 1850.[13] Indeed, for the years between 1812 and 1846, the average of the twelve estimated relative risks for deviations from the trend in oats prices is 1.02, which implies that a 10 percent increase in prices was associated with a 2 percent increase in mortality.[14] Between 1847 and 1899, the average of these estimates is less than one, which would mean that mortality decreased in years of high prices. The disappearance of the mortality responses to prices is probably due to a combination of national and local factors. At the national level, the Belgian government introduced new customs procedures after the Flemish crisis in 1845. On a regional scale, the railroad, which reached Verviers in 1843, and improved roads, which linked eastern Belgium to wider international markets, produced greater uniformity and smoothing of retail prices (Dejongh, Van Campenhout, and Ceusters, 2000; Deprez 1948, 47–54; Oris 1998b, 12–17; Scholliers 1993, 225, 237). Within Sart, agriculture was rapidly improving. Between the agricultural censuses of 1846 and 1895, yields of the two principal crops, oats and rye, increased by nearly two-thirds, and farmers in Sart began to adopt the kind of modern animal husbandry that transformed the Pays de Herve a century earlier (Alter, Oris, and Servais 1999). Furthermore, out-migration reduced population pressure and removed redundant labor.

First, the most general pattern that we observe in table 7.2 is the difference between the first and second halves of the nineteenth century. Mortality was sensitive to oats prices before 1847 but insensitive afterward. Second, there do appear to be differences between males and females in infancy and the adult ages. Since infants who are breast-fed should be less affected by scarcity than others, this may indicate that girls were weaned at an earlier age. Mortality differences in adulthood are discussed in chapter 11. Third, evidence of different responses in different occupational groups is very weak, partly because of data limitations. We would expect that day laborers would be most affected by price fluctuations, because they were both poor and dependent on wages. But these data do not support that conclusion. However, the level of mortality among adult male day laborers was significantly higher than that of farmers. Since day laborers were forced to seek work, they may have experienced much greater exposure to disease in hard times than other groups did.

Thus, the first half of the nineteenth century appears to have been a time of hardship. Opportunities for proto-industrial employment were disappearing, and agriculture remained backward in the Ardennes. Although the population continued to increase until the middle of the century, out-migration to nearby industrial areas had already begun. After 1850, there are a number of signs of improving conditions. The link between mortality and prices largely disappeared in the second half of the century. We also see a clear increase in expectation of life.

Although the inhabitants of Sart were undoubtedly poor and sometimes hungry, they lived longer than inhabitants of neighboring towns. While industrial development and urbanization worsened conditions in places like Verviers, Limbourg, and Tilleur, the deindustrialization of the Ardennes made it somewhat less susceptible to epidemics.

Moreover, mortality began to decline much earlier in this relatively poor rural area (Alter and Oris 2000a). By 1850, Sart was actually benefiting from the industrial revolution in its own way. Prices for agricultural commodities were rising until 1873 (Bruneel et al. 1987, Scholliers 1993), and the expanding coal mines were supported by timber from forests in the Ardennes (Hoyois 1981, 517–518). But Sart probably made its most important contribution to the industrial revolution by sending daughters and sons to work in Verviers and its suburbs. Many of these young people sent some of their earnings home to parents and siblings. Moreover, their departures reduced population pressure, which averted the subdivision of farms. The demographic experience of the Ardennes was quite different from nearby industrializing towns, but the divergent histories of these areas were intimately linked together.

Tilleur: Economy, Society, and Mortality in a Booming Industrial Town

In the booming industrial town of Tilleur, there was a dramatic contrast between the long depression of 1876 to 1893 and the preceding phase of explosive growth in coal and iron production and workers' real wages between 1846 and 1875. From an economic point of view, this marks the transition between the iron and the steel Kondratieff cycles, the latter characterized by fewer and larger industrial enterprises. The effect on industrial workers' short-term incomes appears on figure 7.5, which shows the annual movement of real wages. We calculated this series from nominal wages in the iron and coal sectors in Seraing, the industrial complex neighboring Tilleur (data from De Saint-Moulin 1969, IV–V), and the cost of living index constructed by Peter Scholliers (1993).[15] We see large fluctuations in real wages with crises around 1853 to 1855, 1860 to 1862, 1867, and 1871, but during the first period, the trend is clearly positive. In 1875, the index reaches the remarkable value of 190 but falls sharply to 158 in 1876, and drops to 118 to 123 during the years 1877 to 1879. No less important were deep cutbacks in industrial employment. The main coal and steel enterprise of Tilleur, the Society of Sclessin, started with 838 workers in 1846, employed 1,875 in 1869, 2,410 in 1873, but only 1,768 in 1875 and 1,264 in 1880.

René Leboutte has emphasized the importance of the shift from the ascending to the descending phase of the business cycle in the Basse-Meuse, another part of the industrial agglomeration around Liège. He

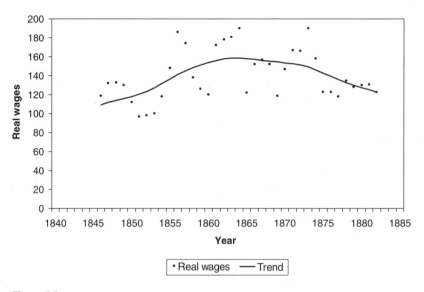

Figure 7.5
Annual real wages in the basin of Seraing, 1846–1882

hypothesizes that the shock of falling real incomes after years of industrial expansion played a decisive role in convincing workers to adopt
birth control (Leboutte 1988). In Tilleur, however, mortality patterns
show another side of this transition. After the "growth sacrifice" of the
years 1846 to 1873, the epidemiological transition emerges during the
economic and social crisis between 1874 and 1880. Figure 7.1 showed
that expectation of life increased during the industrial depression, but
the event-history models demonstrate that the biggest winners were
children aged 0 to 1 and ever-married women 15 to 54 years of age.
Compared to the period 1846 to 1873, young boys benefited from a 42
percent reduction in the risk of death, young girls from a 30 percent
decrease, and their mothers from 26 percent.

Socioeconomic differences within Tilleur appear along two dimensions: occupation and origin (Neven 2000b, Oris 1996). First, we find
that access to resources, as measured by occupation of the household
head, was an important determinant of mortality. Compared to day
laborers, mortality was substantially lower in the households of the
petty bourgeoisie and a proletarian elite, the metal workers. Although
these differences varied by age and sex, risks of death were generally
25 percent lower among the petty bourgeoisie and about 10 percent

lower among metal workers. In contrast, mortality in the households of coal miners was equivalent and sometimes worse than among day laborers, in spite of the higher wages that miners usually received.

Second, we find substantially higher mortality among those living in households headed by migrants, especially those from Flanders and outside Belgium. This effect is particularly large among children, who faced risks 30 to 100 percent higher than urban natives. Clearly, adaptation to the urban epidemiological environment was a serious challenge for migrants to Tilleur, especially for those from different linguistic and cultural origins.

The high mortality in the households of migrants should not be confused with another pattern that we have discussed elsewhere. Oris (1998a) has shown that recent migrants to Tilleur had lower mortality than those who had been in the city a longer time. This pattern is still observable in the results discussed here, because unmarried men between ages 15 and 54 in migrant households had lower mortality than natives. Single migrants were usually a selected group with relatively good health, and we have also observed that those out-migrating from Sart more often came from low-mortality households (Alter and Oris 1997). There was also a possibility that recent migrants would return to their origins when they fell sick. Indeed, in parliamentary debates about the Belgian poor law, some representatives pointed out that local charity offices in the countryside bore unfairly high expenses for the care of migrants whose health had deteriorated in the towns (Neven 2000a, Van Damme 1990).[16] However, the selective effects of migration would have had a short duration in an environment like Tilleur. Migrant households were likely to be in less healthy housing and have fewer social resources to call upon in times of distress.

In the period available for individual-level analysis (1846–1880), mortality in Tilleur did not increase when real wages fell. Indeed, the relationship was in the opposite direction: mortality increased when real wages increased. This is partly due to the higher standard of living after 1850 and the elimination of subsistence crises, which we observed in Sart as well. However, it also reflects the effects of environmental conditions on mortality in a period of explosive growth. High wages attracted additional migrants, who had fewer resources in the community and put additional burdens on already inadequate housing and sanitary facilities. Thus, in short-term fluctuations as well as the "epidemiological depression," Tilleur paid for economic success with higher mortality.

A Death in the Household

Eastern Belgium clearly belongs to the west European area characterized by nuclear family forms as defined by Laslett (1983), Hajnal (1982), and Burguière (1986). In the second half of the nineteenth century, between 68 and 78 percent of the households were formed by a simple family. Solitaries and extended families represented around 10 percent each, the former being a bit more frequent in urban (11 percent) than in rural areas (7 to 8 percent). Multiple families were marginal, between 3 and 5 percent. From an individual point of view, on average 88.6 percent of persons were either head of the household, spouse of the head, or child of the head, and variation around this mean goes from 82 to 95 percent without any clear difference between the towns and countryside.[17] The system also involved neo-locality, the establishment of new households after marriage (Capron et al. 1997, Leboutte 1998). However, life cycle servanthood, the second dynamic associated by John Hajnal (1982) with the nuclear family system, was not a normal pattern in eastern Belgium: servants were present in only 1.0 to 2.4 percent of the households. As in the regions of France studied by Martine Ségalen (1987, 216), children usually stayed at home until marriage (Alter and Oris 1999, Capron et al. 1997).

These features of the family system emerge clearly in the relationships of adults to heads of household shown in table 7.3. In both Sart and Tilleur, married adults usually headed their own households, and young unmarried adults usually lived with their parents. There are some differences related to the rural-urban context. Migrants to Tilleur were often young, unmarried workers who lived with nonkin. While in Sart, young married couples were more likely to live with parents, because establishing a new household was more difficult in a farming community than in a booming city. It is also noteworthy that ever-married old people continued to be heads of households. Unlike some parts of Europe where parents often made retirement contracts with their children (Laslett 1983, 532), farmers in Sart did not yield their farms to their sons.

Housing, Crowding, and Differential Mortality within the Household

A comparison between household composition effects in Sart and Tilleur in table 7.4 reveals the predominance of environmental over family influences. In Sart, the relative risks of dying associated with changes

Table 7.3
Relationship to head of household by age, sex, and marital status, Sart and Tilleur

| | Ages 15–54 | | | | Ages 55 and older | | | |
| | Never married | | Ever married | | Never married | | Ever married | |
	Females	Males	Females	Males	Females	Males	Females	Males
Sart								
Head or spouse	2.6%	2.8%	80.8%	81.0%	50.2%	64.8%	86.6%	88.6%
Stem kin	86.9	85.2	16.4	15.8	17.4	10.9	5.5	4.9
Other	10.5	12.0	2.8	3.2	32.4	24.3	7.9	6.6
Total	100.0	100.0	100.0	100.0	100.0	100.0	100.0	100.0
Tilleur								
Head or spouse	11.1	10.9	90.7	90.0	29.0	44.3	86.8	90.1
Stem kin	62.8	52.7	4.5	3.1	15.4	1.3	3.8	2.8
Other	26.1	36.3	4.8	6.9	55.6	54.3	9.3	7.1
Total	100.0	100.0	100.0	100.0	100.0	100.0	100.0	100.0

in the number of persons in the working (15–54) or nonworking (0–15 or over 55) ages are small and weak. They are mostly under 1.0, which indicates that mortality was lower in larger households, but this pattern does not mean that additional household members reduced mortality. Rather, it can reflect unobserved differences in health-related characteristics among households. For example, the presence of more children tends to identify households with lower mortality in general; it does not necessarily mean that children contribute to the survival of others. If mortality seems more or less indifferent to household composition in Sart, some strong effects appear in Tilleur. This pattern is most likely due to the harmful effects of crowding in the degraded urban environment and, to some extent, to cultural values.

Indeed, mortality in Tilleur was usually higher in households with more children and old people. Two specific subpopulations were sensitive to these factors: female children and young unmarried males. First, the excess mortality of young girls (28 percent for those aged 0–1, 38 percent for those aged 2–14) is not surprising in this coal and iron area. Infectious (such as smallpox or whooping cough) and respiratory diseases (bronchitis, pneumonia, and tuberculosis), which developed in crowded and unhealthy environments,[18] fell more heavily on girls.[19] This may have resulted from different activity patterns of girls and

Table 7.4
Effects of household composition on relative risks of dying, Sart and Tilleur

Relative risks	Ages 0–1		Ages 2–14		Ages 15–54				Ages 55 and older	
					Never married		Ever married		Ever married	
	Male	Female	Male	Female	Male	Female	Male	Female	Male	Female
Sart										
Number of adults	1.04	0.97	0.90	0.95	0.89	0.95	0.92	0.95	0.97	0.89
Proportion below age 15[a]	0.99	1.07	0.86	0.97	0.86	1.00	0.92	0.86	1.09	1.05
Proportion above age 55[a]	0.95	1.18	0.64	1.10	0.96	0.96	1.17	0.91	0.99	0.91
Tilleur										
Number of adults	0.90	0.94	1.05	1.05	0.96	1.09	1.01	0.94	0.91	0.89
Proportion below age 15[a]	1.13	1.28	1.07	1.38	1.23	0.99	1.02	0.90	0.95	0.80
Proportion above age 55[a]	1.22	0.95	0.97	1.03	1.19	1.20	0.84	1.05	0.88	0.87

Note: Controls for socioeconomic status, prices, and time period were also included, but the results are not presented here. Entries in italics are statistically significant at $p < 0.05$.
[a] Effect of a 20 percent change.

boys, but it also may reflect cultural choices and parental investments that were unequally distributed according to gender. For social, cultural, and economic reasons, parents could have favored males, both because sons brought more status to the family and because they promised higher economic returns (Derosas 2000; Klasen 1999; Neven 2000a, 400).

Second, young unmarried men (age 15–54), whose risks of dying increased by 23 percent when the proportion of the household below age 15 increased by 20 percent, were a mixed group. In a coal and iron center such as Tilleur, many single males were migrants, and they contributed to the notorious transiency that characterized Tilleur during the second half of the nineteenth century. However, some single adolescents and young adults were the children of workers living permanently in Tilleur. We have disentangled these two groups: the unstable recent immigrants and the children of established families. The former suffered the worst conditions, living as lodgers in small, crowded houses. They could cope with these terrible circumstances because they did not stay for a long time and probably also because they were a selected and unusually healthy group. It was the young adults raised in Tilleur who were most in danger when the burden of young children rose in their parental households.

To understand this pattern we must transpose Chayanov's (1923/1986) economic model of the family life cycle of peasant families to the proletarian-industrial world of a booming town. After a peak reached soon after marriage and the establishment of an autonomous household, the producer/consumer ratio in the family declined under the burden of successive births (Neven 2000b). Since industrial wages depended on the worker's productivity, the solution was for the male household head to work more (longer days and/or more intensity). According to contemporary local physicians, this resulted in precocious senility, serious weakening, and the appearance of health problems in the 40s and 50s. Indeed, when we compare the age-specific mortality rates of industrial towns to Belgium as a whole, we observe lower mortality of adults aged 20 to 50 and higher mortality for men older than 50 in the urban-industrial areas (Oris 1998a, 293–294, 306–308). When a family reached this turning point, elder sons were forced to enter the labor market, and the higher the number of younger siblings, the stronger the tendency to send sons into the very dangerous working conditions in the mines and factories. Overall, among single men aged 15 to 54 (most of whom were young), those living with their

Table 7.5
Effects of siblings on relative risks of dying, Sart and Tilleur

	Relative risks			
	Ages 0–1		Ages 2–14	
	Male	Female	Male	Female
Sart				
Older brother	0.96	0.92	0.92	0.80
Older sister	0.91	0.91	1.04	0.91
Younger brother			1.05	0.81
Younger sister			0.99	*0.75*
Tilleur				
Older brother	1.12	1.21	1.15	*1.40*
Older sister	1.06	1.14	1.01	1.12
Younger brother			*1.48*	1.01
Younger sister			1.11	1.33

Note: Controls for socioeconomic status, presence of parents, preceding birth interval, prices, and time period were also included, but the results are not presented here. Entries in italics are statistically significant at $p < 0.05$.

families died twice as often as recent in-migrants. When one parent died, the family pressure on these young men became excessive, and they were three or four more times likely to die (Oris and Alter 2001). These results bring a new explanation to the famous "excess mortality in youth" identified by James Riley (1993).

Table 7.5 shows a similar contrast in the effects of siblings in Sart and Tilleur and qualifies these interpretations. Again, the risk of dying was generally lower for children with older or younger siblings in Sart, but siblings raised the risk of death in Tilleur. In this urban environment, unlike the more benign rural environment of Sart, siblings increased crowding and carried infections into the household. As suggested above, the household economy interacted with epidemiological conditions in the urban-industrial context.

Old-Age Mortality and the Nuclear Hardship Hypothesis

To discuss old-age mortality, we will consider only the case of Sart, where we can base our analysis on more than 9,000 person-years and 600 deaths for each sex. A booming industrial town like Tilleur naturally had a young population, and there were too few elderly to analyze successfully.

According to the classic formulation of the nuclear hardship hypothesis by Richard Smith and Peter Laslett, the neo-local establishment of children after their marriages severed intergenerational solidarity, which had often been weakened by separation during life cycle servanthood. Consequently, the old, the widowed, and the sick had very limited opportunities in a nuclear family system: either they endured the deterioration of their strength and health in isolation, or they became the guests of a married child, holding a subordinate position in an extended family household (Laslett 1988). In the first case, their support fell largely on the state or charity. In the second case, the addition of an elderly parent to a household burdened with young children made the downhill slide of the household microeconomic cycle even more severe (Laslett 1991, 125; Smith 1984, 73; Wall 1992, 84). However, Alter (1996) has pointed out the importance of the European system of late marriage in this context. First, late marriage made it more likely that some unmarried children would still be in the household when parents entered old age. Second, many people never married, and some of them remained at home until their parents died. Third, parents could rely on unmarried younger children until their married older children reached a more comfortable stage in the family cycle.

In nineteenth-century Ardennes, the reality was obviously more complicated. Among the ever-married aged 55 and older, 88.6 percent of the men were heads of household, and 86.6 percent of the women were head or spouse of the head. Only 5.0 to 5.5 percent lived under the protection of their children and a slightly higher proportion (6.6 percent of the males, 7.9 percent of the females) in households headed by other kin or nonkin. Moreover, 88 percent of ever-married old men and 85 percent of women lived with at least one child. So, old age in Sart between 1812 and 1900 can certainly not be associated with abandonment, isolation, and loss of position and privilege within the household.

However, the designation of household headship can reflect either the reality of leadership or simply respect for seniority on the part of the local civil servants who compiled the population registers. No less than 35 percent of ever-married old men and 41 percent of women of the same age and status shared a table and a roof with a married child. So more than one-third of old age in nineteenth-century Ardennes was spent in an extended family household, while 53 percent and 44 percent of old men and women, respectively, lived with unmarried children in a nuclear structure. In 1831 in the urban textile center of

Verviers, coresidence with married children was much less common. Old people tended to live in separate households until infirmity made them dependent on their married children (Alter, Cliggett, and Urbiel 1996, 38). However, the group most likely to coreside with married children was elderly widows from the countryside, who migrated to the city to rejoin children who had arrived earlier (Alter 1999, 21–22).

Relationships of authority between generations depended on both the age and health of the old person as well as the marital status and family situation of the children. Our multivariate models provide an important indicator: we do not find strong mortality differences among the elderly related to their position within the household or the presence of children. Unlike in China, being the head of a household brought neither privilege nor penalty (Lee and Campbell 1997). This contrasts with the situation in Verviers, where old people living with married children were twice as likely to die (Alter, Cliggett, and Urbiel 1996, 37–38). Apparently, in the city, where children could live nearby, old people preferred to be independent until failing health forced them to move in with children. In the countryside, household formation decisions were complicated by the need for labor on the farm and the dynamics of inheritance. Farmers in eastern Belgium did not formally retire, as did their counterparts in Japan and Sweden, but the death of a parent began a transition that often involved marriage and migration in the next generation (Alter and Oris 1999, 148).

Another aspect of this problem is the destiny of the "stayers"—those who remained at home until the death of their last parent, which usually occurred when they were beyond the normal age for marriage. Can we say that they paid a price for their filial piety later in their lives? Indeed, among those 55 and older, never-married men had 53 percent higher mortality than married men, and the penalty was 36 percent for never-married women (see the standard Eurasian comparative relationship model for all 55 and older combined). However, this result is quite ambiguous. Single persons normally suffer from higher mortality, because unhealthy individuals are less likely to marry (Kunst, Wolleswinkel-van den Bosch, 1999, 198–200). At the moment, we cannot distinguish between those who chose to remain with parents and those who were unable to marry for other reasons. This question will require further exploration, drawing together individual and family patterns over the entire life course.

Another unsettled point within the nuclear hardship model is the role of kin outside the household in a neo-local regime. In an earlier contribution, we used two approaches to identify the family network beyond the household: an index based on the occurrence of patronyms and a count of "close" kin (father, mother, and siblings) based on genealogical information present in the population registers (see details in Capron 1999). These tools were used for a study focused specifically on the widows. We found that widows with larger kin networks in Sart had lower mortality (−15 percent), and that in both Tilleur and Sart, an increase in the number of kin beyond the household strongly reduced the likelihood of out-migration (−35 percent in both places). The protection of the family network also benefited married women, but its effect was more intense during widowhood. This indicates that the kin network was more active and effective in times of hardship (Alter et al. 2002). These results are another starting point for further investigations.

At this point, our analysis of the nuclear hardship hypothesis is inconclusive, but migration probably holds the key to understanding old age mortality. In her work on the Pays de Herve, Muriel Neven has found higher mobility at older ages among the ever-married, those living alone, the childless, and the very old (age 75 and higher). This results in net out-migration in old age. Many of these migrants left the countryside for the industrial agglomerations centered on Verviers and Liège. In addition, while an average of 10 percent of the population disappeared from the population registers without reporting a destination, this happened to 16 percent of elderly men and 19 percent of elderly women, rising to 29 percent and 35 percent for those who had never married. These people were obviously a marginal population. Not only did they ignore administrative rules about reporting their departures; they also had no kin to tell authorities where they went. Consequently, it is difficult to evaluate the effect of nuclear hardship on old-age mortality, because those who remained in rural areas may have been very different from those who finished their lives in a city (Neven 2000a, chap. 11).

Conclusion

The history of mortality in nineteenth-century eastern Belgium shows that the road to modernization was hard and often unpredictable. Our empirical results stress the contrast between neighboring demographic, social, and economic environments. On one hand, health conditions worsened in the burgeoning cities in spite of rising wages. On the other hand, deindustrialized rural areas combined poverty and rising life expectancies. Sart and Tilleur represent extreme cases on a continuum from rural isolation to rapid urbanization. Such a geographic disparity was not new. As Sheila R. Johansson (2000) has observed for England, "London and other similar capital cities [were] wealthy but unhealthy places," while "remote, economically disadvantaged rural areas— where wages were usually well below average—commonly had the highest life-expectancy levels" (62). However, industrialization created a new type of industrial town where "urban disamenities" (Williamson 1981) were exacerbated by rapid and often chaotic growth. The "paradox of growth" described by Simon Szreter and Graham Mooney (1998) is compounded by our observation that population pressure in rural areas was relieved by sending the healthiest young people to risk their lives in the urban sector.

In Sart, our rural study area in the Ardennes, the multivariate analyses of biographical data highlight the existence of a transition around 1850. The first half of the nineteenth century was a period of intensifying Malthusian pressure, and mortality responded to fluctuations in grain prices (oats). As the discussion in chapter 2 indicated, the burden of hard times was not distributed equally among or within households. Mortality was often higher in the households of landless day laborers, especially for married males who had to move to find work in hard times. Within households, the first victims of short-term economic stress were usually girls and married women, who may have suffered discrimination in the distribution of food. (See chapter 5.) However, mortality in Sart was not much affected by household composition, measured by the number of working adults or the proportions of dependent children and elderly. At younger ages, we found somewhat lower mortality in large households, but in the nuclear family system in Sart, household size was a consequence rather than a cause of differences in mortality. If a child had more siblings, it meant that more of those siblings had survived infancy and early childhood. We also noted little support for the hypothesis that the nuclear family system would leave parents isolated in old age. Most old people in nineteenth-century Sart continued to head households and to have children to support them.

The disappearance of the demographic responses to economic stress after 1850 revealed a qualitative improvement of the living conditions in the East Ardennes. The first significant increases in life expectancy, observed between 1845 and 1875, contrasted sharply with the deepening epidemiological depression in nearby towns. Several explanations have been offered, but the most important is the radical structural change in the economic and demographic geographic system of eastern Belgium. Migration to places like Tilleur solved the population problem in places like Sart. When out-migration climbed after 1851, the effects of grain prices on mortality disappeared. By offsetting population growth, out-migration counteracted tendencies toward subdividing landholdings and increasing landlessness. The result was a reduction of Malthusian pressure on the intergenerational transmission of land within rural families. Migration did not affect all rural areas in the same way. For example, in the Pays de Herve, a neighboring region north of the Ardennes, the proportion of agricultural lands owned by the local peasants fell drastically from 70 or 80 percent around 1800 to 10 to 30 percent in 1860. In Sart, however, this proportion was still 70 percent in 1878–1879, almost exactly the same as the beginning of the nineteenth century.

The young single adults who left Sart came disproportionately from larger families with lower infant and child mortality, and they were presumably healthier than average. As migrants to the rapidly expanding industrial areas, they found new economic opportunities, but the demographic environment was often lethal. We have already evoked the similarity with the postfamine Irish experience, but almost exactly the same process has been observed among the African American population in the late nineteenth century: "It is noteworthy that blacks were slowly migrating out of the comparatively healthier environment of the rural South ... for the much less salubrious urban areas of the South and North. Evidently, economic and social pressures in the South were sufficient to induce migration despite the much less healthy environment into which blacks were moving" (Preston and Haines 1991, 95).

When the industrial revolution shattered the limits of the Malthusian world, the new industrial towns paid a growth sacrifice. Belgian industrial towns experienced a temporary fall in life expectancy, like their counterparts in England and Wales (Reid 1997, Szreter and Mooney 1998, Woods 1994). Our multivariate analyses of longitudinal data draw a sharper picture of the process and identify the victims more precisely. Again the hypotheses posed in chapters 1 and 2 help to organize this evidence.

First, the relationship between mortality and real wages in the industrial towns was just the opposite of what we might expect: increasing incomes were accompanied by rising risks of death. Rising wages in eastern Belgian industrial towns induced rapid in-migration, which undermined both private and public hygiene (Alter and Oris 1997, De Saint-Moulin 1969). In our studies of Tilleur, we see the impact of crowding and poor living conditions on causes of death, epidemics, and the effects of household composition on mortality. In particular, the families of day laborers, coal miners, and long-distance migrants (Flemish and foreigner) were less able to cope with rapid urban growth. However, the main victims were not active adults but rather children, especially girls. Since coal miners were relatively well paid (Neven 2000b, 317), these results suggest that social and economic explanations are overshadowed by ecological conditions.

Working conditions in nineteenth-century cities have been condemned since the first workers' movements (see Haines 1989), and we find some evidence of these dangers in Tilleur. When we distinguish between recent single migrants and unmarried men living with their parents, we find that mortality was higher for the latter. Furthermore, circumstances that increased economic stress within the household, like the death of a wage earner or a large number of young children, affected adults living with their parents. These demographic patterns confirm anecdotal evidence about pressure to send teenagers to work during the early industrial revolution. Although Chayanov's model of the family economy was designed to explain the Russian peasantry, it explains mortality patterns better in industrial Tilleur than in rural Sart (Neven 2000b, 319–322).

The final paradox on the road to modernization in nineteenth-century east Belgium is found in the transition to low mortality. Mortality in Tilleur fell rapidly after 1874, even though a severe industrial depression caused increasing unemployment. From this point on, urban mortality was independent of the economy, a transition that occurred a quarter-century earlier in rural Sart. Of course, neither Tilleur nor Sart can be taken as representative of a process as complex and destabilizing as the industrial revolution, but they show the diverse ways in which the family system of eastern Belgium met the challenges of this new economic and social environment.

Notes

We are grateful to the Belgian National Funds for Scientific Research and the Research Council of the University of Liège for grants in support of our work on eastern Belgium. We also gratefully acknowledge support for the workshop on "Family Systems and

Demographic Responses to Economic Stress" held in Bloomington, Indiana, October 23–25, 1997, from the National Institute of Child Health and Human Development (R13 HD34833-01), the East Asia Regional Research Working Group of the Social Science Research Council, and the Joint Committee on Chinese Studies of the American Council of Learned Societies. George Alter would also like to thank Shannon Kahler for making the Bloomington workshop possible.

1. For a complete list of references, see the bibliography of Belgian historical demography by Oris (1994, esp. 257–270), to be completed by the synthesis of and the works of Devos (1996, 2000), Eggerickx and Tabutin (1994), and Perrenoud (1994).

2. Preliminary communications in Alter et al. (2000), Alter and Oris (1997, 1999b, 2000a), Alter, Oris, and Servais (1999), Capron (1998), Neven (1997, 2000a, 2000b), and Oris (1998a).

3. For example, in the Pays de Herve, 62 percent of the missing children died or out-migrated within the month following their birth.

4. The "false" stillbirths are children who were born alive and died between their birth and its official declaration within the next three days. For a more detailed discussion, see chapter 12.

5. Specifically, when an individual disappeared from our data, we first determined the period of uncertainty surrounding the disappearance. Using the information present in the household (marriage or a child birth, for example), we found dates bracketing the disappearance as tightly as possible. Then we made a list of observed dates of out-migration recorded in the population register within this bracket, and we assigned a randomly selected observed date to terminate the life history with an unobserved end point.

6. In Tilleur, between 1846 and 1880, dates of departure and entry determined according to this method represent 6.5 percent of the observed out-migrations and 5 percent of the in-migrations, respectively. In Sart, however, those proportions are more important, 17.8 and 21.9 percent, due to an obvious underrecording of migration in the late 1830s and early 1840s (Capron et al. 1997, 28–30). Before and after this period, the underrecording is similar to the one observed in Tilleur.

7. For similar developments in other European industrial areas, see Bourdelais and Demonet (1996), Pareja (1997), Szreter and Mooney (1998), and the special issue of the *Annales de Démographie historique*, 1999–2002.

8. From the classic Samuel Preston and Etienne van de Walle (1978) to Sheila R. Johansson (2000) through the demonstration of the "urban penalty" (Kearns 1988), there is a growing international literature on this question.

9. See Alter and Oris (1997), Capron (1998), Neven (1997, 2000b), and Oris (1998a). Szreter (1997) proposes a similar interpretation of the British experience of industrial and urban development.

10. For a recent survey of the anthropometric history and the historical anthropometric data, see Coll and Komlos (1998).

11. We tried price series for rye, wheat, *méteil* (a mix of rye and wheat), potatoes, and a so-called social index, which included all the already cited foods and meat, butter, oil, grease, and tea and coffee. For a detailed description see Oris (1998b, esp. 12–13). Oat prices are taken from the Liège market for the period 1812 to 1830 and the national average prices for 1831 to 1900.

12. In some cases we use this category when the occupation of the head of household was missing.

13. Alter, Oris, and Servais (1999) show that epidemics, which were largely independent of economic conditions, sometimes obscure the relationship between prices and mortality.

14. The average price of oats between 1811 and 1846 was 14.5 francs for 100 kilograms.

15. We have also reconstructed a series of wages for workers of the Society of Sclessin, the main enterprise of Tilleur (Archives générales du Royaume (Bruxelles), Administration du Corps des Mines, no. 180–204), but the information is missing for ten out of the thirty-four years we surveyed. The correlation between the available Sclessin data and the ones about Seraing is 0.9.

16. The Belgian poor laws established that a migrant had to be helped by the charity office of his or her place of immigration only after five years of residence. Before five years, he or she could be helped, but their locality of origin was responsible for reimbursing the costs. It created an incredible number of conflicts between the Belgian communes during the nineteenth century. If we add that the charity offices of most of the industrial towns were poor and completely overrun by the rapid demographic growth and radical change in social structures, it was indeed rational to get back to the countryside for a sick migrant who was able to do it.

17. These observations are based on the authors' calculations for Limbourg, Polleur, Sart, and Tilleur.

18. See Neven and Oris (1995, esp. 228–230) on the housing conditions of tuberculars in late nineteenth-century east Belgium.

19. See Poulain and Tabutin (1981, esp. 114–116, for an overview of the gender differential in causes of death in nineteenth-century Belgium.

8

Mortality and Environment in Three Emilian, Tuscan, and Venetian Communities, 1800–1883

Marco Breschi, Renzo Derosas,
and Matteo Manfredini
in collaboration with James Z.
Lee

Mortality in the past was molded by powerful forces that were largely beyond the control of individuals. The environment was one major constraint, severely affecting the health and well-being of the population. The economy was another: a sudden worsening of conditions could quickly deplete available resources, initiating a process of deprivation that eventually led to sickness and death. Such factors could also have different effects according to the socioeconomic position of individuals. Furthermore, even for persons belonging to the same social group, different household circumstances could enhance or buffer individuals from such external constraints.

This chapter uses event-history analysis of longitudinal individual-level data to examine how climatic and economic variations interacted with social position and family role to affect individual mortality risks in Italy before the demographic transition. Recent studies on mortality in Italy have described its trends and characteristics at an aggregate level, but most factors of individual differentiation are still largely unexplored. The individual approach usually requires use of small population samples. Our study concerns three communities in northern and central Italy during the nineteenth century depicted in map 8.1: the city of Venice and the rural parishes of Madregolo and Casalguidi. These communities are not representative in a statistical sense of the nation or even their respective regions. Nonetheless, we believe that most of the results we present can be extended to other areas where socioeconomic organization and climatic condition were similar.

We divide our chapter into four sections. The first, on national background, summarizes recent research results that show that the development of the population of Italy before unification in 1861 was not homogeneous. The second section describes the regional setting, including the role of mortality in the demographic systems of these

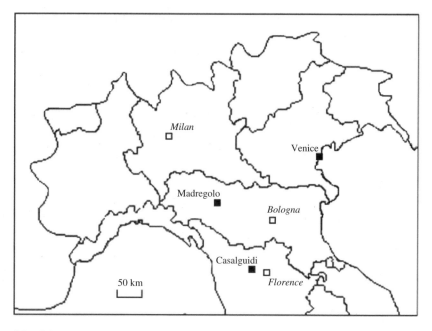

Map 8.1
Northern Italy

three communities. Next, we summarize the data and the differences of the model we estimate from the Eurasia standard comparative models discussed elsewhere in this book. Finally, we present our results and provide evidence, at the individual level, of the influence of such factors on mortality revealed from the estimations of these slightly revised Eurasian models.

Background

Italy has long represented a variegated reality, characterized by different demographic systems. Inverse projection has recently yielded estimates of trends in fertility and mortality for large regional areas that are fairly accurate (Breschi, Pozzi, and Rettaroli 1994; Breschi 1990; Ge Rondi 1998; Rosina and Rossi 1998). They confirm that the years between the mid-eighteenth century and the beginning of the demographic transition in the late nineteenth century were marked by highly diverse demographic systems, each characterized by different levels of fertility and mortality. These studies also show that the prevailing interpretation linking demographic growth in the eighteenth and nineteenth centuries to a reduction in mortality is not appropriate.[1] Rather, population growth in several regions can be attributed to variations in nuptiality and fertility (Breschi, Pozzi, and Rettaroli 1994).

The statistics available on mortality for several Italian areas in the period before unification do not allow for a sufficiently detailed analysis of its levels and structural features.[2] However, partial data at hand suggest that after the high levels of mortality and the epidemics of the seventeenth century, mortality fell in the eighteenth century due to the reduced incidence of plague and other epidemics and of famines (Del Panta 1980). Nonetheless, minor crises were still quite frequent. A 50 percent increase in mortality occurred approximately every twenty-five years. In the nineteenth century, smallpox epidemics gradually disappeared as vaccination became more common.[3] Moreover, the serious, widespread famine of 1816–1817 was the last of its kind. This improvement resulted from an increase in agricultural production, as well as progress in the supply and transportation of farm produce. In addition, the frequent outbreaks of cholera during the nineteenth century affected the overall population growth only marginally (Del Panta 1980).

Despite the reduced frequency of such crises, Italy until the late nineteenth century was nonetheless characterized by high mortality. Although it is difficult to find data for the period before political unification (Pozzi 1995), Italy's position was clearly behind that of several other countries, especially in central and northern Europe. In 1881–1882, in most of Italy, life expectancy at birth was much lower than the national average for northern European countries.[4] By the end of the nineteenth century, infectious or parasitic diseases continued to cause approximately one out of four deaths.[5]

This was most certainly the consequence of the serious backwardness of the socioeconomic development of large areas. Above all, nutritional levels do not seem to have improved at all for most of the Italian population throughout the nineteenth century (Del Panta and Fiorini 1994, Samoggia 1995). Indeed, conditions were as precarious in most cities as they were in the country. Environmental and hygienic conditions in urban areas were often appalling (Ministry of the Interior, General Office of Statistics 1886). Moderate improvement took place only toward the end of the century, when many cities undertook urban renewal.

This situation is mirrored by trends in infant and child mortality, which show no substantial improvement before the 1880s. The risk of dying in infancy and early childhood varied greatly in different parts of the country. This spatial pattern remained almost unchanged throughout the eighteenth and nineteenth centuries. The highest levels of infant mortality were in northern Italy, as well as in the central Adriatic area. This primacy, however, cannot be explained by particularly poor socioeconomic hygienic conditions; these regions were in fact the first to undergo a process of modernization. Rather, the blame should be placed mostly on climatic factors, and especially on cold winters that claimed a large number of victims among infants just a few days or weeks old. Indeed, the Italian peninsula displays a wide variability in climatic conditions, especially as far as winter harshness is concerned, affecting not only infant mortality patterns but also mortality in later ages and the mortality structure overall (Breschi and Livi-Bacci 1986; Breschi, Derosas, and Manfredini 2000; Ferrari and Livi-Bacci 1985). This situation was worsened by a kind of understatement of the dangers of cold winter temperatures, especially for those whose health was most fragile. As the American novelist William Howells, who visited Venice in the 1860s, put it, "Winter is apt to being very severe in mild climates. People do not acknowledge it, making a wretched pretense that it is summer only a little out of humor. The Germans have introduced stoves in Venice, but they are not much in favor with the Italians, who think their heat unwholesome, and endure a degree of cold, in their wish to dispense with fire, which we of the winter-lands know nothing of in our houses" (Howells 1883, 36–37).

Indeed, the effects of an unfavorable climate could be attenuated or worsened by a whole series of factors, such as housing, clothing, the way children were protected from cold, and more generally how babies were cared for. The influence of social and, to a certain extent, cultural factors on infant survival is often mentioned but has rarely been measured in Italy. Only in exceptional cases are mortality estimates according to socioeconomic status available. Where available, they reveal differences in infant mortality by social class, in the cities as well as in the countryside (Breschi and Pozzi 1997, Pinelli and Mancini 1997). Moreover, especially in the cities, married couples of the lower classes regularly resorted to abandonment as a means of disposing of their unwanted children (Corsini 1976, Hunecke 1989, Kertzer 1993). Since 50 percent of abandoned infants died (Ipsen 2000), such a practice resulted in a remarkable increase of overall mortality. On the other hand, there were subpopulations who shared the same or perhaps worse conditions from the socioeconomic and environmental point of view but enjoyed a much more favorable mortality regime. This was the case of the Jewish communities, whose infant mortality rate was around half that of the Catholic population with which they lived, showing that cultural attitudes in child care and lifestyle could significantly overcome the mortality effects of external constraints.[6]

In outlining certain aspects of mortality in Italy in the eighteenth and nineteenth centuries, we have mainly referred to the first years of life. This is due not only to the obvious importance of infant mortality but also to the lack of data on mortality at later ages.[7] Specific studies regarding the mortality of adults and the elderly are rare. Differences in mortality also need to be investigated according to gender and marital status, not to mention differentials related to socioeconomic condition. Moreover, the influence of family context, though often mentioned, has yet to be measured. Death is most certainly conditioned by the characteristics of individuals, but belonging to a particular household and, to a certain extent, to a wider family network could have influenced a person's chances of survival (Poni 1978). Resources were gathered inside the family and redistributed to members, favoring some and discriminating against others. The composition of the family conditioned the lives of each member and might also have affected their level of resistance in the struggle against death.

Northern Italy

Socioeconomic Context

In the following pages, we focus on three different populations: the two rural communities of Madregolo and Casalguidi and a sample from the city of Venice. The time periods covered by our study are 1800 to 1883, 1819 to 1859, and 1850 to 1869, respectively.

Madregolo was a small village, with about 550 inhabitants on average, situated about 20 kilometers from the city of Parma. The territory is completely flat, characterized by the typical structure of the Emilian countryside. The village was composed of a small center with tiny houses, usually occupied by artisans and day laborers, and scattered farmhouses, built on large farms, where sharecroppers and tenants lived.

Madregolo belonged to the duchy of Parma until 1861, when it became part of the Italian Kingdom. This change did not affect the social and economic situation of the village. Agriculture was the main economic activity. The most important crops were wheat and legumes, accounting for 40 and 23 percent of the land, respectively. Fodder plants (16 percent), corn (7 percent), hemp, mulberry, and other crops were present as well. The breeding of dairy cows was practiced for cheese production (Delsante 1982).

The social structure of Madregolo reflects its agricultural orientation. According to the 1849 census, 72 percent of the household heads were involved in farm work, 19 percent were artisans, and the rest were either the better off or the very poor. Of the farmers, 61 percent were sharecroppers and tenants. The rest were farm laborers (Census of Parma 1849). The contracts of sharecropping were stipulated between the landowner and the whole household, represented by the head, and normally lasted one year. The landowners had great power over the sharecropping family and intervened to maintain the proper fit between the farm size and the tenant's household structure and productive capacity, going as far as to allowing or forbidding marriages (Poni 1978). The farm laborers included not only day or seasonal workers but also wage earners (*famigli*), hired for short periods, whose salary included board and lodging but not a share of the crop. They were also hired for a very short time.[8] Overall, the use of short-term contracts, as well as the ignorance and indifference of the landowners, were the main causes of the backwardness of agriculture during the nineteenth century. Together with the proximity to Parma, they also explain the intense population mobility: turnover amounted to one-third every year (Breschi and Manfredini 1998a).

Casalguidi is located in northern Tuscany (central Italy), quite close to the small city of Pistoia. With about 2,400 inhabitants on average during the period under study, Casalguidi depended strongly on Pistoia, to which it was connected by a large carriageway (Breschi and Manfredini 1998b).[9] Unlike Madregolo, the territory is not completely flat, and part of the village is situated on the surrounding hills. The economy of Casalguidi was not based solely on agriculture, though this activity employed the largest part of the population. The Tuscan form of the sharecropping farm (*podere mezzadrile*) was common in Casalguidi and dominant in the area. Though providing for the division of harvest, it was slightly different from Madregolo: whereas in the latter, it was the farmer who had to provide livestock and cattle, in Casalguidi the landowner himself took care of it.

Small independent farmers and farm laborers existed too. On the whole, people devoted to agriculture made up over 72 percent of all the families in the area. The rest of the population included small shopkeepers and artisans, who dwelled in the village center. The crops differed slightly from Madregolo: half of the land was devoted to vine-yards and olive orchards. These allotments were also used to cultivate grain and other cereals. Woods, including stands of chestnut, covered most of the remaining land. Some proto-industrial activities were also present, especially in such textiles as embroidery and silk industries, the production of earthenware goods, and the manufacture of straw hats. Finally, the climate of the two rural areas was similar, with hot summers, frequently over 30°C, and cold winters, often below 0°C.

From 1814 to 1866, Venice was, alongside Milan, one of the two cap-itals of the Lombard-Venetian Kingdom and the seat of state govern-ment. The kingdom was by far the richest province in the Habsburg Empire. Nonetheless, the first half of the nineteenth century turned out to be the most difficult period in the long history of the city. What remained of its leading role in regional and international markets was destroyed with the fall of the aristocratic republic in 1797. The few productive sectors—such as shipbuilding and navigation, glass, and tobacco—all declined considerably in this period, while the number of people making their living by means of temporary or marginal occu-pations increased sharply (Derosas 2002, Franzina 1986, Romanelli 1988, Zalin 1969).

Trends in population in figure 8.1 reflect these difficulties: popula-tion fell from around 140,000 inhabitants at the end of the eighteenth century to fewer than 100,000 in the first quarter of the nineteenth century. In spite of this economic and demographic decay, Venice remained one of the major Italian cities. Its social structure was ex-tremely diverse. Although servants were the modal occupational cate-gory, a large section of the population was employed in small and medium-sized factories. Civil servants, artisans, shopkeepers, fisher-men, sailors, and boatmen were important categories as well (Fran-zina 1986). Moreover, like every other large city, Venice had a large number of public and private institutions—hospitals, old people's homes, orphanages, foundling hospitals, and various kinds of chari-table institutions—whose activities greatly influenced people's lives, especially those of the poor.

Our analysis of Venice focuses on three particular areas of the city: the parishes of Sant'Angelo Raffaele and Santa Eufemia (the latter cov-ering the whole island of Giudecca) and the old Jewish Ghetto. The data concern the households residing there in 1869, although they may

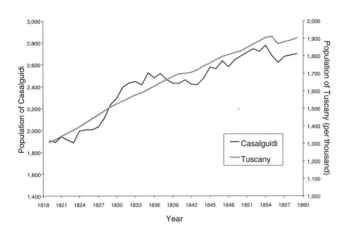

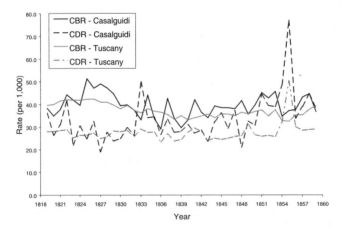

Figure 8.1
Population (top) and birth and death rates (bottom), Casalguidi and Tuscany, 1819–1859
Note: CBR = crude birthrate. CDR = crude death rate.

have moved from elsewhere in previous years. From the social point of view, these areas were all quite depressed. Fishermen and boatmen inhabited Sant'Angelo Raffaele almost exclusively, while porters and hemp workers formed a large part of the population of Giudecca. The composition of the Jewish population was more variegated, but its inhabitants came mainly from low social classes and were mostly involved in the retail trade. Population density was much higher in Sant'Angelo Raffaele (around 170 inhabitants per hectare) than in Santa Eufemia (around 30), since a large part of the island was covered by market gardens and wasteland. The population density in the ghetto was the highest in the city, reaching 1,000 inhabitants per hectare, about four times the average density (Beltrami 1954, 43; Calabi 1991, 235; Derosas 2002; *Municipio di Venezia* 1881, 35).

As one could expect, hygienic conditions were also very bad in the three areas as well as in many other parts of the city. The reports of the sanitary commissions that inspected all the houses in the city after the cholera epidemic of 1873 describe these conditions (Barizza 1987, Federigo 1831–1832).[10] The ghetto, in particular, appeared so unbearably dirty to tourists that they preferred not to visit it (Howells 1883, 192–193). These difficult conditions were often made worse by the climate: rainy, though seldom very cold, winters and hot, humid summers.[11]

Demographic Features

From the demographic point of view, the two villages show trends and patterns quite similar to those characterizing the wider areas where they were located. This is displayed in figure 8.2, which summarizes the population, with crude birthrate and death rate trends for Casalguidi and Tuscany in the period 1819 to 1859, and figure 8.3, which makes the same comparison between Madregolo and the duchy of Modena and Reggio, a small state neighboring the duchy of Parma that was similar to it.

In Casalguidi, the growth of the population was interrupted only by a period of population stability (1836–1843) and the cholera epidemic of 1854 to 1855, which caused a 5.6 percent reduction in the population. The first increase was largely the consequence of a period of recovery following the troubles that marked the Napoleonic years (1800–1815). The overall trend is very similar to that observed for the region as a whole, in both trends and levels, while the annual average

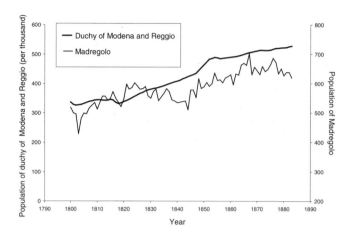

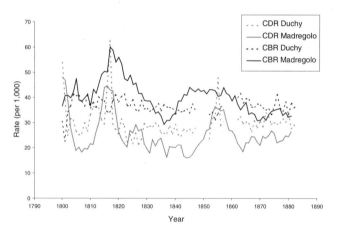

Figure 8.2
Population (top) and birth and death rates (bottom), Madregolo and Duchy of Modena and Reggio, 1800–1883
Note: CBR = crude birthrate. CDR = crude death rate.

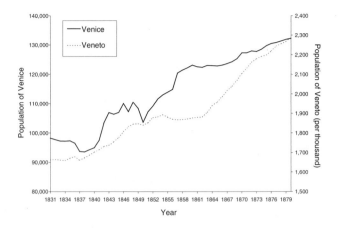

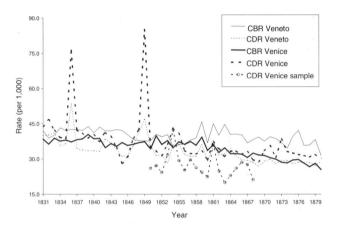

Figure 8.3
Population (top) and birth and death rates (bottom). Venice (total and sample) and Veneto, 1831–1881
Note: CBR = crude birthrate. CDR = crude death rate.

Table 8.1
Life expectancy at birth (e_0) and total fertility rates (TFR), Casalguidi and Tuscany, 1820–1859, Madregolo and Duchy of Modena and Reggio, 1800–1879

Period	Casalguidi		Tuscany		Period	Madregolo		Duchy of Modena and Reggio	
	e_0	TFR	e_0	TFR		e_0	TFR	e_0	TFR
1820–1824	37.4	5.59	37.3	5.55	1800–1809	31.5	5.09	32.7	5.12
1825–1829	43.8	5.88	39.9	5.77	1810–1819	28.7	6.21	28.8	5.32
1830–1834	35.5	5.51	36.6	5.50	1820–1829	41.8	6.32	40.0	5.53
1835–1839	35.2	5.14	38.4	5.34	1830–1839	39.4	5.39	36.4	5.32
1840–1844	39.4	5.73	36.2	5.16	1840–1849	40.6	5.69	36.6	4.96
1845–1849	37.5	5.56	36.7	5.21	1850–1859	31.8	5.64	30.3	4.74
1850–1854	31.9	5.49	36.0	4.97	1860–1869	35.7	5.59	33.6	5.33
1855–1859	25.8	5.09	29.8	4.69	1870–1879	36.4	5.12	31.7	5.12
Total	35.0	5.34	36.2	5.12	Total	35.3	5.63	33.9	5.21

Note: The periods included in this table differ slightly from those reported in the text in order to make them consistent with figures available for Tuscany and the Duchy of Modena and Reggio.
Sources: Casalguidi, Madregolo, and Duchy of Modena and Reggio: our data; Tuscany: Breschi (1990, 283).

growth rate is the same: 8.3 per 1,000.[12] This strong assonance is also confirmed by the estimates of life expectancy at birth and the overall fertility rate, summarized in table 8.1.

Similarities between Madregolo and the duchy of Modena and Reggio are less apparent. The small population size produces wide fluctuations in demographic parameters. For this reason, in figure 8.2, we plotted a five-year moving average rate rather than annual figures, while life expectancy estimates and the overall fertility rate have been calculated over ten-year periods. During the nineteenth century, Madregolo had on average 584 inhabitants, reaching its maximum population in 1867 and the minimum in 1803 (Manfredini 1997). The population grew 19.3 percent overall in the period between 1800 and 1883, with a yearly average growth rate of 2.1 per 1,000, much less than the rate observed in the duchy (5.3 per 1,000). This "limited" growth in the population of Madregolo occurred even in the presence of a higher annual mean value for the crude birthrate (39.9 per 1,000) and a lower crude death rate (25.7 per 1,000) compared to the duchy (respectively, 36.5 and 30.1). These results have direct repercussions on the life expectancy at birth and the total fertility rate summarized in table 8.1. These remain higher in Madregolo than in the duchy of Modena and Reggio, respectively: 35.3 years against 33.9 for the life expectancy at birth and 5.6 children per woman against 5.2 for the total fertility rate. Finally, population mobility stands out as the factor limiting the growth of the population of Madregolo, which had a net out-migration rate of about 12 per 1,000.

After the difficulties of the Napoleonic period and the 1816 to 1817 crisis, the population size recovered quickly from 1820 onward. From 1836, the year of a cholera epidemic, to 1844, the population fell by 12.2 percent, mainly due to a particularly negative out-migration rate. From then on, the increase in population size is steady, interrupted only by cholera epidemics in 1854–1855 and 1867.

From 1820 to 1859, before unification, the two regions show similar figures: life expectancy at birth was around 36 years, and the total fertility rate about 5.1. We find the same values in the Tuscan village, while in Madregolo the total fertility rate was slightly higher (5.7) and life expectancy at birth was 38 years, even if the infant mortality rate of the latter is higher than in Casalguidi (220.8 per 1,000 and 200.7 per 1,000, respectively). This might be related to a possible underregistration of adult deaths in Madregolo due to its high rates of mobility.

Figure 8.3 contrasts the overall population trends of Venice and the Veneto region. From 1830 to 1879, they have the same yearly growth rate: 6 per 1,000. However, the city was heavily affected by particular events.[13] In 1849, the cholera epidemic that hit the city during the siege by the Austrian army was responsible for the deaths of 3,839 people in two months, causing a sharp drop in the population. Venice suffered also from other cholera epidemics, especially in 1836, 1855, and 1873, which were responsible for an increase of at least 10 percent in the number of deaths. Moreover, in 1854 and 1861, there were serious outbreaks of measles (Duodo 1874). Despite the negative demographic balance, population growth was sustained by a fairly strong migratory flow, whereas the region as a whole experienced only a modest increase from 1854 to 1864.

Notwithstanding such differences, mortality and fertility trends, summarized in table 8.2, were broadly similar, even though the city was characterized by a persistently higher mortality than the region. This gap became dramatic when demographic crises reached their peaks, especially during the outbreaks of cholera in 1836 and 1849. As for fertility, the Venetian values were systematically lower than those of the region, declining steadily after 1859. Still, at the end of the cen-

Table 8.2
Crude birthrates (CBR) and crude death rates (CDR), Veneto Region, Venice, and Venice sample, 1850–1869

	Veneto Region		Venice		Venice sample	
Period	CBR	CDR	CBR	CDR	CBR	CDR
1850–1854	38.6	32.6	36.6	35.9	38.8	28.5
1855–1859	39.1	33.3	37.2	34.4	37.5	26.9
1860–1864	41.4	32.5	33.9	33.1	34.7	25.2
1865–1869	39.1	29.1	31.7	31.3	25.8	23.3
Total	39.5	31.8	34.8	33.6	33.7	25.8

Source: Authors' unpublished data for Veneto Region, Venice, and Venice sample.

tury, the city appeared as an outlier, characterized by the highest mortality rate (28.3 percent) among the fifty-six districts of the region, including the other major urban districts, like Padua (23.5), Vicenza (23.6), and Verona (23.5); one of the lowest fertility rates (4.78); and one of the highest permanent celibacy rates, with 10.2 percent of women aged 45 to 49 never married (Dalla Zuanna and Loghi 1997, Franzina 1986).

The crude death rate of the population included in our sample was lower than that for the city as a whole, which was computed from municipal statistics. This is hardly surprising. The presence of hospitals and charitable institutions hosting nonurban residents made the number of deaths artificially higher. Since our sample includes only people resident in Venice, our figures are probably closer to the true levels of Venetian population at that time. Furthermore, we should remember that the Jewish community, whose mortality rate was much lower than that of the Catholic community, is overrepresented in the sample.

Data

For our analysis, we rely on different kinds of source materials. For Madregolo and Casalguidi, we use two kinds of parish registers: (1) lists of births (baptisms), deaths (burials), and marriages and (2) the so-called *Status Animarum* (Manfredini 1996), which supplies information about the vital events that took place in the parish.[14] The acts record names and surnames of the people who experienced them and other information concerning paternity and maternity, as well as the date of the event, the age of the individual concerned, and for Casalguidi, information about his or her socioeconomic status. The available series are almost complete. The *Status Animarum* was a sort of census drawn up by the parson each year, usually during the Easter period, for religious purposes. It organized information by household, listing for each household member name, sex, age, marital status, and relationship to the head. It also included servants and seasonal workers temporarily employed outside the village. For Casalguidi, the complete series from 1819 to 1859 is available.[15] For Madregolo, four years are missing: 1840, 1841, 1859, and 1870.[16]

The *Status Animarum* provide information on household composition and, indirectly, on migration. Moreover, they can be combined with information drawn from parish registers.[17] By linking these two sources, we have been able to reconstruct the biography of each person who spent some part of his or her life in the two villages, as well as the household context within which every vital event took place. Unfortunately, according to the nature of *Status Animarum*, which "photographs" the population at a given moment in time, all events that are not recorded in the parish registers, migrations and nonmarital intrahousehold mobility, cannot be dated precisely.

The data used for Venice were taken from the population register known as *Anagrafe*, which was introduced in 1850 by the Austrian administration and kept up-to-date until 1869. The population register works as a kind of dynamic population census from which variations related to both the individuals and the households to which they belonged could be traced over time. For each individual, family and Christian names, nickname, the names of the parents, marital status at entry, religion, age or date and place of birth, duration of stay in Venice, and profession are recorded, as well as eventual changes along time. The addresses where the households dwelled and the dates of moves are also reported (Derosas 1989).

Our data are drawn from three different quarters and are not statistically representative of the whole city. Several reasons led us to collect data for specific areas rather than create a random sample of the city as a whole. First, this made it possible to cross check the information in the population register with that reported in the parish registers of the same areas. A second reason is that in this way, we have been able to include a large section of the Jewish community in our analysis. The Jewish demographic regime had several unusual features that we think can be usefully contrasted with the non-Jewish majority.

The quality and completeness of the information in the population register are far from perfect. By far the most frequent omission concerns neonatal mortality, but other events might also escape registration. For instance, changes in occupation are seldom reported. Some dates are missing or incomplete. By cross-checking the population and parish registers, we have been able to assess the quality of the former as well as to integrate missing or incomplete pieces of information. Other problems concern the actual composition of the households. In particular, servants were never included in the household they were working for. Traditionally, most servants were young women from the countryside around Venice, and their residence in the city was only temporary. Since we cannot be confident of the data concerning servants, we exclude them from the analysis.

Model

The characteristics of the source material led us to use discrete-time models for the study of the two villages and continuous-time models for the city of Venice. For the villages, we used complementary log-log regression; thus, the nature of the estimates differed slightly. In spite of these differences, the coefficients and associated risk ratios are broadly comparable.

The main difference between our models and the Eurasian standard comparative models is in the first twenty-four months of life.[18] We split this age group, separating the first from the second year of life, in order to analyze in detail the effect of seasons, the main issue of this chapter, on the survival of infants, paying particular attention to the breast-feeding period. This reorganization of age groups implied a different use of some of the variables. We include the presence of both parents in the model for children from 12 to 23 months and consider the effects of presence of father from only 0 to 11 months, since the death of the mother in this phase of life almost always led to the death of the child. Similarly, we include mother's age at birth and previous birth interval only when analyzing infants aged 0 to 11 months since these variables are important largely in the first phase of life.[19]

We also included specific variables measuring aspects of household structure in the analyses of the first two years of life. In order to identify eventual protective or competitive mechanisms deriving from the presence of specific household members, we used modifications of the variables in the standard comparative models. In particular, we examine the effects of the presence of brothers aged 8 or more years old, younger siblings, and unmarried or widowed women aged 15 or more years. The last aims to capture possible protective effects deriving from the help and care that some female members could provide, in some cases substituting for the mother.[20]

Table 8.3 provides a complete list of the variables in the analyses for the different age groups, along with their means. In addition to including many of the variables from the standard comparative models, we added some new ones reflecting characteristics of our sources and the Italian context. We included variables in different age groups to evaluate the role of climate. For the analyses of infants, we adopted a variable for the season of observation since the monthly nature analysis allowed it. This was not possible for the other age groups, whose temporal unit, in discrete-time analyses, was the year. An exception was Casalguidi: since data about mean seasonal values of temperatures were available (Alfani 1920), we used this information to check the influence of particularly hot or cold seasons on the survival of adults.[21]

Another difference between our models and the Eurasia standard comparative models is that we did not estimate different models for males and females and never-married and ever-married individuals. Rather, we took these factors into account simply by introducing the respective variables in the models. This different way of dealing with such data is related to the necessity of increasing the number of observations, especially in the case of Madregolo, in order to make results more reliable.

Results

We organize our discussion of the results from these models, summarized in Tables 8.4 to 8.8, into five sections. The first focuses on biodemographic features of individuals, basically age, at both the household and communal levels. The second focuses on environmental influences, which in this study are considered essentially in terms of seasons. The third is the capacity to respond, and withstand, specific restrictions of nature. This capacity was estimated with respect to the social and economic level of the individuals in the rural village of Casalguidi and with respect to the separation between the Catholic and Jewish population for the three demographic settlements of Venice. This last element allows for the evaluation of the influence of cultural factors in conditioning the risk of individuals' deaths. The fourth

Table 8.3
Means of the variables in the analyses

Variables	Casalguidi (1819–1859)					Madregolo (1800–1883)					Venice (1850–1869)				
	0	1	2–14	15–54	55–74	0	1	2–14	15–54	55–74	0	1	2–14	15–54	55–74
Age (Ref.: 0 months)	9.5					9.5									
1–4 months	34.1					33.8									
5–11 months	56.4					56.7									
Age (Ref.: 16–23 months)		64.3					64.9								
12–15 months		35.7					35.1								
Age (Ref.: 10–14 years)			36.8					32.6							
2–4 years			24.2					28.0							
5–9 years			39.0					39.4							
Age (Ref.: 45–54 years)				18.2					17.8						
15–24 years				32.4					31.4						
25–34 years				27.4					27.9						
35–44 years				22.0					22.9						
Age (Ref.: 65–74 years)					34.6					32.7					
55–64 years					65.4					67.3					
Sex (Ref.: male)	50.3	51.9	50.7	49.9	50.3	51.1	52.5	50.5	51.3	55.6	51.4	51.1	50.7	48.9	49.6
Female	49.7	48.1	49.3	50.1	49.7	48.9	47.5	49.5	48.7	44.4	48.6	48.9	49.3	51.1	50.4
Mother's age at birth (Ref.: 25–29 years)	28.3					30.8					21.6				
25 years or under	16.5					20.4					18.3				
30–34 years	27.7					24.4					21.3				
35 years or more	27.5					24.5					37.9				
Unknown											0.8				

P.B.I. (Ref.: 24 months or more or firstborn)	63.8		53.9		45.5	
Less than 24 months; infant is dead	9.9		11.8		20.5	
Less than 24 months; infant is alive	19.6		21.2		25.5	
Unknown	6.8		13.1		8.5	
Presence of father (Ref.: Present)	99.4		99.6		96.5	
Absent	0.6		0.4		3.5	
Presence of parents (Ref.: Both present)	97.8	82.7	98.3	89.4	94.8	89.1
Only father present	0.9	3.7	0.7	5.3	1.6	3.5
Only mother present	1.3	6.9	1.0	5.3	3.2	6.2
Both absent	—	6.7	—	—	0.4	1.2
Brother aged 8 years or more (Ref.: Absent)	77.3	78.2	78.3	75.1	75.1	71.0
Present	22.7	21.8	21.7	24.9	24.9	29.0
Younger sibling (Ref.: Absent)	93.0		90.9		86.3	
Present	7.0		9.1		13.7	
Unmarried women 15 years or more (Ref.: Absent)	56.5	58.2	56.9	56.7	75.6	77.1
Present	43.5	41.8	43.1	43.3	24.4	22.9

Table 8.3
(continued)

Variables	Casalguidi (1819–1859)					Madregolo (1800–1883)					Venice (1850–1869)				
	0	1	2–14	15–54	55–74	0	1	2–14	15–54	55–74	0	1	2–14	15–54	55–74
Dependency ratio *(Ref.: Normal)*			55.8	82.8	60.8			58.7	82.6	60.1			60.7	84.3	66.2
High dependency			44.2	17.2	39.2			41.3	17.4	39.9			39.3	15.7	33.8
Season of observation *(Ref.: Winter)*	25.2	24.5				25.0	24.4				25.6	25.1			
Spring	25.2	25.3				25.1	25.2				24.9	24.5			
Summer	24.9	25.8				25.0	25.6				26.3	27.0			
Autumn	24.8	24.4				24.9	24.8				23.3	23.4			
Winter temperature *(Ref.: Normal)*			94.9	94.9	95.1										
Very cold			5.1	5.1	4.9										
Summer temperature *(Ref.: Normal)*			96.6	95.7	96.4										
Very hot			3.4	4.3	3.6										
Marital status (Ref.: Currently married)				50.7	59.8				61.3	65.0				38.1	60.6
Unmarried				45.4	9.6				35.0	5.9				58.5	6.2
Widowed				3.9	30.6				3.7	29.2				3.4	33.2

Occupation (Ref.: Day laborer)										
Sharecropper/farmer in general	69.4	68.8	67.1	67.1	67.8	38.5	36.2	33.6	31.3	34.0
Wage earner	14.0	13.4	13.7	13.4	12.3	29.9	31.1	32.5	36.0	28.1
Artisan	13.2	14.1	14.0	14.5	14.8	23.9	24.8	24.8	21.9	22.3
Noble/rich landowner	3.4	3.7	5.2	4.9	5.1	6.8	7.2	8.0	9.0	10.9
Profession unknown						0.8	0.8	1.2	1.8	4.8
Wheat price (logged)	3.1	3.1	3.1	3.0	3.0	2.8	2.8	2.8	2.8	2.8
Religion (Ref.: Catholic)						89.2	88.9	87.1	88.9	90.0
Jew	3.1	3.1	3.1	3.1	3.1	10.8	11.1	12.9	11.1	10.0

Table 8.4
Estimated relative risks of mortality for the three populations: Infants, aged 0–11 months

	Relative risk		
	Casalguidi (1819–1859)	Madregolo (1800–1883)	Venice (1850–1869)
Age in months (Ref.: 0)			
1–4	0.112**	0.053**	—
5–11	0.080**	0.057**	—
Season of observation (Ref.: Winter)			
Spring	0.539**	0.533**	0.820*
Summer	0.390**	0.231**	0.627**
Autumn	0.670*	0.415**	0.702**
Interaction age × season			
1–4 months × spring	2.240**	2.298*	—
1–4 months × summer	2.523**	2.812*	—
1–4 months × autumn	1.547	2.432*	—
5–11 months × spring	1.294	1.301	—
5–11 months × summer	6.357**	4.388**	—
5–11 months × autumn	1.950*	2.031*	—
Sex (Ref.: male)			
Female	0.953	0.901	0.877*
Mother's age at birth (Ref.: 25–29 years)			
25 years or below	0.855	1.297	0.884
30–34 years	1.048	0.811	0.956
35 years or more	1.505**	0.978	1.154
Unknown	—	—	1.796*
Previous birth interval (Ref.: 24 months or more or firstborn)			
Less than 24 months; infant is dead	1.109	0.824	1.529**
Less than 24 months; infant is alive	1.278*	1.106	1.083
Unknown	1.055	1.162	0.758
Presence of the father (Ref.: Present)			
Father absent	0.906	0.674	1.216
Brother aged 8 or more years (Ref.: Absent)			
Present	0.949	1.433*	1.078
Presence of unmarried women 15 years or more (Ref.: Absent)			
Present	0.978	0.826	0.962

Table 8.4
(continued)

	Relative risk		
	Casalguidi (1819–1859)	Madregolo (1800–1883)	Venice (1850–1869)
Father's occupation (Ref.: Day laborer)			
Sharecropper/farmer in general	0.734**	—	—
Artisan	0.984	—	0.751**
Wage earner	—	—	0.824*
Middle class/landowner	0.800	—	0.656**
Profession unknown	—	—	0.869
Religion (Ref.: Catholic)			
Jew			0.449**
Wheat price (10% increase)	1.047	1.069	1.123
Person-years	3,073.3	1,429.8	3,135.3
Number of deaths	628	284	1,002
Degrees of freedom	25	22	20
Log-likelihood	−2,945.3	−1,260.6	−6,746.2

Note: For Casalguidi and Madregolo, results are from a discrete-time event-history analysis using complementary log-log regression. For Venice, results are from a continuous-time event-history analysis using Cox regression.
*Statistical significance at the 5 percent level; **statistical significance at the 1 percent level.

focuses on the family. The dimensions and characteristics of the family, the presence or absence of central figures in this elementary cell of production and consumption, and the internal structure and organization: all these were factors that could influence mortality in many complex ways. In the last section, we consider interactions among all of these factors.

Biological Factors

The expected role of individual biological characteristics, basically sex and age, will be discussed in the comparative chapters, particularly that on gender. We would nevertheless like to point out the interaction between sex and marital status that we included in the analysis of adults and the elderly. The results identify a higher and significant risk of dying for married women between 15 and 54 years in the two rural villages. While the risks associated with childbirth may have

Table 8.5
Estimated relative risks of mortality for the three populations: Infants, aged 12–23 months

	Relative risk		
	Casalguidi (1819–1859)	Madregolo (1800–1883)	Venice (1850–1869)
Age in months (Ref.: 12–15)			
16–23	0.641	2.461	—
Season of observation (Ref.: Winter)			
Spring	0.521	1.886	0.748
Summer	5.183**	4.022*	1.674**
Autumn	3.493**	2.194	1.166
Interaction age × season			
16–23 months × spring	2.208	0.333	—
16–23 months × summer	0.867	0.304*	—
16–23 months × autumn	0.845	0.749	—
Sex (Ref.: Male)			
Female	1.057	1.191	0.940
Presence of parents (Ref.: Both parents present)			
Only father present	2.147	2.008	1.712
Only mother present	0.467	1.255	0.926
Both absent	—	—	0.650
Brother aged 8 or more years (Ref.: Absent)			
Present	0.894	0.955	0.828
Younger sibling (Ref.: Absent)			
Present	0.709	1.937**	1.094
Presence of unmarried women 15 or more years (Ref.: Absent)			
Present	0.764*	0.774*	1.029
Father's occupation (Ref.: Day laborer)			
Sharecropper/farmer in general	0.672**	—	—
Artisan	0.836	—	0.784
Wage earner	—	—	0.664**
Middle class/landowner	0.230**	—	0.573*
Profession unknown	—	—	1.243
Religion (Ref.: Catholic)			
Jew	—	—	0.503**
Wheat price (10% increase)	1.099**	1.026	1.053**
Person-years	1,896.7	1,052.9	2,661.6
Number of deaths	361	149	398
Degrees of freedom	17	14	16
Log-likelihood	−1,731.2	−792.8	−3,087.6

Note: For Casalguidi and Madregolo, results are from a discrete-time event-history analysis using complementary log-log regression. For Venice, results are from a continuous-time event-history analysis using Cox regression.
*Statistical significance at the 5 percent level; **statistical significance at the 1 percent level.

Table 8.6
Estimated relative risks of mortality for the three populations: Children, aged 2–14 years

	Relative risk		
	Casalguidi (1819–1859)	Madregolo (1800–1883)	Venice (1850–1869)
Age in years (Ref.: 10–14)			
2–4	11.199**	9.879**	—
5–9	1.851**	1.601	—
Sex (Ref.: Male)			
Female	1.278*	1.049	0.907
Presence of parents (Ref.: Both parents present)			
Only father present	1.028	1.485	1.290
Only mother present	0.689	2.297**	0.915
Both absent	4.185**	—	1.365
Dependency ratio (Ref.: Normal)			
High dependency	1.163	0.872	0.883
Father's occupation (Ref.: Day laborer)			
Sharecropper/farmer in general	0.961	—	—
Artisan	1.617*	—	0.801*
Wage earner	—	—	0.787
Middle class/rich landowner	0.846	—	0.386**
Profession unknown	—	—	0.686
Religion (Ref.: Catholic)			
Jew	—	—	0.595*
Winter temperature (Ref.: Normal)			
Very cold	0.633	—	—
Summer temperature (Ref.: Normal)			
Very hot	0.688	—	—
Wheat price (10% increase)	1.151**	1.089**	1.013
Person-years	26,709	11,319	25,767.3
Number of deaths	335	167	407
Degrees of freedom	13	7	11
Log-likelihood	−1,590.4	−786.4	−3,145.7

Note: For Casalguidi and Madregolo, results are from a discrete-time event-history analysis using complementary log-log regression. For Venice, results are from a continuous-time event-history analysis using Cox regression.
*Statistical significance at the 5 percent level; **statistical significance at the 1 percent level.

Table 8.7
Estimated relative risks of mortality for the three populations: Adults, aged 15–54 years

	Relative risk		
	Casalguidi (1819–1859)	Madregolo (1800–1883)	Venice (1850–1869)
Age in years (Ref.: 45–54)			
15–24	0.313**	0.268**	—
25–34	0.573**	0.426**	—
35–44	0.654**	0.476**	—
Sex (Ref.: Male)			
Female	1.388**	1.508*	1.099
Marital status (Ref.: Married)			
Unmarried	1.074	0.999	0.895
Widowed	1.521	1.415	1.155
Female × unmarried	0.720	0.921	0.950
Female × widowed	0.430*	0.837	0.833
Dependency ratio (Ref.: Normal)			
High dependency	1.121	0.763	0.933
Profession of head or himself (Ref.: Day laborer)			
Sharecropper/farmer in general	0.890	—	—
Artisan	1.010	—	0.961
Wage earner	—	—	0.917
Middle class/landowner	0.963	—	1.035
Profession unknown	—	—	1.061
Winter temperature (Ref.: Normal)			
Very cold	0.998	—	—
Summer temperature (Ref.: Normal)			
Very hot	0.654	—	—
Religion (Ref.: Catholic)			
Jew	—	—	0.763
Wheat price (logged)	1.151**	1.103**	1.028*
Person-years	53,684	24,624	69,358.9
Number of deaths	524	181	524
Degrees of freedom	15	10	12
Log-likelihood	−2,875.8	−1,030.0	−3,895.0

Note: For Casalguidi and Madregolo, results are from a discrete-time event-history analysis using complementary log-log regression. For Venice, results are from a continuous-time event-history analysis using Cox regression.
*Statistical significance at the 5 percent level; **statistical significance at the 1 percent level.

Table 8.8
Estimated relative risks of mortality for the three populations: Elderly, aged 55–74 years

| | Relative risk | | |
	Casalguidi (1819–1859)	Madregolo (1800–1883)	Venice (1850–1869)
Age in years (Ref.: 65–74)			
55–64	0.457**	0.321**	—
Sex (Ref.: Male)			
Female	1.006	0.883	0.878
Marital status (Ref.: Married)			
Unmarried	1.244	0.711	1.087
Widowed	0.998	0.760	1.403
Female × unmarried	0.932	1.316	0.951
Female × widowed	0.754	1.365	0.867
Dependency ratio (Ref.: Normal)			
High dependency	1.020	1.207	0.934
Profession of head or himself (Ref.: Day laborer)			
Sharecropper/farmer in general	0.949	—	—
Artisan	1.132	—	0.861
Wage earner	—	—	0.752*
Middle class/landowner	0.763	—	0.991
Profession unknown	—	—	0.711
Winter temperature (Ref.: Normal)			
Very cold	0.992	—	—
Summer temperature (Ref.: Normal)			
Very hot	1.971**	—	—
Religion (Ref.: Catholic)			
Jew	—	—	0.917
Wheat price (10% increase)	1.050	1.071*	1.072**
Person-years	10,860	4,403	13,136.7
Number of deaths	448	152	367
Degrees of freedom	13	8	12
Log-likelihood	−1,824.8	−633.0	−2,339.6

Note: For Casalguidi and Madregolo, results are from a discrete-time event-history analysis using complementary log-log regression. For Venice, results are from a continuous-time event-history analysis using Cox regression.
*Statistical significance at the 5 percent level; **statistical significance at the 1 percent level.

accounted for some of this excess, results in chapter 11, on gender, suggest the picture was more complex.

Season

Seasonal variation in mortality risks was pronounced. As expected, table 8.4 reveals that the winter season is responsible for a noticeable increase in the risk of death during the first month of life.[22] Those born in summer show a definite and significant lower risk—even 70 to 80 percent—in the two rural communities. According to table 8.5, however, summer was a dangerous time for children in the second year of life, most likely because they had been weaned. Although the adverse effects associated with the hot season became apparent even as early as 5 months, the most pronounced effects were in the first months of the second year of life, when breast-feeding was normally just finished. In this phase of life, the risk associated with the hot season is four to five times that of winter.

In Venice, the winter carries a clear increase in the risk of death. Its impact, however, is most apparent in the first months of life and less apparent afterward. Similarly, the higher coefficient associated with the weaning period during summer is reduced as well. Indeed, the summer proved to be less risky than the winter. Elsewhere, we have demonstrated that the situation in Venice was wholly similar to that described for Madregolo and Casalguidi (Breschi, Derosas, and Manfredini 2000; Derosas 1999). More precisely, winters were especially dangerous only during the first month of life. From the second to the sixth month, seasons had no significant effects on mortality. Summers became extremely dangerous during the second semester of life. From the second to the fifth year, it was the turn of spring to be associated with higher mortality, reflecting the prevalence of the infectious diseases typical of adolescence.

We also examined the effects of climatic conditions on the health of adult people. For Venice, again we used the season as a proxy. Interestingly enough, winters were quite dangerous for old people, almost doubling their relative risk of dying in comparison with summer and fall. The observations by Howells quoted previously are clearly confirmed: in Venice, people found the relative cost of heating their houses prohibitive. The result was that the weakest, such as the newborn and the elderly, who were obliged to stay at home, easily became sick.

For Casalguidi, we were obliged to follow a different approach. The results for the temperature variable in tables 8.6 through 8.8 demonstrate that very cold winters, unlike very hot summers, did not significantly affect any adult age group. In the years characterized by particularly hot summers, the risk of death rises significantly among elderly people, becoming more than two times higher than in the periods with typical summer conditions. This probably reflects the increase in illnesses related to the digestive system and to the presence of ecological-environmental factors that favor the development of infectious diseases.[23]

It is clear that the ability to defend oneself against the effects of climate, above all during the cold season, is directly related to the availability of the necessary economic means to provide adequate defense: heating, suitable clothing, adequate nutrition, and hygiene. During the nineteenth century, these conditions were not yet available for most of the Italian population, even if the upper classes were probably able to protect themselves from climate harshness.

In order to verify this hypothesis, we run separate and much reduced models, stratified by season of observation, for the first two years of life in table 8.9. The main conclusion from the analyses is the dichotomy between city and countryside. In the countryside, the winter hit all social groups without distinction, while in Venice, the upper class experienced a reduction in the risk of infant death. It is possible to argue that the chances to protect themselves from the cold in the countryside did not differ much between the lower and upper classes. The possibility for farmers to find shelter in the cattle shed during winter may represent a partial explanation for this behavior, as well as the absence of heating even in the houses of the upper class. In Venice, the situation seems different, and day laborers were the most exposed to the rigors of winter.

In contrast, profession seems to play a more important role during summer in the countryside than in the city. The reason would seem clearer in this last case, and it is plausibly connected to the rhythm of work of farm laborers. This category shows an increased risk mainly during summer, during and after weaning, the second year of life. For all the other social categories, the risk of dying during hot seasons was much lower: farmers and other well-off people were 40 to 80 percent less likely to die. We can therefore assume that during that particular period, the laborers' wives had to return immediately to work in order to contribute to the meager income of their husbands, thereby causing

Table 8.9
Estimated relative risks of dying in the first two years of life according to season and father's occupation, Casalguidi (1819–1859) and Venice (1850–1869)

| | Summer | | | | Winter | | | |
| | Casalguidi | | Venice | | Casalguidi | | Venice | |
Variables	0–11 months	12–23 months	0–11 months	12–23 months	0–11 months	12–23 months	0–11 months	12–23 months
Age in months (Ref.: 0)								
1–4	0.234**				0.096**			
5–11	0.412**				0.069**			
Age in months (Ref.: 12–15)								
16–23		0.548**				0.628**		
Father's occupation (Ref.: Day laborer)								
Sharecropper/farmer in general	0.718*	0.599**			0.808	1.075		
Wage earner	0.698	0.855	0.974	0.758	1.028	0.764	0.773	0.544*
Artisan			0.700	0.774		—	0.654**	0.703
Middle class/landowner	0.594	0.197*	0.683	0.780	0.956		0.352**	0.648
Person-years	766.1	497.3			774.6	472.9		
Number of deaths	180	182	215	146	187	37	306	81
Degrees of freedom	5	4	3	3	5	4	3	3
Log-likelihood	−868.0	−800.2	−1,404.6	−958.3	−785.5	−220.5	−1,717.3	−525.3

Note: For Casalguidi, results are from a discrete-time event-history analysis using complementary log-log regression. For Venice, results are from a continuous-time event-history analysis using Cox regression.
*Statistical significance at the 5 percent level; **statistical significance at the 1 percent level.

a decrease in the amount of care and attention devoted to their children. The fact that nearly all laborers had nuclear families increased the problems securing child care, for nobody else was available to look after children.

Socioeconomic Factors

The social and economic status of a family has been classified, as usual, in relationship to occupation. The lowest social class, day laborers, has been adopted as the reference category. In the rural context, this includes all those peasant professions that did not take part in the sharing of harvest, such as daily and paid laborers, plus very poor people, such as beggars, especially in Venice. The category of artisan includes all nonfarmers' occupations, which are sometimes at a lower social level than sharecroppers and tenants, the other peasant category. Finally, the upper class includes landowners as well as smallholders in the countryside and bourgeois and middle-class individuals in Venice.

Our analysis shows that household socioeconomic status is important above all for the younger age group (table 8.4) and becomes fundamental in the early years of life (tables 8.5 and 8.6). This holds true as much for Casalguidi as for Venice, despite the great social, economic, and environmental differences. In both cases, the relative risks follow precisely the social hierarchy. In Casalguidi, the children of farm laborers are subject to a higher risk of infant mortality than their peers in other occupational categories, in particular sharecroppers and the well-to-do, which present lower risks in both the first and second years of life. This is particularly true between 12 and 23 months of life, a period in which endogenous and genetic causes of death play a less important role: sharecroppers and the middle class had, respectively, 33 percent and 77 percent lower risks of death. In Venice, meanwhile, the day laborers are the social group whose children were the most likely to die, while among the other classes, the differences are minimal (table 8.5). The distinction between poorer and better-off classes becomes greater for children between ages 2 and 14, in which the risk of death of a member of the middle class is one-third of a child of a day laborer (table 8.6).

In Casalguidi, the children of craftsmen are, unexpectedly, disadvantaged. This result is not easily interpreted and should perhaps be considered in the light of the fact that the wives of the craftsmen were employed in activities such as weaving and straw hat making. Also,

the families of the craftsmen lived in the town center and were probably more exposed to possible contagious diseases. This model remains
broadly unaltered for all the other age groups, even if the results lose
statistical significance. Nevertheless, it is not only the social differences
that determine different mortality risks.

Social conditions being equal, other more generally cultural factors
could increase or diminish the risk of mortality as they influenced
behaviors noticeably. This fact emerges clearly considering the position
of the Jewish population within the Venice sample. Acting as fore-
runners of behaviors that were to spread later among the rest of the
population, the Jews adopted a lifestyle and were carriers of cultural
models that had a strong impact on mortality. Among the possible
reasons, we can suggest diet, hygiene, and habits: hand washing and
ritual bathing for women, attention to children, a higher level of education, an open and modern approach to medical science, the importance of mutual help, and the presence of a developed system of
welfare and assistance institutions (Derosas 2000).[24] All this was reflected in a risk of mortality that was less than half that of the Catholic
population in the first two years of life (tables 8.4 and 8.5) and about
60 percent in the 2- to 14-year age range (table 8.6). These factors cease
to be important in the adult and old-age groups (tables 8.7 and 8.8).
Here, indeed, other elements intervene to influence the probability of
survival more greatly. This is nevertheless extremely interesting, even
though expected, for it clearly indicates that the key to reducing infant
and adolescent mortality lies primarily in changes in lifestyle rather
than a modification of economic conditions.

Family Context

There is no doubt that, at least in Italy, the family represents the
main environment in which the individual's life and relationships take
place. Thus, the family also became a source of defense and protection
against external processes and events. Within the family, the hierarchy
and roles were rigidly defined. The head of the family, usually a male,
dealt with the allocation of resources among members, though there
were notable differences between the city and the countryside.[25]

In the rural countryside, the way farms were run affected the dimensions and structure of the family, with the tenants and sharecroppers
usually living in complex family structures and the laborers in nuclear
families (Barbagli 1984, Viazzo and Dionigi 1992). The first group

needed a sufficient number of hands to cultivate the holding and to ensure, by the permanent presence of male children, the continuation of the lease contract for the land (Cazzola 1996, Giorgetti 1974, Poni 1982). The laborers could not afford complex or numerous families, as they had to move frequently in search of work. The family organization of laborers and tenants required, however, that the son, if married, remain within the family, thus giving origin to a patrilocal type of marriage (Barbagli 1984, 1990). In the city, the dimensions of the dwellings, the greater costs of children, and the possibility of turning to charity organizations for assistance if needed led inevitably to more streamlined families than those of the countryside. Family organization in Venice is certainly different from and less complex than that in Madregolo and Casalguidi. The average size is decidedly smaller, 3.5 members instead of the 5.7 and 5.2 in Madregolo and Casalguidi, respectively, and the structure is noticeably different. Only 4 percent of the families in Venice were multiple, while this type represented over 21 percent in Madregolo and 16 percent in Casalguidi. Multiple-family households were common in Italy, above all in agricultural areas characterized by sharecropping, precisely as in the case of the rural areas of Tuscany and Emilia. The presence of single people was another distinctive characteristic of Venice city: in Venice, there were four times as many single people as in rural areas.

In a previous study (Breschi et al., 1999), we found that household structure was a determinant of the survival of children in the rural context, in particular for those living in complex families, extended or multiple. It is evident that the richness of relationships within these domestic groups, and the possibility of mutual help offered between the components, represented a flexible structure even in the most difficult situations. Here, we aimed to specify more precisely the household structure, taking into account, on one hand, the ratio between consumers and producers within each family group, and, on the other hand, the presence of some specific members (table 8.3). Regardless of the structure of the family, some of its members could have different influences on the welfare of the others. Once more, this is especially true for children, who were obviously in the most delicate position. From this point of view, it is quite interesting to note that the presence of unmarried or widowed women aged 15 or more years reduced risks in infancy and especially in the second year of life (tables 8.4 and 8.5). The period during and just after weaning is the most at risk for exogenous causes of death, when care and help are particularly required.

Female figures might have helped the mother in carrying out some duties as well as in taking care of the baby. This protective effect is even more interesting given that the presence of older brothers aged 8 years or more does not have a consistent effect, except in Madregolo, where it had an adverse effect in the first year of life of the index child. The rigid labor division between men and women in rural households could therefore play a fundamental role even in the survival of children.

The significant negative effects induced at Madregolo by the presence of older brothers (on newborn children) or younger sibling (on children in their second year of life) are hardly explainable, although they might entail a strong competition among children. In the poor Emilian community, the struggle for care, attention, and resources within the household could reach levels not common in the other two communities.

While a child benefited indirectly from support offered to his or her mother, his or her position could worsen dramatically in the case of a new birth. Indeed, the mother finds herself in a very difficult situation, under pressure to care for both babies. Our analyses, however, do not reveal a distinct pattern. As for the global and synthetic indicator of household age composition, the dependency ratio, no significant results emerged from our analyses. The explanatory power of this factor is very limited in all the age brackets examined (tables 8.4 and 8.5). More precise indicators are probably needed to evaluate this aspect better.

Crisis

All the aspects previously described (biological, familial, and social) had an important role in the struggle for survival. The relevance of these factors could be heightened or attenuated in moments of economic, epidemic, or family crisis. First, the economy could be affected by social or political problems, much in the way as agriculture could be affected by the weather, such as a drought or flooding. We examined the influence of economic factors through the use of the price of wheat as an indicator of relative hardship.[26]

Figure 8.4 shows the movements of the mean annual values of the price of wheat in markets close to the areas studied.[27] There emerges a constant feature from the data despite the geographical distance separating the markets. In particular, there was a sharp rise in wheat prices

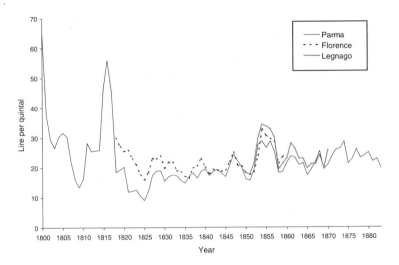

Figure 8.4
Price of wheat, Parma, 1800–1883; Florence, 1819–1859; Legnago, 1850–1869

during the cholera epidemic of 1854–1855 and a less marked rise in 1861, the year of Italy's unification. In Parma and Florence, price changes kept a similar relationship throughout the period. It is interesting to observe, in the case of the Parma market, the sharp and sudden increase in wheat prices during both the 1816–1817 crisis and in the early period of Napoleon's dominion (1800–1805).

Recent studies of Tuscany and Friuli have already demonstrated how the level and fluctuations of prices significantly influence mortality rates, above all in the young and old age groups but not in the infant group (Breschi and Gonano 1998, Gonano 2000). Our analyses broadly confirm these macrolevel results. Among infants, prices do not seem to determine any significant differences in mortality risk in all the three communities studied. The result confirms, on the one hand, the expected role of protection represented by the breast-feeding period, at least in the first year of life, and, on the other hand, the impossibility of further large increases in infant mortality, which was already high in "normal" periods.

As for the remaining age groups, we found evidence of a large and diffuse impact of wheat prices on the risk of death. After the second year of life, price increases reduced the survival chances of individuals. Children and adults are at the most at risk in the rural villages: a 10 percent increase in wheat prices caused an 8 to 10 percent increase in mortality in Madregolo and around 15 percent in Casalguidi, as shown in tables 8.6 and 8.7. In Venice, the elderly were apparently the most exposed to the consequences of price rises. An increase of 10 percent in wheat price implied an increase of 7 percent in the mortality of the old-age group, as shown in table 8.8.

These results must be interpreted very carefully. The coincidence of viral epidemics and rising prices was a common phenomenon in the past, making it difficult to evaluate the specific effect of economic conditions on mortality rates. This study is even more difficult in the absence of any indication about the causes of death, which is the case for Casalguidi and Madregolo. Nevertheless, it is possible with some certainty, and for some specific epidemics, to determine their endogenous origins and the cause-and-effect relationship between rising prices and epidemics. The typhus epidemic of 1817 (whose data are here available only for Madregolo) is a well-known example. It represented without a doubt the conclusive act of a dramatic chain of bad harvests, wars, and political instability that gave origin to rising prices and consequent famine. For these reasons, the typhus of 1817 is regarded as the last subsistence crisis in the Italian population history.

In Casalguidi and Venice, price increases also preceded epidemics. From the few data we have about mean monthly prices in Casalguidi, it would seem that even there, the price rise (peaking in April 1854) preceded the great cholera epidemic, which peaked in August 1855, with fifty-one deaths. The same phenomenon is partially recognizable in Venice for the cholera epidemic of 1855. The price crisis started in July 1853 and lasted until June 1857, while the cholera epidemic became particularly virulent only in May and June 1855. Moreover, the cholera outbreak was preceded and accompanied by a violent crisis in infant and child mortality, raising the infant mortality rate to 444 per 1,000 in 1854 and finally 577 per 1,000 in 1855 in the two parishes of our sample (Derosas 1999).

Even with these clarifications on a possible cause-and-effect relationship, we are not able to distinguish the independent contributions of price increases and epidemics of cholera and typhus to the increased mortality level in, respectively, 1855 and 1817. In the case of Casalguidi, the analysis is even more difficult because the period concerned is quite short, and the mortality crisis (1854–1855) occurred on the occasion of both the last great cholera epidemic and by far the most relevant rise in prices of the period studied. We estimated an exploratory model for the entire population 2 to 74 years of Casalguidi to test the possible interrelationship between wheat price and cholera epidemic. First, we constructed a model with the sole price variable included: the result is a very high and significant relative risk: a 10 percent increase in prices caused an 11.4 percent increase in mortality. Successively, we added a dummy variable for the years of the cholera epidemic. The effect of price on mortality is now much more limited, around 5.4 percent. Therefore, in such particular cases and in the absence of any indication about causes of death, it is quite difficult to distinguish the separate impact of price and epidemics on mortality risks. Economic factors surely triggered epidemics, and even during the crises, bad harvests and unavailability of resources could induce an increase in the risk of dying, but once the epidemic spread out, its direct influence on the mortality pattern is not entirely clear.

Aware of these problems, we assumed anyway that some social groups were better equipped to defend themselves in the face of sweeping economic crises and reduce the risks caused by these events. This relationship has already been commented on and tested in the Eurasian standard models by interacting occupation and wheat price levels (see chapters 3 and 5). But in our case, the adoption of the profession as proxy for the socioeconomic status of families and individuals presents some limits. The most evident is that for some important social categories, the definition and classification of profession is particularly difficult due to the vagueness of the entry in the registers. A useful example is the category of farmer: it is clearly too general and imprecise a classification to clarify the real economic status of the peasant family. To avoid such problems, information concerning the ownership of the house has been taken into account. It represents a better proxy, since it is a real discriminant factor between well-off people and the rest of the population: sharecroppers and farm laborers rarely owned the house in which they lived, while the large majority of landowners did. Unfortunately, these data are available only for Casalguidi. However, by means of a very reduced model, which involves the age groups more sensitive to price variations (2–74 years), it is possible in table 8.10 to prove how protective was the effect induced by house ownership. A 10 percent rise in price seems to affect nonowners much more than owners, causing a 12 percent increase in the risk of death among the former against "only" a nonsignificant 4 percent among the latter.

An especially stressful moment in families occurs on the death of one of the parents.[28] In these situations, children, especially the very

Table 8.10
Effects of home ownership and wheat prices on relative risks of dying, ages 2–74 years, Casalguidi, 1819–1859

Variables	Relative risk
Property of the house (Ref.: Owner)	
Nonowner	0.098*
Wheat price (10% increase)	1.045
Nonowner × 10% increase in price	1.073*
Total effects of prices on mortality 2–74 years by property of the house	%
Owner	1.045
Nonowner	1.121*
Person-years	91,253
Number of deaths	1,307
Degrees of freedom	3
Log-likelihood	−7,407.4

*Statistically significant at the 5 percent level.

young, suffer the most consequences. There is no doubt about the dramatic effects of the mother's death on the survival of infants (0–11 months) for they depend on her milk, but it should not be undervalued that due to the care and attention children needed even after weaning, older children also suffered from her loss. The absence of the mother leads to a noticeable increase in the risk of dying in the second year of life in all the three populations considered, though not statistically significant.

Even the loss, or simply the absence, of the father could bring severe economic hardships for the family. This problem should particularly affect those children no longer dependent on the mother for food.[29] Our results do not suggest a clear or uniform pattern of responses. While the death of the father, as expected, had little effect on the survival of infants, it caused a significant increase in the risk of death among adolescents in Madregolo (more than double compared to those who had both parents alive). Casalguidi and Venice do not seem to respond in the same way. In an earlier work on Casalguidi (Breschi and Manfredini 1998b), we demonstrated how this behavior depended on a differential migration of children who lost their fathers from those losing mothers, which led to their being less looked after. In these situations of stress, the complex family seemed to maintain its protective effect on the child's chances of survival and indeed increased its importance.

In a study dealing with family mobility in Casalguidi (Manfredini forthcoming), we observed that the death of the father, when he was also head of family, not only affected the children's survival possibilities, but also caused an immediate increase in stress within the family. This often spurred the family to emigrate from the village, to either the wife's family of origin or the city, a place better equipped to provide assistance for families in need.

Conclusions

In this chapter we have focused on the effects of climate, social disparity, and economic stress on mortality at different ages. In pretransitional demographic regimes, these factors played a major role in determining dramatic discriminations in health and mortality outcomes within as well as between populations. Though their origin was different, they interacted with each other, cumulating their negative effects. Not only social inequalities were themselves a remarkable factor of differentiation; they also sharpened the impact of adverse climatic and environmental conditions and of negative economic conjunctures. Those sectors of society that were more exposed to unhealthy conditions and characterized by greater frailty were less likely to succeed in improving their standards of living and experience a process of upward social mobility. However, individuals sharing the same socioeconomic and environmental conditions were not affected in the same way. Infants and children and the elderly suffered more from adverse conditions, while nonelderly adults were relatively immune. The buffers offered by the household to its weakest members could provide only a partial shelter from external constraints.

We examined two rural areas in northern and central Italy and a sample of the urban population of Venice during different periods of the nineteenth century. Although these communities experienced remarkable differences from the environmental point of view as well as in socioeconomic organization, we found interesting, if somewhat unexpected, regularities in their response to the major factors differentiating mortality outcomes. In both the urban and the rural areas, social cleavage was mirrored by strong mortality differentials in the first and the last stages of life. A clear seasonal pattern of infant and early childhood mortality is also common to the three populations, winter being extremely dangerous in the neonatal phase as much as summer was in the weaning period. Whereas in Venice, the better-off were able to defend their infants from the winter harshness, no such social differentiation can be detected in Casalguidi, where rich and poor resorted to the same ways of repairing from cold, usually gathering in the stables. In Casalguidi, the higher mortality of children of day laborers during summertime suggests, albeit indirectly, that their mothers were obliged to neglect them while working in the fields. Correspondingly, our analysis shows that children benefited sensibly by the presence of other women in the household. Such a presence, however, was quite unusual in day laborers' households. Overall, mothers could provide only a limited amount of resources to their children, so that a new birth resulted in an increase of the risk of death for the previous child. Whereas the chances of survival of the children who had lost their mother in infancy were dramatically reduced, the absence of the father was more negative in childhood. Finally, while infants and adults were apparently indifferent to short-term economic stresses, at least as far as mortality is concerned, children and the elderly showed a marked sensitivity to price rises, either directly or through the rise of epidemics to which they were frequently associated.

Although the sample that we used for our analysis cannot be regarded as representative at the national or even regional level, we argue that the mechanisms we have outlined may have been apparent in much larger areas and situations in pretransitional Italy. Whereas our results confirm the vulnerability of Italian populations to the elementary forces of environment and socioeconomic conditions, they suggest that the overall process of mortality decline could be seen as the outcome of a progressive attenuation in the power of such constraints, through an improvement of the living standards concerning wider sectors of the populace.

Notes

This research has benefited from the Eurasian Project on Population and Family History, initiated by Akira Hayami and funded by the Japanese Ministry of Education, Science, Sports and Culture, and from the research project *Lo sviluppo demografico tra costrizione, scelta e adattamento. Italia, XVII–XIX secolo,* coordinated by Marco Breschi and funded by the Italian Ministry of University and Scientific Research.

1. Among the few scholars who have analyzed the demographic mechanism underlining the growth of Italian population in the eighteenth and nineteenth centuries are Bellettini (1987) and Cipolla (1965b). Both, with different emphasis, linked population growth to mortality decrease. Recently, new studies, such as Del Panta (1996), have pointed out the combined role of nuptiality and fertility in the demographic evolution of some regions.

2. Deaths by cause are available for the whole Kingdom of Italy only after 1887.

3. The first coordinated and universal health policy was promoted in 1888 by the central Italian government. For historical information on vaccination practices, see Castiglioni (1936). For a debate on the effectiveness of vaccinations against smallpox and a large literature on this subject, see Sköld (1996b).

4. Life expectancy around 1880 was 42.1 years in England and Wales, 42.2 in France, 43.8 in the Netherlands, 47.0 in Sweden, and only 35.4 in Italy (Livi Bacci 1994, 129, 1999).

5. This figure refers to the definition of infectious and parasitic diseases adopted by the International Mortality Committee in 1948. See Caselli (1991).

6. The lower infant and child mortality of Jewish populations in comparison with the wider communities where they lived is one of the most striking constants of historical demography. Among the many studies supplying evidence of the Jewish advantage in a large set of countries and cities from the eighteenth to the twentieth century, see Cohen (1989), Condran and Kramarow (1991), Marks (1994), Preston and Haines (1991), Schmelz (1971), and Woodbury (1926). For Italy, see Della Pergola (1983), Derosas (1999, 2000), Livi (1918–1920), and Livi Bacci (1978).

7. There is a strong link between total and infant mortality, which in the middle of the nineteenth century represents about 25 to 30 percent of total mortality. However, since the factors that influence infant mortality are different from those that influence mortality overall, they are not clearly correlated.

8. For a detailed description of the forms of agricultural contracts from sixteenth- to nineteenth-century Italy, see Giorgetti (1974). For more specific and local studies, see Finzi (1998) and Poni (1982) on Emilia, Spaggiari (1966) on the duchy of Parma, and Pazzagli (1973) on Tuscany.

9. It was also connected by carriageway to the wealthy and populated Arno Valley.

10. There were houses without any sanitary amenities. As a result, human excreta piled up in side alleys, often polluting the wells that collected the rainwater that residents used for their needs.

11. The average day temperature was below 0°C one week a year and below 5°C seven weeks a year. It was above 25°C forty days a year (Venice Municipality, Town Council of Statistics 1881, 10–15).

12. The data for Casalguidi are "real" data, in the sense that values are measured directly, while those for Tuscany and the duchy of Modena and Reggio were obtained by use of inverse projection.

13. The reconstruction of demographic trends in Venice before unification is problematic since statistical publications are unclear on the criteria used in the collection of data.

14. There are some exceptions to this rule. Priests sometimes also recorded the deaths of parishioners that occurred outside the parish. This concerned mainly adult persons rather than young people and children. The death registers of Casalguidi contain a large number of acts regarding foundlings belonging to the foundling hospitals called *Ospedale degli Innocenti* of the main nearby cities. In Casalguidi, many women nursed babies for money, paid by the foundling hospitals. In these acts, the names of those women are sometimes mentioned. Unfortunately, even if this information were always present, we would not be able to determine the entire set of women who used to take foundlings. We would

lose all those women who returned live foundlings to the hospital. Obviously, we do not include the deaths of foundlings in the analysis on infant mortality. Moreover, in these first analyses, we do not distinguish the women who breast-fed at least one foundling.

15. There is an exception for 1822. In this year, the priest did not draw up the complete *Status Animarum* even if he listed all the principal variations that occurred during the year. We have reconstructed the missing *Status Animarum* combining this partial information with those derived from vital registrations.

16. Some problems emerge especially for Madregolo, where great mobility made the registers less precise. For families remaining in the village just one year (or a little more), the relationships among the members are not always indicated or not clear, because the priest did not know the family or the person.

17. For example, we can mention the problem related to patrilocality, which was very common in the two villages. Therefore, marriage acts usually refer to women not living in the village after marriage. On the contrary, for many couples spending their whole life there, we do not have any registration of the marriage. The cross-checking of information with *Status Animarum* makes it possible to fill this gap: we can in fact know the year of marriage, at least for those couples who celebrated their wedding in the bride's parish and then settled in the groom's parish.

18. See the appendix for a summary of the Eurasia standard comparative models.

19. This variable has been slightly changed in comparison with the Eurasian standards. Actually, our reference category includes two Eurasian categories (whether a child was firstborn and whether the previous birth interval was greater than twenty-four months and the child born previously was still alive), in order to avoid possible multicollinearity problems related to the variable concerning the presence of older brothers.

20. The care of children was explicitly one of the major duties for female members of the household. See Barbagli (1984, 445–460). In previous work (Breschi, Derosas, and Manfredini 2000), we found that the presence of grandmothers and/or sisters aged 8 or more years within the household could play a protective role on the survival of children. The inclusion of this last variable is just an extension, which aims to check the existence of a more comprehensive effect connected to a global female presence.

21. We identify from our winter and summer temperature series periods of excessive heat and cold as those that comprise either the hottest or coldest 5 percent.

22. For the purpose of this analysis, we defined winter as the months of December, January, and February; spring as March, April, and May; summer as June, July, and August; and autumn as September, October, and November.

23. The association between severe weather conditions and elderly mortality has been examined and confirmed by many studies. See Galloway (1985), Kalkstein and Davis (1989), and R. Lee (1981).

24. Personal hygiene and cleanliness at home apparently overwhelmed the effects of filthy streets and public places discussed above. For similar conditions, see Condran and Kramarow (1991).

25. In Madregolo, 92.9 percent of heads were male, in Casalguidi, 86.2 percent, and in Venice, 83.4 percent.

26. For Casalguidi, Madregolo, and Venice, respectively, the historical series are made up of average annual values recorded in the markets of Florence (Bandettini 1957),

Parma (Spaggiari 1959), and Legnago (one of the markets close to Venice; data taken from the *Gazzetta Uffiziale di Venezia*), then converted into real lire to make the series comparable over time and to each other. Owing to the quite short periods covered by our analyses (except for Madregolo), which excludes problems of confounding long-term effects, the price series were not detrended. In the case of Venice, monthly series are also available, and these were useful for a more accurate analysis of infant mortality.

27. It is worth noting that annual averages reflect calendar years that average actually over two consecutive harvest years, since new prices were usually fixed after the crop, around July. In the case of particularly high fluctuations of prices from one harvest to the next, the average value could not represent the real economic situation. Some exploratory analyses we carried out with some monthly data did not show particular and significant changes in the estimation of risks.

28. Because of problems with the reliability of data, we have excluded in this study the few orphans who had lost both parents.

29. Other problems connected with the death of the father should not be forgotten, above all those concerning the loss of reference points, social representation, and emotional investment.

9

Mortality and Household in Two Ou Villages, 1716–1870

Noriko O. Tsuya and
Satomi Kurosu
in collaboration with Hideki
Nakazato

This chapter examines the patterns and covariates of mortality in two agricultural villages called Shimomoiya and Niita in northeastern Japan between 1716 and 1870. The northeastern region called Ou, depicted in map 9.1, was one of the least economically developed regions in preindustrial Japan and was the northern boundary of rice cultivation at that time. Using local population registers called *ninbetsu-aratame-cho*, we analyze how short-term economic stress, measured by variations in local rice prices from one year to another, affected the mortality of males and females at different life stages in these preindustrial Japanese villages. As delineated in chapters 1 and 2, we regard the ability to overcome short-term economic stress caused by fluctuations in agricultural output to be a measure of the living standard. Given the setting of our study—two farming villages in preindustrial Japan whose livelihood depended almost solely on agriculture—the use of annual variations in local rice price is appropriate to account for short-term economic stress because rice was the staple food. This chapter also examines, in multivariate contexts, how family and household characteristics influenced the likelihood of death of males and females at different life stages. In a preindustrial society in which public health and social welfare measures were, if not totally nonexistent, underdeveloped, family and household were even more important than today in determining the chances of survival. Like most other enduring human groups, families and households in Japan are never entirely egalitarian. Especially in preindustrial agrarian households, individuals' chances of survival were strongly affected by the structure of their household and the positions they occupied within that structure. Controlling for the effects of family and household contexts (in addition to short-term economic stress), this study

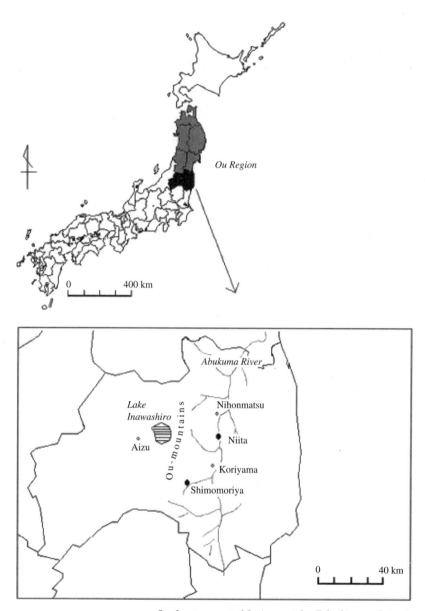

Southeastern part of Ou (present-day Fukushima prefecture)

Map 9.1
Northeastern Japan

seeks to identify who, among different household members, was most or least likely to suffer death at different stages of life.

In the next section, we briefly explain the regional contexts of population, economy, and family systems in which this study is situated. Here, we especially focus on the trends of population change and economic development in northeastern Japan in the eighteenth and nineteenth centuries, fluctuations in agricultural output as measured by annual variations in local rice prices, and characteristics of the household and family systems prevalent in the region. We next turn to explanations of the two communities, Shimomoriya and Niita, and data sources used in this study. We also explain the trends of population size and aggregate death rates in the two villages under consideration. We then examine the levels and patterns of mortality by sex in the two villages, based on life tables. Conducting a series of discrete-time event-history analyses, we analyze how economic stress, family and household contexts, and individual characteristics affected the mortality of males and females at different stages of life. The chapter concludes with a summary of the findings and a discussion of their implications.

Tokugawa Japan, which began in 1603 and ended in 1868, was a society with enormous local differences, not only in demographic patterns but also in socioeconomic development, family systems, and ecological contexts (Cornell and Hayami 1986; Hayami and Kurosu 2001; Kurosu, Tsuya, and Hamano 1999). In this sense, evidence from this study based on two northeastern villages is clearly not sufficient to account for the entire mortality regime in the latter half of Tokugawa Japan. However, the results of the multivariate analysis based on the rich data sources that this study provides should enable us to further our understanding of the nature of the mortality effects of local economic change, household contexts, and individual characteristics in preindustrial rural Japan.

Background

Population Trends and Economic Development

Northeastern Japan experienced a number of famines and crop failures in the eighteenth and nineteenth centuries (Saito 2002).[1] Of these, the Kyoho (1732–1733), Tenmei (1783–1787), and Tempo (1836-1838)

famines, named after reign years, are known as the three major famines in the Tokugawa era. The region also experienced a smaller but
nevertheless serious famine in 1755 known as the Horeki famine. These
major famines and resulting crop failures left a clear imprint on the
population size of the northeastern region. Until the early nineteenth
century, the population in the northeast was in general on the decline,
showing a clear contrast to central Japan, where the population was
in general stable, and to the southwest, whose population increased
(Hayami 1986). The northeastern region, in particular, was devastated
by the Tenmei famine and the long spell of bad weather preceding
it (Koriyama-shi 1981a, 340–341). For example, in the Nihonmatsu
domain in which the two villages of this study were located, the domain population declined by 17 percent in just five years, from 1783
to 1787 (Nagata, Kurosu, and Hayami 1998). The population in the
region also suffered from less serious but nevertheless major population losses during the Tempo famine in the 1830s. We will show later
in the chapter that the trends of population changes in the two villages
were similar to those in the region as a whole.

Among the major regions of Tokugawa Japan, the northeast was
in general the one with the least economic development and proto-
industrialization. Compared to central and southwestern Japan, the
overall level of proto-industrialization in the northeast is considered
to have been much more limited. Officially, the Nihonmatsu domain
authorities discouraged the development of proto-industry during
much of the eighteenth century. Nonetheless, evidence indicates developments of such local industries as sake brewing, paper making, and
cotton and silk textiles in the nineteenth century (Nagata, Kurosu, and
Hayami 1998; Tomobe 1998). Only after the Tenmei famine in the late
1780s, did the domain government adopt a new policy to upgrade
agricultural technologies and increase rice production. In the 1790s, the
authorities then started encouraging local specialized production of
cash crops, resulting in the development of proto-industries in the
domain from the 1800s onward (Nagata, Kurosu, and Hayami 1998).
After the Tempo famine, the region experienced improvements in environmental conditions as indicated by a drastic decline in the occurrence of famines and crop failures. At the same time, the rigid social
structure and social stratification system of Tokugawa Japan became
increasingly slack, leading to the period called *bakumatsu*, the last years
of the Tokugawa shogunate regime.

Rice Prices in the Tokugawa Agrarian Economy

To measure annual fluctuations in local agricultural output, this study employs rice price series in the local market of Aizu, just 40 kilometers to the west.[2] The only available grain price series in Tokugawa Japan covering different parts of the country and with sufficiently long duration are rice prices. However, rice price may not be the best indicator of short-term economic stress for two reasons. First, although rice was the staple food in Tokugawa Japan, farmers and peasants did not subsist solely on it (Kito 1989; Nakagawa 1900, 14, 46–49). Evidence indicates that especially during such economic hardships as harvest failures, dependence on such minor grains as wheat and millet increased to compensate for the increasing scarcity of rice (Nakagawa 1900, 5, 40–41). To measure annual variations in grain harvests accurately, we would therefore have to know price fluctuations not only of rice but also of other grains on which farmers and peasants subsisted. Second, unlike grain prices in many parts of preindustrial Europe, rice prices in Tokugawa Japan were not always determined solely by market factors such as harvests and the demand for consumption, trades, and storage; they were often influenced by political and policy-related decisions of domain governments too. Here, an explanation is in order on the nature of rice price and agrarian economy in Tokugawa Japan.

One major characteristic of Tokugawa economy is the *kokudaka* system (Hayami 1985, 75–107). In the face of the spread of a money economy, the Tokugawa (central) and domain governments adopted this system, under which all agricultural output was measured, taxes on farmers and peasants (not individually but on their villages as a whole) were assessed, and income of domain lords and their warriors (*samurai*) were expressed in terms of one unit (*koku*) of rice.[3] The system was facilitated by the separation, in both the physical and social senses, of *samurai* from farmers and peasants (Hayami 1985, 75–78). Whereas *samurai* lived in the castle town of their domain lord, villages were inhabited by peasants; thus, in Tokugawa Japan, the so-called landed warriors ceased to exist, and *samurai* became a type of salaried officials of domain governments. Meanwhile, villages and peasants were required to pay taxes: in some domains, they were required to pay solely in rice; in others, they were to pay in money (in such a case, it was necessary to have a sort of exchange rate between rice and money).

For example, if the domain government required peasants to pay, say, 500 *koku* worth of taxes, half in rice and half in money, farmers would have to sell rice in the market to pay for the 250 *koku* worth of taxes in money. If crops failed and there were not enough yields to pay for the 250 *koku* of tax rice, they would have to buy rice in the market. Putting it differently, harvested rice had three types of use: self-consumption by peasants, rice to be sold by peasants directly to merchants (commercial rice), and rice to be paid as taxes to domain governments, or to the central government if peasants lived in areas governed directly by the Tokugawa shogunate (tax rice).

In the Aizu domain, adjacent to the Nihonmatsu domain, peasants were required to pay taxes at least in part in money (Harada and Miyamoto 1985, 57–62). In such a system, if the rice price took an abrupt upturn due to a crop failure, the domain government would have had a strong incentive to curb the increase because if the rice price rose too high too quickly, peasants who were already weakened by the harvest failure would not have been able to buy rice in the market to pay for taxes. If the rice price became too low, it would lower the livelihood of *samurai* and put the domain government in a financial bind because the income of the government and salaries of its *samurai* were obtained by selling tax rice in the market.

In this sense, the rice price in the local market of Aizu used by this study is an indicator of harvest variations and played a role as an exchange rate between rice and money. Providing that there are no data available on rice price series based solely on the local market conditions, we use these exchange-rate-based rice price data.[4] Despite the government-controlled nature of rice prices, annual variations in rice prices in the local market of Aizu seem to reflect fairly well crop failures at the time of major famines (see figure 9.1).[5] The local rice price shows an upsurge at around the times of the three major famines of Kyoho, Tenmei, and Tempo, although increases are by no means limited to the years of known famines.

Family System and Household Structure

The ideal and prevalent family form in agricultural villages in pre-industrial Japan was the patrilineal stem family, in which a son (most commonly, an eldest son) continued to live with his parents after marriage, bringing his spouse into his parents' household (Aruga 1943, Otake 1982, Saito 1998). On a broader scale, Nakane (1967) identified

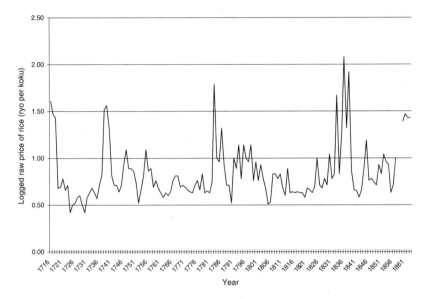

Figure 9.1
Log of raw rice prices (ryo per koku) in the market of Aizu, 1716–1863

three types of succession patterns as regional variations of the Japanese stem family system: areas characterized by eldest son succession, areas characterized by youngest son succession, and the rest, with succession regardless of birth order. According to Nakane, preindustrial northeastern Japan is strongly characterized by eldest son succession. Other studies have classified stem family orientations in preindustrial Japan as the northeastern type (*tohoku-gata*) and conjugal orientations as the southwestern type (*seinan-gata*) (Takei 1971, Naito 1973). The two villages analyzed by this study clearly belong to the former.

Households in preindustrial rural Japan were therefore most likely to have consisted of one married couple, their children, and the parents of the husband (and sometimes nonkin and servants as well). In the course of the family life cycle, nuclear households appeared typically when the couple's parents both died before one of their children married and brought his or her spouse into the household. Only rarely did married siblings of the household head live together under one roof. Such arrangements were often temporary, when married siblings co-resided with the head before forming their own branch household.

Inheritance of property was in principle nonpartible and belonged to the child who continued to live with the parents after his or her marriage. When families had large landholdings, partition of family property was possible, and other siblings, typically male, could receive part of the land and form branch households. Transmission of household headship was in principle by primogeniture and occurred upon either the death or the retirement of a head (Okada and Kurosu 1998). Although it was typically the eldest son who succeeded the headship in the area of our study, the succession by an elder daughter is also reported to have been practiced even when her younger brothers were alive (Narimatsu 1992, 170–182). When no biological son was alive, families often adopted a male heir as either an adopted son (*yoshi*) or the husband of their daughter (*muko-yoshi*).

Under the stem family system, the authorities and responsibilities of the head within an agrarian household and in the community were distinctive and clearly recognized (Kodama 1957, 252–269). The actual decision-making power may not have been concentrated entirely on the head, as farming in preindustrial Japan required toil from every household member (Otake 1982, 297; Saito 1998; Yonemura and Nagata 1998). Nonetheless, it seems plausible to think that household headship, which was normally assumed by adult males, allowed strong control over household resources and awarded ultimate decision-making power in important family and household events such as marriage, adoption, and ancestral rites (Fuse 1993, Torigoe 1985). On the other hand, the statuses and roles of other household members were prescribed by their relationship to the head as well as by such demographic factors as sex, age, and marital status. Thus, the stem family system in preindustrial Japan involved a complex series of well-defined hierarchical relations within the household, based on the rules of supremacy regarding gender (males over females), generation (parents over children), birth order (firstborn over later born), and closeness to main family line (stem kin over nonstem kin).

Although there were considerable regional variations, marriage in Tokugawa Japan was in general universal and early, especially among women, compared to historical Europe (Kurosu, Tsuya, and Hamano 1999). The northeastern region is known especially as a region characterized by very early and universal marriage, with a large majority of men and women marrying by the mid-twenties (Tsuya and Kurosu 1999). Another feature of marriage behavior in our villages is the lack of stability of marital unions, characterized by frequent divorces and quick remarriages. For example, roughly one-third, 34 percent, of all observed first marriages in Shimomoriya and Niita ended in divorce (Kurosu, Tsuya, and Hamano 1999). Women who experienced marital disruption remarried relatively quickly. More than two-thirds, 70 percent, of women whose first marriages were dissolved due to divorce or death of spouse remarried within five years after the dissolution of their first marriage if they survived for that duration. This suggests that despite the instability of first marital unions, women and men in northeastern Tokugawa villages lived most of their lives within the matrices of family relations because while marriage was brittle, remarriage was easy and quick.

The Communities and Data Sources

Topography of the Villages

Our study is based on data from the local population registers in Shimomoriya and Niita, two farming villages in northeastern Japan. During the Tokugawa period, the northeastern region, traditionally known as Ou, consisted of two subregions: Mutsu, facing the Pacific Ocean, and Dewa, facing the Sea of Japan. Both villages under consideration belonged to the Nihonmatsu domain located in the southeastern part of Ou, the southern part of Mutsu (which is now Fukushima prefecture). Situated at the foot of a mountain range, Shimomoriya was susceptible to cold summers and poor harvests resulting from chilly gusts off the Ou Mountains (Narimatsu 1985, 1–3). Because the village was located in a hilly area with severe winter weather, most of its agricultural land was not fertile and was unfit to grow cash crops such as mulberry trees. Niita, located between the capital town of Nihonmatsu and the growing market town of Koriyama, two major population centers in the domain at that time, sat on flat land and had less severe winter weather (Narimatsu 1992, 4–6). Though situated north of Shimomoriya, Niita thus enjoyed a better climate for agriculture.[6] Nonetheless, lying on the banks of the Gohyaku River, the village was vulnerable to frequent floods.

Although somewhat different in their geographical conditions, both villages were almost totally agricultural (Narimatsu 1985, 152–180; 1992, 6). Because of the underdeveloped and unmechanized agricultural technologies at that time, the northeastern region in which the two villages were located was the northernmost boundary of rice farming in Tokugawa Japan. Living standards in the villages are therefore thought to have been low, with the economy being near subsistence level. Since the livelihood of the villagers was often at the mercy of fluctuations in agricultural output, villagers' chances of survival were threatened when crop failures occurred. Later in the chapter, we will look in detail at the trends in the villages' population size, death rates, and rice price fluctuations as related to known famines and crop failures in northeastern Tokugawa Japan.

Data Sources

Our study draws data from the local population registers called *ninbetsu-aratame-cho* (NAC) in the villages of Shimomoriya and Niita.[7] In both villages, the NAC was enumerated annually at the beginning of the third lunar month. Surviving NAC registers in Shimomoriya cover three intermittent years before 1716 (1687, 1699, and 1708) and the 154-year period from 1716 to 1869. During the 154 years, there are nine years (1720, 1729, 1846, 1850, 1858, and 1864–1867) for which NAC records are missing. For Niita, the surviving NAC registers cover the 151-year period from 1720 to 1870, during which there are only five years missing (1742, 1758, 1796, 1857, and 1858). Thus, in the two villages, there exist virtually undisrupted records spanning the latter half of the Tokugawa era. Because our preliminary analysis showed that the causal structure of mortality was not substantially different between the villages, we pool the records from 1716 to 1869 for Shimomoriya and those from 1720 to 1870 for Niita together.

In addition to the continuous coverage of these records, the NACs in the two villages have other advantages as demographic data. First, the registers were compiled using the principle of current domicile; thus, the NAC data are all de facto.[8] Registers compiled in this way give far more exact demographic information than those based on the principle of legal residence although the latter de jure principle seems to have been much more frequently used (Cornell and Hayami 1986).

Second, in the NACs in the two villages, the dates (month and year) of major demographic events such as birth, death, and migration were annotated except for infants who died before they could be registered alive. The dates of occurrence of these events were not usually given in Tokugawa population registers (Saito 1992; Smith 1977, 19). Moreover, exits from the records due to unknown reasons are extremely rare. Such mysterious disappearance consists of merely 0.6 percent (nineteen cases) of all exits during the 154 years covered by Shimomoriya's registers and only 0.3 percent (thirteen cases) of all exits during the 151 years recorded by Niita's registers.

Despite these strengths, the NAC registers also have shortcomings, the most serious of which is the underregistration of infant deaths. Like the population registers in other Tokugawa villages, the registers in the two villages suffer from the omission of unregistered infant deaths. That is, not all births and infant deaths were recorded in the registers—only those who survived from birth to the subsequent registration were entered. Consequently, infants who died before the first registration were excluded and never came under observation.

Except for this inherent problem of unregistered births and infant deaths, the NAC registration data in Shimomoriya and Niita are considered to be of, if not the highest, one of the highest in quality among the surviving local population registers in Tokugawa Japan. Using these NAC records, we can identify in most cases the time of entrance to observation due to birth or immigration, as well as the time of death and other exits, although the population in the two villages had considerable in- and out-migration (Narimatsu 1985, 54–56, 101–120; 1992, 32–38).[9] Hence, for the purposes of mortality analysis, we can both specify the timing of death and accurately define the population at risk.

The original annual NAC records (which were organized into one sheet per year for each household) were first linked into time-series data sheets called basic data sheets (BDSs) for all households. The BDSs were then entered into machine-readable form, from which a relational database was created (for specifics, see Hayami 1979, Ono 1993). From the database, it is possible to derive for each individual and household indices of past, present, and future demographic and life course events, and to link all individuals present in the village to the records of parents, spouses, siblings, and other household members. From the relational database, we constructed a rectangular file for our mortality analysis, using person-year recorded in the population registers as the unit of observation.

It is possible to compute chronological age for all individuals whose births were recorded in the NAC registers, that is, individuals born in the villages during the period for which the NAC registers exist. However, natives (those born in the villages between 1716 and 1870) comprise less than one-half of all persons who appeared in the population registers of the two villages. Further, information used to construct other covariates in the multivariate model is mostly organized in terms of the timing of population registration. We therefore employ as the measure of age a variable indicating the number of registrations each individual went through after birth until his or her exit from the universe of observation due to death or emigration. Thus, in this study, *age* refers to the age measured in terms of the timing of the NAC registration.[10] Being measured in this way, the youngest possible NAC age of individuals included in our analysis is 1.

Trends in Population Size and Death Rates in the Villages

According to the NAC records, Shimomoriya was a relatively small village, whose population in 1716 was 419. As shown in figure 9.2, village population was relatively stable in the first thirty-five years for which the records are available, until it started to decline at around the time of the Horeki famine in the mid-1750s. Devastated by the great Tenmei famine in the mid-1780s, the village population further

Figure 9.2
Changes in population size: Shimomoriya, 1716–1869, and Niita, 1720–1870

declined to 286 in 1786, a drop of 32 percent in the seventy years from 1716. Though the population rebounded somewhat between the 1790s and 1820s, it again took a dramatic downturn during the Tempo famine in the late 1830s, reaching a low of 238 in 1840. The population recovered gradually afterward to 328 in 1869, but it never reached the 1716 level.

Niita was a bigger village, with a population of 538 in 1720. The village population, described in figure 9.2, was also stable, as in Shimomoriya, for the first fifty years, until it began to decline in 1770. Owing mainly to the Tenmei famine in the mid-1780s and a long spell of bad weather preceding it (Koriyama-shi 1981a, 340–341, 1981b, 176–180), Niita's population decreased from 530 in 1770 to 430 in 1786, a decline of 19 percent in fifteen years. Afterward, population fluctuated between 420 and 450 from 1786 to 1800 and then decreased again in the early 1800s. By 1820, population reached the all-time low of 367 and then started a gradual upturn. The population size of Niita was not as seriously affected as Shimomoriya by the Tempo famine; it recovered, and even surpassed, the 1720 level by the late 1860s.

In summary, except for the first few decades of the period under examination in which population growth was stagnant, and for the last few decades in which it showed an upturn, the population size in the two villages was in overall decline. Especially large net population losses occurred at the times of major famines in the mid-1780s and the late 1830s. Hence, though evidence is by no means definitive, these findings seem to imply that the village population was affected by an acute food shortage in the short run, triggered by widespread crop failures.

We can also see at the aggregate level the possible mortality effects of major famines in the two villages. Table 9.1 shows the crude death rates (CDRs) by decade for the pooled population of Shimomoriya and Niita. We can see that the decades covering the Kyoho, Tenmei, and Tempo famines (the 1730s, 1780s, and 1830s, respectively) suffered higher rates. The rate for 1780 to 1789 is especially high, with a CDR of 28.8 per 1,000, indicating the severity of the mortality effect of the Tenmei famine in the region. The upturn in the CDR during the 1830s, the decade of the Tempo famine, is not as distinctive as that in the 1780s.[11]

The death rate shows dramatic downturns in the decades following these two great famines—a CDR of 17.5 for 1790 to 1799 and 17.4 for 1840 to 1849, respectively—implying that the upturn in the CDR in the 1780s and 1830s was crisis mortality caused by the two great famines.

Table 9.1
Crude death rates by sex and decade, Shimomoriya and Niita, 1716–1870

	Crude death rate				Number of deaths		
	Both sexes	Male	Female	Sex ratio	Total	Male	Female
1716–1729	21.8	21.8	21.9	100	206	112	94
1730–1739	26.8	25.7	28.2	91	260	136	124
1740–1749	24.8	26.2	23.1	114	215	121	94
1750–1759	26.4	25.7	27.1	95	225	117	108
1760–1769	20.9	18.7	23.3	80	190	88	102
1770–1779	24.6	27.8	21.0	133	205	123	82
1780–1789	28.8	28.6	29.1	98	217	110	107
1790–1799	18.2	17.4	19.0	91	122	59	63
1800–1809	27.9	27.9	27.8	100	202	105	97
1810–1819	25.9	25.2	26.6	95	175	86	89
1820–1829	25.1	26.8	23.4	114	168	89	79
1830–1839	26.4	27.5	25.3	109	181	94	87
1840–1849	17.4	19.4	15.3	127	107	60	47
1850–1859	21.0	17.6	24.3	72	118	49	69
1860–1870	22.8	25.8	19.9	130	152	86	66
1716–1870	24.1	24.3	23.8	102	2,743	1,435	1,308

Note: Data shown are restricted to the years for which an immediately succeeding register is available.

Because the most vulnerable parts of the population were wiped out by the famines (and in the case of Tempo famine also an epidemic), the death rate decreased sharply in the following decades.[12]

Levels and Patterns of Mortality: Results of Life Table Analysis

Before proceeding to the discrete-time event-history analysis of mortality at different stages of life, we look at overall levels as well as at the sex and age patterns of mortality in the two villages. Table 9.2 presents the abridged life table by sex for the pooled population of Shimomoriya and Niita from 1716 to 1870. The life table is constructed based on person-years recorded in the local population registers. *Age* in this table is NAC age. The use of NAC age instead of chronological age should not be a problem except for the first years of life, in which mortality tends to be high. Since children at the NAC age of 1 could, in an extreme case, be just 2 days old, the probability of dying for NAC ages

Table 9.2
Death rate in the life table population (m_x), probability of dying (q_x), and life expectancy (e_x) by sex, based on person-years recorded in local population registers, Shimomoriya and Niita, 1716–1870

Age interval	Male m_x	q_x	e_x	Female m_x	q_x	e_x
1–4	.060	.211	42.2	.055	.193	42.1
5–9	.018	.086	49.0	.012	.060	47.8
10–14	.006	.030	48.4	.005	.025	45.7
15–19	.007	.036	44.8	.010	.047	41.8
20–24	.010	.047	41.4	.010	.049	38.7
25–29	.006	.031	38.3	:012	.059	35.5
30–34	.006	.032	34.5	.014	.068	32.6
35–39	.009	.043	30.5	.013	.061	29.8
40–44	.012	.059	26.7	.017	.080	26.6
45–49	.014	.067	23.3	.011	.053	23.7
50–54	.018	.088	19.7	.015	.074	19.9
55–59	.028	.131	16.4	.024	.114	16.3
60–64	.026	.120	13.5	.029	.135	13.0
65–69	.055	.245	10.0	.063	.275	9.6
70–74	.094	.382	7.4	.100	.400	7.3
75–79	.150	.539	5.4	.149	.535	5.5
80–	.259	—	3.9	.241	—	4.2

Note: Age here is not chronological age, but *ninbetsu-aratame-cho* (NAC) age, that is, a consecutive number of NAC registrations a person went through after birth.

1 to 4 shown in the table is likely to be higher than the probability of dying for chronological ages 1 to 4.

From table 9.2, we can see that the probability of dying from ages 1 to 4 in the two villages together is 0.211 for males and 0.193 for females and that life expectancy at age 1 is similar: 42.2 for males and 42.1 for females. Comparing these estimates of life expectancy at age 1 to those in other Tokugawa villages (Hanley 1974; Hayami 1973, 204; 1992, 249; Jannetta and Preston 1991; Saito 1992; Smith 1977, 56), the mortality level in the two villages appears to be, if not the highest, one of the highest.[13] Except for males in the village of Yokouchi from 1726 to 1775 and females in Hida villages from 1776 to 1855 with which life expectancies at age 1 in the two villages are almost on a par, other villages in central and western Japan exhibit lower, sometimes considerably lower, levels of mortality.

Turning to age patterns of mortality, as shown in table 9.2, if they survived to age 5, people in the two villages are expected to have lived, on average, roughly 50 more years (49 years for males and 48 years for females). If they were lucky to survive to age 50, they had, on average, a little less than 20 more years to live. We can also see that in childhood until age 15, males had a considerably higher probability of dying than females. From ages 15 to 44, however, females suffered distinctively higher mortality than males, perhaps because of high maternal mortality associated with childbearing. The only exception is the age group 20 to 24, in which males have a nearly equal level of mortality to that of females.[14] After age 44, females had a better chance of survival (lower mortality) than males until they reached age 60, after which females again had higher mortality than males.

In summary, the overall mortality level in Shimomoriya and Niita between 1716 and 1870 was, if not the highest, quite high as a rural population in the latter part of early modern Japan. However, if they survived the periods of high mortality risks such as infancy and early childhood, children in the village could expect to live until the mid- to late 50s. And if women survived their reproductive years, they, like men, could expect to live to around age 70.

Variables for the Multivariate Analysis

The dependent variable of our multivariate analysis is a dichotomous variable measuring whether an individual died within the next year from an NAC registration to the immediately succeeding registration. Out of the 2,468 individuals who appeared in Shimomoriya's registers from 1716 to 1869, 1,273 deaths are recorded. As for Niita, out of the 4,075 individuals who appeared in its registers from 1720 to 1870, there are 1,703 deaths recorded. Altogether, out of the 6,543 individuals who appeared in the population registers in the two villages, there are 2,976 recorded deaths. Because we restrict our multivariate analysis to the years for which an immediately succeeding register is also available and because the analysis of old-age mortality is limited to those aged 55 to 74, the numbers of persons and deaths included in our analysis become smaller. Of 3,155 males and 3,102 females used in our analysis, there are 2,233 recorded deaths (1,147 male and 1,086 female) in the two villages.

Given the annual nature of NAC registration, we employ a discrete-time event-history analysis model. The model is estimated by a series of logistic regressions with robust standard errors (for specifics of the model, see chapter 3). Our model employs six general groups of covariates: (1) current age and residing village, which are always included in the model as control variables; (2) short-term economic stress measured by the log of raw rice price in the local market of Aizu; (3) household characteristics measured by such factors as household landholding, household size, and the proportion of household members over age 54; (4) presence of kin in household such as parents, grandparents, and siblings; (5) household relationships and statuses of index individuals as measured by marital status and relationship to household head; and (6) period. For infant and child mortality, we also include a covariate measuring an interval from previous to index birth.

Table 9.3 shows the means of the covariates used in the discrete-time event-history analyses of infant (age 1), childhood (ages 2–14), adult (ages 15–54), and old–age (ages 55–74) mortality by sex. Some of the covariates are constructed to vary by time at the level of individuals recorded in the NAC, with *time* being the years for which the registers exist. Some other covariates are time dependent at the level of household in which the index individual lived. And some others are time independent (do not vary by time). Conducting a series of the analyses introducing groups of explanatory and control variables by stepwise fashion, we tested the explanatory power of the model, as well as the significance of the effect of each variable. Because some of the covariates were found to be multicollinear, we examined the effects of covariates with multicollinearity by introducing them interchangeably in the model. We also tested the significance of the effects of interaction of rice price with other covariates. To simplify the presentation and interpretation of the results, we present only the most parsimonious models.

Specifically, current age of the index individual is a covariate, the effect of which needs to be controlled because mortality is a function of age. This covariate consists of five-year age groups, except for ages 2, 3, and 4, in which mortality is thought to be high. Using the highest age group for each segment of the life course—ages 10 to 14 for childhood, 50 to 54 for adult, and 70 to 74 for old age—we construct four, seven, and three dummy variables for the three life stages, respectively. Because the records from two villages are pooled in our analysis, a dichotomous variable is also included in the model to control for the possible village-level differentials in mortality. If the index individual

Table 9.3
Means of the covariates used for the discrete-time event-history analysis of mortality in Shimomoriya and Niita, 1716–1870

	Infant		Child	
	Female	Male	Female	Male
Current age (Ref.: Highest age group)				
2	—	—	0.092	0.093
3	—	—	0.085	0.086
4	—	—	0.081	0.081
5–9	—	—	0.376	0.377
Economic stress				
Log of local rice price	−0.218	−0.236	−0.228	−0.229
Household characteristics				
Household landholding	12.340	—	—	—
Landholding × logged local rice price	−2.256	—	—	—
Number of kin household members	—	—	—	5.261
Proportion aged 55 or more	0.135	—	—	—
Presence of parents (Ref.: Both parents present)				
Father only	—	—	0.056	—
Mother only	—	—	0.102	—
No parent	—	—	0.078	—
Presence of grandparents				
Grandmother	0.637	—	—	—
Grandfather	—	—	—	0.375
Presence of siblings[a]				
Older sister	—	—	—	0.325
Previous birth interval less than 24 months	—	—	—	0.084
Period (Ref.: 1716–1759)				
1760–1799	—	—	0.247	0.253
1800–1839	—	—	0.258	0.254
1840–1870	—	—	0.173	0.162
Village (Shimomoriya = 1)	0.413	0.399	0.444	0.410

Table 9.3
(continued)

	Adult			Elderly	
	All female	Married female kin	Male	Female	Male
Current age (Ref.: Highest age group)					
15–19	0.149	0.129	0.145	—	—
20–24	0.144	0.143	0.139	—	—
25–29	0.137	0.140	0.131	—	—
30–34	0.127	0.129	0.129	—	—
35–39	0.118	0.119	0.124	—	—
40–44	0.111	0.115	0.117	—	—
45–49	0.108	0.113	0.111	—	—
55–59	—	—	—	0.323	0.304
60–64	—	—	—	0.285	0.282
65–69	—	—	—	0.232	0.243
Economic stress					
Log of local rice price	−0.235	−0.238	−0.240	−0.247	−0.252
Household characteristics					
Household landholding (in *koku*)	12.566	11.916	12.673	11.266	10.492
Number of kin household members	—	—	—	4.778	—
Number of nonkin/servants	—	0.375	—	—	—
Marital status (Ref.: Currently married)					
Widowed	0.041	0.044	0.027	0.340	0.146
Divorced	0.040	0.041	0.050	0.046	0.065
Never married	0.040	—	0.163	0.000	0.031
Unknown	0.024	—	0.052	0.030	0.030
Household relationship (Ref.: For males, head; for females, spouse of head)					
Head	0.025	0.026	(Ref.)	0.049	—
Spouse of head	(Ref.)	(Ref.)	0.007	(Ref.)	—
Stem kin	0.192	0.182	0.275	0.694	—
Spouse of stem kin	0.143	0.160	0.065	0.000	—
Nonstem kin	0.024	0.021	0.032	0.010	—
Nonkin or servants	0.070	—	0.113	0.016	—
Period (Ref.: 1716–1759)					
1760–1799	0.295	0.289	0.287	0.327	0.321
1800–1839	0.245	0.240	0.234	0.266	0.233
1840–1870	0.148	0.148	0.139	0.090	0.081
Village (Shimomoriya = 1)	0.430	0.421	0.409	0.460	0.439

Note: The unit of observation is person-year.
[a] Including blood-related siblings, adoptive siblings, and in-laws. As for in-laws, older and younger siblings are measured in terms of biological age differences between the index person and in-laws.

resided in Shimomoriya, the value of the variable is 1; it is 0 if he or she was a resident of Niita.

We measure short-term economic stress by the log of the raw rice price in the local market of Aizu. In an earlier analysis of mortality in the two villages, our earlier study (Tsuya and Kurosu 2000) examined the effects of different rice price series—prices in Aizu and in the central market of Osaka—using different specifications: raw prices, detrended prices based on moving averages, and prices detrended using the Hodrick-Prescott filter. We found that short-term economic stress in the local area was best measured by raw prices. Here, we use the logged raw price to facilitate comparisons with other populations. To examine the nature of rice price fluctuations further, we also test the effects of prices time-lagged by one year.

Household characteristics are measured by three factors: household landholding, household size that can be divided by kin members and nonkin or servants, and proportion of household members aged 55 and above.[15] Household landholding (*mochidaka* in *koku*) is a continuous variable indicating the total productive capacity of the land held by the household. This covariate measures not only the amount of household income and economic resources available, but also the wealth and socioeconomic status of the household.[16]

Household size is divided into two components in our analysis: kin members and nonkin or servants. In our earlier analysis (Tsuya, Kurosu, and Nakazato 1997), we found that the mortality effects of the two components differed according to the sex and life stage of individuals. For example, a higher number of servants meant more labor sources for cultivation, but those servants needed to be managed and looked after. Thus, servants may have alleviated the demand of hard labor from household members who had been chiefly responsible for cultivation but may also have been a source of worry and trouble for those who were in charge of taking care of them. Similarly, a higher number of kin members in the household could mean more kin protection at a time of difficulty, though it may also have meant higher exposure to the risk of infectious diseases. We therefore model the effects of household size using these two separate covariates.

Further, high multicollinearity is found between landholding and household size because households with large landholdings were likely to have a large number of servants. The number of servants in turn accounted for a large part of variations in household size. Given the underdeveloped agricultural technologies at that time, households with large landholdings needed many servants for cultivation. Hence, we test the mortality effects of landholding and household size, introducing only one or two of the three covariates into the model at a time.

The proportion of household members aged 55 and above is a covariate measuring the age structure of household and, indirectly, the degree of old-age dependency existing within the household (see chapters 2 and 4 for detailed discussion). Given the relatively small household size and simple household structures prevalent in the villages—a vast majority of households were either simple or vertical stem-type households—this covariate is highly correlated with the presence of grandparents. Thus, we also test this household characteristic variable and the presence of grandfather and grandmother interchangeably.

The effects of coresident kin are measured by three groups of covariates: presence of parents, grandparents, and siblings.[17] Presence of parents is a covariate consisting of four categories: both parents present, only father present, only mother present, and no parent present. Using both parents present as the reference category, we constructed three dummy variables. Presence of grandparents is measured by two dichotomous variables: grandfather present and grandmother present. Since it is vital for the health and survival of young persons, but not adults, to have parents and grandparents living with them, we include presence of parents and grandparents only in the models for infant and child mortality. Presence of siblings is measured by four dichotomous variables: older brother(s) present or not, younger brother(s) present or not, older sister(s) present or not, and younger sister(s) present or not. Siblings include adoptive or step-siblings and in-laws. Older or younger siblings are measured in terms of biological age differences between the index person and his or her siblings under consideration.

The household relationship of the index individual is an important variable affecting the chances of survival in preindustrial societies because the position that each individual occupied within the household strongly influenced the degree of access to household resources and the statuses and roles assigned to him or her. Measured by the relationship of the index individual to his or her household head, this covariate consists of six categories: head, spouse of head, stem kin, spouse of stem kin, nonstem kin, and nonkin or servant. Stem kin members include parents, and grandparents if present, of the head as well as the head's children and grandchildren. For women, spouses of stem kin are mostly wives of the head's sons and grandsons, whereas, for men, they are primarily husbands of the head's daughters who are the heiress. The number of men falling into the latter category is very small. Nonstem kin members are those who are related to the head by blood, marriage, or adoption but are not stem kin. To facilitate easier and more meaningful interpretation of the results, we use different reference categories for males and females in the analyses of adult and elderly mortality: for males, the reference is household head; it is the spouse of the head for females. The analyses of infant and child mortality do not include the household relationship because boys and girls in the two villages spent a vast majority of their infancy and childhood years as stem kin members of household.

Our models for adult and old-age mortality include marital status. This covariate is employed because, similar to household relationship, marital status influenced the statuses and roles each individual was assigned within the household hierarchy in preindustrial Japanese households. Marital status may also capture the effect of marriage protection, an array of social, economic, psychological, and environmental benefits associated with marriage (Gove 1973, Hu and Goldman 1990, Lillard and Panis 1996). Given the prevalence of early and universal marriage in the two villages (Tsuya and Kurosu 1999), marital status may indicate the possibility of marriage selection in the sense that people failed to get or stay married because of their unhealthy conditions. Marital status consists of five categories: currently married, widowed, divorced, never married, and unknown. Using currently married as the reference category, we create four dummy variables.

For infant and child mortality, the model also includes an interval from previous birth to index birth (called *previous birth interval* hereafter), which is a proximate determinant known to affect the likelihood of infant and child death (Hobcraft, McDonald, and Rutstein 1985; Preston 1985). A short interval from previous to index birth, especially less than 24 months, is found to be associated with higher infant and child mortality because a short birth interval tends to result in maternal depletion and children's greater exposure to infectious diseases. When a child is born in a short interval from the previous birth, parental care and attention are also likely to be divided between two small children. Originally, this covariate was a composite variable measuring previous birth interval, combined with the survival status of the previous child. However, because our preliminary analysis indicated that the survival status of the previous child did not have a significant mortality effect, we specify this covariate as a dichotomy. The covariate is 1 if the interval was less than 24 months and 0 if the interval was 24 months or more or if the index child was the firstborn.[18]

Our model also takes into account the possible mortality effects of different periods within the 154-year period under consideration (1716–1870). There were considerable temporal differentials in socioeconomic development and environmental conditions in the northeastern region and the country as a whole during the latter half of Tokugawa Japan. First, the commercialization of agriculture based on family farming started on a full scale in the 1750s (Hayami 1985, 91–92). Then, at around the turn of the eighteenth century, the Nihonmatsu domain government changed its official policy discouraging the development of proto-industries and began to encourage the local production of cash crops (Nagata, Kurosu, and Hayami 1998), resulting in the industrialization of agrarian villages in the domain. Finally, in the late 1830s, after the Tempo famine, the rigid social structure and hierarchy of Tokugawa Japan became increasingly loose, leading to the period called *bakumatsu* (the last decades of the Tokugawa regime). Thus, we divide the 154-year period of 1716 to 1870 into four subperiods, each of which contains a sufficiently large number of years: before 1760, 1760 to 1799, 1800 to 1839, and after 1839. Using the earliest subperiod, 1716 to 1759, as the reference, we construct three period dummies.

The Results of the Discrete-Time Event-History Analyses

Infant (Age 1) Mortality

Table 9.4 shows the odds ratios of the covariates estimated by the discrete-time event-history analysis of mortality for females and males at age 1. We can see from the table that logged raw rice prices in the local market of Aizu are found to have been strongly and positively associated with the likelihood of the death of females at age 1 in the two villages. Household landholding is significantly but negatively associated with the mortality of infant females, with the interaction between rice price and landholding being also significant and negative. These findings suggest that female infants were highly vulnerable to short-term economic stress caused by fluctuations in agricultural output, but that their chances of survival improved significantly if they lived in a household with large landholdings. Moreover, this protective effect of landholding on mortality of infant females was even stronger in times of severe economic stress. That is, differences in the

Table 9.4
Estimated odds ratios of the covariates of the probability of dying in the next year among infants at age 1 by sex, Shimomoriya and Niita, 1716–1870

| | Female infants | | | | Male infants | |
| | Model 1 | | Model 2 | | | |
	Odds ratio	p-value	Odds ratio	p-value	Odds ratio	p-value
Log of local rice price	6.441	0.001	6.467	0.000	0.867	0.708
Household landholding	0.954	0.008	0.960	0.023	—	—
Landholding × logged rice price	0.903	0.018	0.905	0.016	—	—
Proportion of household members aged 55 or older	0.095	0.016	—	—	—	—
Presence of grandmother	—	—	0.528	0.009	—	—
Village (Shimomoriya = 1)	0.785	0.307	0.802	0.345	0.827	0.414
Constant	0.234	0.000	0.233	0.000	0.087	0.000
Number of individuals	1,062		1,062		1,263	
Number of deaths	85		85		98	
−2*Log-likelihood	562.96		561.92		688.27	
Chi-square	22.93		23.90		0.87	
Degrees of freedom	(5)		(5)		(2)	
p-value	0.000		0.000		0.001	

Note: Odds ratios are estimated by the logistic regression with robust standard errors.

chances of survival for infant girls living in households with large landholdings and those living in households with smaller landholdings became larger at the time of harvest failure or famine.

The proportion of household members aged 55 and above is found to have been negatively associated with the mortality of female infants (see model 1 for female infants in table 9.4). Because this covariate is highly correlated with the presence of the grandfather and grandmother, we also estimate the model using coresident grandparents instead (see model 2 for female infants in table 9.4). We find that the presence of the grandfather had no effect but that of the grandmother was negatively associated with the mortality of female infants at the 10 percent level. These findings imply that infant girls benefited by coresidence with the elderly probably because coresiding grandmothers cared for these infant girls, which helped them counter the risk of death. We can see from table 9.4 that none of the covariates, including logged rice prices, considered in this study has a significant mortality effect for male infants.

Childhood (Ages 2–14) Mortality

Table 9.5 shows the results of the discrete-time event-history analysis of mortality of males and females at ages 2 to 14. We can see that the probability of death among female children goes up when local rice prices increase; however, the price effects on female children, which are statistically significant only at 10 percent, are not as highly significant as those on female infants, which are significant at 1 percent. Thus, female children were vulnerable to short-term economic stress caused by local rice price fluctuations, although not as much as infant girls. Moreover, unlike the case of female infants, in which the mortality effect of prices becomes insignificant once prices are time-lagged, the positive mortality effect of price variations on female children remains significant even when prices are lagged by one year (data not shown). This suggests that the effect of price fluctuations on female childhood mortality was not short-lived but lasted into the next year.

Although not definitive, the presence of parents also affected the chances of survival of female children. Compared to those who had both parents living with them, girls whose parents were both absent from the household suffered a somewhat higher likelihood of death. There is also a clear temporal trend in the mortality of female children. Female child mortality fell as time passed, with the decline after 1839 being especially notable. This implies that the mortality of female children improved significantly when the rigid social stratification in Tokugawa Japan became looser. Being the least advantaged and least powerful member under the Tokugawa patriarchal stem family system, female children may have benefited from the increasing instability in this social structure.

Like female children, the mortality of male children is significantly affected by local rice price fluctuations, although the magnitude of the mortality effect on boys is not as much as that on girls. One unit of increase in local rice prices increases the likelihood of death for boys by 30 percent, whereas the corresponding figure for girls is 60 percent. Unlike female children, however, the mortality effects of prices on male children are not long-lasting. Though still positive, the effects become insignificant when lagged by one year (data not shown).

The number of kin household members is positively associated with the mortality of male children (see model 1 for male children in table 9.5). This suggests that male children living in a larger household were more likely to die than those living in a smaller household. We

Table 9.5
Estimated odds ratios of the covariates of the probability of dying in the next year among children aged 2–14 by sex, Shimomoriya and Niita, 1716–1870

| | Female children | | Male children | | | |
| | | | Model 1 | | Model 2 | |
	Odds ratio	p-value	Odds ratio	p-value	Odds ratio	p-value
Current age						
2	14.366	0.000	12.904	0.000	12.049	0.000
3	9.137	0.000	8.284	0.000	7.721	0.000
4	7.094	0.000	5.156	0.000	4.855	0.000
5–9	2.700	0.000	3.033	0.000	2.910	0.000
Log of local rice price	1.649	0.060	1.303	0.071	1.300	0.074
Number of kin household members	—	—	1.089	0.017	—	—
Presence of parents						
Father only	0.748	0.462	—	—	—	—
Mother only	1.152	0.260	—	—	—	—
No parents	1.433	0.100	—	—	—	—
Presence of other kin						
Older sister	—	—	0.765	0.026	—	—
Grandfather	—	—	—	—	1.423	0.002
Previous birth interval less than 24 months	—	—	1.306	0.091	1.300	0.094
Period						
1760–1799	0.893	0.263	0.909	0.272	0.905	0.262
1800–1839	0.804	0.109	0.807	0.093	0.803	0.088
1840–1870	0.689	0.040	0.803	0.128	0.849	0.194
Village (Shimomoriya = 1)	0.728	0.022	0.852	0.203	0.843	0.173
Constant	0.007	0.000	0.005	0.000	0.007	0.000
Person-years at risk	11,981		12,784		12,788	
Number of individuals	1,543		1,524		1,524	
Number of deaths	231		287		287	
−2*Log-likelihood	2,082.76		2,530.84		2,530.34	
Chi-square	164.15		247.28		237.71	
Degrees of freedom	(12)		(12)		(11)	
p-value	0.000		0.000		0.000	

Note: Odds ratios are estimated by the logistic regression with robust standard errors.

interpret this result to imply that this covariate is a proxy for the degree of exposure to various health risks, especially infectious diseases, within the household. If this is the case, boys were clearly vulnerable to such risks.

The presence of an older sister and grandfather in household also influences the mortality of male children, although the effects of these two coresident kin variables are the opposite. The mortality of male children is reduced significantly, by 23 percent, if they have at least one older sister living with them. It may be that older sisters served as baby-sitters to their younger brothers and that the presence of such kin caregivers increased the chances of survival of male children (see model 1 for male children in table 9.5). In contrast, the presence of a grandfather in the household significantly increases the likelihood of death of male children (see model 2 for male children in table 9.5). Because the presence of the grandfather and number of kin in household is found to be multicollinear (positively correlated), the number of kin members is dropped from the model once the presence of the grandfather is introduced. This result may imply that male children and male elderly, who were both dependent on care and support within the household while commanding preferential treatments under the patrilineal stem family system, may have competed for the same household resources. If this was the case, under the stem family system in which a senior generation possessed a definite advantage over a younger generation, it was more likely for elderly males to win such competition over male children. Under this family system, the mortality of female children was not affected by the presence of the grandfather, probably because girls, unlike boys, were not usually entitled to compete for such resources.

A short previous birth interval tends to increase male childhood mortality, though the effect is significant only at the 10 percent level. Relative to children whose previous birth interval was long (24 months or more) or to those who were firstborn, children born with a short previous interval were more likely to die. This suggests that a boy who was born within 24 months of the birth of a previous child was significantly more likely to die than boys who were firstborn or born 24 or more months after the birth of the previous child. This was probably because two (or more) small children would have competed for parental care and other resources. There are also some period differentials in male childhood mortality, though the temporal trend is not as clear and consistent as in the case of female childhood mortality.

Adult (Ages 15–54) Mortality

Table 9.6 presents the estimated odds ratios of the covariates of mortality for men and women at ages 15 to 54. First, looking at all women aged 15 to 54, we can see that household landholding is positively associated with female adult mortality at the 10 percent level (see model 1 for adult females in table 9.6). This suggests that women in households with large landholdings were somewhat more likely to die than were those in households with small landholdings. Because household landholding is thought to measure or proximate different factors according to women's household and marital statuses, we next restrict the analysis to ever-married women with kinship ties to the household head (by excluding never-married women and nonkin or servants). From models 2 and 3 for adult females in table 9.6, we see that both landholding and number of servants in the household, which are used interchangeably, are associated positively with adult female mortality, the mortality-enhancing effect of number of servants being especially significant. This means that the presence of servants and nonkin members significantly increased the mortality of ever-married adult women with kinship ties to the head. Altogether, we interpret these findings to suggest that as landholding increased, housekeeping and household supervisory responsibilities for married adult women increased accordingly, mainly because those women were chiefly responsible for managing and caring for servants. The difficulties and stress associated with such household responsibilities may have exerted detrimental health effects on these women.[19]

Marital status also significantly affected the mortality of women at ages 15 to 54. Relative to currently married women, divorced and never-married women were much more likely to die during adulthood. Focusing on ever-married women, divorced women were much more likely to die than their currently married counterparts. Given that early and universal marriage was prevalent in the two villages (Tsuya and Kurosu 1999), we interpret these results to imply a possible marriage selection. That is, divorced or never-married women were more likely to die not because they were divorced or single; rather, they failed to get or stay married because of their poor physical and mental health. This less healthy subgroup subsequently suffered death at a significantly higher likelihood than their more robust counterparts.

Household relationship also influenced the mortality of adult women significantly. Compared to those who were heads' spouses, women who were spouses of stem kin had significantly higher mortality. Most of these spouses of stem kin being the wives of sons of heads, this result seems to indicate the detrimental health effects of the widely documented low status and hardships of daughters-in-law in pre-industrial Japan (Kodama 1957, 255–260; Tsuya and Choe 1991). Relative to the head's spouse, women who were nonkin were also somewhat more likely to die. Altogether, we interpret the higher mortality of women who were wives of sons or nonkin members to imply the powerlessness and structural vulnerability of those women in agrarian households in preindustrial Japan.[20]

Female adult mortality became significantly lower after 1760, though mortality had a mild upturn between 1800 and 1830. Thus, in the case of adult female mortality, though there is no clear temporal trend, there appears to be a threshold at around 1760, after which it became significantly less.

Unlike the mortality of adult women, the mortality of adult men responds significantly and positively to annual fluctuations of local rice prices (see adult males in table 9.6). And the significant and positive mortality effect remains even when rice prices are lagged by one year (data not shown). This suggests that the mortality of adult men increased significantly as a result of the short-term economic stress caused by crop failure and that the mortality effect remained into the next year. Adult male mortality was also influenced significantly but negatively by household landholding. By contrast, the effect of landholding on adult female mortality is positive, although statistically insignificant (data not shown). We interpret this result to imply that in contrast to adult women, adult men were likely to benefit from income and other resources generated by the land owned by the household to reduce mortality risks. As shown in table 9.6, one additional *koku* of landholding reduced the mortality of adult males by 1.7 percent. Although this may seem small, the effect of landholding could be substantial. For example, compared to landless peasants (comprising around 10 percent of adult men), adult men who lived in households with the average landholding (13 *koku*) had 22 percent lower mortality. If men lived in a household with 28 to 37 *koku* of landholding (the top 5 percent), their mortality was reduced by about one-half to two-thirds (48 to 63 percent).[21]

There are significant differentials in the mortality of adult men by marital status. Relative to those who were currently married, divorced men were much more likely to die. Although not significant at the 10

Table 9.6
Estimated odds ratios of the covariates of the probability of dying in the next year among adults aged 15–54 by sex, Shimomoriya and Niita, 1716–1870

| | Adult females | | | | | | Adult males | |
| | Model 1 | | Model 2[a] | | Model 3[a] | | | |
	Odds ratio	p-value	Odds ratio	p-value	Odds ratio	p-value	Odds ratio	p-value
Current age								
15–19	0.463	0.005	0.523	0.022	0.503	0.013	0.205	0.000
20–24	0.574	0.023	0.593	0.039	0.649	0.075	0.316	0.000
25–29	0.778	0.280	0.770	0.279	0.827	0.407	0.238	0.000
30–34	1.025	0.913	1.021	0.930	0.995	0.982	0.300	0.000
35–39	0.969	0.893	1.043	0.860	1.011	0.961	0.387	0.000
40–44	1.110	0.643	1.127	0.608	1.293	0.238	0.652	0.043
45–49	0.766	0.287	0.737	0.244	0.725	0.200	0.730	0.129
Log of local rice price	1.003	0.499	1.170	0.222	1.128	0.263	1.485	0.020
Household landholding	1.010	0.081	1.010	0.088	—	—	0.983	0.031
Number of nonkin/servants	—	—	—	—	1.063	0.023	—	—
Marital status								
Widowed	1.299	0.193	1.324	0.184	1.186	0.289	1.351	0.144
Divorced	2.697	0.000	3.098	0.000	2.876	0.000	1.584	0.022
Never married	2.028	0.013	—	—	—	—	1.291	0.114
Unknown	0.360	0.171	—	—	—	—	1.050	0.939

	OR	p	OR	p	OR	p	OR	p
Household relationship								
Head	0.893	0.736	0.709	0.354	0.728	0.389	(Ref.)	(Ref.)
Spouse of head	(Ref.)	(Ref.)	(Ref.)	(Ref.)	(Ref.)	(Ref.)	1.267	0.692
Stem kin	0.929	0.706	0.925	0.704	1.018	0.925	1.823	0.000
Spouse of stem kin	1.678	0.004	1.628	0.007	1.491	0.036	1.417	0.265
Nonstem kin	1.730	0.026	1.206	0.296	1.125	0.365	3.028	0.000
Nonkin/servant	0.708	0.269	—	—	—	—	0.705	0.424
Period								
1760–1799	0.691	0.014	0.711	0.031	0.713	0.022	0.883	0.487
1800–1839	0.785	0.113	0.808	0.179	0.838	0.234	1.869	0.000
1840–1870	0.587	0.009	0.618	0.022	0.645	0.029	1.206	0.380
Village (Shimomoriya = 1)	1.244	0.065	1.286	0.042	1.174	0.171	1.233	0.104
Constant	0.013	0.000	0.013	0.000	0.014	0.000	0.016	0.000
Person-years at risk	26,800		23,793		26,196		28,170	
Number of individuals	2,042		1,614		1,646		2,151	
Number of deaths	313		283		313		270	
−2*Log-likelihood	3,349.69		3,025.22		3,347.45		2,926.57	
Chi-square	72.35		53.34		61.39		116.02	
Degrees of freedom	(22)		(19)		(19)		(22)	
p-value	0.000		0.000		0.000		0.000	

Notes: Odds ratios are estimated by the logistic regression with robust standard errors.
[a] Models 2 and 3 for adult females are restricted to ever-married women (aged 15–54) with kinship ties to the household head. The model excludes women who were nonkin or servant, and/or who were never married or whose marital status was unknown.

percent level, never-married and widowed men were also somewhat more likely to suffer death. These results seem to imply clearly the effect of marriage as selection and possibly as protection. Given that marriage was relatively early and widespread in the two villages, divorced and single men are thought to have been physically and mentally unrobust, which resulted in their higher likelihood of death. Although the effects are not significant, we cannot also deny the possibility of marriage protection, as widowed men also show a somewhat higher likelihood of dying.

Household headship was beneficial to the health of adult men. Compared to household heads, adult men who were stem kin or nonstem kin were much more likely to suffer death. Because the age and marital status of index men are controlled for, we interpret these results to imply the importance of power and authority associated with headship, which helped them counter various health risks. Compared with stem kin and nonkin members, household heads are also thought to have had greater control over household resources, so that they could more easily overcome the risks of death by mobilizing those resources.

The effects of period dummies indicate that adult male mortality was significantly higher between 1800 and 1839. A serious local famine occurred in the 1800s, and the great Tempo famine took place in the 1830s, affecting the northeastern region and the country as a whole. Adult males in the two villages may have suffered uncommonly high death tolls during these famines.

Old-Age (Ages 55–74) Mortality

Table 9.7 shows the estimated odds ratios of the covariates of the mortality of women and men at ages 55 to 74. We can see from the table that the effect of local rice prices on the mortality of elderly women is positive but statistically insignificant. However, the effect of landholding is negative and significant (see model 1 for elderly females in table 9.7). Using the number of kin household members instead of landholding, we then find that the size of coresident kin is also significantly and negatively associated with the mortality of elderly women (see model 2 for elderly females in table 9.7).[22] Altogether, these results suggest that elderly women living in households with more economic resources enjoyed a lower risk of death, probably because wealthier households could afford to provide more protection

Table 9.7
Estimated odds ratios of the covariates of the probability of dying in the next year, elderly aged 55–74, Shimomoriya and Niita, 1716–1870

| | Elderly females | | | | Elderly males | |
| | Model 1 | | Model 2 | | | |
	Odds ratio	p-value	Odds ratio	p-value	Odds ratio	p-value
Current age						
55–59	0.205	0.000	0.196	0.000	0.320	0.000
60–64	0.253	0.000	0.250	0.000	0.264	0.000
65–69	0.596	0.000	0.584	0.000	0.573	0.000
Log of local rice price	1.105	0.300	1.153	0.204	2.072	0.000
Household landholding	0.985	0.038	—	—	0.977	0.005
Number of kin household members	—	—	0.955	0.057	—	—
Marital status						
Widowed	1.267	0.031	1.201	0.073	1.533	0.001
Divorced	1.010	0.486	0.990	0.484	1.311	0.067
Never married	—	—	—	—	0.946	0.869
Unknown	0.674	0.415	0.988	0.972	1.640	0.083
Household relationship						
Head	0.665	0.113	0.614	0.050	—	—
Spouse of head	(Ref.)	(Ref.)	(Ref.)	(Ref.)	—	—
Stem kin	0.649	0.006	0.641	0.004	—	—
Spouse of stem kin	—	—	—	—	—	—
Nonstem kin	1.547	0.199	1.048	0.468	—	—
Nonkin/servant	0.414	0.261	0.641	0.429	—	—
Period						
1760–1799	1.095	0.542	1.025	0.855	1.102	0.474
1800–1839	1.275	0.108	1.179	0.230	1.144	0.355
1840–1870	1.676	0.009	1.586	0.015	1.467	0.059
Village (Shimomoriya = 1)	0.888	0.281	0.878	0.218	1.017	0.874
Constant	0.154	0.000	0.183	0.000	0.110	0.000
Person-years at risk	8,107		8,953		8,970	
Number of individuals	762		781		870	
Number of deaths	366		405		390	
-2^*Log-likelihood	2,827.37		3,133.31		3,059.11	
Chi-square	167.70		177.10		143.91	
Degrees of freedom	(16)		(16)		(13)	
p-value	0.000		0.000		0.000	

Note: Odds ratios are estimated by the logistic regression with robust standard errors.

and care to elderly women (many of whom were the heads' mother and grandmothers). Because households with larger landholding tended to be those with more coresident kin, elderly women who lived with a larger number of kin also enjoyed greater kin support and protection. Support and protection provided by coresident kin (most of whom were their children and grandchildren), in turn, helped elderly women counter health risks. The more that such kin protection was available, the better off elderly women were.

Marital status also affected the mortality of elderly women. Widowed women were more likely to die than those whose husbands were alive. This increasing mortality effect of widowhood seems to imply possible marriage protection because those women were strong enough to survive until at least age 55, a ripe old age in a preindustrial population.

Relative to elderly women who were a head's spouse, women who were stem kin of the head were much less likely to die. Given their ages, these stem kin women were mostly mothers and grandmothers of heads. Women who themselves were heads also had a somewhat lower likelihood of death than women who were wives of heads. These results again imply the negative health effects of household responsibilities and roles associated with being heads' wives, resulting from shouldering various responsibilities for managing households.

There is a positive temporal trend in the mortality of elderly women, and this is also the case for the mortality of elderly men (see elderly males in table 9.7). As the time passed, the mortality of elderly women and men increased. Elderly mortality in the last period, 1840 to 1870, was especially high. Although we are not certain why this was the case, the results seem to suggest that the breakdown of the rigid Tokugawa social structure was not beneficial to women and men in old age. This in turn implies that elderly men and women were in general respected and well treated (probably for the sake of their old age), enjoying a relatively high status in the Tokugawa society.

From table 9.7, we can also see that the effect of logged local rice price on elderly men is very significant and positive. The mortality effects of rice prices on elderly men are stronger and more significant than are those on adult men. Further, these positive mortality effects remain when prices are lagged by one year (data not shown). These findings therefore suggest that elderly men were highly vulnerable— more vulnerable than their younger adult counterparts—to short-term economic stress caused by annual fluctuations in local rice prices, and such detrimental health effects lingered into the next year.

Marital status also affected the mortality of elderly men. Widowed elderly men were much more likely to suffer death compared to their currently married counterparts. Divorced men and men whose marital status was unknown were also somewhat more likely to die than currently married men. Although the mortality effect of the divorced state may have been due to marriage selection (their marriage was disrupted because their physical and mental health deteriorated), it seems more likely that the effect of widowhood and divorce for elderly men indicates marriage protection. While they were healthy enough to survive to the ripe old age of 55 and above, these elderly men, feeling desolate and depressed because of the loss of their wife, probably lost their vigor to live, consequently suffering higher mortality. Comparing them with elderly women, we also notice that the positive mortality effect of widowhood was stronger and more significant among men in old age. This implies the importance of marriage protection for elderly men, in the sense that support and protection given by their wives helped them counter mortality risks in old age.

Summary and Discussion

To the extent that annual fluctuations in the local rice price captured short-term economic stress resulting from harvest failure, mortality responses to the short-term economic stress of people who lived in two agrarian villages in northeastern Tokugawa Japan were notable, although they varied considerably by sex and life stage. Female infants were highly vulnerable to the short-term economic stress caused by local rice price fluctuations, and the price effect was also dependent on the household landholding of those baby girls. At the time of harvest failure or famine, the mortality effect of price fluctuations was significantly lower if infant girls lived in wealthy households. In contrast, the mortality of male infants was not responsive to short-term economic stress. Both female and male children were also vulnerable to short-term economic stress caused by crop failure, though child mortality was not as responsive to price fluctuations as was the mortality of female infants. For adults and elders, male mortality responded significantly and positively to rice price fluctuations, whereas female mortality did not. Moreover, the mortality effects of rice price fluctuations for female children and adult and elderly men were not short-lived, lasting into the following year. Although the mortality of adult women was not affected directly by rice price fluctuations, this does not necessarily mean that these women were unaffected by other types of short-term economic stress. For example, our earlier studies found that the mortality of married adult women in these villages increased significantly with the death of the adult male head or their husband (Tsuya and Kurosu 2000, 2002). This suggests that adult women were also vulnerable to stress resulting from a sudden breakdown of the economic and social bases on which they depended. Altogether, people in these two preindustrial Japanese agrarian villages were in general vulnerable to the short-term economic stress caused by annual fluctuations in agricultural output. Since the sensitivity of mortality to short-term economic stress is thought to indicate the extent to which living standards affect mortality (see chapter 2), our results suggest that the likelihood of survival of the residents in agricultural villages in preindustrial northeastern Japan was indeed influenced by fluctuations in living standards, although some gender and age groups were more vulnerable than others.

We also found that in these two northeastern villages, household landholding was strongly associated with large household size, because large households tended to have a large number of servants and more children. Hence, the mortality effects of landholding and household size were multidimensional and could be positive or negative according to the sex and life stage of individuals. On the one hand, because households with larger landholdings and more members had more resources, individuals living in these households benefited from such resources in countering health risks. Larger landholdings and household size also meant more kin household members who provided protection and support, and elderly women seem to have benefited from such kin protection. This health enhancing (mortality-reducing) effect of landholding and household size was the case for female infants, adult men, and elderly men and women. However, larger landholdings and household size also exerted detrimental health effects because more coresident members meant a higher exposure to infectious diseases; male children in particular suffered from such exposure. Large landholdings and household size also meant a large number of servants and nonkin members to be managed and looked after, and the health of married adult women seems to have suffered from the difficulties and stresses caused by heavy household management responsibilities.

Our study also revealed the importance of household relationship for the likelihood of survival of men and women in their adult years (aged 15–54). Women were especially vulnerable when they were in structurally powerless positions within the household such as daughters-in-law or nonstem kin members of head. Nonhead adult men also suffered higher mortality than adult men who were household heads, implying that the power and authority associated with household headship were also important factors for adult men in countering various health risks.

Coresident kin mattered to the chances of survival, especially for persons at the beginning and end of their life course—children and the elderly. Further, although the nature of the mortality effect differed by sex, the mortality of the young and the elderly was influenced in more than one way according to whom they lived with. For example, the chances of survival of female infants were increased by the presence of the grandmother. Likewise, coresiding older sisters increased the survival chances of male children. The presence of the wife improved the chances of survival of elderly men, while elderly women benefited from coresidence with kin in general, especially offspring. However, coresident kin were not always beneficial, as shown by the negative health effect of the presence of the grandfather on the mortality of male children.

This study also showed significant changes over time in the levels of mortality in the two northeastern Japanese villages between 1716 and 1870. An especially notable contrast was seen between changes in the mortality of female children and those of elderly men and women. Whereas the mortality of female children declined almost linearly over time, elderly mortality increased over time. This implies that as the rigid Tokugawa social structure deteriorated, female children, who were the least privileged members in preindustrial agrarian households, enjoyed improved chances of survival. In contrast, the elderly benefited by the rigid social order and stratification in Tokugawa society in the sense that their old age entitled them to respect and privilege. Once this social structure became shaky, their chances of survival also suffered.

This study revealed the intricacies and complexities associated with people's chances of survival in preindustrial agrarian villages in northeastern Japan. People were in general vulnerable to short-term economic stress caused by fluctuations in agricultural output from one year to another, although the level of vulnerability differed by their sex and life stage. In this preindustrial society, household resources and family relations were important in countering health risks. Furthermore, the positions that individuals occupied within the household were vital to their chances of survival. It was not enough to live in a wealthy household. To counter mortality risks, people needed to be in a position that enabled them to mobilize household wealth and resources. Similar to societies today, when people were physically frail in early childhood and in old age, protection and care provided by families were also important in reducing mortality risks.

Notes

We are grateful to Akira Hayami and Saeko Narimatsu for being instrumental in making the original population registration data available, to Masako Unosawa for her assistance in transcribing the original registration records, and to Yoshihiko Ono and Jonathan Chow for creating the data file for multivariate analysis. We also thank Minja Kim Choe, Cameron Campbell, Tommy Bengtsson, and James Z. Lee for helpful comments.

1. Saito (2002) reports that according to one source (Ogashima 1894), there were twenty-eight recorded famines in the Tokugawa period, and according to another (R. Saito 1966), there were sixty-one estimated famines between 1600 and 1900.

2. The northeastern region of Japan is traditionally known as the Ou region. In Tokugawa Japan, Ou consisted of two subregions: Mutsu and Dewa. Roughly dividing the Ou region vertically in the middle, Mutsu was the part facing the Pacific Ocean, and Dewa was the one facing the Sea of Japan.

3. One *koku* equals approximately five bushels.

4. Rice and other grain price data based on local market conditions do exist for other parts of Tokugawa Japan. A typical example is the price series from the local market town of Kariya in the Nobi region in central Japan, which include data on retail rice and some other grain prices in Kariya from the 1750s to 1860s (Iwahashi 1988).

5. Iwahashi (1981) provides rice price series for other parts of Tokugawa Japan, and Miyamoto (1988, 386–430) analyzed the correlation between local rice markets and the Osaka central market in early modern Japan. Feeney and Hamano (1990) also examined the relationship between rice price fluctuations and fertility in late Tokugawa Japan.

6. Sericulture became popular in the region at that time, and mulberry leaves were major cash crops. According to a survey conducted by the domain government in 1828 on the use of agricultural land and local industries, around 30 percent of the dry field in Niita was cultivated as mulberry fields, whereas only 5 to 10 percent of the dry field in Shimo-moriya was for growing mulberry trees (Nihonmatsu-shi 1982, 581).

7. The population registers in Shimomoriya and Niita, like all other localities in the Nihonmatsu domain, were *ninbetsu-aratame-cho* (NAC) rather than the *shumon-aratame-cho* (SAC) more common elsewhere. Although these two types of registers collected similar information, the original purpose of the SAC was to identify hidden Christians and prevent the entry and spread of Christianity. The NAC, although based on the SAC, were, as the name indicates, primarily for population registration and investigation (Narimatsu 1985, 11–14, 1992, 10–12; Nagata, Kurosu, and Hayami 1998).

8. The size of de jure population can also be computed for both villages because records were kept as far as one's permanent (legal) domicile was in the villages. However, for

persons whose legal domicile was in the village but did not reside there, information on individual circumstances, including demographic events that occurred while away from the villages, are generally unavailable.

9. Return migration or repeated migration in and out of the village also seem to have been fairly common, especially among males. For example, Narimatsu (1985, 103–104) cited a case of one male who changed his employer fourteen times, spending altogether thirteen years (out of the twenty-seven years from age 13 to his death at age 40) outside the village as a servant.

10. In addition to chronological age (age according to Gregorian calendar) and NAC age, there is also the traditional Japanese method of counting age. As in the rest of East Asia, it regards a child as age 1 at birth and adds an additional year on each New Year's Day thereafter.

11. According to historical evidence, the Tenmei famine, which hit mainly northeastern and eastern Japan, was by far the most serious famine recorded in early modern Japan (Hayami 1982; Narimatsu 1985, 199–200). The socioeconomic, demographic, and political consequences of this famine were so serious that after the famine, the Nihonmatsu domain government started a system of reserving rice for emergency by each locality (Narimatsu 1985, 52–53). Thus, when the Tempo famine hit the region, many villages and towns in the domain, including Niita, are thought to have been better prepared and protected than in the past. However, presumably because extra rice was hardly available for storage given its poor agricultural land, Shimomoriya may have been devastated again by this famine.

12. The CDR for 1800 to 1809 is also relatively high. Though no large-scale famine is known to have occurred during this period in the northeastern region, a small-scale epidemic may have occurred. For example, there exists a document (*Kyowa-gannen Ekibyo-nin-daka Shirushiage-cho*) that recorded the number of villagers who suffered from infectious and parasitic diseases in Shimomoriya in 1800 and how they were treated. According to that document, twenty-one villagers died of these diseases in that year (Narimatsu 1985, 71–72).

13. Life expectancy at age 1 by sex in other Tokugawa villages estimated by previous studies is as follows: 42.7 years for males and 44.0 years for females in Yokouchi from 1726 to 1765 (Hayami 1973, 204); 43.7 for males and 41.9 for females in Hida villages from 1776 to 1855 (Janetta and Preston 1991); 44.9 for males and 44.8 for females in Nishojo from 1773 to 1869 (Hayami 1992, 249); and 46.1 for males and 50.8 for females in Nakahara from 1717 to 1830 (Smith 1977, 56). The figures for Hida villages are the unweighted averages of estimates for twenty-year periods.

14. Causes for higher-than-expected mortality for males aged 20 to 24 in the two villages are unknown. One possibility is tuberculosis. The life table for Japan from 1921 to 1925 shows a clear bulge in the probability of dying, due mostly to a high likelihood of death by tuberculosis, for ages around 20 (Okazaki 1980, 83). However, even in that life table, sex differential in mortality for ages 20 to 24 is not distinctive. Surviving historical documents on the two villages, translated by Narimatsu (1985, 1992), reveal very little about causes of death and do not show any evidence of the prevalence of tuberculosis in the villages or the surrounding areas in the eighteenth and nineteenth centuries.

15. We also tested such other covariates measuring household characteristics as proportion of household members under age 15 and household type. These variables were found to be statistically insignificant and/or multicollinear to some other variables in the

model. For details of the definitions, measurements, and nature of the effects of these variables, see Tsuya, Kurosu, and Nakazato (1997).

16. According to Hamano (2000), who examined different measures of household economic status, household landholding is the most appropriate and most widely used indicator of household economic status in preindustrial Japanese villages.

17. We also tested the effects of coresident sons and daughters on adult and old-age mortality, first specifying their marital statuses and then without such specification. The mortality effects were found to be insignificant.

18. *Firstborn* here refers to *observed* first birth. For children who were born in the villages, *first birth* means actual first birth. However, for those who appeared in the universe of observation at later ages, first births include eldest surviving children at the time of first registration, who were not necessarily firstborn.

19. Based on data from a 1933 time-use survey of selected farm households by Japan's Imperial Agricultural Association, Saito (1996) found that women aged 31 to 50 in households with large landholdings spent, on the average, the highest number of hours on both agricultural and domestic activities, compared with women in households with smaller landholdings or those in tenant households. He speculated that it was probably the case that nonelderly adult women in large farm households shouldered most of the responsibilities associated with running such large households, taking care of household members. See similar data for household heads in northeastern China reported by Lee and Campbell (1997).

20. G. W. Skinner (1993) also made similar findings in his study of conjugal power, drawing data from population registers of eight villages in central Tokugawa Japan. He argued that the experience of wielding power as an adult within the family increased longevity and that powerlessness and structural vulnerability to oppression had negative health effects in the long run.

21. In terms of person-years, more than 98 percent of adult men under consideration lived in households with landholdings less than 38 *koku*. Hence, net of other factors in the model, virtually nobody in our data of adult men had the likelihood of death near zero.

22. A study by Cornell (1989) on an agricultural village in central Japan in the nineteenth century also found that the life expectancy of elderly women was improved substantially by the presence of children and grandchildren in the household.

10 Mortality and Household in Seven Liaodong Populations, 1749–1909

Cameron Campbell and
James Z. Lee

Household context was a key determinant of individual standard of living in late imperial China. Resource allocation and work assignments of household members determined their consumption and their sensitivity to short-term stress. These allocations were anything but equal: households were highly stratified, with multiple overlapping hierarchies (Lee and Campbell 1997). Senior generations took precedence over junior ones. Within each generation, the older were favored over the younger. Men had priority over women. The least privileged were further differentiated according to whether particular kin who could represent their interests were present in the household (Campbell and Lee 2002).

Previous studies of the standard of living in late imperial China have largely ignored differences within or between households, focusing instead on secular trends and comparisons with Europe. Most have focused on evidence from one region of China, Jiangnan, which during the late imperial era was one of the wealthiest areas in the country. The majority have taken a traditional approach to the measurement of standard of living, drawing inferences from estimates of per capita production or consumption (Li 1998, Pomeranz 2000). Some have assessed trends in standard of living by constructing mortality estimates from data in lineage genealogies (Harrell and Pullum 1995, Liu 1995a, 1995b).

This chapter uses mortality outcomes to examine the role of the household in determining individual standard of living in Liaodong, China, during the Qing (1644–1911). We examine how household socioeconomic status conditioned the mortality risks of individual members, identifying who benefited and who did not when the household prospered. To map the networks of authority and dependency that bound household members together and decided the allocation of resources, we examine how relationship to the head and the presence or absence of particular kin affected mortality risks.

We divide the chapter into five sections. The first reviews the debate on the standard of living in China before the twentieth century and summarizes previous findings on mortality trends and patterns. The second introduces the Liaodong populations. The third describes the model we estimate for Liaodong, detailing its differences from the comparative model. The fourth discusses results from both the standard Eurasian comparative model and the Liaodong-specific model. The fifth concludes with remarks about the implications of our findings for our understanding of mortality and the standard of living in late imperial China, focusing on the role of the household.

The Standard of Living in Qing China

The consensus used to be that living standards were lower in China than in Europe during the Qing dynasty. Influenced by Malthus's portrait of China during the late eighteenth century as a land of misery and poverty where the positive check predominated, a succession of observers argued, and continue to argue, that the nineteenth century was a time of rising population pressure in China and stagnant or declining living standards. The essential problem, in this view, was that the combination of early and universal female marriage and uncontrolled fertility within marriage precluded any role for preventive checks. As a result, China was trapped in a high-pressure equilibrium, with persistently higher death rates and lower standards of living than the western European populations in which the marriage-based preventive check operated (Wrigley and Schofield 1981).

A number of studies have sought to illustrate changes in the standard of living in late imperial China by estimating mortality from genealogical data. The earliest was Yuan I-chin (1931), who used a genealogy to calculate life tables for a Guangdong lineage from the fourteenth century to the middle of the nineteenth. Liu Ts'ui-jung analyzed genealogies from a variety of lineages throughout eastern and southern China (1978, 1981, 1983, 1985, 1992, 1995a, 1995b) to reconstruct trends and age patterns of mortality during the Ming (1368–1643) and Qing. Similar studies have been carried out for lineages in Xiaoshan, Zhejiang (Harrell and Pullum 1995) and Tongcheng, Anhui

(Telford 1990), as well as for a national-level descent group (Zhao 1997b).

From these analyses, scholars claim to have detected evidence of deteriorating living standards. Death rates rose in the first half of the seventeenth century, fell during the second half, and then rose steadily from the eighteenth century until the end of the nineteenth (Harrell 1995b, Liu 1985). Interpretations of these trends typically link them to dynastic decline and renewal. Thus, turmoil associated with the fall of the Ming dynasty in the first half of the seventeenth century allegedly accounted for the initial increase. Pacification by the new Qing dynasty and subsequent prosperity accounted for the subsequent but short-lived decrease. Rising population pressure led to the increase in death rates from the beginning of the eighteenth century to the end of the nineteenth.

Shortcomings in genealogies as sources for demographic analysis indicate caution in evaluating claims about mortality trends (Harrell 1987, Pope 1989). Many Chinese genealogies were compiled retrospectively, with information about lineage members often based on the recollections of descendants. Members with no progeny, because they died young, never married, or were infertile, are accordingly more likely to be omitted. Because this problem is worse for earlier than for later generations, estimates of mortality rates earlier in time are more likely to be biased downward, leading to spurious trends of rising death rates. Moreover, since most genealogies provide few details on men who died before adulthood, it is difficult to use them to study child or adolescent mortality. Since they typically provide no details on women at all, they cannot be used to study female mortality.

Comparison of mortality levels between China and Europe fails to reveal systematic differences indicative of lower living standards in the former. Adult mortality varied considerably within China and does not seem to have been consistently higher than that in historical European populations. Table 10.1 summarizes many of the available estimates of life expectancy in China before the mid-twentieth century. Levels vary because the characteristics and contexts of the populations differed. For example, life expectancy in the imperial lineage was the lowest by far because only lineage members were compelled to live in a large and crowded city, Beijing. In some cases, estimates differed because the methods used to produce them differed. Two estimates of life expectancy for China as a whole between 1927 and 1931 that used the

Table 10.1
Estimates of life expectancy for selected historical Chinese populations

Population	Age		
	0	10	20
Liaodong			
North			
Men, 1789–1909		47.1	39.8
Women, 1789–1909		42.3	37.4
South			
Men, 1789–1909		48.4	41.4
Women, 1789–1909		47.9	41.8
Imperial lineage *(Famlpohei a hall cry ph puty)*			
Men born, 1644–1739	27.2	36.9	29.9
Men born, 1740–1839	33.6	37.2	29.5
Men born, 1840–1899	34.7	37.8	32.2
Women born, 1640–1739	24.6	34.8	30.7
Tongcheng lineages			
Men, 1300–1880	31.0	38.9	32.4
Women, 1300–1880	26.0	38.8	33.5
Chekiang lineages			
Shen lineage			
Men born, 1680–1739		45.5	37.2
Men born, 1740–1829		41.4	33.1
Women born, 1680–1739		47.7	39.8
Women born, 1740–1829		44.8	36.9
Hsu lineage			
Men born, 1680–1739		45.2	36.6
Men born, 1740–1829		38.9	31.1
Women born, 1680–1739		47.2	39.1
Women born, 1740–1829		42.3	35.0
Taiwan 1906			
Males	27.7	33.5	
Females	29.0	27.2	
China 1929–1931[a]			
Males	34.9	47.0	40.7
Females	34.6	40.6	40.1
China 1929–1931[b]			
Males	24.6	34.2	30.1
Females	23.7	33.9	29.3

Sources: Liaodong: Authors' calculations from data analyzed in this chapter. Imperial lineage: Lee, Campbell, and Wang (1992); Campbell (1995). Chekiang lineages: Liu (1985). Tongcheng lineages: Telford (1990).
[a] Notestein and Chiao (1937).
[b] Barclay, Coale, Stoto, and Trussell (1976).

same data differ by ten years because they resulted from application of different methods to the same data (Barclay et al. 1976, Notestein and Chao 1937).

Other studies challenge the received wisdom that living standards in late imperial China were lower than in Europe, and stagnant or declining. Based on estimates of per capita production and consumption, Kenneth Pomeranz (2000) argues that living standards in China were probably comparable to those in Europe at least until the middle of the eighteenth century, though they may have declined during the nineteenth century. Similarly, Li Bozhong (1998) has argued that at least in some parts of China, per capita production and consumption were stable or rose until the middle of the nineteenth century. James Z. Lee and Wang Feng (1999b) have argued that the Malthusian understanding of the Chinese demographic system was fundamentally incorrect, especially when it came to the relationship between living standards and demographic behavior. They claim that the preventive check played a much more important role in China than Malthus and his intellectual heirs realized because married couples adjusted their fertility behavior according to their economic circumstances.[1] The sustained rise in China's population during the Qing was a response to improving living standards, not a reflection of couples' desire to maintain high fertility in the face of stagnant or declining living standards.

New studies have moved beyond reconstruction of aggregate levels and trends to examine the role of the household in determining individual standard of living. Relationship to the household head affected mortality risks because it determined location in the household hierarchy (Lee and Campbell 1997). The presence or absence of particular kin was also important. As is the case in almost all contemporary populations (Hu and Goldman 1990), widows and widowers in China had higher death rates than the currently married (Campbell and Lee 1996). Mothers had sole responsibility for child care; thus children suffered when their mother died but not when their father died (Campbell and Lee 2002). This effect was apparent even when other adult women were present in the household, implying that when a wife in a multiple-family household died, her sisters-in-law did not take care of her children as attentively as they did their own. Sons, meanwhile, were as important to their mothers as their mothers were to them: because married women had to have a son to be fully enfranchised in their husband's family, they had lower death rates if they had a living son.

Examination of mortality levels and their sensitivity to short-term stress yields a complex picture of within-household differences in the standard of living. Lower overall levels of mortality appear to have carried a price in the form of heightened sensitivity to short-term stress. Although the mortality rates of men in Liaodong were lower overall than those of women, they were also more sensitive to price variation (Lee and Campbell 1997). Differentiation of the mortality response to prices by occupation, household context, and other characteristics provides additional examples of situations where individuals whose death rates were lower overall were nevertheless more sensitive to prices (Campbell and Lee 2000). We interpret such findings as consistent with a model of the Chinese household in which each member is entitled to some minimum level of consumption and the privileged members appropriate the surplus that remains. When times were bad and there was no surplus, the consumption of the more privileged fell accordingly.

Data

The populations that we examine were part of a Qing military and administrative system known as the Eight Banners (Ding 1982; Ding et al. forthcoming; Elliott 2001). They were assigned to the Imperial Household Agency and were closely monitored as they were Royal Peasants and of more concern to the Imperial Court than regular population.

The Qing government registered these populations in the "Household and Population Registers of the Eight Banner Han Army" (*Hanjun baqi rending hukou ce*). The Qing devised a system of internal cross-checks to ensure consistency and accuracy. First, they assigned every person in the Banner population to a residential household (*linghu*) and registered them on a household certificate (*menpai*). Then they organized households into clans (*zu*), and compiled annually updated clan genealogies (*zupu*). Finally, every three years the government agents compared these genealogies and household certificates with the previous household register to compile a new register. They deleted and added people who had exited or entered the population in the last three years and updated the ages, relationships, and official titles of those people who remained and recorded any changes in their given names. Each register, in other words, completely superseded its predecessor.

The Banner registers provide far more comprehensive and accurate demographic and sociological data than the household registers and lineage genealogies common elsewhere in China (Harrell 1987; Jiang 1993; Lee and Campbell 1997; Skinner 1987; Telford 1990). This is because Banner populations were under special state jurisdiction, distinct from provincial administration elsewhere. In Liaoning, population registration began as early as 1625, when the Manchus made Shenyang their capital and incorporated the surrounding communities into the banner system. It was not until the establishment of the General Office of the Three Banner Commandry in 1749–1752, however, that a single provincial authority assumed control of the population registration process (Tong and Guan 1994; 1999); and it was not until 1749 that Liaoning population registers assumed a uniform format as well as a uniform triennial schedule.

From 1749 onward, the registers recorded at three-year intervals for each person in the target population the following information in order of appearance: relationship to their household head; name(s) and name changes; adult banner status, including official title, if any; age; animal birth year; lunar birth month, birth day, and birth hour; marriage, death, or emigration, if any, during the intercensal period; physical disabilities, if any, and if the person is an adult male; name of their household group head; banner affiliation; and village of residence.[2] Individuals are listed one to a column in order of their relationship to the head, with children and grandchildren listed first, followed by co-resident siblings and their descendants, and uncles, aunts, and cousins. Wives are always listed immediately after their husbands, unless they are superseded by a coresident widowed mother-in-law.

The data from the Banner registers are also distinguished by the ease with which they can be reorganized longitudinally. Individuals and their households can be followed very easily from one register to the next because they appear in almost the same order in successive registers. Accordingly, it is relatively straightforward to reconstruct life histories and generate variables describing individual and household characteristics as well as outcome measures at particular times or over a specific time interval.

For this analysis, the most important feature of these registers is that they are well suited to the study of mortality. One of the most important strengths of the demographic data is that the population at risk is known precisely. Once individuals entered the household registration system, they were followed until they departed in their last record through death, emigration, or marriage. Thus, daughters and widows who left their households through marriage or remarriage since the previous register are explicitly identified as having done so, as are individuals who died since the previous register. Those who departed the area without permission were annotated as having left illegally.

The data also have some shortcomings. The most important is that children were registered late. On average, children do not make their first appearance in the registers until they are 5 or 6 *sui* (Lee and Campbell 1997). Very few appear before age 3 *sui*, and almost none appears before age 2 *sui*. As a result, we do not analyze infant mortality. The problem is worse for girls than for boys, so that among registered children, there is a pronounced excess of males (Lee and Campbell 1997). It appears that many girls were never registered while in their natal families, and appeared in the registers only once they had married and joined their husband's household. Accordingly, results for female child mortality should be treated with caution. Another shortcoming is that the registers do not identify dates of death, only the three-year period in which death occurs. This requires the use of discrete-time event-history techniques.

The data we analyze here are a subset of a larger population of nineteen distinct state farm subpopulations, which currently includes 938,413 observations of 171,715 individuals who lived in more than 400 largely rural communities in what is now Liaoning province between 1749 and 1909. Map 10.1 summarizes the geographic distribution of this larger population over an area of 6,000 square miles, approximately the size of the contemporary Netherlands, from the coast of the Liaodong Peninsula in the south to the hills of northern Liaoning. In this analysis we distinguish coastal communities from other communities.

The southern state farm systems were all located in or near what is now Gaiping County on the Liaodong Peninsula. They were either on or close to the coast of the Bohai Gulf. They were also close to Yingkou, which became a treaty port open to international trade around 1860. Accordingly, the region was heavily involved in coastal trade and, during the last half of the nineteenth century, international trade as well. As a result, the economy in this region was much more commercialized than in the central or northern regions, at least during the last half of the nineteenth century.

The northern state farms were scattered in a belt that ran from what is now the provincial capital, Shenyang, to a hilly and remote region

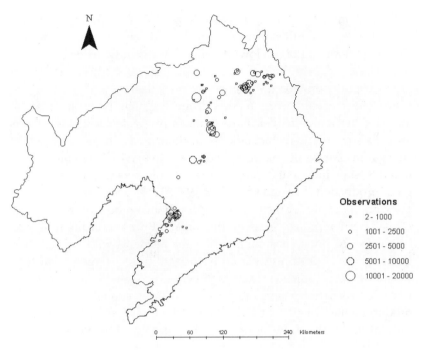

Map 10.1
Northeastern China

in the northeast of the province. The state farms that lay just to the north of Shenyang were situated on an agricultural plain. Previous analysis suggested that they were relatively densely populated (Lee and Campbell 1997). The area in the northeast, in contrast, appears to have remained a sparsely populated frontier for much of the period under consideration. Even today many of the villages in the northeast that were recorded in the registers are poor and inaccessible. While at the time of writing the available data were not sufficient for comparisons within the northern region, in our more recent analyses we have begun to distinguish the area north of Shenyang from the remote and hilly area in the northeast.

To study the influence of economic conditions on mortality outcomes, we use grain price series from an empire-wide system to monitor food conditions that began elsewhere in China as early as the late seventeenth century and were extended to Liaodong into the late eighteenth century (Wu 1996). In this system, county magistrates reported each week the price of five major food grains (rice, wheat, husked and unhusked millet, soybean, and sorghum) to the provincial government. The governor then prepared each month a brief summary for the central government of the lowest and highest county prices by prefecture. These monthly prefectural summaries of the highest and lowest reported prices provide the bulk of our price data.

We use monthly price reports from Fengtian prefecture, which includes the areas in which the state farms were located. Previous analysis suggests that fluctuations in grain prices in this area reflect changes in climate and harvest yields more than changes in market demand or state intervention; thus, prices should be a proxy for regional grain production (Lee and Campbell 1997, 31–35). State farm residents grew grain mainly for their own consumption and bought or sold only a small portion of their grain on the market. Prices accordingly should be a proxy for food consumption. For the residents who did sell their grain on the market, research on historical Europe suggests that they would not have benefited from high prices, because the inverse correlation between production and prices was strong enough that for small producers, the benefits of being able to sell at a higher price were typically offset by the drawbacks of having less to sell (Galloway 1988). Only large producers who had a surplus even when the harvest was poor would have benefited from high prices. We expect high prices to have been associated with poor harvests overall and reduced consumption among subsistence farmers and small producers, but no change in consumption among major producers.

Sorghum was a staple crop; thus, we use sorghum price as an indicator of economic conditions.[3] We use low sorghum price series because we believe they were more reflective of the situation in rural areas than the high price series, which are most likely to have been from urban areas. Figure 10.1 summarizes low sorghum prices from 1768 to 1910. Since the sustained increase that began in the 1880s may have been an artifact of inflation, and may not have reflected actual reductions in consumption or real income, we excluded the period after 1888 from the analysis of price effects. Prices before 1888 were clearly volatile, in some cases doubling or tripling from one year to the next and then remaining high for several consecutive years.[4] Since there was no secular trend in prices before 1888, and regressions using detrended prices series yielded broadly similar results, in our analysis we made use of logged raw prices, not logged detrended prices.

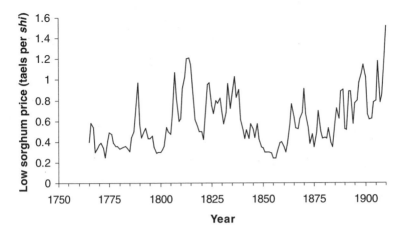

Figure 10.1
Annual sorghum prices in Liaodong, 1765–1910

Models

To illuminate the determinants of standard of living in Liaodong, we have estimated two sets of models using the Liaodong household register data described in the appendix. The first consists of the comparative models defined in chapters 1, 3, and 5. The second set, referred to as the Liaodong models, is based on a modification of the comparative models that includes additional variables of substantive interest only in a Chinese context or available only in the Chinese data. It also omits some variables that were unimportant as determinants of mortality in rural Liaodong. Table 10.2 summarizes these Liaodong model variables.

Here we discuss only the variables unique to the Liaodong models. The variables fall into three categories: contextual, socioeconomic, and household. The contextual variables capture the macrolevel secular trends, regional differences, short-term economic fluctuations, and village characteristics that formed the background against which microlevel variation between and within households occurred. We include such variables not only because they are substantively interesting in their own right, but also because if they were correlated with the microlevel variables for socioeconomic status and household composition, failure to control for them could lead to misleading results.

Table 10.2
Means and standard deviations of the variables used in the analysis, Liaodong, 1789–1909

Variable	Children				Adults				Elderly			
	Female		Male		Female		Male		Female		Male	
	Mean	SD	Mean	SD	Mean	SD	Mean	SD	Mean	SD	Mean	SD
Death in next three years	0.07	0.25	0.04	0.19	0.04	0.20	0.03	0.18	0.13	0.34	0.17	0.37
Age^a	8.77	3.81	8.89	3.88	19.85	10.37	17.41	11.20	7.77	5.44	7.35	5.34
Age^2	91.52	67.43	94.05	69.66	501.53	435.51	428.42	431.58	90.00	98.80	82.45	95.15
Age^3	1,054.6	1,026.4	1,100.8	1,072.0	14,345.8	16,354.3	12,114.8	15,672.1	1,214.6	1,731.7	1,091.1	1,652.7
Context												
(Year–1789)												
North	25.50	15.76	34.20	37.53	33.15	35.80	34.58	36.00	32.96	34.70	36.27	36.21
South			15.83	25.51	14.55	24.38	13.65	23.79	14.28	24.20	13.24	23.93
Low sorghum price (10% increase)												
North	–5.64	3.95	–3.52	3.94	–3.68	3.97	–3.83	3.98	–3.90	4.01	–4.12	4.04
South			–2.40	4.05	–2.24	3.93	–2.12	3.86	–2.22	3.91	–2.07	3.83
South			0.37	0.48	0.36	0.48	0.34	0.47	0.35	0.48	0.32	0.47
Village population (10% increase)	57.89	13.63	54.59	12.79	53.93	13.17	53.92	13.56	51.93	14.20	51.90	15.01
Proportion of men married (observed/expected)	1.01	0.14	1.04	0.17	1.03	0.17	1.01	0.18	1.01	0.19	0.98	0.21

Socioeconomic status												
Father's banner occupation (Ref.: Adult male)												
Artisan	0.02	0.16	0.01	0.10	0.01	0.08	0.01	0.07	0.00	0.06	0.01	0.08
Soldier	0.15	0.35	0.03	0.16	0.02	0.14	0.02	0.12	0.01	0.09	0.01	0.12
Local official	0.03	0.17	0.01	0.11	0.01	0.10	0.01	0.09	0.01	0.08	0.01	0.10
Number of others in household with banner occupation												
Artisan	0.06	0.27	0.03	0.17	0.02	0.16	0.02	0.15	0.02	0.14	0.01	0.12
Soldier	0.28	0.64	0.09	0.41	0.09	0.39	0.08	0.38	0.07	0.34	0.06	0.35
Local official	0.08	0.36	0.07	0.46	0.06	0.42	0.05	0.37	0.04	0.33	0.04	0.35
Working-age adults in household	6.54	5.11	6.86	5.87	6.77	5.74	6.44	5.60	5.04	5.13	4.91	5.27
Household												
Mother alive	0.91	0.29	0.90	0.30	0.46	0.50	0.50	0.50				
Father alive	0.92	0.28	0.89	0.32	0.36	0.48	0.43	0.49				
Grandfather alive	0.32	0.47	0.30	0.46								
Grandmother alive	0.46	0.50	0.38	0.49								
Any older brothers	0.40	0.49	0.38	0.49								
Any older sisters	0.25	0.43	0.10	0.30								
Any younger brothers	0.30	0.46	0.20	0.40								
Any younger sisters	0.16	0.37	0.05	0.21								

Table 10.2
(continued)

Variable	Children Female Mean	Children Female SD	Children Male Mean	Children Male SD	Adults Female Mean	Adults Female SD	Adults Male Mean	Adults Male SD	Elderly Female Mean	Elderly Female SD	Elderly Male Mean	Elderly Male SD
Marital status (Ref.: Currently married)												
Widowed					0.09	0.28	0.29	0.45	0.50	0.50	0.11	0.31
Never married							0.06	0.24	0.21	0.40	0.28	0.45
No living son					0.45	0.50	0.61	0.49	0.11	0.31	0.27	0.45
Widowed × no living son					0.02	0.13	0.02	0.15			0.06	0.24
Daughter-in-law present									0.63	0.48	0.53	0.50
Relationship to head												
Head	0.00	0.03	0.01	0.11	0.01	0.07			0.05	0.21		
Nonstem kin of head	0.39	0.49	0.40	0.49	0.38	0.49	0.39	0.49	0.29	0.45	0.28	0.45
Stem kin of head	0.33	0.47	0.36	0.48					0.30	0.46	0.05	0.21
N	3,541		29,889		52,059		68,650		13,582		12,753	
Deaths	247		1,171		2,281		2,389		1,831		2,417	

[a] Age is entered in the analysis as the number of sui from the beginning of the age group. Thus, in the analysis of child mortality, it is age in $sui - 2$; in the analysis of adult mortality, it is age in $sui - 16$; and in the analysis of elderly mortality, it is age in $sui - 56$. Age^2 = age squared; Age^3 = age cubed.

For socioeconomic status, we use extensions of the comparative models to examine the consequences of agricultural and nonagricultural income separately. As in the comparative model, we measure nonagricultural income with categorical variables for occupation. We distinguish three categories of occupation: artisan, soldier, and local elite. All three had incomes from the state or, as was the case of certain local elites, the resources to purchase an honorary appointment. Artisans also had marketable skills that allowed them to supplement their state incomes. We have demonstrated in an analysis of male marriage that having a banner occupation was an important source of privilege: men with banner occupations married earlier and in far higher proportions than other men (Campbell and Lee 1998).

We test whether the presence of other kin with an occupation affected individual standard of living. Large, multiple-family households were common in Liaodong. Even if someone had no occupation, he may have lived with someone who did. If men typically shared the proceeds of their occupation with household members other than their spouse and children, that should be reflected in their mortality rates. If they shared the proceeds only with their wives and children, then the mortality rates of other household members should be unaffected. We expect the latter to be the case: we have already shown in an analysis of male marriage that while having a father with an occupation or having an occupation of one's own dramatically increased the chances of marrying, coresiding with other kin with occupation had little effect (Campbell and Lee 1998).

We make use of two other indirect measures of socioeconomic status. The first is a new village-level proxy for prosperity calculated from the proportions of men currently married. We construct the index by dividing the observed proportion of males in the village aged 11 *sui* and above who are currently married by the proportion expected if age-specific proportions currently married were identical to those observed for all villages combined. Such an index is informative because in historical China, marriage was a sensitive indicator of prestige and access to resources (Campbell and Lee 1998, Harrell 1985, Lee and Campbell 1997, Lee and Wang 1999b). Men from families of high socioeconomic status consistently married earlier and in higher proportions. The villages in which higher-than-average proportions of men were currently married should have been wealthier. If this assumption holds, then the households within them on average also had to have been wealthier.

As in the standard Eurasian comparative models, we also measure the socioeconomic status of the household by a count of the number of working-age adults. We treat the number of adults as an indicator of socioeconomic status because household size and wealth in rural China were correlated. This association has been noted at least from the time systematic surveys were first carried out in the early part of the twentieth century (Gamble 1954), though it remains unclear whether it derives from the tendency of wealthy households to increase their size through marriage and divide less frequently or the ability of large households to enjoy returns to scale in agriculture. We have already confirmed that household size and wealth were correlated in Liaodong by showing that men who grew up in larger families married earlier (Campbell and Lee 1998).

Measures of household composition, calculated from the perspective of each individual, reveal how the configuration of kin conditioned the allocation of household resources. The Liaodong household was hierarchical, stratified by generation, age, and gender (Lee and Campbell 1997). Thus, access to resources depended heavily on who else was present in the household and how they were related to the index individual. We base the variables on those for the comparative models, but adjust them to test specific hypotheses about the role of particular types of kin in the historical Chinese household.

First, we examine how relationship to the head conditioned access to resources. We distinguish individuals according to whether they are a head, a head's spouse, or stem kin. While we have shown that heads enjoyed a variety of privileges, for example, early marriage (Campbell and Lee 1998, Lee and Campbell 1997), our previous work has also shown that they paid a price for their privilege in the form of higher death rates (Lee and Campbell 1997). We attributed this to more frequent exposure to disease.

Second, to reconstruct networks of dependency within the Liaodong household, we examine the effects of the presence or absence of particular types of kin. In hierarchical households such as in Liaodong, those at the bottom of the hierarchy depended on senior members of the household to represent their interests in household decisions about resource allocation. This was most true for women and children. Adult women had few entitlements in their own right; the claims they could make on household resources grew out of their roles as wives and mothers. Children did not participate as equals in discussions about how to share the resources of the household. Their parents had to represent their interests.

Another major distinction between the Liaodong models and the comparative models is that we do not estimate separate models for adults according to whether they had ever married. That marital distinction had to be made in the comparative models because young European adults who had never married were itinerant and therefore poorly recorded. In Liaodong, this was not an issue. While men who never married were more likely to depart the area illegally, the rates at which they did so were low (Campbell and Lee 2001). Because we knew when they left, moreover, we can censor their observations from the time they depart. To examine whether the mortality of the men who never married differed from that of the men who did, we introduce an indicator variable to identify them.

Results

We organize our discussion of results topically, beginning with contextual factors, proceeding to socioeconomic status, and concluding with household organization. The focus throughout is on findings from the Liaodong models, not the comparative models, since the key comparative findings are discussed in other chapters. The results from the Liaodong models are in tables 10.3 through 10.5. They cover children aged 2 to 15 *sui*, adults aged 16 to 55 *sui*, and elderly aged 56 to 75 *sui*, respectively. Instead of coefficients, we present hazard ratios generated from them by exponentiation. To save space, we present only *p* values from statistical tests on coefficients rather than standard errors and indicators of significance. Finally, to facilitate interpretation of the implications of the results, we use predicted probabilities on certain occasions to estimate survival chances and life expectancies under different scenarios.[5]

Context

Variations in death rates after the first year of life did not help balance population with resources in Liaodong over the long term (Lee and Wang 1999b). There is no evidence from secular trends that mortality was on the rise, even though pressure increased during the nineteenth century and triggered other demographic responses (Lee and

Table 10.3
Effects of community, household, and individual characteristics on the relative risk of
dying in Liaodong, 1789–1909, children aged 2–15 *sui*

Variable	Females		Males	
	Relative risk	*p*-value	Relative risk	*p*-value
Age	0.568	0.01	0.581	0.00
Age^2	1.032	0.33	1.027	0.07
Age^3	1.000	0.72	1.000	0.71
Contextual				
(Year–1789)				
North	0.990	0.04	0.989	0.00
South			0.984	0.00
Low sorghum price (10% increase)				
North	1.020	0.26	1.025	0.01
South			1.000	0.98
South			0.685	0.01
Village population (10% increase)	1.005	0.32	1.006	0.01
Proportion of men married (observed/ expected)	0.792	0.64	0.533	0.00
Socioeconomic status				
Father's banner occupation (Ref.: Adult male)				
Artisan	0.963	0.94	1.116	0.66
Soldier	0.989	0.95	1.112	0.49
Local official	1.179	0.65	1.076	0.78
Number of others in household with banner occupation				
Artisan	0.760	0.35	1.114	0.44
Soldier	1.162	0.19	0.997	0.96
Local official	1.236	0.21	0.946	0.42
Working-age adults in household	0.935	0.00	1.014	0.03
Household				
Mother alive	0.700	0.13	0.750	0.01
Father alive	0.836	0.49	0.992	0.94
Grandfather alive	1.470	0.01	1.165	0.02
Grandmother alive	0.966	0.80	1.092	0.16
Any older brothers	1.060	0.68	1.055	0.40
Any older sisters	1.170	0.31	1.128	0.15
Any younger brothers	0.869	0.45	1.032	0.73
Any younger sisters	0.972	0.90	0.796	0.17

Table 10.3
(continued)

	Females		Males	
Variable	Relative risk	*p*-value	Relative risk	*p*-value
Relationship (Ref.: Head's stem kin)				
Head	3.830	0.20	0.959	0.91
Nonstem kin of head	1.387	0.02	1.013	0.84
N	3,541		29,889	
Deaths	247		1,171	
Degrees of freedom	24		27	
Log-likelihood	−809.29		−4,515.52	

Note: This analysis made use of a complementary log-log regression. See the text for details.
Age^2 = age squared; Age^3 = age cubed.

Campbell 1997). In the northern farm systems, according to tables 10.3 through 10.5, death rates actually decreased over time for everyone except adult males. The pace of change was greatest for male children. The implication, according to table 10.6, is that male life expectancy at age 6 *sui* rose by about seven years in the space of 100 years. In the half-century for which it was possible to calculate mortality rates for females over the entire life span, their life expectancy at age 6 *sui* rose by just under two years. As for the southern state farm systems, only among male children was there a discernible change over time in the chances of dying. Again, the trend was downward, not upward.

Mortality nevertheless responded to short-term economic fluctuations, though only in the northern state farm systems. The patterns of response by sex are basically the same as from the comparative models and from our earlier studies: men were sensitive to price fluctuations and women either less sensitive or not sensitive at all (Campbell and Lee 1996, 2000; Lee and Campbell 1997). For males, the response by age was uniform. According to the hazard ratios in tables 10.3 through 10.5, a 10 percent increase in grain prices raised the risks of dying by 2.5 percent for children, 2.8 percent for adults, and 2.7 percent for the elderly. That male child mortality was more sensitive here than in the comparative model is attributable to the control for secular trends, which brings the relationship between short-term price and mortality fluctuations into sharper relief. The total impact of short-term price variation could be substantial. In table 10.7, life expectancy at age 6 *sui*

Table 10.4
Effects of community, household, and individual characteristics on the relative risk of dying in Liaodong, 1789–1909, adults aged 16–55 *sui*

Variable	Ever-married females		Males	
	Relative risk	*p*-value	Relative risk	*p*-value
Age	1.013	0.59	0.986	0.47
Age^2	1.000	0.88	1.002	0.03
Age^3	1.000	0.80	1.000	0.15
Contextual				
(Year−1789)				
North	1.002	0.05	0.997	0.00
South	1.002	0.22	1.002	0.27
Low sorghum price (10% increase)				
North	1.016	0.03	1.028	0.00
South	0.999	0.89	0.982	0.04
South	0.693	0.00	0.608	0.00
Village population (10% increase)	1.003	0.10	1.002	0.16
Proportion of men married (observed/expected)	0.733	0.02	0.969	0.80
Socioeconomic status				
Own or husband's banner occupation (Ref.: Adult male)				
Artisan	0.743	0.31	1.365	0.14
Soldier	0.636	0.02	1.210	0.22
Local official	0.632	0.08	1.322	0.17
Wald: Artisan = soldier = local official = 0 (3 d.f.)	$\chi^2 = 9.29$	0.03	$\chi^2 = 5.18$	0.16
Number of others in household with banner occupation				
Artisan	0.909	0.49	1.212	0.15
Soldier	0.989	0.86	0.941	0.37
Local official	1.094	0.05	0.988	0.86
Wald: Artisan = soldier = local official = 0 (3 d.f.)	$\chi^2 = 4.61$	0.21	$\chi^2 = 2.95$	0.40
Number of working-age adults in household	1.000	0.93	0.999	0.81
Household				
Father alive	1.103	0.11	0.973	0.68
Mother alive	0.843	0.00	0.822	0.00
Marital status (Ref.: Currently married)				
Widowed	1.212	0.02	0.972	0.75
Never married			1.224	0.00

Table 10.4
(continued)

Variable	Ever-married females		Males	
	Relative risk	p-value	Relative risk	p-value
No living sons	1.122	0.03	0.924	0.17
Widowed × no living sons	1.553	0.00	1.538	0.00
Relationship (Ref.: Female: head's spouse; Male: head)				
Head	0.913	0.71		
Stem kin of head	0.862	0.04	0.903	0.16
Nonstem kin of head	1.025	0.67	0.941	0.26
N	52,059		68,650	
Deaths	2,281		2,389	
Degrees of freedom	25		25	
Log-likelihood	−9,257.356		−9,900.46	

Note: This analysis made use of a complementary log-log regression. See the text for details.
Age^2 = age squared; Age^3 = age cubed.

was 4.8 years lower when prices were at their highest than when prices were at their lowest. As for females, only the death rates of adults were affected by prices. A 10 percent increase in prices raised their chances of dying by 1.6 percent. Life expectancy at age 6 *sui* varied by 3.1 years between the years of highest and lowest prices.

Location affected mortality. Mortality in the southern state farm systems not only exhibited less trend and sensitivity to price but was lower overall. According to life tables calculated directly from the original data in chapter 3, male life expectancy at age 6 *sui* was 48.7 in the northern state farm systems and 51.2 in the southern ones, a difference of 2.5 years. The southern advantage for females was even more pronounced. Female life expectancies at age 6 *sui* in the north and south, respectively, were 43 and 50, a difference of seven years. Although the attenuated response to price in the south may simply reflect the inadequacy of the price series we use as a measure of economic conditions, the weight of the evidence, especially from comparisons of levels and trends, suggests that the mortality environments of the northern and southern state farm systems differed dramatically. For one thing, the south was more prosperous than the north by virtue of its proximity to the treaty port of Niuzhuang. Thus, its residents did not live as close to the margin as their northern counterparts.

Table 10.5
Effects of community, household, and individual characteristics on the relative risk of dying in Liaodong, 1789–1909, elderly aged 56–75 *sui*

Variable	Ever-married females		Males	
	Relative risk	*p*-value	Relative risk	*p*-value
Age	1.041	0.00	1.058	0.00
Age^2	1.005	0.18	1.000	0.27
Age^3	1.000	0.58	1.000	0.00
Contextual				
(Year−1789)				
North	0.996	0.00	0.996	0.00
South	0.998	0.18	0.998	0.27
Low sorghum price (10% increase)				
North	1.005	0.58	1.029	0.00
South	0.989	0.31	0.996	0.66
South	0.686	0.00	0.664	0.00
Village population (10% increase)	1.006	0.00	1.010	0.00
Proportion of men married (observed/expected)	1.264	0.09	1.414	0.01
Socioeconomic status				
Own or husband's banner occupation (Ref.: Adult male)				
Artisan	0.409	0.21	0.856	0.58
Soldier	0.554	0.10	1.391	0.05
Local official	1.331	0.36	1.557	0.03
Wald: Artisan = soldier = local official = 0 (3 d.f.)	$\chi^2 = 5.19$	0.16	$\chi^2 = 9.03$	0.03
Number of others in household with banner occupation				
Artisan	0.790	0.19	1.153	0.37
Soldier	0.917	0.26	0.855	0.04
Local official	0.907	0.22	0.939	0.37
Wald: Artisan = soldier = local official = 0 (3 d.f.)	$\chi^2 = 4.72$	0.19	$\chi^2 = 6.37$	0.09
Number of working-age adults in household	1.014	0.01	1.008	0.16
Household				
Marital status (Ref.: Currently married)				
Widowed	1.169	0.04	1.101	0.08
Never married			0.972	0.77
No living sons	1.074	0.47	1.087	0.32
Widowed × no living sons	1.080	0.52	0.989	0.92

Table 10.5
(continued)

Variable	Ever-married females		Males	
	Relative risk	p-value	Relative risk	p-value
Daughter-in-law present	0.952	0.45	1.045	0.45
Relationship (Ref.: Female: head's spouse; Male: head)				
Head	0.864	0.26		
Stem kin of head	1.055	0.52	0.653	0.00
Nonstem kin of head	1.021	0.78	0.957	0.41
N	13,582		12,753	
Deaths	1,831		2,147	
Degrees of freedom	24		24	
Log-likelihood	−5,158.5		−5,586.0	

Note: This analysis made use of a complementary log-log regression. See the text for details.
Age^2 = age squared; Age^3 = age cubed.

Table 10.6
Secular trends in mortality in the northern state farm systems, Liaodong, 1789–1909

Year	Female				Male			
	$_{10}p_6$	$_{40}p_{16}$	$_{20}p_{56}$	e_6	$_{10}p_6$	$_{40}p_{16}$	$_{20}p_{56}$	e_6
1789	0.87	0.57	0.28	41.79	0.85	0.56	0.19	42.18
1824	0.89	0.55	0.31	42.84	0.89	0.58	0.21	44.52
1849	0.92	0.54	0.34	43.60	0.92	0.60	0.25	46.54
1874		0.53	0.38		0.94	0.62	0.28	48.31
1889		0.51	0.41		0.95	0.64	0.31	49.85

Note: $_np_x$ is the probability that an individual currently age x will die in the next n years. e_x: the life expectancy of an individual currently age x.
Source: Authors' calculations from results in tables 10.3–10.5. See the text for a description of assumptions.

Table 10.7
Grain price effects on mortality in the northern state farm systems, Liaodong, 1789–1909

Low sorghum price	Female				Male			
	$_{10}P_6$	$_{40}P_{16}$	$_{20}P_{56}$	e_6	$_{10}P_6$	$_{40}P_{16}$	$_{20}P_{56}$	e_6
0.32	0.91	0.58	0.35	44.4	0.93	0.66	0.32	49.3
0.39	0.90	0.57	0.35	43.9	0.93	0.64	0.30	48.5
0.47	0.90	0.56	0.35	43.4	0.92	0.63	0.28	47.7
0.56	0.89	0.55	0.34	42.9	0.92	0.61	0.26	46.9
0.68	0.89	0.53	0.34	42.3	0.91	0.59	0.24	46.1
0.83	0.89	0.52	0.34	41.8	0.91	0.58	0.22	45.3
1.00	0.88	0.51	0.33	41.2	0.91	0.56	0.20	44.5

Note: $_nP_x$ is the probability that an individual currently age x will die in the next n years.
e_x: the life expectancy of an individual currently age x.
Source: Authors' calculations from results in tables 10.3–10.5. See the text for a description of assumptions.

Within regions, villages differed. The number of people living in a village affected the chances of dying by influencing the disease environment. In almost all age groups and for both sexes, death rates rose with the number of people living in the village. A 10 percent increase in village population raised the chances of dying by between 0.6 and 1.6 percent, depending on sex and age. We summarize the implications in table 10.8, which presents predicted life expectancies at age 6 *sui* in villages across the range of observed sizes. Boys and girls could expect to live four years longer if they resided in one of the smallest villages instead of one of the largest. Such findings are consistent with those from historical Europe (Humphreys 1885). As a village became more populous, exposure to disease became more frequent. Frequent contacts between residents created more opportunities for the direct transmission of diseases from one person to another. Inadequate procedures for handling waste raised the likelihood of infection by contaminated water and insects.

Socioeconomic Status

Household prosperity, reflected in our village-level proxy, benefited wives and children but not adult males. According to the results for the marriage-based prosperity index in tables 10.3 through 10.5, the death rates of adult women and male children were lower in villages where higher proportions of males were married. While the elderly in

Table 10.8
Effects of village size on mortality, Liaodong, 1789–1909

Village popula-tion	Female				Male			
	$_{10}P_6$	$_{40}P_{16}$	$_{20}P_{56}$	e_6	$_{10}P_6$	$_{40}P_{16}$	$_{20}P_{56}$	e_6
4	0.91	0.57	0.42	45.1	0.93	0.63	0.38	49.1
17	0.91	0.56	0.39	44.2	0.93	0.62	0.33	48.1
73	0.90	0.55	0.36	43.3	0.92	0.61	0.27	47.1
304	0.89	0.53	0.33	42.3	0.91	0.60	0.22	46.1
1,272	0.88	0.52	0.30	41.3	0.91	0.59	0.17	45.0

Note: $_nP_x$ is the probability that an individual currently age x will die in the next n years.
e_x: the life expectancy of an individual currently age x.
Source: Authors' calculations from results in tables 10.3–10.5. See the text for a description of assumptions.

Table 10.9
Effects of village prosperity index on mortality, Liaodong, 1789–1909

Pros-perity index	Female				Male			
	$_{10}P_6$	$_{40}P_{16}$	$_{20}P_{56}$	e_6	$_{10}P_6$	$_{40}P_{16}$	$_{20}P_{56}$	e_6
0.7	0.89	0.51	0.37	41.3	0.90	0.60	0.28	45.8
0.85	0.89	0.52	0.36	41.9	0.91	0.60	0.26	46.2
1	0.89	0.54	0.34	42.5	0.91	0.60	0.24	46.4
1.15	0.90	0.55	0.33	43.1	0.92	0.60	0.23	46.7
1.3	0.90	0.57	0.32	43.7	0.93	0.61	0.21	46.9

Note: $_nP_x$ is the probability that an individual currently age x will die in the next n years.
e_x: the life expectancy of an individual currently age x.
Source: Authors' calculations from results in tables 10.3–10.5. See the text for a description of assumptions.

such villages had higher death rates, most likely because more frail people survived to old age, living in a village with higher proportions of males married raised life expectancy. Households in prosperous communities either allocated larger shares of resources to women and children, or they allocated the same shares but women and children benefited the most from the proportional increase in consumption. According to table 10.9, girls aged 6 *sui* who lived in the most prosperous villages could expect to survive 2.4 years longer than their counterparts in the poorest ones. The advantage for boys in the wealthiest villages was 1.1 years.

Similarly, when men held a banner occupation, their wives benefited more in terms of life expectancy than they did. According to table

10.4, the adult wives of soldiers and officials were one-third less likely to die than the wives of men who were healthy adult males. Among the elderly in table 10.5, the wives of soldiers had substantially lower chances of dying than other women. Once again, it appears that as family income increased, either the share allocated to wives also increased or shares remained constant but the same proportional increase in consumption benefited wives' health the most. For men themselves, the benefits of additional income were more than offset by the increased risks of work and travel associated with such official appointments. This was most readily apparent among the elderly in table 10.5. Men who were still soldiers and officials at these advanced ages were between 1.4 and 1.5 times more likely to die than other men.

Perhaps wives benefited so much because men with occupations did not share their rewards with other household members. In tables 10.3 through 10.5, there were no consistent effects for the counts of other household members holding occupations, only sporadic and contradictory effects of the numbers with specific occupations. This echoes the finding from an earlier analysis of male marriage that prospects were determined largely by their own and their father's occupation, not by the occupations of other household members (Campbell and Lee 1998). Even though in this society men with an outside income supposedly turned the proceeds over to the household head to reallocate, ostensibly with the interests of the whole household in mind, the accumulated evidence indicates that most of the benefits of the banner occupation accrued to the man who held it, his wife, and his children.

Although larger households were wealthier (Campbell and Lee 1998, Lee and Campbell 1997), for most family members the beneficial effects of increased consumption failed to offset the adverse effects of crowding. Just as larger villages had higher death rates, so did larger households. According to tables 10.3 through 10.5, each additional working-age adult raised the chances of dying by 1.6 percent for boys, 1.4 percent for elderly females, and 0.8 percent for elderly males. The net effects, at least for males and ever-married women, were nevertheless small. According to table 10.10, a boy aged 6 *sui* who lived in a household with one or two adults could expect to live only 1.3 years longer than if he lived in one of the very largest households, with twenty adults. Similarly, according to calculations not shown here, the life expectancy of a married woman aged 21 *sui* differed only slightly between the two extremes of household size.

Large households, however, valued daughters so much that the benefits for girls of growing up in a large household outweighed the

Table 10.10
Effects of number of working-age adults in the household on mortality, Liaodong, 1789–1909

House-hold size	Female				Male			
	$_{10}p_6$	$_{40}p_{16}$	$_{20}p_{56}$	e_6	$_{10}p_6$	$_{40}p_{16}$	$_{20}p_{56}$	e_6
0	0.84	0.54	0.37	40.4	0.92	0.60	0.26	46.9
5	0.88	0.54	0.34	42.2	0.92	0.60	0.25	46.6
10	0.91	0.54	0.32	43.4	0.91	0.60	0.23	46.3
15	0.94	0.54	0.29	44.3	0.91	0.61	0.22	46.0
20	0.96	0.54	0.27	44.9	0.90	0.61	0.21	45.6

Note: $_np_x$ is the probability that an individual currently age x will die in the next n years. e_x: the life expectancy of an individual currently age x.
Source: Authors' calculations from tables 10.3–10.5. See the text for a description of assumptions.

drawbacks. Just as larger households allowed more daughters to survive infancy (Wang, Campbell, and Lee forthcoming), they also treated them better in childhood and adolescence. According to table 10.3, every additional adult lowered the chances that a girl would die in the next three years by 6.5 percent. According to table 10.10, a girl aged 6 *sui* living in a household with twenty adults was only one-fourth as likely to die before she reached age 15 *sui* as a girl living in a household with one or two adults. The net benefits of spending her childhood in a large household were so pronounced that a girl aged 6 *sui* could expect to live 4.5 years longer if she was in one of the largest households and not one of the smallest ones.[6] Larger households had more opportunities to diversify production and assign members specialized tasks, and accordingly they were better able to make use of their daughters' skills.

Household

Being a household head may have had perquisites like early marriage and more children, but it also carried a price. Just as an earlier examination of Daoyi revealed that heads had higher death rates than other members of multiple-family households (Lee and Campbell 1997), so in this analysis we also find that heads and their wives in Liaodong had higher death rates than other household members. Thus, among ever-married adult females, heads' wives had higher death rates than the wives of heads' stem kin. Adult male heads also had higher death rates than their stem kin, though this disadvantage was statistically significant only in the comparative Eurasian relationship model, with price interactions not in the Liaodong models. Among elderly males, meanwhile, the heads had higher death rates than their stem kin.

Because less privileged household members depended on senior members to represent their interests, individual well-being depended not only on location within the household hierarchy, but also on whether particular kin were present. Children, for example, relied on their mothers to care for them and represent their interests. As was the case in earlier analyses of smaller samples, the death rates of children increased when their mother, but not their father, died (Campbell and Lee 1996, 2002). Thus, according to table 10.11, girls aged 6 *sui* who lived with both parents were almost one-third less likely to die by age 15 *sui* than girls who lived with their fathers. Similarly, boys who lived with both parents were more than one-quarter less likely to die by age 15 *sui* than their counterparts who lived with their fathers.

Mothers were most important to their young children during times of economic stress: fathers seem to have neglected the interests of their children when times were hard. Not only were the death rates of children without mothers higher overall, but according to the results for northern populations from the comparative Eurasian relationship model, they were much more sensitive to changes in grain prices. A 10 percent increase in sorghum prices increased the chances of dying by 20 percent for girls who lived with their fathers but by only 2 percent for girls who lived with both parents. Similarly, a 10 percent increase in prices raised the chances of dying by 7.8 percent for boys who lived

Table 10.11
Effects of presence of parents on mortality, Liaodong, 1789–1909

Father alive?	Mother alive?	Female		Male	
		$_{10}P_6$	$_{40}P_{16}$	$_{10}P_6$	$_{40}P_{16}$
No	No	0.82	0.52	0.89	0.53
No	Yes	0.87	0.57	0.92	0.59
Yes	No	0.85	0.48	0.89	0.54
Yes	Yes	0.89	0.54	0.92	0.60

Note: $_nP_x$ is the probability that an individual currently age x will die in the next n years.
Source: Authors' calculations from tables 10.3–10.5. See the text for a description of assumptions.

with their fathers but had almost no effect on boys who lived with both parents.

Elderly women remained important advocates for the interests of their children even after they reached adulthood. Adult men benefited from the presence of their mother but not their father. In table 10.11, the presence of a living mother increased the chances that a man would survive from age 16 *sui* to age 55 *sui* by 6 percentage points. A surviving father had little effect. As for adult women, though the relationship between wives and their mothers-in-law is widely regarded as a major source of tension in historical and even contemporary Chinese households, according to table 10.4 adult women were less likely to die if their mother-in-law was alive. According to table 10.11, having a mother-in-law raised the chances of surviving from 16 to 55 *sui* by 5 to 6 percentage points. The presence of a father-in-law had little effect. Women, in turn, needed to bear sons to be fully enfranchised in their husband's household (Campbell and Lee 2002). In Liaodong, as elsewhere in China, one of a wife's most important responsibilities was to produce a son for her husband's family. Mothers were treated differently from barren daughters-in-law. These differences were so great that in Liaodong, according to table 10.4, adult women without surviving sons were more likely to die than those with sons. Men, by contrast, were unaffected by whether they had a son, except in the small proportion of cases where they were also widowed. Predicted survival probabilities in table 10.12 indicate that for adult women, the presence of a son raised the chances of survival from age 16 *sui* to age 55 *sui* by 3 to 4 percentage points, depending on whether she was also widowed.

Adult women also relied on their husbands to represent their interests. According to tables 10.4 and 10.5, widows had higher death rates

Table 10.12
Effects of presence of spouse and living sons on mortality, Liaodong, 1789–1909

Widowed?	Living son present?	Female		Male	
		$_{40}p_{16}$	$_{20}p_{56}$	$_{40}p_{16}$	$_{20}p_{56}$
No	Yes	0.57	0.45	0.64	0.31
No	No	0.54	0.42	0.66	0.28
Yes	Yes	0.51	0.39	0.65	0.28
Yes	No	0.47	0.37	0.67	0.25

Note: $_np_x$ is the probability that an individual currently age x will die in the next n years.
Source: Authors' calculations from tables 10.3–10.5. See the text for a description of assumptions.

than married women. At least in adulthood, the possibility that this was due to bereavement or common exposure to pathogens is ruled out by the absence of an effect for men of losing their wives. From table 10.12, it is apparent, moreover, that having a living husband actually affected well-being more than having a living son. Being widowed raised the chances of dying between ages 16 and 55 *sui* by 6 to 7 percentage points, depending on whether the woman also had a son. The net effect is almost twice as strong as that of not having a son.

The presence of certain types of kin could also be harmful if the claims they made on household resources took precedence. Households, for example, neglected the interests of children in favor of those of their grandfather if he was present. As reported in an earlier study of Daoyi and Gaizhou alone, according to table 10.3, children whose grandfathers were still alive had higher death rates than children whose grandfathers had already died (Campbell and Lee 1996).

Conclusion

Analysis of household registers from Liaodong, here and elsewhere, has demonstrated the importance of household context in determining individual standard of living in historical China. By allowing for differential demography in which the probabilities of demographic events are related to individual, household, and village characteristics, household registers have permitted us to move far beyond the reconstruction of trends, levels, and patterns typical of earlier studies of mortality based on genealogies. By treating demographic outcomes as indicators of access to resources, we have begun to map the contours of privilege between and within households, showing how households favored some members and discriminated against others in the allocation of resources.

This study provides a number of new insights into rural society in late imperial Liaodong. First, we have shown that village and household size affected the epidemiological environment. Second, we have replicated a key finding from an earlier analysis of marriage that men with banner occupations shared little of the proceeds except with members of their immediate family. If they did share the proceeds, it had little impact on the demographic behavior of other household members. Third, we have begun to map the networks of dependence within the Chinese household by which members at the bottom of the hierarchy could nevertheless count on more privileged members to represent their interests in household negotiations about the allocation of resources.

Most important, we have clearly demonstrated that the sharp delineation of gender roles in historical China caused the factors that determined the standards of living of men and women to differ fundamentally. Men's responsibilities lay in the economic sphere, and those of women lay in the domestic sphere. Thus, variations in mortality were longitudinal for men and cross-sectional for women. At least in the northern populations, male mortality was most responsive to short-term economic fluctuations. Price effects were most consistent among adults and the elderly, but also apparent among children. When the household had to cut back on consumption, men reduced theirs the most. Additionally, in several situations, statuses that were sources of privilege, including household headship and attainment of a banner occupation, actually raised mortality. The implication of such results, as we have argued elsewhere, is that the price that men paid for privilege was increased exposure to various forms of risk, and this affected their mortality (Lee and Campbell 1997, Campbell and Lee 2000).

Since women were restricted to the domestic sphere, it comes as no surprise that their well-being depended most heavily on the characteristics of their household. Adult women benefited the most when the household was located in a prosperous village. When a man held a banner occupation, it was his wife who enjoyed a reduction in the chances of dying. Women were also much more sensitive than men to the specific configuration of kin in the household. For a woman, whether children, husband, parents, and parents-in-law were present all mattered. Where men were affected by household characteristics, it generally reflected the importance and influence of women in the domestic sphere. Thus, the death rates of boys and even adult males depended on whether their mother, not their father, was present.

Notes

Cameron Campbell received support from the Chiang Ching-Kuo Foundation for International Scholarly Exchange and the UCLA Academic Senate Council on Research.

1. The positive check also played a role, but not in the way that Malthus thought. Whereas Malthus and others emphasized the adverse effects of misery and poverty on death rates across the age range, Lee, Wang, and Campbell (1994) argue that the calculated use of infanticide by couples to adjust family size and sex composition to their circumstances predominated.

2. Relationship to household head is available only from 1789 onward. Before 1789, the registers distinguish individuals by household group, not household, and provide relationship only to the household group head.

3. The prices of the various grains were actually highly correlated, except for rice, which was a relatively minor crop in Liaodong (Lee and Campbell 1997).

4. Many of the most prominent spikes were associated with extended spells of unfavorable weather such as cold summers (Lee and Campbell 1997).

5. Whenever we calculate predicted probabilities, we set all continuous variables to their mean values and all dichotomous variables to 0. The sole exception to the latter is that when models include variables for the presence of mother and father, we set them to 1.

6. This calculation assumes that women marry into families with the same number of adults as their natal families.

III   Comparative Demographies

11 Gender Differences in Mortality

George Alter, Matteo
Manfredini, and Paul Nystedt
in collaboration with Cameron
Campbell, James Z. Lee,
Emiko Ochiai, and Rosella
Rettaroli

As mortality declined in the twentieth century, female death rates fell faster than male rates, and the female advantage widened. Thus, in developed countries, we have become accustomed to higher female life expectancies, and a number of scholars have proposed biological explanations for lower female mortality. Where excess female mortality persists, such as in South Asia, it is regarded as an exception that requires explanation.

Demographers writing from a historical perspective highlight the recent origin of this female advantage. In his widely cited review, "A Century of International Mortality Trends" (1956), George Stolnitz wrote, "The occurrence of higher male survival rates at some ages, far from being comparatively rare, has in fact been usual over the world during most of the last century" (23). Stolnitz went on to point out that trends in sex differences in mortality differed by age. While the male disadvantage in infancy tended to diminish, excess male mortality above age 50 rose in the twentieth century (26). In 1978, Dominique Tabutin also called attention to historical patterns of excess female mortality in Europe. He concluded, "Under the Old Regime, excess female mortality is indisputable in the procreative ages, is probable at young ages, but weak and more uncertain at the highest ages" (125).[1] Tabutin and his colleagues have continued to study examples of excess female mortality, especially in childhood, in European populations (Devos 1996, Eggerickx and Tabutin 1994). Excess female mortality usually emerged in late childhood and continued into the childbearing ages, and it was typically higher in rural than in urban areas. Where causes of death are available, girls were more susceptible to infectious diseases, particularly respiratory diseases, including tuberculosis (Tabutin and Willems 1998).

Samuel Preston (1976) showed that the sex differential in mortality from various causes of death changed as mortality declined. We might expect males to lose some of their earlier advantage as the composition of mortality changed. Since infectious diseases were more unfavorable to females, lower death rates from these diseases benefit females disproportionately. However, Preston finds that the male "disadvantage *from particular causes of death* increases" (123 emphasis in original). He also links economic modernization and urbanization to increasing excess male mortality, especially for cardiovascular diseases (154–158).

The Eurasia Project provides new opportunities for examining the origins of gender differences in mortality. Results on mortality levels reveal a remarkable similarity in age patterns of gender differences across the five study areas.[2] There is some diversity in very early childhood, but female mortality exceeded male mortality from late childhood until the end of the reproductive years. Male and female mortality levels converged around age 50, so that rates were similar in old age. Although this pattern is familiar from previous studies of the nineteenth century, it is nonetheless striking to find such consistency among such distant and diverse populations. The Eurasia standard comparative event-history models allow us to study this pattern in detail by examining responses to economic stress and household composition.[3] For this chapter, we have also carried out additional analyses of maternal mortality, taking advantage of the detailed information on the timing of births and deaths available for Sart and Scania.

Overall, our results point to a combination of explanations for female mortality excesses. In spite of the clear association between excess female mortality and the reproductive ages, maternal mortality does not explain the entire pattern. In some places, excess female mortality appears well before the average age at marriage. Furthermore, cultural preferences result in subtle differences in responses to household composition.

Explanations of Gender Differences

Biology, behavior, and environment interact to produce unequal mortality by gender. Alternative explanations emphasize different sides of this triangle. We divide our discussion of these explanations into those that emphasize biology, maternal mortality and depletion, economic roles, lifestyle, and resource allocation.

Biology

The widening gap between male and female mortality in the twentieth century stimulated examination of biological factors that might lead to excess male mortality. However, Stolnitz (1956) and more recently Waldron (1986) point out that evidence of excess female mortality in the past argues against biological models, while others suggest that secular trends in the sex ratio of mortality must be due to different lifestyles (Zhang, Sasaki, and Kesteloot 1995). Even studies that found different mortality in seemingly similar male and female populations, such as monks and nuns, have been criticized for failing to account for all of the social and behavioral differences between men and women (Johansson 1987). The most plausible modern theories attribute excess male mortality to an interaction of biological and behavioral factors (Härtel 1988), especially at adult and old ages (Lang, Arnold, and Kupfer 1994). Matthews (1989) found, for example, that females are protected from coronary heart diseases by both behavioral and biological characteristics. The biological aspect derives from female reproductive hormones such as estrogen that could play an important role in the metabolism of lipids and lipoproteins, with positive effects on the survival of women at least up to the end of the fertile period.

While Waldron (1986) considers biological studies of sex differences in adult mortality to be inconclusive, she does favor a biological explanation of excess male perinatal mortality. Male infants appear to be more susceptible to mortality from respiratory infections and accidents of childbirth, but this disadvantage disappears within the first year of life. Most geneticists and biologists also agree on the biological influence of sexual chromosomes (Soliani and Lucchetti 1997, Waldron 1983a). The presence of the Y chromosome (or, better, the presence of only one X chromosome) among men makes the emergence of X-linked diseases easier. Since they are genetically determined, they can also induce congenital malformations, whose effects can be lethal from very young ages.[4] Hemophilia is perhaps the best-known and best-studied disease of this kind, but other more dangerous illnesses have been implicated too. These conditions can attack the nerve system (Hartl 1983) or induce a form of mental retardation, the so-called fragile-X syndrome (Soliani and Lucchetti 1997).

Maternal Mortality and Maternal Depletion

Two frequently cited biological explanations for female mortality excesses are maternal mortality and maternal depletion. Excess female mortality is often greatest in the childbearing ages and disappears around age 50. This obviously suggests a link with childbearing, and there is little doubt that death during or following childbirth played some role. However, maternal mortality, defined in the narrow sense of deaths resulting directly from complications of childbirth, is not sufficient to account for observed levels of excess female mortality. Schofield (1986) estimates that maternal mortality in early modern England claimed about 10 mothers for every 1,000 births, implying a 6 to 7 percent risk of dying over the childbearing years. Estimates from other places are similar (Bardet et al. 1981).

Childbirth may contribute to female mortality in other ways. In poor societies, pregnancy and lactation impose additional demands on women whose nutritional status is already poor. This maternal depletion may make them more susceptible to certain infectious diseases that are more dangerous when the host is poorly nourished. In some places, customs associated with childbirth may have exacerbated the nutritional impact of childbirth and lactation. For example, Ochiai (1999a) described a Japanese practice where mothers were restricted to a diet of rice gruel for twenty-one days after giving birth.[5] These costs of childbearing had very visible signs: Christensen et al. (1998) found that the Danish proverb, "A tooth per child," was very nearly correct for women born early in the twentieth century. Childbearing must have been every bit as costly a century earlier.

Abortion was a potentially important cause of maternal deaths in some of the societies that we are studying. Methods of abortion, both mechanical and chemical, were inherently dangerous, and they probably increased the risk of death in later pregnancies as well. It is impossible to know how widespread abortion was in any historical population; however, there are strong indications that it was used in both China and Japan (Hsiung forthcoming, Li 2000, Ochiai 1999a, Shepherd 1995). Although both religion and law prohibited it in Europe, some authors, such as McLaren (1984), argue that traditional herbal abortifacients were widely known and accepted. However, abortion was probably uncommon in Europe until the late nineteenth and early twentieth centuries, when pressure for family limitation increased (Loudon 1992).

Economic Roles

In all societies, there are gender differences in economic roles. While it would be difficult to show that one gender worked less than the other, there is no doubt that types and locations of work often differed, as did the value attached to work associated with one sex or the other. In both East and West, men were more likely to be responsible for field crops and the care of draught animals, while female activities revolved around child rearing, the preparation of food and clothing, small animals, and gardens.[6] In complex households with three or more generations living together under one roof, roles differed by age and even relationship to the household head, further complicating the impact of gender on mortality.[7]

Differences in economic roles entailed different risks of disease and injury. Men were more prone to accidents, but women's roles may have exposed them to more pathogens over the long term. In particular, time spent by women cooking over open fires in poorly ventilated rooms may have increased the risk of respiratory disease (Fridlizius 1988). In addition, women were often responsible for nursing the sick, which increased their exposure to infectious pathogens.

It is unclear whether there were gender differences in the likelihood of exposure to disease through contacts outside the household. In Europe, both men and women were involved in market activities related to their tasks within the family economy. Women usually sold garden vegetables, eggs, and milk, and these activities would have brought them to markets in nearby towns. In hard times, exposure patterns were likely to change. Pitkänen and Mielke (1993) found that males aged 10 to 29 were most likely to be sent elsewhere to find work in two nineteenth-century Finnish famines, and mortality was particularly high among these migrants.

Lifestyle

Men and women differ in the prevalence of risky behaviors. In the twentieth century, a major source of higher male mortality was the higher rate of cigarette smoking among men. While the importance of tobacco in these historical populations is unclear, other behaviors differentiated men and women. For example, young males are the most likely to engage in behaviors that result in death by violence. Today, they are especially likely to die in motor vehicle accidents, but there were other risky behaviors in the nineteenth century. Riley (1993) has demonstrated the existence of a "trauma bump" in early adulthood due to deaths caused by accidents and violence.

Males were also more likely to abuse alcohol then and now. Fridli-zius (1988) and more recently Willner (1999) attribute the unusual Swedish pattern of excess male mortality in the adult ages to alcohol. The gender difference was particularly large in urban areas, but the male disadvantage decreased during the second half of the nineteenth century. Willner (1999) suggests that stabilizing social conditions and expanding ideals of temperance and respectability reduced the impact of alcohol consumption on male mortality in the late nineteenth century.

Unequal Distribution of Resources Within the Household

Many authors who have examined cases of excess female mortality point to the unequal distribution of nutrition and health care within families. Studies of South Asia, where female excess mortality is par-ticularly pronounced, have found that girls and women receive less food and are less likely to receive medical attention (Das Gupta 1987). Males were often favored in the distribution of food because their tasks were perceived as more physically demanding, because of the author-ity of males within the household, or because of cultural preferences for male children. As Preston (1976) and others have pointed out, excess female mortality tends to be greatest in poor societies, where resources are most limited. There is usually less excess female mortal-ity in urban areas, where women have greater opportunities to make economic contributions to the household.

There is little direct evidence of the distribution of food within households in historical sources, but the existing evidence tends to suggest that girls and women had fewer claims on family resources (Wall 1981). For example, one respondent to a survey of English work-ing women wrote, "A woman with little wage has to go without a great deal at those times, as we must give our husbands sufficient food or we should have them home and not able to work; therefore we have to go without to make ends meet" (Women's Co-Operative Guild 1915, 20). Kennedy (1973) concludes that the preferential treatment of males in Irish households caused excess female mortality in Ireland. Pinnelli and Mancini (1991) point to the correlation between increasing excess female mortality and economic crisis in Italy from 1871 to 1900. During this period, nutrition worsened, emigration increased, especially for males, and the positions of girls and women within the family appear to have weakened. When the economy improved, the relative position of females improved, and excess female mortality began to decline again.

In China, official state ideology and customary practice left girls and women with less access to household resources than boys and men. Families preferred sons because they carried out important ancestor worship rituals, remained in the household after they married, and were perceived as stronger and more productive. After a woman married, she was expected to serve her husband, bear sons for him and raise them, and eventually care for his elderly parents. Low status had many implications. Women had no inheritance rights and very little in the way of property rights, and they laid claim to household resources primarily in their role as the mother of a son (Campbell and Lee 2000). At meals, the females of the household usually ate only after the males, including sons, were finished. Men also had a higher priority when it came to allocating clothing, medical care, and other necessities.

Some authors have linked excess female mortality to changes in the economic roles of women. Johansson (1984), Humphries (1991), and Klasen (1998) argue that the changing value of women's work in agriculture in Sweden, England, and Germany, respectively, affected female mortality. When the relative productivity of female labor was higher, they had more claim on resources within the family and lower mortality.

These explanations are not mutually exclusive, and excess female mortality is most likely to be a result of a combination of interacting causes. For example, environmental conditions that exacerbated respiratory diseases and maternal depletion following childbirth would mostly affect women who suffered from poor nutrition due to an unequal distribution of food within the household.

Age Patterns of Sex Differences

A clear pattern of sex differences in mortality by age can be seen across all five sets of Eurasia Project villages. Since mortality rates for some adult ages are subject to random fluctuations due to small numbers of deaths, table 11.1 and figure 11.1 combine age groups to present this pattern in two different ways. In table 11.1, we calculate mortality sex ratios from life table probabilities of dying between certain ages. In

Table 11.1
Life table values

	China		Japan	Italy		Belgium	Sweden
	Liaodong North, 1789–1909	Liaodong South, 1789–1909	Niita and Shimomoriya, 1716–1870	Casalguidi, 1819–1859	Madregolo, 1800–1883	Sart, 1812–1899	Four Scanian parishes, 1815–1865
Male probability of dying in the interval ($_nq_x$)							
0–1	0.186	0.107		0.202	0.236	0.184	0.202
1–5	0.100	0.075	0.211	0.234	0.224	0.099	0.116
5–15	0.054	0.065	0.113	0.036	0.051	0.052	0.080
15–25			0.081	0.041	0.032	0.064	0.039
25–50	0.266	0.240	0.212	0.223	0.155	0.207	0.217
50–75	0.758	0.722	0.675	0.702	0.660	0.695	0.753
Female probability of dying in the interval ($_nq_x$)							
0–1	0.245	0.123		0.199	0.205	0.142	0.183
1–5	0.149	0.087	0.193	0.258	0.244	0.112	0.120
5–15	0.128	0.102	0.084	0.061	0.055	0.063	0.071
15–25			0.094	0.061	0.066	0.063	0.055
25–50	0.322	0.256	0.283	0.276	0.261	0.267	0.178
50–75	0.685	0.630	0.691	0.641	0.705	0.712	0.745
Ratio of male to female probability of dying (M/F)							
0–1	0.76	0.88		1.01	1.15	1.30	1.10
1–5	0.67	0.86	1.09	0.91	0.92	0.88	0.97
5–15	0.42	0.64	1.36	0.60	0.93	0.83	1.13
15–25			0.87	0.67	0.49	1.02	0.70
25–50	0.83	0.94	0.75	0.81	0.59	0.78	1.22
50–75	1.11	1.15	0.98	1.09	0.94	0.98	1.01

Percentage of those surviving to age 15 who die before age 50

Male	30.6	29.0	27.6	25.5	18.2	25.8	24.7
Female	40.9	33.2	35.0	32.0	31.0	31.3	22.3
Difference (M – F)	–10.3	–4.2	–7.4	–6.6	–12.8	–5.5	2.3

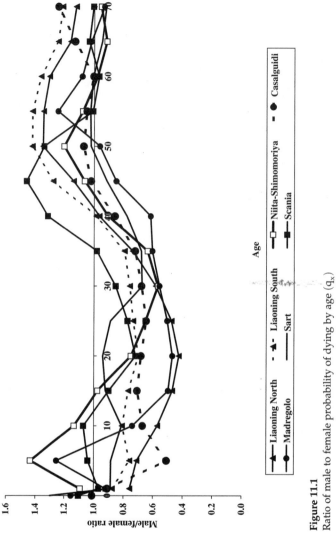

Figure 11.1
Ratio of male to female probability of dying by age (q_x)

figure 11.1, the mortality sex ratios are smoothed by taking a three-point moving average beginning with the age group 10 to 14 to remove random movements due to the small numbers of cases. Limitations in the various data sets, described in the appendix, should be kept in mind. In particular, we note that the data from the Liaodong state farms miss many unmarried women, who were almost all under age 20. Nevertheless, the pattern that emerges from figure 11.1 appears quite robust.

All of our study areas show excess female mortality in the young adult ages. The curves in figure 11.1 diverge in childhood and later adulthood, but there is a remarkably consistent pattern of higher female mortality in the prime childbearing ages. In the three European areas, where it is possible to measure mortality in the first year of life, male infants were more likely to die than female infants. According to Waldron (1986), this is probably due to physiological differences between male and female infants at the time of birth. After age 1, the sex ratio of mortality tends to fall below one, indicating lower male than female mortality. This pattern is not uniform, however. For example, the Scanian parishes tended to have higher female mortality at ages 1 to 5 but higher male mortality between ages 5 and 15.

Even though preference for sons is widely considered stronger in China and Japan than in Europe, excess female mortality in childhood was not greater in our Asian samples. In fact, the Japanese villages of Niita and Shimomoriya are the only ones that show a consistent female advantage from age 1 to 15. However, the data in table 11.1 do not reflect the incidence of infanticide, which was practiced to some extent in both China and Japan. While parents in China were more likely to use infanticide on girls than boys, they did not necessarily discriminate against the girls they allowed to survive (Lee, Wang, and Campbell 1994). Evidence in the event-history models discussed below does suggest that the competition for resources within the household affected girls differently in China and Japan than in our European samples.

Males in a number of our study populations have higher-than-expected mortality between ages 15 and 25, the "trauma bump" (Riley 1993). However, there is a similar phenomenon in several of the female populations as well. Furthermore, the upturn in female mortality is earlier in the populations that married earlier: those in Liaodong, Ou, and possibly northern Italy. Differences in the timing of this turning point between males and females result in a variety of patterns in the sex ratio of mortality between ages 15 and 25.

The excess female mortality that we see in young adulthood disappears entirely at older ages. With remarkable consistency, female and male mortality curves converge between ages 40 and 50. This convergence appears to be a little earlier in the Scanian data, but that is partly due to the smoothing procedure used in figure 11.1. After age 50, we find excess male mortality in some of our populations, but the Liaodong state farms are the only place where higher male mortality persists into the oldest ages.

Figure 11.1 makes clear the coincidence between excess female mortality and the reproductive ages. In addition, the mortality curves for women in Liaodong and Ou turn upward at earlier ages and converge to male mortality at earlier ages than the curves for European women. Since women in the Asian villages married earlier and had their last children younger than the European women, these turning points also point to the importance of childbearing. The last panel of table 11.1 shows the difference between male and female probabilities of dying between ages 15 and 50. Only in Scania were men less likely than women to survive the childbearing years, and even this result would have been different had we considered the age interval from 15 to 40.

Responses to Short-Term Economic Stress

Famines can transform sex differences in mortality. Male mortality often rises more than female mortality during famines, but this is not universally the case (Kane 1987, Ó Gráda 1999, Sen 1981, Watkins and Menken 1985). Explanations of male susceptibility to famine mortality range from differences in physiology to behaviors during famine, including the loss of privileges experienced during normal times. Ó Gráda (1999) suggests that females have a physiological advantage during food shortages because of their smaller body size and higher percentage of body fat. Pitkänen and Mielke (1993) attribute excess male mortality in Finnish famines to migration patterns, which were more likely to expose males to epidemic diseases. Arriaga and Way (1988) link higher male mortality during famines in Sri Lanka to male advantages in normal times. Although women were more likely to be poorly nourished in normal years, suffering was shared equally during famines. Thus, the loss of privileges for males when times were bad accounts for their stronger mortality response during crisis. Campbell and Lee (2000) make a similar argument about responses to economic stress in northeastern China.

Table 11.2
Ratio of relative risks for effects of prices (male/female)

Country	Site	Infants	Chil-dren	Ever-married adult	Never-married adult	Ever-married elderly	Never-married elderly
China	Liaodong North		[a]	1.11		[b]	
	Liaodong South		[a]			[a]	
Japan	Niita and Shimomoriya	[c]	0.73	1.35		1.98	
Italy	Casalguidi	2.25	0.81	1.30	1.88	[c]	
	Madregolo	[b]	1.95	2.15	3.03	0.67	
	Venice	1.28	1.04	0.94	1.28	0.75	[c]
Belgium	Sart	[c]	1.70	0.54	2.30	[a]	[b]
Sweden	Four Scanian parishes	0.98	0.95	0.70	0.91	0.90	

Note: Based on Eurasia standard comparative individual model.
[a] Both relative risks below 1.
[b] Male relative risk above 1; female relative risk below 1.
[c] Male relative risk below 1; female relative risk above 1.

It is even less clear how periods of less severe economic stress affect gender differences in mortality. The measure of economic stress used in this book captures fluctuations in food supply that fall far short of the famines examined by most previous studies. To be sure, serious famines did occur, particularly in the villages of Ou, and even small increases in prices could cause hunger among the poor and landless. Nevertheless, as explained in chapter 2, the focus here is on smoothing consumption across good and bad years, not the response to periods of extreme distress.

Bengtsson and Saito (2000b) have previously pointed out that gender differences in responses to economic stress varied among the Eurasia Project communities. Table 11.2 compares the responses of males and females to economic stress by computing ratios of the relative risks to price fluctuations in the Eurasia standard comparative individual model.[8] These ratios show differences in the effect of higher prices on males and females. Ratios greater than one suggest that male mortality responded to higher prices more than female mortality did. Since we are interested in positive correlations between prices and mortality, a ratio is not computed when the effect of prices is negative. If we look for gender differences in these responses, we do not find a single compelling pattern. There are often pronounced differences between males and females, but they tend to vary across age groups and among villages.

The ratios in table 11.2 referring to infancy and childhood are quite diverse. The records from Liaodong do not show a relationship between prices and childhood mortality. Other evidence, however, suggests that infanticide was more prevalent in bad years (Lee, Campbell, and Tan 1992), so our records underestimate the effects of economic stress on children. In Niita and Shimomoriya, girls were much more affected by price fluctuations than boys, but five of the six estimates from northern Italy suggest that prices affected boys more strongly than girls. In Sart, infant girls appear to have been at a disadvantage in bad years, but boys were affected more strongly between ages 2 and 15. Finally, in Scania, the responses of boys and girls were about the same.

Responses among adults depended on age, gender, and marital status. Married men were more responsive to prices than married women in Liaodong, Ou, and northern Italy and less responsive in Sart and Scania. The relatively strong responses of ever-married males continued into old age in Liaodong and Ou, but older women were affected more in the three northern Italian samples. Not surprisingly, prices affected unmarried men aged 15 to 54 more than they did unmarried women. Unmarried adult women were so rare in the Asian data that estimates are not possible, but prices had strong effects on unmarried men in both Liaodong and Ou. Again, the Scanian data do not show much difference between men and women.

The diversity of responses to economic stress shown in table 11.2 suggests that there is no single explanation for sex differences in mortality responses to short-term economic stress. The strongest case for a biological explanation may be the high ratio of male to female mortality responses among ever-married adults in Ou. If female physiological advantages were important in cases of severe malnutrition, we would expect them to be most apparent in these data. Northeastern Japan experienced severe famines in the 1730s, 1780s, and 1830s. In contrast, we do not find a consistent female disadvantage in our European data, which are mostly from the nineteenth century after subsistence crises had disappeared.[9] High food prices in Scania and the Ardennes affected ever-married adult men less than ever-married women, and this effect was even more unbalanced among landless laborers, the poorest occupational group. However, it is noteworthy that the typhus epidemic that struck Sart in 1816 disproportionately affected males. Although 1816 was not the year of highest prices, it was in the middle of a severe crisis caused by bad harvests on the heels of the Napoleonic Wars.

Crisis behaviors that increased exposure to disease may explain the higher male responsiveness to economic stress among never-married adults in northern Italy and eastern Belgium. Unmarried males would be the first group sent out of the household in search of work during hard times. We see a similar pattern among ever-married adults who were not stem kin of the head of household in the results from Liaodong and Ou, where marriage was early and universal.[10] However, this differential does not appear among the never married in the Scanian parishes. Since Scania had a much more extensive system of life cycle servanthood, the experiences of young men and women may have been more similar there.

The "loss of privilege" hypothesis also appears to fit the overall findings for ever-married adults. Although none of our study populations professed sexual equality, traditions of male dominance were arguably strongest in China and perhaps Japan and somewhat weaker in Belgium and Sweden. In table 11.2, responses do divide along these lines, with the northern Italian populations in between. Furthermore, there is a striking reversal in the sex pattern of responses to economic stress between childhood and adulthood. In Ou, girls were affected more than boys, but women were affected less than men. In Sart, girls were affected less than boys, but women were affected more than men.

In sum, we cannot point to a single pattern of gendered responses to economic stress or a single model that will explain why gender differences varied by age in different places. Biological differences between males and females may have emerged in some cases, but they were not a major factor in most of our study areas. Rather, these results highlight differences in the intensity of food shortages, changes in the distribution of resources within the households in bad times, and age-sex patterns of activity outside households during crises.

Household Composition

Even in normal times, family members had to compete for limited resources, and associations between household composition and mortality may reveal differences in gender preferences. The standard models estimated for all Eurasia Project research sites include variables describing each household in broad age and sex categories. We expect that additional family members in the prime working ages, 15 to 55, would have increased resources available to the family, possibly making more food available and mortality lower for the least favored groups. In contrast, children and the elderly were in competition for resources, and households with more dependents may have distributed resources and the risk of dying unequally by age and gender.

In table 11.3, we examine the effects of changes in household composition on mortality, as measured by the number of persons aged 15 to 54, the proportion of persons under age 15, and the proportion of persons aged 55 and older.[11] Entries in table 11.3 are relative risks of death broken down by age, sex, and marital status. The relative risks in the first panel show the effect of adding one more working-age person to the household. In the second and third panels, we show the effects of a 20 percentage point change in the proportion under age 15 or age 55 and older. Such a change is equivalent to a difference of one person in a five-person household.

We begin by noting that most of the estimates in table 11.3 probably have a bias toward showing lower mortality in larger households. This is likely to occur when there are unobserved differences in mortality among households. Households that are healthier will tend to be larger simply because they experience fewer deaths. This effect should be particularly strong when we look at infant and child mortality. A high proportion of young children will usually be an indicator of conditions within the household that lowered infant and child mortality. Infants should be less likely to die in households where more of the preceding children survived. Thus, we should treat relative risks below 1.0 with caution.

The first panel of table 11.3 suggests that the size of the household in terms of the number of persons of working age had little effect on mortality. All of the relative risks for the number of persons 15 to 54 are close to 1.0, and few of them are statistically significant. There is a general tendency in the European results for mortality to be lower in larger households, but we cannot point to a gender differential with any confidence.

When we look at the presence of the young and old in the household, a pattern emerges, especially in Liaodong and Ou. The presence of other persons in the household adversely affected girls much more often than it did boys. For example, an additional child under age 15 adversely affected girls aged 2 to 14 in six of our eight cases. In comparison, two of the eight estimates for boys imply higher mortality in households with more children. Persons older than age 55 also affected boys and girls differently. In the European populations, there is only one case where persons 55 and older had a more beneficial effect on infant girls than on male infants. At ages 2 to 14, the effect of another elderly person is beneficial for most boys but neutral or harmful for most girls. The largest effects in this age group are for girls in Liaodong and Ou. In both cases, an additional person aged 55 or older increased the risk of death for a girl by 30 percent.

Figures 11.2, 11.3, and 11.4 present these household composition effects for children aged 2 to 14 in a visual form. The implication is that girls had to compete for resources within the household, but boys did not. The effects of elderly persons in Liaodong and Ou households are particularly suggestive. These results fit our expectations that families protected boys because they were likely heirs and that girls ranked below the elderly in the household hierarchy. We should point out, however, that persons over age 55 meant different things in Asia and Europe. Marriage was so much earlier in Liaodong and Ou that the average age of childbearing was about five years younger than in the European samples. Liaodong and Ou households were also more likely to be complex, although there were complex households in the Italian villages. As a result, elderly persons in Asia were usually grandparents, but persons over age 55 in the European villages were usually a child's own parent.

These results suggest that inequality in the distribution of resources within households mattered. It is very interesting to find the most consistent evidence of competition for resources among girls aged 2 to 14. As we saw, girls had higher mortality than boys of this age, and the results presented in table 11.3 suggest that they were in a more vulnerable position than their brothers.

Widowhood

Another important aspect of household composition, especially in older ages, is the presence or loss of a spouse. The death of a spouse adversely affects the surviving partner in a number of ways, and the mortality of the newly widowed individual usually increases during a period of grief and adjustment. As early as 1912, March estimated that the widowed and the never married were twice as likely to die as married people in France, Prussia, and Sweden, and recent studies have confirmed this finding. Moreover, the impact of bereavement is usually

Table 11.3
Effects of changes in household composition on the relative risks of dying

		0–1		2–14		15–54 Ever-married		15–54 Never-married		55+ Ever-married		55+ Never-married	
		Female	Male	Female	Male	Female	Male	Female	Male	Female	Male	Female	Male
Number of persons in household aged 15–54 (estimated effect of adding one person)													
China	Liaodong	0.85	0.90	0.98	1.01	1.01	0.99		0.99	1.00	1.00		1.06
Japan	Niita and Shimomoriya	0.96	0.94	1.08	1.00	1.05	1.00		1.13	0.98	1.08		
Italy	Casalguidi	0.98	0.97	0.89	0.93	0.93	0.95	1.02	0.99	1.08	0.91		
	Madregolo			1.01	1.00	1.02	0.99	0.93	0.99	1.04	0.98		
	Venice	0.97	0.88	0.95	0.89	0.82	0.88	1.03	0.89	1.04	0.91	0.02	0.29
Belgium	Sart	0.97	1.04	0.95	0.90	0.95	0.92	0.95	0.89	0.89	0.97	1.32	0.74
Sweden	Four Scanian parishes	0.96	0.98	1.07	0.99	1.04	0.95	0.98	1.00	1.06	1.07		
Proportion of household under 15 years old (estimated effect of a 20% increase)													
China	Liaodong	0.88	0.80	1.16	1.14	0.98	0.96		0.96	1.03	0.99		1.17
Japan	Niita and Shimomoriya		1.05	1.13	0.88	0.98	0.93		1.07	0.94	1.07		
Italy	Casalguidi	1.16	1.05	1.25	0.98	0.91	1.15	1.24		1.18	0.86		
	Madregolo	0.96	0.93	0.98	1.05	0.79	1.29	1.26	0.70	1.22	1.17		
	Venice	0.88	0.75	1.03	0.85	0.83	1.04	1.00	0.78	1.06	0.85	7.34	0.16
Belgium	Sart	1.07	0.99	0.97	0.86	0.86	0.92	1.00	0.86	1.05	1.09	1.23	0.88
Sweden	Four Scanian parishes	0.89	0.93	1.15	0.96	1.12	1.11	1.04	0.88	0.92	1.04		

Proportion of household aged 55 or more (estimated effect of a 20% increase)

Country	Region											
China	Liaodong	0.54		1.30	0.99	1.06	1.01	*0.86*	0.98	0.96	1.12	
Japan	Niita and Shimomoriya		1.02	*1.30*	*0.95*	1.09	0.98	*1.34*	1.01	*1.13*		
Italy	Casalguidi	*1.43*	0.86	*1.13*	*0.52*	1.06	1.16	1.26	1.20	*0.86*		
	Madregolo	1.04	0.84	0.96	*0.70*	0.92	1.29	*1.37*	1.18	*1.05*		
	Venice	1.00	0.92	0.90	*1.09*	0.91	0.86	*0.93*	1.00	*0.85*	0.13	*0.31*
Belgium	Sart	1.18	0.95	*1.10*	*0.64*	0.91	1.17	*0.96*	0.91	0.99	1.15	
Sweden	Four Scanian parishes	*0.58*	0.93	1.06	*0.84*	0.94	1.31	0.65	1.06	*1.13*		*0.73*

Notes: Based on Eurasia standard comparative household model. Italicized numbers indicate *p*-value < .05.

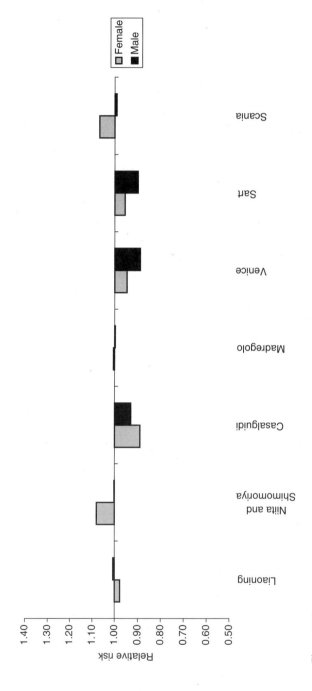

Figure 11.2
Relative risk of death to children aged 2–14 for an increase in persons aged 15–54 by sex

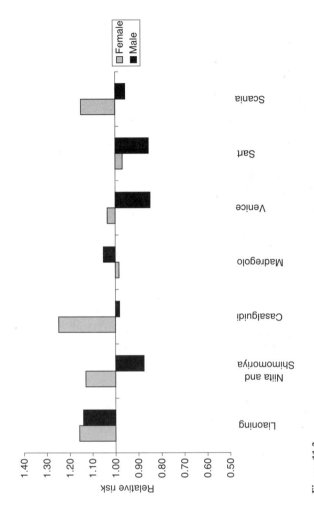

Figure 11.3
Relative risk of death to children aged 2 to 14 for an increase in persons aged 0–15 by sex

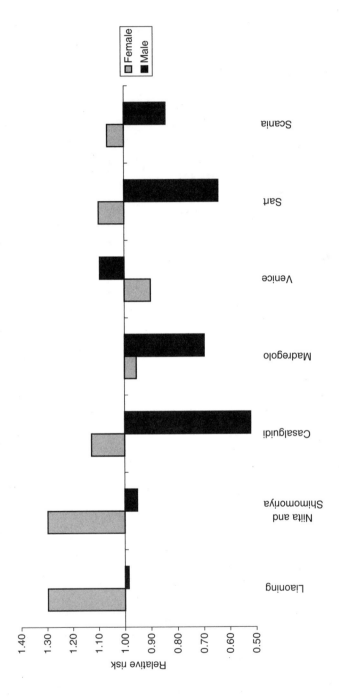

Figure 11.4
Relative risk of death to children aged 2–14 for an increase in persons aged 55 and over by sex

Table 11.4
Ratio of male to female relative risks due to widowhood

		Adults (ages 15–54)	Elderly (ages 55 and over)
China	Liaodong	0.82	0.89
Japan	Niita and Shimomoriya	0.95	1.14
Italy	Casalguidi	**	**
	Madregolo	0.43	**
	Venice	0.45	0.74
Belgium	Sart	1.49	1.10

Note: Based on relative risks for widows and widowers in Eurasia standard comparative relationship model.
**One or both estimated relative risks is less than 1.

greater for widowers than for widows (Gove 1973, Rogers 1995). Men appear to be more dependent on their wives for basic support in daily life, while widows may be better able to draw on social support (Bowling 1987).

Within the Eurasia Project, Nystedt (2002) has used time spent in widowhood as a time-varying covariate to separate the transitory and persistent effects of bereavement on the mortality of surviving elderly spouses in Scanian parishes. He found that the spousal bereavement penalty was larger for men. Whereas the risk of dying doubled for women during the first six months after the death of the spouse, the corresponding risk for men almost tripled. After six years, this excess risk decreased to 19 percent for widows and 34 percent for widowers.

Although it is not possible to duplicate Nystedt's precise approach with results from the Eurasia standard comparative models, the relationship model does include an estimate of the difference in mortality risks between widows and widowers and the currently married. Although these estimates control for age, they do not control for time since bereavement. This may be important, because widows are usually much less likely to remarry than widowers. In addition, migration may affect these estimates. For example, if women were more likely to out-migrate after the loss of a spouse, we may be comparing subgroups that differ in important respects.

Table 11.4 presents male/female ratios of the relative risks associated with being a widower/widow in two age groups, 15 to 54 and 55 and older. Somewhat surprisingly, only three of the nine ratios indicate that men were more affected by widowhood than women, and

Sart is the only place where men were more strongly affected in both age groups. This is especially noteworthy because Sart is the only rural area included in table 11.4 to have a predominantly nuclear family system. The more complex family forms in Liaodong, Ou, and northern Italy may have blunted the effects of widowhood for men, at least while they remained heads of households.[12]

The Consequences of Childbirth

Childbirth poses a number of risks for the mother, and the convergence between female and male mortality at the close of the childbearing years suggests that childbearing must be part of the explanation for excess female mortality in the adult ages. Nevertheless, previous studies have found that the amount of maternal mortality resulting directly from childbirth is not sufficient to explain the difference between the mortality of married women and married men. The same appears to be true in our data. In Sart, we found only forty-four women (7.6 per 1,000) who died within forty-two days of giving birth and sixty-six (11.3 per 1,000) within the first six months among 5,824 births. Results for the first six months in Casalguidi and the Scanian villages are similar: 7.9 per 1,000 (28 deaths among 3,553 births) and 7.4 per 1,000 (41 deaths among 5,508 births), respectively. These levels match estimates from England (Schofield 1986, Wrigley et al. 1997) and Germany (Knodel 1988). Assuming six births per woman, this implies that between 4 and 7 percent of women would have died from maternal mortality.

The most common causes of maternal death were puerperal fever, toxemia, and hemorrhage (Loudon 1992). Puerperal fever, the most important of these in the nineteenth century, was most often the result of streptococcal infections. Recognition of the contagiousness of puerperal fever was increasing, especially after Semmelweis's well-known experiments in the Vienna Maternity Hospital in the 1840s, but it took many years for physicians to accept his emphasis on disinfection (Loudon 1992). Pregnancy also affects the mother's immune system in complex ways. Weinberg (1984) introduced the term *pregnancy-associated immune deficiency syndrome*. Others reject the characterization of these changes as an immunodeficiency (Stirrat 1994), but there is general agreement that the mother's immune system must adjust to the presence of the fetus (Reid 1998). These adjustments appear to make mothers more susceptible to some diseases, including smallpox and malaria (Hart 1988).

Maternal mortality is not the only possible link between child-bearing and mortality. The physical demands of pregnancy, breast-feeding, and taking care of young children may have had other effects on mothers. Miller, Rodriguez, and Pebley (1993) found that breast-feeding women in Bangladesh lost weight for more than a year after each birth, and women with more previous births and shorter intervals between births were less able to recover before their next birth. Pebley and Davanzo (1993) also found that breast-feeding affected a woman's weight, but they did not find that the length of the interval between births affected weight at the next birth. If maternal depletion was oper-ating in our historical populations, the number of children ever born or the number of young children present in the household should have affected it.

We have examined the effects of both maternal mortality and mater-nal depletion with additional event-history models for the commune of Sart, Belgium, and the Scanian parishes in southern Sweden. These data sets have continuous observation of vital events and migra-tion, which makes it easier to examine the consequences of childbirth. Tables 11.5 and 11.6 show event-history models for currently married women who have had at least one birth. In these Cox partial likelihood models, the baseline hazard accounts for the effect of age on mortality.

Both the Sart and the Scanian data show the effects of maternal mor-tality. In Sart, according to table 11.5, mortality was more than twice its normal level during the first six months following a birth. Table 11.6 reveals that in Scania, the relative risk of dying was more than five times normal in the first year after a birth. A more detailed analysis of the Sart data suggests that this effect was even more concentrated in the first few months after a birth. Survival curves fall quickly after a birth but converge to their long-run slope after forty-two days.[13]

There is little evidence of a general maternal depletion effect. We examined this hypothesis in three different ways with the Sart data. Model 1 in table 11.5 has two variables: number of surviving children and number of child deaths. Model 2 looks at numbers of persons in the household in three age groups: under 15, 15 to 54, and 55 and older. Finally, model 3 uses dummy variables by number of children ever observed to detect nonlinear effects. None of these models shows higher mortality for mothers with more children. Indeed, we find the

Table 11.5
Estimated relative risks of dying for currently married women aged 15–44 with at least one child, Sart, 1812–1899

Covariates	Mean	Model 1 Relative risk	p-value	Model 2 Relative risk	p-value	Model 3 Relative risk	p-value	Model 4 Relative risk	p-value	Model 5 Relative risk	p-value
Price of oats	0.00	1.06	0.02	1.06	0.03	1.06	0.02	1.06	0.02	1.06	0.04
Time period											
1812–1846	0.43	1.00		1.00		1.00		1.00		1.00	
1847–1875	0.33	1.05	0.76	1.05	0.73	1.00	0.98	1.00	0.99	1.01	0.96
1876–1900	0.24	0.54	0.00	0.52	0.00	0.50	0.00	0.50	0.00	0.51	0.00
Time since last birth											
0–6 months	0.26	2.39	0.00	2.48	0.00						
6–12 months	0.24	0.82	0.49	0.86	0.60						
12–18 months	0.15	0.95	0.85	0.99	0.96						
18–24 months	0.11	1.17	0.58	1.20	0.51						
2–3 years	0.10	1.00		1.00							
3–4 years	0.05	1.36	0.30	1.35	0.31						
4–5 years	0.03	1.03	0.93	1.02	0.96						
5+ years	0.05	1.35	0.26	1.26	0.38						
Surviving children	3.16	0.88	0.00								
Child deaths	0.80	1.42	0.00								
Persons aged 0–14	2.87			0.91	0.06						
Persons aged 15–54	2.41			0.94	0.39						
Persons 55 and older	0.17			0.91	0.56						
Children ever observed											
1	0.16					1.12	0.64	1.11	0.67	1.12	0.65
2	0.17					0.89	0.61	0.86	0.55	0.89	0.62

	(1)	(2)	(3) RR	(3) p	(4) RR	(4) p	(5) RR	(5) p
3	0.16		1.00		1.00		1.00	
4	0.14		0.70	0.16	0.71	0.18	0.70	0.16
5	0.12		1.16	0.53	1.15	0.56	1.16	0.52
6	0.09		0.74	0.29	0.72	0.27	0.75	0.30
7	0.07		1.04	0.90	1.05	0.86	1.04	0.89
8	0.10		0.90	0.71	0.93	0.79	0.91	0.73
Interval 0–6 months	0.26		2.22	0.00	1.62	0.26	2.25	0.00
Interaction: Interval 0–6 months × children ever observed								
1					2.41	0.10		
2					0.75	0.66		
3					1.00			
4					1.10	0.88		
5					0.87	0.82		
6					3.32	0.06		
7					1.13	0.86		
8					1.80	0.34		
Interaction oats × interval 0–6 months							0.87	0.02
Max log-likelihood	−1,527.5	−1,544.6	−1,546.5		−1,541.4		−1,543.7	
−2*log-likelihood	3,054.9	3,089.2	3,092.9		3,082.7		3,087.4	
Overall test of model, Chi-square	87.8	53.5	49.8		60.0		55.3	
Degrees of freedom	12	13	11		18		12	
Overall p-value	0.00	0.00	0.00		0.00		0.00	

Note: Unit numbers below "Children ever observed" signify birth order.

Table 11.6
Estimated relative risks of death for currently married women aged 18–49, Scania, 1800–1895

Covariates	Relative risk	*p*-value
Time since last birth (years)		
0–1	5.63	0.00
1–2	1.22	0.54
2–3	1.00	(Ref.)
3–4	0.68	0.38
4–5	1.05	0.90
5–6	1.15	0.74
6 or more	0.65	0.26
Household size	1.07	0.01
Age at first birth		
Under 20	1.00	(Ref.)
20–24	0.66	0.18
25–30	0.63	0.14
Over 30	0.58	0.10
Unknown	0.49	0.51
Birthdate (continuous)	1.00	0.39
Number of own children in household younger than 15 (continuous)	0.83	0.00
Time at risk		24,441.1
Deaths		134
Log likelihood		−870.74
Chi-square		81.65
Degrees of freedom		13

opposite: women with more surviving children were less likely to die. This pattern is clearest in model 1, which shows that mothers were 12 percent less likely to die for each surviving child but 42 percent more likely die for each child who had died. The most probable explanation is that mothers tend to die from the same social and environmental conditions that kill their children. We see a similar pattern with different covariates in the results from Scania. In table 11.6, women living in larger households were more likely to die, but each child under age 15 reduced the relative risk of death by 17 percent. A similar pattern is apparent in table 11.3, where an additional child under age 15 reduced the relative risk of dying for ever-married women in every location except Scania.

Family size, however, affected maternal mortality in a more complex way. Earlier studies have found that maternal mortality was high at very low and very high parities but low in between. Knodel (1988) found this J-shaped pattern in his study of eighteenth- and nineteenth-century German villages. Table 11.5 shows a similar pattern in Sart. Model 4 includes an interaction between the period less than six months after a birth and the number of children ever observed. This interaction is very large after the first birth and low between births two and five, and it rises suddenly after six births. Table 11.6 shows a similar effect in a somewhat different way. In Scania, we find that women who had their first birth under age 20 were 30 to 50 percent more likely to die. This variable captures both ends of the J described by Knodel. Practically all births under age 20 in Scania were first births, and women who began childbearing earlier reached higher parities than other women of the same age.

Model 5 suggests that economic stress did not affect maternal mortality. This model includes an interaction between prices and the period less than six months after a birth. The estimated relative risk for this interaction term is less than one, suggesting that maternal mortality decreased during bad times. However, this pattern is probably due to selection effects. High prices also reduced fertility, and women who were at greater risk of maternal mortality were probably less likely to give birth in years of high prices.

Conclusion

Although the areas studied by the Eurasia Project differed in a number of fundamental social, economic, and cultural respects, sex differences in mortality were remarkably similar. All of the women in our samples experienced higher risks of death from late adolescence until the end of their childbearing years. There was much less consistency at other ages. Boys had generally higher mortality in childhood, especially before age 1, and old-age mortality was roughly the same for men and women.

The age pattern of excess female mortality strongly suggests an association with childbearing, and maternal mortality explains a large part, but not all, of the difference between men and women. Marriage was late in our European study areas, and excess female mortality emerged at ages when few people were married. Although the outcome was the same, it is highly likely that there were two different processes leading to high female mortality rates: one affecting girls and another affecting married women.

The evidence on household composition presented suggests that girls were more likely than boys to compete for resources with other household members. These effects are noticeably stronger in the two sets of Asian populations, but they appear to be present in the European populations as well. Differences in training for future careers would also have become apparent in this age group. Boys would be spending more and more time working beside their fathers in the fields, while girls would have assisted their mothers in the home. Both differential access to resources and emerging differences in work environments probably contributed to higher female susceptibility to tuberculosis and other respiratory diseases.

Maternal mortality was clearly an important contributor to the excess mortality of married women, and the risks associated with childbirth rose rapidly after five births. However, it would be incorrect to focus solely on the dangers of childbirth. The evidence suggests that women continued to have weaker claims on resources than men after as well as before marriage. This shows up most clearly in our data from the Ardennes and Scania, where the overall level of mortality was lowest. Married women in these two communities showed much more responsiveness to economic stress than married men. Ironically, the most serious famines tended to reverse the fortunes of men and women. Whether it was due to female physiology or loss of male privileges, or more likely both, male, not female, mortality increased the most when times were bad in Liaodong, Ou, and the villages of Casalguidi and Madregolo.

Notes

We thank Sheila Ryan Johansson for her suggestions on an earlier draft of this chapter. Previous versions of this chapter were presented at the Department of Statistics, University of Udine, Italy (February 23, 1999); Department of Health and Society, Linköping University, Linköping, Sweden (March 25, 1999); Centre for Population Studies, Umeå University, Umeå, Sweden (May 18, 1999); and Centre for Advanced Study, Norwegian Academy of Science and Letters, Oslo, Norway (June 14, 1999). We are grateful to participants in those seminars for their helpful comments. George Alter thanks the Swedish Collegium for Advanced Study in the Social Sciences for a fellowship that supported his work on this chapter. Paul Nystedt acknowledges support from the Swedish Council for Working Life and Social Research, the Swedish Council for Social Research, and the Bank of Sweden Tercentenary Foundation.

1. Our translation from the French.

2. See chapter 3 for a brief discussion of mortality levels in the Eurasia populations.

3. See chapter 1 and the appendix for introductions to these models and chapters 3 and 5 for summaries of results.

4. It is important to note that the decline of mortality allowed many individuals to reach reproductive ages even if they carried genes that predisposed them to disease. This produced a "relaxation" of biological selection and an increase in the prevalence of "dangerous" genes (Lucchetti 1978).

5. Some societies did recognize the demands that childbearing placed on mothers. In China, women who had just given birth were supposed to rest for a month in almost complete isolation, eating special foods believed to help restore their health. The practice was called *zuo yuezi* (Hsiung forthcoming). Of course, not every family had the means to practice this.

6. See, for example, Segalen (1983).

7. See chapters 4 and 5 for a discussion of household organization and an analysis of its implications for mortality levels and sensitivity to short-term stress.

8. See tables 3.3 and 3.4 for the original results from the Eurasia standard comparative individual model. For adults, those tables present the results only for ever-married adults.

9. The potato blight in 1846 did have severe consequences in certain places, like Ireland and Flanders, but none of our study populations depended primarily on potato cultivation.

10. We computed these estimates (not shown) from results in the Eurasia standard comparative relationship model with price interactions.

11. These results are from the Eurasia standard comparative household model.

12. See chapter 5 for additional results on household composition.

13. The International Federation of Gynecology and Obstetrics and the World Health Organization both define death within forty-two days of childbirth as maternal mortality (Schofield 1986). The survival curves for Sart suggest exactly the same dividing line.

Infant and Child Mortality

Michel Oris, Renzo Derosas,
and Marco Breschi
in collaboration with George
Alter, Tommy Bengtsson,
Cameron Campbell, Satomi
Kurosu, and Matteo
Manfredini

For several reasons, infant and child mortality occupies a major place in the analysis of mortality and of demographic regimes. The most obvious one is that in pretransitional demographic systems, infant and child deaths accounted for the majority of all deaths. Infants and children are frailer than adults since they need nutrients not only to maintain their bodies but also to develop them. During the period of our study, they are also more vulnerable to epidemic diseases than adults are. For access to food and help against epidemics, children are entirely dependent on families and their larger communities.[1] This chapter extends the analysis of chapter 3 with a more detailed analysis of infant and child mortality for the locations where data are available.[2] A number of studies have been devoted to infant and child mortality, particularly for the eighteenth and nineteenth centuries.[3] Ambitious collective inquiries have reconstructed levels and trends from vital statistics.[4] In this line of research, a great deal of attention has been paid to issues related to the age pattern of mortality before the age of 1. Seasonality was explored as another decisive time dimension (Breschi and Livi-Bacci 1986, Vilquin 1978). However, geography also fascinated demographers, and many works explored the differentials of levels and trends between regions or the peculiar history of an area.[5] Along this line, several explanatory models have been constructed. Good examples are the analysis of the forty-six Belgian *arrondissements* in the second half of the nineteenth century by Lesthaege (1977), focusing on a socioeconomic and cultural perspective, or, focusing on an epidemiological orientation, the model of exposure and resistance used by Johansson and Mosk (1987) in their study of mortality in Japan between 1900 and 1960 and generalized by Perrenoud and Bourdelais (1998, 60).

Even though many important studies have been published, empirical research still lags behind theoretical frameworks.[6] Reher and Schofield pointed out that the key question when working on mortality is how to separate the effects of its main determinants (1991, 2). They are often difficult to isolate because aggregate analyses are necessarily based on averages (Johansson and Kasakoff 2000, 56). However, previous analyses of microdata, at the familial or individual level, are often much more descriptive than explanatory. For example, even for such easier-to-detect aspects as mortality differentials by social and economic status of the family, still very little is known (Bengtsson 1999, 120–125; Breschi and Pozzi 1997; Perrenoud 1997, 300–303; van Poppel and Mandemakers 1997, 298). Collecting such nominal data is very time-consuming, and classical methods only allow the examination of the effects of one or two variables.[7] This is why the microhistorical demography based on nominal data often describes but seldom explains. While we know a great deal about levels and trends, we know much less about differentials (Johansson and Kasakoff 2000, 56; Pozzi and Robles Gonzáles 1996; Reher and Schofield 1991, 2).

Biological, environmental, economic, social, and cultural factors interact to influence the survival chances of the youngest members of society. Mosley and Chen (1984) have explored this in their analysis of infant mortality in developing countries. Their work focuses on the specification of such determinants linking the risks introduced by a disease to the death of the child. Diseases and malnutrition no longer are mere causes of death, but the consequence of an interaction between social and biological contexts. This conceptual framework and its elaborations by Mosley (1985), Schultz (1984), and van Norren and van Vianen (1986) have received a great deal of attention and influenced research on child mortality in developing countries (Ruzicka 1989) as well as in historical studies (Kok, Van Poppel, and Kruse 1997; Rollet 1994; Williams and Galley 1995; Woods, William, and Galley 1997).

We use a similar theoretical framework to construct our own explanatory model, which is close to the comparative relationship model described in chapter 2 and the appendix. There is, however, an important difference. We divide infant and child life into four stages: the first ten days of life, the tenth day to the end of the sixth month, the beginning of the seventh month to the first birthday, and the first to the fourth year. There are technical and substantive reasons behind this division. Essentially, we expect that the direction and importance of the factors affecting children's health change very rapidly at the beginning of life, with genetic and familial factors declining in importance and social, economic, and environmental ones increasing. Failing to take such variations into account can produce misleading or scarcely interpretable results. In this chapter, we show something slightly different though in part unexpected: similar causal patterns can be found in regimes of high as well as low mortality.

Infant and Child Mortality: Estimates, Levels, and Trends

Sources, Data, and the Limits of Comparability

A full comparative analysis of mortality at young ages faces some serious obstacles. The Asian data do not permit the direct computation of infant mortality. The Liaodong data are based on household listings updated every three years. Consequently, most children born after one update who die before the next are not recorded.[8] As for the local population registers of the Japanese villages of Shimomoriya and Niita, or *ninbetsu-aratame-cho*, they were collected annually in the third lunar month of the year and suffer from similar omissions of unregistered infant births and deaths (Cornell and Hayami 1986). The NAC of the Nihonmatsu domain include some children who died before the registration day, thus reflecting this domain's pronatal policies, which started in the late seventeenth century. Studies of northeastern villages using other sources estimate the underregistration of births ranged between 12 and 8 percent (Kinoshita 1999, Kito 1996, Tsuya and Tomobe 1998).

In the European cases, all the data sets have been built up either linking annual household lists (*Status Animarum* in Italy, religious examination registers in Sweden) with parish registers of baptisms, burials, and marriages or relying on population registers (*anagrafe* in Venice, *registres de population* in Belgium), eventually integrated or cross-checked with information drawn from parish registers. In these cases, we have been able to gather a very accurate data set, though, of course, we cannot pretend they are perfect.[9] There is a distinction between the places where migrations were directly recorded—Belgium, Sweden, Venice—and the Italian villages where immigrants are inferred indirectly, by their appearance in the next annual list. Whereas in Sweden and Belgium more than 96 percent of the birth acts or baptisms have been linked (Bengtsson and Dribe 1997, 4; Neven 2000a,

13–14), in the Italian villages "many births and deaths do not appear among the population listed in the registers" (Breschi, Derosas, and Manfredini 2000). These were mostly deaths that occurred shortly after arrival in the village. Wet-nursing is also a cause: the village of Casalguidi in Tuscany, for instance, received from the cities nearby a large number of babies sent there for nursing. Although many died and were recorded in the parish registers, they are not included in our analyses because we usually ignore the date of their arrival and, consequently, their exact time of exposure to the risk of dying; moreover, no reliable information is available about those who returned alive to the foundling institutions after weaning. Nevertheless, simply ignoring these children may be problematic since they competed with the native infants and children for parental care, especially breast-feeding.

A more general problem concerns stillbirths, including so-called false stillbirths, that is, children born alive who died before the registration of their birth or baptism. In the Belgian communities, where counting them is possible, stillbirths were respectively 3.59 percent of all births in Tilleur (1847–1880) and 3.57 in Sart (1812–1900). Excluding or including even such small numbers has a large impact on neonatal and infant mortality rates.[10] In table 12.1, which includes stillbirths, the eastern Belgian rates are comparable to the Scanian and northern Italian ones. This may partly be an artifact of differences in religious attitudes. Catholics frequently reported stillbirths as live births in order to allow the baptism to take place. Protestants did not share such views and went so far as to condemn the behavior of Catholics in this matter.[11] In Catholic Belgium, different practices for the baptism of dead children were observed in the eighteenth century; it even seems that these "stillbirth miracles" were particularly frequent in the Ardennes region, where Sart is located (Gélis 2000, 121). However, for both Sart and Venice, we draw on population registers that were organized and maintained by the state or the communal administrations. In this case, we can assume that parents had no motivation to declare a stillbirth as a living birth at the official registration system. If anything, under-recording of neonatal deaths was more frequent.

Beyond these cultural differences, Bengtsson (1999, 123–124) has argued that neonatal mortality "can be used as an indicator of severe under-recording since any possible under-registration is more likely to take place in the few weeks after birth than later on in childhood." From this point of view, only international comparisons are adequate to scale the results in table 12.1. In fourteen eighteenth- and nineteenth-

Table 12.1
Sex ratio at birth and neonatal mortality rate in six European settings

	Scania	Sart	Tilleur	Venice	Casalguidi	Madregolo
Births	3,300	5,718	3,928	3,773	3,554	1,909
Sex ratio at birth	1.11	1.07	1.02	1.07	1.02	1.03
Deaths by month						
0 month	213	426	326	504	276	185
1 month	46	85	59	75	49	21
2 months	47	62	56	50	41	24
3 months	23	36	58	46	35	14
4 months	17	44	32	39	35	8
5 months	21	33	43	33	22	15
6 months	24	39	34	38	31	15
7 months	14	31	36	43	23	16
8 months	19	26	36	42	31	15
9 months	23	42	33	44	40	13
10 months	13	34	27	53	44	16
11 months	16	44	33	35	53	18
Total infant deaths	476	902	773	1,002	680	360
Neonatal mortality rate	64.55	74.50	82.99	133.58	77.66	96.91
Infant mortality rate	144.24	157.75	196.79	265.57	191.33	188.58

century German villages, Knodel (1988, 48) found that neonatal mortality varied between 67 and 190 per 1,000, with an average of 108 (including stillbirths). Although high, the level observed in mid-nineteenth-century Venice, 134 per 1,000, is moderate compared to the three villages of Bavaria, where between 140 and 190 babies per 1,000 died during the first month of life. Ganiage (1988, 206–207) found also in the eighteenth-century French rural region of Beauvaisis mortality above 140 or even 160 per 1,000. At the opposite end are the 42 per 1,000 observed in the English village of Colyton between 1750 and 1799, the 41 per 1,000 calculated in the Swedish mining and metal-working parish of Västanfors between 1841 and 1850, the 48 per 1,000 of Sundsvall city (1815–1849), while in Linköping city and surrounding rural areas, neonatal mortality was always 70 to 95 per 1,000 between 1750 and 1848 (Bengtsson 1999, 124). Rates were a bit higher, 80 to 110 per 1,000, in eighteenth-century Geneva (Perrenoud 1979, 416). Our case studies are in between. The lowest neonatal mortality, which is in Scania, is only slightly lower than Sart and Casalguidi. They are all above the level for which we can be sure of underrecording problems. The infant mortality decline was also well underway in Scania in the first half of the nineteenth century, which explains the low figures.[12]

Globally, the differential demography we observed could be due to two factors: the wide cultural, ecological, and socioeconomic differences between Europe and Asia, as well as within Europe and within Asia, and the smaller local environment of the rural or urban communities we analyze. We assume this ambiguity since it reflects the reality of life, which is constructed both from the top by socialization and integration of cultural norms and from the bottom by complex interactions between individuals, households, families, and communities in peculiar ecotypes.

Moreover, our observations encompass time periods of different length, some very long (1716–1870 for the Japanese villages) and others rather short (1850–1869 for Venice). We control for this in the event-history models by introducing dummy variables for periods corresponding to different stages of structural changes. But for an analysis of levels, we must keep in mind that we are looking at localities that were at early but slightly different stages in the demographic transition and that averages can hide trends.

Infant Mortality in the European Settings

Figure 12.1 summarizes trends in infant mortality rates.[13] Although broken by brutal accidents, especially in the early 1830s, the trend in Scania is clearly declining, reflecting accurately the national tendency observed in Sweden. Elsewhere, the variations are quite chaotic, without clear reductions until the very end of the nineteenth century. These trends correspond to the well-known distinction between a "northern" model of infant mortality decline with early reductions and a "western" model with later reductions (Perrenoud and Bourdelais 1998, 78–80).

The differences in level are also striking. Infant mortality, summarized in table 12.2, was higher in the northern Italian countryside than in eastern Belgian or southern Sweden. In Sart, the percentage dying

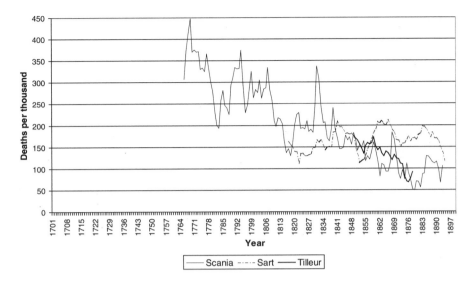

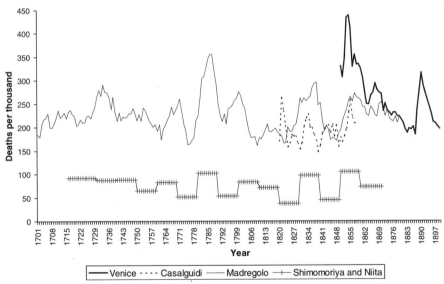

Figure 12.1
Infant mortality trends in seven settings, 1700–1900
Note: Venice = two parishes from 1850 to 1874, the city from 1875 to 1900.

Table 12.2
Mortality risks by sex and age in nine Eurasian settings

Place	Sex	Age			
		0	1–4	5–9	10–14
Sart, 1812–1900 (Belgium)	Male	0.1837	0.0989	0.0348	0.0176
	Female	0.1416	0.1118	0.0394	0.0242
Tilleur, 1846–1880 (Belgium)	Male	0.2261	0.1931	0.0543	0.0418
	Female	0.1664	0.1874	0.0790	0.0286
Scania, 1829–1867 (Sweden)	Male	0.1757	0.1102	—	—
	Female	0.1454	0.1118	—	—
Casalguidi, 1819–1859 (Italy)	Male	0.2019	0.2339	0.0211	0.0154
	Female	0.1995	0.2579	0.0415	0.0200
Madregolo, 1800–1883 (Italy)	Male	0.2361	0.2240	0.0368	0.0148
	Female	0.2047	0.2435	0.0294	0.0264
Venice (Catholics), 1850–1869	Total	0.2849	0.2541	0.0559	0.0252
Liaoning North, 1789–1909 (China)	Male	—	0.1855	0.0685	0.0334
	Female	—	0.2445	0.0964	0.0579
Liaoning South, 1789–1909 (China)	Male	—	0.1072	0.0435	0.0328
	Female	—	0.1225	0.0573	0.0314
Shimomoriya and Niita (Japan), 1716–1870	Male	—	0.2110	0.0860	0.0300
	Female	—	0.1930	0.0600	0.0250

during the first year of life varied between 14 and 18 percent, while it was between 20 and 24 percent in Casalguidi and Madregolo. In Belgium, as well as in Italy, infant mortality did not start its decisive decline before the turn of the twentieth century; therefore, we can consider this gap as a real one. Among the urban sites, the expected urban excess mortality is present in Italy: in Venice, 28.5 percent died before their first birthday. Similarly, in Belgium, the growing industrial town of Tilleur experienced higher infant mortality than the remote village of Sart, and Belgium as a whole,[14] but the gap is clearly smaller than the one in Italy.

The general difference between Italy, on one hand, and Belgium and Sweden, on the other, is not easy to explain. Several authors have stressed the importance of climatic conditions. We also suspect that breast-feeding was more frequent or longer in east Belgium and southern Sweden than in northern Italy, although Livi-Bacci (1977, 261) describes long breast-feeding as customary in Italy. Improved maternal health status could reduce endogenous mortality among infants. Later in the chapter, we test these hypotheses.

The size of the urban-rural differential is somewhat unexpected. In accounting for the "urban penalty," chapter 8 suggested a role for poor hygienic conditions and the higher costs of child rearing in urban areas. In the booming town of Tilleur, however, the overall situation was probably similar, and yet infant mortality there was much lower.[15] Other factors were probably at work. In Venice, around 10 percent of newborns, most of them legitimate, were abandoned at the local foundling institution, suggesting a low level of parental concern for child welfare and health (Derosas 2000, Grandi 1991). On the contrary, abandonment was quite unusual in nineteenth-century east Belgium and practically nonexistent among the proletarian population of Tilleur, whose adult males highly valued a large number of children as proof of their virility, the good health of their women, and family wealth, as well as a form of old-age security (Leboutte 1988, 179–180; Oris 1995b, 374; Spagnoli 1983). Also, married women had fewer employment opportunities in a coal and iron town like Tilleur than in Venice and could focus more on child care and housekeeping.[16] Moreover, a contemporary physician noted that in the Liège area, women used prolonged breast-feeding (fourteen to fifteen months) to space births (Oris 1995b, 374). Venetian women faced a much more diversified labor market and this could affect the duration and the continuity of breast-feeding, with dramatic consequences for infant mortality.[17]

Child Mortality from South to North Europe

The difference between northern Italy and the Belgian East Ardennes remained steady during early childhood. However, for children between ages 1 and 5, Tilleur had relatively high mortality, with almost one child out of five dying. This is not a surprise. In a study of mortality in nineteenth-century French towns, Preston and Van de Walle (1978) considered mortality between ages 1 and 4 as a better indicator of living conditions, especially sanitary conditions, than infant mortality itself, since the latter depended heavily on cultural attitudes toward child care, especially breast-feeding.[18] Eggerickx and Debuisson (1990) and Kearns (1993) have demonstrated that child mortality between the ages of 1 and 4 indeed varies more than infant mortality in the first year of life, which is confirmed also by table 12.2. Mortality between the first and the fifth birthday was around 10 percent in the Belgian East Ardennes and in Scania, but the risks were twice as high, between 22 and 26 percent, in Casalguidi and Madregolo. The gap between

Tilleur and Venice was narrower: while one child in five died in Tilleur, in Venice the rate was one out of four.

We find here a double differential. The first one is between urban and rural areas, less clear in infancy, but very strong from the age of 1 until 15 (see table 12.2 for the risks between ages 5 and 14). This is a confirmation of Preston and van de Walle's (1978) interpretation. The second differential is between northern and southern Europe. These patterns are actually very much in line with the typology of European patterns in Caselli (1991).[19]

Asian Uncertainties

Estimating infant mortality has long been a challenge for historical demographers of Japan. Studies utilizing model life tables suggest high mortality of infants and children under age 10 relative to other ages (Kito 1993, Saito 1997b). Infant mortality estimates, however, vary from 125 to 288 per 1,000, and life expectancy at birth ranges from 24 to 55 years (Saito 1997b). The variations arise from regional differences—geographical and social environments—as well as the method and assumption of estimation. At the higher end lies the estimation by Jannetta and Preston (1991): about 277 per 1,000 in a village in central Japan between 1776 and 1875. This appears too high and may reflect their strong assumption of zero migration (Saito 1997b). Infant mortality of peasants in northeastern Japan, where Ou is located, was generally higher than in southwestern Japan (Kinoshita 1999).

According to estimates by Tsuya and Kurosu (2000), low, medium, and high levels of infant mortality of the villages of Shimomoriya and Niita were 180, 200, and 230 for males and 150, 180, and 200 for females. The estimated high, medium, and low, respectively, life expectancies at birth were 35.7, 34.9, and 33.6 for males and 36.5, 35.2, and 34.4 for females. Figure 12.1 shows the chances of dying in the next year for infants recorded for the first time in the population register (NAC age 1), which is clearly too low, 40 to 50 percent lower than the next lowest estimate; this is due to underregistration as well as age counting. On the other hand, the mortality risks in childhood in Shimomoriya and Niita were quite high. Between 1716 and 1870, about one child in five died in the four years after their first registration (table 12.2). Levels in north Liaodong between 1789 and 1909 appear similar.

In the Asian data, according to table 12.2, there is a clear break after age 5 when the estimates become quite accurate and the mortality risks fall dramatically. However, the values observed in Liaodong and Ou are quite high compared to the European ones: among those who survived until their fifth birthday, between 4.4 and 9.6 percent died in the next five years. In the age group 10 to 15, the risks stayed above 3 percent. Considering the problems in the estimations of these values, especially at young ages, this demonstrates at least that variations in living conditions of children could have been as pronounced in Asia as in Europe.

Models of Infant and Child Mortality

To move beyond description, we look at theoretical frameworks that have been constructed to synthesize at least sixty years of intense multidisciplinary research on the mortality of infants and children. Like Mosley (1985) and Mosley and Chen (1984), van Norren and van Vianen (1986) in their model emphasize the malnutrition-infection syndrome: "In the great majority of the cases, infant and child death is the ultimate outcome of a combined process of multiple recurrent infections and nutritional deficiencies which cumulatively retard growth, lead to excessive loss of weight and progressively wear down the individual's resistance until finally an ordinary illness such as respiratory infection, diarrhea or measles results in death" (1–2). In other words, they reiterate the existence of a "road to death" for the majority of diseases.[20] Figure 12.2 outlines this process through an abbreviated scheme with five levels.[21]

Such elaborate models are difficult to apply in contemporary studies, let alone historical ones. A major limitation is imposed by the practical conditions of research that can logically reduce the number of variables in the model for which data may be gathered (De Vries 1991). The collection of adequate information for the third level, which focuses on

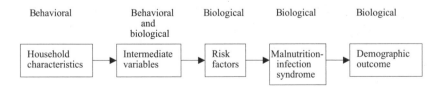

Figure 12.2
Schematic description of the van Norren–van Vianen model
Source: van Norren and van Vianen (1986, 8).

the four biological risk factors, shown in figure 12.2, is especially problematic. Some indicators, for example, premature birth, weight at birth, anthropometric state, and vitamin A levels, are available only when the children are born in health centers. Moreover, some factors, such as the "susceptibility to infections," are difficult, if not impossible, to measure directly. Finally, the model focuses on the malnutrition-infection syndrome. It does not consider any other factors unrelated to such a syndrome that can nonetheless be a direct cause of death. These include, for instance, congenital malformations, traumas at birth, and several infectious diseases of the acute type. This is why the four risk factors are often replaced by a single concept, frailty, that has been defined and elaborated in statistical terms (Mosley and Becker 1991, Riley and Alter 1996). Because of the practical difficulties associated with related empirical work, such models, including the one in Schultz (1984), have not had the impact on the demographic literature they deserve. No doubt, this explains why the gap dividing theoretical framework and empirical research, especially in historical demography, is so wide.

Indeed, we do not pretend to be able to develop fully the "complex equation including social, economic, cultural, geographical, and even climatological variables" that Reher and Schofield (1991, 16–17) advocated. We can, however, use proxies to capture the effect of such factors that cannot be directly measured as attitudes toward health, hygiene, and child care. For this purpose, we pay particular attention to the age pattern of the effects of such factors. Although they do not develop this idea, van Norren and van Vianen point out that their model must be adapted appropriately to the age considered (1986, 15). The main feature of our analyses is indeed a more refined segmentation of the different stages of infant and child life.

Standard infant mortality analysis usually does not go beyond the distinction between neonatal and postneonatal mortality, variously fixed at different points during the first month, sometimes with further distinctions at the very first moments of life.[22] While maintaining a place for neonatal mortality, here considered occurring in the first ten days, we propose to keep separated also the first semester from the second one, in the hypothesis, supported by the contemporary medical literature, that in some settings, the breast-feeding period was rather short at the time. We therefore have four different age brackets—0 to 9 days, 10 to 179 days, 180 to 365 days, and 1 to 5 years—which we presume are characterized by different risk profiles. Such an approach is particularly important from both a substantial and a technical point of view. From a substantial point of view, we expect in particular that the effect of some factors on the risk of dying will remain substantially unchanged through the various stages, while others might change direction and become protective or dangerous. Even more interesting, we expect that some factors, while unimportant when examined over a longer age span, actually play an important role only in specific and more restricted circumstances.[23] Table 12.3 summarizes our variables and hypotheses.

We do not want to repeat a detailed discussion of the variables taken into account, which can be found in chapters 2 and 3. From the model of van Norren and van Vianen (1986, 11), we note that the risk factor "constitution at birth" is the essential determinant of death in the first days of life, and we associate this risk with biological variables such as sex, parity, previous birth interval, and mother's age. Breast-feeding plays a major role since it directly affects three of the four risk factors: the nutritional intake of course, but also exposure to disease and susceptibility to contamination. The newborn has a very weak immune system, although the active biological substances in the mother's milk are highly protective (Livi Bacci 1999, 179). We expect, consequently, that biological factors remain a primary determinant until weaning, which is the real transition between infancy and childhood. Childhood is the period where we expect mortality to become more sensitive to the standard of living, measured here through economic fluctuations, climatic conditions, social status, and household composition.[24]

Such a transition from biology to society and economy should not be considered from a simplistic point of view. Indeed, as van Norren and van Vianen (1986) point out, most biological factors (especially all those related to fertility history) depend on social behaviors. Other variables reflect this ambiguity. The excess mortality of children who were firstborn or born to a young mother is usually related to endogenous factors, associated with the difficulty of a first delivery, while the excess mortality of those born to aged mothers is related to exogenous factors, such as the nutritional deprivation of the mother and her reduced capacity to breast-feed (Bideau 1981, 231–234). Similarly, from empirical studies, we suppose that the absence of both parents, although extremely rare at a very young age, was always a disaster. The absence of the mother had a very negative impact before weaning but not so much after. The father's absence directly affected household incomes, increasing the risks of mortality among children but not

Table 12.3
Expected effects of individual, household, and intermediate variables on mortality by stages of life during infancy and childhood

	0–9 days	10–179 days	180–365 days	1–4 years
Biological variables				
Sex				
Female	–	–	±	+
Male	Ref.	Ref.	Ref.	Ref.
Previous birth interval by survivorship				
Firstborn	+	+	(+)	
Short and alive	+	+		
Short and dead	+	+	(±)	
Long and alive	Ref.	Ref.	Ref.	Ref.
Long and dead	(±)	(±)	(±)	
Mother's age				
Young	+	+		
Medium	Ref.	Ref.	Ref.	Ref.
High	+	(+)	(+)	
Household characteristics				
Head social status				
High			(–)	–
Medium	Ref.	Ref.	Ref.	Ref.
Low			(+)	+
Presence of parents				
None	++	++	+	+
Mother only	(+)	(+)	(+)	+
Father only	++	++	+	(+)
Both	Ref.	Ref.	Ref.	Ref.
Presence of siblings				
Older brother				(±)
Older sister				+
Younger brother	/	/	/	–
Younger sister	/	/	/	–
External variables				
Food prices			(+)	+
Season				
Winter	+	+	(–)	–
Spring			(–)	–
Summer	Ref.	Ref.	Ref.	Ref.
Autumn			(–)	–

Note: + = higher risks. – = lower risks. / = variables not included in the model for a given age group. ( ) or ± = some uncertainty about the direction of the effect.

necessarily among breast-fed infants (Beekink, van Poppel, and Lief-broer 1999, 22–27; Oris and Ochiai 2002).

From a technical point of view, the use of semiparametric multi-variate regression methods, such as the Cox regression, is based on the assumption that the effects of the covariates do not vary with the variable used to capture the baseline hazard—in this case, age. Clearly, this contradicts the general hypothesis of a change in the earliest stages of life from biological determinants of death to socioeconomic ones (van Poppel and Mandemakers 1997, 292). Our segmentation of the beginning of life in four age groups is intended as an answer to this technical problem.

Even so, the van Norren and van Vianen (1986) model is important. Though perhaps less precise and deep than Schultz's (1984) contribution, their work is more pedagogical. As a good topo-geography of our knowledge, it gives us the chance to evaluate which part of the gap between theoretical framework and empirical research we have a chance to fill through multivariate analyses using the segmentation approach and the proxy variables that we can calculate from our data. Examination reveals that we miss three components. The first is related to the education of the parents, knowledge about health and nutrition, and use of health service. This is the cultural dimension that we will return to. The second missing component is public and private hygiene. Since we deal with pre-Pasteurian societies, it is not likely that this absence could affect our results, as far as we control for the effects of climatic conditions by using the current season as a proxy. Finally, and related to the first point, when the risk factors or frailty produced a malnutrition-infection syndrome, medical interventions could slow or sometimes accelerate the road to death, but we know nothing about that part of the story, at least not at an individual level. However, especially if we focus on the two first levels of the van Norren and van Vianen (1986) model, the household characteristics and the intermediate variables, it remains clear that our model represents an important step forward, covering most of the components they identified and even improving notably the description of the household composition.

For reasons already mentioned, our comparative analysis will focus on the European populations and make use of some partial results for Shimomoriya and Niita in Ou summarized later in table 12.6.[25] Table 12.4 presents the number of births, person-years, and deaths by setting and period of life.[26] The segmentation approach proposed here implies that we work on small populations for which event-history methods

Table 12.4
Deaths, person-years, and mortality rate by age group, in six European settings

Settings	Scania	Sart	Tilleur	Venice	Casal-guidi	Madre-golo
Births	3,300	5,718	3,928	3,773	3,554	1,909
Deaths at:						
0–9 days	154	317	221	345	171	113
10–179 days	212	346	343	400	284	146
180–365 days	110	209	209	257	225	99
1–4 years[a]	476	221	575	663	595	270
Person-years						
0–9 days	87	145	97	89	94	50
10–179 days	1,406	2,432	1,685	1,509	1,494	743
180–365 days	1,464	2,485	1,734	1,536	1,639	812
1–4 years[a]	10,319	4,728	8,701	9,593	8,348	4,307
Death rates[b]						
0–9 days	46.7	55.4	56.3	91.4	48.1	59.2
10–179 days	64.2	60.5	87.3	106.0	79.9	76.5
180–365 days	33.3	36.6	53.2	68.1	63.3	51.9
1–4 years[a]	144.2	38.6	146.4	175.7	167.4	141.4

[a] Ages 1–2 for Sart.
[b] Death rates are computed as deaths in the age range per 1,000 live births.

are well suited (Allison 1984). Each coefficient estimate comes with an assessment of its statistical significance, the p value. Since Cox regression is time transformation invariant, time at risk does not matter. What matters are risk set sizes and the number of deaths at each observed age. The amount of information in the sample is approximately proportional to the total number of observed deaths. In this study, the concentration of so many deaths at young ages in historical populations facilitates our segmentation approach.

Starting Life: The Baby and the Family

Table 12.5 summarizes our results but presents only estimates that were statistically significant at the 90 percent level. Most of the results confirm our expectations regarding the different effects of variables in various age groups. By looking through the results for the different models, the importance of the mother's role for the survival of the newborn emerges quite clearly. During the neonatal period, the mother's age at childbirth, her health conditions, approximated through her age and birth spacing, and her presence in the child's life after birth are extremely important. Medical literature provides evidence that accounts for the relevance of the strictly "biological" variable and the "congenital" weakness of children born to mothers of advanced age (Katwijk and Peters 1998). In the past, however, such "biological" risks were amplified (Thornton and Olson 1992, 20; van de Walle 1986, 233) by the precarious and compromised conditions of working mothers who were exhausted by many pregnancies as well as the working hardships in certain rural areas (Rollet 1995).

Table 12.5 shows that mother's age at birth, though relatively unimportant later in the first two years of life, plays a relevant role for the survival of the child during the very first days after birth. Mortality among infants born to mothers aged 35 or more is much higher than that of children born to younger mothers. The relative risk is on the order of 1.5 to 3.6 in Sart, Tilleur, Scania, and the two Italian villages. This strong effect of mother's age observed in Scania and Tilleur has important implications for the plausibility of the hypothesis advanced above that the link between mother's health and children's survival helped explain the differential between north and south Europe.

Only in Ou, as shown in table 12.6, was mother's age at birth not significant as a determinant of infant and child mortality, since women in the villages of Shimomoriya and Niita married as early as 14, and childbearing was also concentrated at ages 15 to 34. Because women in Europe married later, close to or above 25, more European children were born to older mothers, which increased their risk of dying in infancy and childhood. The obvious effects of this link go far beyond the specified conditions considered here. In fact, it is evident that the diffusion of birth control behaviors, more often through stopping than spacing practices (Alter 1992), would have had a considerable role in the lowering of infant mortality rates.[27]

The effect of mother's age has been discussed elsewhere. Lynch and Greenhouse (1994) point out that age is associated with other risk factors: high birth order, large number of children in the household, and short birth interval.[28] The nature of our data precludes us from controlling for all of these, especially birth order, but our multivariate models do include previous birth interval.[29] Even when the age of the mother is controlled for, children born in families where another child had been born in the previous two years run a significantly higher risk

Table 12.5
Summary of the multivariate analyses of mortality risks in infancy and childhood by age group in six European settings

Covariates	0–9 days						10–179 days						180–365 days						1–4 years					
	Sc	Sa	Ti	Ve	Ca	Ma	Sc	Sa	Ti	Ve	Ca	Ma	Sc	Sa	Ti	Ve	Ca	Ma	Sc	Sa[a]	Ti	Ve	Ca	Ma
Female			0.45				0.78	0.72	0.71														0.43	
Previous birth interval and survivorship																								
Firstborn	—						—						—			1.58		0.29	—				0.69	
Less than 24 months, dead	—		3.11	1.70			—	2.13	2.71	1.38			—						—					
Less than 24 months, alive	—	2.03			1.88		—	1.86	1.77				—				1.40		—		2.06		0.70	
More than 24 months, dead	—			*	*	*	—			*	*	*	—	*		*	*	1.86	—			*	*	*
More than 24 months, alive	—	*		*	*	*	—	*	*	*	*	*	—	*	*	*	*	*	—			*		*
Mother's age (years)																								
Less than 20	*						*						*						*					
20–24		*						1.49									0.68	*					0.67	*
25–29		*	*	*	*	*		*	*	*	*	*	*	*		*	*	*				*	*	*
30–34								1.46							1.47									
35–40	3.65		2.34		2.68	1.49		1.57		1.81	1.44				1.83						1.29			
40 or more		1.70						1.52						1.72										
Social status																								
High	*	*					*	*		0.45	*		*	*		0.75	—	—	*	*	0.52	0.49	0.33	—
Medium		*	1.06		*		*	*		0.80			*	*		0.60	*	—	*	*	0.76	0.70	*	—

Low		*	*		1.79	—		*	*	0.78	1.56	—		*	*	0.72		—		*	*	0.64		—
Lowest		1.51		*		—	0.64			*	1.32	—				*	1.35	—		1.64	*	*	1.58	—
Parents																								
Only father	—	3.61		4.20	3.85	2.06	—	3.22		2.85	2.60		—	2.54					—			1.61	2.61	
Only mother	—					2.00	—	1.67	1.54				—						—	2.26				
Neither	—						—						—						—	3.17	2.67			
Siblings																								
Older brother				1.49						1.37	0.74										1.30			
Older sister						0.61	0.76		1.40	0.63						0.64						0.81	0.71	
Younger brother	—	—	—	—	—	—	—	—	—	—	—	—	—	—	—	—	—	—		—				1.96
Younger sister	—	—	—	—	—	—	—	—	—	—	—	—	—	—	—	—	—	—		—				1.96
Season																								
Winter		2.14		4.23	4.08	4.32				*		2.32	2.16	2.65		*	0.35		2.01	1.60		*	0.21	0.62
Spring		1.85		3.13	1.83	2.34	1.53			0.75			3.13	1.68			0.26		2.66				0.16	0.55
Summer	*	*	*	*	*	*	*	*	*	0.57	*	*	*	*	*	2.16	*	*	*	*	*	1.39	*	*
Autumn		2.10		1.63	2.18					0.69		1.68				1.49	0.49						0.68	
10% increase in price[b]																	1.06		1.05		1.03	1.03	1.11	

Note: Sc = Scania; Sa = Sart; Ti = Tilleur; Ve = Venice; Ca = Casalguidi; Ma = Madregolo. For the definition of the social groups, see note 21. * = reference category. — = a variable was not included in the model.

[a] For Sart, the age group is 1–2 years.

[b] For Scania and Tilleur, the relative risk reflects the effects of a 10 percent reduction in real wages.

Table 12.6
Estimated odds ratios of the covariates from the discrete-time event-history analysis of the probability of dying in the next year, infants and children, Shimomoriya and Niita, 1716–1870

Covariates	Infant (aged 1)		Child (aged 2–9)	
	Odds ratio	p-value	Odds ratio	p-value
Female	1.009	0.954	0.876	0.184
Previous birth interval and survivorship				
Firstborn	1.207	0.314	—	—
Less than 24 months, dead	1.339	0.707	—	—
Less than 24 months, alive	2.025	0.005	—	—
More than 24 months, dead	1.153	0.705	—	—
Parents' presence				
Only father	—	—	0.672	0.203
Only mother	—	—	1.108	0.572
Neither	—	—	1.679	0.030
Siblings				
Older sister	—	—	0.843	0.114
Landholding	0.987	0.374	1.003	0.691
Number of kin household members	0.943	0.236	1.092	0.004
Rice price, 10% increase	1.119	0.017	1.011	0.466
*Price*landholding*	0.994	0.068	—	—
Current age (years)				
2	—	—	14.148	0.000
3	—	—	9.238	0.000
4	—	—	6.095	0.000
5	—	—	5.271	0.000
6–8			2.810	0.004
Period				
1716–1799	0.750	0.184	0.760	0.035
1800–1839	0.748	0.190	0.668	0.003
1840–1870	0.753	0.307	0.680	0.011
Village (Shimomoriya = 1)	0.841	0.297	0.788	0.021
Number of observations	2,190		14,223	
Number of deaths	193		379	
Log-likelihood	−591.19		−101.11	
Chi-square	21.22		213.27	
Degrees of freedom	(13)		(17)	
p-value	0.015		0.000	

of dying in the neonatal period, at least for Venice, Sart, Tilleur, and Casalguidi. In Tilleur and Venice, this risk was multiplied two or three times when the older child had died.[30] Actually, an opposite result might have been expected, since the death of the previous child would have relieved the family of a burden, benefiting the survivors, and especially the other children. Instead, we observe here what Knodel (1978) called the "physiological effect of mortality on fertility": that mortality of the preceding sibling interrupted his or her breast-feeding and could shorten the birth interval, increasing the risk of death for the next baby.[31]

The phenomenon of death clustering at the family level is an essential but until recently neglected component of mortality research, especially at young ages. As far as we know, among historical demographers, Alain Bideau (1981) was the first to carry out a systematic analysis of what he called "family heterogeneity," followed by Lynch and Greenhouse (1994). The existence of the clustering has been pointed out several times (Bengtsson et al. 1998, 129–130; Breschi et al. 1999, 204–207; Das Gupta 1990; Duer 1992; Knodel 1988, 89–90; Nault, Desjardins, and Légaré 1990). Recently Sastry (1997) and Alter, Oris, and Broström (2001) have tried to estimate a "family effect" using a statistical approach. According to the latter study, in nineteenth-century Sart, "the risk of dying for children in the healthiest quartile of families was less than half the risk in the least healthy quartile."[32]

An example that explicitly illustrates one of the mechanisms of death clustering can be seen in the extreme case of the mother's death, taking into account that her death means maternal mortality when we consider the survival of the children during their ten first days of life. In most of the communities analyzed, the mother's death meant a further risk for her child's survival, particularly if so tragic an event took place immediately after birth. In such a circumstance, the mother's death, often related to an advanced age at pregnancy, finds clear explanations in the biomedical field but may as well be related to the condition of the family.

With regard to the strictly biological and genetic interpretation, it is surprising to note that a clear differential in the risk profile of gender is absent. Only for Tilleur do the values of the parameters show lower mortality for females, what is usually observed at an aggregated level. They are more apparent between 10 and 179 days in the north European settings but not in the three Italian ones.

Biological or Social? The Data Challenge

Such results could reflect cultural differences in the parental investment on children but also raise the issue of critical problems in the registration of births and deaths, which can be crucial for assessing a
social effect on survival in the first days of life. Bengtsson (1999, 120–
125) noted that several studies have shown a neonatal mortality differential according to the social status of the parents that does not fit our
initial hypothesis of a domination of biogenetic factors at the very beginning of life. When a relationship is found, it is a positive one, not a
negative one: the babies of the wealthy people died more. Several case
studies in Germany have observed higher infant mortality among
peasants than among the landless (Imhof 1984; Sundin and Tedebrand
1981; Bengtsson 1999, 121). We already noted that working hardships
were extreme for mothers in certain rural contexts. For Imhof (1981),
the proto-industrial period and the transition from the preindustrial to
the industrial world were characterized by rising pressure on married
women in rural households. For early twentieth-century Japan, original data from a survey allowed Saito (1996) to demonstrate that
women of the wealthy peasant families accumulated significantly more
hours of work than the women of poorer families. Such findings might
account for an effect of debility that could result in a higher neonatal
mortality due to maternal depletion, but could also affect the capacity
to breast-feed and care for the younger children.

However, as Bengtsson (1999, 121, 123) points out, many other case
studies conclude that there is an absence of social differentials in infant
mortality.[33] At least for the very first days of life, table 12.5 indeed does
not reveal significant differentials in Scania and Venice. In Tilleur, we
found a modest but statistically significant 6 percent excess mortality
among the babies of iron and steel workers compared with the children of the coal miners. The effect is stronger in the Belgian rural municipality of Sart and the Italian village of Casalguidi, and this effect is
"normal," in the sense that in the poorest part of the society, newborns
were 51 to 79 percent more likely to die during the ten first days of life.

Bengtsson (1999) speculates that social selectivity in the accuracy of
the registration could be a simple explanation for the results cited at
the beginning of this section, the births and infant deaths of the wealthy being better recorded.[34] Catherine Rollet recognizes that the question is fundamental: according to the investigation by Louis Henry of
the eighteenth-century French population, 31 percent of infant deaths

Table 12.7
Classification of occupations used in comparison of data quality by social class

Status	Scania	Sart	Tilleur	Venice	Casalguidi
High	Freeholders	—	Petty bourgeoisie	Middle class	Landlords, nobles, bourgeois
Medium	Noble tenants	—	Iron and steel workers	Artisans, shopkeepers	Sharecroppers, tenants, artisans
Low	Semilandless	—	Coal miners	Wage earners	Journeymen, farm laborers, beggars
Lowest	Landless	Day laborers	Day laborers	Day laborers	—

were omitted (Rollet 1994, 9). We know that the situation was even worse in England during the seventeenth, eighteenth, and early nineteenth centuries (Wrigley and Schofield 1981). According to the results just presented, we do not expect to find a social bias in the registration in Sart or Casalguidi, but it could be the case in the three other settings. It might even explain the absence of significant results in any direction. Table 12.8 displays the same indicators of data quality as table 12.1, but broken down by social status. We constrained each team to use its knowledge of the context of each area to classify the occupations according to a simple, even simplistic, social hierarchy, with three to four groups, summarized in table 12.7.[35]

The village of Casalguidi in Tuscany is the only one where, according to table 12.8, neonatal mortality is negatively associated with social status. However, the numbers in the "high" classes—landlords, nobles, and bourgeois—are low, and their sex ratio at birth is definitely too high. The children of journeymen, farm laborers, and beggars have relatively low mortality rates in the first month of life, but the sex ratio at birth in this group also appears too low: 85 boys for 100 girls. Since boys are more at risk during the very beginning of life, this may be a symptom of underregistration. But it implies again that there was higher mortality among the poor. This pattern is also apparent in the Belgian village of Sart and in Venice, with a very clear progression of the risks of neonatal mortality from the wealthiest to the poorer. However, when integrated in a multivariate model with several other variables, as in table 12.5, the effect of social status diminishes in Sart and ceases to be significant in Venice. The sex ratio at birth, meanwhile,

Table 12.8
Indicators of data quality by social status in five European settings

Settings	Scania	Sart	Tilleur	Venice	Casalguidi	Scania	Sart	Tilleur	Venice	Casalguidi
Social status	High					Medium				
Births	401	204	479	236	125	429	4,861	911	897	2,913
Sex ratio at birth	1.02	0.98	1.06	0.93	1.06	1.17	1.09	1.00	1.14	1.04
Deaths by month										
0 month	25	14	39	21	11	39	348	66	101	227
1 month	9	3	5	3	2	4	74	17	20	40
2 months	6	0	6	3	1	6	54	11	5	31
3 months	3	1	5	2	2	3	31	6	10	26
4 months	0	6	4	1		5	33	4	8	24
5 months	4	2	8		1	3	29	8	6	17
6 months	4	1	3	2	1	2	31	2	12	26
7 months	2	2	4	4	2	2	26	5	5	16
8 months	4	0	7	2	1	4	22	6	13	21
9 months	2	1	2	7	1	6	33	9	5	32
10 months	2	1	1	1	1	0	30	3	8	37
11 months	2	2	1	1	2	0	37	7	4	43
Total infant deaths	63	33	85	47	25	74	748	144	197	540
Neonatal mortality rate	62.34	68.63	81.42	88.98	88.00	90.91	71.59	72.45	112.60	77.93
Infant mortality rate	157.11	161.76	177.45	199.15	200.00	172.49	153.88	158.07	219.62	185.38

Social status	Low					Lowest				
Births	829	653	807	1,128	516	1,641	—	1,731	1,512	—
Sex ratio at birth	1.13	0.98	1.03	1.05	0.85	1.10	—	1.01	1.06	—
Deaths by month										
0 month	47	64	84	145	38	102	—	137	236	—
1 month	15	8	12	25	7	18	—	25	26	—
2 months	11	8	18	15	9	24	—	21	25	—
3 months	8	4	17	13	7	9	—	30	21	—
4 months	1	5	5	11	11	11	—	19	18	—
5 months	4	2	5	10	4	10	—	22	16	—
6 months	9	7	7	12	4	9	—	22	12	—
7 months	4	3	11	11	5	6	—	16	22	—
8 months	4	4	8	9	9	7	—	15	18	—
9 months	5	8	10	7	7	10	—	12	24	—
10 months	4	3	5	18	6	7	—	18	26	—
11 months	0	5	13	10	8	14	—	12	19	—
Total infant deaths	112	121	195	286	115	227	—	349	463	—
Neonatal mortality rate	56.69	98.01	104.09	128.55	73.64	62.16	—	79.15	156.08	—
Infant mortality rate	135.10	185.30	241.64	253.55	222.87	138.33	—	201.62	306.22	—

is too high among the Venetian middle classes: 114 for 100 girls.[36] Normally this "petty bourgeoisie" is seen as a social group under pressure, living just above the poverty line and always worried about falling below it (Leboutte 1988); thus, such a sex ratio might reflect use of female abandonment.

It seems that it is in the data of the Belgian village of Sart that stillbirths are the most clearly distinguished from living births. Since event-history analyses require a measure of duration, stillbirths cannot be included in the analysis. As far as Sart and Tilleur are concerned, the analyses in table 12.5 include only living births. In the other data, it is quite clear that several children born dead were recorded as live births with duration of life of at least one day.[37] Table 12.9 displays the estimates of the same multivariate model of neonatal mortality, using only the "official" living births on one side and all the recorded births on the other, with stillbirths being assigned one day of life.

It is important to stress that we are moving from our starting question about the respective importance of biology, economy, and society on children's survival to a rather different one. In fact, we find very coherent patterns of mortality in settings characterized by remarkably different levels of infant mortality. Calculated as a ratio of deaths over births, the mortality rate during the first ten days of life was 47 per 1,000 in Scania but 91 per 1,000 in Venice. As we already noted, excluding stillbirths has a very large impact: in Sart, the rate falls from 55.4 to 20.1 per 1,000. However, as far as we are concerned with the patterns of risk factors, as is the case in table 12.9, it is quite surprising to see that most of the results are unchanged. While it seems that the importance of definitions and recording is overstated, even if there are few differences, each one is instructive.

In Sart as well as in Scania, the effect of seasons, especially the springtime, appears stronger when stillbirths are excluded. Unexpectedly, it is when stillbirths are included that 40 percent overmortality among the children of the poorest inhabitants of Sart, the day laborers, becomes statistically significant: we find here the confirmation that the so-called endogenous mortality was a social construction. However, including stillbirths does not solve the problems of social class biases in the registration of births and infant deaths. Indeed, in Scania, when stillbirths are included, the excess mortality of the children of noble tenants becomes even more pronounced. Their chances of dying are 59 percent higher than those of the children of the freeholders. We also see in Sart that a short birth interval when the previous child is alive increases substantially the mortality risk of the index child, but this impact is even stronger—a 103 percent increase instead of a 69 percent increase—when stillbirths are excluded. This difference can be attributed to the competition for care from the mother between the two most recent babies. In Scania, as far as living births are concerned, only a short previous birth interval combined with the death of the preceding child increases substantially neonatal mortality, by 57 percent. However, when stillbirths are included, the effect becomes even stronger: an 85 percent increase. Even when the interval is long, the death of an elder sibling doubles the chances of a rapid death. The influence of the mother's age (35 and more) is the same, but only when all the births are taken into account. So in Scania, not only are the fertility-mortality link and the clustering of deaths clearer when stillbirths are part of the analysis, the influence of the biological factors increases as well.

At this stage, we can provisionally conclude that survival in the very first days of life depended largely on family effects such as the presence of parents, the mother's age, and the previous births interval. Maternal depletion was obviously an important factor, and we found evidence in an Italian and a Belgian village that the poorest mothers were the most affected. Once again, there is no simple boundary that divides the effects of biology and society.

The Causality Transition: When Children Become Vulnerable to Economic Conditions

As the child grows up, biological and genetic factors become less important, while social and cultural factors become more important. It does not seem to be the case in table 12.5, at least not at first glance, because the direct dependence of the child on the mother during the first six months of life is always evident. Between days 10 and 179, the absence of the mother multiplies the risks of death by between 2.6 and 3.2. The influence of the mother's age declines but remains strong, with a 44 to 81 percent penalty for the infants born to women aged 35 and more.[38] The impact of a short previous birth interval is as adverse as during the ten first days of life, and this effect becomes even more common, observed everywhere except in Casalguidi. However, after the ten first days of life, the strictly biological are no longer plausible.

The protection due to breast-feeding is evident when comparing the risk factors for this age range with those for the second semester, and especially with the period following the first birthday. With the partial

Table 12.9
Comparison of the mortality patterns during the ten first days of life, stillbirths included or excluded

Variables	Sart, 1812–1899: Stillbirths included			Sart, 1812–1899: Stillbirths excluded			Scania, 1766–1867: Stillbirths included			Scania, 1766–1867: Stillbirths excluded		
	Mean	Relative risk	p-value	Mean	Relative risk	p-value	Mean	Relative risk	p-value	Mean	Relative risk	p-value
Parents present												
Both	0.915	1.000		0.932	1.000		0.990	1.000		0.990	1.000	
Mother only	0.055	1.254	0.373	0.055	1.202	0.674						
Father only	0.013	3.847	0.000	0.012	3.609	0.013						
Neither	0.017	1.202	0.690				0.010	1.469[a]	0.408	0.010	0.948[a]	0.941
Previous birth interval and child survival[b]												
25+ and alive	0.415	1.000		0.418	1.000		0.403	1.000		0.405	1.000	
Firstborn	0.192	1.557	0.053	0.187	1.158	0.706	0.219	1.519	0.056	0.219	1.225	0.470
24 or below and dead	0.041	1.565	0.119	0.041	1.349	0.533	0.104	1.846	0.001	0.103	1.571	0.066
24 or below and alive	0.234	1.694	0.000	0.235	2.033	0.002	0.121	0.961	0.848	0.123	1.271	0.309
25 and over and dead	0.119	1.337	0.141	0.118	0.837	0.621	0.071	2.030	0.000	0.070	1.433	0.198
Mother's age												
Below 20	—	—		—	—		0.060	1.000		0.061	1.000	
20–24	0.104	0.941	0.794	0.102	0.645	0.281	0.340	0.866	0.592	0.342	0.749	0.354
25–29	0.234	1.000		0.236	1.000		0.320	1.267	0.369	0.320	1.066	0.836
30–34	0.275	1.086	0.631	0.275	0.846	0.537	0.169	1.262	0.405	0.168	0.859	0.654
35–39	0.232	1.269	0.194	0.232	0.778	0.414	0.069	2.061[c]	0.015	0.067	1.459[c]	0.301
40–49	0.155	1.797	0.003	0.155	1.700	0.078						

Siblings												
Older brother present	0.600	1.125	0.442	0.610	1.222	0.427	0.540	1.153	0.312	0.540	1.082	0.668
Older sister present	0.580	1.060	0.690	0.580	0.936	0.773	0.510	1.160	0.280	0.510	0.901	0.551
Sex												
Male	0.520	1.000	—	0.520	1.000	—	0.518	1.000	—	0.517	1.000	—
Female	0.480	0.800	0.051	0.480	0.727	0.094	0.482	0.818	0.072	0.483	0.865	0.315
Social status												
Freeholder	—	—	—	—	—	—	0.129	1.000	—	0.131	1.000	—
Noble tenants	—	—	—	—	—	—	0.214	1.529	0.042	0.213	1.200	0.450
Semilandless	—	—	—	—	—	—	0.134	1.318	0.264	0.134	1.155	0.633
Landless or day laborer	0.090	1.402	0.059	0.090	1.356	0.331	0.523	1.268	0.226	0.522	0.951	0.823
Quarter												
January–March	0.250	1.335	0.083	0.250	2.143	0.012	0.264	1.000	—	0.264	1.000	—
April–June	0.250	1.237	0.215	0.250	1.854	0.050	0.224	1.301	0.086	0.223	1.496	0.048
July–September	0.250	1.000	—	0.250	1.000	—	0.228	0.878	0.441	0.229	0.970	0.891
October–December	0.250	1.387	0.060	0.250	2.099	0.020	0.283	1.180	0.271	0.284	1.412	0.081
Prices and period												
10% increase in price of oats, 1812–1899	0.000	0.999	0.751	0.000	1.004	0.532						
10% decline in real wages, 1847–1899	0.600	1.588	0.000	0.600	0.966	0.862	-2.3	0.984	0.438	-2.3	0.956	0.077
Events	315			115			330			197		
Person-years at risk	144.753			142.659								
Maximum log-likelihood	-1,641.05			-788.70			-1,768.50			-1,255.05		

a Neither parent present.

b In months.

c Mother's age 35 or more.

exception of the mother's absence, the variables describing the mother and her recent reproductive behavior lose most of their significance in the second semester of life. Conversely, during the first semester of life, children were protected from the consequences of short-term economic stress. The variables meant to capture such effects—cereal prices in Italy and Sart, real wage in Scania and Tilleur—begin to have influence after the first semester, and particularly after the first birthday, by which time large numbers of children were no longer breast-fed. Although the protective influence of breast-feeding cannot be ruled out, a selection effect must be taken into account. Aggregate studies showed that fertility was highly responsive to prices (Galloway 1988), much more than infant mortality (Bengtsson and Ohlsson 1985), and longitudinal analyses of individual data demonstrated that such sensitivity was especially strong among the poorest segments of the society (Alter and Oris 1999, Bengtsson and Dribe, forthcoming). We are not able at this point to identify the sources of the association between economic conditions, socioeconomic status, and fertility, but such results suggest that one reason for the lower sensitivity of infant mortality was that the infants who would have been most affected by adverse economic conditions were less likely to be born in the first place, because their parents had curtailed their fertility.

Between their first and fifth birthdays, children in the rural parishes of Scania, the village of Casalguidi, the city of Venice, and the booming town of Tilleur show a pronounced reaction to the coincidence of adverse economic conditions and a cholera epidemic.[39] The influence of the economic dynamics, however, is marked even when the effects of epidemics are controlled for. In Venice, according to table 12.5, a 10 percent increase in the price of wheat can cause a 3 percent increase in mortality among children aged 1 or more. A decline in the real wages has a similar impact in Scania (a 4 percent increase) and Tilleur (3.1 percent). It is in Casalguidi that the sensitivity of children to prices is the highest: with an 11 percent rise in mortality for a 10 percent increase in food prices. This is also the only place where a strong effect is apparent in the second semester of life.

The influence of social status was even more pronounced, at least in the two Italian settings where such information is available. In Casalguidi as well as Venice, infants born to the poorest segments of the population were 30 to 55 percent more likely to die than the infants of the highest social group. The same pattern, although less pronounced, is also observed in the second semester, but again it is really between the first and the fifth birthday that the social hierarchy is an important determinant of mortality. Children born from poor families pay a heavy toll: being the son of a day laborer in Casalguidi, Venice, Tilleur, or Sart means a risk one and a half times that of the children of share-croppers, wage earners, or any other social class. Being the child of a small landowner or a professional reduced by half the risk of dying, in comparison to the children of sharecroppers.

In dividing the beginning of life into four stages, we had two ambitions: to observe a transition from biology to society and economy in terms of the factors affecting mortality and to identify the approximate time of weaning. Regarding our first objective, we obtained a complex picture. In the first few days of life, social and economic influences are far from absent; they act through selection effects (for example, the impact of prices on fertility) and cannot be separated from biological factors within the concept of maternal depletion. After the first ten days of life, the continued influence of "biological" variables can reflect long-lasting effects of maternal depletion on child care or delayed effects, in which children who weakened in the first days of life died later. These issues are at the heart of ongoing research that must also deal with the crucial and difficult questions of heterogeneous frailty and clustering of deaths (Alter, Oris, and Broström 2001; Vaupel et al. 1998). Nevertheless, if a strict chronological distinction between endogenous and exogenous causes seems definitively outdated, it remains that both a clear and a floating boundary separated infancy from childhood, with clearly different patterns of causalities. In particular, social status and economic conditions became dominant in the latter period, as has often been observed in historical and contemporary demographic research (Preston 1996).

How such a distinction relates to weaning is far from clear. In Venice and Casalguidi, social status was a determinant of death already after the first ten days of life, but food prices were a determinant only after a semester of life or even after the first birthday. We can conclude that obviously breast-feeding was shorter in the Italian settings than in the Belgian ones and probably in Scania, but no more.

Same Pattern, Different Levels: From Culture to Ecology

It is also obvious that when we started a multivariate analysis based on the careful construction of an explanatory model, we hoped to understand why more or fewer people—infants and children in our peculiar case—died in pretransitional societies. From this point of view, we are far from our expectations since the most striking lesson from table 12.5 is that similar mortality patterns can be found in regimes of both high and low mortality. The immediate temptation is to look at the gap between the "ideal" van Norren and van Vianen (1986) framework and the real model we have been able to construct with our data. Let us remember that this gap has three dimensions: culture, public hygiene, and medical therapy.

As far as culture is concerned, we included some control variables in two models. In Venice, the sample includes the population of the Jewish ghetto, whose poor economic and hygienic conditions were noted by contemporary foreign visitors (Derosas 2003). Nevertheless, their infant mortality rate was half that of Venetian Catholics: 140 per 1,000 compared to 310 to 320 per 1,000. When biological, social, economic, and climatic variables are taken into account in a multivariate model, Jewish babies were 74 percent less likely than Venetian Catholics to die during the first month of life, 49 percent less likely between one and six months, and 27 percent less during the second semester of life.[40] In Tilleur, the children of the Flemish immigrants suffered from a real epidemiological shock and faced risks 55 percent higher than the children born to native families, though this penalty only affected the age group 1 to 4 years.

While these differences are outside the focus of this chapter and are examined in detail elsewhere (Derosas 2000, 2003; Oris and Alter 2001), we want to stress that beyond such cultural indicators are hidden at least two dimensions: one concerning health education and behavior, the other the adaptation to environmental constraints. Preston and Haines (1991) have interpreted the evolution of child mortality differentials in late-nineteenth-century America according to the timing of the diffusion of germ theory among different social classes and ethnic groups. What is important, however, is not so much the knowledge but the attitudes of prevention in daily life and the contacts with the health system—the "instrumental rationality" (Thornton and Olson 1992) or the "know-how" (Woods and Williams 1995, 130). Even before Pasteur and Koch, the Jews (Meffre, forthcoming) and at least some Protestant denominations (Head-König 2000, Sköld 1996a) supported active health attitudes, while some Catholic orientations tended toward acceptance and resignation. The critical debate on the registration of stillbirths partly reflects this difference, as well as the discussions around systems of "economy of life" and "waste of life" initiated by Imhof (1984). However, in any case, it was a simple differential.

Rutten (1997, 337–347) shows, for example, how the most conservative part of the nineteenth-century Dutch Protestant church rejected vaccination against smallpox as an offense to God. It is a complicated story, and here we just want to point out that it is essential to look beyond the statistical result, especially when a cultural indicator is concerned.

Moreover, culture is not everything. As Johansson (2000, 62–63) noted recently, "Studies of eighteenth century British Quakers, a Protestant sect that encouraged members to lead virtuous and healthy lives suggest that, even in their case, health-promoting attitudes and values were overwhelmed by local environmental considerations." The local environment is also a crucial element whose importance has long been stressed. In the early 1970s, Pierre Chaunu developed the theory of the "molecular territorial structuration of demographic behaviors," arguing that ecology overwhelmed almost always social and economic differentials (Chaunu 1972). Bideau (1981, esp. 226) and Smith (1991) also considered ecological conditions the most important determinant of mortality prior to the health transition. The recent detailed inquiries of Blum and Bringe (1992), Breschi et al. (1999), Dobson (1997), Viazzo (1989), and others lend support to this view. For example, British historical demographers, stimulated by developments in historical geography, showed that even during the industrial revolution, disease environment remained more important than class (Reid 1997, 151; Williams and Galley 1995; Woods 1994).

It is not easy to deal with this issue in an analysis of individual data. At an aggregate level, we can analyze the pattern of urbanization, institutions and policies, and so on. It is more difficult to do so for rural parishes. Moreover, an isolated approach of half a dozen cases scattered throughout the European continent would have little interest. What we are able to do is to include in our models the season as a pertinent indicator of how families and individuals were able to cope with a common environmental condition, the climate. Breschi and Livi Bacci (1994, 173–174) showed how the nineteenth-century Russian population avoided a winter peak of mortality among infants because of their high capacity for adaptation. A winter peak was common in many climates with milder winters. Moreover, the interpretation of seasonal variations is related, among other things, to housing conditions and food hygiene (Breschi and Livi-Bacci 1994; Knodel 1988, 60–68; Perrenoud 1979, 429–432), important issues that we cannot address directly but can approach indirectly through analysis of seasonality.

Table 12.5 shows that whatever the stage of life, climatic conditions had a decisive impact on the risk profile of the five populations in the analysis.[41] For the period from birth to the fifth birthday, this is clearly the most important determinant of death. Interestingly enough, their effect is far from homogeneous in both the different age groups and the different case studies considered. Normally, winter is a dangerous period at the beginning of life, although clothes, heating, good housing, and so forth can blunt its effects. In keeping with the Russian results, Scania shows no significant seasonal pattern during the 10 first days of life and only a spring peak between 10 and 179 days.

In more temperate regions, as in Sart, babies were twice as likely to die in winter as summer, and it was an immediate effect since no significant seasonal variations are noted between 10 and 179 days. It is, however, in the three Italian settings that the winter peak was the cruelest: during the first 10 days of life, a newborn was four times more likely to die than in the summer. And it was true in a large city like Venice as well as in two villages with very different agricultural and social structures like Casalguidi and Madregolo. The strong protective effect of summer for neonatal deaths leads us to suppose that in many cases, these might be due to the insufficient heating systems of the houses or to the exposure of the newborn to cold during the baptism ceremony. This last hypothesis could explain why the effect was so strong in Italy.[42] In Sart, the first explanation is the most plausible since excess mortality during winter remains marked in the second semester of life and between 1 and 4 years, but a winter peak is apparent in the same age groups in Scania. It could be related to changes in the clothes and the exposure to cold and harsh conditions when the babies progressively leave the cradle and start to discover the world.

In the second semester of life, the relative positions of summer and winter are reversed in Venice and Casalguidi. It is now summer that becomes extremely dangerous for the health of the children, more than doubling their risk of dying. Such a transition after six months of life was also observed at the national level in Italy (Breschi and Livi Bacci 1994, 178). Though attenuated, the negative influence of summer continues through early childhood in Venice; the effect is more persistent in Casalguidi and appears in Madregolo. Summer and fall have a strong relationship with diarrhea and other gastric diseases, while the relationship with chronic malnutrition exists only in summer. These pathologies affect children only after weaning, when they have lost the protection of the mother's milk and are susceptible to contamination through the ingestion of infected food. If we link this result with those on the impact of social hierarchy, it is apparent that breast-feeding in Venice was not as short in duration as the two or three months noted by the contemporary physicians cited earlier. It seems more likely that weaning was carried out at around six months of age, thereby inverting the seasonal pattern. The same calendar was observed in Casalguidi, while the later transition in Madregolo is an indication that breast-feeding there was more prolonged. The difference between these two Italian villages is driven chiefly by the large number of babies sent to Casalguidi for nursing who, as was discussed earlier, competed with native babies for maternal care.

The environmental constraints acted, therefore, in the opposite direction. The warm summers of the Mediterranean triggered infectious diseases of the digestive system among children made vulnerable by early weaning. Winter's cold and spring's rainy weather favored the spread of respiratory diseases that exerted their influence only later. Generally our results clearly support Caselli's (1991) emphasis on the importance of climatic conditions and food hygiene in accounting for differences between Northern and Southern Europe. Obviously, different pathologies required different answers and cures.

In Sweden, as in Belgium, an economic influence is also apparent. It is not a coincidence that in Scania and in Sart children aged 6 months and older suffered not only during winter but also during the spring, especially in Scania. In poor rural societies, food supplies are most scarce in the spring, when the previous harvest has been exhausted but new crops are not yet available for harvest (Alter, Oris, and Servais 1999). Food availability could directly affect not only weaned children but also breast-feeding children, via their mothers. Indeed, at least in Sart, we observed that married women aged 20 to 55, practically speaking most mothers, were highly sensitive to fluctuations in the price of foods. Even in the second part of the nineteenth century, when the influence of prices on mortality largely disappeared, women in that age group are the only people who died at a higher rate when food became more expensive. As we noted above, the same was true of fertility, which was directly linked with adult married women's health status in pretransitional time (Alter, Neven, and Oris 2000).

Conclusions

In this chapter, we developed a comparative analysis of mortality amongst the frailest, the least valuable, the easiest-to-replace members of pretransitional populations and families: the children.

Through comparison of the results from our case studies, we showed that the transition from biology to society and economy, or from infancy to childhood, is not uniform. Treating neonatal mortality as equivalent to endogenous mortality is clearly misleading, as already pointed out by John Landers (1993, 139–141). Of course, we cannot deny that families, especially mothers, helped protect babies from the influence of short-term economic stress. The only exception is found in Casalguidi, but only in the second semester of life, and is likely to be accounted for by the frequency of wet-nursing in this village. It is an important result since infants are the only ones who benefited from such complete protection from economic fluctuations, while children aged 1 to 5 are very responsive to price fluctuations, as well as to the social status of the household head. Conversely, it remains true that in our results, the survival chances of newborns are clearly dependent on their mother's health status, as reflected in age and birth spacing, or even more explicitly through mother's survival. However, such a biological causality is modulated by social, economic, and cultural determinants.

First, there is a selection effect: young babies are not sensitive to short-term economic stress, but adult married women and their fertility are adversely affected by food price increases. Second, even after such a selection, a detailed critical analysis of stillbirths and living births shows that contrary to some previous findings, neonatal mortality is higher among the poorest classes. Third, at the intersection of society, economy, and culture, the European system of late marriage postpones both the beginning and the end of the fertile life and is clearly the source of the relationship between mother's age and higher risks of neonatal death. Although imperfect, the comparison with a Japanese case is illuminating. Generally, the concept of maternal depletion offers a chance to synthesize these new results and to look at the interactions between biology and society.

So, examining the transition from biological to social and economic determinants of infants and children deaths over the life course, we find a more complicated story than expected, where interactions are decisive. Another point has been a surprise: at this stage of the research, we observe much more heterogeneity in mortality levels than in the patterns of determinants. We understand much better the differentials in the risks of dying before age 5 within each of the populations we are studying, but these patterns have more similarities than differences. This means that compositional differences between populations in terms of biology or economy do not account for why mortality levels were higher in some places than in others.

This is why, in the final section of the chapter, we analyzed seasonality as a proxy for environmental dimensions. Starting from a rich tradition of historical research in both France and England, we assumed that local ecology almost always overwhelmed social and economic differentials in mortality. The influence of seasonality on young children's survival is indeed impressive, seasons being the strongest factors of differentiation among all those we tested. But again, it is in fact precisely when an independent variable like seasonality is taken into account that difference appears in the ways of living and dying in southern and northwestern Europe. From that point of view, our microdata perfectly fits the macroview proposed by Caselli (1991) and enriches and elaborates it.

Confirming previous findings, an inverse relationship existed between the winter peak in neonatal mortality and the severity of the weather. Social and cultural adaptations, in other words, overwhelmed the climatic conditions. Second, two different structures emerge. On one hand, mortality in the spring peak among weaned children, in Scania and in the Belgian Ardennes, reflects the Malthusian tension among rural populations, which were particularly at risk in the period between two harvests. On the other hand, pronounced excess mortality during the summer reveals that Italian populations suffered from structural problems in housing conditions and food hygiene, especially when specific circumstances shortened the duration of breast-feeding. Again, there is no simple boundary or simple overwhelming causal factor; rather, constructions and interactions produce distinct patterns. In other and perhaps more explicit words, infant and child mortality *levels* are not really predicted by the social and biological composition of each population; levels appear more as a product of social and family organizations in peculiar ecotypes.

Notes

We thank Alfred Perrenoud, Chris Wilson, Michael Haines, Alessandro Rosina, Peter Sköld, James Lee, and many other members of the Eurasia Project for their helpful comments and suggestions.

1. See chapters 2 and 4.

2. See also the appendix.

3. In the CD of the *International Bibliography of Historical Demography, 1977–1995* (by Serge Nekrasof), we count 773 references for infant mortality alone.

4. See Boulanger and Tabutin (1980), or the synthesis of the Princeton inquiry by Francine van de Walle (1986).

5. See the recent special issue of *Historical Methods*, 33:2, on "Spatial Variations in Mortality."

6. See, for example, the special issue of the *Annales de Démographie Historique* in 1994 and two volumes edited, respectively, by Bideau, Desjardins, and Pérez-Brignoli (1997) and by Corsini and Viazzo (1997).

7. See the complaint by Perrenoud (1993, 384–385).

8. According to Lee and Campbell (1997, 66), "roughly one-third of male births and two-thirds of female births were never registered; presumably because they died before the mean age at registration, that is approximately 6 *sui*." Six *sui* corresponds roughly to 4.5 Western years of age.

9. For example, in the *Status Animarum* of Madregolo and Casalguidi, the Italian villages, some 800 persons had been recorded with an age 0, against 1,200 to 1,300 with an age of 1. This kind of age heaping, typical at very young age, could result in an important over-estimation of infant mortality because of the underestimation of the population at risk, but it has been corrected thanks to the linkage with the parish registers of baptisms (Breschi, Derosas, and Manfredini 2000).

10. In Sart, the neonatal mortality rate is 74.5 per 1,000 births, when stillbirths are included in the deaths at less than 1 month of life, and 38.5 per 1,000 when stillbirths are excluded. In Tilleur, the values are, respectively, 83 and 43.3. In Sart, the infant mortality rate is 152.5 per 1,000, or 117.2 with or without the stillbirths; in Tilleur the rate is 196.8, or 157.1.

11. See Gélis (2000) for the theological debates and Knodel (1988, 480–502) for demographic evidence.

12. The neonatal mortality rate for Scania from 1766 to 1867 is 103.5, excluding stillbirths and 119.2 including stillbirths. Thus, neonatal mortality was declining as infant mortality declined.

13. The lines are moving averages of infant mortality with windows of 3 to 11 years, depending on the size of the population at risk in seven settings.

14. The infant mortality rate was around 15 percent in rural Belgium in the second third of the nineteenth century. Calculated by Masuy-Stroobant (1983, 447).

15. See chapter 7.

16. Similarly, Perrenoud and Bourdelais (1998, 71–72) point out the contrast between the textile areas of north France where infant mortality was between 20 and 25 percent at the end of the nineteenth century, and the coal and iron areas, where infant mortality did not exceed 13 percent, which is perfectly consistent with the levels observed in Tilleur.

17. "According to contemporary physicians, some Venetian mothers used to wean their children even after two or three months, adopting some awful methods of mixed feeding" (Derosas 2000).

18. See also the comparison of infant and child mortality in Bavaria and Italy for the period 1876 to 1885 conducted by Francine van de Walle (1986, 209).

19. Summarizing Caselli's (1991) work, Reher and Schofield wrote: "As Caselli points out, infant and especially child mortality patterns in Europe show considerable similarities with summer climate: areas of hot, dry summers seem to be plagued by high levels of child mortality where diarrhea and other intestinal diseases are relatively more important than in other parts of the continent. The peculiar structure of pretransitional childhood mortality patterns, which can be seen in Coale and Demeny's 'South tables' where child mortality ($_4q_1$) is as high or higher than infant mortality ($_1q_0$), may well be related to summer climate and its consequence for food and water purity" (Reher and Schofield 1991, 16).

20. See historical examples in Perrenoud (1997, 30) as well as the discussion in chapter 2.

21. The van Norren and van Vianen (1986) model is much more complex than figure 12.2 suggests. Specifying each level, they define seven characteristics at the household level, from the demographic composition to the use of health services; thirteen intermediate variables, which are both behavioral and biological, from mother's age at birth to accidents; and four risk factors: nutritional intake, constitution at birth, exposure, and susceptibility. They also try to establish the complex web of effects and connections.

22. See, for example, Knodel (1988), Lynch and Greenhouse (1994, 125), and van Poppel and Mandemakers (1997, 292–298).

23. Here we are making references to the comparative models, which have been calculated by each team in this book. To include our Asian data, we calculate these models for ages 0 to 1 and 2 to 14.

24. For Samuel Preston (1996, 534–535), the idea that "socio-economic differentials in mortality tended to increase during the first five years of a child's life" emerges in the demographic literature from the first analyses of the *World Fertility Survey* in the early 1980s.

25. For these last cases, "age" in terms of the timing of NAC registration is used. Therefore, the youngest possible NAC age of individuals included in our analysis is 1, which is considered "infants." "Child" is defined as those with NAC ages 2 to 5, seen as the Western equivalent of ages 1 to 4. Due to the Japanese counting system, one should be careful, however, to see these age differences (particularly the difference between one and two) as an exact equivalent of Western counterparts. See chapter 9.

26. The number of deaths for Sart and Tilleur does not include the stillbirths.

27. This point was made by Knodel (1988, 85) and further developed by Woods, Watterson, and Woodward (1988, 1989).

28. See also Miller (1989), Preston (1996, 535), and van Poppel and Mandemakers (1997, 294).

29. Family forms reconstructed through the Fleury and Henry (1985) method are well suited to deal with these issues as Knodel (1988, 86), Lynch and Greenhouse (1994), and Bengtsson (1999) have shown. However, they do not include the mobile families that we can identify through population registers. Nevertheless, we must always take into account in our analyses such left truncations. For immigrant families, we can only count the number of children ever observed. It is consequently impossible to establish birth order strictly. The problem exists also for the calculation of the previous birth order and survival of the elder sibling but is more contained. We create for these variables a category "unknown" for the first observed births of immigrant families.

30. For comparable results in developing countries, see Alam and David (1998) and Alam (1995).

31. "A previous birth interval of less than 730 days indicates that the next elder sibling was breast-fed for a fairly short period of time since breast-feeding tends to prolong birth intervals" (Bengtsson 1999, 134).

32. Similarly, in Madregolo (1800–1883), 65 percent of the deaths came from 19 percent of the families, while in Casalguidi (1819–1859) and Venice (1850–1859), 75 percent of the deaths came from 31 percent of the families (Breschi et al. 1999, 204–207).

33. For more details and references, see Breschi and Pozzi (1997), van Poppel and Mandemakers (1997, 298), and Perrenoud (1997, 300–303).

34. Bengtsson (1999) suggests that a neglected explanation of possible excess mortality among the children of the wealthy classes could be that landless and poor people were more scattered, living in more isolated parts of the parish. But such a social geography could also make it more difficult for the latter to declare a birth promptly and also more difficult for the pastor to monitor these families.

35. It was not possible for Madregolo because information on occupation is too sparse.

36. The sex ratio in the "high" classes is too low (93) but the number of cases for this social group (236 births, 47 deaths) is too low.

37. The participants working with Scanian data ran a special calculation for the period 1766 to 1867, observing 197 deaths between one and ten days and 133 stillbirths.

38. In the two Belgian settings, the children of the very young mothers (aged 15 to 19 in the booming town of Tilleur, where the Malthusian brake was precociously broken, and aged 20 to 24 in Sart, where the control on the access to marriage remained severe and the age at first union high) suffered from 50 percent higher risks of dying between 10 and 179 days of life. Such excess mortality of infants of young women is relatively commonly observed, more as a part of a J than a severe U pattern (Knodel 1988, 88). The explanations are complex, since biological aspects (first births are more at risk as well as adolescent conceptions) interacted with sociocultural ones (illegitimate children are much more frequent among the infants of young mothers).

39. Although the results are not shown on table 12.5, the models ran on Venice and Tilleur include as control variables a dummy variable identifying the years of cholera epidemics.

40. See tables 1 through 3 in Derosas (2003).

41. Tilleur is a peculiar case: epidemics are so important in its epidemiological landscape that the seasonal pattern is completely chaotic.

42. See Derosas (2003), which cites an eighteenth-century Italian physician's description of the "custom of exposing the newborns to cold and harsh weather during the baptism ceremony." Landers (1993, 139–141) offers a detailed discussion of English and French cases where the incidence of respiratory infection at the very beginning of life poses problems for the "law" proposed by Bourgeois-Pichat (1951) to disentangle endogenous and exogenous deaths in infancy.

13　Old-Age Mortality

Noriko O. Tsuya and
Paul Nystedt
in collaboration with Matteo
Manfredini, Muriel Neven,
and Cameron Campbell

Old-age mortality is an underexplored topic in studies of historical populations and societies. The primary reason for the scarcity of historical studies on mortality in old age is the difficulty in obtaining data on the population at risk: all the elderly present in the area and at risk of experiencing a death. Historical studies of mortality responses of the elderly to economic variations and household factors are even scarcer because they require longitudinal microlevel records in which not only the population at risk, but also demographic, socioeconomic, and household characteristics of individual elders are documented.[1] Even for contemporary populations, multivariate analyses of mortality among the elderly are of fairly recent vintage, since they are possible only with longitudinal data such as those from the Health and Retirement Survey.

Using longitudinal, nominative household registers in five pre-industrial societies in the Eurasia Project has a unique advantage in conducting such multivariate studies in comparative historical perspective. Based on the results of the Eurasia standard comparative models (see the appendix), this chapter examines the socioeconomic, demographic, and household determinants of mortality of males and females in old age in different parts of Belgium, Sweden, Italy, China, and Japan.

Historians have long engaged in studies of differences in demographic and social behavior between, as well as within, the East and West. Such demographic studies date back from the monumental study by Malthus (1803) to the now-classic study by Wrigley and Schofield (1981) and the recent reappraisal of these Malthusian and neo-Malthusian accounts by Lee and Wang (1999b). East-West differences in the family systems were also the subject of inquiry by many family historians and demographers such as Hajnal (1965, 1982), Laslett (1977, 1983), and Saito (1998).

From the contemporary perspectives of gerontology and demography of aging, studies on patterns and factors of old-age mortality in past times are also valuable and useful. All the societies under consideration have already undergone the first demographic transition. For example, between 1995 and 2000, life expectancy at birth in the five societies under consideration ranged between 68 and 77 for men and 72 and 83 for women (United Nations 1998). Under such circumstances, roughly 70 to 90 percent of men and women are expected to survive until age 65. As shown in chapter 3 of this book, however, average expectancy of life at birth in our populations ranged from the low 30s to the low 40s. In those circumstances, the proportion surviving to age 65 was around 30 percent or less.

In this chapter, focusing on ever-married men and women aged 55 to 74 in rural communities in eighteenth- and nineteenth-century Belgium, Sweden, Italy, China, and Japan, we examine the mortality effects of variations in local economic conditions and household and individual characteristics in comparative and multivariate context. We pay special attention not only to the differences between and within Europe and Asia but also to gender differentials as well. As little cross-cultural or historical evidence was previously available, the Eurasia Project is uniquely suited to examine such issues.

In preindustrial agrarian societies, as noted in chapter 4, the public systems of social security and welfare for the elderly were underdeveloped at best. Chances of survival in old age were therefore affected strongly by local economic conditions. Elderly men and women, however, are thought to have responded differently to short-term economic stress, depending on local economic development and social organizations. At the same time, their mortality responses would also have differed, depending on the economic resources and structural features of households in which they resided. Given economic and demographic constraints, the vulnerability of the elderly was further differentiated by their status and position within the household.

In the next section, we discuss theoretical backgrounds on old-age mortality in historical perspective by synthesizing major hypotheses and findings of existing studies. This enables us to situate the results of our analyses in larger theoretical contexts. We also explain briefly the data and measurements pertaining to the analyses of old-age mortality. We next examine and compare the levels and gender patterns of mortality of elderly men and women in rural communities in the five countries. We then discuss the results of the event-history analyses of old-age mortality for men and women separately. Specifically, through event-history analyses, we first look at mortality responses to fluctuations in local grain prices or wages. Controlling for local economic fluctuations, we next compare the effects of household socioeconomic status and age composition on the mortality of elderly men and women. To identify which elderly men and women were most or least likely to die, we further examine the mortality effects of demographic and household factors measured at individual levels. Through these analyses, we seek to elucidate, in comparative Eurasian perspective, the patterns and causal mechanisms of old-age mortality, an important but underexamined aspect of mortality in past times.

Theoretical Background

In this chapter, we examine three aspects of mortality among the aged in rural communities in five Eurasian societies: responses to local economic conditions, how aggregate characteristics of the household such as its labor capacity and dependency ratio affected mortality, and how positions of individual elders within the household affected their likelihood of death.

In preindustrial agrarian settings, living standards were influenced strongly by agricultural output, and chances of survival were affected, often seriously, by income fluctuations caused by variations in harvest yields.[2] Local economic downturns may have had especially harsh effects on persons and households in poverty. The mortality effects of local economic fluctuations are thought to have been especially strong for elderly men and women, especially those in the least well-to-do households, who were likely to be frailer and more vulnerable to deterioration in living standards in the community.

Characteristics of household in which the elderly lived are also thought to have affected their chances of survival. Postulated originally by Chayanov (Thorner, Kerblay, and Smith 1966, 53–69) for peasant families in pretransitional Russia, the size and age composition of the household is argued to have influenced its economic well-being. Specifically, the consumer-worker ratio within the preindustrial agrarian household was negatively associated with the general volume of its economic activity and productivity. Based on this Chayanov rule, providing that household size and the amount of household resources did not drastically change in the short run, the ratio between consumers (children and elderly) and producers (working-age adults) within a household is hypothesized to have adversely affected the health and survival chances of its elderly members.

Old-age mortality would also have been affected by the overall socioeconomic status of household in which the elderly lived. Results from contemporary studies on socioeconomic differentials in mortality show that persons with higher socioeconomic status, reflected in higher education, social class, or occupational status, are likely to have lower mortality in old age (Kitagawa and Hauser 1973; Preston and Elo 1995; United Nations 1982, 42–82; Valkonen 1998). Providing that the public social security and welfare systems were underdeveloped in preindustrial societies, the health and survival of the elderly would have been strongly influenced by the availability of economic resources within the household.

Chances of survival of individual elders were also affected by their marital status as well as their positions and relationships within the household. Mortality differentials by marital status and sources of such differentials are the focus of a number of studies on contemporary populations (Goldman 1993a, 1993b; Goldman and Hu 1993; Gove 1973; Hu and Goldman 1990; Lillard and Panis 1996). Although the number of studies on factors of old-age mortality in preindustrial populations is much more limited, a substantial portion of existing studies discusses the effects of marital statuses, especially the relationship of widowhood to mortality (Cornell 1989, March 1912, Neven 1998, Nystedt 2002, Tsuya and Kurosu 2002, Uhlenberg 1980). These studies commonly found that compared to currently married individuals, those without a spouse (widowed, divorced, and never married) were more likely to die and that the mortality effect of the loss or lack of spouse was generally stronger among men than among women.

This association between the loss or lack of spouse and mortality can be explained by the competing or complementary hypotheses of marriage selection and marriage protection.[3] According to the hypothesis of marriage selection, widowed, divorced, or single individuals (especially men) are more likely to die because they failed to marry or stay married because of their poor health.[4] The marriage protection hypothesis postulates that married persons are less likely to die because an array of social, economic, psychological, and environmental benefits associated with marriage enhances their health and helps them counter mortality risks. Though we cannot rule out the possibility of marriage selection, as widowed elderly could and did remarry and healthy elderly probably had a higher chance of remarriage than unhealthy ones, marriage protection seems to be a more plausible explanation. Existing evidence uniformly suggests that due to either psychological difficulties or economic and social deprivation, the mortality of ever-married elderly men and women in preindustrial populations increased significantly with the loss of their spouse.

Their mortality may also have varied by living arrangements, especially the presence of adult children. While historical studies of the effects of coresident kin on mortality in old age are rare, Cain's studies (1981, 1983) on fertility in contemporary South Asia offer important theoretical implications. According to Cain, children not only contribute labor to their parents' household, but also offer longer-term economic benefits, such as insurance against the risk of income insufficiency in old age. Given the virtual absence of old-age pension systems and health insurance in preindustrial agrarian communities, coresident adult children must have been even more important for the well-being and health of elderly parents. Previous historical demographic studies of Belgium and Japan indeed found that the elderly enjoyed support and protection from adult children living with them (Alter 1996; Alter, Cliggett, and Urbiel 1996; Alter et al. 1997; Cornell 1989; Tsuya and Kurosu 2000).

At the same time, marital statuses of coresiding adult children may also have important implications for mortality in old age in preindustrial communities. In the context of preindustrial western European nuclear households, unmarried children are thought to have been more valuable to their parents because the parents could enjoy a larger share of time and care from the children. In the East Asian context of extended family households, however, married children may have been more beneficial to their parents as their spouses (especially sons' wives) were supposed to care for the older generation.[5]

In preindustrial rural societies, chances of survival in old age may also have been enhanced or reduced by the positions that individual elders occupied within their household, especially their relationships to the head of household. For example, in the context of stem family households in preindustrial Japan, nonstem kin and nonheirs were likely to have suffered structural vulnerability and powerlessness, whereas heads and heirs are thought to have enjoyed more structural advantages (Skinner 1993). Lee and Campbell (1997) also found that in communities in Liaodong, the likelihood of dying in old age differed according to relationship within the household. As discussed in chapter 4, the five specific Eurasian societies under consideration in this study had different household systems. Our analysis of these societies seeks to shed light on the workings of household systems and their differential impact on the survival of men and women in old age.

Data and Measurements

The analyses in this chapter focus on ever-married men and women aged 55 to 74. The lower age boundary (age 55) was selected because this is the age at which a substantial proportion of household heads in Sweden and Japan began to retire (see chapter 4; Okada and Kurosu 1998). It was also the age at which men in the Chinese household registers began to be annotated as "old" or "retired," and the age that the Belgian population census between 1866 and 1910 regarded as the beginning of old age. The upper age boundary was chosen primarily to avoid the estimation bias caused by increasingly selective populations who survived to very old ages.[6] The decision to make age 74 the upper limit is also due to concern over the quality of data for some of the populations under consideration.[7]

The five sets of analyses presented in this chapter use different age measures: chronological age in the three European populations, traditional age in *sui* in the northeastern Chinese populations, and the number of annual population registrations that an index individual survived after birth—referred to as the *ninbetsu-aratame-cho* (NAC) age—in northeastern Japan.[8] Given that the focus of our analysis is the last phase of life, these differences in measurements of age do not seriously affect our results.

Our analyses draw the data from sixteen rural communities in different regions of five Eurasian societies: the commune of Sart in eastern Belgium; four parishes in Scania in southern Sweden; two parishes—Casalguidi in Toscana and Madregolo in Emilia-Romagna—in northern Italy; seven state farms in Liaodong in northeast China; and two farming villages of Shimomoriya and Niita in Ou in northeast Japan (for specifics, see the appendix).[9] Table 13.1 presents the sex- and country-specific numbers of person-years and deaths that were included in our comparative analyses of mortality in old age. Though there are differences in the duration and size of data among the five countries, the overall quality and depth of data that we use are considerable. The number of person-years recorded is 68,497 for Liaodong,

Table 13.1

Summary of data used in the analyses of old-age mortality: Ever-married males and females aged 55–74 in rural communities: Five historical societies in Europe and Asia

Country and community	Person-years			Deaths		
	Male	Female	Total	Male	Female	Total
China						
Liaodong	30,971	37,526	68,497	1,915	1,815	3,730
Japan						
Shimomoriya and Niita	8,229	7,712	15,941	361	343	704
Italy						
Casalguidi	4,901	4,913	9,814	210	188	398
Madregolo	2,257	1,887	4,144	81	64	145
Belgium						
Sart	9,473	8,401	17,874	609	543	1,152
Sweden						
Four Scanian parishes	3,449	3,089	6,538	158	155	313
Total	59,280	63,528	122,808	3,334	3,108	6,642

15,941 for Shimomoriya and Niita, 13,958 for Casalguidi and Madregolo together, 17,874 for Sart, and 6,538 for the four Scania parishes; the number of deaths is 3,730 for Liaodong, 704 for Shimomoriya and Niita, 543 for Casalguidi and Madregolo, 1,152 for Sart, and 313 for the Scania parishes. The total number of person-years and deaths used in our analyses are 122,808 and 6,642, respectively.

We next turn to measurements of community, household, and individual factors. Since detailed explanations of the Eurasia standard comparative models are given in chapter 1 and the appendix, we explain these measures in a summary fashion and give detailed explanations only when they relate to issues of aging and old age. As explained in chapter 2, our analyses test structures of mortality responses to variations in local economic conditions, household context at the household level, and household context at the individual level. Table 13.2 presents descriptive statistics for the household contextual variables used in our multivariate analyses of old-age mortality. To examine the effects of changes in local economic conditions, the analyses employ the local price series of staple grains or wages of agricultural day laborer, as described in the appendix.

To account for the effects of household characteristics, our analyses employ household socioeconomic status, number of adult household members, and age composition. To measure household economic

Table 13.2
Means of the socioeconomic and household variables used for the event-history analysis of mortality of ever-married elderly in rural communities: Five historical societies in Europe and Asia

| | China | | Japan | | Italy | | | | Belgium | | Sweden | |
| | Liaodong | | Shimomoriya and Niita | | Casalguidi | | Madregolo | | Sart | | Scania | |
Variables	Male	Female	Male	Female	Male	Female	Male	Female	Male	Female	Male	Female
Socioeconomic status												
Head's occupation/status												
Adult male farmer/peasant	.965	.977										
Artisan	.007	.004										
Soldier	.016	.011										
Functionary	.012	.008										
Household landholding (in *koku*)			10.561	11.122								
Head's occupation/status												
Sharecropper/farmer					.690	.653						
Paid farm laborer					.142	.116						
Artisan/other non-farm worker					.117	.191						
Middle-class					.051	.040						
Cultivator									.826	.747		
Functionary									.024	.028		
Artisan and industrial workers									.058	.052		
Day laborers									.057	.057		
Miscellaneous									.117	.117		
Freeholder/Crown tenant											.165	.100

	(1)	(2)	(3)	(4)	(5)	(6)	(7)	(8)	(9)	(10)	(11)	(12)
Tenant on noble land											.229	.191
Semilandless											.225	.227
Landless											.447	.417
Household characteristics												
No. of adults in household	5.712	5.413	2.323	2.277	3.053	2.724	3.705	3.554	2.435	2.375	4.162	3.900
Proportion below age 15	.141	.141	.181	.194	.192	.166	.216	.204	.209	.135	.230	.210
Proportion above age 55	.321	.322	.408	.421	.323	.373	.303	.355	.337	.380	.240	.250
Marital status												
Currently married	.682	.503	.774	.600	.807	.517	.754	.614	.556			.408
Widowed	.318	.497	.155	.353	.193	.483	.246	.386	.444			.592
Divorced			.045	.015								
Unclear if widowed/divorced			.026	.032								
Household relationship												
Head	.671	.492		.227	.050	.927	.281	.943	.177	.886	.121	.000
Spouse of head	.000	.003		.300	.232	.000	.493	.000	.598	.000	.531	.866
Stem kin of head	.045	.482		.076	.699	.007	.158	.038	.168	.049	.209	.055
Nonstem kin of head	.284	.009		.366	.007	.066	.056	.016	.056	.068	.139	.079
Servant/other	.000	.014		.031	.012	.000	.012	.003	.002	.000	.000	.000
Presence of children												
None	.187	.208	.244	.183	.300	.263				.334	.121	.154
Only unmarried	.226	.164	.353	.490	.334	.320				.236	.531	.435
Only married	.437	.497	.037	.120	.166	.200				.223	.209	.246
Both	.150	.131	.344	.207	.200	.217				.207	.139	.164
Child's marital status unknown		.031	.022									
Any marital statuses	.579											.505

Note: Means are computed based on the number of person-years observed and recorded.

status, we use occupation of household head for the European populations,[10] occupation of elderly men themselves or husband of elderly
women for the Chinese analysis, and household landholding (in *koku*)
for Japan.[11]

Household-level characteristics are also measured by three structural
variables: the number of working-age adults (those aged 15 to 55) in
the household, the proportion of household members under age 15
(children), and the proportion of those above age 55 (the elderly). The
average number of working-age adults in the elder's household varies
considerably among the five Eurasian societies under consideration—
from around 2.3 in northeastern Japan to over 5.4 in northeastern
China—reflecting in part differences in dominant household types.
However, there are not as much intercountry differences in the proportions of children and the elderly. The proportion of children ranges
from 14 to 23 percent, while the proportion of elderly is roughly in the
25 to 40 percent range.

To account for the mortality effects of household context experienced
by individual elders, our analyses use three indicators: elders' marital
status, their relationship to household head, and presence of children
in household. Providing that this chapter focuses on ever-married
elderly, marital status consists of the currently married and the formerly married, with the exception of Sweden, for which such a distinction is not possible. As shown in table 13.2, in all populations
except for Ou in northeastern Japan, the formerly married consist of
widows and widowers with the virtual absence of divorced persons.
Even in the two northeastern Japanese villages where marital disruption due to divorce was substantial (Kurosu, Tsuya, and Hamano
1999), widowhood was much more prevalent among the formerly
married in old age. The divorced consisted of only a small proportion
of the formerly married.

To measure relationship to household head, we grouped elderly
men and women into five categories: head, spouse of head, stem kin of
head, nonstem kin of head, and nonkin or servant.[12] The five populations under consideration varied in the composition of household
relationships of men and women in old age, probably reflecting differences in the patterns of headship transfer and dominant household
types. In Ou, in which the ideal family system was the patrilineal stem
family, retirement of heads before death was frequent (Okada and
Kurosu 1998). In contrast, retirement of household head rarely happened in Sart (Alter and Oris 2000a), northern Italy (Lagazio, Martelli,

and Rettaroli 1998), and Liaodong (Lee and Campbell 1997, 109–119). In northeastern China, complex households were also much more prevalent than in the other communities, whereas in eastern Belgium, most households were simple (see chapters 7 and 10). In northern Italy, simple households and multiple family households seem to have coexisted, as multigenerational households were relatively common among sharecroppers (see chapter 8; Kertzer and Karweit 1995).

Consequently, in eastern Belgium, an overwhelming majority of elderly men and women were household head and head's wife, respectively. In northern Italy, as in eastern Belgium, a large majority of elderly men were head, and the largest category among elderly women was head's spouse. However, it is also notable that a considerable proportion of elderly women in northern Italy were head or stem kin (mother) of head, probably reflecting the prevalence of multifamily households among sharecroppers' households in Madregolo. Nonstem kin (mostly uncles, aunts, and cousins of head) were much more common in Liaodong than in the other four populations, whereas both spouse and stem kin (mother) of head were common among elderly women. In Ou, as expected, head and stem kin (father) of head were equally prevalent among elderly men, whereas head's spouse and stem kin (mother) of head were common among elderly women.

Presence of children in household is also a factor thought to have strongly affected mortality in old age in preindustrial rural communities. Marital statuses of coresident children could also have been important from the standpoint of the protection and support that elderly parents receive from coresident children. To capture the possible non-linear effect of coresident children by their marital status, our analyses specify presence and marital status of children by four categories: no children present, only unmarried children present, only married children present, and both unmarried and married children present. Somewhat unexpectedly, according to table 13.2, in all Eurasian populations, ever-married men and women spent a large part (70–85 percent) of their elderly years with their coresident children, except for southern Sweden, in which about half of the elderly years were spent living with children. However, given the differences in household systems and marriage timing among these populations, the proportion of the elderly whose coresident children were all married was by far the highest in northeastern China. By contrast, the proportion of the elderly living only with unmarried children was highest in eastern Belgium.

Mortality Levels

Before we discuss the results of the event-history analyses, we compare the levels and patterns of rural old-age mortality in the five pre-industrial Eurasian societies under consideration. Through this, we seek to situate survival to and through old age in the overall mortality regimes in comparative perspective. Table 13.3 presents the life table estimates by sex of the proportions surviving to old age and the life expectancies by age in old age.[13]

Looking at the overall levels of survival, there appears to be a divide between the two western European populations, Sart and Scania, and the two East Asian populations, Liaodong and Ou, with the Mediterranean population, northern Italy, in the middle. The levels of survival to and through old age in the five historical Eurasian populations therefore form an almost perfect continuum with eastern Belgium at one end and northeastern China at the other. In Sart, in eastern Belgium, roughly half of persons born are estimated to have survived to age 55 and around one-third to age 65. In northern Liaodong in northeastern China, only around one-third of births are estimated to have survived to age 55 and roughly 20 percent of them to age 65.

Furthermore, in Sart, the level of old-age mortality declined significantly during the last period, 1875 to 1899 (see chapter 7). There were no significant period differentials in Liaodong, whereas old-age mortality increased significantly between 1840 and 1870 in Niita and Shimomoriya in Ou (see chapter 9). Given these, if we are to compare the western European and the East Asian populations during the latter half of the nineteenth century, East-West differences in the level of elderly mortality are likely to be even larger.

Within the two world regions (Europe and East Asia) and within each country, there are also differences in the level of survival by environmental conditions and economic development. Within western Europe, Sart had a higher proportion surviving to and through old age than Scania, possibly a reflection of early industrialization and more favorable climate. Within Liaodong, the northern state farms clearly had lower levels of survival than the southern ones, a reflection of their harsher climate and less prosperous economy.

However, there are no consistent regional or country patterns in sex differentials in the overall level of survival. In the four Scania parishes and in southern Liaodong, the estimated proportion surviving tends to be higher for females than for males. By contrast, the proportion surviving is in general higher for males than females in Sart, the two northern Italian communities, northern Liaodong, and the two northeastern Japanese villages.

Though there are clear East-West and inter- and intracountry differences in the level of survival to and through old age, there are no distinguishable patterns in life expectancy in old age. Rather, the age patterns of life expectancy in old age were similar between and within the East and the West. If anything, life expectancy at age 55 was somewhat lower in western European populations than in populations in Mediterranean Europe or East Asia. As shown in the right panel of table 13.3, having survived to age 55, men and women in these five historical societies could expect to live roughly fifteen to seventeen more years. If they survived to age 65, they could expect to live roughly nine to twelve more years. Hence, if they survived until their mid-50s, the elderly in these five historical societies survived on average to around age 70. And if they survived the first ten years of the elderly years (until their mid-60s), they could expect to live to their mid-70s.

In summary, whereas the proportion of persons who managed to survive to and through old age differed clearly between the East and the West and also within each region, life expectancy during the elderly years did not show distinctive differences. In these five historical societies, elderly men and women in rural communities were members of a robust minority who managed to win the race of survival. Once they survived through the years of high mortality risks, they enjoyed life expectancies not so different from those of contemporary posttransitional populations.[14]

Mortality Determinants

This section first compares the patterns of mortality responses of rural men and women in old age to short-term economic stress caused by fluctuations in local grain prices or real wages in the five historical societies. Controlling for variations in local economic conditions, we next examine the mortality effects of household socioeconomic status as measured by occupation of the household head or household landholding. We then move to the analysis of the mortality effects of household contexts measured at the household level, such as the number of adults present in the household and the compositions of children and elderly in the household, net of the effects of price fluctuations and

Noriko O. Tsuya and Paul Nystedt

Table 13.3
Life table estimates of the percentage of survivors and life expectancy by age and sex among the elderly in rural communities: Five historical societies in Europe and Asia

Country, community, and period	Percentage surviving to age					Life expectancy at age				
	55	60	65	70	75	55	60	65	70	75
China[a]										
Liaodong North, 1789–1909										
Male	35.6	29.0	22.7	16.0	9.9	14.5	12.2	9.9	8.0	6.4
Female	27.4	24.1	19.8	14.6	9.6	16.4	13.3	10.6	8.5	6.6
Liaodong South, 1789–1909										
Male	40.7	34.0	26.6	19.1	13.0	16.0	13.6	11.6	10.3	8.9
Female	39.2	34.5	28.8	22.9	15.8	17.3	14.3	11.7	9.0	6.9
Japan[b]										
Shimomoriya and Niita, 1716–1759										
Male	37.6	32.7	28.8	21.8	13.6	16.5	13.6	10.0	7.4	5.4
Female	36.8	32.6	28.1	20.3	11.7	16.0	12.7	9.3	6.9	5.2
Italy										
Casalguidi, 1819–1859										
Male	38.5	33.4	27.2	20.3	12.2	15.9	13.0	10.4	8.1	6.7
Female	33.7	29.7	23.9	18.4	12.9	17.4	14.4	12.2	10.1	8.4
Madregolo, 1800–1883										
Male	40.3	36.2	29.7	22.2	14.6	16.8	12.4	9.5	6.9	4.1
Female	35.6	32.1	27.8	20.3	10.7	16.1	12.6	9.2	6.7	5.4

Belgium										
Sart, 1812–1899										
Male	47.5	40.9	34.3	25.6	15.8	16.2	13.4	10.5	8.1	6.7
Female	45.0	39.5	32.9	23.8	14.2	15.8	12.7	9.7	7.4	5.7
Sweden										
Four Scanian parishes, 1815–1865										
Male	43.3	37.4	28.9	20.5	12.1	15.2	12.2	10.1	8.1	6.7
Female	46.9	39.2	30.4	22.0	13.2	14.8	12.2	9.9	7.6	5.7

[a] Assuming the probability of dying during infancy is .200 for both sexes.
[b] Assuming the probability of dying during infancy is .200 for males and .180 for females.

Table 13.4
Estimated effects of a 10 percent increase in prices on the mortality of ever-married elderly males and females in rural communities: Five historical societies in Europe and Asia

Country and community	Male		Female	
	Relative risk	p-value	Relative risk	p-value
China				
Liaodong North, 1789–1909	2.05	0.01	−0.12	0.88
Liaodong South, 1789–1909	−1.51	0.13	−0.24	0.82
Japan				
Shimomoriya and Niita, 1716–1870	7.59	0.00	0.81	0.64
Italy				
Casalguidi, 1819–1859	−0.22	0.96	15.69	0.00
Madregolo, 1800–1883	4.20	0.27	8.24	0.047
Belgium				
Sart, 1812–1899	−5.50	0.11	−3.72	0.35
Sweden				
Four Scanian parishes, 1829–1867	5.32	0.13	6.23	0.08

Notes: The values are estimated by controlling for the effects of age, household or household head's socioeconomic status (except for Madregolo), time period (in Belgium and Japan), and community (in Sweden and Japan). Prices used: for Belgium, one-year logged difference between logged oat price and trend; for Sweden, inverse of logged real wages; for Italy, log of raw wheat and corn prices; for China, logged raw sorghum prices; and for Japan, log of raw rice price. In the models for Belgium, the trends in oat prices are also controlled.

household socioeconomic status. Finally, controlling for local economic fluctuations, household socioeconomic status, and other household-level characteristics, we examine the mortality effects of individual-level characteristics such as marital status, household relationships, and presence of children.

Economic Conditions

Table 13.4 presents the results of the event-history analysis of the effects of local price fluctuations on the mortality of rural men and women aged 55 to 74 in the five historical Eurasian populations. Controlling for age, household socioeconomic status, time period (Sart and Ou), and community (Scania and Ou), the estimated risk ratios indicate the mortality effect of a 10 percent increase in prices or, in Scania, a 10 percent decrease in logged real wages.[15]

We can see from table 13.4 that with the exception of Sart in eastern Belgium, old-age mortality in the other four preindustrial Eurasian rural populations was in general vulnerable to price fluctuations. When local grain prices went up, the likelihood of death among the elderly also had a tendency to increase; however, the magnitude of responsiveness differed by sex and community. In four Scania parishes in southern Sweden, mortality of men and women was highly responsive to fluctuations in real wages caused by grain price variations, and the magnitude of the mortality effect was similar between the sexes, though women seem to have been somewhat more responsive.

In the Tuscan village of Casalguidi in northern Italy, elderly women were extremely vulnerable to economic stress caused by harvest failure, but elderly men were largely unaffected. In the Emilian village of Madregolo in the same region, both men and women were affected by local economic fluctuations, but women were much more vulnerable than were men. By contrast, in the rural communities in the northeastern part of the two East Asian countries (northern Liaodong and Shimomoriya and Niita), it was men who were likely to suffer death, whereas women were largely unaffected by changes in local economic conditions.

These findings seem to suggest that similar to the situations in contemporary developing populations, gender differentials in the mortality responses to price fluctuations captured differences in the status of men and women in the larger society.[16] If this was the case, however, we cannot find a plausible explanation for the vulnerability of elderly men to economic variations in the two East Asian populations. Rather, these gender differentials in northeastern China and northeastern Japan could have been due not only to the generally low status of women but also to differences in power over finite resources within the household in the context of patriarchal family systems. Under the patriarchal family system in East Asian societies, males, especially adult and elderly men, ordinarily enjoyed a much greater share of household resources. When the local economic conditions took abrupt downturns because of widespread harvest failure, however, men suffered more because the degree of economic deprivation they experienced in crisis times was much greater than was the case for females.[17] It was not that women did not suffer in times of economic hardships. They probably did. Nonetheless, their life conditions did not deteriorate as drastically as did men's because women faced more limited economic opportunities to begin with.

Socioeconomic Status

Table 13.5 presents the estimated effects (relative risks) of household socioeconomic status on mortality of ever-married elderly men and women in rural communities. We can see that there are no clear patterns in the mortality effects of household socioeconomic status in the preindustrial Eurasian rural populations under consideration, with an exception of northeastern Japan.

In both Sart in eastern Belgium and Casalguidi in northern Italy, elderly women in households headed by artisans or industrial workers (many of whom were wives of artisans or industrial workers) were more likely to die than women who were wives of farmers or share-croppers, whereas the mortality of elderly men was virtually unaffected by their occupational status. In Sart, relative to women whose household head (mostly whose husband) was a cultivator, women whose head was a functionary had significantly lower mortality, whereas elderly men faced similar mortality independent of whether the head of household (usually an elderly man himself) was a cultivator or a functionary. For both of these societies, it seems that the occupation of head or husband influenced the mortality of the wife in old age more than it did the mortality of the husband.

In Liaodong, elderly men who were soldiers were 35 percent more likely to die than men who were farmers. On the other hand, in this northeastern part of the Qing China, elderly women married to soldiers were *less* likely to die than those married to farmers. In other words, being a soldier and being married to one affected the mortality of elderly men and women in opposite directions in rural Liaodong. In addition, according to table 3.6, elderly men who were functionaries also suffered higher mortality at the time of local economic hardship, as the main effect of this occupational category was insignificant but its interaction with grain price was significant and positive. Male soldiers and functionaries in the Eight Banner state farm system traveled frequently and were therefore away from home often (chapter 10; Lee and Campbell 1997, 159–176). Those soldiers and functionaries might have been more frequently exposed to infectious diseases, as they certainly had more interactions with people from other areas. This frequent travel and wider exposure to health risks apparently had harmful effects on the survival of soldiers and functionaries in old age. On the other hand, while those elderly soldiers were away from home, their wives enjoyed better health possibly because they did not have to

Table 13.5
Estimated effects of socioeconomic status of the household or household head on the mortality of ever-married elderly males and females in rural communities: Five historical societies in Europe and Asia

Country and community	Indicator	Male Relative risk	Male p-value	Female Relative risk	Female p-value
China					
Liaodong	Occupation of self, husband, or father				
	Adult male farmer	1.00	—	1.00	—
	Artisan	0.91	0.74	0.41	0.12
	Soldier	1.35	0.06	0.55	0.06
	Functionary	1.30	0.16	1.04	0.90
Japan					
Shimomoriya and Niita	Household landholding (in *koku*)[a]	0.98	0.02	0.98	0.01
Italy					
Casalguidi	Head's occupation				
	Sharecropper/farmer	1.00	—	1.00	—
	Paid farm laborer	1.13	0.55	1.03	0.91
	Artisan/blue collar	0.89	0.62	1.42	0.05
	Middle class	0.76	0.44	0.55	0.25
Belgium					
Sart	Head's occupation				
	Cultivator	1.00	—	1.00	—
	Functionary	1.01	0.98	0.39	0.04
	Artisan/industrial worker	0.87	0.46	1.39	0.09
	Day laborer	0.98	0.92	1.24	0.22
	Miscellaneous	1.53	0.02	1.02	0.89
Sweden					
Four Scanian parishes	Head's occupation				
	Freeholder	1.00	—	1.00	—
	Tenant on noble land	0.88	0.74	0.94	0.88
	Semilandless	0.66	0.17	0.67	0.26
	Landless	0.94	0.82	0.82	0.53

Notes: The values are estimated by controlling for the effects of age, price variations, time period (for Belgium and Japan), and community (for the pooled populations in Sweden, China and Japan).
[a] Given that the villages were exclusively agricultural, the head's occupation was almost totally farmers and peasants. Landholding being zero means landless peasants; landholding of around 12 *koku* is the average; and landholding of 30 to 36 *koku* belonged to the top 5 percent.

work as hard taking care of their husband. Putting it differently, the absence of a husband may have improved the survival chances of certain women. This finding is tied closely to the mortality effect of marital status that we discuss later in the chapter.

In contrast to the other four Eurasian populations, household socioeconomic status exerted strong and consistent mortality effects in Shimomoriya and Niita, two farming villages in northeastern Japan. As shown in table 13.5, the chances of survival of both elderly men and women were affected significantly by their household landholding, and the magnitudes of the effect were very similar between the sexes. An increase of landholding by one *koku* reduced their mortality by 2 percent. Though this may seem small, the effect could be substantial. Compared to elders whose households did not own any land (roughly 10 percent of the households in the villages), if elderly men and women lived in a household with 12 *koku* worth of land (which was the median), their likelihood of death was reduced by about 24 percent. If the elderly was in a household with 30 to 36 *koku* worth of land (top 5 percent), their likelihood of death was 60 percent lower than that of the landless elderly.[18]

In summary, the findings of this section suggest that whereas a household's socioeconomic status had some effects on the chances of survival of individual elderly in some of our populations (especially in East Asia), the effects were in general neither strong nor consistent. Further, none of the interactions between household socioeconomic status and prices was statistically significant (results not shown) in all of the rural populations under consideration. This lack of consistent effects and insignificant interaction with grain prices implies that in many of our populations, household socioeconomic status did not generally have strong effects on the likelihood of death among men and women who survived to old age. This was the case even at the times of economic hardship.

Household Composition

Table 13.6 presents the estimated effects of household composition on the mortality of ever-married elderly men and women in the rural Eurasian communities under consideration. Focusing first on the mortality effect of the number of working-age adults, we do not see any systematic differences between or among the European and the East Asian populations. In fact, the directions of the effects are the opposite

Table 13.6
Estimated effects of household characteristics measured at the household level on the mortality of ever-married elderly males and females: Five historical societies in Europe and Asia

Country and community	Characteristics	Male		Female	
		Relative risk	p-value	Relative risk	p-value
China					
Liaodong	Number of adults	1.00	0.39	1.00	0.62
	Proportion below age 15	0.94	0.74	1.14	0.50
	Proportion above age 54	0.80	0.11	0.92	0.54
Japan					
Shimomoriya and Niita	Number of adults	1.08	0.05	0.98	0.75
	Proportion below age 15	1.42	0.28	0.72	0.62
	Proportion above age 54	1.88	0.00	1.04	0.92
Italy					
Casalguidi	Number of adults	0.91	0.15	1.08	0.22
	Proportion below age 15	0.45	0.18	2.22	0.11
	Proportion above age 54	0.50	0.24	2.45	0.10
Madregolo	Number of adults	0.98	0.69	1.04	0.54
	Proportion below age 15	2.22	0.33	2.70	0.21
	Proportion above age 54	1.22	0.32	2.22	0.32
Belgium					
Sart	Number of adults	0.97	0.49	0.89	0.05
	Proportion below age 15	1.49	0.16	1.25	0.49
	Proportion above age 54	0.93	0.82	0.64	0.17
Sweden					
Four Scanian parishes	Number of adults	1.07	0.01	1.06	0.18
	Proportion below age 15	1.19	0.73	0.67	0.45
	Proportion above age 54	1.81	0.37	1.34	0.66

Notes: The values are estimated by controlling for the effects of age, price variations, socioeconomic status of household or household head (except for Madregolo), time period (for Belgium and Japan), and community (for the pooled populations in Sweden, China and Japan). "Adults" in the table refers to persons aged 15 to 55.

between the two West European populations—eastern Belgium and southern Sweden. In Sart, the mortality of elderly women went down significantly as the number of adult household members increased, suggesting that the more adults an elderly woman had living with her, the better was her chance of survival. By contrast, the mortality of elderly men and women in Scania increased as the number of household members aged 15 to 55 went up. In Shimomoriya and Niita, male old-age mortality also increased as the number of working-age adults in the household increased.

The number of working-age adults in the household measures its labor capacity. There is also a possibility that this factor was measuring the degree of support and protection that elders received from co-resident adults. Whichever effects this variable captures, their mortality effect is hypothesized to be negative, and it seems to be the case in rural eastern Belgium. But this is clearly not the case for southern Sweden and northeastern Japan. Instead, if this factor was a proxy of crowding, the findings suggest that the elderly in Scania and elderly men in northeastern Japan were vulnerable to health risks caused by crowding in the household. No matter which the explanation is, however, we cannot find consistent explanations to account for the whole picture. It is probably the case that in different family systems and economic contexts, the number of working-age adults in a household meant and measured different factors of old-age mortality.

Turning to the effects of the two variables of household age composition (the proportions below age 15 and above age 55), we can see that these compositional factors did not significantly affect the mortality of elderly men and women in our rural populations in Europe and East Asia. The only exception was men in Shimomoriya and Niita. The likelihood of death of elderly men in these two Japanese villages increased significantly as the proportion of household members above age 55 went up. Because many of the households with a high proportion of members above age 55 were those in which elderly men lived alone or only with their wife, it is possible that this variable captures the deteriorating effect on old-age mortality of the lack or absence of adult children and other adults in household.

As discussed earlier in the chapter, Chayanov (Thorner, Kerblay, and Smith 1966) postulated the mortality-lowering effect of household labor capacity and the mortality-enhancing effect of consumer/worker ratio within household. Our findings fail to provide strong empirical support for these theoretical arguments, at least from the viewpoint of microlevel analysis. Number of working-age adults and age composition within a household did not have strong and consistent effects on mortality of elderly men and women in any of the preindustrial rural communities in Europe and East Asia under consideration. As discussed in chapter 5, household structure and composition did not seem to matter much even during an economic downturn, as interactions of these factors with local grain prices were all insignificant.

Individual Status within the Household

We next turn to the effects of marital status and household relationships—demographic and household characteristics measured at individual levels. Table 13.7 presents the estimated effects of marital status

Table 13.7
Estimated effects of marital status on the mortality of ever-married elderly males and females in rural communities: Five historical societies in Europe and Asia

Country and community	Marital status	Male Relative risk	Male p-value	Female Relative risk	Female p-value
China					
Liaodong	Currently married	1.00	—	1.00	—
	Widowed	1.10	0.06	1.23	0.00
Japan					
Shimomoriya and Niita	Currently married	1.00	—	1.00	—
	Widowed	1.50	0.00	1.31	0.01
	Divorced	1.30	0.15	0.82	0.71
	Unclear if widowed or divorced	1.35	0.14	1.26	0.35
Italy					
Casalguidi	Currently married	1.00	—	1.00	—
	Widowed	0.97	0.56	0.82	0.15
Madregolo	Currently married	1.00	—	1.00	—
	Widowed	0.69	0.20	0.23	0.17
Belgium					
Sart	Currently married	1.00	—	1.00	—
	Widowed	1.21	0.03	1.09	0.37

Note: The values are estimated by controlling for the effects of age, price variations, socioeconomic status of household or household head (except for Madregolo), household relationship, presence of children, time period (for Belgium and Japan), and community (for the pooled populations in China and Japan).

on the mortality of elderly men and women in rural settings in the five historical societies.[19] As expected, in most of our populations, widowhood was associated strongly with mortality. In Sart, the mortality of widowed men was significantly higher than that of currently married men. In the two East Asian populations, the mortality of widowed elderly of both sexes was significantly higher than that of men and women whose spouse was alive. Especially in the two northeastern Japanese villages, the loss of spouse for any reason (not only by the death of spouse but also by divorce) seems to have increased the likelihood of death of elderly men.[20]

Turning to the other measures of individual household status, namely, household relationships of individual elderly men and women, we can see from table 13.8 that in the European populations, household relationships did not result in significant mortality differences. On the other hand, in Niita and Shimomoriya, being stem kin of head significantly reduced the mortality of elderly women.[21] Relative to women who were spouse of the head, women who were stem kin (mothers and grandmothers) of the head had much better chances of survival in old age. Studies of mortality in preindustrial Japanese villages found that during adulthood (ages 15–54), women who were the spouse of the stem kin of head (most of whom were daughters-in-law of the head) suffered a much higher mortality compared to women who were the head's wives (Skinner 1993, Tsuya and Kurosu 2000). These results together imply the structural advantage brought about by the privileged status of mothers-in-law in preindustrial rural Japanese household. In these Japanese villages in which marriage was early and universal (Tsuya and Kurosu 1999), if women were robust enough to survive through their years as daughters-in-law and were lucky enough to have their children succeed the headship, they enjoyed a much better chance of survival.[22]

Presence of Children

Table 13.9 presents the estimated effects of presence of children on old-age mortality in the five historical societies. As shown in the table, although the effects are not necessarily significant and consistent, the presence of adult children in general helped elderly men and women counter health risks. The mortality-reducing effects of the presence of children were especially strong and notable in Casalguidi and Madregolo. In Sart, the presence of only married or only unmarried children

Table 13.8
Estimated effects of individual household relationships on the mortality of ever-married elderly males and females in rural communities: Five historical societies in Europe and Asia

Country and community	Relationships	Male Relative risk	Male p-value	Female Relative risk	Female p-value
China					
Liaodong	Head	1.00	—	0.87	0.28
	Spouse of head	—	—	1.00	—
	Stem kin of head	0.53	0.00	1.03	0.70
	Nonstem kin of head	0.92	0.11	1.02	0.84
Japan					
Shimomoriya	Head	1.00	—	0.65	0.29
and Niita	Spouse of head	—	—	1.00	—
	Stem kin of head	1.15	0.21	0.58	0.07
	Nonstem kin of head	0.70	0.60	1.13	0.82
	Servant/other	0.95	0.92	0.46	0.63
Italy					
Casalguidi	Head	1.00	—	1.15	0.75
	Spouse of head	—	—	1.00	—
	Stem kin of head	2.44	0.25	0.98	0.96
	Nonstem kin of head	0.78	0.43	0.75	0.52
	Servant/other	—	—	1.65	0.42
Madregolo	Head	1.00	—	4.40	0.20
	Spouse of head	—	—	1.00	—
	Stem kin of head	0.98	0.97	4.25	0.19
	Nonstem kin of head	1.64	0.64	2.47	0.22
Belgium					
Sart	Head	1.00	—	—	—
	Spouse of head	—	—	1.00	—
	Stem kin of head	0.90	0.58	0.85	0.37
	Nonstem kin of head	1.04	0.82	1.03	0.85
Sweden					
Four Scanian	Head/kin of head	1.00	—	—	—
parishes	Servant/other	1.20	0.57	—	—

Note: The values are estimated by controlling for the effects of age, price variations, socioeconomic status of household or household head (except for Madregolo), marital status (except for Sweden), presence of children, time period (for Belgium and Japan), and community (for the pooled populations in Sweden, China, and Japan).

Table 13.9
Estimated effects of presence of children on the mortality of ever-married elderly males and females in rural communities: Five historical societies in Europe and Asia

Country and community	Presence of children	Male Relative risk	Male p-value	Female Relative risk	Female p-value
China					
Liaodong	None	1.00	—	1.00	—
	Only unmarried	0.85	0.04	0.78	0.00
	Only married	1.02	0.73	0.90	0.10
	Both	1.01	0.92	0.82	0.02
Japan					
Shimomoriya and Niita	None	1.00	—	1.00	—
	Only unmarried	0.92	0.75	1.45	0.08
	Only married	0.78	0.26	1.13	0.44
	Both	0.92	0.75	0.99	0.97
	Child's marital status unknown	1.29	0.32	0.88	0.84
Italy					
Casalguidi	None	1.00	—	1.00	—
	Only unmarried	0.32	0.00	0.37	0.00
	Only married	0.27	0.00	0.46	0.00
	Both	0.33	0.00	0.40	0.00
Madregolo	None	1.00	—	1.00	—
	Only unmarried	0.17	0.00	0.23	0.00
	Only married	0.22	0.00	0.37	0.01
	Both	0.25	0.00	0.35	0.01
Belgium					
Sart	None	1.00	—	1.00	—
	Only unmarried	0.98	0.83	0.89	0.34
	Only married	0.95	0.71	1.01	0.94
	Both	1.17	0.23	1.10	0.46
Sweden					
Four Scanian parishes	No	1.00	—	1.00	—
	Yes	0.87	0.61	1.26	0.29

Note: The values are estimated by controlling for the effects of age, price variations, socioeconomic status of household or household head (except for Madregolo), marital status (except for Sweden), household relationship (except for Swedish females), time period (for Belgium and Japan), and community (for the pooled populations in Sweden, China, and Japan).

reduced the mortality of elderly men with a significant interaction with grain price fluctuations (results not shown). This suggests that the presence of children helped elderly men counter health risks at the time of economic hardships, though coresiding children did not make a notable difference in the likelihood of their survival in ordinary times.

In the East Asian populations, the effects of presence of children on old-age mortality were more limited yet still significant. In Liaodong, the presence of unmarried children helped improve the chances of the survival of elderly men, and the presence of children of any marital status helped reduce the mortality of elderly women. In Shimomor-iya and Niita, in clear contrast to the case of Liaodong women, the mortality of elderly women who had only unmarried children living with them was significantly higher than that of women who had no coresident children, but there was no effect when all or some of the coresident children were married. Given the patrilineal stem family system (not stem family households) prevalent in preindustrial north-eastern Japan, having only unmarried children at home probably indi-cated poverty or disability, whereas in Europe this was a normal consequence of the marriage system. At least, this meant that elderly women in these northeastern Japanese villages did not have any co-resident children-in-law, especially daughters-in-law who could have taken over some of household tasks and responsibilities. This suggests that women with only unmarried children were worse off than women without any children living with them, probably because the burden of taking care of unmarried children without the help from married chil-dren and their spouse outweighed the benefits associated with chil-dren's labor and support.

Summary and Discussion

Life in preindustrial societies was unsure. Only a minority succeeded in surviving to old age. This chapter shows that elderly men and women in rural communities in five historical Eurasian societies were a selected minority who managed to win the race to survive. Once they survived through the years of high health risks such as infancy and childhood and, for women, the reproductive years, they enjoyed life expectancies not so different from those in contemporary posttransi-tional populations.

This study also identified significant East-West differences in the likelihood of survival to and through old age, with the Western European populations (eastern Belgium and southern Sweden) at the high end and the East Asian populations (northeastern China and northeastern Japan) at the low end, with a Mediterranean population, northern Italy, in the middle. We also found that within the two regions (Europe and East Asia) and also within each country, there were differences in the level of survival by environmental conditions and economic development. The likelihood of survival was in general higher in countries and communities with more favorable economic and geographic conditions.

Event-history analyses of mortality responses to local economic variations reveal that old-age mortality in these preindustrial rural populations in Europe and East Asia was in general vulnerable to price fluctuations. When local grain prices increased, the likelihood of death among the elderly also tended to increase, though the degree of mortality responses differed by sex and community.

The multivariate analysis of the mortality effects of household socioeconomic status showed no consistent patterns in the preindustrial European and East Asian populations under consideration. There were no notable differences in old-age mortality by household socioeconomic status, with the exception of two northeastern Japanese villages in which household resources as measured by landholding clearly helped old men and women avoid mortality risks in old age. Similarly, none of the three household structural variables—the number of working-age adults in the household and the compositions of members below age 15 and above age 55—were found to have strong and systematic effects in terms of mortality differences between or among the European and the East Asian populations. This suggests that contrary to what Chayanov argued (Thorner, Kerblay, and Smith 1966), labor capacity and consumer/worker ratio within the household did not strongly affect the mortality of elderly men and women in rural communities, at least in multivariate contexts.

We found stronger and more consistent effects of individual-level demographic and household characteristics on old-age mortality. In most of our preindustrial rural populations, widowhood significantly raised mortality in old age, consistent with findings from many existing studies on the mortality effects of marital statuses in historical and contemporary populations (Cornell 1989; Goldman 1993a, 1993b; Hu and Goldman 1990; March 1912; Neven 1998; Nystedt 2002; Tsuya and

Kurosu 1999). As Cain (1981, 1983) argued in studies of contemporary South Asia, our findings also show that the presence of adult children helped elderly men and women counter mortality risks under various situations in preindustrial rural communities. This was especially the case for the elderly in three European populations.

The life of the elderly in pretransitional rural societies was vulnerable to changes in local economic conditions. However, having coresident spouse and adult children helped these rural men and women survive health risks in old age. In preindustrial Europe and East Asia, the systems of social welfare and social security in the public domain were underdeveloped. Under such circumstances, it was very important for the elderly to have spouse and children living with them, because coresident kin was probably the most important and readily available source of support and protection in old age. Clearly, more studies are needed to account for what old age meant in comparative historical perspective. Intricacies of the causal mechanisms of mortality at the last stages of life also need to be further examined in a multilevel comparative context.

Notes

An earlier version of this chapter was presented at the 2000 annual meeting of the Population Association of America, Los Angeles, March 23–25. Paul Nystedt acknowledges the Swedish Council for Working Life and Social Research, the Swedish Council for Social Research, and the Bank of Sweden Tercentenary Foundation for their support. The authors are especially grateful to Cameron Campbell, Tommy Bengtsson, James Z. Lee, George Alter, Shigemi Kono, and Kiyomi Morioka for helpful comments, and Satomi Kurosu, Hideki Nakazato, and Aoi Okada for assistance and information.

1. Most published quantitative studies of the elderly in the past appear to be descriptive, focusing on living arrangements and presence of kin either with cross-sectional data or simulation (Alter 1996, Hareven 1996, Kertzer and Laslett 1995, Okada and Kurosu 1998).

2. See chapter 2, as well as Bengtsson and Ohlsson (1985) and Galloway (1988).

3. For specifics of these hypotheses, see Goldman (1993a, 1993b).

4. By contrast, according to Lillard and Panis (1996), in the contemporary United States, unhealthy men tend to marry or remarry sooner than healthy men, suggesting the possibility of "adverse selection" in the sense that men in poor health have a stronger incentive to marry.

5. Hermalin, Ofstedal, and Chang (1992) found that in contemporary Taiwan, daughters-in-law play a key role in providing assistance to the elderly.

6. Inclusion of elders at very old ages introduces the selectivity bias because as the upper cut-off age goes up, individual genetic and socioeconomic characteristics of a small minority of robust elderly have increasingly strong influences on the results.

7. For example, in Liaodong, many people who appear to have survived past age 75 were actually people who were dead but whose deaths were not registered. Consequently, their records were carried forward from one register to the next for some years after a death actually took place, but then at some point the record in question was removed from the sequence of registers. Unfortunately, it is impossible to estimate how often this occurred.

8. For details on the definitions and measurements of the Chinese age *sui* and the Japanese NAC age, see chapters 9 and 10 of this book, respectively.

9. The Eurasian Project also covers the city of Venice in Italy. However, because urban-rural differences in the geographic, economic, and socioeconomic features and contexts were too large to allow comparison, this chapter excludes Venice from the analysis.

10. The exception is Madregolo in northern Italy, for which no information on head's occupation or any other household socioeconomic indicators is available.

11. Because the two villages under consideration were almost exclusively agricultural, almost all households were those of peasants. Given the absence of objective criteria to group household landholding, it was measured by a continuous variable. The average landholding of households in which the elderly lived was around 12 to 13 *koku*, while 30 to 36 *koku* represented the top 5 percent. One *koku* is equivalent to approximately five bushels.

12. In the Scania data, household relationship was not recorded in the original sources and therefore had to be inferred from the results of family reconstitutions. Because of this, the only possible distinction for elderly males was between head and nonhead (including former owners of the land, lodgers, and servants). Similarly, for elderly females, the only distinction was between heads' spouses and others. Because the proportions of elderly men and women who fell into the latter categories (nonheads for men and others for women) were very small, household relationship was not included in the analysis for Scania.

13. Given the nature of data, direct estimates of the proportion of dying during infancy are not available for northeastern China and northeastern Japan. See the appendix. Thus, based on previous studies (Lee and Campbell 1997, 58–70; Tsuya and Tomobe 1998), the probability of dying during infancy was assumed to be 0.200 for both sexes in northeastern China and 0.200 for males and 0.180 for females in northeastern Japan.

14. For example, in contemporary Sweden, life expectancy at age 65 is 15.6 for males and 19.2 for females in 1993 (United Nations 1996). In Japan in 1985, life expectancy at age 65 was 15.5 for males and 18.9 for females (National Institute of Population and Social Security Research 2000, 82).

15. Because the expected effects of changes in real wages are opposite those in grain prices (wages went down when prices went up), table 13.4 presents the inverse of the estimated effects (relative risks) of fluctuations in real wages for Scania to make the estimation results comparable.

16. See chapter 11.

17. Campbell and Lee (2000) made a similar point about reasons for the vulnerability of elderly males in Liaodong.

18. In terms of person-years, more than 99 percent of elderly men lived in a household with landholding less than 30 *koku*, whereas more than 99 percent of elderly women lived

in a household with less than 37 *koku*. Hence, virtually no elderly in the two Japanese villages enjoyed mortality near or equal to zero, a logical impossibility.

19. As found by a number of previous studies (Helsing and Szklo 1981, Martikainen and Valkonen 1996, Niemi 1979, Nystedt 2002), the mortality effect of widowhood tends to decrease through time from the death of the spouse. Our analyses estimate the average (general) effect of widowhood.

20. Given the high geographical mobility of the population in Madregolo (Lagazio, Martelli, and Rettaroli 1998), it is likely that widowed elderly women in the community were a highly selective group, as many elderly women would have moved out of the community upon the loss of their husband.

21. Lee and Campbell (1997) found that compared to other male household members, household heads had significantly higher mortality in rural Liaodong.

22. In Liaodong, men who were stem kin of head had significantly lower mortality than men who were heads. Unlike in preindustrial villages in northeastern Japan, in which male household heads passed the headship to their sons and sons-in-law in their mid-50s and early 60s (Okada and Kurosu 1998), men in Liaodong were likely to retain the headship until their death. Under this context, elderly men who were stem kin of head (who were retired fathers or sons of head) were a small minority in exceptional situations. We therefore do not interpret this finding in the text.

14

Agency and Demography: Eurasian Comparisons of Life under Pressure

James Z. Lee, Cameron Campbell, and Tommy Bengtsson

While the immediate causes of all deaths are, by definition, biological, *Life under Pressure* illuminates the important influence of social and economic background on such events. Mortality levels and short-term mortality responses were strongly linked to family and social organization and to political and economic systems. In spite of considerable differences in exposure, resource allocation, and work responsibilities, the overall mortality levels in our widely disparate communities were surprisingly similar. They differed considerably, however, in their mortality responses to short-term stress. Differences in mortality responses by socioeconomic status during bad times were the consequence of differential resources, different entitlements, and differing welfare policies from community to community. Differences in mortality responses by age and gender were similarly the product of microlevel decisions made by parents and families during bad times as to whom to favor or whom to protect. Because these choices were political in the sense that they were negotiated, even contested, decisions by different interested parties, they yield insight into important differences in preferences and politics—into the different aspects of what we call human agency.[1]

It is now commonly recognized that these demographic decisions affect and in turn are affected by the cultural context in which they are made (Carter 1995, Hammel 1990). Culture is not simply an unchanging program that dictates beliefs and practices to passive populations from one generation to the next. Instead, culture provides guides to individuals, families, and communities to interpret their surroundings and defines the range of options normally available to respond. Individuals and families are agents who evaluate and act. The choices they make and their evaluations of the outcomes alter the cultural context experienced by others, expanding or erecting boundaries. Because of this constant feedback—what Giddens (1979) calls "the reflexive

monitoring and rationalization of a continuous flow of conduct"—
cultural context evolves according to human agency, not only across
but within generations.

The agency that affects mortality levels and responses can be conscious or unconscious (Leibenstein 1981).[2] While existing institutions
and customs may constrain or define the range of possible choices, it is
important to distinguish between decisions that require active choices
on how to act and decisions that do not. In *Life under Pressure*, we
describe how many of the differences in mortality levels and mortality responsiveness by socioeconomic status were the product of passive actions in accordance with existing customs and institutions. We
also explain why differences in mortality responsiveness by household
composition and relationship, in contrast, required active decisions by
parents and family about resource allocation and work assignments.
Our holistic approach illuminates the complexity that resulted from the
exercise of passive and active agency and distinguishes in particular
between the more active agency of individuals as household members
from their more passive agency as members of communities and states.

By relating mortality levels and responses to household composition,
and family relationships in our household and relationship models, we
identify and compare how households resolved the competing claims
of different members. Even when patterns of mortality levels and
responses by such broad categories as age and gender were broadly
similar and therefore unrevealing, patterns of differentials between and
within households varied tremendously from one community context to another. Such similarities and differences between communities
point to differences in social and family organization that conditioned
the exercise of agency.

Socioeconomic differences in mortality responses between communities, by contrast, reveal the importance of passive agency and demonstrate how community and state institutions could condition the
impact of economic stress. These actions required proactive efforts by
individuals, communities, and polities but did not require conscious
choices about how to act. Western states organized to protect property
at the expense of the poor, while Eastern states promoted stability even
at the expense of the powerful. The socioeconomic gradient in mortality responses to economic stress was accordingly more pronounced
in the West than in the East. For example, in Casalguidi, according to
table 8.10, homeowners in this Tuscan community were much less vulnerable to rising prices than those who did not own homes. In Scania,

according to table 6.2, a decrease in real wages by slightly more than half after 1815 would increase mortality among the landless by 79 percent, but produced no statistically significant effect on the landed.

Even within the same community, levels and responses varied because household characteristics, especially wealth or more broadly socioeconomic status, defined and constrained the choices to be made. Rising food prices due to poor harvests had opposite consequences for rich and poor households and different consequences even for members of the same household. Poor farmers had nothing to sell and less to consume, and the landless faced lower wages and higher prices. But large landowners could sell their surplus for greater profits. As a result, and as we have seen repeatedly in our analyses, when prices rose, poor and landless households had to decide whose consumption to reduce, while rich households had to choose whom to favor.

Sudden stress, in other words, forced household members to act decisively in ways that were unnecessary in normal times, revealing hitherto unnoticed preferences. In virtually all our communities, with the exception of Scania, most households forced to make choices about the allocation of increasingly scarce resources chose to do so unequally according to unexpected patterns of age and gender bias. In Tilleur, according to table 7.4, as the proportion of children in the household increased and pressure on resources rose, the bias of parents for sons meant that the death rates of female infants and children increased, whereas the death rates of male infants and children did not. Similarly in Ou, according to table 9.4, households confronted by rising rice prices discriminated against their infant daughters but not their infant sons. In Ou as well as Liaodong, such discrimination or protection depended on the presence or absence of maternal intervention. According to table 5.10, children whose mothers were dead were affected disproportionately by rising grain prices.

But while some families, faced with unexpectedly reduced circumstances, might choose to save sons rather than daughters, others faced with unusually favorable circumstances might choose to favor daughters over sons. When grain prices in Casalguidi rose, table 3.5 reveals that middle-class households used their new wealth to benefit female infants and male children, whose mortality actually declined. Similarly, in Liaodong households, according to table 10.10, female child mortality fell as the number of adults increased, while male child mortality remained the same. In Ou, according to table 9.4, wealthier households used their resources to improve the survival chances of infant females and better insulate them against economic stress. Indeed, according to this same table, when a grandmother was available in Ou to provide child care, female infants, but not males, benefited.

Moreover, when times were unusually bad, many patriarchal societies forced men to bear the brunt of such short-term stress. In Liaodong, for example, households responded to poor times by reducing the consumption of males disproportionately. Thus, tables 10.3, 10.4, and 10.5 reveal that when prices rose in Liaodong, male death rates increased more than female death rates, except, of course, among children.[3] Table 9.4 reveals a broadly similar pattern of heightened male sensitivity to short-term stress in Ou. Rice price increases affected male mortality more than female mortality at all ages except infancy. Such behavior was hardly confined to East Asia. In Madregolo in northern Italy, according to tables 3.3 and 3.4, male mortality was much more sensitive than female mortality. In Tilleur in eastern Belgium, males suffered from another form of economic stress. Families facing the pressure of supporting a large number of children sent their eldest sons off to work at unhealthy and even dangerous occupations. As a result, in table 7.5, as the proportion of children in the household increased, so did the mortality of young, unmarried men. Gender roles could cut both ways. Privileges could carry prices that were paid only in bad times.

Not all differences in mortality levels within the household were necessarily the result of conscious decision. Some were simply the unintended consequences of traditional household roles. In Ou, the higher mortality of spouses of stem kin relative to spouses of the head, apparent in table 9.6, was a consequence of the disadvantaged position of daughters-in-law in Japanese society. Conversely, in Liaodong, the higher mortality of household heads or their spouses in tables 10.4 and 10.5 was a likely by-product of the additional exposure to disease that Chinese household heads faced in their role as household leader and representative (Lee and Campbell 1997). Neither Japanese daughters-in-law nor Chinese household heads were required in this respect to think consciously about their behavior. Neither of them therefore necessarily displayed passive or active agency, just acquiescence to customary behavior and institutions.

These new insights comprise the core of our new understanding of life under pressure in Eurasia. We have demonstrated that gender bias was pervasive but subtle. Dichotomization between a patriarchal East and a more gender egalitarian West is no longer appropriate. Mortality responses to short-term economic stress were not merely a function of local ecology and human biology. The exercise of agency by families in both the East and West resulted in unexpectedly gendered patterns of mortality levels and responses. We have also demonstrated that while ageism was universal, age preferences were just as complex as gender preferences. While the mortality responses to economic stress varied by age in every context, the age patterns of response differed dramatically, reflecting differences in priorities. Finally, we have reaffirmed the particularism of power and property. The strength of socioeconomic differences in the West relative to the East reflect the different orientation of states, with Western states focused on the protection of property, and Eastern states focused on power and stability. Such findings demonstrate the importance of the comparative approach, for it is only through such comparison that we can identify similarities and differences in human behavior.

Our approach combines the analytic strengths of demographic and economic history. Previously, demographers have analyzed in detail the role of proximate determinants as mechanisms in shaping demographic outcomes, but have treated the more distal determinants as fixed elements of a static culture that can be taken for granted. Economic historians, meanwhile, have focused on the influence of economic conditions on demographic outcomes, ignoring the intervening mechanisms by which individual and family choices translated economic stress into impacts on specific individuals. In contrast, our holistic, more inductive analysis allows us to distinguish the contentious and, above all, contingent nature of demographic decision making, which was never inevitable, never simply the result of customary practice or the inherent consequence of some universal rationality or principles of human behavior.

At the same time, *Life under Pressure* also reaffirms the importance of systematic empirical comparisons in social scientific discovery.[4] Several of our most important discoveries, in fact, were unanticipated. While we had sought to contrast the favoritism typical of the hierarchical joint Asian family with the reputed egalitarianism of the simple European family, we discovered that at least under pressure, such displays of favoritism were almost universal. While we had designed our individual, household, and relationship models to identify the use of active agency by individuals and households, we also discovered the importance of passive agency due to the different cultural orientation of community practices and actions under pressure. In other words, while we had hypothesized that Eurasian contrasts in mortality behavior would be the result of active agency and microsocial and economic conditions, we instead discovered that passive agency and macro-differences in institutions and customary practices at the community, regional, and even national level were just as important.

This contrast between active and passive agency is demonstrated in our analysis of orphan mortality presented in tables 5.4 and 5.10. While we had expected our results to confirm that orphans in the East survived in larger numbers than their Western counterparts because of the protection afforded them by the Asian joint family system, this turned out to be not the case. If anything, children who had lost a parent were more vulnerable in complex Asian families than they were in simpler Western family systems. Western concepts of charity singled out such orphan children for protection and evidently did a better job than the much-vaunted Asian family safety net. The passive agency of Western charity, in other words, surpassed the active agency of family decision making in protecting this vulnerable population. This is a good example of the social demographic consequences of ideological and institutional contrasts.

Although we ultimately were able to produce a parsimonious, indeed binary, narrative of comparative geographies, this narrative is fundamentally different from what we had initially expected. In contrast to the active and passive agency we had thought were characteristic of Eastern collectivism and Western individualism, we ended up with the discovery of universal patterns of active and passive agency on both sides of the Eurasian continent. In contrast to the reaffirmation of heavy gender bias in the East and less gender discrimination in the West, we ended up identifying examples of age or gender bias in virtually every Eurasian community we studied. We had expected our analysis to confirm the existence of gender bias in the East and gender egalitarianism in the West, not transform our understanding by revealing unexpected patterns of bias in both. We had expected our analysis to reveal as important a role for household size and composition in the West as in the East, not overturn our understanding of familial altruism. Had we used assertion and illustration as our research method, we would have been much less likely to realize that these hypotheses were incorrect. Even had we done so, we would have been hard put to identify an alternative pattern.

Our discovery of these underlying regularities differentiates our work from other efforts to account for complexity and contingency in social history.[5] The traditional approach in social history is to refute generalizations and theories through what amounts to a historical narrative that emphasizes uniqueness and difference (Wong 1997). But while this approach may challenge existing theories, it does not suggest new ones to replace them, only additional confirmation that reality is complex. Our approach, by contrast, not only uncovers exceptions that undermine existing theories; it reveals underlying similarities necessary for the formulation of new ones.

Our results illustrate the importance of formulating and testing hypotheses in comparative historical sociology. Had we carried out a qualitative comparison of the quantitative results from the local histories in chapters 6 through 10, we would have produced a narrative of contrasts that emphasized contingency, explaining the results for each location in terms of its special characteristics. This narrative would very likely have been eminently plausible in the light of the received wisdom about the differences between East and West, if only because our interpretation of the results for each location would have been guided by the received wisdom. By carrying out quantitative comparisons specifically designed to test and possibly reject our hypotheses, not illustrate our theories, we made possible the findings described earlier on the role of agency in accounting for the patterns by age and sex described earlier and the importance of institutional context to patterns of socioeconomic differences.

The process of hypothesis, empirical testing, and revised hypotheses that produced such insights was necessarily iterative. We translated hypotheses about community and household organization into predicted patterns of differentials in mortality responses to economic stress. We then specified the event-history models that would reveal or refute such patterns. To estimate these models, participants had to reorganize their data to construct needed variables. When the data for a community did not allow for the construction of a needed variable, we had to adjust the model. Only when we had estimated models for all communities could we review the results for evidence for or against our initial hypotheses. And when results refuted or at least failed to support our original hypotheses, we proceeded through several more cycles of hypothesis development, model specification, estimation, and interpretation to arrive at our conclusions.

The results of this empirical process, however, demonstrate the dangers of overreliance on deduction or reasoning from first principles to construct or validate social scientific theories.[6] In chapter 5, for example, we discuss the received wisdom from many distinguished social scientists who had deduced from similarities in Eurasian domestic organization a variety of similar demographic behavior (Das Gupta 1997, 1998; Davis 1955; G. W. Skinner 1997). Assuming that similarly structured households behave similarly, they thought that the preponderance of joint households in the East and simple households in the West meant that household savings and household safety nets would be more common in Asia than Europe. Although they provided a variety of quantitative evidence, these consisted of illustrative findings from individual communities rather than rigorous comparison of multiple Eurasian contexts. They used quantitative evidence, in other words, largely as qualitative illustrations. In *Life under Pressure*, we use quantitative evidence systematically to test the underlying assumptions of these claims and show that as in the case of the comparative mortality of orphans, local traditions and institutions often produce different outcomes than these theories would predict.

The Eurasian Project in Population and Family History confirms as well the continuing need for new data and new quantitative and qualitative methods of analysis to produce new social science knowledge and advance new social science theory. Previously, the superficial similarity across contexts in the level and sensitivity of mortality in aggregated analysis had concealed remarkable variation by age, gender, socioeconomic status, household composition, and relationship. Thus, although the data were sufficient to reveal aggregate demographic responses to short-term economic stress, they could not illuminate the role of human agency that produced these responses. No amount of reanalysis and reinterpretation could have overcome these data limitations. That we could do so in *Life under Pressure* was largely a function of research design and the application of event-history analysis on individual-level longitudinal data. These data and techniques, however, also have their own limitations. Overcoming them will require even larger and more ambitious comparisons with more data and finer sieves.

For the moment, our understanding of *Life under Pressure* remains constrained in at least two respects: our data are still insufficient, and our methods are limited. A more refined and therefore more revealing analysis requires far more data than were available for these analyses. While the data presented here were sufficient to demonstrate the broad outlines of the differences between East and West and illuminate the roles of active and passive agency in shaping mortality responses, they were not enough to support the finely grained comparisons within and across populations required to test more hypotheses about the mechanisms underlying specific phenomena.[7] More data would allow for more detailed categorizations, better accounting for the interactions among multiple influences, and more conclusive statistical tests. This is not simply an issue of number of observations. We need data from additional communities to better understand the role of macrolevel context and assess the importance of passive agency. The relatively small number of communities in this analysis limited us to broad comparisons between East and West and precluded more detailed comparisons of communities according to their social organization and economic basis.

The methods we applied in comparisons within and between communities are equally limited. Our inability to pool data from different countries when estimating models restricted our analysis to broad patterns in the directions of effects and precluded detailed comparisons of the strengths of effects. Pooling the data not only from different communities but also from different countries would have allowed finely grained comparisons of the magnitudes of effects. Such comparisons would have provided insight into the mechanisms that underlay the phenomena we observed by yielding definitive conclusions about the relative importance of different influences in different contexts.

Nevertheless, these initial results from a much larger project on Eurasian Population and Family History allow us to appreciate the diversity of human experience, not the fictitious uniformity of classic grand social theory. In contrast to the classic preference for sweeping, often monocausal narratives of inevitability, we have produced alternative narratives that emphasize the importance of specific institutions or configurations of relationships and thus highlight the contingency of human history. In contrast, therefore, to their emphasis on the uniformity of history, our narrative emphasizes the diversity of human experience. Our work, in other words, brings back the importance of history and empirical historical research for social science and social theory.

In future volumes, we will identify similar patterns of universal agency in the reproductive culture, spatial mobility, and marital patterns of our communities. Deliberative demographic decision making was a crucial element in marriage, reproduction, and migration patterns.

Notes

We thank George Alter and Noriko O. Tsuya for their comments on previous drafts of this chapter.

1. We distinguish agency from action in the sense that agency implies a conscious decision to act. We also distinguish active from passive agency in the sense that active agency requires a decision how to act, while passive agency does not.

2. Leibenstein (1981) was among the first to make this distinction in demography. While we recognize that this distinction can create an artificial separation between norms and institutions, on the one hand, and so-called active decision making, on the other, we think that Leiberstein's categories are useful: they reinforce the degree to which institutions and elites can have a major impact on mortality responses to economic pressure, and they distinguish the microlevel of conscious choice and contested decisions from actions that are more closely tied to the macrolevel of institutions and norms. See Carter (1995), however, for a sweeping critique of Leibenstein (1981) and our approach.

3. In Lee and Campbell (1997), we describe in detail how female children died in far larger numbers than male children during periods of high grain prices due to sex-selective infanticide.

4. Little (1995) reaffirms this case, "What [the social sciences] must share in common is a commitment to the requirements of empirical evaluation. For to offer a scientific account of a domain of phenomena is implicitly to claim that the account is truthful and justified; and in order to provide rational support for a body of theory. We need to make skillful use of available empirical data in evaluation of our hypotheses and interpretations. Science is not simply a set of competing interpretations; it is rather a set of positive assertions about the world which must be justified on the basis of rigorous interrogation of empirical evidence."

5. See, for example, the discussion in Little (2000).

6. *Life under Pressure* nevertheless relies on deduction, but in the form of statistical theory, for the tools used to measure relationships and assess results. We use quantitative methods not to describe phenomena but to measure the relationships between variables within communities, which we then compare. Measurement of the relationship between mortality and economic stress requires application of estimation techniques originally developed by statisticians. Assessment of the chances that a relationship apparent in the data is real, and not an artifact of chance variation in the data, requires the use of hypothesis tests derived by statisticians from probability theory. In future work, we expect to make use of related but more advanced techniques to carry out definitive comparisons of patterns of coefficients between communities.

7. We need more and also better data. More refined measures of socioeconomic status, for example, would help clarify its role in conditioning the mortality impacts of short-term stress. In these analyses, we relied on a crude categorization of occupation. Direct measures of household income, wealth, or consumption obviously would have been preferable. Better measures of community-level context would also have facilitated analysis. Local harvest yields, for example, might be a better measure of short-term stress than grain prices, since local prices do not necessarily reflect local conditions.

Appendix   Sources and Measures

Cameron Campbell
in collaboration with Satomi
Kurosu, Matteo Manfredini,
Muriel Neven, and Tommy
Bengtsson

Reconstruction of household strategies for responding to stress and smoothing consumption by the analysis of differentials in vital rates requires detailed data on economic conditions, household characteristics, and individual demographic behavior. Such data are rare, even for contemporary societies. Data from different societies similar enough in organization and content to permit direct comparisons are even more unusual. A distinguishing feature of the Eurasia Project in Population and Family History is that participants have located appropriate sources from the eighteenth and nineteenth centuries for communities in Belgium, China, Italy, Japan, and Sweden; transcribed them into databases; and generated comparable measures of socioeconomic status, household context, and demographic behavior.

In this appendix, we describe these sources. We begin by identifying requirements for data content and organization implied by our interest in the substantive questions in chapters 1 and 2. Next, we review the sources commonly used for the study of household context and demographic behavior in past times, and show that only longitudinal, nominative household registers meet the requirements of the study. We then introduce the household registers from eastern Belgium, northeast China, northern Italy, northeast Japan, and southern Sweden. We summarize their origins and administrative purposes, as well as the procedures by which they were compiled. We also identify known shortcomings relevant to the analysis of mortality, including problems with the recording of the population at risk and the recording of demographic events.

We then describe the measures that participants constructed from these data to investigate the issues raised in chapters 1 and 2. Although population registers in the five societies were originally established for different reasons and therefore varied in terms of format and content, we have identified measures of socioeconomic and household context that can be constructed from the available data and meaningfully compared. For each measure, we specify the hypotheses about household behavior that it is intended to test and describe the conclusions that could be drawn from possible outcomes. In situations where the interpretation of a measure varies from one society to the next, we provide clarification.

Needs

Longitudinal data are necessary for the analysis of demographic responses to economic stress because they permit measurement of the influence of current economic conditions on future demographic behavior. For data to be considered longitudinal, they must track members of the population through time and record changes in their characteristics as they take place. The time at which demographic events occurred should also be available, either directly from the original data or by supplementation from other forms of data. From such data, the characteristics of the population at risk of a demographic event at any point in time may be reconstructed and rates for different segments of the population computed. Ideally, the data should be updated on a continual basis, so that the dates of events are recorded as they occur. In practice, by making use of the methods for analyzing longitudinal microdata, it is possible to analyze less detailed data that specify only whether an event occurred in a particular time interval.

To test hypotheses about strategies for response to economic stress in past times, the longitudinal data must be at the level of the individual. Each possible strategy leads to a distinct set of expectations about the pattern of differentials in the demographic effects of changing economic conditions. Though aggregate longitudinal data such as series of prices and vital rates may be used to document relationships between economic conditions and demographic behavior, they do not have the resolution needed for finely grained comparisons of the responses of different segments of the population. In contrast, application of the event-history techniques to data on individuals allows differentiation of demographic responses to economic stress. We may compare responses by socioeconomic status and household characteristics.

Details on the households in which individuals live are also necessary. The household, the most basic unit of social and economic organization in the past, typically had primary responsibility for responding to short-term economic stress. Individual standard of living accordingly depended on aggregate characteristics of the household such as size, income, wealth, and age and sex composition. Since decisions about the allocation of resources and responsibilities resulted from interactions between household members, standard of living also depended on location in the household and the nature of relationships to other members. Differentials in the response to economic stress by household context reveal which members households favored or discriminated against when it became necessary to reduce consumption and adjust allocations.

To measure stress, time series describing economic conditions in the community covered by the social and demographic data must be available. Series may consist of prices or wages, or both. If a price series is available, it should be for a locally important necessity, for example, a staple grain. Such series serve as indicators of economic conditions in past times because fluctuations in the prices of staple foods and other necessities were the main source of short-term variations in real income. If a wage series is available, it should be for a locally important form of labor. In a rural setting, for example, a series consisting of the wages of agricultural day laborers would be preferred. Ideally, it should also be deflated by a price series to produce an estimate of real incomes.

Additional community-level measures of stress are useful. Winter temperatures, for example, conditioned household needs for fuel for heating. Comparison of the mortality response to winter temperature reveals which social groups were especially vulnerable because they could not afford adequate heating. Supplementation of agricultural price data with climatic data on temperatures and rainfalls, meanwhile, helps establish whether price fluctuations were due to harvest variations or other changes in the market induced by external events such as war or changes in trade policy.

The data must be geographically specific, at least to the extent that demographic events are known to have taken place in the area covered by the economic time series. If it is not possible to determine whether the events recorded in the data actually took place in the area covered by the economic time series, then results from the analysis of the effects of economic fluctuations are not meaningful.

Coverage of the population must be complete in at least three respects. First, the data must record the entire community, not members of particular socioeconomic strata. Since we test hypotheses by examination of demographic responses to economic fluctuations by socioeconomic status, household context, and individual characteristics, data that record only segments of the population are inadequate. Second, for any given time, it must be possible to determine from the data the population that is actually present in the area and at risk of experiencing a demographic event. The population accordingly either has to be closed, or entries and exits have to be recorded. Third, recording of the timing of demographic events must be complete. Incomplete recording of demographic events leads to inaccurate estimates of rates. The count of deaths in the numerator will be too low. If records of vital events are used to exclude individuals who have died, departed, or disappeared otherwise from further consideration, incomplete recording of deaths and other may also inflate the denominator.

Comparison of Sources

Studies of economic historical demography typically make use of one of five types of sources. Parish registers have been used extensively to reconstruct time series of demographic rates for a variety of mainly European populations. Vital statistics have also been used extensively to study demographic trends in Europe and elsewhere, especially during the mortality and fertility declines. Censuses have proved to be a rich source for the study of households in past times. In some cases, application of indirect methods of demographic estimation to them has yielded estimates of demographic rates as well. Genealogies have been used most commonly to estimate long-term trends in demographic rates in parts of China. They have also been used extensively to study relationships between family structure and demographic behavior in nineteenth-century Germany. More recently, household registers have been used to study relationships between household organization and demographic behavior in a variety of Asian and European countries in the eighteenth and nineteenth centuries. In this section, we describe each of these five sources and assess their strengths and weaknesses for the purposes of this study.

Parish Registers

Parish registers typically consist of records of the baptisms, marriages, and burials in a community. They are remarkable for their time depth. In some locations, they were compiled on a continuous basis from the sixteenth century well into the nineteenth. At the very least, they provide counts of vital events in a community. Since the population at risk tends not to vary much from year to year, time series constructed directly from these counts have been used to study short-term fluctuations in demographic behavior as well as seasonality. Where the population at risk is known or can be approximated, time series of rates may be estimated and used to study long-term trends in demographic behavior.

Family reconstitution has allowed analysis of parish register data to move well beyond the analysis of trends and fluctuations in demographic rates. Records often provide sufficient detail to link together the entries for an individual's baptism, marriage, and burial if they took place in the same community. Information from one entry can be used to supplement another; for example, the date from an individual's baptismal record can be used to calculate ages of that person at marriage and death. Where baptismal records provide sufficient detail on parentage, links can be made from one generation to the next, and fertility histories constructed.

Parish registers alone do not meet our criteria. As summarized in table A.1, they have two major weaknesses. First, although they allow for family reconstitution, they almost never provide details on households. In other words, though they may identify who is related to whom, they do not specify who lives with whom. Second, they almost never include details on movements into and out of the area. Since the communities they cover are rarely closed to migration, it is often difficult to determine who is actually present in the community and at risk of experiencing a demographic event. Studies of mortality are typically restricted to infancy and childhood, when it can be safely assumed that

Table A.1
Comparison of features of sources for historical demography

	Parish registers	Vital statistics	Censuses	Geneal-ogies	Household registers
Longitudinal	×	×		×	×
Individual level	×		×	×	×
Detail on households			×		×
Geographic specificity	×	×	×		×
Complete community	×	×	×		×
Population at risk		×	×	×	×
Timing of vital events	×	×		×	×

the recently baptized are still present, or else to adults for whom both baptismal and marriage records exist (Wrigley et al. 1997, 210–211).[1] Analysis of the mortality of more mobile segments of the population, including adolescents and unmarried adults, is usually impossible.

Vital Statistics

In the last half of the nineteenth century and the first half of the twentieth, many governments established systems to register births, deaths, and other demographic events, largely replacing parish registers.[2] Because vital statistics generated from these new systems typically summarize the demographic behavior of complete national, regional, and in some cases local populations, they have proved an invaluable resource. For example, most attempts to model the age pattern of human mortality have relied on vital statistics data (Coale and Demeny 1983, United Nations 1982). Such data have also been used in studies of the demographic transition in developed countries, providing a basis for systematic international comparisons of the declines of fertility and mortality (Coale and Watkins 1986, Preston 1976).

Vital statistics series, however, are not useful for the purposes of the study. Although they are longitudinal and cover complete communities, they provide no detail on individuals and households. Since event-history approaches are impossible, comparison between population subgroups is limited to categories defined by statistical bureaus in their original tabulations. Typically, rates were tabulated by gender, age, and region. In some cases, they were tabulated by ethnicity, marital status, or occupation. Only rarely were rates tabulated by combinations of characteristics.

Censuses

A census is a snapshot of an entire population taken at a specific point in time. Though the efforts of states to enumerate their populations have a long history, censuses in their current form began to appear only in the eighteenth century. As governments recognized their value, the practice spread quickly, and by the end of the late nineteenth century, most of what are now the developed countries carried them out on a regular basis, usually every ten years. Censuses typically attempt to gather such basic information as name, age, sex, and occupation for all members of a target population. They usually organize individuals by residential household and record relationship to the household head. In some cases, they include details on past demographic events, for example, timing of marriage or the survivorship of a mother's births.

Analyses of censuses have advanced our knowledge of social and household organization in the past. They have been used extensively to compare distributions of occupation, education, and household structure and other characteristics along dimensions such as region and ethnicity (Watkins 1994). In some cases, where questions were asked about past demographic behavior, application of indirect methods has yielded estimates of cross-sectional variation in infant and child mortality (Preston and Haines 1991). Where series of censuses exist, tabulations from them have been used to construct time series. For example, Preston and McDonald (1979) and Ruggles (1998) have studied long-term trends in divorce in the United States by making use of census data.

Censuses, however, are inappropriate for our study. At heart, they are not longitudinal. Time intervals between censuses tend to be so long and migration rates so high that it is rarely possible to follow individuals and households through time. Further complicating record linkage is the tendency on the part of individuals to change their name or report other information such as age inconsistently. Conversely, multiple individuals often share the same name or have other characteristics in common. An additional problem with censuses is that they rarely provide detail on the timing of demographic events. While in theory this problem may be resolved by linking individual records to birth and death certificates (Kitagawa and Hauser 1973), in practice such linkage is difficult.

Genealogies

Genealogies record ancestry. In their most basic form, they consist of little more than names of family members arranged by generation and parents' identity. Typically, they also include information on the dates of birth and death. Such data allow for the reconstruction of fertility histories. In some cases, they provide dates of marriage. Occasionally, they also include additional details on migration, occupation, and notable achievements, for example. They are typically retrospective, compiled based on the recollections of family members. Only rarely are they prospective, in the sense that events are recorded as they occur. In terms of time depth, they vary considerably. While most cover only the most recent seven or eight generations, roughly two centuries, some follow families for many centuries.

Because of their time depth, genealogies have proved especially valuable for analysis of time trends during periods when census and vital statistics are not readily available. In China, for example, they have been used to reconstruct trends in the demographic rates of lineage members, usually from the Ming dynasty (1368–1644) onward (Liu 1981, 1983, 1985, 1992, 1995b), but in some cases from several hundred years earlier (Liu 1995a, Yuan 1931, Zhao 1997b). Where genealogies from different locations in the same country are available, they also allow for regional comparisons. Thus, Knodel (1988) used German genealogies not only to study trends in demographic behavior during the eighteenth and nineteenth centuries, but also to link regional variations to differences in social, cultural, and economic context.

Genealogies are nevertheless inappropriate for our study. Most important, they do not provide details on household context. Like the results of family reconstitutions from parish registers, they reveal how individuals were related to each other, but they almost never specify with whom they lived. Because they usually do not specify residence, it is not always possible to be confident that individuals are actually in the location covered by the economic and other time series used in the analysis. Finally, they often neglect to record certain types of individuals. This problem is especially serious in Chinese genealogies (Harrell 1987). Those who died young, never married, or never had children were less likely to be recorded. Daughters are typically omitted, and details on wives are often sketchy.

Household Registers

Household registers are continuous records of the residential context and demographic behavior of the members of a community. Although registers have existed in one form or another in China for at least two thousand years, they began to appear in other countries only in the seventeenth and eighteenth centuries. Typically, they appear in one of two forms. In some situations, a master document exists containing entries for each household. As events occur in a household, annotations are made to its entry. After annotations have accumulated to the point where further updates to entries are difficult, a new document is created with the most current information from the existing document. In other situations, the population was repeatedly enumerated, usually annually but in some cases at less frequent intervals. Each new enumeration included details on demographic events that had occurred since the previous one. Individuals and households were listed in roughly the same order in successive enumerations, allowing them to be followed over time.

They also typically record details on the current socioeconomic status of the household. Commonly, registers record the occupation of the household head. In some cases, they may also record the occupations of other household members. In some societies, they even include details on tenure arrangements and landholding. In other societies, it is possible to link to other sources that contain such information.

Household registers combine elements of parish registers, genealogies, and censuses. Like parish registers and genealogies, they are inherently longitudinal. They follow individuals through time, recording the timing of demographic events such as marriage, childbirth, and death. Like parish registers, they usually record only the events that occur within the community. Like censuses, household registers provide detail on residence. Individuals can be linked to their households, and contextual variables may be constructed. Household registers also resemble censuses in that they attempt to provide complete records of entire communities. They are superior to censuses, however, in that they record the composition on a continuous basis, not an occasional one. For this reason, they avoid one of the most serious problems of parish registers, because they allow the population at risk of experiencing a demographic event to be reconstructed with confidence.

These sources do suffer from limitations that affect their suitability for certain types of analysis. The most serious is that they often fail to record short-term migrations into and out of the target population. Thus, registers may not always provide a completely accurate picture of the population present in the community. Individuals who are in the area for only a few weeks or months may never appear in the register. Similarly, those who reside in the area but are absent for a short time may never be identified as having been away. Infants who die soon after they are born may also be missing, for similar reasons, so that there is no record of their existence. While such problems are most common in the registers that record the population at fixed intervals, they occur sometimes in registers updated continuously.

They sometimes also fail to provide precise information on the timing of demographic events. Again, although this problem is especially common in registers updated at fixed intervals, it also exists in some of the registers that are updated continuously. Registers updated at fixed intervals may simply show that an event has occurred since the last update but not specify when. Continuous registers may record the year or month of an event but not the day. Such problems are often dealt with by supplementing the material in the household registers with data from other sources that record exact dates, for example, parish registers.

In spite of such limitations, household registers are the only source suitable for this study. Because registers record the characteristics of both households and individuals on a continuous basis, they allow for differential demography through the application of event-history techniques. The hazard of mortality is treated as an outcome measure, and a regression approach used to measure its association with characteristics of the individual and his or her household and community. Depending on what additional data are available, demographic rates and responses to economic stress may be differentiated by such social and economic characteristics as occupation, landholding, and religion. The ability to link individuals to other members of their household, meanwhile, makes it possible to study the effects of contextual features of the household.

Household registers may perhaps best be thought of as the historical demographic analogue of contemporary longitudinal or panel surveys. Decades ago, sociologists recognized that the cross-sectional nature of the surveys that were then the mainstay of the field imposed numerous serious limitations on the types of inferences that could be drawn from the collected data. To test key theories of social stratification, socialization, and attitude formation, it would be necessary to follow individuals through time. The longitudinal studies initiated in response, most notably the Wisconsin Longitudinal Study (WLS), have proved to be rich sources for the analysis of American society and continue to this day, in spite of the narrow geographic focus evident in their names. The massive, nationally representative panel studies that followed, including the National Longitudinal Surveys of Youth (NLSY), the Panel Study of Income Dynamics (PSID), and the National Survey of Families and Households (NSFH), are now among the most commonly used sources in empirical, quantitative economic and sociological research.

Available Data

The authors of this book have identified eighteenth- and nineteenth-century household registers from eastern Belgium, northeast China, northern Italy, northeast Japan, and southern Sweden that meet all of the above criteria. Either all of the necessary information is available in the original source, or additional details could be added by linking to auxiliary sources. Though it has been laborious and time-consuming, teams have transcribed the contents of the registers and related sources into databases, checked and corrected the information, and organized everything to produce the variables necessary for analysis.

The locations for the study were selected based on the availability of data. For a variety of reasons, including the complexity of maintaining a registration system, historical household register data are rare. Beyond the countries already involved in this study, eighteenth- and nineteenth-century registers exist in only a few other locations, mainly in northern Europe. Countries in which register data for a few communities had already been transcribed into a database around the time when the study was initiated were rarer still.

Although all teams began entry and analysis of data before they became involved in the project, participation has nevertheless entailed a substantial additional commitment of time and resources. Each team has spent a considerable amount of time on exploratory analysis, estimation of proposed and final standard models, and the write-up of results. In most cases, they have had to generate new variables from their existing databases to meet the requirements of the models. In several cases, they even had to supplement existing data by transcribing new material. Either information necessary to construct specified variables was not in the original database and had to be added to existing observations, more observations were necessary to estimate the models successfully, or more study sites were felt necessary to increase confidence in results.

Although registration systems covered entire countries or, in the case of Liaodong in northeast China, a country-sized region, this study could analyze data on only a small number of populations in each country. The reasons for this are again practical, not theoretical. First, although registers were supposed to be compiled for every community in the countries or regions that had them, not all of the register series survive intact. Because gaps in a series create problems for demographic analysis and examination of the effects of economic fluctuations requires reliable data for many years, only communities for which largely unbroken sequences of registers were available were eligible for entry and analysis. In most of the countries, this narrowed the field of possible sites considerably.

Second, transcribing the contents of the original registers into computer databases is labor and resource intensive. Since it is only in the past two decades that statistical methodology and computer technology have advanced to the point where creation of databases is worthwhile, most efforts to transcribe data began only recently. As a result, even in countries where large numbers of registers have survived intact, coding is complete for only a small number of populations. All of the participants are currently engaged in the transcription of additional register series, and future comparative analysis will make use of much larger numbers of populations from each country.

The samples are, accordingly, not representative of entire countries in a statistical sense. We do not intend for calculations made from their data to be treated as point estimates of parameter values for the populations of their respective countries. For that to be possible, far more communities would have to be in each country's sample. Moreover, the communities would need to have been selected at random, and every community would need to have had a chance of ending up in the sample. As it stands, the numbers of communities in each sample are so small and geographically concentrated that not even by application of weights would it be possible to generate plausible estimates for entire countries.

The registers are nevertheless valuable for comparative analysis. They provide examples of the behavior of households in known geographic, economic, and social contexts, summarized in chapter 4 and described in detail in the local history chapters. Household systems can be treated as another community contextual feature, like topography, climate, land tenure, and so forth. We can identify the roles of such contextual features in conditioning responses to economic stress by comparing communities and tying variations in demographic behavior to variations in context. For example, differences in the demographic behavior of two communities that are similar on every dimension of context but household system must be attributable to differences in household system.

Individual-level household register data are far superior to aggregate data for comparative analysis. Hypotheses about the response of households to changing economic conditions in past times typically generate predictions about how differentials in demographic rates in a community will evolve. Since register data allow for differentiation of demographic responses by socioeconomic status and household characteristics, they allow for such predictions to be tested. Aggregate data, by contrast, allow comparison of responses only between communities, not within them.

The time depth of available data, summarized in table A.2, varied. In general, the period immediately before the demographic transition is covered, while the transition itself is not. Thus, available registers cover the early or mid-nineteenth century for all of the populations and the eighteenth or nineteenth century for some of them. In northern Italy, registers for earlier periods exist but are not used in this analysis because they are still being entered. In the Scanian parishes in southern Sweden, many socioeconomic and demographic data for both earlier and later periods have already been entered and the results from their analysis published elsewhere (Bengtsson 1989, 1993b, 1999; Dribe 2000; Lundh 1995), but key details on household composition so far have been entered only for the period specified in the table. In the Liaodong region in northeast China, registers from before 1789 exist and have been entered but were not used in this analysis because they organize individuals by lineage, not residential household (Lee and Campbell 1997).

The total amount of data available for each country, measured in person-years in table A.2, also varied. One person-year of observation corresponds to one person observed for one year. For example, coverage of 500 people for 50 years would yield 25,000 person-years of observation. Differences between countries reflect variation between them in the time depth of the available data, the number of populations coded, and the size of each population. The large numbers of person-years and deaths available are useful primarily for the finely grained analysis they permit of the factors that influenced mortality. For most of the populations under consideration, sufficient person-years of observation and deaths were available to differentiate death rates and their sensitivity to economic conditions by socioeconomic status and household context. Problems may still arise for certain socioeconomic groups and never married who simply are too few to be included into the analyses. Adding them with other groups is not an alternative, since the groups will then be too heterogeneous.

Table A.2
Household register data used in the analysis

Population	Time Period Begin	End	Total years[a]	Average population size	Person-years	Deaths	Frequency of update
Belgium							
Sart	1812	1900	89	2,133	189,798	3,754	Continuous
Polleur	1847	1900	54	1,324	71,477	1,361	
Tilleur	1847	1866	20	3,541	70,830	1,291	
Limbourg	1847	1866	20	3,343	66,856	849	
China							
Dami	1789	1909	45	759	34,169	951	Triennial
Daoyi	1792	1906	72	3,013	216,939	4,896	
Feicheng Yimiancheng	1792	1909	69	1,587	106,172	2,227	
Gaizhou	1789	1885	54	1,384	74,715	1,350	
Gaizhou Manhan	1792	1837	12	1,417	16,500	338	
Gaizhou Mianding	1792	1858	27	1,640	43,070	807	
Niuzhuang Liuerbao	1789	1825	27	2,156	56,810	937	
Italy							
Casalguidi	1819	1859	40	2,402	95,398	2,485	Continuous for vital events; annual for household data
Madregolo	1800	1883	80	572	42,735	999	Same as for Casalguidi
Venice	1850	1869	19	5,361	101,864	2,546	Continuous

Japan							
Niita	1720	1870	146	472	68,844	1,643	Annual
Shimomoriya	1716	1869	145	346	50,197	1,199	
Sweden[b]							
Hög	1829	1867	39	456	18,258	302	Continuous
Kävlinge	1829	1867	39	492	19,672	399	
Halmstad	1829	1867	39	618	24,727	506	
Sireköpinge	1829	1867	39	581	23,252	424	

[a] Total years may be smaller than the difference between begin and end years because of missing data.
[b] Data for Scania extend further back but give fewer details about household size and composition. The analysis in the local history chapter goes back to 1766.

Origins

Although the household registers from these five societies recorded very similar information, their origins and purposes varied, as did the procedures for updating them. As a result, each country's registers have distinct strengths and weaknesses for the study of mortality that need to be taken into consideration in the comparison of results. To provide context for the later discussion of these strengths and weaknesses, here we summarize the basic features of the registers from each country. Note that here we focus on the registers themselves, not the communities they cover.

The Japanese registers are from Niita and Shimomoriya, two villages in the Ou region in the northeast of the country. The registers came from a system first established in 1638 to prevent the entry and spread of Christianity by ensuring that village residents were all associated with approved temples. These registers, generally known as *shumon-aratame-cho* (SAC), were updated on an annual basis by copying entries from the previous one and editing them as necessary. Updates appear to have been carried out in the third lunar month, usually in March or April. The SAC had a number of uses, and in many locations they were maintained until 1872, when the Meiji government recognized religious freedom and replaced the SAC with the new *koseki* registration system.

In Niita and Shimomoriya in Ou, the SAC were used almost entirely for administrative purposes. Indeed, they did not even record information on religious affiliation. They were actually referred to as *ninbetsu-aratame-cho* (NAC). While SAC registers in many locations were compiled on a de jure basis, identifying locations of legal but not necessarily actual residence for individuals, the ones used for Niita and Shimomoriya were de facto.

The Chinese registers recorded residents of seven state farm systems in Liaodong in what is now Liaoning province in the northeast of the country (Lee and Campbell 1997). They were primarily descended from Han Chinese who had migrated from Shandong province in the seventeenth century. All were members of the Eight Banner system, a civil and military organization that was part of the Qing state. The registers were first compiled in the early eighteenth century and were updated every three years until after the fall of the Qing in 1911. The Qing relied heavily on the registers for administration of the state farms. The state used them to limit population movements onto or out of state lands. The state also used them to identify men eligible for military service, corvee labor, and occupations or special privileges available only to members of the Eight Banner system.

As a source, the Eight Banner registers were distinct from and superior to the *baojia* registers used elsewhere in China (Skinner 1987). Because the state relied on the registers for administration of its farms, it devised a remarkable system of internal cross-checks to ensure consistency and accuracy. First, it assigned every person in the population to a residential household (*linghu*) and registered them on a household certificate (*menpai*). Then it organized households into clans (*zu*) and compiled annually updated clan genealogies (*zupu*). Finally, every three years, it compared these genealogies and household certificates with the previous register to compile a new register. During these updates, which took place after the Lunar New Year, they deleted and added people who had exited or entered in the last three years and updated the ages, relationships, and occupations of those people who remained. Each register, in other words, completely superseded its predecessor.

Data for the northern Italian populations were derived from two different sources. Data for the villages of Casalguidi and Madregolo come from *Status Animarum*, local censuses drawn up for religious purposes by the parish priest on an annual basis, usually around Easter. They appear to have been de facto records of the resident population at the time of compilation. Although they exist from as early as the sixteenth century onward in some locations, in the communities studied they are usable only from the mid-eighteenth century on because of large gaps in the earlier years. At least in some cases, compilation continued until the beginning of the twentieth century. Although the analysis in chapter 8 ended in 1883, the last *Status Animarum* in Madregolo was actually compiled in 1914.[3] Since the census-like *Status Animarum* recorded household composition, occupation, and certain other characteristics, the Italian participants obtained exact dates of vital events such as birth, marriage, and death by linking to entries in parish registers. Linkage between successive *Status Animarum* identified individuals who entered or exited the population between compilations, as well as changes in the composition of households and the characteristics of individuals. Since precise dates were not available for events inferred from linkage of *Status Animarum*, relevant analyses made use of discrete-time methods.

The data from the city of Venice are from a population register known as the *anagrafe*, maintained for administrative purposes by the local government from 1850 to 1869. In the registration system, each household was represented on a form, a *fogli di famiglia*. It listed household members and included socioeconomic characteristics such as religion and occupation. The forms were updated with annotations on a continual basis to reflect entrances and exits of household members, as well as changes in status for those remaining in the household. Although registers were compiled for the entire city, only the material for certain districts has been entered and analyzed.

The data for Belgium are from a series of population registers compiled during the nineteenth century. So far, series are available for two villages in the Ardennes, Sart and Polleur, a small town, Limbourg, and an industrial suburb of Liège, Tilleur. In terms of their organization and content, the Belgian registers most closely resemble the ones from Venice. In a particular year, a register was opened. It recorded details on households and the individuals living in them, including their socioeconomic characteristics. Information in the register was updated on a continual basis by adding annotations to each household's entry. When annotations accumulated to the point that further updates became awkward, the register was closed, and a new one containing only current information was opened. For example, new registers were opened for Sart in 1843, 1846, 1866, 1880, and 1890. To supplement the data on the timing of vital events, the Belgian team linked in additional information from birth and death registers.

The data from the Scanian parishes in southern Sweden are in some ways the most complex, having been created by the integration of several different sources. The core of the Scanian data used in the analysis here consists of catechetical examination registers from 1829 onward. These were essentially household registers. Clergymen relied on them when examining parishioners' knowledge of the Bible to identify who was eligible to be tested. They provide details, updated at least once a year, on household and family characteristics, as well as on migration. The registers also list place and time of birth of all individuals and include the numbers of servants and lodgers present in each household. In a few cases, they also describe retirement contracts. They do not, however, include details on the size and type of the farm held by a household. They also underreport births that followed by an early death.

These core data have therefore been supplemented from several other sources. Data on the occurrence of vital events were supplemented from records of baptisms, burials, and marriages recorded in local parish registers from the mid-seventeenth century until the end of the nineteenth century. Additional information regarding farm size and tenure arrangements was added from poll tax registers (*mantalslängder*) and land registers (*jordeböcker*). These were available from the seventeenth century onward, though their quality was poor in the early years.

Completeness

In spite of the compilation procedures just described, none of the household registration systems completely succeeded in recording its entire target populations. Especially in the Asian populations, registers were most likely to exclude the very young. In the registers from the Japanese region of Ou, children were typically not recorded until they survived to the time of the first annual update of the registers following their birth. The registers accordingly provide little information on children in their first few months of life. This problem was not unique to the Asian populations: the Italian *Status Animarum* appear to have missed babies who were born and died in between compilations. Information for such infants, however, could be obtained by linkage to information on baptisms and burials in parish registers.

Such problems were more serious in the Liaodong registers (Lee and Campbell 1997). Children typically first appeared in the second or third triennial register following their birth, by which time they were already several years old. If they died before they were registered, they left no record of their existence. Additionally, even though coverage of females appears to have been complete after marriage, many of them were never recorded while they were daughters. If they died without ever marrying, in many cases there was no record of their existence. Analysis of daughters is therefore restricted to the populations where their records were more complete.

In the European populations, there were two types of problems. First, in certain locations, infants may not have been recorded in the household registers until they were old enough to be baptized. There is strong reason to think that this was the case in Sweden (Bengtsson 1999, Bengtsson and Lundh 1994). This problem has been dealt with by linking to birth and death entries in parish registers. Fortunately, baptism typically occurred fairly soon after a birth, within weeks or at most a few months; thus, the numbers of alive but unrecorded infants are much smaller than in China and Japan. In Sweden, the possibility of emergency baptism (*nöddop*) of an apparently unhealthy infant also contributed to the completeness, though not all births and deaths were recorded.

Second, older adolescents and young adults were often covered poorly from the time they left their parents' household to the time they settled down and formed a household of their own. If during this time they were servants or hired hands, their record in the household where they worked was cursory, and the information might not be sufficient to establish a link to their natal household. It could be difficult to tell, therefore, whether a boy or girl who had left his or her parents' household was still in the area but serving in another household, or had left the area completely and therefore no longer at risk. For this reason, analysis was carried out separately for adults who had married and those who had not.

Certain types of deaths were less likely to be recorded. One limitation common to all de facto household registers was that when individuals died outside the community, their deaths were not recorded. This does not pose a serious problem, however, because household registers also allow individuals who have left the community to be excluded from consideration from the time of their departure. The caveat remains that if the individuals who left were selected according to some characteristic that was also related to their health, death rates computed for the population remaining in the community might differ from the ones that would be observed if no one was able to leave.

A second common problem was with the recording of mortality in the first years of life. In the Japanese registers from Ou and the Chinese registers from Liaodong, those who died before their parents registered them left no record of their existence. Infant mortality rates from the Ou household registers therefore reflect the experience of infants who have already survived the first few months of life, and are lower than the ones that would be observed if infants were recorded from the time of birth. Similarly, infant mortality rates cannot be calculated at all from the Liaodong household registers, and child mortality rates tend to be based on the small numbers of children who were registered at a relatively early age. In the Scanian data, meanwhile, there may be no records of infants who died before they could be baptized. Because baptism tended to take place shortly after birth, however, this would affect estimates of neonatal mortality.

In Liaodong, China, an additional problem was that there were small numbers of individuals who survived to absurdly advanced ages. Apparently the deaths of certain individuals were never recorded, so that they were carried forward in the registers indefinitely as if they were still alive. Such individuals accounted for only a small fraction of observations in the age ranges where analysis was actually carried out; thus, excluding their records from consideration does not affect the results.

Recording of the timing of death was also less precise in the Asian populations than in the European populations. While exact dates of death were recorded for many individuals who survived infancy in certain Japanese registers, in particular the NAC from Ou, such precision was not universal. In other Japanese registers, it was known only that an individual had died in the year between updates of the register. As a result, the Ou analysis uses discrete-time event-history methods in which the dependent variable is the likelihood of dying between the current and the next register.

The Liaodong registers have a similar problem. They do not provide a precise date of death, only an annotation—the Chinese character *gu*—to indicate that an individual had passed away in the three years since the previous update. The Liaodong analysis, accordingly, also makes use of discrete-time event-history methods. In this case, the dependent variable is the likelihood of dying in the three years between the current register and the next one. The length of the time interval necessitates the use of what is referred to as a complementary log-log link to yield coefficients comparable to those from the continuous-time methods applied to the European data and the logistic regression applied to the Ou data.

Models

The strength of the household registers is that in addition to recording deaths and the population at risk, they allow for the construction of variables that describe the community and household contexts of individuals, as well as their socioeconomic status. Here we describe the variables constructed for use in the analysis. We begin with the measures common to all of the models: age, sex, and short-term economic stress. We cover the remaining variables in order of appearance in the individual, household, and relationship models. We start with the measures of socioeconomic status in the individual model, proceed to the aggregate characteristics of the household in the household model, and conclude with the individual measures of household context in the relationship model.

Age and Sex

Teams carried out separate analyses for eight combinations of age group and sex. We defined four age groups. The first consist of infants in the first 24 months of life. There is considerable empirical evidence to suggest that mortality determinants during this period differ from those later in childhood. The second consists of children between the ages of 2 and 15. We chose 15 as the upper boundary because that is the age at which children in European societies began to leave the natal household in large numbers to work elsewhere. In the Asian societies, it was often the age at which large numbers of individuals began to marry. The third age group consisted of adults aged 15 to 55. The upper boundary was selected because that is the age at which many household heads in Scania began to retire. Probably not entirely by coincidence, it was the age at which men in the Liaodong registers began to be annotated as "old" or "retired."

In all populations, European and Asian, there is strong reason to think that ages used in the analysis are exceptionally accurate by the standards of much historical and even contemporary demographic data. Because individuals were followed through time—in many cases, all the way from birth—their birth date or age at time of first observation could be used as the basis for calculating their age at every subsequent point in time. The ages used in the analysis, in other words, are not self- or kin reported. They are not subject to the problems of erroneous recollection common to self-reported ages in censuses or kin-reported ages on death certificates.[4]

The populations differed in the way age was measured. In the Liaodong populations, age was measured in the customary manner in *sui*. In this system, individuals were 1 *sui* at the time of their birth. Afterward, their age was incremented annually at the time of the Lunar New Year. In the study of Ou, the age used in the analysis, referred to as the NAC age, was based on the number of registers an individual had appeared in. Individuals were 1 year old in the first register after their birth and aged 1 year in every subsequent register. In the European study populations, in contrast, age was measured by the number of birthdays an individual had survived through. Individuals were aged 0 for the first 12 months of life, 1 for the next 12, and so on.

Age-specific death rates and other life table values are accordingly not precisely comparable because it is impossible to compute them for exactly identical ranges in all countries. For example, $_nq_x$, the probability of dying within n years for an individual currently aged x, has slightly different interpretations in the life tables for the Liaodong, Ou, and European populations. In a life table based on Chinese *sui*, it represents the chances of dying within the next n years for someone currently aged x *sui*. Such an individual could be x − 2 or x − 1 Western years of age, depending on when during the year they were born. In a life table for the Ou populations, $_nq_x$ refers to the probabilities of death within five years of people whose NAC age is x. Such individuals could be x − 1 or x Western years of age.

Such considerations turn out to be serious ones in only very specific situations. For the Liaodong analysis, to produce age ranges approximately equivalent to the Japanese and European ones, it sufficed to define age groups to begin and end at ages in *sui* one year higher than in the Western age groups they are to be compared to. Adulthood, for example, lasts from ages 16 to 55 *sui* in the Liaodong analysis. Old age lasts from 56 to 75 *sui*. As long as mortality changes slowly with age, such an approximation is adequate to produce results that can be compared to the European ones. The Japanese age ranges may also be treated as reasonable approximations to the Western ones. It is only when mortality changes very rapidly with age and the age range of interest is narrow that serious problems arise. For that reason, even though we compare patterns of differentials and price effects in childhood mortality between our Asian and European populations, we avoid detailed comparisons of the underlying mortality levels.

Short-Term Economic Stress

Table A.3 summarizes the measures of short-term stress. In four of the five countries, price series for key local crops, usually grains, were used. In Liaodong, sorghum prices were used.[5] In Ou, rice price series were used.[6] In Italy, wheat and in one case corn prices from nearby cities were used. For the eastern Belgian populations, the prices of both oats and rye were used. Oats were the grain of choice for the poor, especially in hard times. Rye, however, was an important commercial

Table A.3
Economic data

Population	Content of series	Geographic area covered	Frequency of reporting	Coefficient of variation (SD/Mean)	% of crisis years (> 2 × Median)
Belgium					
Sart	Basket of staple foods	Verviers and Liège prices, completed with Belgian prices when missing	Annual (1811–1900)	0.042	0
Tilleur and Limbourg	Real wages	Belgium	Annual (1840–1900)	0.213	0
China					
Liaodong farm systems	Sorghum prices	Prefecture	Monthly	0.394	3.4
Italy					
Casalguidi	Wheat	City market	Three times weekly	0.188	0.0
Madregolo	Wheat and corn	City market	Monthly	0.392	4.8
Venice	Wheat				
Japan					
Niita and Shimomoriya	Rice	Neighboring domain	Yearly	0.354	9.8
Sweden					
Four Scanian parishes	Real wages	Local	Yearly	0.089	3.3

crop. In Scania, the price of rye, the most important local crop, was used to deflate a wage series described later.

Prices were usually from nearby markets, and therefore are likely to reflect local conditions. The rice prices used for Niita and Shimomoriya in Ou were from the neighboring domain of Aizu. The prices for the Tuscan village of Casalguidi came from Pistoia. Those for Madregolo came from Parma, which was only 20 kilometers away. The Belgian prices were also local, although prices from the city of Verviers and for the country as a whole were also experimented with. The Liaodong prices were from Fengtian prefecture, the administrative district in which the populations were located, which partly corresponds to the contemporary province of Liaoning.[7]

In Scania, a local real wage series was constructed to measure short-term economic stress. It is derived from locally reported wages and prices that were to be used for government-constructed market price scales to value payments in kind for the various counties. They recorded the prices of important crops in the various locations in each county, including rye and wages for day laborers. On the assumption that fluctuations in day laborer real wages were generally reflective of fluctuations in income for the landless populations as a whole, the real wage series was constructed by deflating them with the price of rye.[8] Since nominal wages varied only very slowly, the short-term changes stem from price variation. We therefore expect the farmers to respond in the opposite way as the landless.

Teams mostly used annual prices measured at the time of the fall harvest or prices averaged over the harvest year. For example, the rice prices used in the analysis of Ou were collected each year in October or November. During the period analyzed in this book, the rye prices used for Scania were collected each year in the fall (Jörberg 1972, 12). The eastern Belgian oat prices were a calendar year average, as were the northern Italian prices. They were lagged so that the effects of future harvests were being used in an analysis of current behavior. In Liaodong, three-year averages of monthly prices were used. The population was enumerated on a triennial basis, and it could be determined only whether individuals died between one interval and the next.

When appropriate, participants experimented with detrended time series, usually with a Hedrick-Prescott filter.[9] Removal of trends serves two purposes. If long-term trends reflect secular increases or decreases in real income, failure to remove them would make it difficult to identify the mortality effects of short-term fluctuations. A statistical association between prices or income and mortality might reflect either short-term mortality increases caused by fluctuations in economic conditions or a secular mortality trend associated with rising or falling living standards. For the countries for which prices alone are available as a measure of stress, detrending also helps account for currency inflation or deflation. Without detrending, the same price level at different points in time might correspond to different standards of living.

To compare the effects of proportional changes in wages or prices, natural logs are used instead of raw prices. Estimated relative risks were adjusted to reflect the changes in the chances of dying when grain prices rose or real wages fell by 10 percent. Raw prices and wages are not used because estimated relative risks for them would reflect the effects of a one-unit change in their level. These would not be comparable from one society to the next because the units used to measure prices and quantities of grain vary. For example, the relative risk of mortality associated with a one tael per *shi* increase in grain prices in the Liaodong populations could not be compared meaningfully to the one associated with a one lire per quintal increase in the price of wheat in the Italian populations.

Participants also experimented with other measures of short-term stress. For Italy, the effects of seasonal and year-to-year variation in climate have been investigated. For Belgium, the influences of temperatures, which are expected to have had a major effect on harvest outcomes, have been studied. A variety of price series from both nearby Verviers and for the country as whole were experimented with. In both northern Italy and eastern Belgium, the consequences of epidemics were studied through the introduction of variables indicating whether or not one was under way. Care was taken, of course, to ensure that epidemics were identified from external evidence, not from the data themselves. For Japan, the short-term effects on the mortality of household members of the loss of a household head were examined. Results from these investigations are discussed in the local history chapters or in other published work.

We estimated three sets of models: the individual, the household, and the relationship. Table A.4 presents the variables in each model, while A.5 presents the variables included in each age group. Broadly speaking, the individual model focused on the effects of socioeconomic status, where possible of the individual, the spouse, or the parent, but in some cases the household. The household model included aggregated characteristics of the household, in particular, the number of working-age adults and the proportion young and old. The relationship model described household context from the perspective of the individual. Below, we discuss each of these models in more detail.

Individual Model

In most of the populations, the occupation of the household head was the major measure of socioeconomic status. Preferable measures of socioeconomic status, for example, education or household income, were not available. Because neither prestige scores nor average incomes were available for these historical populations, occupation was specified categorically. To the extent possible, the categories were constructed so that the occupations within them were reasonably homogeneous in terms of both skill requirements and type and level of income.

In the Liaodong analysis, occupation of self, husband, or father was used instead of occupation of head. Four categories were constructed from the dozens of statuses that appeared in the registers. In ascending order of status, they were adult male, artisan, soldier, and local official. Adult males were a residual category that accounted for the vast majority of men. They are presumed to have engaged largely in agriculture.[10] Artisans were individuals whose title indicated the mastery of a craft. In addition to receiving some income from the state, they had marketable skills.[11] Soldiers were the equivalent of enlisted men in the Eight Banner military hierarchy. They had incomes in cash and in kind from the state that should have helped insulate them from economic fluctuations. Local officials consisted mainly of leaders in the local Banner administrative and military hierarchies who had substantial state incomes in cash and in kind and who held power over the disposition of state resources. This category also includes a small number of individuals with purchased official titles indicative of substantial wealth, as well as some individuals such as scribes whose job titles indicated difficult-to-acquire skills such as literacy.

For Italy, occupations were available in Casalguidi and Venice, but not in Madregolo. For Casalguidi, chapter 8 identified four additional categories. The remaining categories, in roughly ascending order of socioeconomic status, were day laborer, sharecropper or other farmer, artisan or shopkeeper, and nobleman or rich landowner. Day laborers worked as hired hands on land owned by others. Sharecroppers rented their land and paid in kind. The remaining farmers were a mixture

Table A.4
Variables used in each model

	Individual		Household		Relationship	
	Level	Re-sponse	Level	Re-sponse	Level	Re-sponse
Socioeconomic status (SES)	×	×	×	×	×	×
Period	×	×	×	×	×	×
Real prices or wages	×	×	×	×	×	×
SES × price or wage interactions		×		×		×
Household characteristics						
Number of adults			×	×		
Proportion less than age 15			×	×		
Proportion older than age 55			×	×		
Household characteristics × price interactions				×		
Individual characteristics						
Parents						
Father present					×	×
Mother present					×	×
Neither present					×	×
Siblings						
Number of older brothers age 1 or older					×	×
Number of older sisters age 1 or older					×	×
Number of younger brothers age 1 or older					×	×
Number of younger sisters age 1 or older					×	×
Previous birth interval						
First birth					×	×
Missing/uncertain					×	×
24 months or less, infant dead					×	×
24 months or less, infant alive					×	×
24 months or more, infant dead					×	×
Age of mother						
Unknown					×	×
Below 20					×	×
20–25					×	×
30–34					×	×
35–39					×	×

Table A.4
(continued)

	Individual		Household		Relationship	
	Level	Re-sponse	Level	Re-sponse	Level	Re-sponse
Marital status						
Widowed					×	×
Divorced					×	×
Previously married, can't tell if widowed or divorced					×	×
Household relationship						
Head					×	×
Spouse of head					×	×
Stem kin of head					×	×
Nonstem kin of head					×	×
Servant/other					×	×
Presence of children						
Only unmarried					×	×
Only married					×	×
Both married and unmarried					×	×
Individual characteristics × price interactions						×

of small landowners and renters with other land tenure arrangements. Artisans earned their living independently, by practicing a craft that required learned skills. In terms of their economic standing, they were highly heterogeneous; some were poorer than sharecroppers and tenants. Noblemen and rich landowners are self-explanatory. In the estimation of the standard models, the latter three categories were collapsed together because the total numbers of observations were small. As for Venice, the analysis distinguishes day laborers, wage earners, artisans and shopkeepers, and finally the wealthy. Both Casalguidi and Venice included additional categories for individuals whose occupations were not recorded.

In eastern Belgium and Scania, it was possible to construct a number of distinct occupational categories. In eastern Belgium, five were created. In ascending order of status, they were cultivator, day laborer, artisan or industrial worker, and functionary. Additionally, there was a very small residual category consisting of miscellaneous occupations.

Table A.5
Variables included in the models for each age group

	0–1	2–14	15–54 Ever married	15–54 Never married	55–75 Ever married	55–75 Never married
Socioeconomic status (SES)	×	×	×	×	×	×
Period	×	×	×	×	×	×
Real prices or wages	×	×	×	×	×	×
SES × price or wage interactions	×	×	×	×	×	×
Household characteristics						
Number of adult members	×	×	×	×	×	×
Proportion less than age 15	×	×	×	×	×	×
Proportion older than age 55	×	×	×	×	×	×
Price interactions	×	×	×	×	×	×
Individual characteristics						
Grandfather present	×	×				
Grandmother present	×	×				
Parents						
Father present	×	×				
Mother present	×	×				
Neither present	×	×				
Siblings						
Number of older brothers age 1 or older	×	×				
Number of older sisters age 1 or older	×	×				
Number of younger brothers age 1 or older	×	×				
Number of younger sisters age 1 or older	×	×				
Previous birth interval						
First birth	×	×				
Missing/uncertain	×	×				
24 months or less, infant is dead	×	×				
24 months or less, infant is alive	×	×				

Table A.5
(continued)

	0–1	2–14	15–54		55–75	
			Ever married	Never married	Ever married	Never married
Age of mother						
Unknown	×					
Below 20	×					
20–25	×					
30–34	×					
35–39	×					
Marital status						
Widowed			×		×	
Divorced			×		×	
Previously married, can't tell if widowed or divorced			×		×	
Household relationship						
Head	×	×	×	×	×	×
Spouse of head			×		×	
Stem kin of head	×	×	×	×	×	×
Nonstem kin of head	×	×	×	×	×	×
Servant/other		×	×	×	×	×
Presence of children						
Unmarried only			×		×	
Married only			×		×	
Both married and unmarried			×		×	
Interactions of above with price	×	×	×	×	×	×

In the primarily rural Scanian parishes, individuals were distinguished according to the nature of their tenancy and the size of their farms. Farm size was measured in *mantal*.[12] The Swedish team created four separate categories: the landless; the semilandless, tenants on noble land, and freeholders and Crown tenants. The semilandless were those who had less than one-sixteenth of a mantal, while freeholders and Crown tenants had at least one-sixteenth of a *mantal*. The landless and semilandless paid rent in several different ways, the most important of which appears to have been labor but to some extent in cash as well. Freeholders and Crown tenants generally paid their taxes or rent in cash, while the noble tenants quite often paid rent in kind, usually with labor.

In Ou, socioeconomic status was represented by household land-holding. The land owned by the household (*mochidaka*) was measured in *koku*. Japanese *koku*, like Swedish *mantal*, actually measured the productive capacity of a piece of land, not its area. According to a national standard, one *koku* was supposed to be enough to support one person. For landowners, *honbyakusho*, this variable was a measure not only of wealth but also of social status and potential income. Tenant farmers who worked land held by others, *mizunomi*, had 0 recorded for this variable.

Household Model

Analysis examined the effects of the number of working-age adults, the proportion of household members aged 15 or below, and the proportion of household members aged 55 or above. These measures were not in the original data; they had to be generated after linking together the records of coresident individuals. In the Liaodong, northern Italian, and Ou cases, the populations were recorded completely at regular intervals, and it was a simple matter to count the individuals in each household and compute the proportions in the age groups of interest. In the European populations, where the populations were enumerated infrequently but the timing of entrances into and exits from the household was recorded, constructing these measures was more complex. Essentially, every time the household structure changed, the variables for household characteristics had to be recomputed. These new variables values were used until the composition changed again.

Relationship Model

To examine effects of relationship to household head, we categorized individuals according to whether they were household heads, their stem kin, their nonstem kin, or other coresident but unrelated individuals. Which category served as the reference depended on the age group and sex under consideration. The indicator variables were generally easy to construct because relationship to the household head was recorded in the original data in most registers. Of course, countries varied in the diversity of relationships. Nonstem kin of the head were more common in the societies that had more complex households: northern Italy, Ou, and especially Liaodong. In eastern Belgium and Scania, most households were simple, and nonstem kin of the head were rare. In the Scanian data, household relationship was not even recorded in the original sources and had to be inferred from the results of family reconstitutions. Our expectation is that heads and their stem kin were more privileged than nonstem kin.

To measure marital status, we introduced categorical variables indicating whether individuals were currently married, divorced, or widowed. The reference category consisted of the currently married. These variables were straightforward to construct since marital status was either recorded in the original data as a characteristic of the individual or could be inferred easily by examining whether a spouse was also present in the household. In Liaodong and some of the European populations, whether women were daughters, wives, or widows was specified in the original data. Whether men were currently married could be determined by checking to see if they had a spouse present. Whether an unmarried man was a widower could be determined only by examining his past marital history. The Ou data were similar. In general, we expected the currently married to be less vulnerable than the widowed and divorced.

Measures of the presence or absence of particular kin varied by age group. In every case, they were not in the original data and had to be constructed by record linkage. For children, the emphasis was on measuring the effects of presence of parents and siblings. For each of the four combinations of father and mother present or absent, one indicator was constructed. The omitted category was both parents present. We expected children to be adversely affected by the absence of one or both parents. As for sibling composition, indicators were constructed for whether older sisters, older brothers, younger sisters, and younger brothers were absent.[13] We do not have strong priors for the effects of these variables. Older siblings may have helped provide care. Both they and younger siblings, however, may have competed for limited resources.

We also investigate the importance of biomedical factors in infant and child mortality with categorical variables for the length of the previous birth interval and the outcome of the previous birth. We distinguish six situations. The reference consists of situations where the preceding birth interval is longer than 24 months and the infant is still alive. There is one category each for infants who are first births and infants for whom the preceding birth interval cannot be constructed. The remaining three categories consist of infants born after birth intervals longer than 24 months where the preceding birth has died, and infants born after short birth intervals according to whether the pre-ceding birth is still alive. We expect infants born after short birth inter-vals to be more vulnerable than those born after long ones.

For adults and the elderly, the effects of the presence of children were examined. Rather than assume linear effects of number of chil-dren, we specified four categorical variables. These corresponded to the situations where no children were present, only married children were present, only unmarried children were present, and a mixture of married and unmarried children were present. The reference category consisted of adults with no children present. In general, we expected the elderly with unmarried children to have been best off because they did not need to compete with a child-in-law or grandchildren for attention and care. Those with no children present should have been worst off because they had no one coresident to provide care and support.

Conclusion

In this appendix, we began with a review of the data needs for a study of relationships between economic conditions, household organization, and demographic behavior in past times. We argued that such a study required longitudinal, individual-level nominative data that included information about household characteristics and socioeconomic status. It also had to be possible to link such data to measures of stress, most likely time series of prices or wages. We argued that of the five types of sources commonly used for economic historical demography, only household register data met the specified needs.

Household registers are unique as a source in many respects. Like censuses, they record characteristics of the household and allow mem-bers to be linked together. Unlike censuses, registers follow individuals and households through time. In contrast with genealogies and other sources, they often provide data on socioeconomic status, in the form of occupation or else land tenure and farm size. Such data, of course, tend to be less detailed, and there are almost never any data on income or consumption. Registers can also be linked to community-level infor-mation on local conditions, economic or otherwise.

The participants in this study have already assembled and tran-scribed a prodigious quantity of household register data, setting the stage for an empirical analysis focused on the issues in chapters 1 and 2. Using the event-history methods to estimate the models just described, we differentiate demographic responses to stress by household context and socioeconomic status. From the results, we can test hypotheses about how households dealt with stress in past times. By taking such an approach and comparing responses within communities, we avoid the ecological fallacy that plagues attempts to make inferences by comparing aggregate responses of communities with different characteristics.

Notes

1. In the latter cases, the baptismal record is necessary to calculate age. The marriage record, meanwhile, establishes presence in the community since migration after the formation of a household was relatively uncommon.

2. Some countries had established vital registration systems even earlier. Sweden's began in 1749.

3. Gaps in the data for Madregolo between 1883 and 1914 precluded their use.

4. The tendency of individuals to misreport their own age in censuses, or the ages of their deceased kin on death certificates, has led to such peculiar phenomena as a spurious racial crossover in mortality rates at later ages in the United States (Preston et al. 1996). In the United States, age-specific death rates calculated from numerators based on kin-reported ages on death certificates and denominators based on self-reported ages in the census suggest a pattern in which white death rates are lower than black ones in infancy, childhood, and adulthood but higher in old age. Analysis of mortality among the elderly using death certificates linked to earlier census and other records suggests that the apparent black advantage at later ages is the spurious result of race differences in the prevalence of age misreporting.

5. While previous work has shown that the prices of several major grains including wheat, millet, corn, and sorghum were highly correlated with each other and with birth and death rates (Lee, Campbell, and Tan 1992), sorghum was the most important of these crops according to sources on local history.

6. Strictly speaking, these are not market prices but rather exchange rates between rice and silver set by the domain government. See chapter 9 for details.

7. Unlike the series used for most of the other populations, the Fengtian prices used for Liaodong were not from a single, specific market. They are from a system that recorded the lowest and highest market prices for key grains observed every month in the prefecture. Low prices were used in the analysis because they are likely to have reflected conditions in producer areas, while high prices reflected conditions in consumer areas. See Lee and Campbell (1997).

8. For a discussion of alterative measures, see Bengtsson and Dribe (1997).

9. See the local history chapters for discussions of which, if any, techniques were applied for each. Detrending with an unweighted moving average was avoided because the entrance into and exit from the window of extreme values can have a strong effect. An apparent fluctuation in a smoothed series may be due simply to proximity to an extreme value, and their application may introduce new and spurious cycles into the smoothed

series. The Hedrick-Prescott filter has the attractive property series in this respect though is not free from problems (Harvey and Jaeger 1993).

10. Only occupations connected to service in the Eight Banners were identified. If an individual had a private occupation, whether as a merchant, moneylender, or craftsman not in Banner service, it was not recorded. In the predominantly rural populations that make up most of the Liaodong data, this is unlikely to have been much of a problem. Even today, the vast majority of the populations in these areas are engaged exclusively in agriculture, and interviews with elderly residents suggest that nonagricultural occupations were even rarer in the distant past.

11. Some of the more common occupations in this category were blacksmith (*kezijiang*), dyer (*ranjiang*), tailor (*caifeng*), and bowmaker (*gongjiang*).

12. This was not a measure of actual surface area but rather productive capacity. Two pieces of land of the same size might have different *mantal* ratings depending on a number of factors. The same piece of land at different points in time might also have different *mantal* ratings if there had been changes in productivity.

13. Counts were not used because preliminary investigations on the data from Liaodong and other countries suggested effects were not linear.

References

Aalen, Odd O. 1978. "Nonparametric Inference for a Family of Counting Processes." *Annals of Statistics* 6:534–545.

Abel, Wilhelm. 1966/1980. *Agricultural Fluctuations in Europe: From the Thirteenth to the Twentieth Century.* London: Methuen.

Alam, Nurul. 1995. "Birth-Spacing and Infant and Early Childhood Mortality in a High Fertility Area of Bangladesh: Age-Dependent and Interactive Effects." *Journal of Biosocial Science* 27.4:393–404.

Alam, Nurul, and Patricia H. David. 1998. "Infant and Child Mortality in Bangladesh: Age-Specific Effects of Previous Child's Death." *Journal of Biosocial Science* 30.3:333–348.

Alfani, Guido. 1920. *Un secolo di osservazioni meteoriche: contributo allo studio della climatologia italiana.* Florence: Tipografia Barbera.

Allen, Robert. 2000. "Economic Structure and Agricultural Productivity in Europe, 1300–1800." *European Review of Economic History* 3:1–25.

———. Forthcoming. "Real Wages in Europe and Asia: A First Look at the Long-Term Patterns." In *New Evidence of the Standard of Living in Pre-Industrial Europe and Asia*, eds. Robert Allen, Tommy Bengtsson, and Martin Dribe. Oxford: Oxford University Press.

Allen, Robert, Tommy Bengtsson, and Martin Dribe, eds. Forthcoming. *New Evidence of the Standard of Living in Pre-Industrial Europe and Asia.* Oxford: Oxford University Press.

Allison, Paul D. 1984. *Event History Analysis: Regression for Longitudinal Event Data.* Beverly Hills, Calif.: Sage.

Alter, George. 1988. *Family and the Female Life Course: The Women of Verviers, Belgium, 1849–1880.* Madison: University of Wisconsin Press.

———. 1992. "Theories of Fertility Decline: A Nonspecialist's Guide to the Current Debates." In *The European Experience of Declining Fertility, 1850–1970: The Quiet Revolution*, eds. John R. Gillis, Louise Tilly, and David Levine. Oxford: Basil Blackwell, 13–27.

———. 1996. "The European Marriage Pattern as Solution and Problem: Households of the Elderly in Verviers, Belgium, 1831." *History of the Family* 1.2:123–138.

———. 1999. "Vieillir dans les ménages d'une ville industrielle: l'impact de l'âge de migration (Verviers, début du XIXe siècle)." *Annales de Démographie Historique* 2:9–29.

————. Forthcoming. "Reproductive Strategies in Europe and Asia before the Demographic Transition." In *Prudence and Pressure: Reproduction in Europe and Asia, 1700–1900*, eds. George Alter, Noriko O. Tsuya, and Wang Feng. Unpublished ms.

Alter, George, Catherine Capron, Muriel Neven, and Michel Oris. 2002. "When Dad Died: Household Economy and Family Culture in Nineteenth Century East Belgium." In *When Dad Died*, eds. Renzo Derosas and Michel Oris. Berlin: Peter Lang, 401–432.

Alter, George, Lisa Cliggett, and Alex Urbiel. 1996. "Household Patterns of the Elderly and the Proximity of Children in a Nineteenth Century City, Vervier, Belgium, 1831–1846." In *Aging and Generational Relations over the Life Course*, ed. Tamara K. Hareven. Berlin: Walter de Gruyter, 30–52.

Alter, George, Laurel L. Cornell, Hideki Nakazato, Cheryl S. Jamison, and Michel Oris. 1997. "Household Formation Systems Matter for the Lives of Older People." Paper presented at the annual meeting of the Social Science History Association, Washington, D.C., October 17–19.

Alter, George, Muriel Neven, and Michel Oris. 2002. "Individuals, Households and Communities Facing Economic Stresses: A Comparison of Two Rural Areas in 19th Century Belgium." In *Family Structures, Demography and Population: A Comparison of Societies in Asia and Europe*, eds. Muriel Neven and Catherine Capron. Liège: Laboratoire de Démographie, 185–210.

Alter, George, and Michel Oris. 1997. "Mortality and Migration in East Belgium during the Industrial Revolution: Town and Countryside Perspectives." Population Institute for Research and Training Working Paper 97-11. Bloomington: Indiana University.

————. 1999. "The Access to Marriage in 19th Century East Belgium." In *Marriage and Economic Conditions in the North European Countryside since 1400*, eds. Isabelle Devos and Liam Kennedy. Tielt: Brepols, 133–151.

————. 2000a. "Mortality and Economic Stress: Individual and Household Responses in a Nineteenth-Century Belgian Village." In *Population and the Economy*, eds. Tommy Bengtsson and Osamu Saito. Oxford: Oxford University Press, 335–370.

————. 2000b. "Early Life Conditions and the Decline of Adult Mortality in the Belgian Ardennes, 1812–1890." Paper presented at the Max Planck Institute for Demographic Research, Rostock, April 28, 1999. Revised May 29, 2000.

Alter, George, Michel Oris, and Göran Broström. 2001. "The Family and Mortality: A Case Study from Rural Belgium." *Annales de Démographie Historique* 1:11–31.

Alter, George, Michel Oris, and Paul Servais. 1999. "Prices, Crises and Mortality in 19th Century East Ardennes." Indiana University Population Institute for Research and Training Working Paper 99. Bloomington: Indiana University.

Alter, George, Noriko O. Tsuya, and Wang Feng, eds. Forthcoming. *Prudence and Pressure: Reproduction in Europe and Asia, 1700–1900*, George Alter, Noriko O. Tsuya, Wang Feng, et al. Book manuscript submitted to MIT Press.

Åmark, Klas. 1915. *Spannmålshandel och spannmålspolitik i Sverige 1710–1830*. Stockholm: Isaac Marcus.

————. 1961. *Sveriges statsfinanser 1719–1809*. Stockholm: P. A. Norstedt & Söners Förlag.

André, Robert, and José Pereira-Roque. 1974. *La démographie de la Belgique au XIXe siècle.* Brussels: Université Libre de Bruxelles.

Arriaga, Eduardo E., and Peter O. Way. 1988. "Determinants of Excess Female Mortality." *Population Bulletin of the United Nations* 21–22:45–54.

Aruga, Kizaemon. 1943. *Nihon no kazoku-seido to kosaku-seido* (Tenant farming and family system in Japan). Tokyo: Miraisha.

Balassa, Bela. 1981. *The Newly Industrializing Countries in the World Economy.* New York: Pergamon Press.

Bandettini, Pierfrancesco. 1957. *I prezzi sul mercato di Firenze dal 1800 al 1890.* Turin: Industria Libraria Tipografica Editrice.

Banggaard, Grethe. 2002. "Fattigforsorgen på landet 1763–1894: Fem sogne i Skåne." Lund Papers in Economic History No. 75. Lund: Lund University, Department of Economic History.

Banti, Alberto M. 1989. *Terra e denaro: una borghesia padana dell'Ottocento.* Venice: Marsilio.

Barbagli, Marzio. 1984. *Sotto lo stesso tetto: mutamenti della famiglia in Italia dal XV al XX secolo.* Bologna: Il Mulino.

———. 1990. "Sistemi di formazione della famiglia." In *Popolazione, società e ambiente: temi di demografia storica italiana (secc. XVII–XIX).* Bologna: Cooperativa Libraria Editrice Universit di Bologna, 3–43.

Barclay, George W., Anley J. Coale, Michael A. Stoto, and James Trussell. 1976. "A Reassessment of the Demography of Traditional Rural China." *Population Index* 42.4:606–635.

Bardet, Jean Pierre, Katherine A. Lynch, Geraldine P. Mineau, Michael Hainsworth, and Matthew Skolnick. 1981. "La mortalité maternelle autrefois: une étude comparée (de la France à l'ouest de l'Utah)." *Annales de Démographie Historique*: 31–48.

Barizza, Sergio. 1987. "Il comune di Venezia. 1806–1946. L'istituzione. Il territorio." *Guida-inventario dell'Archivio municipale.* Venice: Comune di Venezia.

Bauman, Kurt J. 1999. "Shifting Family Definitions: The Effect of Cohabitation and Other Nonfamily Household Relationships on Measures of Poverty." *Demography* 36:315–324.

Beekink, Eric, Frans van Poppel, and Aart C. Liefbroer. 1999. "Surviving the Loss of the Parent in a Nineteenth-Century Dutch Provincial Town." *Journal of Social History* 32:641–670.

Bellettini, Athos. 1987. *La popolazione Italiana: un profilo storico.* Turin: Einaudi.

Beltrami, Daniele. 1954. *Storia della popolazione di Venezia dalla fine del secolo XVI alla caduta della Repubblica.* Padua: CEDAM.

Bengtsson, Tommy. 1984. "Harvest Fluctuations and Demographic Response, Southern Sweden 1751–1859." In *Preindustrial Population Change*, eds. Tommy Bengtsson, Gunnar Fridlizius, and Rolf Ohlsson. Lund: Almqvist & Wiksell, 329–356.

———. 1987. "Migration och löner. Tillämpning av Todaros migrationsteori på 1800-talets svenska urbanisering." In *Ekonomisk-historiska vingslag.* Lund: Ekonomisk-historiska föreningen.

————. 1989. "Real Wage Variation and Adult Mortality: Life Events in Västanfors, 1750–1859." Paper presented at the IUSSP General Conference, New Delhi.

————. 1990. "Migration, Wages, and Urbanization in Sweden in the Nineteenth Century." In *Urbanization in History: A Process of Dynamic Interactions*, eds. Ad van der Woude, Jan de Vries, and Akira Hayami. Oxford: Clarendon Press, 186–204.

————. 1993a. "A Re-Interpretation of Population Trends and Cycles in England, France and Sweden, 1751–1860." *Histoire et Mésure*, VIII.1, 93–115.

————. 1993b. "Combined Time-Series and Life Event Analysis: The Impact of Economic Fluctuations and Air Temperature on Adult Mortality by Sex and Occupation in a Swedish Mining Parish, 1757–1850." In *Old and New Methods in Historical Demography*, eds. David Reher and Roger Schofield. Oxford: Clarendon Press, 239–258.

————. 1999. "The Vulnerable Child, Economic Insecurity and Child Mortality in Pre-Industrial Sweden: A Case Study of Västanfors, 1757–1850." *European Journal of Population* 15:117–151.

————. 2000. "Inequality in Death. The Effects of the Agrarian Revolution in Southern Sweden: 1765–1865." In *Population and the Economy*, eds. Tommy Bengtsson and Osamu Saito. Oxford: Oxford University Press, 301–334.

Bengtsson, Tommy, and Martin Dribe. 1997. "Economy and Demography in Western Scania, Sweden, 1650–1900." Eurasian Project on Population and Family History Working Paper Series, No. 10. Kyoto: International Research Center for Japanese Studies.

————. Forthcoming. "New Evidence on the Standard of Living in Sweden during the 18th and 19th Centuries: Long-Term Development of the Demographic Response to Short-Term Economic Stress among Landless in Western Scania." In *New Evidence of Standard of Living in Pre-Industrial Europe and Asia*, eds. Robert C. Allen, Tommy Bengtsson, and Martin Dribe. Oxford: Oxford University Press.

Bengtsson, Tommy, and Gunnar Fridlizius. 1994. "Public Intergenerational Transfers as Old-Age Pension Systems: A Historical Interlude?" In *The Family, the Market and the State in Ageing Societies*, eds. John Ermisch and Naohiro Ogawa. Oxford: Oxford University Press, 198–215.

Bengtsson, Tommy, Gunnar Fridlizius, and Rolf Ohlsson, eds. 1984. *Preindustrial Population Change: The Mortality Decline and Short-Term Population Movements*. Lund: Almqvist & Wiksell.

Bengtsson, Tommy, and Christer Gunnarsson. 1994. "Population, Development, and Institutional Change: Summary and Analysis." In *Population, Economic Development, and the Environment: The Making of our Common Future*, eds. Kerstin Lindahl-Kiessling and Hans Landberg. Oxford: Oxford University Press, 1–24.

Bengtsson, Tommy, and Lennart Jörberg. 1975. "Market Integration in Sweden During the 18th and 19th Centuries: Spectral Analysis of Grain Prices." *Economy and History* 18.2:93–106.

Bengtsson, Tommy, and Martin Lindström. 2000. "Childhood Misery and Disease in Later Life: The Effects on Mortality in Old-Age of Hazards Experienced in Early Life, Southern Sweden, 1760–1894." *Population Studies* 54.3:263–277.

Bengtsson, Tommy, and Christer Lundh. 1994. "La mortalité infantile et post-infantile dans les pays Nordiques avant 1900." *Annales de Démographie Historique*: 23–43.

Bengtsson, Tommy, and James Oeppen. 1993. "A Reconstruction of the Population of Scania, 1650–1760." Lund Paper in Economic History, No. 32. Lund: Lund University, Department of Economic History.

Bengtsson, Tommy, and Rolf Ohlsson. 1978. "Befolkning och konjunkturer." *Meddelande från Ekonomisk-historiska institutionen* nr 1. Lund: Lund University, Department of Economic History.

————. 1985. "Age-Specific Mortality and Short-Term Changes in the Standard of Living: Sweden, 1751–1859." *European Journal of Population* 1:309–326.

Bengtsson, Tommy, and Osamu Saito, eds. 2000a. *Population and the Economy: From Hunger to Modern Economic Growth*. Oxford: Oxford University Press.

————. 2000b. "Introduction." In *Population and the Economy*, eds. Tommy Bengtsson and Osamu Saito. Oxford: Oxford University Press, 1–20.

Bengtsson, Tommy, Osamu Saito, David Reher, and Cameron Campbell. 1998. "Population and the Economy: From Hunger to Modern Economic Growth." In *Debates and Controversies in Economic History: Proceedings of the Twelfth International Economic History Congress*, ed. Clara-Eugenia Núñez. Madrid: Fundacion Ramon Areces, 69–144.

Berkner, Lutz. 1972. "The Stem Family and the Development Cycle of the Peasant Household: An Eighteenth Century Austrian Example." *American Historical Review* 77:398–418.

Berlin, Isaiah. 1958. *Two Concepts of Liberty*. Oxford: Clarendon Press.

Bernhardt, Eva. 1992. "Crowding and Child Survival in Stockholm, 1895–1920." Paper presented at the UIESP, Séminaire sur la mortalité des enfants dans le passé, Montréal, Oct. 7–9.

Bideau, Alain. 1981. "Variables familiales de la mortalité infantile." In *Les Hommes et la santé dans l'histoire. Mensch und Gesundheit in der Geschichte*, ed. Arthur E. Imhöf. Husum: Matthiesen Verlag, 223–250.

Bideau, Alain, Bertrand Desjardins, and Hector Pérez-Brignoli, eds. 1997. *Infant and Child Mortality in the Past*. Oxford: Clarendon Press.

Blayo, Yves. 1975. "La mortalité en France de 1740 à 1829." *Population* 30 (Numéro spécial):123–142.

Blum, Alain, and Arnaud Bringe. 1992. "Mortalité locale et générale en France 1670–1829." In *Modèles de la Démographie Historique*, eds. Alain Blum, Noël Bonneuil, and Didier Blanchet. Paris: INED, 11–43.

Bongaarts, John. 1980. "Does Malnutrition Affect Fecundity? A Summary of Evidence." *Science* 108:564–569.

Boulanger, Paul-Marie, and Dominique Tabutin. 1980. *La mortalité des enfants dans le monde et dans l'histoire*. Liège: Ordina.

Bourdelais, Patrice, and Michel Demonet. 1996. "L'évolution de la mortalité dans une ville industrielle: Le Creusot au 19e siècle." In *Les systèmes démographiques du passé*, eds. Alain Bideau, Guy Brunet, Katherine Lynch, and Alfred Perrenoud. Lyon: Programme de Recherches en Sciences Sociales, 335–356.

Bourgeois-Pichat, Jean. 1951. "La mesure de la mortalité infantile." *Population* 6:233–248, 459–480.

Bowling, Ann. 1987. "Mortality after Bereavement: A Review of the Literature on Survival Periods and Factors Affecting Survival." *Social Science and Medicine* 24.2:117–124.

Brenner, Robert, and Christopher Isett. 2002. "England's Divergence from China's Yangzi Delta: Property Relations, Microeconomics and Patterns of Development." *Journal of Asian Studies* 61.2:609–662.

Breschi, Marco. 1990. *La popolazione della Tosacana dal 1660 al 1960: Un'ipotesi di ricostruzione.* Florence: Universitá Degli Studi Di Firenze, Dipartimento Statistico.

———. 1999. *Vivere in Friuli. Saggi di demografia storica (secc. XVI–XIX).* Udine: Forum.

Breschi, Marco, and Renzo Derosas. 2000. "The Contribution of the Eurasian Project to the Italian Demographic History: The Example of Infant and Child Mortality." In *Family Structures, Demography and Population. A Comparison of Societies in Asia and Europe,* eds. Muriel Neven and Catherine Capron. Liège: Laboratoire de Démographie, 211–234.

Breschi, Marco, Renzo Derosas, Corrado Lagazio, and Matteo Manfredini. 1999. "L'influenza del contesto familiare sulla sopravvivenza dei bambini. Risultati di indagini microdemografiche sull'Italia dell'Ottocento." *Bollettino di Demografia Storica* 30:187–211.

Breschi, Marco, Renzo Derosas, and Matteo Manfredini. 2000. "Infant Mortality in Nineteenth-Century Italy: Interactions between Ecology and Society." In *Population and the Economy,* eds. Tommy Bengtsson and Osamu Saito. Oxford: Oxford University Press, 457–490.

Breschi, Marco, and Giovanna Gonano. 2000. "Relazioni di breve periodo tra decessi per età, prezzi e clima: Toscana 1818–1939." In *Salute e malattia fra '800 e '900 in Sardegna e nei paesi dell'Europa mediterranea,* eds. Lucia Pozzi and Eugenia Tognotti. Sassari: Editrice Democratica Sarda, 81–119.

Breschi, Marco, and Massimo Livi Bacci. 1986. "Saison et climat comme contraintes de la survie des enfants: The Experience of Italy during the Nineteenth Century." *Population* 41.1:9–36.

———. 1994. "Le mois de naissance comme facteur de survie des enfants." *Annales de Démographie Historique*: 169–185.

Breschi, Marco, and Matteo Manfredini. 1997. "A Rural Village of the Plain: Madregolo in the Nineteenth Century." Area Report manuscript presented at the Eurasian Project Fertility Conference, Bloomington, Ind.

———. 1998a. "Individual and Family Mobility: First Results from an Analysis on Two Italian Rural Villages." Dipartimento di Scienze Statistiche, Università degli Studi di Udine, Research notes, 12.

———. 1998b. "A Tuscany Village: Casalguidi in the 19th Century." Eurasian Project on Population and Family History Working Paper Series, No. 21. Kyoto: International Research Center for Japanese Studies.

———. 2002. "Parental Loss and Kin Networks: Demographic Consequences on Children in an Italian Village." In *When Dad Died,* eds. Renzo Derosas and Michel Oris. Bern: Peter Lang, 381–400.

Breschi, Marco, and Lucia Pozzi. 1997. "Un problema di demografia differenziale: mortalità infantile e condizione socio-economica." In *Disuguaglianze: stratificazione e mobilità sociale nelle popolazioni Italiane (dal sec. XIV agli inizi del secolo XX)*, Vol. 1. Bologna: CLUEB, 285–310.

Breschi, Marco, Lucia Pozzi, and Rosella Rettaroli. 1994. "Analogie e differenze territoriali nella crescita della popolazione Italiana, 1750–1911." *Bollettino di demografia storica* 20:41–94.

Broström, Göran, Anders Brändström, and Lars Persson. 1984. "The Impact of Breastfeeding Patterns on Infant Mortality in a 19th Century Swedish Parish." *Journal of Tropical Pediatrics* 30:154–159.

Bruneel, Claude, Frank Daelemans, Michel Dorban, and Christian Vandenbroeke. 1987. "Population et subsistances dans l'espace belge (XVIe–XIXe siècles)." In *Evolution agraire et croissance démographique*, ed. Antoinette Fauve-Chamoux. Liège: Derouaux Ordina, 293–324.

Buck, John Lossing, ed. 1937. *Land Utilization in China*. 3 vols. Chicago: University of Chicago Press.

Burguière, André. 1986. "Pour une typologie des formes d'organisation domestique de l'Europe moderne (XVIe–XIXe siècle)." *Annales, ESC* 41:639–655.

Cain, Mead T. 1977. "The Economic Activities of Children in a Village in Bangladesh." *Population and Development Review* 19.3:201–227.

———. 1978. "The Household Life Cycle and Economic Mobility in Rural Bangladesh." *Population and Development Review* 4.3:421–438.

———. 1981. "Risk and Insurance: Perspectives on Fertility and Agrarian Change in India and Bangladesh." *Population and Development Review* 7.3:435–474.

———. 1982. "Perspectives on Family and Fertility in Developing Countries." *Population Studies* 36.2:159–176.

———. 1983. "Fertility as an Adjustment to Risk." *Population and Development Review* 9.4:688–702.

Calabi, Donatella. 1991. "Il ghetto e la città." In *La città degli Ebrei. Il ghetto di Venezia: architettura e urbanistica*, eds. Ennio Concina, Ugo Camerino, and Donatella Calabi. Venice: Albrizzi, 201–301.

Campbell, Cameron. 1995. "Chinese Mortality Transitions: The Case of Beijing, 1700–1990." Ph.D. dissertation, University of Pennsylvania.

Campbell, Cameron, Wang Feng, and James Lee. 2002. "Pretransitional Fertility in China." *Population and Development Review* 28.4 (December):735–750.

Campbell, Cameron, and James Lee. 1996. "A Death in the Family: Household Structure and Mortality in Rural Liaoning, Life-Event and Time-Series Analysis, 1792–1867." *History of the Family: An International Quarterly* 1.3:297–328.

———. 1998. "Economic and Household Constraints on Male First Marriage in Northeast China, 1789–1909." Unpublished manuscript.

———. 2000. "Price Fluctuations, Family Structure, and Mortality in Two Rural Chinese Populations: Household Responses to Economic Stress in Eighteenth and Nineteenth

Century Liaoning." In *Population and the Economy*, eds. Tommy Bengtsson and Osamu Saito. Oxford: Oxford University Press, 371–420.

————. 2001. "Free and Unfree Labor in Qing China: Emigration and Escape among the Bannermen of Northeast China, 1789–1909." *History of the Family: An International Quarterly* 6.4:455–476.

————. 2002. "When Husbands and Parents Die: Widowhood and Orphanhood in Late Imperial Liaoning, 1789–1909." In *When Dad Died*, eds. Renzo Derosas and Michel Oris. Bern: Peter Lang, 313–334.

Cao Shuji. 2001. *Zhongguo renkou shi: vol 5, Qing shiqi* (Chinese population history: vol. 5, the Qing). Shanghai: Fudan daxue chubanshe.

Cao Shuji and Chen Yixin. 2002. "Maersasi lilun he Qingdai yilaide Zhongguo renkou: ping Meiguo xuezhe jinnianlai de xiangguan yanjiu (Malthusian theory and Chinese population since the Qing: A critique of recent American scholarship)." *Lishi yanjiu* (Historical research) 1:41–54.

Capron, Catherine. 1996. "La population de Limbourg au milieu du 19e siècle: un essai de démographie différentielle." Master's thesis, University of Liège.

————. 1998. "Mortalité différentielle et causes de décès à Limbourg au milieu du XIXe siècle." *Bulletin du Crédit communal* 52.203:45–62.

————. 1999. "Essai de reconstruction automatique des parentés à partir du registre de population belge." In *Revue Informatique et statistique dans les Science Humaines*. Liège: Centre Informatique de Philosophie et Lettres, Université de Liège, 9–49.

Capron, Catherine, and Michel Oris. 1997. "Demography, Family Systems, and Economy in Nineteenth-Century East Belgium." Area report manuscript presented at the EurAsian Project Mortality Conference, Kyoto.

————. 2000. "Ruptures de cohabitation entre parents et enfants dans les villes et les campagnes du Pays de Liège au XIXe siècle." In *De l'Usage des seuils. Structures par âge et âges de la vie*, eds. Alain Bideau, Patrice Bourdelais, and Jacques Légaré. Paris: Société de Démographie Historique, 229–270.

Capron, Catherine, Michel Oris, George Alter, Muriel Neven, and Etienne van der Straten. 1997. "Demography, Family System, and Economy in 19th Century East Belgium: A Report for the Eurasian Project." Paper presented at the Eurasian Project Meeting, Tokyo, Japan, Jan. 12–14.

Carlsson, Gösta. 1970. "Nineteenth Century Fertility Oscillations." *Population Studies* 24:413–422.

Carter, Anthony T. 1995. "Agency and Fertility: For an Ethnography of Practice." In *Situating Fertility: Anthropology and Demographic Inquiry*, ed. Susan Greenhalgh. Cambridge: Cambridge University Press, 55–85.

Caselli, Gabriella. 1991. "Health Transition and Cause-Specific Mortality." In *The Decline of Mortality in Europe*, eds. Roger Schofield, David Reher, and Alain Bideau. Oxford: Clarendon Press, 68–96.

Castiglioni, Arturo. 1936. *Storia della medicina*. Milan: Arnoldo Mondadori.

Cazzola, Franco. 1996. *Storia della campagne padane dall'Ottocento ad oggi*. Milan: Bruno Mondadori.

Chao, Kang. 1986. *Man and Land in China.* Stanford: Stanford University Press.

Chaunu, Pierre. 1972. "Malthusianisme démographique et Malthusianisme économique. Réflexions sur l'échec de la Normandie à l'époque du Démarrage." *Annales E.S.C.* 27.1:1–19.

Chayanov, Aleksander Vasil'evich. 1923/1986. *The Theory of Peasant Economy.* Madison: University of Wisconsin Press.

Christensen, Kaare, David Gaist, Bernard Jeune, and James W. Vaupel. 1998. "A Tooth per Child?" *Lancet* 352.9123:204.

Cipolla, Carlo M. 1965a. *Guns, Sails, and Empires: Technological Innovation and the Early Phases of the European Expansion, 1400–1700.* New York: Pantheon.

———. 1965b. "Four Centuries of Italian Demographic Development." In *Population in History,* eds. V. D. Glass and D. E. C. Eversley. London: E. Arnold 570–587.

Citro, Constance F., and Robert T. Michael. 1995. "Unit of Analysis and Presentation." In *Measuring Poverty: A New Approach,* eds. Constance F. Citro and Robert T. Michael. Washington, D.C.: National Academy Press, 301–316.

Clapham, John H. 1926. *An Economic History of Modern England: The Railway Age, 1820–1850.* Cambridge: Cambridge University Press.

Coale, Ansley, and Paul Demeny. 1983. *Regional Model Life Tables and Stable Populations.* 2nd ed. New York: Academic Press.

Coale, Ansley, and Susan C. Watkins, eds. 1986. *The Decline of Fertility in Europe.* Princeton, N.J.: Princeton University Press.

Cohen, Robert. 1989. "Health and Mortality among the Jews of Surinam in the Eighteenth Century." In *Papers in Jewish Demography 1985,* eds. Uziel O. Schmelz and Sergio Della Pergola. Jerusalem: Hebrew University of Jerusalem, Institute of Contemporary Jewry, 187–198.

Coll, Sebastian, and John Komlos. 1998. "The Biological Standard of Living and Economic Development: Nutrition, Health and Well-Being in Historical Perspective." In *Debates and Controversies in Economic History: Proceedings of the Twelfth International Economic History Congress,* ed. CI.-E. Núñez. Madrid: Proceedings Twelfth International Economic History Congress, 219–282.

Comune di Venezia, Giunta di statistica. 1889–1890. *Bollettino mensile.* Venice.

Condran, Gretchen A., and Ellen A. Kramarow. 1991. "Child Mortality among Jewish Immigrants to the United States." *Journal of Interdisciplinary History* 22:223–254.

Cooper, Frederick, Thomas C. Holt, and Rebecca J. Scott. 2000. *Beyond Slavery: Explorations of Race, Labor, and Citizenship in Postemancipation Societies.* Chapel Hill: University of North Carolina Press.

Cornell, Laurel. 1987. "Hajnal and the Household in Asia: A Comparative History of the Family in Preindustrial Japan, 1600–1870." *Journal of Family History* 12.1–3:143–162.

———. 1989. "Yome, shutome, Ubasteyama: 19-seiki Nihon noson ni-okeru rojin-josei no sabetsu shiboritsu (Daughters-in-law, mothers-in-law, and the 'Ubasteyama' Legend: Differential mortality of elderly women in an agricultural village in 19th century Japan)."

In *Tokugawa shakai kara-no tenbo* (Perspectives from the Tokugawa Japanese society), eds. Akira Hayami, Osamu Saito, and Shinya Sugiyama. Tokyo: Dobunkan, 191–213.

Cornell, Laurel L., and Akira Hayami. 1986. "The *shumon-aratame-cho*: Japan's Population Registers." *Journal of Family History* 11.4:311–328.

Corsini, Carlo. 1976. "Materiali per lo studio della famiglia in Toscana nei secoli XVII–XIX: gli esposti." *Quaderni Storici* 33:998–1052.

Corsini, Carlo, and Pier Paolo Viazzo, eds. 1997. *The Decline of Infant and Child Mortality: The European Experience: 1750–1990*. The Hague: Martinus Nijhof.

Cox, David R. 1972. "Regression Models and Life Tables (with Discussion)." *Journal of the Royal Statistical Society Series B* 34:187–220.

Crafts, Nicholas F. R. 1996. "The Human Development Index: Some Historical Comparisons." Working Papers in Economic History, No. 33/96. London: London School of Economics.

Crouzet, François. 1966. "Croissances comparées de l'Angleterre et de la France au XVIIIe siècle." *Annales, E.S.C.* 21:254–291.

Czap, Peter. 1982. "The Perennial Multiple Family Household, Mishino, Russia, 1782–1858." *Journal of Family History* 10:5–26.

———. 1983. "'A Large Family: The Peasant's Greatest Wealth: Serf Households in Mishino, Russia, 1814–1858." In *Family Forms in Historic Europe*, eds. Richard Wall, Jean Robin, and Peter Laslett. Cambridge: Cambridge University Press, 105–152.

Dalla Zuanna, Gianpiero, and Marzia Loghi. 1997. *Popolazione e popolazioni: studi territoriali preliminari alla storia della popolazione veneta 1856–1911*. Padua: Cooperativa Libraria Editrice Universit di Padova.

Das Gupta, Monica. 1987. "Selective Discrimination against Female Children in Rural Punjab, India." *Population and Development Review* 13.1:77–100.

———. 1990. "Death Clustering, Mother's Education and the Determinants of Child Mortality in Rural Punjab, India." *Population Studies* 44.3:489–505.

———. 1995. "Fertility Decline in Punjab, India: Parallels with Historical Europe." *Population Studies* 49.3:481–500.

———. 1997. "Kinship Systems and Demographic Regimes." In *Anthropological Demography*, eds. David Kertzer and Tom Fricke. Chicago: University of Chicago Press, 36–52.

———. 1998. "Lifeboat versus Corporate Ethic: Social and Demographical Implications of Stem and Joint Families." In *House and Stem Family in Eurasian Perspective*, eds. Antoinette Fauve-Chamoux and Emiko Ochiai. Kyoto: International Research Center for Japanese Studies, 444–466.

Dasgupta, Parta. 1993. *An Inquiry into Well-Being and Destitution*. Oxford: Oxford University Press.

Dasgupta, Parta, and Martin Weale. 1992. "On Measuring the Quality of Life." *World Development* 20.1:119–131.

Davenant, Charles. 1699. *An Essay upon the Probable Method of Making a People Gainers in the Balance of Trade*. London.

Davis, Kingsley. 1955. "Institutional Factors Favoring High Fertility in Underdeveloped Areas." *Eugenics Quarterly* 2:33–39.

———. 1963. "The Theory of Change and Response in Modern Demographic History." *Population Index* 29:345–366.

Davis, Kingsley, and Blake, Judith. 1956. "Social Structure and Fertility: An Analytical Framework." *Economic Development and Cultural Change* 4 (April):211–235.

Deaton, Angus, and John Muellbauer. 1980. *Economics and Consumer Behavior*. Cambridge: Cambridge University Press.

Dejongh, Guy, Bjorn Van Campenhout, and Michel Ceusters. 2000. "In de greep van de markt. De integratie van de regionale landbouwmarkten in België, 1700–1850." *Revue Belge d'histoire contemporaine/Belgisch Tijdschift voor Nieuwste Geschiedenis* 29.1-2:5–47.

Del Panta, Lorenzo. 1980. *Le epidemie nella storia demografica Italiana (secoli XIV–XIX)*. Turin: Loescher.

———. 1996. "Dalla metà del Settecento ai nostri giorni." In *La popolazione Italiana dal Medioevo ad oggi*, eds. Lorenzo Del Panta, Massimo Livi Bacci, Giuliano Pinto, and Eugenio Sonnino. Rome-Bari: Laterza, 131–212.

Del Panta, Lorenzo, and Maria E. Fiorini. 1994. "Disponibilità alimentari e tendenze della mortalità in Italia: un tentativo di analisi per il periodo 1861–1921." *Bollettino di Demografia Storica* 20:111–121.

Della Pergola, Sergio. 1983. *La trasformazione demografica della diaspora ebraica*. Turin: Loescher.

Delsante, Ubaldo. 1982. *Collecchio. Strutture rurali e vita contadina*. Collecchio (PR): Italia Nostra.

Deprez, Marcel. 1948. "Essai sur le mouvement des prix et des revenus en Belgique au début du 19e siècle (1789–1830)." Ph.D. dissertation, University of Liège.

Derosas, Renzo. 1989. "A Database for the Study of the Italian Population Registers." *Historical Social Research/Historische Sozialforschung* 52:59–65.

———. 1999. "Appesi a un filo: I bambini veneziani davanti alla morte (1850–1900)." In *La scoperta dell'infanzia a Venezia: Cura, educazione e rappresentazione Venezia 1750–1930*, eds. Nadia Filippini and Tiziana Plebani. Venice: Marsilio, 39–53.

———. 2000. "La fortuna di nascere ebrei: Fattori culturali nei differenziali di mortalità infantile." In *Per Marino Berengo: Scritti degli allievi*, eds. Livio Antonielli, Carlo Capra, and Mario Infelise. Milan: Franco Angeli, 743–777.

———. 2002. "La demografia dei poveri. Pescatori, facchini e industrianti nella Venezia di metà Ottocento." In *Storia di Venezia. 8. L'Ottocento*, ed. Stuart J. Woolf. Venice and Rome: Fondazione Treccani, 711–770.

———. 2003. "When Culture Matters: Differential Infant Mortality of Jews and Catholics in Nineteenth-Century Venice." *Historical Methods* 36.4.

———. Forthcoming. "A Family Affair: Marriage, Mobility, and Living Arrangements in Nineteenth-Century Venice." In *The Road to Independence: Leavers and Stayers in the House-*

hold in Europe and Asia, eds. Frans van Poppel, James Lee, and Michel Oris. Bern: Peter Lang.

Derosas, Renzo, and Michel Oris, eds. 2002. *When Dad Died: Individuals and Families Coping with Family Stress in Past Societies*. Bern: Peter Lang.

De Saint-Moulin, Léon. 1969. *La construction et la propriété des maisons expressions des structures sociales. Seraing depuis le début du 19e siècle*. Brussels: Crédit Communal.

Desama, Claude. 1976. "L'expansion démographique du XIXe siècle." In Hasquin (dir.), *La Wallonie. Le Pays et les Hommes. Histoire-économies-sociétés*, vol. 2: *De 1830 à nos jours*. Paris: La Renaissance du Livre, 139–156.

———. 1985. *Population et révolution industrielle. Evolution des structures démographiques à Verviers dans la première moitié du 19e siècle*. Paris: Les Belles Lettres.

Desama, Claude, and Catherine Bauwens. 1995. "Une petite ville au coeur de la révolution industrielle: Verviers et le travail de la laine." In *La Belgique industrielle en 1850*, eds. Bart Van der Herten, Michel Oris, and Jan Rogiers. Brussels: Crédit Communal, 87–128.

Devos, Isabelle. 1996. "La régionalisation de la surmortalité des jeunes filles en Belgique entre 1890–1910." *Annales de Démographie Historique*: 375–407.

———. 2000. "Te jong om te sterven. De levenskansen van meisjes in België omstreeks 1900." *Tijdschrift voor Sociale Gerschiedenis* 26.1:55–75.

De Vries, Henny F. 1991. "The Malnutrition-Infections Syndrome Model: A Preliminary Study for Nigeria and Zimbabwe." In *Studies in African and Asian Demography: CDC Annual Seminar, 1990*. Cairo, 677–711.

Ding Yizhuang. 1992. *Qingdai baqi zhufang zhidu yanjiu* (Research on the Eight Banner garrison system during the Qing). Tianjin: Guji chuban she.

Ding Yizhuang, Guo Songyi, James Lee, and Cameron Campbell. Forthcoming. *Liaodong yimin de qiren shehui* (Banner Society and the Settlement of Eastern Liaodong). Shanghai: Shanghai shehui kexue chubanshe.

Dobson, Mary. 1997. *Contours of Death and Disease in Early Modern England*. Cambridge: Cambridge University Press.

Doi, Takeo. 1973. *Anatomy of Dependence*. Tokyo: Kodansha Press.

Dribe, Martin. 1995. "Migration, Security and Economic Fluctuations, Family Migration from Halmstad 1801–1860." Lund Papers in Economic History, No. 40. Lund: Lund University.

———. 2000. *Leaving Home in a Peasant Society: Economic Fluctuations, Household Dynamics and Youth Migration in Southern Sweden, 1829–1866*. Södertälje: Almqvist & Wiksell.

Duara, Prasenjit. 1995. *Rescuing History from the Nation: Questioning Narratives of Modern China*. Chicago: University of Chicago Press.

———. 1998. "Why Is History Antitheoretical?" *Modern China* 24.2:105–120.

Duer, Michel. 1992. "Les unes croissent et multiplient, les autres non. La reproduction différentielle des familles." In *La société française au 19e siècle: tradition, transition, transformations*, eds. Jacques Dupâquier and Denis Kessler. Paris: Fayard, 439–459.

Du Halde, Jean-Baptiste. 1674–1743. *A Description of the Empire of China and Chinese-Tartary: Together with the Kingdoms of Korea and Tibet: Containing the Geography and History (Natural as Well as Civil) of those Countries* .... From the French of P. J. B. Du Halde, Jesuit; with notes geographical, historical, and critical and other improvements, particularly in the maps, by the translator Imprint London: Printed by T. Gardner for E. Cave, 1738–1741.

Duodo, Giovanni. 1874. *Prospetti dimostranti l'andamento diviso per decadi di tutte le nove epidemie choleriche avutesi in Venezia e fra di esse confrontate negli anni 1835, 36, 37, 49, 51, 55, 66, 67, 73.* Venice: Giunta Comunale.

Dupâquier, Jacques. 1989. "Demographic and Subsistence Crises in France." In *Famine, Disease, and the Social Order in Early Modern Europe*, eds. John Walter and Roger Schofield. Cambridge: Cambridge University Press, 189–199.

Dyson, Tim, and Cormac Ó Gráda, eds. 2002. *Famine Demography: Perspectives from the Past and the Present.* Oxford: Oxford University Press.

Eggerickx, Thierry, and Marc Debuisson. 1990. "La surmortalité urbaine, le cas de la Wallonie et de Bruxelles à la fin du 19e siècle." *Annales de Démographie Historique*: 23–41.

Eggerickx, Thierry, and Michel Poulain. 1995. "Croissance et déclin des communes industrielles dans le contexte de l'industrialisation et de la désindustrialisation de la Wallonie." In *Passé et avenir des bassins industriels en Europe*, eds. René Leboutte and Jean-Paul Lehners. Luxembourg: Centre Universitaire du Luxembourg, 269–288.

Eggerickx, Thierry, and Dominique Tabutin. 1994. "La surmortalité des filles en Belgique vers 1890. Une approche régionale." *Population* 49.3:657–683.

Elliott, Mark. 2001. *The Manchu Way: The Eight Banners and Ethnic Identity in Late Imperial China.* Palo Alto: Stanford University Press.

Elvin, Mark. 1973. *The Pattern of the Chinese Past.* Stanford: Stanford University Press.

Fang, Xing. 1996. "Qingdai Jiangnan shi zhen tanwei (Cities and towns in Qing Jiangnan)." *Zhongguo jingji shi yanjiu* (Research in Chinese economic history), 11.3:91–98.

Fauve-Chamoux, Antoinette, and Emiko Ochiai, eds. 1998. *House and Stem Family in Eurasian Perspective.* Kyoto: International Research Center for Japanese Studies.

Federigo, Gaspare. 1831–1832. *Topografia fisico-medica della città di Venezia, delle sue isole, estuari e lagune, dei cangiamenti nati e dei mezzi profilattici d'igiene.* Padua: Tipografia del Seminario.

Feeney, Griffith, and Kiyoshi Hamano. 1990. "Rice Price Fluctuations and Fertility in Late Tokugawa Japan." *Journal of Japanese Studies* 16.1:1–30.

Ferrari, Guido, and Massimo Livi Bacci. 1985. "Sulle relazioni tra temperatura e mortalità nell'Italia unita, 1861–1914." In *La popolazione italiana nell'Ottocento. Continuità e mutamenti.* Bologna: CLUEB, 273–298.

Finegan, Michael. 1988. "Inheritance and Family Structure in Qing China: Evidence from Taiwan and Fujian." Unpublished manuscript.

Finzi, Roberto. 1998. *Civiltà mezzadrile: la piccola coltura in Emilia-Romagna.* Rome-Bari: Laterza.

Fleury, Michel, and Louis Henry. 1985. *Nouveau manuel de dépouillement et d'exploitation de l'état civil ancien*, 3rd ed. Paris: Institut Nationald'études demographiques.

Flinn, Michael W. 1981. *The European Demographic System, 1500–1820*. Baltimore: Johns Hopkins University Press.

Fogel, Robert W. 1992. "Second Thoughts on the European Escape from Hunger: Famines, Chronic Malnutrition, and Mortality Rates." In *Nutrition and Poverty*, ed. Siddiqur R. Osmani. Oxford: Clarendon Press, 243–286.

Fogel, Robert W. 1994. "The Relevance of Malthus for the Study of Mortality Today: Long-Run Influences on Health, Mortality, Labour Force Participation, and Population Growth." In *Population, Economic Development, and the Environment: The Making of our Common Future*, eds. Kerstin Lindahl-Kiesling and Hans Landberg. Oxford: Oxford University Press, 231–284.

———. 1996. "The Escape from Hunger and Premature Death, 1700–2100: Europe, America and the Third World." 1996 Ellen McArthur Lectures, Cambridge University, Nov. 12–20.

———. 1997. "New Findings on Secular Trends in Nutrition and Mortality: Some Implications for Population Theory." In *Handbook of Population and Family Economics*, eds. Mark R. Rosenzweig and Oded Stark. Amsterdam: Elsevier, Vol. 1A, 433–481.

Fourastié, Jean. 1959. "De la vie traditionelle à la vie 'tertiaire.'" *Population* 14:417–432.

Frank, Andre Gundar. 1998. *Re-orient: Global Economy in the Asian Age*. Berkeley: University of California Press.

Franzina, Emilio, ed. 1986. *Venezia*. Rome-Bari: Laterza.

Freedman, Maurice. 1958. *Lineage Organization in Southeastern China*. London: Athlone Press.

———. 1966. *Chinese Lineage and Society: Fukien and Kwangtung*. London: Athlone Press.

Fridlizius, Gunnar. 1979. "Population, Enclosure, and Property Rights." *Economy and History* 22.1:3–37.

———. 1984. "The Mortality Decline in the First Phase of the Demographic Transition: Swedish Experiences." In *Preindustrial Population Change*, eds. Tommy Bengtsson, Gunnar Fridlizius, and Rolf Ohlsson. Lund: Almqvist & Wiksell, 71–114.

———. 1988. "Sex-Differential Mortality and Socio Economic Change, Sweden 1750–1910." In *Society, Health and Population during the Demographic Transition*, eds. Anders Brändström and Lars-Göran Tedebrand. Stockholm: Almqvist and Wiksell, 237–272.

Fridlizius, Gunnar, and Rolf Ohlsson. 1984. "Mortality Patterns in Sweden, 1751–1802: A Regional Analysis." In *Preindustrial Population Change*, eds. Tommy Bengtsson, Gunnar Fridlizius, and Rolf Ohlsson. Lund: Almqvist & Wiksell, 299–328.

Frisch, Rose E. 1978. "Nutrition, Fatness and Fertility: The Effect of Food Intake on Reproductive Ability." In *Nutrition and Human Reproduction*, ed. Henry W. Mosley. New York: Plenum, 91–121.

Fukutake, Tadashi. 1967. *Japanese Rural Society*. Oxford: Oxford University Press.

Fuse, Akiko. 1993. *Kekkon to kazoku* (Marriage and the family). Tokyo: University of Tokyo Press.

Gadisseur, Jean. 1990. *Le produit physique de la Belgique, 1830–1913.* Brussels: Palais des Académies.

Galloway, Patrick R. 1985. "Annual Variations in Deaths by Age, Deaths by Cause, Prices and Weather in London, 1670–1830." *Population Studies* 39.3:487–505.

———. 1986. "Differentials in Demographic Responses to Annual Price Variations in Pre-Revolutionary France: A Comparison of Rich and Poor Areas in Rouen, 1681 to 1787." *European Journal of Population* 2:269–305.

———. 1988. "Basic Patterns in Annual Variations in Fertility, Nuptiality, Mortality, and Prices in Pre-Industrial Europe." *Population Studies* 42:275–303.

———. 1993. "Short-Run Population Dynamics among the Rich and Poor in European Countries, Rural Jutland, and Urban Rouen." In *Old and New Methods in Historical Demography,* eds. David Reher and Roger Schofield. Oxford: Clarendon Press, 84–108.

Gamble, Sidney D. 1954. *Ting Hsien: A North China Rural Community.* Stanford: Stanford University Press.

Ganiage, Jean. 1988. *Le Beauvaisis au 18e siècle: la campagne.* Paris: INED.

Gaunt, David. 1983. "The Property and Kin Relationships of Retired Farmers in Northern and Central Europe." In *Family Forms in Historic Europe,* eds. Richard Wall, Jean Robin, and Peter Laslett. Cambridge: Cambridge University Press, 249–279.

Gélis, Jacques. 2000. "Les pratiques de 'répit' et l'attitude de l'église en Belgique. XIVe–XVIIIe siècles." In *Sixième Congrès de l'Association des Cercles francophones d'Histoire et d'Archéologie de Belgique, Congrès de Mons, 25–27 août 2000,* Vol. 1. Mons, 121.

Ge Rondi, Carla. 1998. "La dinamica demografica delle province lombarde tra Sette e Ottocento." *Bollettino di Demografia Storica* 28:63–87.

Ghai, Dharam P., et al. 1977. *The Basic-Needs Approach to Development: Some Issues Regarding Concepts and Methodology.* Geneva: International Labour Office.

Giddens, Anthony. 1979. *Central Problems in Social Theory: Action, Structure and Contradiction in Social Analysis.* Berkeley: University of California Press.

Gillberg, Lorents. 1765. *Beskrifning öfver Malmöhus lähn uti hertigdömmet Skåne.* Lund: Carl Gustav Berling (Facsimile. 1980. Lund: Bröderna Ekstrands Tryckeri).

Giorgetti, Giorgio. 1974. *Contadini e proprietari nell'Italia moderna: rapporti di produzione e contratti agrari dal secolo XVI a oggi.* Turin: Einaudi.

Glass, David V., and Eversley, David E. C., eds. 1965. *Population in History.* London: E. Arnold.

Godding, Phillipe. 1987. *Le droit privé dans les Pay-Bas.* Brussels: Credit Communal de Belgique.

Goldman, Noreen. 1993a. "The Perils of Single Life in Contemporary Japan." *Journal of Marriage and the Family* 55.1:189–208.

———. 1993b. "Marriage Selection and Mortality Patterns: Inferences and Fallacies." *Demography* 30.2:189–208.

Goldman, Noreen, and Yuanreng Hu. 1993. "Excess Mortality among the Unmarried: A Case Study of Japan." *Social Science and Medicine* 36.4:533–546.

Goldstone, Jack. 1986. "The Demographic Revolution in England: A Reexamination." *Population Studies* 40:5–33.

———. 2000. "The Rise of the West—or Not? A Revision to Socio-Economic History." *Sociological Theory* 18.2:175–194.

Gonano, Giovanna. 1998. "Fluttuazioni economiche di breve periodo e comportamenti demografici in Friuli." In *Economia e popolazioni in Friuli dalla caduta della Repubblica di Venezia alla fine della dominazione austriaca*, eds. Marco Breschi and Paolo Pecorari. Udine: Forum, 145–164.

Goody, Jack. 1976. *"Production and Reproduction": A Comparative Study of the Domestic Domain*. Cambridge: Cambridge University Press.

———. 1983. *The Development of the Family and Marriage in Europe*. Cambridge: Cambridge University Press.

———. 1990. *The Oriental, the Ancient, and the Primitive: Systems of Marriage and the Family in the Pre-Industrial Societies of Eurasia*. Cambridge: Cambridge University Press.

———. 1996. *The East in the West*. Cambridge: Cambridge University Press.

Goubert, Pierre. 1960. *Beauvais et le Beauvaisis de 1600 à 1730*. Paris: S. E. V. P. E. N.

Gove, Walter R. 1973. "Sex, Marital Status, and Mortality." *American Journal of Sociology* 79.1:45–67.

Grandi, Casimira, ed. 1991. *Benedetto chi ti porta maledetto chi ti manda. L'infanzia abbandonata nel Triveneto (secoli XV–XIX)*. Treviso: Fondazione Benetton.

Guinanne, Timothy W. 1997. *The Vanishing Irish: Household, Migration, and the Rural Economy in Ireland, 1850–1914*. Princeton, N.J.: Princeton University Press.

Gutman, Myron P. 1988. *Toward the Modern Economy: Early Industry in Europe, 1500–1800*. Philadelphia: Temple University Press.

Gutman, Myron P., and Etienne van de Walle. 1978. "New Sources for Social and Demographic History: The Belgian Population Registers." *Social Science History* 2:124–143.

Haesenne-Peremans, Nicole. 1981. *La pauvreté dans la région liégeoise à l'aube de la révolution industrielle. Un siècle de tension sociale (1730–1830)*. Paris: les Belles-Lettres.

Haines, Michael. 1989. "Déclin de la mortalité et conditions de travail." *Annales de Démographie Historique*: 139–155.

Hajnal, John. 1965. "European Marriage Patterns in Perspective." In *Population in History*, eds. V. D. Glass and D. E. C. Eversley. London: 101–146.

———. 1982. "Two Kinds of Pre-Industrial Household Formation System." *Population and Development Review* 8:449–494.

Hamano, Kiyoshi. 2000. "Meiji-shonen Noka-betsu Bussan Tokei ni tsuite: Tama-gun, Shinmachi-mura Shiofuna-mura no Sanbetsu-torishirabe-cho (Statistics on Agricultural Products in Early Meiji Japan: Registers of Products in the Villages of Shinmachi and Shiofuna in Tama County)." *Komonjo Kenkyu* 52:22–32.

Hamano, Kiyoshi, Satomi Kurosu, and Shuma Morimoto. Forthcoming. "Universal Marriage in Tokugawa Society: A Reconsideration of Celibacy in Nishijo." In *The Demography of Traditional Japan, 1600–1870*, ed. Osamu Saito. Oxford: Oxford University Press.

Hammel, Eugene A. 1990. "A Theory of Culture for Demography." *Population and Development Review* 16.3:455–485.

Hammel, Eugene A., and Patrick R. Galloway. 2000. "Structural Factors Affecting the Short-Term Positive Check in Croatia, Slavonia, and Srem in the Eighteenth and Nineteenth Centuries." In *Population and the Economy*, eds. Tommy Bengtsson and Osamu Saito. Oxford: Oxford University Press, 255–278.

Hammel, Eugene A., and Peter Laslett. 1974. "Comparing Household Structure over Time and between Cultures." *Comparative Studies in Society and History* 16:73–111.

Hammond, John L. 1930. "The Industrial Revolution and Discontent." *Economic History Review* 1st ser. 2.2:215–228.

Hanley, Susan B. 1974. "Fertility, Mortality, and Life Expectancy in Pre-Modern Japan." *Population Studies* 28.1:127–142.

———. 1997. *Everyday Things in Pre-Modern Japan: The Hidden Legacy of Material Culture.* Berkeley, California: University of California Press.

Hanley, Susan B., and Arthur P. Wolf, eds. 1985. *Family and Population in East Asian History.* Stanford: Stanford University Press.

Harada, Toshimaru, and Matao Miyamoto. 1985. *Rekishi no nakano Bukka* (Commodity prices in historical context). Tokyo: Dobunkan.

Hareven, Tamara K., ed. 1996. *Aging and Generational Relations over the Life Course.* Berlin: Walter de Gruyter.

Harrell, Steven. 1985. "The Rich Get Children: Segmentation, Stratification, and Population in Three Chekiang Lineages." In *Family and Population in East Asian History*, eds. Susan Hanley and Arthur Wolf. Stanford: Stanford University Press, 81–109.

———. 1987. "On the Holes in Chinese Genealogies." *Late Imperial China* 8.2:53–79.

———. 1995a. *Chinese Historical Microdemography.* Berkeley: University of California Press.

———. 1995b. "Introduction: Microdemography and the Modeling of Population Process in Late Imperial China." In *Chinese Historical Microdemography*, ed. Steven Harrell, 1–20.

———. 1997. *Human Families.* Boulder, Colo.: Westview Press.

Harrell, Steven, and Tom Pullum. 1995. "Marriage, Mortality, and the Developmental Cycle in Three Xiaoshan Lineages." In *Chinese Historical Microdemography*, ed. Steven Harrell. Berkeley: University of California Press, 141–162.

Hart, C. Anthony. 1988. "Pregnancy and Host Resistance." *Baillière's Clinical Immunology and Allergy* 2.3:735–757.

Härtel, Ursula. 1988. "Die unterschiedliche sterblichkeit von mannern und frauen, mit beispielen aus der Bundesrepublik Deuthschland." *Sozial und Praventivmedizin/Medecine Sociale et Preventive* 33.3:135–139.

Hartl, Daniel L. 1983. *Human Genetics.* New York: Harper and Row.

Harvey, A. C., and A. Jaeger. 1993. "Detrending, Stylized Facts and the Business Cycle." *Journal of Applied Econometrics* 8:231–247.

Hayami, Akira. 1973. *Kinsei Noson no Rekishi-Jinkogakuteki Kenkyu* (A historical demographic study of agricultural villages in early modern Japan). Tokyo: Toyo Keizai Shinposha.

———. 1979. "Thank You Francisco Xavier: An Essay in the Use of Microdata for Historical Demography of Tokugawa Japan." *Keio Economics Studies* 6.1-2:65–81.

———. 1982. "Kinsei Ou-chiho jinko no shiteki-kenkyu joron (An introductory study on the population history of the Ou region in early modern Japan)." *Mita Gakkai Zasshi* 75.3:298–320.

———. 1985. *Nihon ni okeru Keizai-Shakai no Tenkai* (Socioeconomic development in Japan). Tokyo: Keio Tsushin.

———. 1986. "Population Changes." In *Japan in Transition: From Tokugawa to Meiji*, eds. Marius B. Jansen and Gilbert Rozman. Princeton: Princeton University Press, 280–317.

———. 1992. *Kinsei Nobi-chiho no Jinko Keizai Shakai* (Population, economy and society in early modern Japan: a study of the Nobi region). Tokyo: Sobunsha.

Hayami, Akira, and Satomi Kurosu. 2001. "Regional Diversity in Demographic and Family Patterns in Pre-Industrial Japan." *Journal of Japanese Studies* 27.2:295–321.

Hayami, Akira, and Emiko Ochiai. 2001. "Family Patterns and Demographic Factors in Pre-Industrial Japan." In *Asian Population History*, eds. Tsui-jung Liu, James Lee, David Reher, Osamu Saito, and Wang Feng. Oxford: Oxford University Press, 395–415.

Head-König, Anne-Lise. 2000. "Frontières culturelles et régime démographique catholique et protestant dans la vallée de la Linth (canton de Glaris) en Suisse aux 18e et 19e siècles." In *Régimes démographiques et territoires: les frontières en question*, ed. Association internationale des démographes de langue française. Paris: P.U.F., 215–224.

Heckscher, Eli. 1949. *Sveriges ekonomiska historia, II: 1*. Stockholm: Albert Bonniers Förlag.

Hélin, Etienne. 1960. "La genèse et la disparition des isolats. Remarques méthodologiques et sondages préliminaires dans la province de Liège." Master's thesis, University of Liège.

Hellstenius, Johan. 1871. "Skördarna i Sverige och dess verkningar." *Statistisk tidskrift* 29:77–119.

Helsing, Knud, and Moyses Szklo. 1981. "Mortality after Bereavement." *American Journal of Epidemiology* 114:41–52.

Hermalin, Albert, Mary Beth Ofstedal, and Ming-cheng Chang. 1992. "Types of Supports for the Aged and Generational Relations over the Life Course: A Historical and Cross-Cultural Perspective." PSC Comparative Study of the Elderly in Asia Research Report No. 92-14. Ann Arbor: Population Studies Center, University of Michigan.

Heuschling, Xavier. 1841. "Doubles emplois ... dans la statistique des décès." *Bulletin de la Commission centrale de Statistique* 1:540–554.

Hill, Martha. 1992. *The Panel Study of Income Dynamics: A User's Guide*. Newbury Park, Calif.: Sage.

Ho, Ping-ti. 1959. *Studies on the Population of China, 1368–1953*. Cambridge, Mass.: Harvard University Press.

Hobcraft, John, J. McDonald, and S. O. Rutstein. 1985. "Demographic Determinants of Infant and Child Mortality." *Population Studies* 39:233–250.

Hoch, Steven. 1986. *Serfdom and Social Control in Russia: Petrovskoe, a Village in Tambov.* Chicago: University of Chicago Press.

Hoffmann, Philip T., David Jacks, Patricia A. Levin, and Peter H. Lindert. Forthcoming. "Sketching the Rise of Inequality in Early Modern Europe." In *New Evidence of the Standard of Living in Pre-Industrial Europe and Asia,* eds. Robert Allen, Tommy Bengtsson, and Martin Dribe. Oxford: Oxford University Press.

Hollingsworth, T. H. 1964. "The Demography of the British Peerage." *Population Studies* 18.2: Supplement.

Hosmer, David W., and Stanley Lemeshow. 1999. *Applied Survival Analysis: Regression Modeling of Time to Event Data.* New York: Wiley.

Howells, William D. 1883. *Venetian Life.* Leipzig: Bernard Tauchnitz.

Hoyois, Giovanni. 1981. *L'Ardenne et l'Ardennais.* 2 vols., Brussels and Paris: Editions Universitaires.

Hsiung Ping-chen. Forthcoming. "More or Less: Cultural and Medical Factors behind Marital Fertility in Late Imperial China." In *Abortion, Infanticide, and Reproductive Behavior in Asia,* eds. James Lee and Osamu Saito. Oxford: Oxford University Press.

Hu, Yuanreng, and Noreen Goldman. 1990. "Mortality Differentials by Marital Status: An International Comparison." *Demography* 27.2:233–250.

Huang, Philip. 1985. *The Peasant Economy and Social Change in North China.* Stanford: Stanford University Press.

———. 1990. *The Peasant Family and Rural Development in the Yangzi Delta, 1350–1988.* Stanford: Stanford University Press.

Huang, Philip. 2002a. "Development or Involution in Eighteenth-Century Britain and China? A Review of Kenneth Pomeranz's *The Great Divergence: China, Europe, and the Making of the Modern World Economy.*" *Journal of Asian Studies* 61.2:501–538.

———. 2002b. "Beyond the East-West Binary: Resituating Development Paths in the Eighteenth-Century World." *Journal of Asian Studies* 61.2:539–590.

———. 2003. "Further Thoughts on Eighteenth-Century Britain and China: Rejoinder to Pomeranz's Response to My Critique." *Journal of Asian Studies* 62.1:157–167.

Hudson, Pat, and William R. Lee, eds. 1990. *Woman's Work and the Family Economy in Historical Perspective.* Manchester: Manchester University Press.

Humphreys, Noel A., ed. 1885. *Vital Statistics: A Memorial Volume of Selections from the Reports and Writings of William Farr.* London: Royal Sanitary Institute.

Humphries, Jane. 1991. "'Bread and a Pennyworth of Treacle': Excess Female Mortality in England in the 1840s." *Cambridge Journal of Economics* 15:451–473.

Hunecke, Volker. 1989. *I trovatelli di Milano. Bambini esposti e famiglie espositrici dal XVII al XIX secolo.* Bologna: Il Mulino.

Huntington, Samuel P. 1995. *The Clash of Civilizations and the Remaking of World Order.* New York: Simon & Schuster.

Imhof, Arthur. 1981. "La surmortalité des femmes mariées en âge de procréation: un indice de la condition féminine au 19e siècle." *Annales de Démographie Historique*: 81–87.

———. 1984. "The Amazing Simultaneousness of the Big Differences and the Boom in the 19th Century: Some Facts and Hypotheses about Infant and Maternal Mortality." In *Preindustrial Population Change*, eds. Tommy Bengtsson, Gunnar Fridlizius, and Rolf Ohlsson. Lund: Almqvist & Wiksell, 191–222.

Ipsen, Carl. 2000. "Legal Infanticide: Foundling Mortality and Its Measurement in Turn-of-the-Century Italy, with Special Reference to the Casa dell'Annunziata of Naples." *Popolazione e storia* (special issue), 123–150.

Iwahashi, Masaru. 1981. *Kinsei Nippon Bukka-shi no Kenkyu* (A study of the history of price in early modern Japan). Tokyo: Ohara Shinseisha.

———. 1988. "Kouiki-Nobi-chihoken no bukka hendo, 1756–1867: Kariya-bukka wo chushinto-shite (Price variations in the greater Nobi region 1756–1867: With special references to Kairya prices)." *Matuyama Shodai Ronshu* 39.2:335–366.

Jannetta, Ann B., and Samuel Preston. 1991. "Two Centuries of Mortality Change in Central Japan: The Evidence from a Temple Death Register." *Population Studies* 45.3:417–436.

Jevons, W. Stanley. 1871/1970. *The Theory of Political Economy*. Bungay, Suffolk: Penguin Books.

Jiang, Tao. 1993. *Zhongguo jindai renkou shi* (Modern population history of China). Hangzhou: Zhejiang renmin chubanshe.

Johansson, Sheila Ryan. 1984. "Deferred Infanticide: Excess Female Mortality during Childhood." In *Infanticide*, eds. Glenn Hausfater and Sarah B. Hrdy. New York: Aldine, 463–485.

———. 1987. "Neglect, Abuse, and Avoidable Death: Parental Investment and the Mortality of Infants and Children in the European Tradition." In *Child Abuse and Neglect: Biosocial Dimensions*, eds. Richard J. Gelles and Jane B. Lancaster. New York: De Gruyter, 57–93.

———. 2000. "Macro and Micro Perspectives on Mortality History." *Historical Methods* 33.2:59–72.

Johansson, Sheila R., and Alice B. Kasakoff. 2000. "Mortality History and the Misleading Mean." *Historical Methods* 33.2:56–58.

Johansson, Sheila R., and Carl Mosk. 1987. "Exposure, Resistance and Life Expectancy: Disease and Death during the Economic Development of Japan, 1900–1960." *Population Studies* 41:207–235.

Jörberg, Lennart. 1972. *A History of Prices in Sweden, 1732–1914*, Vols. 1–2. Lund: Gleerups.

Kalbfleisch, John D., and Ross L. Prentice. 1980. *The Statistical Analysis of Failure Time Data*. New York: Wiley.

Kalkstein, Laurence S., and Robert E. Davis. 1989. "Weather and Human Mortality: An Evaluation of Demographic and Interregional Responses in the United States." *Annals of the Association of American Geographers* 79.1:44–64.

Kane, Penny. 1987. "The Demography of Famine." *Genus* 43.1-2:43–58.

Kaplan, Hillard. 1994. "Evolutionary and Wealth Flows Theories of Fertility: Empirical Tests and New Models." *Population and Development Review* 20.4:753–791.

Katwijk C., and L. L. Peters. 1998. "Clinical Aspects of Pregnancy after the Age of 35 Years: A Review of the Literature." *Human Reproduction Update* 4.2:185–194.

Kearns, Gerry. 1988. "The Urban Penalty and the Population History of England." In *Society, Health and Population during the Demographic Transition*, eds. Anders Brändström and Lars-Göran Tedebrand. Stockholm: Almqvist and Wiksell, 213–236.

———. 1993. "Le handicap urbain et le déclin de la mortalité en Angleterre et au Pays de Galles, 1851–1900." *Annales de Démographie Historique*: 75–105.

Kennedy, Robert E. 1973. *The Irish: Emigration, Marriage, and Fertility*. Berkeley: University of California Press.

Kertzer, David I. 1993. *Sacrificed for Honor: Italian Infant Abandonment and the Politics of Reproductive Control*. Boston: Beacon Press.

Kertzer, David I., and Tom Fricke, eds. 1997. *Anthropological Demography: Toward a New Synthesis*. Chicago: University of Chicago Press.

Kertzer, David I., and Nancy Karweit. 1995. "The Impact of Widowhood in Nineteenth-Century Italy." In *Aging in the Past: Demography, Society, and Old Age*, eds. David I. Kertzer and Peter Laslett. Berkeley: University of California Press, 229–248.

Kertzer, David I., and Peter Laslett, eds. 1995. *Aging in the Past: Demography, Society, and Old Age*. Berkeley: University of California Press.

Kinoshita, Futoshi. 1999. "Shumon Aratame-cho ni okeru shussei to nyujishibo no kashou touroku: nihon rekishijinkogaku no nokosareta kadai (Underregistration of births in Shumon Aratame-cho: A longstanding unsolved issue in Japanese historical demography)." *Jinkogaku Kenkyu* 25:27–39.

Kitagawa, Evelyn M., and Philip M. Hauser. 1973. *Differential Mortality in the United States: A Study of Socioeconomic Epidemiology*. Cambridge, Mass.: Harvard University Press.

Kito, Hiroshi. 1989. "Kinsei-nihon no shushoku-taikei to jinko-henka (Types of staple food and population change in early modern Japan)." In *Tokugawa shakai karano tenbo: Hatten, kouzo, kokusai-kankei* (Perspectives from Tokugawa society: development, structure, and international relations), eds. Akira Hayami, Osamu Saito, and S. Sugiyama. Tokyo: Dobunkan, 33–56.

———. 1993. "Rekishijinkogaku ni okeru shibo dotai (Mortality in historical demography)." Economic Research Society of Sophia University, Discussion Paper Series No. 93-3. Tokyo: Sophia University.

———. 1996. "Shumon Aratame-cho to Kainin Kakiage-cho: 19 seiki kitakanto noson no nyuji shibo (Shumon Aratame-cho and pregnancy registers: infant mortality in nineteenth century agricultural villages in north Kanto)." Working Paper Series No. 2. Kyoto: International Research Center for Japanese Studies, Eurasian Project on Population and Family History.

Klasen, Stephan. 1998. "Marriage, Bargaining, and Intrahousehold Resource Allocation: Excess Female Mortality among Adults during Early German Development, 1740–1860." *Journal of Economic History* 58:432–467.

————. 1999. "Family Composition, Gender Preference, and Parental 'Investment': Selective Gender Bias in Mortality among Infants and Children during Early German Development." Paper presented at the European Science Foundation Workshop on Leaving Home in Historical Eurasian Societies. The Hague, June 18–20.

Knodel, John. 1978. "Natural Fertility in Pre-industrial Germany." *Population Studies* 32.3:481–510.

————. 1988. *Demographic Behavior in the Past: A Study of Fourteen German Village Populations in the Eighteenth and Nineteenth Centuries.* Cambridge: Cambridge University Press.

Kodama, Kota. 1957. *Kinsei nomin seikatsu-shi* (A historical study on life conditions of peasants in early modern Japan). Tokyo: Yoshikawa Kobunkan.

Kok, Jan, Frans van Poppel, and Ellen Kruse. 1997. "Mortality among Illegitimate Children in Mid-Nineteenth Century The Hague." In *The Decline of Infant and Child Mortality*, eds. Carlo A. Corsini and Pier-Paolo Viazzo. The Hague: Martinus Nijhof, 193–211.

Kolchin, Peter. 1987. *Unfree Labor: American Slavery and Russian Serfdom.* Cambridge, Mass.: Harvard University Press.

Koriyama-shi. 1981a. *Koriyama-shi shi 2: Kinsei*, Jyo (The history of Koriyama City 2: Early modern period), Vol. 1, 2nd ed. Tokyo: Kokusho Kanko Kai.

————. 1981b. *Koriyama-shi shi 2: Kinsei, Ge* (The history of Koriyama City 2: Early modern period), Vol. 2, 2nd ed. Tokyo: Kokusho Kanko Kai.

Kousser, Morgan. 1980. "Quantitative Social Scientific History." In *The Past before Us*, ed. Michael Kammen. Cambridge: Cambridge University Press, 433–456.

Kunst, Anton, Judith Wolleswinkel-van den Bosch, and Johan Mackenbach. 1999. "Medical Demography in the Netherlands: Recent Advances, Future Challenges." *Population Issues: An Interdisciplinary Focus*, eds. Leo J. G. van Wissen and Pearl A. Dykstra. New York: Kluwer Academic/Plenum Publishers, 187–228.

Kurosu, Satomi. 1998. "Marriage in a Stem Family System: Inheriting Daughters and Non-Inheriting Daughters in Two Northeastern Villages, 1716–1870." In *House and Stem Family in Eurasian Perspective*, eds. Antoinette Fauve-Chamoux and Emiko Ochiai. Kyoto: International Research Center for Japanese Studies, 245–269.

Kurosu, Satomi, and Emiko Ochiai. 1995. "Adoption as an Heirship Strategy under Demographic Constraints: A Case from Nineteenth-Century Japan." *Journal of Family History* 20.3:261–288.

Kurosu, Satomi, Noriko O. Tsuya, and Kiyoshi Hamano. 1999. "Regional Differentials in the Patterns of First Marriage in the Latter Half of Tokugawa Japan." *Keio Economic Studies* 36.1:13–38.

Kuznets, Simon. 1971. *Modern Economic Growth: Rate, Structure, and Spread.* New Haven, Conn.: Yale University Press.

Lach, Donald F., and Edwin Van Kley. 1993. *Asia in the Making of Europe*, Vol. III. Chicago: University of Chicago Press.

Lafosse, Arlette. 1977. "Epidémies de choléra à Verviers (1833–1834, 1849, 1866)." Master's thesis, University of Liège.

Lagazio, Corrado, Cristina Martelli, and Rosella Rettaroli. 1998. "Italian Mortality Report: Madregolo during the 19th Century." *Eurasian Project on Population and Family History Working Paper Series*, No. 17. Kyoto: International Research Center for Japanese Studies.

Landers, John. 1993. *Death and the Metropolis: Studies in the Demographic History of London, 1670–1830*. Cambridge: Cambridge University Press.

Landes, David S. 1983. *Revolution in Time: Clocks and the Making of the Modern World*. Cambridge, Mass.: Harvard University Press.

———. 1998. *The Wealth and Poverty of Nations: Why Some Are So Rich and Some So Poor*. New York: Norton.

Lang, Erich, Klaus Arnold, and Peter Kupfer. 1994. "Frauen werden alter. Biologische, medizinische und soziologische ursachen." *Zeitschrift fur gerontologie und geriatrie* 27.1:10–15.

Laslett, Peter. 1977. "Characteristics of the Western Family Considered over Time." *Journal of Family History* 2.2:89–116.

———. 1982. "Family and Household as Workgroup and Kin Group: Areas of Traditional Europe Compared." In *Family Forms in Historic Europe*, eds. Richard Wall, Jean Robert, and Peter Laslett. Cambridge: Cambridge University Press, 513–563.

———. 1988. "Family, Kinship and Collectivity as Systems of Support in Pre-Industrial Europe: A Consideration of the 'Nuclear Hardship' Hypotheses." *Continuity and Change* 3:153–175.

———. 1991. *A Fresh Map of Life*. Cambridge, Mass.: Harvard University Press.

Laslett, Peter, and Richard Wall, eds. 1972. *Household and Family in Past Time*. Cambridge: Cambridge University Press.

Lavely, William, and R. Bin Wong. 1998. "Revising the Malthusian Narrative: The Comparative Study of Population Dynamics in Late Imperial China." *Journal of Asian Studies* 57:714–748.

Leboutte, René. 1988. *Reconversions de la main-d'œuvre et transition démographique: Les bassins industriels en aval de Liège, 17e–20e siècles*. Paris: Les Belles-Lettres.

———. 1996. "Adaption, reconversion, mutation. Le rôle de la proto-industrialisation dans la genèse du bassin industriel liégeois." In *Proto-Industrialization. Recent Research and New Perspectives*, ed. René Leboutte. Genève: Droz, 262–290.

———. 1998. "La dynamique des ménages aux 18e–19e siècles: L'exemple de la Basse-Meuse liégeoise." In *Dix essais sur la démographie urbaine de la Wallonie au XIXe siècle*, eds. Claude Desama and Michel Oris. Brussels: Crédit Communal, 163–196.

Lee, James Z., and Cameron Campbell. 1997. *Fate and Fortune in Rural China: Social Organization and Population Behavior in Liaoning, 1774–1873*. Cambridge: Cambridge University Press.

———. 1998a. "Headship Succession and Household Division in Three Chinese Banner Serf Populations, 1789–1909." *Continuity and Change* 13.1:117–142.

———. 1998b. "Getting a Head in Northeast China: Household Succession in Four Banner Serf Populations, 1789–1909." In *House and Stem Family in Eurasian Perspective*, eds.

Antoinette Fauve-Chamoux and Emiko Ochiai. Kyoto: International Research Center for Japanese Studies, 403–430.

Lee, James, Cameron Campbell, and Tan Guofu. 1992. "Infanticide and Family Planning in Rural Liaoning, 1774–1873." In *Chinese History in Economic Perspective*, eds. Lillian Li and Thomas Rawski. Berkeley: University of California Press, 149–176.

Lee, James, Cameron Campbell, and Wang Feng. 1993. "The Last Emperors: An Introduction to the Demography of the Qing (1644–1911) Imperial Lineage." In *Old and New Methods in Historical Demography*, eds. David Reher and Roger Schofield. Oxford: Clarendon Press, 361–382.

————. 2002. "Positive Check or Chinese Checks." *Journal of Asian Studies* 62.2:591–608.

Lee, James, and Jon Gjerde. 1986. "Comparative Household Morphology of Stem, Joint and Nuclear Household Systems: Norway, China, and the United States." *Continuity and Change* 1.1:89–112.

Lee, James (Li Zhongqing), Guo Songyi, and Ding Yizhuang. 2000. *Hunyin jiating yu renkou xingwei: Dongxi bijiao* (Marriage, family, and population behavior: East-West comparisons). Beijing: Peking University Press.

Lee, James, and Osamu Saito, eds. Forthcoming. *Abortion, Infanticide, and Reproductive Behavior in Asia: Past and Present*. Oxford: Oxford University Press.

Lee, James, and Wang Feng. 1999a. "Malthusian Models and Chinese Realities: The Chinese Demographic System, 1700–2000." *Population and Development Review* 25.1:33–65.

————. 1999b. *One-Quarter of Humanity: Malthusian Mythology and Chinese Realities, 1700–2000*. Cambridge, Mass.: Harvard University Press.

Lee, James, Wang Feng, and Cameron Campbell. 1994. "Infant and Child Mortality among the Qing Nobility: Implications for Two Types of Positive Check." *Population Studies* 48.3:395–412.

Lee, Ronald D. 1981. "Short-Term Variation: Vital Rates, Prices, and Weather." In *The Population History of England, 1541–1871*, eds. Edward Wrigley and Roger Schofield. Cambridge: Cambridge University Press, 356–401.

————. 1990. "The Demographic Response to Economic Crisis in Historical and Contemporary Populations." *Population Bulletin of the United Nations* 29:1–15.

————. 1993. "Inverse Projections and Demographic Fluctuations: A Critical Assessment of New Methods." In *Old and New Methods in Historical Demography*, eds. David Reher and Roger Schofield. Oxford: Clarendon Press, 7–28.

————. 1997. "Population Dynamics: Equilibrium, Disequilibrium, and Consequences of Fluctuations." In *Handbook of Population and Family Economics*, Vol. 1B, eds. Mark R. Rosenzweig and Oded Stark. Amsterdam: Elsevier, 1063–1115.

Lefebvre, Louis. 1947. "Une expérience inutile et injuste: l'application à l'Ardenne de la loi du 25 mars 1847 sur le défrichement des bruyères." In *Miscellanea Historica in honorem Leonis van der Essen*, vol. 2. Brussels: Presses Universitaires, 1039–1048.

Leibenstein, Harvey. 1981. "Economic Decision Theory and Human Fertility Behavior: A Speculative Essay." *Population and Development Review* 7.3:381–400.

Le Roy Ladurie, Emmanuel. 1974. *The Peasants of Languedoc*. Urbana: University of Illinois Press.

———. 1975. "Famine Amenorrhoea (Seventeenth–Eighteenth Centuries)." In *Biology of Man in History*, eds. Robert Forster and Orest Ranum. Baltimore: John Hopkins Press, 163–178.

Lesthaege, Ron. 1977. *The Decline of Belgian Fertility, 1800–1970*. Princeton, N.J.: Princeton University Press.

Levine, David. 1987. *Reproducing Families: The Political Economy of English Population History*. Cambridge: Cambridge University Press.

Lewis, Martin, and Karen Wigen. 1997. *The Myth of Continents: A Critique of Metageography*. Berkeley: University of California Press.

Li, Bozhong. 1998. *Agricultural Development on Jiangnan, 1620–1850*. New York: St. Martin's Press.

———. 2000. "Duotai, biyun yu jieyu: Song Yuan Ming Qing Jiangzhe diqu de jieyu fangfa jiqi yunyong yu chuanbo (Abortion, contraception, and sterilization: Birth control methods and their dissemination in Song-Yuan-Ming-Qing Jiangsu and Zhejiang)." In *Hunyin yu jiating: Dongxi bijiao shi* (Marriage and family: East–West comparative history), eds. Ding Yizhuang, Guo Songyi, and James Lee. Peking: Peking University Press, 172–196.

———. Forthcoming. "Farm Productivity in Liangnan, 1620–1850." In *New Evidence of the Standard of Living in Pre-Industrial Europe and Asia*, eds. Robert Allen, Tommy Bengtsson, and Martin Dribe, eds. Oxford: Oxford University Press.

Lillard, Lee A., and Constantijn W. A. Panis. 1996. "Marital Status and Mortality: The Role of Health." *Demography* 33.3:313–327.

Lindahl-Kiessling, Kerstin, and Hans Landberg. 1994. *Population, Economic Development, and the Environment: The Making of our Common Future*. Oxford: Oxford University Press.

Little, Daniel. 1995. "Objectivity, Truth, and Method: A Philosopher's Perspective on the Social Sciences." *Anthropology Newsletter* (Nov.), 42–43.

———. 2000. "Explaining Large-Scale Historical Change." *Philosophy of the Social Sciences* 30.1:89–112.

Liu, Ts'ui-jung. 1978. "Chinese Genealogies as a Source for the Study of Historical Demography." *Studies and Essays in Commemoration of the Golden Jubilee of the Academia Sinica*. Taibei: Academia Sinica, 849–870.

———. 1981. "The Demographic Dynamics of Some Clans in the Lower Yangtze Area, ca. 1400–1900." *Academia Economica Papers* 9.1:115–160.

———. 1983. "Ming Qing renkou zhi zengzhi yu qianyi—Changjiang zhong xiayou diqu zupu ziliao zhi fenxi (Population growth and migration in the Ming and Qing—analysis of genealogical materials from the Middle and Lower Yangzi)." In *Dierqu Zhongguo shehui jingjishi yanjiuhui lunwen ji* (Papers from the second seminar on Chinese social and economic history), eds. Cho-yun Hsu, Han-kuang Mao, and Ts'ui-jung Liu. Taibei: Chinese Research Materials and Service Center, 283–316.

———. 1985. "The Demography of Two Chinese Clans in Hsiao-shan, Chekiang, 1650–1850." In *Family and Population in East Asian History*, eds. Susan Hanley and Arthur Wolf. Stanford: Stanford University Press, 13–61.

———. 1992. *Ming Qing shiqi jiazu renkou yu shehui jingji bianqian* (Lineage population and socioeconomic changes in the Ming and Qing periods). 2 vols. Taibei: Institute of Economics, Academia Sinica.

———. 1995a. "Demographic Constraint and Family Structure in Traditional Chinese Lineages, ca. 1200–1900." In *Chinese Historical Microdemography*, ed. Steven Harrell. Berkeley: University of California Press, 121–140.

———. 1995b. "Historical Demography of South China Lineages." In *Chinese Historical Microdemography*, ed. Steven Harrell. Berkeley: University of California Press, 94–120.

Livi, Livio. 1918–1920. *Gli ebrei alla luce della statistica*. 2 vols. Florence: Libreria della Voce.

Livi-Bacci, Massimo. 1977. *A History of Italian Fertility during the Last Two Centuries*. Princeton, N.J.: Princeton University Press.

———. 1978. "Una comunità israelitica in un ambiente rurale: la demografia degli ebrei di Pitigliano nel XIX secolo." In *Studi in memoria di Federigo Melis*, Vol. 5. Naples: Giannini, 99–137.

———. 1991. *Population and Nutrition*. Cambridge: Cambridge University Press.

———. 1994. *Manuale di demografia*. Turin: Loescher.

———. 1999. *La population dans l'histoire de l'Europe*. Paris: Le Seuil.

Loudon, Irvine. 1992. *Death in Childbirth*. Oxford: Clarendon Press.

Lucchetti, Enzo. 1978. "Aspetti genetici e demografici nello studio delle popolazioni umane." *Antropologia contemporanea* 1:41–57.

Lundh, Christer. 1983. "Levnadsstandarden—indikatorer och mått: engelsk och svensk debatt om lönearbetarnas villkor 1750–1850." Meddelande från Ekonomisk-historiska institutionen, No. 29. Lund: Lunds universitet.

———. 1995. "Households and Families in Pre-industrial Sweden." *Continuity and Change* 10.1:33–68.

Lundh, Christer, and Mats Olsson. 2001. "Godsens bönder och ålderdomen. Undantagssystemet under 1800-talet." In *Skånska godsmiljöer*. Lund: Skånes hembygdsförbund, 117–134.

———. Forthcoming. "The Institution of Retirement at Scanian Estates in the Nineteenth Century." *Continuity and Change* 17.2.

Lundsjö, Olle. 1975. *Fattigdomen på den svenska landsbygden under 1800-talet*. Stockholm: Almqvist & Wiksell.

Lynch, Katherine A. 2000. "Infant Mortality, Child Neglect, and Child Abandonment in European History: A Comparative Analysis." In *Population and Economy: From Hunger to Modern Economic Growth*, eds. Tommy Bengtsson and Osamu Saito. Oxford: Oxford University Press, 133–164.

Lynch, Katherine A., and Joël B. Greenhouse. 1994. "Risk Factors for Infant Mortality in Nineteenth-Century Sweden." *Population Studies* 48.1:117–133.

Macfarlane, Alan. 1978. *The Origins of English Individualism: Family, Property, and Social Transition.* Oxford: Oxford University Press.

———. 1986. *Marriage and Love in England: Modes of Reproduction, 1300–1840.* Oxford: Basil Blackwell.

———. 1987. *The Culture of Capitalism.* Oxford: Oxford University Press, 1987.

———. 1997. *The Savage Wars of Peace: England, Japan and the Malthusian Trap.* Oxford: Basil Blackwell.

Macfarlane, Alan, and Gerry Martin. 2002. *Glass: A World History.* Chicago: University of Chicago Press.

Maddison, Angus. 2001. *The World Economy: A Millennial Perspective.* Paris: Organisation for Economic Co-operation and Development, Development Centre.

Mahoney, James. 1999. "Nominative, Ordinal, and Narrative Appraisal in Macro-Causal Analysis." *American Journal of Sociology* 104.4:1154–1196.

Malthus, Thomas Robert. 1798/1986. *An Essay on the Principle of Population, First Edition,* ed. Antony G. Flew. London: Penguin English Library.

———. 1803. *An Essay on the Principle of Population,* 2nd ed., ed. Donald Winch. Cambridge: Cambridge University Press.

———. 1826/1986. "An Essay on the Principle of Population." In *The Works of Thomas Malthus,* ed. E. A. Wrigley and David Souden, Vol. 2. London: William Pickering.

Manfredini, Matteo. 1996. "L'utilizzo degli Status Animarum nelle ricostruzioni nominative: miglioramenti informativi qualitativi e quantitativi. Il caso di Madregolo (1629–1914)." *Bollettino di Demografia Storica* 24–25:113–129.

———. 1997. "A Rural Population of Northern Italy: Madregolo during the XIX Century." Eurasian Project on Population and Family History, Working Paper Series, No. 12. Kyoto: International Research Center for Japanese Studies.

———. Forthcoming. "Families in Motion: Role and Characteristics of Household Migration in a Nineteenth Century Rural Italian Parish." *The History of the Family: An International Quarterly* 8.2.

March, Lucien. 1912. "Some Researches Concerning the Factors of Mortality." *Journal of the Royal Statistical Society* 75:505–538.

Marks, Lara. 1994. *Model Mothers: Jewish Mothers and Maternity Provisions in East London, 1870–1939.* Oxford: Oxford University Press.

Martikainen, Pekka, and Tapani Valkonen. 1996. "Mortality after the Death of a Spouse." *American Journal of Public Health* 86:1087–1093.

Marx, Karl. 1853. "The British Rule in India." In *The Portable Karl Marx,* ed. Eugene Kamenka. New York: Penguin Books, 329–341.

Masuy-Stroobant, Godelieve. 1983. *Les déterminants individuels et régionaux de la mortalité infantile. La Belgique d'hier et d'aujourd'hui.* Louvain-la-Neuve: Ciaco.

Matthews, Karen A. 1989. "Interactive Effects of Behaviour and Reproductive Hormones on Sex Differences in Risk for Coronary Heart Disease." *Health Psychology* 8.4:373–387.

McLaren, Angus. 1984. *Reproductive Rituals: The Perception of Fertility in England from the Sixteenth to the Nineteenth Century.* London: Methuen.

McMahon, Brian, Thomas F. Pugh, and Johannes Ipsen. 1960. *Epidemiologic Methods.* Boston: Little, Brown.

Meffre, Véronique. Forthcoming. "La sous-mortalité infantile des communautées juives européennes et américaines au XIX siècle: un essai de synthèse critique." In *La démographie des minorities*, eds. Guy Brunet, Michel Oris, Alain Bideau. Bern: Peter Lang.

Menken, Jane, and Cameron Campbell. 1992. "Implications for Long-Term Population Growth of Age Patterns of Famine-Related Mortality Increase." *Health Transition Review* 2.1:91–101.

Meuvret, Jean. 1946. "Les crises de subsistence et la démographie de la France d'Ancien Régime." *Population* 1:643–650.

———. 1965. "Demographic Crises in France from the Sixteenth to the Eighteenth Century." In *Population in History: Essays in Historical Demography*, eds. D. V. Glass and D. E. C. Eversley. London: Edward Arnold, 507–522.

Miller, Jane E. 1989. "Is the Relationship between Birth Intervals and Perinatal Mortality Spurious? Evidence from Hungary and Sweden." *Population Studies* 53:479–495.

Miller, Jane E., Germán Rodriguez, and Anne Pebley. 1993. "Lactation and Mother's Post-Partum Weight Change." In *International Population Conference. Montreal 1993*, Vol. 1. Liège: International Union for the Scientific Study of Population, 579–591.

Ministero dell'Interno, Direzione generale di statistica (Ministry of the Interior, General Office of Statistics). 1886. *Risultati dell'inchiesta sulle condizioni igieniche e sanitarie nei comuni del Regno.* Rome.

Miyamoto, Matao. 1988. *Kinsei Nippon no Shijo-Keizai: Osaka Kome-shijo Bunseki* (Market economy in early modern Japan: An analysis of the Osaka rice market). Tokyo: Yuhikaku.

Montulet, Marius. 1955. "Essai d'évolution d'un terroir récemment herbager. Sart-les-Spa: étude de géographie humaine." Master's thesis, University of Liège.

Morris, Morris D. 1979. *Measuring the Conditions of the World's Poor: The Physical Quality of Life Index.* New York: Pergamon Press.

Mosk, Carl. 1983. *Patriarchy and Fertility: Japan and Sweden, 1880–1960.* New York: Academic Press.

Mosley, W. Henry. 1985. "Will Primary Health Care Reduce Infant and Child Mortality? A Critique of Some Current Strategies, with Special Reference to Africa and Asia." In *Health Policy, Social Policy, and Mortality Prospects*, eds. Jacques Vallin and A. Lopez. Liège: International Union for the Scientific Study of Population, 103–138.

Mosley, W. Henry, and Stan Becker. 1991. "Demographic Models for Child Survival and Implications for Health Intervention Programmes." *Health Policy and Planning* 6:218–233.

Mosley, W. Henry, and Lincoln C. Chen. 1984. "An Analytical Framework for the Study of Child Survival in Developing Countries." In *Child Survival: Strategies for Research*, supplement to Vol. 10 of *Population and Development Review*, 25–48.

Muellbauer, John. 1987. "Professor Sen and the Standard of Living." In *The Standard of Living*, ed. G. Hawthorn. Cambridge: Cambridge University Press, 39–58.

Muhuri, Pradip K., and Samuel H. Preston. 1991. "Effects of Family Composition on Mortality Differentials by Sex among Children in Matlab, Bangladesh." *Population and Development Review* 17.3:415–434.

Municipio di Venezia. Giunta Comunale di Statistica. 1881. *Statistica del settennio 1874–80*. Venice: Tipografia Antonelli.

Myrdahl, Gunnar. 1933. *The Cost of Living in Sweden, 1830–1930*. London: P. S. King and Sons.

Nagata, Mary Louise, Satomi Kurosu, and Akira Hayami. 1998. "Shimomoriya and Niita of the Nihonmatsu Domain in the Northeastern Region of Tokugawa Japan." Eurasian Project on Population and Family History Working Paper Series, No. 20. Kyoto: International Research Center for Japanese Studies.

Naito, Kanji. 1973. *Basshi-sozoku no kenkyu* (A study of ultimogeniture). Tokyo: Kobundo.

Nakagawa, Eisuke, ed. 1900. *Shindatsu Nigun Son-shi* (Village history of two counties in the Shindatsu region), Vol. 2. Sendai: Kosetsu Shoja.

Nakane, Chie. 1967. *Kinship and Economic Organization in Rural Japan*. London: Athlone Press; New York: Humanities Press.

———. 1973. *Japanese Society*. London: Penguin Books.

———. 1990. "Tokugawa Society." In *Tokugawa Japan*, eds. Chie Nakane and Shinzaburo Oishi. Tokyo: University of Tokyo Press, 213–231.

Narimatsu, Saeko. 1985. *Kinsei Tohoku Noson no Hitobito: Oshu Asaka-gun Simomoriya-mura* (People in a northeastern agricultural village in early modern Japan: The village of Shimomoriya, Asaka County, Ou Region). Kyoto: Mineruva Shobo.

———. 1992. *Edo-jidai no Tohoku noson: Nihonmatsu-han Niita-mura* (Agricultural villages in northeastern Tokugawa Japan: The village of Niita in Nihonmatsu Domain). Tokyo: Dobunkan.

National Institute of Population and Social Security Research. 2000. *Latest Demographic Statistics 2000*. Tokyo: National Institute of Population and Social Security Research (in Japanese).

Nault, François, Bertrand Desjardins, and Jacques Légaré. 1990. "Effect of Reproductive Behaviour on Infant Mortality of French Canadians during the 17th and 18th Centuries." *Population Studies* 44.2:273–285.

Neven, Muriel. 1997. "Epidemiology of Town and Countryside: Mortality and Causes of Death in East Belgium, 1850–1910." *Revue Belge d'Histoire Contemporaine* 27.1-2:39–82.

———. 1998. "Intensity and Consequences of Widowhood in Nineteenth Century East Belgium." *Revue: Informatique et Statistique dans les Sciences humaines* 34:125–190.

———. 2000a. "Dynamique individuelle et reproduction familiale au sein d'une société rurale: Le Pays de Herve dans la seconde moitié du 19e siècle." Ph.D. dissertation, University of Liège.

———. 2000b. "Mortality Differential and the Peculiarities of Mortality in an Urban-Industrial Population: A Case-Study of Tilleur, Belgium." *Continuity and Change* 15.2:297–329.

Neven, Muriel, and Michel Oris. 1995. "Les statistiques des dispensaires antituberculeux et des hôpitaux au service de l'histoire sociale et de l'épidémiologie de la 'peste blanche' fin 19e–début 20e siècle." *Annales de Démographie Historique*: 225–240.

———. 1998. "Les industries rurales dans l'Est de la Belgique au 19e siècle. Une histoire d'ambiguïtés." Unpublished ms.

Niemi, Timo. 1979. "The Mortality of Male Old Age Pensioners Following Spouse's Death." *Scandinavian Journal of Social Medicine* 7:115–117.

Nihonmatsu-shi. 1982. *Nihonmatsu-shi shi, Dai-6-kan: Kinsei III* (The history of the City of Nihonmatsu, Vol. 6: Early modern period, No. 3). Nihonmatsu-shi.

Notestein, Frank W., and Chiao Chiming. 1937. "Population." In *Land Utilization in China*, ed. John Buck. Chicago: University of Chicago Press, Vol. 1, 358–399.

Nystedt, Paul. 2002. "Widowhood-Related Mortality in Scania, Sweden during the 19th Century." *History of the Family* 7.3:451–478.

O'Brien, Patrick K., and Stanley L. Engerman. 1981. "Changes in Income and Its Distribution during the Industrial Revolution." In *The Economic History of Britain since 1700, Vol. 1: 1700–1860*, eds. Richard Floud and Donald McCloskey. Cambridge: Cambridge University Press.

Ochiai, Emiko. 1996. *The Japanese Family System in Transition: A Sociological Analysis of Family Change in Postwar Japan*. Tokyo: LTCB International Library Foundation.

———. 1998. "Two Types of Stem Household System in Japan: The *Ie* in Global Perspective." In *House and Stem Family in Eurasian Perspective*, eds. Antoinette Fauve-Chamoux and Emiko Ochiai. Kyoto: International Research Center for Japanese Studies.

———. 1999a. "Modern Japan through the Eyes of an Old Midwife: From an Oral Life History to Social History," trans. Mio Neuse. In *Gender and Japanese History*, eds. Wakita Haruko, Anne Bouchy, and Ueno Chizuko. Osaka: Osaka University Press, 235–296.

———. 1999b. "The Reproductive Revolution at the End of Tokugawa Period." In *Women and Class in Japanese History*, eds. Hitomi Tonomura, Anne Walthall, and Wakita Haruko. Ann Arbor: University of Michigan Press, 187–215.

Odén, Birgitta. 1987. "Planering inför ålderdomen i senmedeltidens Stockholm" (Retirement Planning in Stockholm in the Late Middle Ages). In *Manliga strukturer och kvinnliga strategier: en bok till Gunhild Kyle, december 1987* (Male Structures and Female Strategies: A book to Gunhild Kyle, December 1987), eds. Birgit Sawyer and Anita Göransson. Gothenburg: Historiska Institutionen, Univ.

Ogashima, Minoru, ed. 1894. *Nihon Saii-shi* (The history of natural disasters in Japan). Tokyo: Nihon Kogyokai.

Ó Gráda, Cormac. 1993. *Ireland before and after the Famine: Explorations in Economic History, 1808–1825*, 2nd ed. Manchester: Manchester University Press.

————. 1999. *Black '47 and Beyond: The Great Irish Famine in History, Economy, and Memory.* Princeton, N.J.: Princeton University Press.

Okada, Aoi, and Satomi Kurosu. 1998. "Succession and the Death of the Household Head in Early Modern Japan: A Case from a Northeastern Village, 1720–1870." *Continuity and Change* 13.1:143–166.

Okazaki, Yoichi. 1980. *Jinko Tokeigaku* (Methods for statistical analysis of population). Tokyo: Kokinshoin.

Olofsson, Jonas. 1996. *Arbetslöshetsfrågan i historisk belysning. En diskussion om arbetslöshet och social politik i Sverige 1830–1920.* Lund: Lund University Press.

Olsson, Mats. 2002. *Storgodsdrift. Godsekonomi och arbetsorganisation i Skåne från dansk tid till mitten av 1800-talet* (Manorial Economy and Corvée Labor in Early Modern Scania). Stockholm: Almqvist and Wiksell.

Ono, Yoshihiko. 1993. "Bunkakei no Keisanki-riyo II: Deita nyuryoku no Yuzaa Intaafeisu (Rekishi-jinkogaku no Baai) (Computer utilization for humanities II: User interface for data entry, the case of historical demography)." *Nihon Kenkyu* 8:165–182.

Ooms, Herman. 1996. *Tokugawa Village Practice: Class, Status, Power, and Law.* Berkeley: University of California Press.

Oris, Michel. 1988. "Choléra et hygiène publique en Belgique. Les réactions d'un système social face à une maladie sociale." In *Peurs et terreurs face à la contagion*, eds. Jean Pierre Bardet, Patrice Bourdelais, Pierre Guillaume, François Lebrun, and Claude Quetel. Paris: Fayard, 83–106.

————. 1990. "L'urbanisation de la province de Liège, 1800–1970. Sur un concept, son approche et son usage." *Bulletin trimestriel du Crédit Communal*, no. 172:77–92.

————. 1994. *Bibliographie de l'histoire des populations belges: Bilan des travaux des origines à nos jours.* Liège: Derouaux.

————. 1995a. "L'histoire des apports migratoires, une clé pour lire le temps long des bassins industriels." In *Passé et avenir des bassins industriels en Europe*, eds. René Leboutte and Jean-Paul Lehners. Luxembourg: Centre Universitaire du Luxembourg, 289–312.

————. 1995b. "La transition de la fécondité légitime dans le milieu urbain wallon et bruxellois." In *Transitions démographiques et sociétés: Chaire Quetelet 1992*, eds. Dominique Tabutin, Thierry Eggerickx, and Catherine Goubin. Louvain-la-neuve: Académia l'Harmattan, 359–379.

————. 1996. "Fertility and Migration in the Heart of the Industrial Revolution." *History of the Family* 1.2:169–182.

————. 1998a. "Mortalité, industrialisation et urbanisation au 19e siècle. Quelques résultats des recherches liégeoises." In *Dix essais sur la démographie urbaine de la Wallonie au 19e siècle*, eds. Desama Claude and Michel Oris. Brussels: Crédit Communal, 289–321.

————. 1998b. "A Brief Discussion on the Economic Series in 19th Century Belgium." Eurasian Project on Population and Family History Working Paper Series, No. 19. Kyoto: International Research Center for Japanese Studies.

————. 2002. "Le poids des réseaux familiaux dans les migrations en Belgique orientale au 19e siècle? Peut-on quantifier?" In *Life in Town: Vivere in Citta*, ed. Eugenio Sonnino. Rome: Universita La Sapienza.

Oris, Michel, and George Alter. 2001. "Paths to the City and Roads to Death: Mortality and Migration in East Belgium During the Industrial Revolution." In *Recent Work in Belgium Historical Demography 19th and Early 20th Centuries*, eds. Isabelle Devos and Muriel Neven. Special Issue of the *Revue Belge d'Histoire Contemporaine* 31.3–4:453–495.

Oris, Michel, and Emiko Ochiai. 2002. "Family Crisis in the Context of Different Family Systems: Frameworks and Evidence on 'When Dad Died.'" In *When Dad Died*, eds. Renzo Derosas and Michel Oris. Bern: Peter Lang, 27–89.

Ota, Motoko, and Mikako Sawayama. Forthcoming. "From Infanticide to Abortion." In *Abortion, Infanticide, and Reproductive Behavior in Asia*, eds. James Lee and Osamu Saito. Oxford: Oxford University Press.

Otake, Hideo. 1982. *Hoken-shakai no nomin kazoku* (Peasant families in a feudal society). Tokyo: Sobunsha.

Palloni, Alberto, Hector Perez-Brignoli, and Elizabeth Ariàs. 2000. "Malthus in Latin America: Demographic Responses during the Nineteenth and Twentieth Centuries." In *Population and the Economy*, eds. Tommy Bengtsson and Osamu Saito. Oxford: Oxford University Press, 213–253.

Pareja, Alonzo A. 1997. "Immigracion y condiciones de vida en la villa de Bilbao, 1825–1935." Doctoral thesis, Faculdad de Ciencias Sociales y de la Informacion, Bilbao.

Parenti, G. 1942. *Prezzi e mercato a Siena (1546–1765)*. Florence.

Parthasarathi, Prasannan. 1998. "Rethinking Wages and Competitiveness in the Eighteenth Century: Britain and South India." *Past and Present* 158:79–109.

———. Forthcoming. "Agriculture, Labor and the Standard of Living in Eighteenth Century India." In *New Evidence of the Standard of Living in Pre-Industrial Asia and Europe*, eds. Robert Allen, Tommy Bengtsson, and Martin Dribe. Oxford: Oxford University Press.

Pazzagli, Carlo. 1973. *L'agricoltura toscana nella prima meta dell'800: tecniche di produzione e rapporti mezzadrili*. Florence: Olschki.

Pebley, Anne R., and Julie Davanzo. 1993. "Maternal Depletion and Child Survival in Guatemala and Malaysia." RAND Labor and Population Program, Working Paper Series 93-118. Santa Monica, Calif.: RAND.

Perkins, Dwight H. 1969. *Agricultural Development in China, 1368–1968*. Chicago: Aldine.

Perrenoud, Alfred. 1979. *La population de Genève, 16e–19e siècles*. Geneva: Société d'Histoire et d'Archéologie de Genève.

———. 1981. "Surmortalité féminine et conditions de la femme (17e–19e siècles): Une vérification empirique." *Annales de Démographie Historique*: 104–117.

———. 1993. "Histoire démographique et histoire sociale." *Annales de Démographie Historique*: 383–389.

———. 1994. "La mortalité des enfants en Europe francophone: état de la question." *Annales de Démographie Historique*: 79–96.

———. 1995. "Transitions épidémiologiques et transitions de fécondité dans le passé occidental." In *Transitions démographiques et sociétés: Chaire Quetelet 1992*, eds. Dominique Tabutin, Thierry Eggerickx, and Catherine Goubin. Louvain-la-neuve: Académia l'Harmattan, 239–255.

————. 1997. "La mortalité." In *Histoire des populations de l'Europe*, eds. Jean-Pierre Bardet and Jacques Dupâquier, Vol. 1. Paris: Fayard, 289–316.

Perrenoud, Alfred, and Patrice Bourdelais. 1998. "Le recul de la mortalité." In *Histoire des populations de l'Europe*, eds. Jean-Pierres Bardet and Jacques Dupâquier, Vol. 1. Paris: Fayard, 57–101.

Pinnelli, Antonella, and Paola Mancini. 1991. "Différences de mortalité par sexe de la naissance à la puberté en Italie: un siècle d'évolution." *Population* 46.6:651–676.

————. 1997. "Gender Mortality Differences from Birth to Puberty in Italy, 1887–1940." In *The Decline of Infant and Child Mortality*, eds. Carlo Corsini and Pier Paolo Viazzo. The Hague: Martinus Nijhof.

Pitkänen, Kari J., and James H. Mielke. 1993. "Age and Sex Differentials in Mortality during Two Nineteenth Century Population Crises." *European Journal of Population* 9.1:1–32.

Pomeranz, Kenneth. 2000. *The Great Divergence: Europe, China, and the Making of the Modern World Economy*. Princeton, N.J.: Princeton University Press.

Pomeranz, Kenneth. 2002. "Beyond the East-West Binary: Resituating Development Paths in the Eighteenth-Century World." *Journal of Asian Studies* 19.2:539–590.

————. 2003. "Facts Are Stubborn Things: A Response to Philip Huang." *Journal of Asian Studies* 62.1:167–181.

————. Forthcoming. "Standards of Living in 18th Century China: Regional Differences, Temporal Trends, and Incomplete Evidence." In *New Evidence of the Standard of Living in Pre-Industrial Europe and Asia*, eds. Robert Allen, Tommy Bengtsson, and Martin Dribe. Oxford: Oxford University Press.

Poni, Carlo. 1978. "Family and Podere in Emilia Romagna." *Journal of Family History* 1:201–234.

————. 1982. *Fossi e cavedagne benedicon le campagne*. Bologna: Il Mulino.

Pope, Clayton. 1989. "Adult Mortality before the Twentieth Century: Current Evidence and New Sources." Paper presented to the UCLA Von Gremp Workshop in Economic History, Los Angeles.

Poulain, Michel. 1977. "Une épidémie de choléra et ses répercussions démographiques: un mécanisme autorégulateur suite à une crise de mortalité." *Population et Famille* 41.2:73–90.

Poulain, Michel, and Dominique Tabutin. 1977. "Mortalité aux jeunes âges en Belgique de 1840 à 1970." *Population et Famille* 42.3:49–86.

————. 1981. "La surmortalité des petites filles en Belgique au 19e et au début du 20e siècle." *Annales de Démographie Historique*, 105–118.

Pozzi, Lucia. 1995. "La transizione della mortalità in Italia: strumenti di analisi ed ipotesi interpretative." In *Continuità e discontinuità nei processi demografici: l'Italia nella transizione demografica*. Soveria Mannelli (CZ): Rubbettino, 263–274.

————. 2000. *La lotta per la vita. Evoluzione e geografia della sopravvivenza in Italia fra '800 e '900*. Udine: Forum.

Pozzi, Lucia, and Elena Robles Gonzáles. 1996. "L'analisi della mortalità infantile negli anni della transizione: una riflessione sull'esperienza italiana e spagnola." In *Studi di popolazione. Temi di ricerca nuova.* Rome: Secondo Convegno dei Giovani Studiosi dei Problemi di Popolazione, 147–171.

Preston, Samuel H. 1976. *Mortality Patterns in National Populations: With Special Reference to Recorded Causes of Death.* New York: Academic Press.

———. 1985. "Mortality in Childhood: Lessons from the WFS." In *Reproductive Change in Developing Countries: Insights from the World Fertility Survey,* eds. John Cleland, John Hobcraft, and Betzy Dinesen. Oxford: Oxford University Press, 253–272.

———. 1996. "Population Studies of Mortality." *Population Studies* 50.3:525–536.

Preston, Samuel H., and Irma T. Elo. 1995. "Are Educational Differentials in Adult Mortality Increasing in the United States?" *Journal of Aging and Health* 7.4:476–496.

Preston, Samuel H., Irma T. Elo, Ira Rosenwaike, and Mark Hill. 1996. "African-American Mortality at Older Ages: Results of a Matching Study." *Demography* 33.2:193–209.

Preston Samuel H., and Michael Haines. 1991. *Fatal Years: Child Mortality in Late 19th Century America.* Princeton, N.J.: Princeton University Press.

Preston, Samuel H., Patrick Heuveline, and Michel Guillot. 2001. *Demography: Measuring and Modeling Population Processes.* Oxford: Basil Blackwell.

Preston, Samuel H., and John McDonald. 1979. "The Incidence of Divorce Within Cohorts of American Marriages Contracted Since the Civil War." *Demography* 16.1:1–25.

Preston, Samuel H., and Etienne van de Walle. 1978. "Urban French Mortality in the 19th Century." *Population Studies* 32:275–297.

Quetelet, Adolphe. 1869. *Physique sociale ou essai sur le développement des facultés de l'homme.* Brussels: Muquardt. 2 vols.

Reher, David S. 1990. *Town and Country in Pre-Industrial Spain: Cuenca, 1550–1870.* Cambridge: Cambridge University Press.

———. 1991. "Population et économie dans le Mexique du XVIIIêne siècle: Une analyse des fluctuations annuelles." *Population* 5:1185–1207.

———. 1997. *Perspectives on the Family in Spain, Past and Present.* Oxford: Oxford University Press.

———. 1998. "Family Ties in Western Europe: Persistent Contrasts." *Population and Development Review* 24.2:203–234.

———. 1999. "Back to the Basics: Mortality and Fertility Interactions during the Demographic Transition." *Continuity and Change* 14.1:9–33.

Reher, David S., and Roger Schofield. 1991. "The Decline of Mortality in Europe." In *The Decline of Mortality in Europe,* eds. Roger Schofield, David Reher, and Alain Bideau. Oxford: Clarendon Press, 1–17.

———, eds. 1993. *Old and New Methods in Historical Demography.* Oxford: Clarendon Press.

Reid, Alice. 1997. "Locality or Class? Spatial and Social Differentials in Infant and Child Mortality in England and Wales, 1895–1911." In *The Decline of Infant and Child Mortality,* eds. Carlo Corsini and Pier-Paolo Viazzo. The Hague: Martinus Nijhof, 129–154.

Reid, Thomas M. S. 1998. "Striking a Balance in Maternal Immune Response to Infection." *Lancet* 351.9117:1670–1671.

Reuterswärd, Elizabeth, and Franceska Olsson. 1993. "Skånes Demografiska Databas." Lund Paper in Economic History, No. 33. Lund: Lund University.

Richards, Toni. 1984. "Weather, Nutrition and the Economy: The Analysis of Short Run Fluctuations in Births, Deaths, and Marriages, France 1740–1909." In *Preindustrial Population Change*, eds. Tommy Bengtsson, Gunnar Fridlizius, and Rolf Ohlsson. Lund: Almqvist & Wiksell, 357–390.

Rilievo degli abitanti di Venezia 1869. 1871. Venice.

Riley, James C. 1993. "Excess Mortality in Youth." In *Old and New Methods in Historical Demography*, eds. David Reher and Roger Schofield, 394–410.

Riley, James C., and George Alter. 1996. "The Sick and the Well: Adult Health in Britain during the Health Transition." *Health Transition Review* 6 Suppl.:19–44.

Rogers, Richard G. 1995. "Marriage, Sex, and Mortality." *Journal of Marriage and the Family* 57.2:515–526.

Rollet, Catherine. 1994. "La mortalité des enfants dans le passé: au-delà des apparences." *Annales de Démographie Historique*: 7–22.

———. 1995. "La construction d'une culture internationale autour de l'enfant." In *Comment peut-on être socio-anthropologue? Autour d'Alain Girard.* Paris: L'Harmattan, 143–167.

Romanelli, Giandomenico. 1988. *Venezia Ottocento: L'architettura l'urbanistica.* Venice: Albrizzi.

Rosina, Alessandro, and Fiorenzo Rossi. 1998. "Il Veneto." *Bollettino di Demografia Storica* 28:89–114.

Rotberg, Robert, and Theodore K. Rabb, eds. 1985. *Hunger and History: The Impact of Changing Food Production and Consumption Patterns on Society.* Cambridge: Cambridge University Press.

Ruggles, Steven. 1998. "The Rise of Divorce and Separation in the United States, 1880–1990." *Demography* 34.4:455–466.

Rutten, Willibrord. 1997. *De vreselijkste aller harpijen. Pokkenepidemieën en pokkenbestrijding in Nederland in de 18de en 19de eeuw . . . .* Wageningen: Landbouwuniversiteit.

Ruzicka, Lado. 1989. "Problems and Issues in the Study of Mortality Differentials." In *Differential Mortality: Methodological Issues and Biosocial Factors*, eds. Lado Ruzicka, Guillaume Wunsch, and Penny Kane. Oxford: Clarendon Press, 3–17.

Saito, Osamu. 1978. "The Labor Market in Tokugawa Japan." *Explorations in Economic History* 15.1:84–100.

———. 1992. "Jinko-tenkan-izen no Nihon ni okeru mortality: pataan to henka (Mortality in pretransitional Japan: Patterns and changes)." *Keizai Kenkyu* 43.2:248–267.

———. 1996. "Gender, Workload and Agricultural Progress: Japan's Historical Experience in Perspective." In *Proto-Industrialization: Recent Research and New Prospects. In Memory of Franklin Mendels*, ed. René Leboutte. Geneva: Librairie Droz, 129–151.

————. 1997a. *Hikakushi no enkinho* (Perspectives on comparative history). Tokyo: NTT.

————. 1997b. "Infant Mortality in Pre-Transition Japan: Levels and Trends." In *Infant and Child Mortality in the Past*, eds. Alain Bideau, Bertrand Desjardins, and Hector Perez Brignoli. Oxford: Clarendon Press, 135–153.

————. 1998. "Two Kinds of Stem Family System: Traditional Japan and Europe Compared." *Continuity and Change* 13.1:167–186.

————. 2002. "The Frequency of Famines as Demographic Correctives in the Japanese Past." In *Famine Demography: Perspectives from the Past and Present*, eds. Tim Dyson and Cormac O'Grada. Oxford: Oxford University Press, 218–239.

Saito, Ren'ichi, ed. 1966. *Fukenbetsu Nenbetsu Kisho Saigai Hyo* (Tables of climatic and natural disasters by year and prefecture). Tokyo: Chijin Shokan.

Samoggia, Alessandra. 1995. "Alimentazione e mortalità in Italia alla fine del XIX secolo." In *Continuità e discontinuità nei processi demografici: L'Italia nella transizione demografica*. Soveria Mannelli (CZ): Rubbettino, 275–282.

Sastry, Narayan. 1997. "Family-Level Clustering of Childhood Mortality Risk in Northeast Brazil." *Population Studies* 51.3:245–261.

Schmelz, Uziel O. 1971. *Infant and Early Childhood Mortality among the Jews of the Diaspora*. Jerusalem: Institute of Contemporary Jewry, Hebrew University.

Schofield, Roger. 1984. "Population growth in the century after 1750: The role of mortality decline." In *Preindustrial Population Change*, eds. Tommy Bengtsson, Gunnar Fridlizius, and Rolf Ohlsson. Stockholm: Almqvist and Wiksell, 17–39.

Schofield, Roger. 1985a. "English Marriage Patterns Revisited." *Journal of Family History* 10:2–20.

Schofield, Roger. 1985b. "Through a Glass Darkly: *The Population History of England* as an Experiment in History." *Journal of Interdisciplinary History* 15:571–593.

————. 1986. "Did the Mothers Really Die? Three Centuries of Maternal Mortality in the 'The World We Have Lost.'" In *The World We Have Gained*, eds. Lloyd Bonfield, Richard M. Smith, and Keith Wrightson. Oxford: Blackwell, 231–260.

————. 1989. "Family Structure, Demographic Behavior and Economic Growth." In *Famine, Disease, and the Social Order in Early Modern Society*, eds. John Walter and Roger Schofield. Cambridge: Cambridge University Press, 279–304.

————. 2000. "Short-Run and Secular Demographic Response to Fluctuations in the Standard of Living in England, 1540–1834." In *Population and the Economy*, eds. Tommy Bengtsson and Osamu Saito. Oxford: Oxford University Press, 49–71.

Schofield, Roger, David Reher, and Alain Bideau, eds. 1991. *The Decline of Mortality in Europe*. Oxford: Clarendon Press.

Scholliers, E. 1960. *De levensstandaard in de XVe en XVIe eeuw te Antwerpen; loonarbeid en honger*. Antwerp: De Sikkel.

Scholliers, Peter. 1993. "The Cost of Living in Nineteenth Century Belgium." In *Studia Historica Oeconomica. Liber Amicorum Herman Van der Wee*, Leuven: Universitaire Pers, 221–238.

Schultz, T. Paul. 1984. "Studying the Impact of Household Economic and Community Variables on Child Mortality." In *Child Survival: Strategies for Research*, eds. Henry W. Mosley and C. Lincoln Chen. *Population and Development Review*, Suppl. to Vol. 10, 215–236.

Scrimshaw, Nevin S. 1985. "The Value of Contemporary Food and Nutrition Studies for Historians." In *Hunger and History*, eds. Robert Rotberg and Theodore Rabb. Cambridge: Cambridge University Press, 331–336.

Ségalen, Martine. 1983. *Love and Power in the Peasant Family: Rural France in the Nineteenth Century*. Chicago: University of Chicago Press.

———. 1987. "Life Course Patterns and Peasant Culture in France: A Critical Assessment." *Journal of Family History* 12.1-3:213–224.

Sen, Amartya. 1981. *Poverty and Famines: An Essay on Entitlement and Deprivation*. Oxford: Clarendon Press.

———. 1987. "The Standard of Living." In *The Standard of Living*, ed. G. Hawthorn. Cambridge: Cambridge University Press.

———. 1992. *Inequality Reexamined*. New York: Russell Sage Foundation.

Servais, Paul. 1982. "Industries rurales et structures agraires: le cas de l'Entre-Vesdre-et-Meuse aux XVIIIe et XIXe siècles." *Revue Belge d'Histoire contemporaine* 13.2–3:179–206.

Shepherd, John. 1995. *Marriage and Mandatory Abortion among the 17th Century Siraya*. Arlington, Va.: American Anthropological Association.

Skinner, Quentin. 1997. *Liberty before Liberalism*. Cambridge: Cambridge University Press.

Skinner, G. William. 1987. "Sichuan's Population in the Nineteenth Century: Lessons from Disaggregated Data." *Late Imperial China* 8.1:1–79.

———. 1993. "Conjugal Power in Tokugawa Japanese Families: A Matter of Life or Death." In *Sex and Gender Hierarchies*, ed. Barbara Diane Miller. Cambridge: Cambridge University Press, 236–270.

———. 1997. "Family Systems and Demographic Processes." In *Anthropological Demography*, eds. David Kertzer and Tom Fricke. Chicago: University of Chicago Press, 53–95.

Skoglund, Anna-Maria. 1992. *Fattigvården på den svenska landsbygden år 1829*. Rapport i socialt arbete, nr 58. Stockholm: Stockholm University, School of Social Work.

Sköld, Peter. 1996a. "From Inoculation to Vaccination: Smallpox in Sweden in Eighteenth and Nineteenth Centuries." *Population Studies* 50.3:247–262.

———. 1996b. "Escape from Catastrophe: The Saami's Experience with Smallpox in Eighteenth and Early Nineteenth Century Sweden." *Social Science History* 21.1:1–25.

———. 1997. *"The Two Faces of Smallpox: A Disease and Its Prevention in Eighteenth and Nineteenth Century Sweden."* Demographic Data Base Report No. 12. Umeå: Umeå University.

Smith, Adam. 1776/1970. *An Inquiry into the Nature and Causes of the Wealth of Nations*. Bungay, Suffolk: Penguin Books.

Smith, Daniel Scott. 1991. "Mortality Differences before the Health Transition." *Health Transition Review* 4:235–237.

Smith, Richard S. 1984. "The Structured Dependence of the Elderly in the Middle Ages and Thereafter." *Ageing and Society* 4:409–428.

Smith, Thomas C. 1977. *Nakahara: Family Farming and Population in a Japanese Village.* Stanford: Stanford University Press.

Söderberg, Johan. 1978. *Agrar fattigdom i Sydsverige under 1800-talet.* Stockholm: Almqvist & Wiksell.

Soete, Antoon. 1995. "De Cockerill à Bessemer: l'industrie métallurgique lourde." In *La Belgique industrielle en 1850*, eds. Bart Van der Herten, Michel Oris, and Jan Rogiers. Brussels: Crédit Communal, 145–176.

Solar, Peter M. 1995. "Poor Relief and English Development before the Industrial Revolution." *Economic History Review* 48.1:1–22.

Soliani, Lamberto, and Enzo Lucchetti. 1997. "I fattori genetici della mortalità." In *Démographie: analyse et synthèse. Causes et conséquences des évolutions démographiques*, Vol. 1. Rome: Università degli Studi di Roma La Sapienza, Dipartimento di Scienze Demografiche; Paris, France: Institut National d'Études Démographique; Louvain-la-Neuve, Belgium: Université Catholique de Louvain, Institut de Démographie, Départment des Sciences de la Population et du Développment, 71–83.

Somogyi, S. 1973. "L'alimentazione dell'Italia." In *Storia d'Italia*, Vol. 5. Turin: Einaudi, 893.

Spaggiari, Pier Luigi. 1959. *I prezzi di generi alimentari sul mercato di Parma.* Turin: Industria Libraria Tipografica Editrice.

———. 1966. *L'agricoltura negli stati parmensi dal 1750 al 1859.* Milan: Banca Commerciale Italiana.

Spagnoli, Paul G. 1983. "Industrialization, Proto-Industrialization and Marriage: A Reconsideration." *Journal of Family History* 8.3:230–247.

Statistiska Centralbyrån. 1969. *Historisk statistik för Sverige. Del 1. Befolkning, 1720–1967.* 2nd ed. Stockholm.

Staunton, George L. 1797. *An Authentic Account of an Embassy from the King of Great Britain to the Emperor of China.* 2 vols.

Stirrat, Gordon M. 1994. "Pregnancy and Immunity." *British Medical Journal* 308.6941:1385–1386.

Stolnitz, George. 1956. "A Century of International Mortality Trends: II." *Population Studies* 10.1:17–42.

Sundin, Jan, and Lars-Göran Tedebrand. 1981. "Mortality and Morbidity in Swedish Iron Foundries 1750–1875." In *Tradition and Transition*, eds. Anders Brändström and Jan Sundin. Umeå: Demographic Data Base, 105–159.

Svensson, Patrick. 2001. *Agrara entreprenörer. Böndernas roll i omvandlingen av jordbruket i Skåne 1800–1870.* Lund: Almqvist and Wiksell.

Szreter, Simon. 1997. "Economic Growth, Disruption, Deprivation, Disease, and Death: On the Importance of the Politics of Public Health for Development." *Population and Development Review* 23.4:693–728.

Szreter, Simon and Graham Mooney. 1998. "Urbanization, Mortality, and the Standard of Living Debate: New Estimates of the Expectation of Life at Birth in Nineteenth Century British Cities." *Economic History Review* 51.1:84–112.

Tabutin, Dominique. 1978. "La surmortalité féminine en Europe avant 1940." *Population* 33:121–148.

Tabutin, Dominique, and Michel Willems. 1998. "Differential Mortality by Sex from Birth to Adolescence: The Historical Experience of the West (1750–1930)." In *Too Young to Die: Genes or Gender?* eds. United Nations, Department of Economic and Social Affairs, and Population Division. New York: United Nations Department of Economic and Social Affairs, Population Division, 17–52.

Takei, Masaomi. 1971. "Seinan-Nihon-gata kazoku ni okeru sozoku to fuyo (Succession and dependency in families in southwestern Japan)." In *Hoshakaigaku no Gendaiteki Kadai* (Contemporary issues in legal sociology), eds. T. Ushiomi and Y. Watanabe. Tokyo: Iwanami Shoten, 225–253.

Telford, Ted. 1990. "Patching the Holes in Chinese Genealogies: Mortality in the Lineage Populations of Tongcheng County, 1300–1880." *Late Imperial China* 11.2:116–136.

Thestrup, Paul. 1971. *The Standard of Living in Copenhagen, 1730–1800: Some Methods of Measurement.* Copenhagen: Københavns Universitet, Institut for Økonomisk Historie.

Thomas, Dorothy S. 1941. *Social and Economic Aspects of Swedish Population Movements: 1750–1933.* New York: Macmillan.

Thorner, Daniel, Basil Kerblay, and R. E. F. Smith. 1966. *A. V. Chayanov on The Theory of Peasant Economy.* Madison: University of Wisconsin Press.

Thornton, Patricia, and Sherry Olson. 1992. "Familles montréalaises du 19e siècle: trois cultures, trois trajectoires." *Cahiers Québeçois de démographie* 21.2:51–75.

Thunberg, C. P. 1791–1793. *Resan til och uti Kejsardömet Japan åren 1775 och 1776.* Fascimile ed. Stockholm 1980: Rediviva Publishing House.

Tien, Ju-kang. 1988. *Male Anxiety and Female Chastity: A Comparative Study of Chinese Ethical Values in Ming-Ch'ing Times.* Leiden: Brill.

Tilly, Louise A., and Joan W. Scott. 1975. "Women's Work and the Family in Nineteenth Century Europe." *Contemporary Studies in Society and History* 17:36–64.

Todd, Emmanuel. 1990. *L'Invention de l'Europe.* Paris: Seuil.

Tomobe, Ken'ichi. 1998. "Kinsei-kindai Nihon ni okeru kazoku rousaku keiei no bunseki (An analysis of peasant household economy in early modern and modern Japan)." *Mita Gakkai Zasshi* 90.4:15–55.

Tong Yonggong, and Guan Jialu. 1994. "Qianlongchao Shengjing zongguan neiwufu de sheli (The Establishment of the Central Office of the Imperial Household Agency During the Qianlong Period)." *Gugong bowuyuan yuankan* 2:19–23.

———. 1999. "Shengjing neiwufu de shezhi yange jiqi lishi zuoyong (The Establishment of the Shengjing Imperial Household Agency and Its Historical Functions)." In *Qingzhu Wang Zhonghan jiaoshou bashiwu ji Wei Qingyuan jiaoshou qishi huayan xueshu lunwen heji* (Joint festschrift for Wang Zhonghan and Wei Qingyuan) Bo Di, ed. Hefei: Huangshan shushe, 326–331.

Torigoe, Hiroyuki. 1985. *Ie to Mura no Shakaigaku* (Sociology of the Ie and Villages). Kyoto: Sekaishisosha.

Triandis, Harry C. 1995. *Individualism and Collectivism*. Boulder, Colo.: Westview Press.

Trussell, James and Timothy Guinnane. 1993. "Techniques of Event-History Analysis." In *Old and New Methods in Historical Demography*, eds. David Reher and Roger Schofield. Oxford: Clarendon Press, 181–205.

Tsuya, Noriko O., and Minja Kim Choe. 1991. "Changes in Intrafamilial Relationships and the Roles of Women in Japan and Korea." NUPRI Research Paper Series No. 58. Tokyo: Nihon University Population Research Institute.

Tsuya, Noriko O., and Satomi Kurosu. 1998. "Patterns and Covariates of Fertility in Eighteenth and Nineteenth Century Rural Japan: Evidence from Two Northeastern Villages." Paper presented to the Eurasian Project Fertility Conference, Bloomington, Indiana.

———. 1999. "Reproduction and Family Building Strategies in 18th and 19th Century Rural Japan: Evidence from Two Northeastern Villages." Paper presented at the annual meeting of the Population Association of America, New York, Mar. 25–27.

———. 2000. "Mortality Responses to Short-Term Economic Stress and Household Context in Early Modern Japan: Evidence from Two Northeastern Villages." In *Population and the Economy*, eds. Tommy Bengtsson and Osamu Saito. Oxford: Oxford University Press, 421–456.

———. 2002. "The Mortality Effect of Adult Male Death on Women and Children in Agrarian Household in Early Modern Japan: Evidence from Two Northeastern Villages." In *When Dad Died*, eds. Renzo Derosas and Michel Oris. Bern: Peter Lang, 261–299.

Tsuya, Noriko O., Satomi Kurosu, and Hideki Nakazato. 1997. "Mortality in Early Modern Japan: Patterns and Correlates." Eurasian Project on Population and Family History Conference Papers Series, No. 20. Kyoto: International Research Center for Japanese Studies.

Tsuya, Noriko O., and Ken'ichi Tomobe. 1998. "Infant Mortality and Underregistration of Births in a Nineteenth Century Japanese Village: An Analysis of Pregnancy Registers." Paper presented at the Eurasian Project Nuptiality Conference, Beijing, Nov. 25–29.

Tuvestrand, Birgitta, Anna-Brita Lövgren, and Bengt Danielson, eds. 1995. *Biskopsvisitationerna i Skåne 1698–1880*. Skriftserie, No. 5. Lund: Landsarkivet.

Uhlenberg, Peter. 1980. "Death and the Family." *Journal of Family History* 5:313–320.

United Nations. 1982. *Levels and Trends of Mortality since 1950*. New York: United Nations.

———. 1994. *World Development Report*. New York: United Nations.

———. 1996. *Demographic Yearbook 1996*. New York: United Nations.

———. 1998. *Demographic Yearbook 1998*. New York: United Nations.

United Nations Department of International Economic and Social Affairs. 1982. *Model Life Tables for Developing Countries*. New York: United Nations.

Utterström, Gustaf. 1957. *Jordbrukets arbetare*. Stockholm: Tidens Förlag.

Valkonen, Tapani. 1998. "The Widening Differentials in Adult Mortality in Socio-Economic Status and Their Causes." In *Symposium on Health and Mortality, Brussels, Belgium, 19–22 November 1997*, ed. Population Division of the United Nations. New York: United Nations, 189–217.

Van Damme, Dirk. 1990. "Onderstandswoonst, sedenterisering en stad-plattelandtegenstellingen. Evolutie en betekenis van de wetgeving op de onderstandswoonst in België (einde achttiende to einde negentiende eeuw)." *Belgisch Tijdschrift voor Nieuwste Geschiedenis*, 21:483–534.

Vandenbroeke, Chris, Frans van Poppel, and Ad Van der Woude. 1983. "Le développement séculaire de la mortalité aux jeunes âges dans le territoire du Bénélux." *Annales de Démographie Historique*: 257–289.

van de Walle, Francine. 1986. "Infant Mortality and the European Demographic Transition." In *The Decline of Fertility in Europe*, eds. Ansley J. Coale and Susan C. Watkins. Princeton, N.J.: Princeton University Press, 201–233.

van Norren, Bert, and Harrie van Vianen. 1986. *The Malnutrition-Infections Syndrome and Its Demographic Outcome in Developing Countries*. The Hague: Programming Committee for Demographic Research.

van Poppel, Frans, and Kees Mandemakers. 1997. "Differential Infant and Child Mortality in the Netherlands, 1812–1912: First Results of the Historical Sample of the Population of the Netherlands." In *Infant and Child Mortality in the Past*, eds. Alain Bideau, Bertrand Desjardins, and Hector Pérez Brignoli. Oxford: Clarendon Press, 276–300.

van Poppel, Frans, Michel Oris, and James Lee, eds. Forthcoming. *The Road to Independence: Leavers and Stayers in the Household in Europe and Asia*.

van Zanden, Jan L. Forthcoming. "What Happened to the Standard of Living before the Industrial Revolution?" In *New Evidence on the Standard of Living in Pre-Industrial Europe and Asia*, eds. Robert Allen, Tommy Bengtsson, and Martin Dribe. Oxford: Oxford University Press.

Vaupel, James W., James R. Carey, Kaare Christensen, Thomas E. Johnson, Anatoli I. Yashin, Niels V. Holm, Ivan A. Iachine, Väinö Kannisto, Aziz A. Khazaeli, Pablo Liedo, Valter D. Longo, Yi Zeng, Kenneth G. Manton, and James W. Curtsinger. 1998. "Biodemographic Trajectories of Longevity." *Science* 280.5365:855–860.

Verstraelen, Jean. 1972. "Transformations agricoles et démographiques d'un village pendant l'industrialisation. Jalhay de 1805 à 1913." Master's thesis, University of Liège.

Viazzo, Pier Paolo. 1989. *Upland Communities: Environment, Population and Social Structure in the Alps since the Sixteenth Century*. Cambridge: Cambridge University Press.

Viazzo, Pier Paolo, and Albera Dionigi. 1992. "La famiglia contadina nell'Italia settentrionale, 1750–1930." In *Storia della famiglia Italiana*, eds. Marzio Barbagli and David I. Kertzer. Bologna: Il Mulino, 159–190.

Vilquin, Eric. 1978. "La mortalité infantile selon le mois de naissance: Le cas de la Belgique au 19e siècle." *Population* 33.6:1137–1153.

Wakefield, David. 1998. *Fenjia: Household Division and Inheritance in Qing and Republican China*. Honolulu: University of Hawaii Press.

Waldron, Ingrid. 1983a. "Sex Differences in Human Mortality: The Role of Genetic Factors." *Social Science and Medicine* 17.6:321–333.

————. 1983b. "The Role of Genetic and Biological Factors in Sex Differences in Mortality." In *Sex Differentials in Mortality: Trends, Determinants, and Consequences,* eds. Alan D. Lopez and Lado T. Ruzicka. Canberra: Australian National University, Department of Demography.

————. 1986. "What Do We Know about Causes of Sex Differences in Mortality? A Review of the Literature." *Population Bulletin of the United Nations* 18:59–76.

————. 1987. "Patterns and Causes of Excess Female Mortality among Children in Developing Countries." *World Health Statistics Quarterly* 40:194–210.

Wall, Richard. 1981. "Inferring Differential Neglect of Females from Mortality Data." *Annales de Démographie Historique*: 119–140.

————. 1992. "Relationships between the Generations in British Families, Past and Present." In *Families and Households: Divisions and Change,* eds. Catherine Marsh and Sara Aber. New York: St. Martin's Press.

————. 2002. "Families in Crisis and the English Poor Law as Exemplified by the Relief Programme in the Essex Parish of Ardleigh 1795–7." In *The Logic of Female Succession: Rethinking Patriarchy and Patrilineality in Global and Historical Perspective.* International Symposium 19:101–127. Kyoto: International Research Center for Japanese Studies.

Wall, Richard, Jean Robin, and Peter Laslett, eds. 1983. *Family Forms in Historic Europe.* Cambridge: Cambridge University Press.

Walter, John, and Roger Schofield, eds. 1989. *Famine, Disease, and the Social Order in Early Modern Society.* Cambridge: Cambridge University Press.

Wang, Feng, Cameron Campbell, and James Lee. Forthcoming. "Fertility, Household Context, and Economic Fluctuations in Eighteenth and Nineteenth Century Rural China." In *Reproductive Regimes,* eds. George Alter, Noriko Tsuya, and Wang Feng. Cambridge, Mass.: MIT Press.

Wang, Feng, and James Lee. 1998. "Adoption among the Qing Nobility and Its Implications for Chinese Demographic Behavior." *History of the Family* 3:411–427.

————. 2002. "Zhaidiao renkou juedinglun de guanghuan (Correcting population determinism)." *Lishi yanjiu* (Historical research) 1:55–61.

Wargentin, Pehr. 1976. "De l'homme; mortalité de l'homme en Suède, comparée à celle de la femme. Du nombre des naissances et des morts dans tous les mois de l'année." In *Mémoires (abrégés) de l' Académie Royale des Sciences de Stockholm.* Paris.

Watkins, Susan C., ed. 1994. *After Ellis Island: Newcomers and Natives in the 1910 Census.* New York: Russell Sage Foundation.

Watkins, Susan Cotts, and Myron P. Gutman. 1983. "Methodological Issues in the Use of Population Registers for Fertility Analysis." *Historical Methods* 6.3:109–120.

Watkins, Susan Cotts, and Jane Menken. 1985. "Famines in Historical Perspective." *Population and Development Review* 11.4:647–675.

Weibull, Carl G. 1923. *Skånska jordbrukets historia intill 1800-talets början.* Lund: Gleerups.

Weinberg, Eugene D. 1984. "Pregnancy and Resistance to Infectious Disease." *Reviews of Infectious Diseases* 6:814–831.

Weir, David. 1984a. "Rather Late Than Never: Celibacy and Age at Marriage in English Cohort Fertility, 1541–1871." *Journal of Family History* 9:340–354.

———. 1984b. "Life under Pressure: France and England, 1670–1870." *Journal of Economic History* 44:27–47.

Will, Pierre-Etienne, and R. Bin Wong, with James Lee, eds. 1991. *Nourish the People: The State Civilian Granary System in China, 1650–1850*. Ann Arbor: University of Michigan, Center for Chinese Studies.

Williams, Naomi. 1992. "Death in Its Season: Class, Environment and Mortality of Infants in 19th Century Sheffield." *Social History of Medicine* 5.1:71–94.

Williams, Naomi, and Chris Galley. 1995. "Urban-Rural Differentials in Infant Mortality in Victorian England." *Population Studies* 49:401–420.

Williams, Naomi, and Graham Mooney. 1994. "Infant Mortality in an 'Age of Great Cities': London and the English Provincial Cities Compared, 1840–1910." *Continuity and Change* 9.2:185–212.

Williamson, Jeffrey G. 1981. "Urban Disamenities, Dark Satanic Mills, and the British Standard of Living Debate." *Journal of Economic History* 41.1:75–84.

———. 1998a. "Real Wages and Relative Factor Prices in the Third World, 1820–1940: The Mediterranean Basin." HIER Discussion Paper No. 1842, Department of Economics, Harvard University, July.

———. 1998b. "Real Wages and Relative Factor Prices in the Third World 1820–1940: Asia." HIER Discussion Paper No. 1844, Department of Economics, Harvard University, Aug.

Willner, Sam. 1999. *Det svaga könet? Kön och vuxendödlighet i 1800-talets Sverige* Linköping studies in art and science 203. Tema hälsa och samhälle, Linköpings universitet.

Winberg, Christer. 1981. "Familj och jord i tre västgötasocknar." *Historisk tidskrift* 3:278–310.

Wolf, Arthur. 1985. "Chinese Family Size: A Myth Revitalized." In *The Chinese Family and Its Ritual Behavior*, eds. Jih-chang Hsieh and Ying-chang Chuang. Taibei: Institute of Ethnology, Academia Sinica, 30–49.

———. 1995. *Sexual Attraction and Childhood Association: A Chinese Brief for Edward Westermarck*. Stanford: Stanford University Press.

———. 1998. "Two Kinds of Patriarchy." Manuscript.

Wolf, Arthur P. 2001. "Is There Evidence of Birth Control in Late Imperial China?" *Population and Development Review* 27:133–154.

Wolf, Arthur, and Susan Hanley, eds. 1985. "Introduction." In *Family and Population in East-Asian History*. Stanford: Stanford University Press, 1–13.

Wolf, Arthur P., and Chieh-shan Huang. 1980. *Marriage and Adoption in China, 1845–1945*. Stanford: Stanford University Press.

Women's Co-operative Guild. 1915. *Maternity: Letters from Working-Women* London: G. Bell and Sons.

Wong, R. Bin. 1997. *China Transformed: Historical Change and the Limits of European Experience.* Ithaca, N.Y.: Cornell University Press.

Woodbury, Robert M. 1926. *Infant Mortality and Its Causes.* Baltimore: Williams and Wilkins.

Woods, Robert. 1994. "La mortalité infantile en Grande-Bretagne: un bilan des connaissances historiques." *Annales de Démographie Historique*: 119–134.

Woods, Robert, Patricia A. Watterson, and Jennifer A. Woodward. 1988, 1989. "The Causes of Rapid Infant Mortality Decline in England and Wales, 1861–1921." *Population Studies* 42.3:343–366; 43.1:113–132.

Woods Robert, and Naomi Williams. 1995. "Must the Gap Widen before It Can Be Narrowed? Long-Term Trends in Social Class Mortality Differentials." *Continuity and Change* 10:105–137.

Woods, Robert, Naomi Williams, and Chris Galley. 1997. "Differential Mortality Patterns among Infants and Other Young Children: The Experience of England and Wales in the Nineteenth Century." In *The Decline of Infant and Child Mortality*, eds. Carlo A. Corsini and Pier Paolo Viazzo. The Hague: Martinus Nijhof, 57–72.

Woolf, Stuart. 1986. *The Poor in Western Europe in the Eighteenth and Nineteenth Centuries.* London: Methuen.

World Bank. 1994. *World Development Report 1994: Infrastructure for Development.* Oxford: Oxford University Press.

Wrigley, Edward A. 1978. "Fertility Strategy for the Individual and the Group." In *Historical Studies of Changing Fertility*, ed. Charles Tilly. Princeton, N.Y.: Princeton University Press, 135–154.

———. 1987. *People, Cities and Wealth: The Transformation of Traditional Society.* Oxford: Basil Blackwell.

Wrigley, Edward A., and Roger Schofield. 1981. *The Population History of England, 1541–1871: A Reconstruction.* Cambridge: Cambridge University Press.

Wrigley, Edward A., Ros S. Davies, James E. Oeppen, and Roger Schofield. 1997. *English Population History from Family Reconstitution, 1580–1837.* Cambridge: Cambridge University Press.

Wu, Chengming. 1996. "Liyong liangjia biandong yanjiu Qingdai de shichang zhenghe (Grain price studies of market integration during the Qing)." *Zhongguo jingji shi yanjiu* 2:88–94.

Yan, Yunxiang. 1996. *The Flow of Gifts: Reciprocity and Social Networks in a Chinese Village.* Stanford: Stanford University Press.

Yonemura, Chiyo, and Nagata, Mary L. 1998. "Continuity, Solidarity, Family and Enterprise: What Is an *ie*?" In *House and Stem Family in Eurasian Perspective*, eds. Antoinette Fauve-Chamoux and Emiko Ochiai. Kyoto: International Research Center for Japanese Studies, 193–214.

Yuan, I-chin. 1931. "Life Tables for a Southern Chinese Family from 1365 to 1849." *Human Biology* 3.2:57–79.

Zalin, Giovanni. 1969. *Aspetti e problemi dell'economia Veneta dalla caduta della Repubblica all'annessione.* Vicenza: Comune di Vicenza.

Zhang, X. H., Satoshi Sasaki, and Hugo Kesteloot. 1995. "The Sex Ratio of Mortality and Its Secular Trends." *International Journal of Epidemiology* 24.4:720–729.

Zhao, Zhongwei. 1997a. "Demographic Systems in Historic China: Some New Findings from Recent Research." *Journal of the Australian Population Association* 14.2:201–232.

———. 1997b. "Long-Term Mortality Patterns in Chinese History: Evidence from a Recorded Clan Population." *Population Studies* 51.2:117–128.

———. 2002. "Fertility Control in China's Past." *Population and Development Review* 28.4 (December):751–757.

Index